MEDIÆVAL HISTORY

THE HARPER HISTORICAL SERIES

Under the Editorship of

GUY STANTON FORD

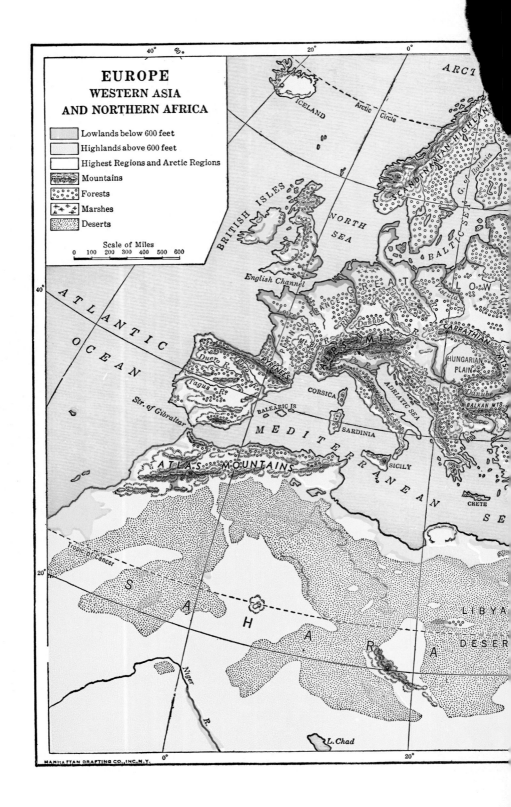

EUROPE
WESTERN ASIA
AND NORTHERN AFRICA

Lowlands below 600 feet
Highlands above 600 feet
Highest Regions and Arctic Regions
Mountains
Forests
Marshes
Deserts

Scale of Miles
0   100   200   300   400   500   600

ARCT

ICELAND   Arctic   Circle

SCANDINAVIAN HIGHLAND

BRITISH ISLES

NORTH SEA

G. of Bothnia

BALTIC SEA

English Channel

GREAT

LOW

FRANCE

Danube

Vistula

40°

ATLANTIC

OCEAN

Duero R.

Tagus

Str. of Gibraltar

PYRENEES

Mt.

ALPS MTS

Danube

CARPATHIAN MTS

HUNGARIAN PLAIN

BALKAN MTS

CORSICA

BALEARIC IS

SARDINIA

MEDITERRANEAN

ADRIATIC SEA

ATLAS   MOUNTAINS

SICILY

CRETE

SE

Tropic of Cancer

S   A

H   A

R   A

LIBYA

DESER

Niger

R.

L. Chad

20°

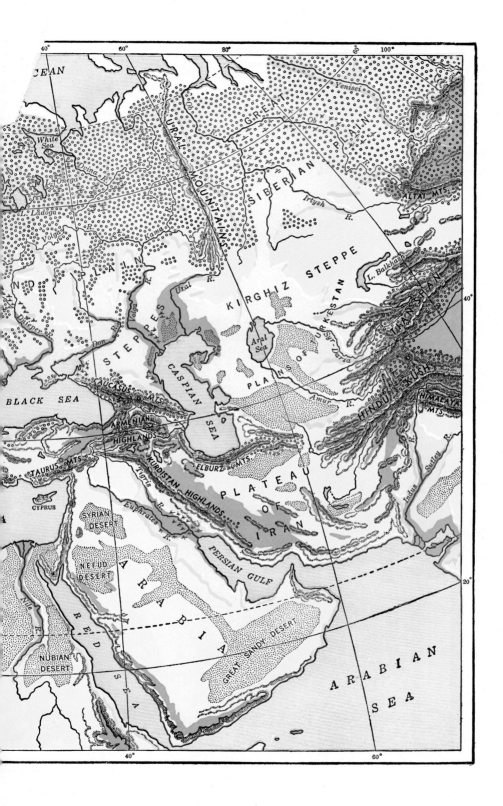

MEDIÆVAL HISTORY

EUROPE FROM THE SECOND TO THE SIXTEENTH CENTURY

Third Edition

by

CARL STEPHENSON

Professor of History · Cornell University

HARPER & BROTHERS · PUBLISHERS · NEW YORK

Library of Congress catalog card number: 51-11957

To the Memory of
a Revered Master

CHARLES HOMER HASKINS

Contents

Maps

Figures

Genealogical Tables

(*beginning p. 495*)

Plates

(*between pp. 232 and 233*)

Editor's Foreword

As a student primarily of what is called modern European history, the editor of this series has found himself more and more reluctant to capitalize and underline the word modern. He has never shared the idea that the only history worth while is that of the day before yesterday or since Watt patented a steam engine in 1769. With regret he has faced year after year the massed products of secondary schools whose growing numbers are in inverse ratio to what the secondary-school history courses taught them of the beginnings of their own civilization and the origin of the economic, political, and social institutions that shape their lives. The narrow view in the schools of what is significant in the evolution of western Europe forces the college teacher of modern history to explain the church, the beginnings of self-government, the rise of the middle class, the historic bases of democracy in education by the printed word, the origins of the scientific spirit and of the university he attends. Even such terms as Renaissance and Reformation are often words for something as vague to these young people fresh from high school as is the quantum theory.

I am therefore as a teacher of modern history and an editor glad to co-operate with a publishing house and with authors of known scholarship who make it possible for the college student and teacher to learn something of the historic heritage upon which this and coming generations must build what in time may be justly called modern history. This volume is my third opportunity and the justification of the volume may well rest upon what its author says in his concluding note. I commend it to student and teacher alike as prologue rather than epilogue.

But the justification would fail if Professor Stephenson had not preceded his conclusion by an exceptionally well-organized and clearly written text. He has steadily and sturdily kept as the core of his work the great historic and persisting institutions that take shape in the period we call mediæval. These he has clothed with an interest that prepares the student to understand the succeeding centuries. As a student and teacher I am happy to see this volume take its place beside the other sound and teachable volumes in this field in this and other series. They are a promising effort to give roots to a generation in danger of floating purposelessly like plankton in the shallow shoals of today.

GUY STANTON FORD

Preface to the Revised Edition

In the preface to the first edition of this book, which was published eight years ago, I pointed out that it was arranged according to a chronological plan in the hope that it would be more than a narrative of political history with a series of postscripts on other phases of life. Such chronological arrangement has been followed even more rigorously in the present revision. By reducing the chapters from twenty-eight to twenty-six, and by thoroughly reorganizing their contents, I have tried to make the book clearer as well as briefer. A good many names of persons and places have been ruthlessly deleted; a considerable mass of other detail has been drastically cut down. Should anyone feel that in certain respects the condensation has been carried too far, he will, I trust, obtain some recompense from the new material that has been added. The sections dealing with economic developments, social conditions, arts, letters, and education have been greatly enlarged. In particular, more adequate attention has been given to science, technology, and material civilization generally. A better emphasis has thus been placed on the original contributions of the Roman Empire, and on the later contributions of the Byzantine and Arab Empires, to the culture of mediæval Europe.

The maps of the earlier edition remain with little change, as do the genealogical tables and the chronological charts. On the other hand, a number of substitutions have been made in the plates, and many more figures have been inserted to illustrate points in the text. For the majority of the plates I continue to be indebted to the College of Architecture, Cornell University. For others I have to thank

Professors F. O. Waagé and P. A. Underwood of the Department of Fine Arts, as well as the persons and firms to whom certain photographs are individually ascribed. Acknowledgments of permission secured from various publishers to quote from their editions of mediæval authors will be found in the footnotes.

Directly or indirectly, many friends have aided me in preparing this revised edition. Parts of the manuscript have been read and criticized by my colleagues, Professors M. L. W. Laistner and A. H. Detweiler, and by Professor Henry Guerlac of the University of Wisconsin. In so far as much is here reproduced from the first edition of the book, or from my *Brief Survey of Mediæval Europe,* I am also under obligation to Professors G. H. Sabine and Harry Caplan of Cornell University and to Professor E. A. J. Johnson, now of New York University. Two scholars who earlier helped me— Nathaniel Schmidt and G. L. Hamilton—are no longer with us. Without repeating what I have said on previous occasions, I wish once more to express my gratitude to Dr. Guy Stanton Ford, editor of Harper's Historical Series, and to Dr. H. H. King, Faculty Research Assistant in the Cornell University Library. My wife has again been the principal author of the index. Others have given me advice and encouragement which I shall always remember, but which I cannot begin to appreciate in writing.

As a final word, I should like to record a hope. When peace brings a return of sanity to our distracted world, may our students even more fully realize that much we cherish was the product of years antedating 1914, or even 1492!

CARL STEPHENSON

March, 1943

Preface to the Third Edition

This Third Edition of my *Mediæval History* remains fundamentally the same as the one preceding. However lazily, I have seen no reason for a drastic reorganization of the chapters or for a complete rewriting of them. I have merely tried, in the light of recent historical criticism, to improve various sections of the older book—especially those dealing with social developments and with the advance of learning, whether academic or non-academic.

The Maps and Genealogical Tables have been reprinted as they were, but the Chronological Charts have been considerably changed and the Suggested Readings brought up to date. Besides, a number of new Figures and Plates are here included. For most of them due acknowledgment is given in the pertinent footnotes. For Plate XVI, however, I have particularly to thank M. Édouard H. Seyrig, of the *Institut français d'archéologie,* Beyrouth. Professor Henry Guerlac, now my colleague in Cornell University, has again given me much useful advice. And for all the other friendly co-operation I have had I remain deeply grateful; not only to the persons mentioned in the earlier preface, but to those who have since been kind enough to suggest alterations of my text.

Whatever I have written should not, of course, be taken as definitive; my best hope is to encourage other students to continue work on the many unsolved problems that confront the historian of the Middle Ages. So I once more quote Abelard: *Dubitando enim ad inquisitionem venimus; inquirendo veritatem percipimus* (see p. 263).

CARL STEPHENSON

July, 1951

MEDIÆVAL HISTORY

INTRODUCTION

Preliminary Definitions

The student who takes up a history of the mediæval period, or of the Middle Ages, may properly want to know what is meant by those conventional terms. "History," as here understood, is the study of man's past rather than everything man did in the past. However fascinating conjecture on the latter subject may seem, it is one on which we, as historians, can have nothing to say. For an event that left no trace to be studied must remain unknown to us. The historian, like the scientist, is supposed to rely on ordinary human faculties and not to offer supernatural explanations. In other words, whatever is stated as historical fact should be verifiable by actual evidence—by something that anyone, properly trained, may himself examine. How scanty such evidence is for earlier centuries, and how difficult to appraise, is known to every mature student of history. But to introduce advanced research is not the purpose of the following chapters; they are intended merely to present a little of what has come to be accepted as fact by most historians, together with a few suggestions as to its significance. If truly interested, the reader should not hesitate to question any statement here made. Inquiry, after all, is the essence of history.

The term "history"

Next we come to the term "mediæval." For it we especially have to thank, or blame, Italian writers of the fourteenth and fifteenth centuries. Convinced that their own civilization marked the rebirth of Græco-Roman civilization, they popularized the concept of a "mediæval" (or "dark") age between an ancient and a modern age. That their interpretation of history was far from accurate is now generally recognized. Yet their terminology continues to govern the teaching of history in our schools, and the present textbook keeps to established convention in its title. As the reader will see, no more is thus implied than particular attention to the history of Europe

The term "mediæval"

1

from Roman times to the opening of the sixteenth century. During that period the emphasis placed by any historian necessarily depends upon his own point of view. In the following pages the emphasis will be placed on developments in western Europe because, as the author believes, what we Americans call civilization seems to have developed there—though greatly influenced by cultural advances in the near east. Asiatic history, whatever its intrinsic value, will here be considered a matter of secondary importance.

How the age called mediæval differed from that called ancient should be clear from what is said in the first few chapters; whether a sharp distinction can be drawn between the age preceding 1500 and the one following is a question which can hardly be answered until that date has been reached. Meanwhile there is no need for worry about any marked peculiarity of mediæval men in general. They will be found to have varied quite as much as the men of more recent centuries. Fortunately, we do not have to begin with an abstruse definition of the mediæval. It should, however, be realized that, while attempting to describe the past, we must use a modern vocabulary. And although most of our current words can be expected to have a reasonably precise connotation, a number of those in constant use by historians, as well as by journalists, are all too often misunderstood. Three— "state," "nation," and "race"—are especially apt to be confused in popular writing. Before we apply them to the Roman world, accordingly, we should be careful to explain what we mean by them.

"State" and "nation" Today, as in ancient times, a state has a territorial basis. It not only can be named; it also can be drawn on a map. All residents of such a territory, without regard to personal likes and dislikes, are subject to the supreme authority of the government there established. For example, when a citizen of Mexico crosses an imaginary line to the north, he ceases to be bound by Mexican law and becomes bound by that of our country. Yet, normally, he will still be considered a Mexican. Although he leaves his state behind, he bears with him his nationality—a matter that is not so easy to define. Speech is sometimes a guide to nationality, sometimes not. Frenchmen and Germans, we know, are likely to speak respectively French and German. But a man who speaks French may be a Canadian; a man who speaks German may be a Swiss. A person whose native tongue is Spanish may belong to any one of a dozen nations. Descent, furthermore, is not the determining factor in nationality, or there would be—to mention a single instance—no American nation. Here, as in Europe, nationalism is ultimately resolved into little more than the feelings of a people. Men who declare themselves a nation are one; a nation is said to be self-determined. In more recent centuries there has been a tendency for every nation to demand a government of its own, to insist on being also a state. This sort of nationalism, however, is a late development; it does not appear in the early centuries of European history. The Romans, though quite familiar with the territorial state, had no concept of the national state. To them a nation (*natio*) was merely a people whose common origin was indicated by a common custom which had nothing to do with political status or aspiration. Therefore, when nations are referred to in the chapters immediately following, the term should be understood thus vaguely—as having no significance other than what it had for the Romans.

The word "race" has a very different meaning. A man may change his state by moving away from it, or his nation by transferring his affections; but he cannot change his race, for that is born with him. Properly understood, a race is a people marked off from others by hereditary characteristics—for instance, the black skin of the Negro. Although, up to a certain point, color is a useful guide in identifying race, it utterly fails when we come to consider the white inhabitants of Europe. The question of primary interest to us is whether these peoples can be classified in distinct races according to some other scheme. *Alleged races of Europe*

It is still the confirmed habit of many authors to speak of a Latin, Celtic, Slavic, Germanic, or even an Anglo-Saxon race. Yet such differentiation is based on language; and language, however significant in the history of civilization, is not inherited. We cannot be safe in assuming that two groups were related by blood descent because they spoke kindred tongues; there are too many known instances of a population that changed its language as the result of conquest or intermarriage. So, of more recent years, it has become fashionable to divide Europeans into other races—such as Mediterranean, Alpine, and Nordic. Men of the first type are short and slender, with dark complexions, black eyes, and skulls that measure more from back to front than from side to side. Those of the second have medium complexions, brown eyes, round heads, and thick-set frames. The Nordics are tall, fair, blue-eyed, and, like the first group, long-headed. As a matter of fact, a traveler crossing the continent of Europe from south to north can readily perceive these three types predominating in the regions for which they are named. But are they, as a popular school of writers would have us believe, the three fundamental races of Europe through whose antagonisms and interminglings the entire history of the western world can best be explained?

The more closely that theory is examined, the weaker it appears. In the first place, it rests almost solely on modern observation of physical characteristics and takes for granted the primitive invasion of the continent by three races bearing those characteristics. Aside from a few scattered bones and certain vague remarks by ancient authors, we have no evidence concerning the appearance of early European peoples. Secondly, the theory assumes that stature, complexion, skull-formation, and the like are purely hereditary. But this is denied by many scientists, who point out that climate, diet, and other environmental factors may produce radical alterations of *Race and culture* human physique within a relatively short period. Thirdly, the selection of three races, as set forth above, is quite arbitrary from the mathematical point of view. People classified according to one pair of opposites—e.g., tall and short—fall into two groups. If a second test is then applied—such as complexion—four groups are defined. And as each added distinction doubles the number, five tests result in thirty-two groups. Of all these, which are the original races and which are mixtures?

Although there obviously are superior breeds of men, as there are of domestic animals, we cannot in the former case be sure how the better strains were produced. Presumably they are all the result of intermixture. As far as the known history of Europe is concerned, the biologically pure race is a figment of the imagination—and so is the alleged relation between a particular set of physical characteristics and various intellectual, spiritual, or moral traits. Even if we admit that certain features of coloring and bone-formation are the true marks of an original race, we are still left to wonder precisely what they may have to do with political genius, commercial shrewdness, artistic skill, or any of the other qualities that make a people great. The historian's pre-eminent task, at any rate, is to deal with cultures; for the relative superiority of a people can be judged only from what it has accomplished.

CHAPTER I

The Roman World

1. GOVERNMENT AND LAW

Our study of European history begins with the Roman power at its height. This starting-point is convenient for several reasons. Although it excludes direct consideration of the more ancient period, it enables us to review the developments of that period in their culminating stage—when for the first time the entire Mediterranean world was organized as a political unit. And for the ensuing age such a review is of prime importance. To understand the salient features of European history for the next thousand years and more, the student must have a knowledge of the Roman Empire and its civilization.

The germ from which the Roman Empire sprang was a settlement of Latin-speaking people on the Tiber in Italy. To the contemporary Greeks these early Romans could have appeared hardly more than a rude farmerfolk. Yet, from the time we first hear of them, they displayed a surpassing genius for military and political organization. By the end of the third century B.C. the Romans had secured undisputed control of the Italian peninsula; within another hundred years they had conquered Spain, northern Africa, and southern Gaul. Being drawn into the troubled waters of the east, the Romans then crushed the monarchies of Syria and Macedon, made Egypt a protectorate, and so rounded out their dominion of the Mediterranean shores. Most of the territories that were to comprise the Roman Empire were thus in some fashion brought together, but their integration was a long and troublesome process.

Rome, now commanding a host of allied and subject peoples, remained essentially what it had been before—a city-state on the Tiber, formally styled the republic (*res publica*, or commonwealth). Its citizens were the privileged body of Italians who alone enjoyed equal rights under the

5

Roman law, and upon whom in theory the government ultimately depended. Actually, the effective power was restricted to the senatorial aristocracy, the few families who, by controlling the elections, named the magistrates and dictated their policies. The supreme direction of the republic—civil, military, and religious—was called the *imperium* (whence eventually our word "empire"), but as yet it was held by a group of officials styled consuls and prætors. Some of them ruled at home; others administered outlying regions (*provinciæ*, provinces) designated by the senate. For a long time the ancient constitution had worked efficiently, as the amazing success of the republic bore witness; then, in the closing century of the pre-Christian era, the system broke down. Devised for a small city-state, it proved inadequate for the Mediterranean world.

The principate of Augustus

Nearly a hundred years of political disorder, marked by a bitter conflict between the old senatorial aristocracy and its popular opponents, ended with a new settlement carried out by Augustus. At least officially, he avoided the precedent set by his uncle, Julius Cæsar. The latter, after conquering Gaul, had championed the popular cause against the senate and so gained the life dictatorship, which was virtually monarchy without a royal crown. Augustus made it appear that he preferred a political compromise—joint rule by the senate and himself, the first man (*princeps*, eventually "prince") of the state. But newly discovered records show that, in case of conflict, Augustus exercised supreme authority and tended to become more, rather than less, autocratic. His régime, though referred to by modern historians as the empire, is more properly called the principate, for as yet the title *imperator* was little more than the designation of a victorious general.

Theoretically, therefore, the administration of Augustus made no sudden change with the past; the republic remained unaltered, except that it now had a principal magistrate and commander-in-chief elected for life. The senate was kept, not merely as an order of supreme social honor, but as a governing council for the city of Rome and for those of the provinces that required no large body of troops. The highest officials, both civil and military, were normally landed aristocrats. For a while they were still chosen by the ancient assemblies, which also voted formal laws; later these functions in one way or another came to be exercised by the senate and the *princeps*. Although Roman citizenship thus lost much of its political significance, in other respects it continued to be a valuable privilege, the more highly prized because Augustus opposed any lavish extension of the right into the provinces. And since membership in the Roman legions had always been restricted to citizens, this policy placed an inevitable check on territorial expansion. Failing to secure the line of the Elbe, Augustus made the Rhine and the Danube his northern defense. To the east the Parthians were held along the upper Euphrates and the edge of the Arabian desert. In Africa the Sahara provided a natural frontier to the south. These were to remain the principal boundaries of the Roman Empire until its collapse in the fifth century.

Another primary concern of Augustus was the municipal system, on which the whole imperial structure rested. Roman dominion had never been a matter of sheer military occupation. First in Italy and then outside it, the Romans had extended their sovereignty by means of perpetual leagues. Each city-state, while recognizing the superior authority of Rome in some particulars, remained autonomous in all else. Except as specified by solemn treaty, every community was free to govern itself and to develop its own native institutions. Following what had already become an established Roman policy, Augustus now sought, as rapidly as was practical, to organize new city-states throughout all the more backward territories. In the east the Romans generally constructed their municipalities after Greek models, merely continuing the process of Hellenization begun by Alexander the Great. In the west, where Roman dominion had been imposed on more barbarous countries, the urban plan together with the civilization that accompanied it was thoroughly Latin. By the opening of the Christian era the shores of Gaul, Spain, and Africa were dotted with flourishing colonies of Italian settlers and with native communities that rivaled them in prosperity and culture. To advance this work of Romanization to the frontiers on the north and south continued to be a primary object of the principate.

The rule of Augustus has been emphasized in the foregoing pages because it was one of the great political successes in history. Two hundred years after his death the principate remained very much as he had designed it. But with the passage of time the power of the senate had come, more and more obviously, to be overshadowed by that of the *princeps*. To the unforgiving remnant of the old aristocracy this was tyranny and usurpation. As the honor passed from Augustus to unpopular members of his house, the ancient feud blazed up again and various Cæsars wreaked their vengeance in bloody deeds which famous historians have delighted to recount. Such narratives are now being corrected by the study of more sober records that reveal a smoothly running government controlled by experts, and millions of provincials thankful to it for the boon of an undisturbed life. To the Mediterranean world at large the prince who assured the blessings of the great Roman peace was indeed the master of the state. The opposition of a few senatorial families led merely to their extermination and to the advancement of more subservient men to fill the gaps in the ranks. By the second century after Christ the transformation was complete. Public opinion had recognized the prince as the actual ruler of the whole Roman territory; the title *imperator*, like the names Cæsar and Augustus, had come to mean "emperor."

Even the problem of the succession now appeared to have been solved.

Succession to the principate

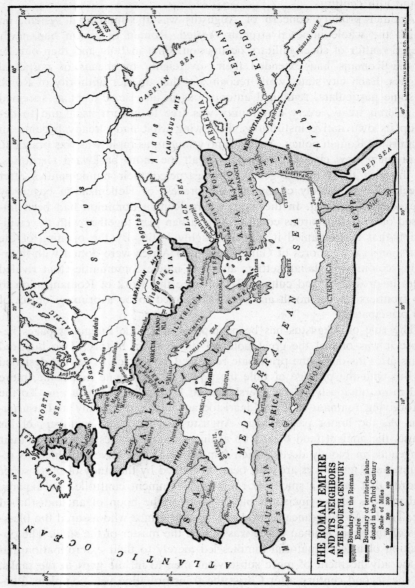

THE ROMAN EMPIRE
AND ITS NEIGHBORS
IN THE FOURTH CENTURY

Boundary of the Roman
Empire
Boundary of territories aban-
doned in the Third Century

Scale of Miles
0   100 200 300 400 500

MAP II.

In 68, on the death of Nero without heirs, the senate had shown itself incompetent to meet such an emergency, merely ratifying whatever nomination was made by the nearest military force and thereby encouraging the various armies to advance on Rome in support of their rival candidates. In 96, however, the senate took advantage of a similar opportunity to install a worthy man named Nerva. He designated the illustrious Trajan as his heir and successor; and according to the same plan Trajan was followed by Hadrian, Antoninus Pius, and Marcus Aurelius (d. 180). These were the five "good emperors," under whom the Roman world enjoyed unbroken calm for over seventy years.

Judged by our best historical standards, the empire of the second century was in a healthful condition. Its military system, especially to modern eyes, seems a marvel of efficiency; for, without the mechanical aids of today, it kept an enormous expanse of territory in a peace that has since remained proverbial. Thanks to the virtually continuous efforts of the emperors, the frontiers had been greatly strengthened since the time of Augustus. Tremendous lines of fortification were thrown across wild regions where neither desert nor river afforded adequate protection—as in the newly acquired provinces of Britain and Dacia, and in Germany, to connect the Rhine and the Danube (see Map II). Along the frontiers were distributed small fortresses (*castella*) held by permanent garrisons, and at wider intervals the great legionary camps (*castra*), which often attracted a considerable urban population. In the earlier period most of this construction had been of earth and timber, but in the course of time masonry was substituted—of such massive strength that much of it has lasted even to our own day. Of equal strength and of much greater utility were the paved roads that paralleled the frontiers and connected them with the great cities of the interior. Primarily designed to facilitate the movement of troops and the transport of supplies, these highways also served as official lines of communication. By means of post-horses stationed at regular intervals, imperial messengers carried dispatches and reports at the highest speed then attainable. *The empire in the second century*

To defend what had come to be the established boundaries of the empire, there were upwards of thirty legions, each of which, containing about five thousand men, bore a peculiar designation and was assigned to a particular region. The legionaries, though still required to be Roman citizens, were now professional soldiers who served for twenty-five years or so in return for regular pay, a share of captured booty, and a pension on retirement. Besides, there were the auxiliary divisions (*auxilia*), which were of about the same strength and included the same kind of troops—except for the technical requirement of Roman citizenship, which auxiliaries commonly acquired on being discharged. Virtually the entire force was infantry, for only small units fought as light-armed cavalry. The imperial soldier thus *The army* continued to resemble his republican predecessor. Next his skin he wore a woolen tunic and military boots, which in a northern climate were supplemented by trousers of barbarian pattern. For defensive armor he was supplied with a helmet and cuirass. His weapons consisted of a spear, either for thrusting or for hurling, a sword, and a dagger. Discipline was well maintained even during the long intervals of peace. When not engaged in drill or maneuvers, he was employed at useful construction. For many of its roads, as well as for most of its fortifications, the empire was indebted to the army.

The municipal system　　Further evidence of Roman vigor in the second century is provided by the remains of countless cities in what had recently been semi-barbarous country. Throughout the west in particular the progressive extension of the city system marked an increasing population and an advancing frontier of civilization. According to the normal pattern, the *civitas* was not precisely a city in our sense of the word, but a city-state that included a considerable territory about an urban center (*urbs*). Its governing body was a miniature senate, usually termed *curia*, which elected the necessary magistrates from its own number. Every citizen of the local community, on acquiring a certain amount of property, was officially enrolled in the list of *curiales*, persons eligible for membership in the *curia* and so for other political honors. During the second century, as is attested by many inscriptions, such rank was highly prized and competition for city offices remained keen, although to hold one might entail the expenditure of a small fortune. The social importance of this municipal aristocracy—the curial class of the west together with its eastern counterpart—can hardly be exaggerated. Constantly increased by the rise of successful men from below, it constituted a sort of imperial bourgeoisie, from which the more exalted orders of the state were in turn recruited.

Administration and finance　　It is characteristic of the age that four of the "good emperors" were by origin Spaniards, and under their rule, very naturally, provincials more and more came to enjoy equality with Italians. By the time of Marcus Aurelius full Roman rights had been granted to better-class communities on all sides. Nothing remained for his successors but the logical completion of a system under which every free inhabitant might be a citizen both of the empire and of his local municipality. Through a similar development the senatorial order became imperial in scope, to include the more distinguished families of provincial cities as well as the old Italian aristocracy. Senators were induced to accept not only high military commands but also great administrative offices in the gift of the prince, such as memberships on the boards that looked after the supplying of the capital with food and water. Financial and secretarial duties in connection with the government had earlier been performed by freedmen of the imperial household. Now, on the contrary, positions of this sort were regularly held by equestrians (*equites*), gentlemen of less than senatorial rank who enjoyed a high property qualification. The civil service, in other words, had become an honorable career—one that, as in a modern state, attracted a host of loyal and efficient subordinates. Long past were the days when any soldier-politician of the republic was thought fit to rule a conquered province.

The substitution of professional for amateur administrators naturally involved the payment of many more salaries by the state. But the provincials were only too glad to support an honest government; and as general prosperity seemed to accompany the improvement of conditions, the emperors did not have to worry about ways and means. Taxation remained somewhat haphazard, being still determined by ancient distinctions among the provinces and among their constituent communities. Some sort of impost was commonly assessed on the land, and occasionally a poll tax or personal-property tax on the inhabitants. Special contributions might be taken from particular trades or professions, and there were numerous indirect taxes, such as customs on goods carried across certain boundaries or brought by ship to certain ports. Besides, every city had the right of charging toll on articles imported for sale within its limits and of using the proceeds for the maintenance of local government. The financial administration of the principate was assuredly a great improvement over that of the republic; yet it continued to lack all systematic planning, for even the best statesmen of that day had little understanding of economic principles.

For a truly great contribution of the Romans we must turn from the realm of finance to that of law. The original law of the republic was a traditional system that applied only to Roman citizens. It protected relatively few rights and for every legal action prescribed a rigid set of forms. Inevitably, as Rome became the metropolis of the Mediterranean world, the courts were led to supplement the ancient law of citizens (*ius civile*) with a new and more flexible law of non-citizens (*ius gentium*). The latter, in particular, governed the contractual relationships of men from all countries and so came to include many sensible provisions with regard to conveyance, partnership, marriage, testamentary succession, and the like. All such amendment was regularly announced in a formal edict by the prætor who held jurisdiction over foreigners at Rome. And as similar edicts were promulgated by the other prætors for the benefit of citizens, the *ius civile* gradually took over many of the speedy and effective remedies that had characterized the *ius gentium*. Although the republican magistrates lost much of their old authority under the principate, the development of the law by prætorian edict was vigorously continued—to culminate in Hadrian's official summary, which could be altered by the emperor alone.

The amalgamation of the *ius civile* and the *ius gentium* was further aided by the rapid extension of Roman citizenship throughout the empire and by the growing devotion of the educated class to the cosmopolitan ideals of

Law and jurisprudence

Stoicism.[1] According to that philosophy, the dictates of reason constituted a natural law (*ius naturale*), morally binding on all men and therefore superior to the enactments of a particular state. But since the *ius gentium* was based on the customs of various peoples, might it not be considered a body of equity from which the *ius civile* could draw continuous improvement? Such, at any rate, became the general conviction of the jurists, the men that made a profession of studying and teaching the science of law. In the ordinary Roman trial the judge (*iudex*) was a private citizen who, by the agreement of the two parties, was supposed to determine the facts and render a decision to comply with the law as previously stated by the magistrate. Often, however, it proved very difficult to apply the known precedents to the case in hand, and the judge would then call upon a jurist for expert advice. At first a consultant of this kind had no official standing; later, under the principate, the government came to designate certain jurists whose opinions, perforce asked in many cases, should be authoritative. The institution was remarkably successful; for it permitted the law, without interruption of its practical working, to be brought into harmony with theoretical principles. Among the achievements of the ancient world none has had a greater or a better-merited permanence.

2. GRÆCO-ROMAN CULTURE

The Latin west and the Greek east

A fact of prime significance for the cultural development of mediæval Europe was the distinction between the eastern and western halves of the Roman Empire. In the latter the extension of Roman dominion generally implied the Latinization of the inhabitants. Throughout Illyricum, the upper Danubian provinces, Gaul, Spain, northern Africa, Britain, and all Italy, except the Greek colonies of the south, Latin became the ordinary speech of the educated classes. And together with the language, they tended to acquire an outlook on life, a mental discipline, a mold of character, that can only be described as Roman. It should, however, be remembered that the Greeks of southern Italy had originally taught the Romans the elements of civilization and that, as long as the Roman Empire persisted, it remained under direct Greek influence. Further description of Latin culture may therefore be postponed until the nature of that influence is better understood.

To the deathless glory of ancient Greece no feeble tribute need be attempted in these pages. By the time of the principate the classic age of Hellenism was long past; the old homeland was depopulated; Athens had yielded pre-eminence in art and letters to the new-grown cities of Syria and Egypt. Those countries, ever since the triumphant campaigns of Alexander, had been progressively Hellenized. While much of the peasant population might retain its native speech and custom, the urban aristocracy became

---

[1] See below, pp. 17-18.

Greek. To be accepted by educated persons, whatever their descent, books had to be written in Greek; ideas had to conform to Greek habits of thought; works of art had to follow the Greek canons of taste. And these æsthetic and intellectual standards were left unchanged by the Romans, who had little to teach the easterners except in matters legal and military.

Numberless critics have commented on the exquisite beauty—a beauty **Sculpture** of grace and simplicity—achieved by the earlier Greeks, whether they wrought in words or in marble. Thus the sculptors of ancient Athens excelled in depicting humanity at its noblest. Avoiding the imperfections of the individual, they sought to represent ideal persons, and did so with a magic touch that the subsequent world has never quite recovered. But though the artists of the Hellenistic age—the period following Alexander—abandoned the antique standards of beauty, they maintained great skill with less exalted themes, such as the pathetic and the comic; and they brought portrait sculpture to a new height of perfection. The continued excellence of this art may be judged from the statues of the early Roman emperors, which were presumably by Greek hands. For in such work —as in the engraving of gems, the designing of coins, the carving of reliefs, or any of the finer crafts—the supremacy of the Greeks was recognized throughout the Mediterranean world. To a certain degree the same truth holds in the sphere of architecture; yet in it the Romans made original contributions of lasting importance.

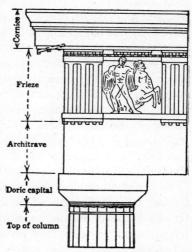

FIG. 1. Greek Entablature.

The classic architecture of ancient Greece is best exemplified by the **Archi-** Doric temple, and pre-eminently by the Parthenon of Athens. There the **tecture** primary unit of construction is a horizontal slab, or architrave, supported by columns. In the Doric temple the architrave bears a decorative frieze with a projecting cornice above it, and these three parts are together called an entablature (see Figure 1). Greek buildings of the Hellenistic period remained structurally the same, though more elaborate capitals came to be used on the columns. The Ionian order is characterized by volutes at the corners of the capital; the Corinthian by a larger capital decorated with acanthus leaves. But the Corinthian style was not invented till late and was popular mainly in the west. For the Romans, evidently, the loveliness of the Parthenon had no appeal. Their temples, though constructed on the

Greek plan, were chiefly noteworthy for magnificence of size and ornamentation. All too often the Roman taste preferred the florid and the pretentious, was willing to combine incongruous elements for the sake of a grandiose effect. These failings are especially prominent in the great monuments erected by the later emperors.

It is not such buildings that entitle the Romans to distinguished rank in the history of architecture. Rather it is their more utilitarian works—forts, aqueducts, amphitheaters, basilicas, and the like—in which for the first time the principles of arch-construction were well developed. Upon these principles a number of great architectural styles were to be evolved by later generations. Yet to the Romans of the early empire, apparently, a mere arch was not a thing of beauty. When putting up a bridge, they thought of it as no more than a useful piece of masonry, and so left the arches plain—and to our eyes charming (see Plate II, Pont du Gard). But when they employed the same structural method in a more formal edifice, they sought to embellish the exterior by framing the arches with quite unnecessary columns and entablatures superficially attached to the walls. In the famous Colosseum (Plate II), for example, the three tiers of arches are thus set off by the Doric, Ionian, and Corinthian orders one over the other —a bit of ostentation never found in the works of ancient Greece. And similar criticism may be applied to the Roman triumphal arches.

Greek literature and science

In imaginative literature, as in the other Greek arts, there had been a distinct falling-off even before the advent of the conquering Romans. The famous books of antiquity continued to be studied with passionate zeal, but too commonly without the production of anything that might in turn deserve such study. So, in the field of poetic composition, it is chiefly the preservation of the old classics for which we have to thank the Greeks of the Hellenistic age. Prose writing, on the other hand, remained noteworthy, and with the establishment of the principate gained actual brilliance. The period from Nero to Marcus Aurelius (58-180) witnessed the careers of Dio Chrysostom, rhetorician and moralist; Plutarch, author of the enormously popular *Parallel Lives*; Arrian, scholarly biographer of Alexander the Great; and Lucian, a clever and original satirist. And although the schools of philosophy produced no such towering genius as Plato, they were still thronged with students who not infrequently made important contributions to intellectual life.

For the majority of educated men philosophy retained its traditional interest—as a system of thought purporting to explain the universe and man's place in it. Yet in the later age an increasing number of scholars turned their attention to that phase of the ancient study which we know as science. The change was largely due to the influence of Aristotle who, in preference to metaphysical speculation, had come to emphasize the observation of natural phenomena and the formulation of general principles from the data thus learned. He had produced a large number of important books; not only on the more usual divisions of philosophy, but also on what we should classify as psychology, literature, government, physics, and biology. Particularly in his work on the last of these subjects Aristotle approached the modern understanding of scientific method—to show that science is valid only in so far as its generalizations are verified and cannot advance without fresh research. It was not his fault that later scholars, regarding the master's words with exaggerated reverence, failed to continue what he had merely begun. In certain fields, nevertheless, admirable results were still achieved.

The Greeks had long excelled in mathematics. Their earlier philosophers had all been interested in problems of arithmetic and geometry, and had demonstrated the fundamental importance of mathematical theory in music and astronomy. Throughout such investigations the Greeks were handicapped by the fact that, like the Romans after them, they used letters for numerals and without regard to place value. The meaning of this remark will be quite evident to anyone who writes a series of Roman numerals in a column and then tries to add them—or, better still, tries to multiply or divide one Roman number by another. Yet the Greeks were able to do all this with apparent ease, and we are thus led to the conclusion that for routine work they commonly employed some device like the abacus, which had long been familiar to the merchants of both Asia and Europe. By means of counters arranged in columns to represent units, tens, hundreds, and the like, arithmetical computation was greatly facilitated; for the inconvenient numerals could be disregarded until it became time to set down the result.

Mathematics: Ptolemy

However this may be, the triumphant advance of Greek mathematics was continued throughout the Hellenistic period, as is proved by the writings of Euclid, Aristarchus, Eratosthenes, Archimedes, Apollonius, Hipparchus, and others in the third and second centuries B.C. Adding the first principles of trigonometry to an exhaustive treatment of geometry, they applied their knowledge, not only to such practical arts as mechanics and surveying, but also to a description of the physical universe. The earth, they agreed, was round and, like the sun and the planets, was contained in the sphere of the fixed stars. With regard to the center of this revolving universe, on the contrary, there was dispute. The unorthodox Aristarchus tried to prove that it was the sun; Hipparchus defended the traditional opinion that it was the earth. And since the latter theory, by much ingenious figuring, was made to explain the observed facts, it came to be accepted by Ptolemy, the last great mathematician of the ancient world. His principal book, written about A.D. 150, combined the best work of his predecessors on astronomy and added much that was original, including a masterly exposition of trigonometry. The *Almagest*, as this book came to be called by the Arabs, was to remain a standard text for over a thousand years. In his *Geography*, furthermore, Ptolemy mapped the known earth by means of circles designating latitude and longitude—a practice that, as will be seen below, greatly influenced the cartographers of the later Middle Ages.

Comparable service to medicine was rendered by Galen, a native of Pergamon contemporary with Ptolemy. Galen, too, wrote towards the close of a long and honorable tradition; for Greek medicine had been illustrious since the time of Hippocrates, the late fifth century B.C. From that day to this the Hippocratic writings—partly by the master, partly by followers— have enjoyed high renown for their sanity and fine ideals. The older physicians, however, generally suffered from a lack of technical information; and this failing was in some part corrected by the medical schools of the Hellenistic age, which extended the list of useful drugs and, through dissection, greatly advanced the science of anatomy. Thus, when Galen wrote his monumental treatise, he could incorporate a relatively large amount of new material. To the modern student, of course, Galen's physiology appears absurd—with its acceptance of three spirits (physical, animal, and natural) resident in the brain, heart, and liver, and of four humors (blood, phlegm, yellow bile, and black bile) giving rise to the sanguine, phlegmatic, choleric, and melancholic temperaments. Yet Galen had an encyclopædic knowledge of medical practice and, for his age, an excellent understanding of the pertinent sciences. Even the mystic reverence for a divine plan that pervades his writing recommended it the more strongly to the learned world of the next fifteen centuries.

Music among the Greeks was at once a science and an art. From the former point of view, as already remarked, it could be considered a branch of mathematics; for scholars had long known that musical tones could be arranged in an arithmetical series according to the lengths of strings that were vibrated or of pipes that were blown through. Furthermore, the Greek study of music involved an elaborate theory of æsthetics—a philosophic appraisal of the various emotions customarily evoked by various kinds of singing or playing. The subject is a highly technical one which remains somewhat controversial. Here it may be passed over with the statement of a very simple conclusion. All musical composition in the Græco-Roman world was based, not on the sounding of different notes simultaneously, but on the sounding of individual notes in sequence. The stringed instruments in common use included the harp, the lyre, and the cither; the wind instruments a variety of oboes, flutes, and horns, as well as a sort of pipe-organ in which water was used to compress the air. Although on some of these instruments it was quite possible to sound more than one note at a time, such was not the regular practice. Only a single melody, indeed, would be played by an entire orchestra, or sung by an entire chorus. The harmony that delighted the Greek was a pattern of successive tones; what we call harmony would have seemed to him a mere chaos of noise.

In richness of content as in artistic perfection Greek literature is unquestionably superior to the Latin. Indeed, the Romans generally admitted that in the finest of composition the Greeks remained their masters. Nevertheless, by the time of the principate, Latin had been developed into one of the world's great literary languages. Such poets as Catullus, Horace, Vergil, and Ovid, while borrowing their meters from Greece, produced immortal verse. And Latin prose attained classic excellence in the work of Cæsar, Cicero, Sallust, Livy, and Seneca. During the period between Nero and Marcus Aurelius poetry somewhat declined, being represented by two specialized forms: the light epigrams of Martial and the heavy satires of Juvenal. But the earlier standard of prose writing was well maintained in the elegantly turned letters of Pliny the Younger, Quintilian's famous book on rhetoric, the popular *Lives of the Cæsars* by Suetonius, and the distinguished works of Tacitus.

As a whole, this literature clearly displays the Latin genius for the practical. The Romans were always more successful in discussion of law, politics, and morals than in the loftier flights of imaginative thought. Compared with the Greeks, they produced little great poetry. The best of their historians cannot be ranked with Thucydides. They contributed nothing to mathematics or natural science. The only philosophy to be adopted by many Latin writers was the later Stoicism, which, divorced from metaphysical argument, provided the educated Roman with a sort of ethical religion. The keynote in the Stoic doctrine is will power—self-control through reason, the divine element implanted in man by the Creator. All men, having in this respect the same original endowment, are equally the sons of God and so brothers to one another. The parts assigned them in the world's drama may vary, but human character remains constant. If a man is true to his real self, he is true to nature; he will then understand the divine order that governs the universe and will ask no other reward.

Stoic ideas gained widespread popularity through the writings of Cicero and Seneca, and, as we have seen, came to pervade the works of the jurists. But the two best expositions of western Stoicism are the *Discourses* of Epictetus, a slave at the court of Nero, and the *Meditations* of the emperor Marcus Aurelius—both of which, very significantly, were written in Greek. All things, says Epictetus[2] are of two sorts: those which are in our power and those which are not. Outside our power are worldly fame and fortune —wealth, office, family, even our bodies. He who concentrates his devotion on such matters is truly the slave, for he is always at the behest of others. Our reason, on the contrary, is our own. The free man is one who has steeled himself to cherish only that which he can himself control, for he is beyond all hurt. "I must die. But must I die groaning? I must be imprisoned.

[2] *Discourses*, bk. i, ch. i.

But must I whine as well? I must suffer exile. Can anyone hinder me from going with a smile, with a good courage, and at peace?"

Epictetus was a slave and a cripple, but he is quoted by the emperor Marcus Aurelius,[3] who tells himself: "You are a little soul burdened with a corpse." A spider, he meditates, is vastly proud of itself when it has caught a fly; one type of man when he has netted a small fish; another—referring to one of his own campaigns—when he has routed the Sarmatians. Marcus reminds himself that all things happen in accord with universal nature; that before long he, like Hadrian and Augustus, will be nothing. And he concludes: "Let it be your hourly care to do stoutly what your hand finds to do, as becomes a man and a Roman." Such was the creed of the men who ruled imperial Rome while it was at its height. But could that creed survive in an age of mounting ignorance and despair?

3. MATERIAL CONDITIONS OF LIFE

The necessities of life:

In the present connection it is not intended to give a comprehensive sketch of how men lived in the ancient world, but merely to note certain elementary facts that may serve to introduce the economic history of the Middle Ages. Our attention will therefore be concentrated on the western provinces and, within them, on such aspects of human existence as were of general significance. The study of a nation's artistic and intellectual accomplishments necessarily deals with the work of the few rather than of the many. The study of a nation's wealth, on the contrary, must chiefly consider the needs and activities of the masses. In seeking to determine the factors that truly governed Roman life, we may well begin by asking what most people had to have.

Food and drink

Then as now the prime necessity was food and, from the modern point of view, the average Roman demanded little. His staple article of diet was bread—either a baked loaf of wheaten flour or, in the case of the very poor, a meal-cake of a cheaper grain like spelt or barley. Meat he could afford to have only rarely, and then it was likely to be pork rather than beef or mutton. But fish—including eels, mussels, and the like—were comparatively plentiful, as were pigeons, chickens, and other domestic fowls. Although milk was hard to transport and preserve, cheese of one kind or another was to be had everywhere. Butter was almost never used by the Mediterranean peoples who, instead, consumed enormous quantities of olive oil. Among the commoner vegetables were peas, beans, lentils, onions, garlic, cabbage, pumpkins, turnips, and other edible roots. Various fruits were cultivated—apples, pears, plums, cherries, peaches, figs, and grapes—together with walnuts, hazelnuts, chestnuts, and almonds. Salads, particularly lettuce and chicory, were in good demand. Honey was the universal sweetening and such native seeds as mustard, poppy, and anise were avail-

[3] *Meditations*, iv, 41; x, 10; ix, 29; viii, 5; ii, 5.

able for seasoning, as well as salt. Everyone, finally, could drink at least some grade of wine, often mixing it with water.

Among all classes in the Roman Empire the standard article of dress was **Dress** the tunic (see Figure 2), which was worn next the skin—with due allowance for very scanty underclothing. The latter, especially when designed for feminine use, might be of linen; but cotton and silk were considered luxurious fabrics of no practical worth. The tunic was regularly made of wool, and so were all outer garments. There was, for example, the toga, a kind of ceremonial blanket that was draped across a man's shoulders to hang in conventional folds. No Roman gentleman would be seen on the street without his toga, but he quickly discarded it on reaching home and thenceforth appeared in his tunic like anybody else. For the sake of warmth he might put on another tunic or a heavy mantle, perhaps fitted with a hood as protection against the weather. Over a short undertunic the Roman woman wore a second and more ample tunic, which in the case of a matron became the dignified *stola* —a sweeping robe that was gathered at the waist by a girdle (see Figure 5).

So far as costume was concerned, the rich were thus left to be distinguished from the poor by the quality of the cloth, the gracefulness of its cut, and, we may suspect, by its rela-

FIG. 2.   Roman Wearing a Tunic.

tive cleanliness. The masses commonly dressed in coarse homespun of a naturally dark wool that would not easily show dirt. The superior person, on the contrary, had to dress in fine white wool, and this—in the absence of good soap and other domestic facilities—meant that his clothes made frequent trips to the cleaner for rinsing, beating, fulling, and pressing. Dyed stuffs, it will be noted, were little used. Only high officials and noblemen were permitted to adorn their tunics with "purple" (probably crimson) stripes. And although bright-colored robes might be thought proper at a fashionable banquet, such articles were in a class with the embroideries, golden ornaments, gems, and perfumes that could be afforded by none but the very wealthy. It may be added that, while the toga was supposed to be accompanied with leather shoes, ordinary footwear consisted of sandals and slippers or, among peasants and laborers, of wooden clogs; and that only such people as worked in sun and rain commonly wore hats.

With regard to the homes of the greater Romans we are very well informed. Thanks to actual remains, we can be quite familiar with a town house of the better sort in Italy. Largely built of stone, brick, or concrete, it would compare favorably with any modern structure of the same size. It would have a good tile roof and solid walls and pavements, often adorned with mosaic or fresco. Though devoid of glass windows, it would be excellently fitted with doors and shutters. In addition to sleeping-rooms and

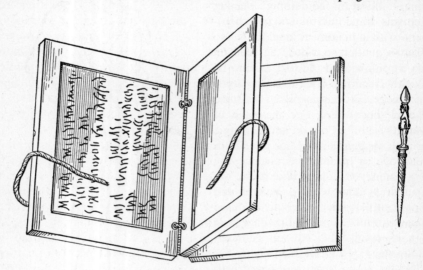

FIG. 3.   Wax Tablets and Stylus.

sun-porches, usually on an upper floor, there would be a hall, reception room, courtyard, dining-room, kitchen, bath, and latrine. Rain-water, to supplement what was furnished by the local aqueducts, would be collected in a cistern. Heat would be supplied by movable stoves for burning charcoal; light by the simple lamps of antiquity—mere dishes of oil with perforated covers through which wicks could be inserted. Ovens and fireplaces for cooking would be found in the kitchen, as well as a variety of pots, pans, and utensils, whether of wood, earthenware, or metal. Plates, bowls, and goblets might be displayed on a sideboard or on shelves. An elaborate table equipment would hardly be needed, for all food was cut up and served by slaves; the diner merely had to use the fingers of one hand. Nor would much additional furniture be demanded; tables and couches for meals, chests and cabinets for storage, an occasional chair, and the necessary beds would about complete the list.

Among the more personal belongings to be found in any comfortable home would be a large assortment of toilet articles: mirrors, combs, scissors, razors, unguents, and the various other things needed for the customary bath. Available writing materials would include, for notes or brief messages, wax tablets and stylus (see Figure 3); for more permanent records, pens, ink, parchment, and papyrus. The pens would probably be pointed reeds rather than quills. Parchment was a specially prepared sheepskin, papyrus the pith of the Egyptian papyrus plant compressed into thin sheets. For keeping track of the time the householder would have to depend on a sundial or, for more general use, a water-clock. The latter was a simple device based on the same principle as the hour-glass: from one receptacle water was allowed to drip into another, on which the passage of time was indicated by a scale. The Roman and Greek practice, however, was to divide the day—i.e., the period between sunrise and sunset—into twelve hours, and the night similarly. So their hour was a variable quantity and the reading of their clock had to be corrected to accord with a change of season, as well as of temperature or barometric pressure. Yet, such as it was, the water-clock ranked high among the scientific contrivances of that day.

This description, of course, applies to the urban dwelling of a wealthy The life man, which he might duplicate, in so far as he could, for a residence in of the the country. Not many persons, we may be sure, could afford to live in poor such style. The average shopkeeper would be fortunate to have a separate house of his own. The bulk of the city population had rooms in tenements —mere cubicles in ramshackle buildings unprovided with heat, light, or other conveniences. But the typical member of the proletariat needed no more than a place to sleep in. He spent his days on the street, wore cast-off clothing, begged his food from a well-to-do patron or bought it for a few coppers from a sidewalk dealer, attended the free shows for recreation, and went to the public baths for relaxation if not for cleanliness. The life of the average peasant must have been infinitely harder. His food, since he produced it himself, may have been better, and he enjoyed the blessing of unlimited fresh air. To earn a livelihood, however, he had to work in the fields throughout the day, and his home was likely to be a mean hut, with walls and floors of pounded clay and with a roof of thatch. Even the small independent farmer could have possessed only what we should consider the most primitive of household necessities.

Having seen what the bulk of the people commonly used, we may now Methods turn to the question of how it was produced. Agriculture, for obvious of pro- reasons, was of first importance. To supply the armies, as well as the popu- duction lace of Rome and other cities, enormous quantities of grain had to be raised and regularly transported to the centers of distribution. By the second century a considerable portion of the necessary wheat was brought by ship from Egypt. But the demand was so great that the owners of fertile land throughout the western provinces continued to find a good profit in growing wheat, together with the oats and barley that were primarily used for feeding livestock. Olive groves, vineyards, and orchards also provided opportunities for the development of large-scale business, as did the pasturing of animals for the sake of wool, hides, and dairy produce. Market-gardening, bee-keeping, fishing, salt-working, and the raising of hogs and poultry flourished in the neighborhood of every large city. And beside these enterprises, which were mainly concerned with the production of food and clothing, may be mentioned those which had to do with the production of other raw materials: mining, lumbering, quarrying, and the like.

Agri-culture

Within the limitations imposed by primitive tools and hand labor, the methods of production were generally efficient. In some instances, notably the growing of olives and grapes, the technique has remained much the same down to the present. And if agriculture was usually unprogressive, it was not through lack of careful study; for this was the one phase of economics to which Roman writers devoted the greatest attention. In the raising of grain and various other crops the fundamental operation was of course plowing. Because most of the cultivated soil was light and dry, the ordinary plow of the Mediterranean countries was a simple iron blade attached to a wooden frame.[4] The wheeled plow, though mentioned by Latin authors, seems to have been used only in the northern provinces, where a heavier soil tended to prevail. In any case, traction would be supplied by yokes of oxen. Criss-cross plowing was generally preferred to harrowing and was followed by continuous hoeing—to prepare the ground for planting and, after the crop was up, to keep down weeds and conserve moisture. The grain, when ripe, was cut off with sickles, dried in the sun, thrown on a threshing floor to be beaten with sticks or trampled by animals, and finally separated from straw and chaff by being tossed into the wind.

The writers on agriculture well understood how to prevent the exhaustion of the soil by the spreading of manure, the plowing under of certain plants, or, to some extent, the rotating of crops. But in actual practice a much simpler process was almost universal. In any year half the arable land was allowed to lie fallow; that is to say, it was used for pasture with an occasional plowing to cover the weeds. Only in this way, apparently, could the productivity of a field be preserved; for compost and manure, however carefully they might be stored, were never available in large quantities. Hay was scarce and grain was expensive; merely to keep the necessary beasts alive, they had to be fed on twigs and fallen leaves. Large flocks of sheep, because of their destructive habits, were commonly pastured in

[4] See Plate XII. The plow here represented is of eleventh-century Italy, but it closely resembles that of antiquity. We are told that a similar plow is still used in Sardinia. Note the "tiller" to guide the plowshare.

regions unsuited to agriculture. Horses were little used except as mounts or for pulling light vehicles. The herding of cattle on a large scale remained unprofitable as long as they could not be fattened for the market. Goats, which would eat anything, were of slight value aside from their milk and wool. The pig was unique among domestic animals in being raised primarily for the sake of meat; the rest, however puny according to modern standards, were prized for other reasons. The result was a chronic shortage of livestock, which led to a chronic shortage of manure and a consequent restriction of crops—and so on round in a vicious circle.

Fig. 4.   Roman Flour
            Mill.

Fig. 5. Spinning with
Distaff and Spindle.

The secondary processes of manufacture tended to be equally primitive. **Common** We are told that the grain for the Roman populace was ground by water- **manu-** power in mills along the Tiber, but the ordinary flour-mill was a much **factures** simpler contrivance. Over a conical stone another stone, hollowed to fit rather tightly, was rotated by draft animals hitched to a shaft; the grain, poured through a hole in the upper stone, came out as flour in a groove about the lower (see Figure 4). Olives were pressed in somewhat the same way. Grapes were trodden by barefooted peasants, and the juice, collected in jars, was allowed to become wine by fermentation. Raw wool, after washing and carding, was twisted into thread by means of the age-old distaff and spindle[5] and was then woven into cloth on a hand loom. Throughout the building trades the Romans maintained the best traditions of the ancient world and, in certain respects, set new standards. Their carpentry was much the same as ours and was carried out with much the same tools, if we consider only those which the manual laborer commonly owns. A similar generalization holds for masonry and bricklaying; to some extent even for concrete-mixing—a technique which the Romans first adapted to construction on a large scale. In other industrial arts, notably

[5] See Figure 5; cf. Plate XIII.

those demanding a more delicate touch, they were likely to be surpassed by the Greeks.

Naviga-
tion

For example, it was Greek craftsmen who excelled in all the finer work of stone-carving, metal-working, gem-cutting, glass-making, ceramics, and the like. Nor had the Romans ever taken kindly to seafaring. Even after they had extended their empire round the Mediterranean, they left the Greeks to build and man the ships, to conduct most of the voyages, and so to dominate maritime trade. Ancient ships, it may be noted here, were of two principal kinds: galleys, which were long narrow boats propelled by oar and on that account used for swift transport as well as warfare, and the round sailing-vessels, which served as the ordinary means of carrying men, animals, and heavy cargoes. Navigation in such a ship, however, was very difficult except under favorable conditions. The fact that it was square-rigged—i.e., fitted with square sails which extended to equal distances on both sides of the mast—prevented its being effectively tacked against the wind. And since the magnetic compass was as yet unknown, mariners feared to lose sight of land. Even on the Mediterranean, therefore, it was customary to suspend all traffic during the winter months.

Engineer-
ing and
applied
science

Within the sphere of military and civil engineering the Romans had a better record. The skill with which they applied the principles of surveying is well attested by their highways, their fortifications, and their well-planned cities. Following the example of their predecessors, whether Greek or Etruscan, they were able to build sea-walls and lighthouses, shafts for mines, irrigation ditches, tunnels, canals, sewers, bridges, and other public works of considerable magnitude. They developed siegecraft to a point beyond which it could not be improved as long as it had to depend on wooden towers, scaling-ladders, battering-rams, catapults, and the like. Yet the scientific achievement implied by such engineering should not be exaggerated. The typical Roman aqueduct, for instance, demanded no more than a practical knowledge of hydraulics. Having figured the height at which the water had to be introduced for the maintenance of adequate pressure throughout a town, the Romans simply constructed an open channel to a higher source, tunneling hills and bridging valleys whenever necessary. While they may have understood the syphoning of a liquid in a sealed conduit, they had no means of applying the theory except when a pipe of lead could be used to carry water into a wealthy man's house. So it was with many other inventions. A system of central heating might be installed in a public bath or a palace; but the cost of an innovation like this was usually held to exceed its real worth. Accordingly the suction pump, the hydraulic screw, and the primitive steam-engine, though described in learned books, were never brought into common use.

The factor of decisive importance seems to have been the cheapness of human energy. Under the republic it had been possible, thanks to the sale

of captives in war, to develop large-scale projects by employing gangs of
slaves. Under the principate, as general peace made the cost of such gangs
prohibitive, the owners of great estates came to depend on *coloni*—theoretically free settlers who were willing to accept small plots of land in return
for part of the produce and, perhaps, a certain amount of labor. But it was
still customary for wealthy men to keep numerous slaves, who performed
all necessary tasks in the master's household—from scrubbing and cooking
to educating children and producing works of art. Therefore, in all the
trades that supplied the demand for luxurious articles the free artisan
could never escape the competition of slave labor. And the market for
whatever was consumed in large quantities by the masses was dominated
by landowners and contractors who could always hire unskilled workmen
at the level of mere subsistence. It was relatively unimportant whether the
employee cultivated grain, tended a vineyard, herded animals, dug in a
mine, manufactured brick, or wove cloth; he was apt to be an economic
dependent but one degree removed from slavery.

Cheap labor and its effect

To supplement our knowledge of applied science among the Romans,
we have, in addition to actual remains, various sculptured representations.
One of them shows a derrick, designed to hoist building materials by
means of a compound pulley; and for that reason it has been said to look
very modern. In this connection, however, we should note one significant
fact: the power for the derrick is supplied by men, presumably slaves,
working a treadmill. To the owners of the legs who revolved the circular
cage such employment was hardly superior to being driven like oxen.
And the average builder, we may be sure, would find little economic
advantage in thus "modernizing" his equipment. While most men had
nothing better to do than drag stones up an inclined ramp, why should he
bother with mechanical cranes? It was not until the later Middle Ages
that happier conditions came to prevail for the ordinary laborer.

CHAPTER II

The Decline of the Roman Empire

1. FROM PRINCIPATE TO ABSOLUTE MONARCHY

The Severi (193-235)

Even before the end of the second century the waning prosperity of the empire was indicated by reports of financial distress in certain municipalities and by the increasing difficulty of checking the barbarians on the northern frontier. To contemporaries these seemed minor troubles, but they were symptomatic of the desperate conditions to follow. Commodus, the unworthy son and designated heir of Marcus Aurelius, was murdered in 193, and the succession to the purple again became an ugly problem. In the armed conflict that ensued the victor proved to be an African general, Septimius Severus, who founded a short-lived dynasty ending in 235. One of the Severi, Caracalla, is famous for a decree extending Roman citizenship to virtually all free inhabitants of the empire—the formal culmination of a process begun long before. A much more significant change effected during the same period was the transformation of the principate into a military despotism. Terrorizing the senate into subservience, the Severi lavished money and privilege upon the army. High civil offices tended to be filled with soldiers, and their point of view determined the chief policies of state. Such an administration, it must be admitted, was not unjustified; the absolute necessity of strengthening the imperial defenses was soon to be fully appreciated. But the legions needed no encouragement in the belief that they were the masters of Rome. With no law governing the succession, every popular commander was a potential emperor awaiting a good opportunity for advancement. It is no wonder that assassination so often provided one.

Civil war (235-70)

When such a fate claimed the last of the Severi in 235, the result was a prolonged civil war in which none of the contestants seemed able to win a decisive victory. While one emperor held the city of Rome, others

26

dominated the provinces. And as the legions followed their champions to distant battlefields, the frontiers were left open to hordes of wandering barbarians. For the first time the Roman populace became familiar with tribal names that future centuries were to make increasingly formidable. Alamans and Franks seized coveted lands along the Rhine and carried their pillaging raids far into Gaul. Goths broke into the Danubian provinces, slew an emperor who tried to stop them, and, taking to the sea, looted the ancient cities of the Ægean. Meanwhile Roman dominion in Asia all but collapsed before the attack of a reconstituted Persian kingdom. Thus, by the second half of the third century, the Roman Empire had actually disintegrated. In the absence of any central authority, the provinces were organized into shifting groups under local chieftains—a condition resembling that which became chronic a century and a half later.

For the moment, however, the disorder was merely the prelude to a new era of stabilization. The work was begun by Aurelian, who rose from the ranks to be hailed as the Restorer of the Empire. In five short years (270-75) he disposed of all rival princes and re-established the old frontiers, except that he abandoned to the barbarians all land to the north and east of the Rhine and the Danube (see Map II). Aurelian's murder by a petty conspirator was a calamity that threatened once more to plunge the world into chaos; fortunately, another soldier-emperor soon took up the unfinished task and brought it to a successful conclusion. This was Diocletian, a Dalmatian of humble birth, who attained the purple in 284 and ruled without serious opposition until 305, when he abdicated. His enactments, formally recognizing the principle of absolute monarchy, so strengthened the empire that it remained intact for another hundred years. The problem of the succession, it is true, continued to cause trouble in spite of Diocletian's attempted solution; for the legions persisted in their ancient habit of installing emperors by force. Yet there were no prolonged civil wars. During most of the fourth century the government was in the hands of such able soldiers as Constantine (306-37), Valentinian (364-75), and Theodosius (379-95), who well maintained the traditions of Aurelian and Diocletian.

Aurelian, Diocletian, and their successors

The policy of these emperors with regard to religion and certain other matters will be considered below. It need only be noted here that, like Diocletian, they found the task of personally governing the whole empire too great for one man. So they generally followed his example in having a co-emperor to share the responsibility. Established precedent fully justified such an administrative division, and a natural line of demarcation separated the Latin west from the Greek east. In the former, of course, Rome continued to be the imperial city; but in the latter, profiting by his experience in civil war, Constantine built a new capital on the site of the ancient Byzantium—a peninsula at the entrance of the Bosphorus (see

The foundation of Constantinople

Map III). To the south is the Sea of Marmora; to the north a narrow inlet, the Golden Horn, which constitutes a magnificent harbor. The position is tremendously strong, for it controls the strait between the Black Sea and the Mediterranean and can hardly be attacked from either side. Here Constantine laid out what he intended as a second Rome, with an imperial palace, a forum, a senate-house, baths, and an enormous hippodrome. He

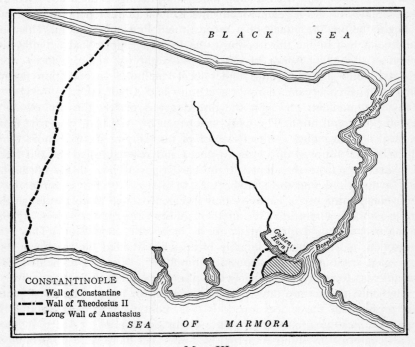

MAP III.

built better than he knew. His city has proved to be one of the world's greatest, a source of inestimable wealth and power to every government that has since held it.

The absolute monarchy
On the whole, Diocletian's monarchy must be recognized as an honest effort to cope with realities. Believing that the preservation of political unity depended on military absolutism, he subordinated everything and everybody to the one consideration. Henceforth the emperor was the sovereign lord and master, officially invested with the regal insignia: the diadem, orb, and scepter, together with the purple robe of the earlier princes. His person and all that belonged to him were sacred. His will, expressed in formal edicts, was the supreme law of the empire—overruling the customary *ius civile* which, with the final extension of citizenship, had

completely absorbed the *ius gentium*. And it was only logical that the ancient practice of adjudication through laymen advised by professional jurists should be superseded by a despotic system under which the judges were imperial servants. This change, however, by no means abrogated the established principles of the Roman law. Judicial action continued to be based on precedent. The legislation of the emperors, as will be seen when we come to the reign of Justinian, naturally resulted in the codification of the old jurisprudence.

Beginning under Diocletian, civil officials were generally stripped of military power and combined in an elaborate hierarchy that, from the lowest of municipal functionaries, extended upward to the emperor. The provinces, now much smaller than they had once been, were grouped in thirteen dioceses, each under a vicar; the dioceses in four prefectures, each under a prefect. The heads of all these districts were appointed by the emperor, shifted about at his pleasure, and held directly responsible to him. Special agents (*agentes in rebus*) were constantly employed to supervise the administration of the post-roads, investigate complaints, spy on local magistrates, and make reports to the master of offices, the super-intendent of the emperor's secretarial bureaux. The head of the legal department, responsible for the drafting of laws and the supervision of the whole judicial system, was the quæstor of the sacred palace. The provost of the sacred bedchamber governed the imperial household. Finance was controlled by the count of the private estates and the count of the sacred largesses. These ministers, together with other great dignitaries, made up the advisory council, or *consistorium*, of the emperor. **Civil administration**

The military administration was dominated by a similar hierarchy. At the top were the masters of horse and the masters of foot, exalted persons who were commonly to be seen at the imperial court. Below them, in actual command of the troops, were the generals (*duces*), divisional commanders, and other subordinate officers. The rank and file of the army, as remarked above, had long been professional soldiers, traditionally separated into two groups: the legions proper, which were restricted to Roman citizens, and the auxiliary units, which were drawn from allied nations. But by the fourth century this ancient distinction had come to have little meaning. The emperors, faced with a chronic lack of men and money, recruited their armed forces as best they could. Sections of the frontier were entrusted to whole tribes of barbarians, who were officially recognized as allies (*fœderati*) and rewarded with allotments of land. The legionaries too, despite their theoretical citizenship, were generally of barbarian descent and accepted the same kind of pay. Maintenance of the old Roman discipline and tactics thus became impossible. The imperial army tended to break up into units of local militia which, either on foot or on horseback, fought in the barbarian fashion. **Military administration**

Although the frontiers had been greatly strengthened under the later principate, experience had proved that they could not always be effectively held—especially by the kind of troops then available. Aurelian had been forced to abandon the regions beyond the Rhine and the Danube, and had taken the ominous step of building a wall round the city of Rome. Diocletian sought to provide better protection for the interior provinces by establishing a field army—a mobile force that could be used wherever he ordered it to go. But the defense of the empire remained so precarious that urban fortification was systematically continued. Before the end of the fourth century every important town had been encircled with masonry and provided with a resident garrison. How inadequate these provisions were will be seen when we come to study the events of the tragic years that followed.

Among the other troubles of the Roman state during the third century was that of a financial crisis. Numerous emperors, to secure temporary relief from bankruptcy, had debased the currency. The inevitable result was that good coins disappeared from circulation and that prices of all commodities rose to an unprecedented level. On attaining power, Diocletian tried to remedy the situation by two principal measures: the re-establishment of sound money and the limitation of amounts at which various articles could be sold. The latter measure, because it could not be enforced, was repealed by Constantine; but he continued Diocletian's monetary policy with noteworthy success. In addition to smaller pieces, he minted a gold *solidus* whose weight was one seventy-second of a Roman pound (*libra*), and a silver coin that, weighing the same, was worth about a fourteenth as much. For many centuries the standard currency of western Europe was to remain on this basis.

To restore the monetary system, however, was not to restore the prosperity of the state. Bureaucratic administration and improved defense meant an increase in the cost of government, and there was no proportionate increase in wealth. Instead, the great majority of the people became progressively poorer; so that receipts from taxation constantly fell off. Although the leveling of the provinces made it possible to establish a uniform system of imposts throughout them, the burden was never equalized among the various classes. Men were divided into a series of ranks, the higher of which were normally exempt from ordinary taxes. The services which they rendered to the emperor were held to free them from the more ignoble charges; and although each privileged group had characteristic obligations, the latter were not oppressive. For example, members of the senatorial aristocracy, being theoretically liable for the expensive luxury of the consulship or prætorship at Rome, merely gave the emperor an occasional "offering" of gold, which they could well afford. And they, like all the great holders of power and place, were immune from the customary tyranny of officials. It was principally the lower and middle classes who bore the crushing weight of the government.

During the fourth century, as earlier, all sorts of indirect taxes continued to be levied. While trade flourished, none of them could be thought exorbitant; but conditions had changed. As times became hard, the state increased its demands, exacting a percentage of the urban tolls and placing special obligations, in money or in service, on every trade and profession. The less the revenue which could be got from commerce, the greater that which had to be got from agriculture. Although certain old contributions of the rural classes persisted into the later period, their heaviest fiscal burden was now the *annona*, Diocletian's tax in kind. For this every district, in proportion to the fertility of the soil and the number of the inhabitants, was assessed in units called *iugera* (yokes) and *capita* (heads). The produce—grain, wine, oil, meat, and the like—was collected by state employees and put into central warehouses, whence it was distributed among the soldiers and officials of the locality. A reapportionment was supposed to be made every five years; but since it was easier to juggle the figures than to carry out a thorough survey, the assessed valuations tended to become more and more arbitrary, and so to bear harder on the unprivileged. The tax, because of chronic waste and thievery, was very inefficient. That it became the chief resource of the imperial administration is eloquent testimony to the economic retrogression of the age.

2. Social Deterioration

It was characteristic of the absolute monarchy that, as service of the state was identified with service of the emperor, nearness to his sacred person came to be the test of all social eminence. On working up the ladder of civil or military preferment, men acquired increasing honor, as well as resonant titles that were scrupulously defined in official registers. Members of the imperial family and a few other grandees could alone be called *nobilissimi* (most noble). The prætorian prefects, the masters of horse and foot, the master of offices, and the rest of the ministers who regularly attended the *consistorium* were *illustres* (illustrious). Their immediate subordinates, such as the vicars and the heads of secondary departments, together with the governors of the more important provinces and the *duces* of the armies, were *spectabiles* (admirable). Senators, lesser provincial governors, and their military peers were *clarissimi* (most distinguished), while local functionaries and the like were only *perfectissimi* (most perfect). A very exalted person might in addition acquire the rank of *patricius* (patrician) and so be addressed by the emperor as "kinsman." Merely to be a "friend of Cæsar" had long been a source of pride, and that especial honor was now reflected in the designation of *comes* or count (literally companion). The two counts in charge of finance have already

The imperial court

been noted. There were many others, such as the count of the sacred vestment and the count of the stable (constable). From the court the title eventually spread to the provinces where, as we shall see, it remained in general use throughout the Middle Ages.

Growth of a caste system

From this nobility of court and imperial service the lower classes were separated by an ever-widening gulf; for unless a man was born to wealth and privilege, his chance of enjoying them became steadily less. That the emperors deliberately sought to depress the bulk of their subjects is hard to believe. Rather, we must suppose, they took what then seemed to be logical and necessary steps for the avoidance of common destruction. While the Roman peace was yet unbroken, the government had begun to suffer from a shortage of troops and from dwindling revenues. Then came protracted civil war, and to its ravages were added those of pestilence. The population sharply declined and the loss was not made up. Lands ceased to be cultivated; urban properties stood vacant; taxes remained unpaid. The state, with frontiers insecurely held, was virtually bankrupt. Cash was so scarce that taxes had to be collected in kind, and many imperial employees had to accept produce for at least part of what was owed them. Even land was used for paying wages—as, for example, those of the troops. In a frantic effort to check the encroaching ruin, Diocletian and his successors resorted to desperate measures. The result was what amounted to an official system of castes.

Trade and industry

As the consequence of a long development, service in the army had now been turned into a largely hereditary profession followed by rude frontiersmen, who were usually of barbarian descent and would accept land as their remuneration. Meanwhile the state's financial difficulties had led it to extend the ancient system of requisitioning animals, conveyances, materials, and labor. Such exactions, left to be enforced by unscrupulous officials, became a never-ending plague for the people of the countryside. But the merchant and the artisan were by no means exempt from similar oppression. For a long time various essential trades had been organized under strict control of the state—among them the millers, bakers, and others who supplied the capital with food; the carpenters, masons, and metal workers who constructed public buildings; the craftsmen who furnished arms to the legions; and the carriers who transported all these things by sea or land. As times grew worse and the credit of the government declined, men naturally hesitated to accept contracts on the usual terms. So edicts were issued to compel the performance of the customary duties and, finally, to prohibit the members of these trades, or their heirs, from quitting their occupations. What had been privileged callings thus tended to become hereditary servitudes and all prospect of commercial revival through private initiative was destroyed.

Agriculture, which was much more important in the Roman world than industry, was inevitably affected also. According to the fiscal plan of Diocletian, each assessment district was liable for a certain quota of tax. The arrangement, it is true, was not supposed to be immutable, but the tendency was to avoid reapportionment and so to keep each territory under a fixed charge. And since the land was worthless without cultivators, they too had to be made into stable assets. The landlord was held responsible for the obligations of his dependents. He levied their taxes, forced them to repair the roads and other public works, and helped to punish them for their misdeeds. Under the established law, the *colonus* who found his position becoming intolerable had been free to abandon his lease;[1] now, on the contrary, he was forbidden by imperial decree to leave the estate. He and his children after him were attached to the soil, to be bought and sold along with it. He became, in other words, what men in the Middle Ages called a serf. *Agriculture*

An equally bitter fate befell the landlord if he happened to be enrolled as a *curialis* in the local *civitas*. That rank carried with it responsibility for whatever taxes were laid on the urban district. As collections fell off, the mounting deficit had to be met by the unfortunate dignitary. The law would not permit him to resign his wretched honor. If in despair he ran away, he might, like a fugitive *colonus*, be captured and brought back. His only escape was, through imperial favor, to attain the senatorial order. As a senator, of course, he would have no share in the government of the empire or even, unless he lived at Rome, in the administration of the capital. But he would be blissfully relieved of liability for other municipal office. Leaving the town to its evil destiny, he could retire to a fortified estate in the country. There, supported by his peasants and protected by his retainers, he could defy official tyranny and spend his days in the society of friends like himself. *The ruin of the cities*

The culmination of these unhappy developments was the ruin, in all but exceptional regions, of urban life and culture. Through the multiplication of cities the frontier of civilization had for hundreds of years steadily advanced; through the influence of the cities the east had tended to become Greek and the west to become Latin. As the reverse process set in during the third century, it naturally brought a relapse towards more primitive conditions—in the east oriental, in the west barbarian. The decrees of the later emperors thus betray a much graver deterioration than the passing of the semi-republican principate; they show that vitality had somehow gone out of the state. And if we compare the culture of the third and fourth centuries with that of the preceding age, the same fact is brought home to us even more convincingly. *The decay of culture*

The decay of the arts during the period between Marcus Aurelius and

[1] See above, p. 25.

Diocletian is no less than shocking. Although the princes strove to maintain the Roman tradition of magnificent building, their structures were little more than piles of inferior masonry devoid of architectural beauty. The fine series of imperial portraits came to an end. All skill in the carving of relief seems to have been lost. Such realistic panels as, for example, could be put on the arch of Titus gave way on that of Septimius Severus to crudely scratched designs; later, when Constantine erected his arch, he was reduced to filching decorations from the monuments of his predecessors. The decline of Latin literature, except in the field of jurisprudence, was equally abrupt. No historian arose to take the place of Tacitus, no poet to take that of Juvenal. Towards the end of the second century we encounter the names of Aulus Gellius, a collector of anecdotes, and Apuleius, a collector of stories; after them ensues a blank. And in the meantime Greek thought had been overwhelmed by the wave of oriental mysticism that will be considered in the following section.

Alleged causes of Roman decline

What was the cause of this degradation, which was to culminate in the so-called fall of Rome? All sorts of answers have been given to the question. Learned writers have attributed the decay of the empire to such diverse influences as sin, slavery, barbarian attack, official tyranny, racial deterioration, epidemics, exhaustion of the soil, lack of applied science, and Christianity. To repeat the arguments that have been marshaled against these and similar contentions is impossible in a brief review of the subject. Suffice it to say that none of them has been generally accepted by historians. The discussion has, however, made one point increasingly plain: the vitality of the empire was intimately connected with that of its component city-states, the centers of political and cultural life throughout the Mediterranean world. Accordingly, if we could identify some internal malady that began to affect the city-state towards the close of the second century, we should have a good explanation for the ultimate collapse of the imperial structure. On the other hand, it may be plausibly argued that the ruin of the city-state was due to some vicious and suicidal policy of the government itself. The bewildered student is thus left to wonder what was cause and what was result, and how much importance, if any, should be attributed to economic factors.

The essential poverty of the west

In this connection it is well to remember a very significant fact: that the eastern half of the empire not only survived the crash of the fifth century but seemed thereafter to enjoy renewed strength. In the east most city-states were far older than the Roman dominion and were not economically dependent on it; whereas in the west most city-states were created and continuously supported by the imperial government. Except in such matters as tax-farming and money-lending, the Romans developed slight talent for commerce. Even after they had become rulers of the Mediterranean, shipbuilding, sea trade, and the more important manufactures remained in

the hands of Greeks. As noted in the preceding chapter, large-scale production throughout the Latin provinces was restricted to raw materials,
the market for which was almost wholly maintained by the state. Aside
from those nourished from public funds—the urban proletariat, the troops,
the officials, and the other imperial employees—who would consume the
food and drink that were such important articles of trade? Or, if we leave
out of account the demand of these same persons for clothing, arms, tools,
and materials, who would buy any great quantity of wool, leather, metal,
timber, stone, brick, and the like?

The truth is that the west, for lack of self-supporting inhabitants, was
an essentially poor country. And, according to modern standards, it was
thinly populated. Most of the western cities, being centers of military and
civil administration rather than of economic production, were relatively
small. In this respect the remains of walls constructed in the third and
fourth centuries provide indisputable evidence. At Rome Aurelian's fortifications enclose a little more than 3000 acres,[2] which may be compared
with the 2000 acres of Alexandria, the metropolis of the east. But Rome
was a parasitical growth, a mere agglomeration of consumers; and none of
the provincial towns in the west extended beyond 1000 acres. Nîmes, the
greatest city of Gaul, covered 790 acres; Trier, the greatest city of the
Rhineland, 704; London, the greatest city of Britain, 330. And these places
were quite exceptional. Throughout Gaul, for example, most cities contained less than 75 acres, many less than 50. The significance of such
figures will be better appreciated if it is remembered that the legionary
fortress, built to accommodate about five thousand men, normally covered
about 50 acres—much the same ratio that we find in a densely populated
town of today. The Roman city, however, was primarily residential rather
than industrial. So we have to consider half a million inhabitants the maximum for the capital and estimate the other cities at proportionally less.
Judged by the standard of the western provinces, London, with perhaps
25,000, was a huge town, certainly five times as big as the average.

Under these conditions it should be quite apparent why the bankruptcy
of the imperial government might ruin the west but relieve the east. And
although there may be dispute as to how the government went bankrupt,
there can be none as to the fact that it did so. Various historians have
argued that the whole political structure of the Roman conquerors depended
on confiscated treasure from the eastern provinces and that, when it was
drained to the east by extravagant purchase of imported goods, the emperors
had no adequate resources for maintaining their grandiose structure. However this may be, we cannot mistake the final outcome. Throughout the
west generally, all but petty commerce disappeared with the imperial

The origin of medi- æval society

---

[2] There are 640 acres in a square mile; a plot measuring half a mile on each side
contains 160 acres.

administration. The cities lost what mercantile population they had ever had. The owners of great estates retired to a life of agrarian isolation. The rural masses, already reduced to serfdom, continued to exist as before. Society became such as we find it for many centuries to come.

3. The New Religions

The failure of Greek philosophy

From the very outset Greek thought had been remarkable for its rejection of traditional authority and its insistence upon fresh research. Not infrequently, as we now realize, Greek scholars had tended to reason on the basis of insufficient data, had allowed fancy to outstrip observation. The validity of their method, nevertheless, was amply demonstrated by the most brilliant advance in science that the world had yet seen. And although their schools of philosophy differed in the solutions offered to various problems, all believed in man's capacity to learn about himself and the universe through the normal human faculties. This attitude was in sharp contrast to the prevalent mysticism of the orient. In all ages the typical mystic has despaired of man's unaided capacities. Truth, he believes, can be reached only by contemplation, by shutting oneself off from the world and communing with the infinite through the medium of the soul. Regarded from this point of view, the acceptance of Neoplatonism by the scholarly world of the third century was equivalent to a declaration of intellectual bankruptcy.

Neoplatonism is a modern term used to distinguish the system of Plotinus (d. 270) and his followers from the original teachings of Plato. Divorcing Plato's "idealism" from its context, Plotinus combined it with various non-Greek elements to form the alleged quintessence of philosophy and religion. But the conclusion of all his labor was to deny what the Athenian philosophers had held most dear; for he came to preach the ultimate futility of thought and the consequent need of inner revelation through ecstatic vision. Neoplatonism thus tended to justify the acceptance of any religion that appealed to the emotions. Although a select few might remain loyal to the metaphysics of Plotinus, most men would find an easier way to reach the same goal. By this time, indeed, many an oriental mystery had come to attract the learned as well as the illiterate.

The oriental mysteries

In an earlier age, presumably, the Romans had found spiritual exaltation in the worship of their ancient deities; yet, long before the establishment of the principate, the official cult had ceased to be more than legal formalism. Educated men regarded the traditional stories of gods and goddesses —whether Greek or Latin—as sheer myth, and rejected all religious doctrines that could not be embraced under such a creed as Stoicism. On the other hand the uneducated, to whom philosophy could offer slight consolation, naturally turned to the new faiths imported from the east. They offered what the legalistic ceremonial of the official temples could not provide: the emotional appeal of a highly sensuous ritual, the certainty of truth mystically revealed, and the assurance to the purified initiate of life in a blessed hereafter. They demanded only what every man could give—faith. And to all alike they promised a reward more precious than wealth could buy. It is no wonder that, with the progressive ruin of state and society, they numbered their converts by the million.

Eventually one of these oriental faiths was to gain supremacy throughout the Roman world, but for several centuries it had to strive against many rivals for popular favor. Earlier mysteries—such as those associated with Bacchus, god of wine, and Demeter, goddess of the harvest—celebrated the principle of fertility and, by depicting the return of vegetation to the earth, symbolized the initiate's entrance into a new spiritual existence. These elements, together with many others, were combined in the worship of the Phrygian Cybele, whom the west knew as Magna Mater. According to the sacred legend, she restored the slain Attis to life through the power of her love; and about this theme of death and resurrection was developed a cult that became widely influential under the principate. Meanwhile a similar myth concerning the resuscitation of Osiris by Isis, an Egyptian goddess, had become the germ of another religion, remarkable for its hierarchy of priests, its elaborate liturgy, and its positive doctrine of immortality. A third popular mystery was that of Mithras, which originated from Persian sun-worship. According to the latter system, known as Zoroastrianism, man's nature, like the universe, is the scene of perpetual strife between the two gods of light and darkness, the forces of good and evil. The individual, to escape the realm of darkness after death, must hold to the light, must follow a strict code of morality. As an aid in the struggle for righteousness, the cult of Mithras offered constant spiritual fortification. To gain admission to it, the candidate had to be purified through an elaborate ceremony. Thereafter he was said to be reborn.

By the third century these mystic religions had borrowed much from one another. To all of them, for example, a sacrificial meal, in which the participant symbolically partook of the divine substance, had become a common feature. All, likewise, tended to absorb the ancient astrology of the Babylonians and Egyptians, such as the lore connected with the signs of the zodiac and the division of time into periods of seven days, each named for a heavenly body or its presiding deity. Some of these cults had originally been marked by license rather than restraint; but, with the passage of time, all came to emphasize ethical teaching. Barbarous ritual was softened and crude mythology was explained in terms of Hellenistic philosophy. All gods could thus be regarded as manifestations of one supreme power, and all dogmas as reflecting the same essential truths. The greatest appeal of the new religions, however, lay in the fact that each offered a divine intermediary through whom the individual could obtain

Common elements

salvation. The Christian faith was but one of many; how it came to receive universal acceptance is a story of truly epic character.

The Christian religion

According to the Christian gospels, Jesus was born—while Augustus still ruled at Rome—in the Judæan town of Bethlehem. Having been recognized by John the Baptist as the prophesied Christ, the Messiah of the Hebrews, He devoted His life to preaching the kingdom which God was about to restore to His people. But this kingdom, said Jesus, was not the earthly monarchy that the Jews had dreamed of re-establishing; it was a spiritual kingdom, to enter which a man must be born again in the spirit. Precise observance of the traditional law was of no avail; the outward act was less than the inward thought. In heaven the faith of a little child was of greater worth than all the learned holiness in the world. Finally, because of His bitter attack upon sacred tradition and vested interest, Jesus was sent to death on the cross—a punishment commonly assigned to thieves and other criminals. The martyrdom served only to advertise an obscure cause. The small band of the faithful proclaimed that Christ had risen from the dead and that, through His abiding spirit, they were able to perform all wondrous works. Their fervor rapidly made converts, one of whom was the apostle Paul. In his own vivid words he tells us how he had never known the man Jesus; how he preached the gospel of the risen Christ. And as the result of his preaching, the Christianity that spread across the Roman Empire was Pauline Christianity. Thanks to his Greek education, Paul was able so to present an essentially Jewish religion that it could be understood throughout the Mediterranean world.

The four gospels and the book of Acts

The character of the primitive Christian Church has been a highly controversial subject for many centuries. We have very few sources regarding the early Christians aside from the writings contained in the New Testament;[3] and since they fail to give a complete picture, the way is left open for a great variety of supplementary interpretation. An introductory textbook that hopes to avoid dogmatic assertions can hardly attempt the description of something that remains a matter of faith rather than of historical evidence. The student who wishes to have any understanding of the subject should himself turn to the early Christian writings, which are neither long nor, in the main, obscure. At the beginning of the Testament the life of Christ is sketched in the four gospels that bear the names of Matthew, Mark, Luke, and John. Three of these men were of Hebrew descent: Matthew and John, who were among Christ's original disciples, together with the younger Mark, who was closely associated with the famous disciple Peter. Luke, on the contrary, was a Greek physician, who accompanied Paul on some of his missionary journeys and also wrote the *Acts of the Apostles*. All scholars agree that Mark and Luke were the authors of the second and third gospels, but many believe that the first

[3] See below, pp. 60-61.

and fourth could not have been composed by the disciples to whom they have been attributed.

However this may be, both *Matthew* and *John* are very remarkable. The former has always been the most popular of the gospels. In simple language it gives not only the narrative of Christ's life that is found in Mark but also a full report of His sayings on many occasions, notably the Sermon on the Mount. Although *Matthew*, like the rest of the New Testament, has come down to us in Greek, it would appear that at least the sayings of Christ were originally recorded in Aramaic[4]—strong evidence, for anyone who demands it, of their authenticity. The fourth gospel is a very different kind of book, being not so much a biography of Christ as a metaphysical explanation of His career and teaching. That such an essay should be less popular than a more straightforward account is quite understandable. Yet, because of its philosophical approach and symbolic language, *John* has had the greater influence upon Christian theology. Since Luke's gospel contains very much the same material as its two predecessors in the Testament, it is distinctly less valuable to the historian than the *Acts of the Apostles*, which stands in a class by itself. Only here do we obtain precise information about the Christians at Jerusalem after the death of their Savior—how they continued to expect His second coming, how in that expectation they established a community of goods, and how they were comforted by various manifestations of the divine presence. Only here, furthermore, do we learn in detail of Stephen's martyrdom and of the persecutor Saul who, having seen the risen Christ in blinding glory on the road to Damascus, became illustrious as Paul the Apostle. And without Luke's graphic description, what could we know of Paul's great work among the Gentiles—his journeys by land and sea, which ended at Rome with his appeal to Cæsar?

To supplement Luke's recital, we have Paul's own letters to the various *Paul's* Christian communities that he had founded. In these famous epistles we *epistles* find, not an account of the author's experiences, but constant reference *and the* to them; not a summary of his original preaching, but an eloquent com- *Apoca-* mentary on its results. Whatever the faith of the reader, he can hardly fail *lypse* to appreciate the sincerity and vigor of Paul's words, which stated the essentials of world-wide Christianity as it has since remained. Compared with the epistles of Paul, those attributed to other apostles are of secondary importance. Passing over them, we come to the *Apocalypse* or *Revelation of John the Divine*. According to tradition, this book and the fourth gospel were composed by the same disciple, though any such authorship has been denied by a large number of critics. The *Apocalypse*, in any case, is a strangely moving work. Obviously inspired by Hebraic prophecy, it sets

---

[4] The language of the Aramæans, which had become the common vernacular of Syria and, as such, was spoken by Christ and the disciples. See below, p. 101.

forth the present vicissitudes and future triumph of the Christian religion in language so mysterious as to call forth endless discussion. For every student of thought and literary expression the *Apocalypse* must always have profound significance. Merely to enumerate a few of its phrases is to demonstrate its influence on the English language: for example, Armageddon, Gog and Magog, Alpha and Omega, the Whore of Babylon, the New Jerusalem, and the Lamb of God. And in what age has the incomparable picture of the Four Horsemen—War, Conquest, Famine, and Death—ceased to have a dreadful meaning? Certainly not in ours.

Christianity and the Roman state

Compared with its rivals, Christianity had many points of superiority. In the first place, the story of Jesus is compellingly beautiful—vastly superior, as a mere story, to the theme of any other oriental mystery. And it is itself the expression of a religious idea. Telling of a savior who died to redeem all men, it requires no symbolic interpretation. Furthermore, the ethical teachings of Jesus lay at the heart of His gospel; they were not a supplement borrowed from Greek philosophy, intelligible only to the learned. Christianity, as the event proved, appealed to all. It did not, like the cult of Mithras, exclude women; nor did it, like the cults of Cybele and Isis, exalt a feminine principle at the expense of others. Lastly, the Christian religion took over from Judaism an uncompromising monotheism. It was a religion that declared every other to be false, a religion at once exclusive and aggressive. Therein lay an avowed hostility to the Roman imperial system that was to invite persecution; yet therein lay also the strength that was to bring triumph.

Roman religious policy

The concept of a church distinct from the state was originally foreign to Roman, as it had been to Greek, thought. Under the constitution of the republic and of the principate, one set of magistrates held all political functions—civil, military, and religious. Any man legally elected was considered competent to ascertain the will of the gods by formal divination or to preside over the public ceremonial of worship; no especially sanctified priesthood was necessary. And as long as the Roman citizen outwardly submitted to the official deities, he was free to believe anything he pleased. Citizens of other communities were permitted to maintain any faith that did not conflict with the general peace of the empire; yet, as a sign of their proper reverence for the dominant state, they were commonly required to recognize by solemn act the cult of its living embodiment, Augustus—a formality as ordinary to that age as an oath of allegiance is to ours.

Polytheism and Judaism

Such requirements, in a polytheistic world, could be expected to offend nobody. The believer would willingly admit one more god to the Pantheon; the skeptic would regard an additional ceremony as a matter of no importance; even the devotee of an oriental mystery, while preferring one manifestation of divine truth, would normally concede that there might be many others. In this polytheistic world the Jew was an exception. To him all faiths except his own were sheer idolatry, an abomination in the sight of the Lord; he would never conform to the official system of Rome. But since the Jewish religion, with its strict observance of a peculiar law, could never be popular enough to be dangerous, the Romans wisely accepted it as a national institution and exempted its followers from emperor-worship. Even after the destruction of the Jewish state (A.D. 70) and the consequent dispersion of the Jews throughout the provinces, their religious beliefs and practices were still tolerated.

To the Christians no such liberty was extended. Although the Roman **Early** government seems for a time to have considered Christianity a mere sect **Christian** of Judaism, by the close of the first century the distinction between the **persecu-** two had become eminently clear. Most of the Jews would have nothing **tions** to do with the new faith, which, on the other hand, had spread rapidly through the Gentile population. The Christians held that they had been freed from the Hebrew law and, to emphasize the fact, celebrated the first day of the week in place of the Jewish sabbath. Yet in their monotheism they remained as intolerant of other creeds as the Jews. In Roman eyes, consequently, the Christians were no better than seditious conspirators. Their associations were declared illegal; to be a Christian was to commit a crime. Thus it came about that the Christians were persecuted, not merely by notorious tyrants, but also by the very best of the emperors. Trajan, Hadrian, Antoninus Pius, and Marcus Aurelius, in so far as they tried to enforce the law, were necessarily hostile to those proscribed by it.

One of our earliest and best sources on the Christian persecutions is the letter written to Trajan by Pliny the Younger, then governor of Bithynia.[5] He reports that he has discharged all suspects who have made offerings of wine and incense to the statue of the emperor. Those who refused he has handed over to execution.

Nevertheless, they affirmed that this was the sum total of their guilt. On a certain day they would meet before dawn and sing in alternate verses a song to Christ as a god. They would bind themselves by oath, not for the sake of criminal acts, but as an engagement not to commit fraud, theft, or adultery, not to break faith and not to refuse the surrender of a pledge when it was demanded. It was their habit then to disperse, although they reassembled later in order to partake of food.

Trajan replies that Pliny has acted very properly. The governor should not himself undertake to ferret out these people, nor should he listen to anonymous accusations. But when Christians are regularly denounced and found guilty, they should be punished according to law.

History has often proved that, merely as a matter of policy, a little persecution is worse than none. The fact that the Roman government was so

[5] Pliny, *Letters*, x, 96-97.

moderate prevented its staying the progress of the outlawed cult. And the joyous courage with which the condemned welcomed martyrdom proclaimed the quality of their faith and converted many a spectator. Then, with the paralysis of the state in the third century, the Christians gained a prolonged respite. Even when the emperors found time to devote to the religious problem, their edicts were chiefly directed against the making of Christian converts—a tacit confession that the task of punishing the offenders was becoming arduous. This was a period in which many oriental mysteries made rapid progress; Christianity was one of them. Heretofore it had gained support mainly from the poor and uneducated; henceforth, on the other hand, we hear more and more of Christians in wealthy and prominent families. But with its enhanced position, Christianity encountered a graver peril than the half-hearted persecution of provincial governors: it was threatened with the loss of its original character through absorption into some other mystic system that promised to be all-embracing.

By the third century the more learned Christians had thus found it necessary to defend their traditional faith against the so-called Gnostics. The latter were an ill-defined group of writers who, after lifting the Christian story from its Hebrew context, combined it with metaphysical speculations of their own. Christ, they declared, was never really human; He was a spirit who merely pretended to die on the cross. Through this redemption those men in whom the spiritual prevailed over the material could obtain salvation, while others, hopelessly dominated by the flesh, could not. A select few, by ascetic practices and meditation, could reach a state of perfection in this life and so provide a holy example for the rest of mankind. Eventually, much of Gnosticism was absorbed into Manichæism—a peculiar blending of Christian and Zoroastrian elements that came to be preached by a certain Mani in Persia. Spreading westward into the Roman Empire, the cult gained numerous adherents on both shores of the Mediterranean and there remained a formidable antagonist of Christianity for over two centuries. In a later chapter it will be seen how the Christians, to combat such enemies as the Gnostics and Manichæans, were led to strengthen their own organization and perfect their own doctrines. For the moment we are concerned rather with their attainment of official recognition and support.

Diocletian, as was to be expected of an autocrat who enjoyed divine honor, resumed the traditional campaign for the suppression of Christianity. By a series of edicts he proscribed the holding of Christian services and ordered the razing of Christian churches, the burning of the Christian scriptures, the imprisonment of the Christian clergy, and the removal of all Christians from public office. Ultimately he commanded that every Christian, under pain of death, should perform the sacrifices established by law. But during the civil war that followed Diocletian's abdication the enforcement of his decrees generally lapsed, and within ten years the illustrious

Constantine had granted complete toleration to the persecuted sect. The son of Constantius, who had earlier been proclaimed emperor by the legions in Britain, Constantine was at first merely one of many rivals for the purple. In 312, by defeating Maxentius at the Milvian Bridge, he gained possession of Rome and became co-emperor with Licinius, the ruler of the east. A dozen years later, when the two associates came to blows, it was again Constantine who triumphed—to remain sole master of the Roman world until his death in 337. Constantine, like most of the soldier-emperors, seems originally to have been a devotee of Mithraism, the favorite religion of the army. Gaul and Britain, where he rose to power, were among the least Christian of the provinces. Nor is there any evidence that, through family connections, he had obtained any Christian teaching. Therefore, if Constantine became a convert to the faith, we may well suppose that it was because he believed himself the recipient of a special revelation.

According to the famous story, which Eusebius reports as having been told by the emperor himself, Constantine was leading his army against Maxentius when he beheld in the sky a blazing cross with the motto IN HOC VINCE (In This Conquer). Whatever may be thought of this alleged vision, Constantine had the name of Christ inscribed on the shields of his troops before the battle of the Milvian Bridge and, having won the victory, spent the rest of his life as a fervent, if not ethically perfect, Christian. The design ✳[6] was placed on his military standards and similar emblems regularly appeared on his coins and monuments. He not only granted freedom of worship to all Christians but also recognized their church as a corporation which might hold property and perform other legal acts. Besides, Constantine brought up his children in the Christian faith, favored Christians in public office, and actively concerned himself with problems of Christian doctrine. Finally, to celebrate his defeat of Licinius, he founded his new capital as a sort of mystic offering—unlike Rome, to be a purely Christian city.

The final step of making Christianity the state religion was taken by Constantine's successors, especially Theodosius,[7] who formally proscribed pagan rites. Thus was completed a revolution of momentous import for the future.

[6] The Greek letters Chi Rho, standing for *Christos*.
[7] See below, pp. 50, 63.

CHAPTER III

The Barbarization of the West

1. THE BARBARIANS BEFORE THE INVASIONS

Frontier
peoples

The more important peoples inhabiting lands beyond the Roman frontiers in the third century were, in Africa, the Moors or Berbers; in western Asia, the Arabs and the Persians; on the central Asiatic plateau and the Caspian steppe, the Ural-Altaic nomads; and to the northwest of them in Europe, the Slavs, the Germans, and the Celts (see Map II). Of these language groups, the first three can be taken up more conveniently in a following chapter. The others must now receive a few words of introduction; for, beginning in the fifth century, they vitally affected the destinies of the European provinces.

The no-
mads of
central
Asia

The Ural-Altaic group, named after a vague expanse of desert and plain extending from the Ural to the Altai Mountains (see Map I), has included such famous peoples as the Scythians, Sarmatians, Huns, Bulgars, Avars, Magyars, Mongols, Tartars, and Turks. Originally these peoples were all nomadic (i.e., wandering); because, as far back as our information extends, agriculture has been impossible throughout their homeland and man has remained dependent on his flocks and herds. If they die, he dies; so where they have to go he goes. In the winter the slopes of the southern mountains provide the necessary pasturage and shelter, but with the advent of the summer drought the nomad is forced to take his animals to the northern grasslands. Thence, in turn, he is driven by the snows of the succeeding winter, to repeat the process interminably year in and year out. Having no settled habitation, the nomads restrict their household belongings to tents, rugs, and a few utensils that can easily be carried on horseback. And they have, of course, no need of any political organization beyond the customary discipline of the tribe, enforced by its chief.

Until very recent times the nomad's wealth consisted of his animals—

principally, among the central Asiatics, horses and sheep. His food, aside from a little wild grain and occasional game or fish, was almost exclusively dairy produce; and this was reduced, in case of a military expedition, to the milk of a few mares which the warrior drove along with him. The animals also supplied their owners with skins to be made into leather and with wool to be woven into cloth or, mixed with hair, to be beaten into felt—an article which, time out of mind, the nomads had used for tents and rugs. Although a sheep might occasionally be slaughtered for the sake of a festive meal, horses were too valuable to be eaten. Whenever the tribe moved its quarters, the horse provided the indispensable means of transportation. And while the women attended to all necessary labor in and about the camp, the men devoted themselves to hunting and raiding on horseback. Thanks to his small but indefatigable mount, the Asiatic nomad covered amazing distances in wastes that others found impassable. Being trained from infancy, the youth soon acquired uncanny skill in riding bareback or on his primitive saddle, as well as in fighting with spear or with bow and arrows. The nomads never delivered a frontal attack, but preferred to gallop round and round the enemy, hurling their weapons and seeking to intimidate him by a show of ferocity. Often they feigned retreat, only to turn on the backs of their horses and riddle their pursuers with a deadly flight of arrows—the so-called Parthian tactics which the Romans learned to their cost in the plains of Mesopotamia.

To the ordinary occupations of pastoral life, accordingly, the Asiatic nomads added those of professional marauders. Throughout all exposed regions the scourge of their raids was unceasing. Normally these raids were merely for loot; but occasionally, as the result of political or economic pressure in the homeland, a migrating horde would bring ruin to far-distant lands. Such episodes are familiar in the history of China, India, Persia, Syria, and even Egypt. Nor did Europe escape, for the Caspian steppe gave the nomads an easy highway to the heart of the continent. In the fourth century it was the Huns who, driving westward along this route, terrorized the peoples then dwelling across the Roman frontier. The Huns, we are told by the chroniclers of the empire, resembled beasts rather than men— with their squat bodies, bowlegs, and ugly faces marked by prominent ears, flat noses, slanting eyes, swarthy skins, and bristling hair. And behind their repulsive exterior, enhanced by the filthiness of their habits, lay a stark ferocity that daunted their more civilized antagonists. Yet most of these physical traits were quickly lost when the invaders, whose numbers were relatively small, settled in the midst of a subject population. Having left their women behind, they took mates from the conquered territory. So their descendants, although the ancient name and perhaps the ancient language might be kept, would inevitably be assimilated to the type of the masses.

Their raids and conquests

Prominent among the victims of these nomads were the Slavs, first mentioned as a fair-haired people living to the north of the Pontic steppe in what is now central Russia. We know remarkably little about the Slavs in ancient times, but in the early Middle Ages their role was generally that of the hunted and the oppressed. Probably their geographic position—between Asiatic raiders from the south and Germanic raiders from the north—had much to do with their misfortunes. Thousands were driven by alien conquerors to till distant lands. Other thousands were carried into captivity and sold throughout the markets of the west; so that the name that by derivation meant "glorious" eventually became our word "slave." Yet through it all, developing a marvelous power of endurance, they lived and multiplied. As more warlike nations killed one another off or pushed westward to despoil the Roman provinces, the Slavs took over the vacated lands. Without a single battle to win the attention of chroniclers, they made the plains of eastern Europe almost solidly Slavic.

In a much earlier age the Celts—or, as the Romans called them, the Gauls—had inhabited the forests of northern Europe as far east as the Elbe. Thence, in a great migration that for a time threatened to wipe out the little republic of Rome, they swept over the Alps into Italy and across the Rhine into the country which was thereafter known as Gaul. A first wave of invaders, the Gaels, occupied the islands off the northwest coast; then the better part of the principal island, which thereby got a permanent name, was conquered by a second wave, the Britons. The languages of these two peoples have persisted as Gaelic and Welsh; but with the Latinization of Gaul the Celtic dialects of that region disappeared, except for an occasional place name. And meanwhile the Gauls, whom all the ancient writers describe as of the Nordic type, had lost their original traits through mingling with the native Mediterranean stock.

The peoples whom the Romans knew as *Germani* are first heard of in the lands bordering on the Baltic. Moving south behind the Celts, they took over the country between the Elbe and the Rhine, where they were held in check by the military defenses of the Roman Empire. For the early Germans we have two principal sources: the *Commentaries* of Cæsar (55 B.C.) and the *Germania* of Tacitus (*c.* A.D. 100). And of the two the latter is the more valuable, although the author wrote with an eye to reproving his luxury-loving compatriots. Thus, when Tacitus paints an idyllic picture of the German marriage customs and family life, we may suspect a little exaggeration for the sake of a moral lesson. The actual Germans whom we encounter in the pages of history—even the most primitive of them—were by no means so pure. Yet, on the whole, Tacitus gives us a reliable account, in many respects confirmed by later records.

With regard to the appearance of the Germans he repeats the general verdict: "fierce blue eyes and reddish hair; great bodies, especially powerful for attack, but not equally patient of hard work; little able to withstand heat and thirst, though by climate and soil they have been inured to cold and hunger." Cæsar describes them as depending mainly on pasturage, together with fishing and hunting; Tacitus emphasizes rather their agriculture. None of the German tribes, he says, lived in cities; even within their villages each man's home was surrounded by a considerable open space. They used no masonry or tile; their houses were built of rude lumber, sometimes smeared with colored earth. Land, being plentiful, was occupied by the villages as needed and was distributed among the inhabitants according to their rank. With regard to social classes Tacitus remains somewhat vague. Besides hereditary noblemen, he constantly refers to chiefs (*principes*), who were largely supported by gifts of produce and cattle. And his typical warrior was by no means an agricultural laborer. During intervals of peace the bravest and most admired spent their time in sleeping, eating, hunting, and loafing, while all necessary tasks about the house or in the fields were left to those who could not fight: women, children, and other dependents. Most of the German slaves, he reports, were not domestic servants like the Roman slaves, but peasants (*coloni*) holding plots of land from which they paid shares of what they raised. There were also freedmen, who were not much better off than slaves.

Wealth among the Germans consisted mainly of livestock: cattle, horses, and other animals of inferior breed. Such property commonly served as money, although Roman coins had come into circulation along the frontier, and although silver cups, golden bracelets, and the like were highly prized everywhere. The man ordinarily wore a tight-fitting garment about his legs (obviously breeches or hose), together with a sort of cloak fastened at the throat by a clasp; and these clothes were often made of skins taken from wild beasts. Women were likely to be dressed in much the same way, or perhaps in flowing robes of striped linen. The men allowed their beards to grow long, as well as their hair, which was sometimes twisted into knots on top of the head. Food was simple: principally fruit, game, and curdled milk in addition to cultivated grain. Except along the Roman border, the Germans were unacquainted with wine; instead they drank a liquid made by fermentation of wheat or barley "into a certain similitude of wine." This beverage, which of course was beer, the warriors consumed in huge quantities, often prolonging their bouts for as much as a day and a night. They were also addicted to gambling; it was not unusual for a man to stake his liberty on a last throw of the dice, to be sold into slavery if he lost. By way of compensation for these vices, Tacitus praises the Germans for their lavish hospitality, their unostentatious funerals, and their strict observance of the marriage bond. The rule everywhere was one husband, one wife; but we may suspect the influence of an economic factor, because we are told that such noblemen as practiced polygamy had no trouble in finding plenty of wives.

Warfare
and the
comitatus

On attaining man's estate, the free German received a gift of arms, which, as Tacitus remarks, corresponded to the *toga virilis* of the Romans. In the presence of the tribe the youth was formally invested with a spear and a shield by one of his relatives or some other prominent person. These arms he thenceforth bore on all occasions; for to lose them was to lose his honorable status. To have thrown away one's shield in battle was considered the depth of infamy. Among the Germans every assembly was a military gathering. Proposals were then submitted by the chief men to the rest of the warriors; if they approved, they clashed their weapons. Political organization was slight. The kings recognized by some of the tribes were little more than leaders in war; they had no arbitrary power of formulating laws or administering punishments. The kindred group remained powerful, defending its members by prosecution of the blood-feud and collecting compensations for injuries done them. Even homicide could be atoned for by a payment of cattle to the injured family. When it came to battle, the average German had no extra equipment to put on; he fought in his ordinary clothes and with his customary arms. Very few had either breastplates or helmets, and cavalry tactics were little developed except among one or two tribes. According to Tacitus, only the Suiones (Swedes) were distinguished as seafarers, and they used mere skiffs not fitted with sails.

Very characteristic of this barbarian society was the institution described by Tacitus as the *comitatus*. Through the offer of warlike adventure and booty, any famous chief might attract a band of companions (*comites*). The relationship was highly honorable to both parties: the men received military equipment and food, while in return they provided their leader with an effective retinue and made possible his greater exploits. The companion might or might not be of noble birth; within the retinue no such distinction could equal that of valor and loyalty on the field of battle. The chief must never be excelled in bravery by his followers and they constantly strove to be as brave as he. Any one of them who survived him in a fight was doomed to lifelong disgrace. To stand by him to the death was their sacred obligation.

Germanic
peoples
of the
third
century

Tacitus gives an extensive catalogue of German tribes, but few of them are ever heard of outside his pages. By the time of Marcus Aurelius the Marcomanni and the Quadi had become dangerous on the upper Danube, and their power was broken only with the utmost difficulty. Then, in the third century, a new series of Germanic peoples came to threaten the whole imperial frontier in Europe. The Goths, striking south from the Baltic, crushed the Sarmatians and overran the Danubian provinces. There, as remarked above, they were finally checked by Aurelian, though he was forced to leave them in possession of Dacia. To the north, meanwhile, had emerged three powerful confederations: the Alamans ("all men"), to whom Aurelian abandoned the triangle between the two great rivers; the Franks ("the free") on the lower Rhine; and to the east of them the piratical Saxons ("dagger-men"), feared on both sides of the British Channel. This was the situation when, in the fourth century, the terrific onslaught of the Huns brought increasing pressure on the already weakened defenses of the empire.

The Roman government had long been suffering from a shortage of troops. Diocletian's military system called for a total force of possibly half a million men; if enough Romans could not be found, the emperors had to hire barbarians. So, in one way or another, streams of Moors in Africa, of Arabs in Syria, and of Germans in Europe entered the imperial service. The auxiliary divisions had from the earliest time been non-Roman; by the fourth century even the citizens in the legions were such as Augustus would never have recognized. Besides, through extension of another ancient precedent, whole tribes had been admitted to the empire as allies (*fœderati*), to whom lands had been assigned in return for an engagement to patrol the frontier. Thus Valentinian's successor in the west, Gratian, formally established large bodies of Franks in what is now Flanders. And about the same time Valens, emperor in the east, made a similar bargain with various chieftains of the Visigoths, or West Goths who had appealed to him for protection against the Huns.

Germans in the Roman service

All this was ordinary enough; it was merely an unfortunate accident that the latter arrangement had tragic consequences. While the Goths were crossing the Danube, they became involved in a violent quarrel with certain high-handed officials. Both sides called in reinforcements, and the result was the battle of Adrianople (378), in which Valens was slain. But for the moment there was no further trouble. The new emperor, Theodosius, quickly restored peace by carrying out the original agreement, and during the rest of his reign the Goths faithfully guarded the frontier, as thousands of other *fœderati* were already doing. The affair hardly marks the beginning of an epoch either for the Romans or for the barbarians.

2. The Imperial Collapse

To explain the history of the fifth century it is necessary first of all to make clear the distinction between Roman and barbarian. Today in America we all know of prominent men who are commonly referred to as Swedes, Italians, Poles, or the like; but who, nevertheless, are American citizens and worthy members of the community. Legally their descent is of no importance. Culturally it may or may not be, according to the degree of their Americanization. The situation was very much the same in the Roman Empire. A man was often called a Frank or a Goth because he came of a Frankish or a Gothic family, although he was quite as Roman as the law could make him, and although the better Romans of his day themselves

Roman and barbarian

had dubious ancestries. The really significant question was the extent to which a particular citizen had absorbed Latin culture. As a matter of fact, the empire of the fourth century was filled with semi-barbarous Romans. The only difference between the armed forces on the two sides of the frontier was that the one was paid by the emperor and, presumably, was better equipped and better disciplined. And since the military service was the surest road to political preferment, the higher offices of the state were frequently held by men of recent barbarian extraction. No one doubted their ability, or their desire to be good Romans. Acquiring wealth and power, they intermarried with the noblest families of the empire; for German blood, in particular, was no social disgrace. On the contrary, the admiration of Roman ladies for Nordic beauty had stimulated a brisk trade in blond wigs made of imported barbarian tresses.

Honorius, Stilicho, and Alaric

Thus we find a Vandal soldier named Stilicho rising to high favor under Theodosius and his incompetent son Honorius, who succeeded as western emperor in 395. Stilicho—*patricius*, master of troops, and eventually father-in-law of the new emperor—became actual ruler of the west. Yet he remained unsatisfied, longing also to control the east, which had been placed under the sovereignty of Arcadius, the second incompetent son of Theodosius. In that design he failed, for the main consequence of his intrigue was to encourage another adventurer like himself. This was Alaric, king of the Visigoths, i.e., the elected chief of the Gothic *fœderati* whom Theodosius had stationed along the Danube. Having extorted some sort of military commission from Arcadius, Alaric led his Goths towards Italy, where Stilicho was already faced by a number of other rebels. By calling all available troops from the northern frontiers, however, Stilicho succeeded in holding off his enemies until, in 408, the jealous Honorius had him executed on a charge of treason. The result was chaos, for the emperor merely shut himself up in the impregnable fortress of Ravenna and let happen what would. So, although Alaric invaded Italy, his negotiations with Honorius came to nothing. In revenge he then starved Rome into submission and gave the proud city to his troops for three days' pillage (410). Shortly afterwards he died in the midst of plans for transporting his army to Africa.

The ruin of the western empire

The succeeding events may be passed over in still briefer review. Under the weakling sons of Honorius and Arcadius the two halves of the empire drifted farther and farther apart. The east, as will be seen in a later chapter, continued much as before and even recovered strength; but the west sank to irretrievable ruin. Before the death of Honorius the imperial administration, and with it the imperial defense, had utterly collapsed. Across the frontiers, now stripped of regular troops, poured hosts of barbarians, to do what they pleased with the unfortunate provinces. Britain, early abandoned to its fate, was overrun by Picts from beyond the northern wall, Scots from Ireland, and Saxons from the continent. Northern Gaul was occupied by Franks, Alamans, and Burgundians, while the Vandals and their allies took Aquitaine and Spain. The Visigoths, in the meantime, had entered a sort of Roman alliance through the marriage of their new king, Alaric's brother, to a sister of Honorius. Acting under an official commission, they now invaded southern Gaul and inflicted so terrific a defeat on the Vandals that the latter abandoned Spain and crossed the strait to Africa (429). There Gaiseric, recently elected king of the Vandals, quickly secured the whole territory west of Tripoli, organized it as an independent state, and made it the base for piratical expeditions to the north and east.

Meanwhile the Huns had extended their ruthless dominion from the Caspian to the Rhine, and had respected the Roman territory only because the eastern emperor had regularly paid them blackmail. Now, under a new and vigorous leader named Attila, they decided on wider operations, and it was fortunate for the government at Constantinople that they struck at Gaul rather than Greece. Although the western emperor, Valentinian III, could be expected to do nothing, his able master of troops, Aëtius, took the field against the invaders. And, thanks to the aid of the warlike Visigoths, he won the famous battle of the Catalaunian Fields, in the region now called Champagne (451). That battle, however, merely diverted Attila towards Italy; the decisive event was his sudden death two years later. Thereupon his horde broke up and the Huns ceased to be a menace. *The Huns under Attila*

At Constantinople, meanwhile, the dynasty of the great Theodosius had ended in 450 with the death of his grandson. The latter, Theodosius II, deserves mention solely because a collection of imperial edicts issued since the accession of Constantine happened to be completed during his reign and so to be called the Theodosian Code.[1] So far as the military situation was concerned, his death brought a decided improvement in the situation; for his successors, though hardly to be listed among the greatest of Romans, were fairly able soldiers. There was, for example, the one who gained power by leading a troop of Isaurians, wild mountaineers from Asia Minor, and who was first known as Tarasicodissa. Then, having gained the favor of Leo I and married the emperor's daughter, he changed his name to Zeno and as such was elevated to the purple in 474. Whatever his origin, he was at least no German barbarian and for that reason, as we shall see, made the best of an opportunity to rid the eastern empire of the Goths. *Zeno and the end of the western emperors (476)*

In spite of the respite provided by the dissolution of Attila's horde, conditions in the west became steadily worse. Valentinian III, the last of the Theodosian house, had Aëtius put to death and was himself assassinated by the retainers of the latter (455). Gaiseric, seizing the favorable moment, brought his Vandals up the Tiber and sacked the capital for the second time—an incident that has unfairly identified their name with wanton destruction; for, like Alaric's Goths, they restricted themselves to systematic

[1] See below, p. 92.

looting. After the murder of Valentinian III the government of Italy fell to a series of military bosses, the local commanders of German mercenaries, who set up and pulled down emperors at pleasure until, in 476, one Odoacer decided that it was a useless formality. Deposing the last of the puppets, a mere boy ironically called Romulus Augustulus, he sent the insignia of the vacant office to Zeno, who in return allowed him the customary title of ‘patricius. Theoretically the empire was again to be ruled by one sovereign; but what was the actual situation?

3. THE GERMANS IN THE EMPIRE

Nature of the barbarian invasions

From the facts noted above it should be quite clear that the Roman Empire did not fall through the shock of foreign conquest or become barbarized through any deliberate attack on its ancient culture. One who makes a careful study of the so-called barbarian invasions finds them very hard to define. In the later fourth century the empire already contained thousands of Germans, but they were not invaders. They were men recruited by the government to serve in the regular army or settled as auxiliaries along the frontiers. The former, especially, often attained full Roman rights and rose to high position in state and society. If they failed to become thoroughly Latinized, it was not because of antagonism on their part. The case of Alaric was fundamentally nothing new. In spite of attendant disorders, the Visigoths were officially admitted to the empire and there enjoyed a definite legal status. Alaric, like Stilicho, became master of troops in the imperial army. And although his methods were somewhat crude, he did not introduce civil war and rapine as novelties to the Roman troops. Then came the great barbarian inroads into Gaul. Franks, Alamans, Burgundians, Vandals, and others poured across the border. Yet their occupation of Roman soil was eventually legalized and their position became indistinguishable from that of the older *fœderati*.

Accordingly, if we allow ourselves to become fascinated by the forms of law, we may decide that there were neither invasions nor barbarians; that there was neither a western empire nor a fall of Rome. The truth is, of course, that by the fifth century legal theory was utterly belied by actuality. Under Aurelian Dacia had been definitely abandoned to the Goths; under Valentinian III Britain was no less definitely abandoned to the Angles and Saxons. For a while the imperial government kept up a pretense of authority in Africa; but in the face of Gaiseric's deeds it could deceive no-one. By more gradual stages Spain and Gaul were also lost. Whatever the official explanation, these provinces were conquered and organized into kingdoms by various Germanic peoples. After 476, although Zeno might be said to hold the administration of an undivided empire, and although his sovereignty was specifically recognized by Odoacer, he had as little real power in Italy as in Dacia. Nor was the reality hidden from Zeno. When the opportunity arose, he did what he could to reassert his authority.

Among the Germanic peoples freed by the death of Attila were the Ostrogoths, or East Goths, who were then admitted to the empire as *fœderati* in the station earlier held by the Visigoths. They were under several kings, one of whom had a son named Theodoric. The boy, being sent as a hostage to Constantinople, there acquired a warm admiration for Roman ways and absorbed at least a modicum of Greek and Latin culture. And there, after his elevation as king, he continued to enjoy imperial favor, acquiring the rank of Roman citizen, *patricius*, and master of troops. He was even designated as one of the two consuls for the year 484. But as Theodoric united all the Ostrogoths under his command and displayed ambitions like those of his predecessor Alaric, Zeno determined to get rid of him by commissioning him against Odoacer. In 489, consequently, Theodoric led his Ostrogoths to Italy, which he conquered and, after the treacherous murder of Odoacer, ruled without challenge until his death in 526.

Theodoric the Ostrogoth

To the west, meanwhile, the Visigoths had extended their control over most of Spain and southern Gaul, including Aquitaine and Provence (see Map IV). The Burgundians, pushing south from the country of the Alamans along the Rhine, had occupied the territory that has since been called Burgundy. And in northern Gaul the Franks had now become a formidable power under the vigorous Chlodovech, or Clovis, of the family known as Merovingian. Originally he was only one of many Frankish kings—the leader of a heathen band that had settled in and about the city of Tournai. A thoroughly cruel and unscrupulous barbarian, Clovis soon proved himself to be also a remarkably able commander. An initial victory at Soissons over a local chieftain gave him possession of the region between the Seine and the Loire. Then, turning against the Alamans, he defeated them near Strasbourg and seized the upper Rhinelands. About this time, through the influence of his Burgundian wife, he was converted to Christianity—a momentous step in his career, for the church now hailed him as the champion of the true faith against his heathen or heretic neighbors.[2] To Clovis the role was entirely congenial. Forcing the Burgundians to join with him, he marched against the Visigoths and crushed them in a decisive battle near Poitiers (507). The Ostrogothic king, it is true, intervened to keep the Franks away from the Mediterranean, preserving Septimania for the Visigoths and taking Provence for himself. But Clovis annexed the rest of Aquitaine and, before his death in 511, rounded out his dominions to the north by murdering or deposing all the other Frankish kings.

The Franks under Clovis (481-511)

By the opening of the sixth century the Roman world had thus come to present a very confused picture. One important aspect, Christianity, will be separately considered in the next chapter. And it will be convenient to leave

[2] On the Arian heresy and its spread among the Goths see below, p. 63.

Roman
and Ger-
manic
insti-
tutions

any further appraisal of the eastern empire as an introduction to the reign of Justinian. In the present connection only a few statements have to be made about the mixture of institutions that henceforth characterized the western provinces. However meager our sources generally, we may at least be certain that throughout most of their subjected territories the Germans were a small minority whose dominion rested on military strength. Once that was broken, the conquerors vanished—to be absorbed into the conquered population, to whom they had already tended to be assimilated. Biologically, the result was negligible; culturally, it merely served to accelerate a process of barbarization begun long before. As will be apparent from the events of later centuries, this was certainly true of the Vandals in Africa and of the Goths in Spain and Italy. Elsewhere, particularly in Gaul and Britain, the permanence of the Frankish and Saxon kingdoms assured the persistence of the invading nations, together with much of their custom. Even there, however, we find a deep Roman influence that became increasingly significant with the passage of time.

The gov-
ernment of
Theodoric

The most thoroughly Roman of all the barbarian kingdoms was that of the Ostrogoths in Italy. Under Theodoric the old administrative system continued without a break. He was surrounded by officials bearing the traditional titles of Diocletian's empire. At Rome the consuls and other magistrates were annually installed and the senate still enjoyed its accustomed prestige. To enforce the Roman law, Theodoric promulgated his famous *Edict*, which was modeled after the Theodosian Code.[3] His taxes were the same as had been collected by his predecessors. He even distributed grain to the populace and gave the traditional shows. All military power, however, was reserved to the Goths, who were settled on the lands assigned to them and, having no protection from the Roman law, were governed by their ancient customs. In strict theory the kingship of Theodoric was a personal command recognized by a group of Germans domiciled in the empire; his authority in Italy rested upon an office conferred by Zeno. When dealing with barbarian princes of the west, Theodoric acted as one sovereign among others; but he always treated the emperor with great deference. In every respect he tried to be a good Roman. Although he is said to have been illiterate, the greatest Latin writers of the day served at his court: Cassiodorus as his secretary and Boëthius as his master of offices.[4] He repaired the aqueducts and other Roman monuments, and himself erected a number of splendid buildings.[5] Aside from the rather mysterious execution of Boëthius on a charge of treason, his reign ended in general tranquillity and good feeling—a bright interlude in a gloomy age.

[3] See above, p. 51.
[4] See below, p. 71.
[5] See below, p. 95.

The
Salic Law
and the
Anglo-
Saxon
dooms

Like Theodoric, the Burgundian and Visigothic kings issued collections of laws for their Roman subjects, which were therefore drawn in large part from the Theodosian Code. Following the example of his royal neighbors, Clovis then published the *Salic Law*. But the principal source of his compilation, as the title implies, was the custom of the Salian Franks, the particular group of peoples that had first recognized him as king. In this connection it should be noted that the *Salic Law*, like the other records of the continental Germans, was composed in Latin. Except for an occasional word, these records tell us nothing about the Germanic languages. To gain a knowledge of the latter, we must turn to actual writings in German, of which the earliest were the Gothic Bible of Ulfilas and the Anglo-Saxon dooms.

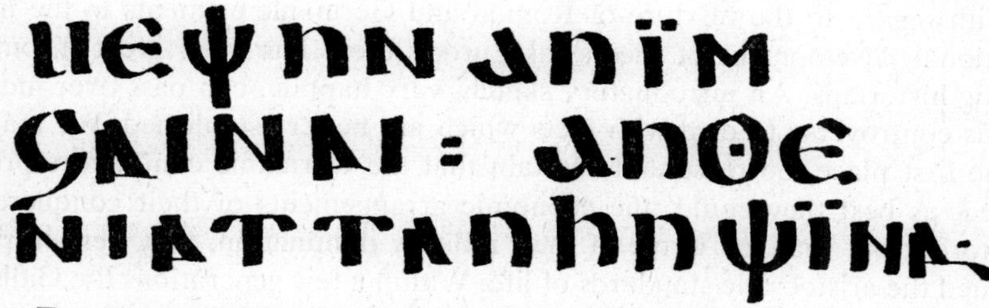

FIG. 6.   Example of Gothic Writing. QVETHUN DU IM JAINAI: DU HVE NI ATTAUHUTH INA. This is *John,* vii. 45: "[and they] said unto them, Why have ye not brought him?"

Even before the Visigoths were permitted to cross the Danube in the fourth century, most of them had been converted to Christianity through the preaching of their first bishop, Ulfilas (d. 383). Desiring to translate the Scriptures for the benefit of his countrymen, he adapted the Greek alphabet to the purpose (see Figure 6). And thanks to his accomplishment, we may be sure of many Gothic words—not only what they meant but also how they were pronounced. To find a similar development in western Europe, we have to wait until the seventh century. By that time the Germanic conquerors of southeastern Britain had been generally Christianized by Roman missionaries.[6] It was their introduction of the Latin alphabet that made possible the writing of the language which we know as Old English or Anglo-Saxon, and which was soon used for the dooms, statements of customary law drawn up by the local kings (see Figure 17).

Mixture of
Roman and
Germanic
custom

The Anglo-Saxons, having settled in a province that had been only partially Latinized and remaining isolated for a long time thereafter, preserved a relatively large proportion of their Germanic customs. The same truth will perhaps hold for the Franks in the extreme north of Gaul. Elsewhere,

[6] See below, pp. 124-25.

however, they tended to be absorbed into the native population and to adopt the institutions of the latter. After conquering most of Gaul, Clovis attempted to reign as the lawful successor of the Roman emperors. He assumed the imperial regalia and surrounded himself with household ministers whose titles were at least reminiscent of Diocletian's court. In so far as possible he maintained the Roman administration, collecting taxes, enforcing justice, and promulgating official documents according to the ancient forms. Nor were his Frankish subjects at all unwilling to accept any Roman usages that seemed profitable: the ownership of agrarian estates, the enjoyment of aristocratic privileges, and the like. Yet the persistence of Roman custom was necessarily restricted by the actualities of life. Clovis, at best, could be only a crude imitation of a Cæsar; the bulk of his warriors, for all their admiration of Roman ways, continued to be thoroughly barbarian.

With regard to the mixture of Roman and Germanic elements in the institutional development of mediæval Europe there has been great dispute among historians. An introductory sketch, very happily, can pass over most of this controversy to deal with facts which are better established. We may, in the first place, be reasonably certain that the Germanic conquerors preserved, as best they could, the economic arrangements of their conquered territories; but that, by virtue of their military domination, they henceforth dictated the aristocratic standards of life. Within a few generations the Gallo-Roman gentleman, even a member of the senatorial nobility, had adopted the warlike habits, together with the costume and arms, of the barbarian tribesman. To maintain his social position, in other words, he had to be a Frank; he married his daughters to Frankish warriors and gave his sons Frankish names. The inevitable result was the disappearance of Romans, as such, throughout the Merovingian kingdom; though still differentiated in the *Salic Law*, they cease to appear in the later enactments. And below this semi-barbarous military and agrarian aristocracy a similar amalgamation produced an economically dependent peasantry. Roman slaves and *coloni,* unfree or half-free Germans, captives in war, and other subjected persons were merged to form the villein class of the Middle Ages.

Judicial organization

Under these conditions it was quite impossible to enforce any uniform system of law. Generally throughout the barbarian states counts (*comites*) were appointed by the kings to act as their subordinates in the local administrative districts, which usually corresponded to the *civitates* of the late empire. Such a count was likely to be a professional warrior rather than a trained civil servant; and in lieu of a salary he was regularly permitted to keep a share of his official perquisites. Within a particular territory the count raised the king's military forces, collected his revenues, and held his courts. As long as Romans could be distinguished from Goths, Burgundians, Franks, and others, each people was supposed to enjoy its own law. But the ultimate result was merely that in every region the majority of the wealthier inhabitants determined whatever judicial procedure was to prevail. The count or his subordinate presided over the court and saw to the king's financial interests; the court itself, consisting of the more substantial persons of the vicinity, declared the law and supervised all trials. Often, for the sake of convenience, much of the routine work was delegated to a select group of judgment-finders—such as the Anglo-Saxon doomsmen or the Frankish *rachimburgi*. In any case the actual law which was thus administered would be based on the unwritten custom of the countryside.

Theoretically, such older provinces as Italy and southern Gaul remained faithful to the Roman law. But even there the absence of professional judges, as also of literate suitors, led to a rapid decay of the ancient system. Legal education was virtually restricted to the training of notaries—men who could draw up wills, deeds, contracts, and other necessary instruments. The study of jurisprudence flourished only in the eastern empire; throughout the west even the more learned could be expected to master only the poor summaries and adaptations issued by the authority of barbarian princes. To live under the Roman law thus became a matter of accepting certain traditional forms with regard to marriage, testamentary succession, conveyance of land, and the like. Judicial procedure ceased to be Roman in any proper sense of the word. More particularly, the ancient method of trial—with its strictly enforced rules for the conduct of plaintiff and defendant, for the admission of evidence, and for the establishment of proof —fell into complete abeyance. On all sides men found it easier to adopt the more primitive custom of the barbarians. During many centuries, accordingly, the common practice of the western European courts came to be dominated by Germanic rather than by Roman precedent.

As provided by the *Salic Law*, the Anglo-Saxon dooms, and similar compilations, any man (A) who wished to bring suit against another (B) first had to summon him, in the presence of witnesses, to attend the local court and there reply to a particular charge. If B failed to appear within a certain time, the court would authorize A, with whatever aid he could muster, to take forcible action against the delinquent. Suppose, however, that B saw fit to defend the suit. A, by means of a prescribed formula, would pronounce his accusation, and B in the same way would deny it. The court, or a select group of doomsmen, would then order some kind of trial to be held on a future day. Normally the burden of proof would rest on B and he would be allowed to clear himself by compurgation. That is to say, he would take a solemn oath that he was innocent and present a definite number of associates to swear that his oath was pure. This entire procedure, it should be noted, was highly ritualistic. To make his accusation stick, A had to be letter-perfect in all required oaths and affirmations; if, on the other hand, B or any of his oath-helpers made the slightest verbal slip, his defense collapsed.

Germanic trials

Much always depended on the character of the persons concerned. A man's "swearing-worth" varied according to his rank; the oath of a nobleman would counterbalance the oaths of at least six ordinary freemen. Besides, anyone of bad reputation would hardly be permitted to bring a valid charge in court or, when accused, to clear himself by compurgation. In case a defendant was barred from that mode of proof, or was unable to find the necessary oath-helpers, he generally had to fall back on the ordeal. After solemn prayer, he plunged his arm into a pot of boiling water or with his bare hand carried a heated bar of iron for a certain distance. He was acquitted if the arm or hand, having been bound up for three days, was officially pronounced clean—i.e., apparently, not infected. Other varieties of ordeal were sometimes used, as well as the judicial combat. In the latter procedure, which was especially popular among the Franks, the two parties, or perhaps their lawfully appointed champions, fought a duel in some prescribed way. And since God had been invoked to defend the right, the victor would be held to have proved his case. Germanic trials thus regularly implied an appeal for divine intervention—to determine the outcome of a fight, the result of a physical test, or the validity of an oath. It was only occasionally that facts were established by what we should call legal evidence, as when a charter was produced to show title to land or when the purchase of an ox was attested by a witness to the transaction.

Wergelds and other compensations

From one or the other of the parties to a suit the king always collected some kind of fee in return for his guarantee of justice; and whenever the case involved a breach of the king's personal protection or special privilege, he might exact a very heavy fine. None of the Germanic peoples, however, had arrived at a clear idea of crime as distinct from civil injury. The custom described by Tacitus still prevailed: homicide, assault, theft, and the like remained primarily offenses against the individual and his kinsmen. If the latter were not bought off, they were lawfully entitled to seek revenge by prosecuting a blood-feud. So the killing of a man regularly necessitated the payment to the relatives of his wergeld, a sum determined by his social rank. Wounding called for compensation in proportion to the value of the part affected, and other wrongs, whether physical or moral, had to be atoned for in the same way. The codes of the barbarian kings thus tended, in the main, to be tariffs of the amounts charged for every kind of injurious action. Here are a few examples.

In case of conviction, the *Salic Law* provides the following compositions. For stealing a sucking pig, a calf, a sheep, or a goat, 3s.;[7] an ox or a cow with a calf, 35s.; a bull, 45s. (double that if it belonged to the king); a dog, a hive of bees, a boat, a fence, or flour from a mill, 15s.; a trained hawk or stag hound, 45s.; a slave or a horse, (minimum) 30s. For housebreaking

[7] The coin here represented by *s.* was the gold *solidus* of Constantine (above, p. 30), the English shilling and the later French *sou*.

without theft, 35*s.*; with theft, up to 35*s.* extra. For carrying off the wife of a freeman, 200*s.* For arson, either of a house with people in it or of a stable with animals in it, 63*s.* For slaying a Roman, 100*s.*; a free Frank, 200*s.*—penalties that were tripled if the slain man was in the royal service or if the slayer attempted to hide the body. For assault and robbery of a Roman, 35*s.*; of a free Frank, 63*s.* For unjustly accusing a freeman before the king, 63*s.* For binding a freeman, 30*s.* For destroying the use of a hand, a foot, or an eye, 63*s.* For stabbing or for striking with bloodshed, 15*s.*; for striking without bloodshed, 3*s.* For slanderously calling a woman a whore, 45*s.*; calling a man a spy or a perjurer, 15*s.*; calling a man a fox or a hare or saying he had thrown away his shield (cf. Tacitus), 3*s.*

The early dooms of the Anglo-Saxons contain many similar enactments. We thus find that in seventh-century Kent the ordinary freeman's wergeld was 100*s.*, normally paid in unblemished livestock: one-fifth "at the open grave" and the rest within forty days. Compensation for breaking the fence round a man's house, for slanderously calling him a perjurer, or for unjustifiably taking his ale-cup away from him, was 6*s.*; for binding him, 20*s.*; for seducing his wife, his entire wergeld—and the offender had to "get another wife with his own money and bring her to the other man's home"! An elaborate list of payments for all kinds of wounds includes the following compensations for total loss: an eye or a foot, 50*s.*; an ear, 25*s.*; a tooth, 1*s.* to 6*s.*, according to its prominence; a thumb, 20*s.* (its nail, 3*s.*); other fingers, from 4*s* to 11*s.* (their nails, 1*s.* each); toes, half the rate for the corresponding fingers.

For over five hundred years it was barbarous custom of this sort that superseded the majestic law of Rome throughout most of the western world.

CHAPTER IV

The Church After Constantine

1. ECCLESIASTICAL GOVERNMENT

Christian tradition and the Bible

Christianity, as remarked above, was one of several mystic faiths that, originating in the east, swept through the Roman Empire. In the first century it remained very obscure; in the second century it gained sufficient prominence to awaken an increasing hostility on the part of the government; in the third century it grew so strong that persecution of its followers came to be recognized as useless; and, finally, in the fourth century it became the official religion of the state. Meanwhile—in the course of bitter conflict with the Jews, with the empire, and with pagan sects—the church had developed a powerful organization. Whatever the controversies that were to arise over this development a thousand years later, there were none in the fourth century. So, without raising the question of absolute truth, which must remain a matter of faith, we may restrict our attention to the theory and practice of the church as it then was.

The ultimate authority, to which appeal was made for the settlement of all disputes, was the sacred tradition of the faithful. Part of that tradition was contained in the Scriptures, but the acceptance of such writings as divinely inspired was itself traditional. In ecclesiastical history a collection of authoritative books is called a canon. The Christian Bible includes two such canons, known as the Old and New Testaments. The Old Testament of the Christians was not the original Hebrew canon, but a Greek version called the Septuagint, which had been drawn up for the use of Hellenized Jews in Alexandria, and which included various books that had never been written in Hebrew.[1] The New Testament was a subsequent compilation that took form as the result of Christian usage. As late as the time of Con-

---

[1] Such as *Esdras, Tobit,* and *Maccabees,* which, if printed in a Protestant Bible, are labeled *Apocrypha.*

stantine, although Paul's epistles, the four gospels, and the *Acts of the Apostles* were universally recognized, opinions were still divided with regard to the *Apocalypse*, the epistles attributed to other disciples, and certain additional writings. The final determination of the canon came only with the formal organization of the church in the period immediately following.

In the meantime, however, all Christian communities had come to hold **The sacra-** certain fundamental doctrines: especially that Christ, the Son of God, had **mental** founded His church on earth to provide men with a new means of salva- **system** tion—the holy sacraments. A sacrament, to use the phrase that was to become official, is the "outward sign of an inward grace." The outward sign is the ceremonial; the inward grace is the grace of God spiritually transforming the recipient. According to this view, every sacrament is a mystery, which supernaturally produces results otherwise unobtainable.[2] The sacrament of baptism, for example, has been held to wash away the sin inherited by the child from his first parents, Adam and Eve. The sacrament of confirmation follows and completes that of baptism. The sacrament of matrimony binds together a man and his wife. On becoming old enough to know right from wrong, the Christian should confess his sins and, on proving his repentance, receive absolution together with a penalty of prayer, fasting, or the performance of other holy works—the sacrament of penance. Rather in the nature of a communal service has been the sacrament of the eucharist, popularly known as the mass. In it the congregation meets to commemorate the last supper of the Lord and through the sacramental bread and wine enters into mystic communion with Him.

To administer sacraments like these the ordinary person was held to be **Theory** obviously incompetent; the supernatural powers of the church had been **of the** entrusted to a sacerdotal class, admission to which was itself a sacrament— **apostolic** that of ordination. The justification of this idea was the theory of the apos- **succession** tolic succession. The apostles, it was affirmed, had received divine authority from Christ, who had laid His hands upon them and so commissioned them to continue the work He had begun. They in turn, by the same ceremony, had commissioned others; and upon their successors, the ordained clergy, devolved the power of administering the sacraments and governing the church. But the apostolic authority, by this doctrine, was given in its entirety only to the bishop (*episcopus*). The priest (*presbyter*) was his subordinate, empowered to administer only some of the sacraments.[3] And below the priesthood a number of lesser grades came to be recognized, of which the highest was that of deacon.

[2] In the early Christian centuries there was considerable variation of sacramental practice (e.g., as to the proper age for baptism) and theological interpretations of particular ceremonies have continued to differ. In such matters the Greek and Roman Churches have never entirely agreed. Clear definition of the "seven sacraments" was first made by Peter Lombard in the twelfth century (see below, pp. 265-66).

[3] Practice in the west excluded both confirmation and ordination.

Territorial organization

It was only after the legalization of Christianity that ecclesiastical government came to be based on a territorial plan borrowed from the Roman Empire. The unit was the *civitas*, the bishop's diocese or see (from *sedes*, seat), in which stood his cathedral church (from *cathedra*, the episcopal chair). The diocese was subdivided into parishes, both urban and rural, each of which was entrusted to a priest named by the bishop. Earlier, on the death of a bishop, the man to be consecrated in his place had been chosen through a somewhat informal election, in which popular acclaim was frequently a decisive factor. Later, as the episcopal office gained prominence in society and politics, it became a prize to be secured through influential patrons, or even to be fought over by rival factions. So the actual choice of a bishop was gradually taken over by the clergy of the diocese, and little was left to the populace beyond a sort of confirmatory applause.

A much more troublesome problem concerned the relative dignity of bishops. For both civil and ecclesiastical administration a number of *civitates* were combined to form a province. One city in each province served as the metropolis, and the bishop of such a city, styled metropolitan or archbishop, normally enjoyed the right of consecrating all bishops within his jurisdiction. Thus far there was general agreement, but the higher grades were a subject of dispute. Applying the imperial system of organization in its entirety would demand prelates corresponding to the vicars and prefects. And would not the supreme rank then have to be shared by the bishops of Rome and Constantinople? Although such a rigorous hierarchy of ecclesiastical offices was never actually established, it might well have been if the empire had not disintegrated. As long as the emperors ruled the Roman world, the church tended to be governed according to their ideas. And they unquestionably regarded it as a department of state, administered by public officials under the sovereignty of Augustus. The peculiar authority of the clergy extended only to matters of faith and religious discipline; their acts, like those of other subjects, depended for legality upon imperial decree.

The empire and heresy

In this connection the policy of the fourth-century emperors with regard to heresy is very illuminating. The concept of heresy had already become clearly defined in the earlier period—as a doctrine advanced in the name of Christianity but denounced by the church as contrary to the orthodox faith. Thus the attempt of the so-called Gnostics[4] to combine Christianity with Neoplatonic mysticism had been rejected by the general agreement of the Christian leaders. In the time of Constantine, however, more serious controversies arose within the organized church itself. In 314 a council of western bishops called by the emperor at Arles condemned the Donatists —a fanatical group which, rebelling against the bishop of Carthage,

[4] See above, p. 42.

asserted that the validity of a sacrament depended on the personal character of the minister.[5] Then, a few years later, a priest of Alexandria named Arius began a dispute that was to have much graver consequences. With what seemed to him unescapable logic he argued that Christ, being the Son of God, must have been younger than the Father; must, indeed, have been a creature rather than a divinity in the absolute sense. Otherwise, said Arius, Christians would have to admit that they were worshiping two gods. Eloquent champions, notably Athanasius, at once arose to defend the traditional faith. They insisted that, although the doctrine of the Incarnation necessitated belief in the humanity of Jesus, Christians must also believe that He was truly God as well, or their customary worship of Him would be no better than idolatry.

In 325, accordingly, Constantine summoned the bishops from all Christendom to decide the question of Arianism in a great meeting at Nicæa, the first general council in the history of the church. Before the assembled prelates, perhaps three hundred in all, the emperor appeared in person to urge the cause of unity. The result was a nearly unanimous declaration condemning the views of Arius and prescribing the formula of Christian belief that, with later amendments, is known as the Nicene Creed. Nevertheless, in one form or another Arianism persisted in the eastern provinces and was thence carried to the Germans by missionaries —among them the famous Ulfilas, translator of the Bible into the Gothic language.[6] The conversion of the Goths to unorthodox Christianity caused them much trouble when they came to rule parts of the empire; for in the meantime Theodosius had secured the final outlawry of Arianism in a council at Constantinople (381) and had established severe penalties to crush heresy throughout the Roman territory. The troubles of the fifth century naturally prevented any rigorous enforcement of the law. Yet the leaders of the church could not forget that the Visigothic and Ostrogothic kings were Arian heretics and in preference to them supported the barbarous Clovis, who had been baptized in the orthodox faith.

The Council of Nicæa (325)

We have seen that, according to the imperial theory, the normal government of the church rested with a hierarchy of bishops corresponding to the hierarchy of civil officials, and that any major cause of dispute should be submitted to a general council of the bishops and settled by the emperor's promulgation of their decision. But from an early time this theory had been opposed by another, to which the calamitous events of the fifth century inevitably gave fresh prominence. Christian tradition, said the upholders of the latter theory, was essentially that handed down by the

Theory of the Petrine supremacy

[5] This doctrine, revived by many later sects, was quite incompatible with the teaching of the organized church, that a sacrament is a divine miracle which is efficacious without regard to the merit of the person who administers it or to that of the recipient.

[6] See above, p. 55.

apostles and preserved in the churches which they had founded: especially Antioch, Alexandria, and Rome. By the test of apostolic foundation, of course, Constantinople had no claim to superior rank. Rome, on the other hand, was the city where, by ancient tradition, the apostles Peter and Paul had both been martyred, and where Peter had been the first bishop. Furthermore, according to the gospel of Matthew (xvi, 18-19), Peter was the rock on which Christ had built His church, the keeper of the keys to the kingdom of heaven, the holder of the power to bind and loose. As Peter had been the head of the apostles, so his successor, the bishop of Rome or pope,[7] was the head of all bishops, the supreme authority of Christendom.

The early papacy

To state this theory was one matter, to enforce it quite another. Of the popes during the first two Christian centuries little more is known than a list of their names. It is only after the time of Constantine that the sources begin to reveal certain popes as distinct individuals who play an active part in the affairs of the universal church. Thus Damasus I (366-84) appears as the author of a digest setting forth the beliefs and practices of the Roman see, including a definite assertion of the papal supremacy. He also proclaimed what was thereafter to be the official canon of the New Testament and, as will be explained below, commissioned the illustrious Jerome to revise the Latin translation of the Bible. From his successor, Siricius (384-99), come the oldest extant papal decretals, formal letters on questions of law and doctrine submitted to Rome for decision. And with Leo the Great (440-61)—a distinguished writer, an eloquent preacher, and an inspiring leader in an age of political ruin—control by the papacy was accepted by most local churches of the west.

Religious divergence between east and west

In the east, on the other hand, the papal sovereignty was bitterly opposed. There the emperor remained powerful, summoning councils to decide religious disputes and warmly supporting the claim of Constantinople to equality with Rome in ecclesiastical privilege. This, assuredly, was one important cause of dissension between east and west. Another was the fundamental incompatibility of Greek and Latin theologians. An earlier council, that of Ephesus (431), had condemned the Syrian Nestorius for so far distinguishing the divine from the human nature in Christ as to deny to the Virgin Mary the title, Mother of God. Since then a number of clergymen, led by the prelates of Egypt, had gone to the opposite extreme of attributing only one nature to Christ. Then, in 451, the views of the latter group—or monophysites, as they came to be called—were rejected by an imperial council at Chalcedon in favor of Pope Leo's judgment as to the combination in Christ of both the human and the divine nature.

---

[7] This title is merely a form of the Latin *papa* (father). It could be used in addressing any priest, but in the west, as a mark of special honor, it came to be reserved for the Roman bishop.

Yet, in spite of the decision thus rendered and generally agreed to in the west, controversy on the same subject continued to rage throughout the east and so, as will be seen in the following chapters, to determine the course of many famous events.

Whatever may have been the theory, it is obvious that in practice the church of the fifth century was very different from what it.had been in the days of Roman persecution. Christianity then was not a faith for the ease-loving and indifferent; there was no worldly advantage in holding ecclesiastical office. But the conversion of Constantine made Christianity fashionable. The clergy attained social and political prominence. The local churches, through gifts and bequests, acquired extensive property. Finally, the decrees of Theodosius compelled all Roman subjects, except the tolerated Jews, to become ostensibly Christian. In reality, many of them remained pagan, especially throughout the country districts—as the word itself implies (*paganus*, a rustic). And even more of them, although they assumed the Christian name, remained pagan at heart; for the earlier situation had been reversed. To be a Christian was now a matter of law, rather than of religious fervor. Being a practical institution, the church had to take the people as they came and mold its requirements to suit the great majority; but in so doing it could hardly satisfy those who demanded a more rigorous Christianity. For them—"the religious," as they were significantly called—the church came to provide an ascetic life primarily devoted to worship and meditation.

Problems of the official church

2. MONASTICISM

Religion in all ages has carried with it a certain element of mysticism, an unending search for hidden truth through some form of supernatural revelation; and in this search men have very generally believed that they have been aided by asceticism, the denial to themselves of lawful pleasures or the infliction upon themselves of unnecessary hardships. Ascetic practices have commonly included celibacy, fasting, prolonged prayer at the expense of sleep, and the renunciation of such luxuries as bathing, soft beds, and comfortable clothes. For priests the church came to prescribe a fairly rigorous standard that, at least in the west, contained the prohibition of marriage. And at particular times all Christians were required to observe a stricter discipline than normal; on Fridays and during Lent, for example, they ought to abstain from eating meat. To many, however, these ordinary requirements seemed inadequate. They felt that, to attain salvation, they must escape from the world and pursue a still more ascetic life. So a woman might abandon her family ties and vow perpetual chastity; a man might give his wealth to the poor and retire into solitude for the sake of acquiring merit through continual prayer and the mortification of the flesh. Such

Mysticism and asceticism

a woman was called a nun; such a man was called a monk (*monachus*), which literally means one living alone, a hermit.

The original monk thus found a cave or built himself a hut where, relying on the offerings of the faithful, he could hope to enjoy the necessary leisure for the perfection of holiness. Since existence is relatively easy in a climate·like that of Egypt, it was hardly strange that this country should witness the first noteworthy development of Christian monasticism. St. Anthony of Egypt, we are told, was inspired by the reading of a text in the Gospel to adopt an ascetic life in the outskirts of his native town and then to go into the desert, where he spent many years as a hermit. Gaining a great reputation for sanctity, he was imitated by a host of others and finally, at their request (about 305), established for them a sort of common discipline. The Antonian system, which thenceforth prevailed in Lower Egypt, prescribed no community life. Each monk had his own cell and there continued whatever practices he liked, meeting with the rest for ecclesiastical service on Saturday and Sunday. It was consequently left for St. Pachomius, about ten years later, to draw up the first rule for cenobites, monks living in true communities. Although each brother occupied a separate dwelling, he was supposed to follow a definite schedule of divine worship, reading of the Scriptures, and manual labor. By the end of the fourth century, it is said, there were no less than seven thousand Pachomian monks in Upper Egypt and a similar plan had been successfully applied to colonies of nuns.

Spreading into Asia, both systems of monastic life attained remarkable popularity. In Syria, where the climate was especially favorable, hermits continued to enjoy great renown. Among them the most famous was St. Simeon Stylites (d. 459), who took up his abode on top of a pillar just wide enough to lie on. There he lived without descending for thirty years, and in the course of that time increased the height of his perch from six to sixty feet, getting needed supplies by lowering a basket on the end of a rope. Meanwhile a more sensible development of monasticism had been made by St. Basil, a Greek of Pontus, in the later fourth century. After studying the Antonian and Pachomian customs, he rejected them for his country and substituted what we still know as a monastery—a house where the monks all live together under one roof, sharing common quarters and participating in a common routine of existence. Under the Basilian rule no trace remained of the old individualism; the monk found each day taken up with a prescribed order of activity, which left nothing to personal caprice. The principal object, of course, was divine worship; but the many services were interspersed with hard work, which Basil thought preferable to exaggerated asceticism. The Basilian system rapidly spread from the Hellenized provinces of Asia and Europe to the newly converted kingdoms of the Slavs—throughout all of which it has remained the standard form of monasticism down to the present.

In the west, meanwhile, the example of the Egyptian monks had come to be widely followed before the end of the fourth century. It became increasingly common for persons of good birth, both men and women, to renounce the world and adopt some form of ascetic life. Hermits appeared on all sides and many of them formed religious communities of the Pachomian type. Those at Tours and Lérins were especially famous in fifth-century Gaul, and it was from there that monastic institutions were carried to Ireland by the illustrious St. Patrick (d. 461). The latter, according to the traditional story, was born of Christian parents in Britain and was originally named Sucat. As a youth, he was captured by Irish pirates and held by them for about six years. Having escaped in a ship bound for Gaul, he became a monk at Lérins and later took holy orders under the Latin name of Patricius. But his great ambition had always been to convert the wild people who had enslaved him; so, in 432, he was consecrated bishop and formally dispatched on a mission to Ireland. Spending there the rest of a long life, he had the satisfaction of seeing the bulk of the Irish enrolled under the standard of the Cross. How the ecclesiastical organization which he thus established was extended by zealous Irish missionaries to Britain and thence to the continent will be seen in a later chapter.

Monasticism in the west: St. Patrick

The system that was to win lasting success in western Europe, however, was not Egyptian monasticism but the more peculiarly Latin monasticism of St. Benedict. According to the *Dialogues* of Pope Gregory I,[8] Benedict was born of a noble family in the Roman municipality of Nursia and, like other youths of his class, was sent to be educated in the capital. There he became disgusted with the vicious life of the fashionable world and decided to become a hermit. For a number of years he lived in a cave overlooking the valley of Subiaco, being scantily fed by a friend from a nearby monastery. As the fame of his holiness spread abroad, disciples thronged to the vicinity, so that Benedict soon found himself the spiritual director of a large community. Then came persecution from various rival establishments devoted to a laxer code of morals; and finally, about 520, Benedict led a band of his most ardent followers to a new abode on the summit of a commanding hill called Monte Cassino, where he composed the rule that was to dominate the religious life of the west. It has often been said that his rule was drawn up for the monks at Monte Cassino, but Benedict's own language proves that from the outset he contemplated a reformed discipline for monasteries generally. Indeed, anyone who carefully reads the rule may easily perceive that it takes the ideals of monasticism for granted and restricts its emphasis to the means by which they can best be attained.

St. Benedict and his rule

Benedict, his prologue declares, "is about to institute a school for the

[8] See below, p. 128.

service of God." He intends to ordain nothing severe or oppressive
although, "to amend vice and preserve charity," certain matters have to
be regulated "somewhat strictly." At the end the author warns the reader
not to be satisfied with what he has just perused. To attain a greater perfection of learning and virtue, he should study the Scriptures and the works
of the holy fathers; Benedict himself has composed "merely a little rule for
beginners." And it applies only to cenobites, "the best kind of monks."
After long training in a monastery one may safely become a hermit, but
without such experience the solitary life is dangerous. There can be no
true holiness without law; one who shuts himself up without a shepherd
is in his own fold, not the Lord's.

The Bene-
dictine
vows

A man desiring admission to the Benedictine community must first serve
for a time as a novice, and so prove his determination and sincerity.
Finally, after demonstrating his fitness to be a brother, he is to sign in
writing a solemn vow of stability, conversion of life, and obedience. Thus
he promises to give up his old life and adopt that of the monk; he resigns
his own will and becomes subject in all ways to the abbot, the elected head
of the monastery; and he swears to remain permanently inside it, for without special authorization he may not set foot beyond its walls. The monastic
life implies the obligations of chastity and poverty. The first Benedict
hardly refers to; the second he dwells on at length.

Let no-one presume to give or receive anything without the command of the
abbot, or to have anything of his own: neither book, nor tablets, nor pen—
nothing whatsoever. For those who are not permitted to have even their bodies
and wills under their own authority should look to the father of the monastery
for all necessary things; they should have nothing but what the abbot has given
or allowed. And all things are to be common to all.

The
abbot

Under these circumstances, the responsibility of the abbot is a heavy
one; he is answerable to God not merely for his own acts but also for those
of his subordinates. In his keeping are the souls of the brethren, as well
as their bodies, the house which they inhabit, and everything of which they
enjoy the use. Before deciding any weighty matter he must call the monks
together for consultation; then, when he has heard their advice, he must
do whatever he considers right, acting always "in the fear of God and
according to the rule." Within the monastery he shall make no distinction
of persons, whether freeborn or servile, except as one or another may excel
in humility and good works. To suit the capacities and deserts of the
brothers, he shall fill all offices in the monastery, apportion all routine
work, and assign special tasks as the need for them may arise. He is to
enforce the prescribed monastic discipline; yet, in doing so, he is to exercise
wide discretionary powers. So the abbot's character is of supreme importance for the well-being of the monastery. When a vacancy occurs in the

abbacy, the monks shall elect a man distinguished for virtue and wisdom, even if by order of seniority "he be the last in the community."

As to the daily life of the monastery, Benedict's régime, compared with the prevalent Egyptian system, is eminently moderate and sensible. The chief duty of the brotherhood is divine worship, "the work of God," and primarily consists in the chanting of psalms. There are to be eight regular services, or offices, beginning with matins "at the eighth hour of the night,"[9] followed by lauds at daybreak and ending with compline at dusk, so that the brothers may retire without the aid of artificial light. This arrangement would permit an unbroken sleep of over eight hours in the winter; and since it would be somewhat less in the summer, compensation is made by a siesta after the midday meal. The monks are to sleep in their clothes—the common tunic and cowl, bound at the waist with a cord—but each is to have a separate bed in the dormitory, together with a mattress, a blanket, and a pillow. The principal meal of the day is to include two cooked dishes besides green vegetables and fruit; and each brother shall in addition receive a pound of bread, part of which he ought to keep for supper. Except in the case of invalids, the eating of meat, like bathing, is generally forbidden, but it should be remembered that, according to Benedict's definition, meat is only the flesh of four-footed beasts. And he is equally generous in the matter of drink. In our time, he states, monks cannot be persuaded that, as some have written, they should have no wine at all; and so he authorizes each to have a daily portion, with an extra allowance because of specially hard work or hot weather.

Most of the monk's day, outside the four or five hours of religious service, is taken up with manual labor; for "idleness," says Benedict, "is the enemy of the soul." In the summer the brothers are to begin their assigned work shortly after sunrise and are to continue until the fourth hour; then they are to engage in reading, meditation, or prayer until the sixth hour (about noon), when they have their first meal. Afterwards they are again to rest for somewhat over two hours, when the afternoon office is celebrated and all return to work until evensong, followed by supper, the final office, and bed at dark. In the winter, when everybody would rise later, the reading period comes first; then labor until dinner, which is had at the ninth hour and is again followed by reading. Sunday is normally to be devoted to the regular worship, attendance at mass, and reading; yet if any brother is unable or unwilling to occupy his time profitably in this way, he may be set to work. Benedict thus prescribes six to seven hours of daily labor. The abbot, however, is to moderate this routine for the benefit of the aged and infirm, and there are many tasks to be assigned besides agriculture—such as cooking and serving at table, care of the monastic property, skilled crafts, clerical work, and the teach-

The daily routine

[9] See above, p. 21.

ing of younger monks or of boys who have been placed there by their parents. Lastly, Benedict provides that certain monks shall always be appointed to look after any guests who may arrive, for hospitality is a sacred obligation. Whoever knocks at the gate, whether rich or destitute, must be received in love and humility as if he were Christ Himself.

The secular and the regular clergy

This was and is Benedictine monasticism. Its direct influence on the religious life of Europe was incalculable, because it set a new and eminently practical standard not only for monks but also, with certain modifications, for nuns. Its more indirect contributions to European civilization, including the advancement of scholarship, will be discussed below in connection with its official adoption by the Roman Church. Here it need only be remarked that, as the result of this adoption, the regular clergy—i.e., persons living under a monastic rule (*regula*)—were sharply distinguished from the secular clergy—i.e., those properly ordained as bishops, priests, deacons, and others to serve the church in the world (*sæcula*).

3. EDUCATION AND LEARNING

Traditional rhetoric and Latin letters

A fact of primary significance for the intellectual history of Europe is that, with the decay of the Roman Empire, education in the west came under control of the church, which naturally changed the older system to accord with Christian ideals. In the time of the principate it had still been customary for Romans of good birth to learn Greek as a matter of course, and even to attend schools in Greece for advanced work. By the fifth century this was no longer true. Most western scholars were thenceforth ignorant of Greek and to them, accordingly, the finest thought of the ancient world became inaccessible. Meanwhile, too, the other Roman studies had lost all contact with the realities of life. Traditionally the mark of a gentleman was training in grammar and rhetoric—what we should recognize as literature and public speaking. But the goal of his ambition was now merely to compose and pronounce declamations on conventional subjects in a conventional way. According to the accepted standard, the truly cultured should never be interested in practical questions, should never say anything simply and directly. Themes had to be drawn from classical sources; argument had to proceed by the weaving together of literary allusions; the style had to be elevated, intricate, and ornate. The more difficult it was to understand what the author was driving at, the more necessary it was for the refined audience to applaud the product; and the narrower the group that could play the game according to the rules, the greater the distinction of belonging to it. Such was the circle of elegant conversationalists pictured for us in the pages of Macrobius (d. 423), and still reflected in the letters of Apollinaris Sidonius (d. 488) while the Goths were completing their conquest of southern Gaul.

Under such circumstances, little could be expected of Latin literature in the fourth and fifth centuries. Although there were many writings, they all suffered from the blight of artificial rhetoric. The best historian of the age was Ammianus Marcellinus. As a literary artist, he was greatly inferior to Tacitus, whose work he sought to bring down to date; yet we are grateful to him for his straightforward account of the events leading up to the battle of Adrianople, where his narrative ends. The compositions of Symmachus, regarded by contemporaries as a peerless stylist, now seem only a mass of turgid phrases, quite empty of meaning. Much the same criticism can be made of Ausonius, whose poetry, while occasionally giving us a valuable glimpse of the author's native Gaul, is generally wearisome. Claudian is better. He at least knew how to compose musical verse in the true classical manner—enough to mark him as a genius in that age—but his subjects were unworthy. Adulation of such men as Honorius and Stilicho could hardly make great literature.

Of more lasting influence were the compilers. Martianus Capella's *Marriage of Philology and Mercury* (early fifth century) consecrated for the Middle Ages the notion of the seven liberal arts, of which we shall subsequently hear much. The *Grammatical Art* of Donatus (fourth century) and Priscian's *Institutes of Grammar* (late fifth century) long remained the standard texts in that field. And the works of Boëthius were of even greater importance. That distinguished man, as already noted, was executed by Theodoric the Ostrogoth on a charge of treason in 524. While in prison he composed the very popular *Consolation of Philosophy*—an allegorical *mélange* of verse and prose that, strangely enough, contains no word of Christianity. For this reason the mediæval tradition to the effect that the author was a holy martyr has become somewhat discredited. Yet, pagan or not, Boëthius performed a memorable service for western Christians by translating into Latin a portion of Aristotle's work on logic, as well as Porphyry's *Isagoge*, an introduction to the study of philosophy. These books, together with the editor's own essays on the same subjects and on the mathematical sciences, were to provide the most advanced education that was known to the schools of the west for the next five hundred years. *Famous textbooks*

Such men as those mentioned above still maintained the tradition of pagan letters, but they had no successors. By the sixth century the intellectual leadership of their world had passed to the great ecclesiastical writers whose works, though not always elegant in style, had the greater merit of practicality. During the earlier period the outstanding exponents of Christian thought had all been Greeks. The first important Latin author to devote himself to the defense of the church was Tertullian, who lived in the time of the Severi. A prolific and eloquent writer, he undertook the refutation of various heresies, only himself to fall under the ban of the orthodox for upholding an ultra-rigorous standard of Christian discipline. Lactantius, who flourished about a hundred years later, was famous for *Latin church fathers* the perfection of his literary style but was decidedly lacking in intellectual stature. Not until the eve of the barbarian invasions did Latin Christendom produce three of its illustrious Four Doctors:[10] St. Ambrose, St. Jerome, and St. Augustine, whose lives may fittingly be sketched as a conclusion to the present chapter.

St. Ambrose (d. 397)

In an earlier age Ambrose might well have risen to command armies and perhaps to wear the purple, for he was the son of a high Roman official and himself possessed the talent and training for a distinguished civil career. After obtaining a good education in both Greek and Latin, Ambrose spent a number of years in the study of law. He then entered the imperial service and was named by Valentinian I as a provincial governor with headquarters in Milan, which had become the favorite residence of the emperor. At that time the bishop of the city happened to be an Arian; so, on his death in 374, there was general rejoicing among the orthodox, mingled with foreboding as to the coming election, for the situation was such as might easily lead to conflict. On the appointed day it was Ambrose who, in his official capacity, had to preside over the assembly of the clergy and laity in the local cathedral. The people had already been excited by rumors of impending strife when, according to the appealing story, a child's voice cried "Ambrose bishop!" And the whole congregation united in acclaiming their youthful president. Ambrose protested his incompetence; although a sincere Christian, he had followed the common practice of postponing his baptism. But the popular demand bore him down and he was duly baptized and consecrated, having been pushed through all the holy orders in the course of a week.[11]

Bishop Ambrose, as would be expected in the case of a man with his background, was essentially an ecclesiastical statesman. In spite of conscientious devotion to the theological studies which he had hitherto neglected, he was never outstanding for his scholarship. Aside from official correspondence, his writings were restricted to practical essays on religion. He took an active part in the suppression of paganism and in the stimulation of zeal for a truly Christian life. Through the eloquence of his sermons, we are told, hundreds of men and women were inspired to renounce the world and assume the garb of ascetics. Yet Ambrose remains chiefly famous for his role of spiritual director to princes. Because his see was in Milan, he had as parishioner first Valentinian and then Theodosius, who completed the series of acts that proscribed all pagan and heretical sects throughout the empire. In this connection the bishop's crowning victory—and it was one on which later generations loved to dilate—came in the year 390. A riot at Thessalonica had greatly incensed the emperor who,

---

[10] I.e., teachers. The fourth, Pope (St.) Gregory the Great, will be considered in Chapter VII.

[11] See above, p. 61.

unmindful of ecclesiastical advice, ordered his troops to make an example of the city. The result was a massacre that filled Ambrose with horror. So, when Theodosius returned to Milan, the bishop refused to perform divine service in his presence and demanded that he publicly show contrition for his sin. Seized with remorse, Theodosius yielded; as a humble penitent he appeared in the cathedral before the assembled court and made submission to God. Thus the lesson was driven home for all to understand, that even Augustus was only human and therefore subject to the authority of the church.

In Jerome we find a very different sort of person—one of the few men **St.** canonized[12] by the church primarily on account of scholarly endeavors. **Jerome** Coming to Rome from his native Dalmatia, he received the ordinary **(d. 420)** rhetorical education and, like so many of his contemporaries, found the charms of pagan literature quite irresistible; for, although he had been brought up as a Christian, he did not at first take the faith very seriously. Later, as the result of an illness and what he accepted as a miraculous vision, he abandoned his sinful passion for rhetoric and vowed exclusive devotion to the church. For a number of years he lived as a hermit in Syria, spending part of his time in the study of Hebrew. In 379 he was ordained priest at Antioch, but three years later was brought to Rome by Pope Damasus, throughout whose pontificate he served as papal secretary. Then, on the accession of Siricius, Jerome again turned eastward and, after extensive travel in Palestine and Egypt, settled in a monastery at Bethlehem, where he died in 420.

During all these years Jerome had constantly engaged in literary work, and his output was truly prodigious. He was a great letter-writer, giving us in his correspondence vivid information concerning all the great religious problems of the age and their bearing upon the daily life of particular men and women. He was an enthusiastic advocate of asceticism, and on that account became embroiled in bitter disputes with certain friends and relatives of his converts. Such argument was never shunned by Jerome, who was quick to take up his pen on any controversial subject. Much of his writing, therefore, was marred by haste and violence. Yet, in spite of these faults, Jerome produced many scholarly books—among them some remarkable investigations of Christian archæology. And it was this interest in antiquities that led him to make numerous translations from the Greek and the Hebrew, including his famous Latin version of the Bible.

Various translations of the Scriptures already existed in the west, but they **The** were known to be corrupt and defective. So Damasus entrusted to Jerome **Vulgate** the task of a complete revision. For the New Testament he naturally

[12] By the ceremony of canonization the church came to recognize as saints those exceptionally holy persons who were deemed worthy of special honor. Prayer might be addressed to a saint for his aid in securing divine grace.

employed Greek manuscripts, and this portion was soon completed. The Old Testament caused him much more trouble; for he realized the importance of using the Hebrew Bible in preference to the Greek Septuagint, and he was not proficient enough in the former language to proceed without assistance. Consequently it was not until after Jerome had taken up his residence in Palestine that, with the help of learned Jews, he was able to complete his undertaking. The result of his labors was the Latin text of the Scriptures which, with the addition of certain translations from the Septuagint, was made official in the western church and eventually became known as the Vulgate. Thus Jerome played an important part in the work to which the papacy was then devoting its chief attention—the definition of Christian doctrine and the establishment of a practical organization through which it could be made effective.

St. Augustine (d. 430)

Almost exactly contemporary with Jerome was the African bishop Augustine, one of the greatest ecclesiastics and one of the most interesting characters in history. He was born at Thagaste in Numidia just after the middle of the fourth century. His father Patricius was a member of the local *curia* and a pagan. His mother Monnica, on the contrary, was a Christian. Through her influence the boy was instructed in the faith and early designated as a candidate for baptism—though for him, as for many at that time, the ceremony was long postponed, and in the meantime he drifted farther and farther from the church. Preparing to follow his father's profession of the law, he received a sound education in Latin grammar and rhetoric. But Greek was already tending to disappear from the African schools and Augustine, to his later regret, learned very little of it. To complete his legal training he was eventually sent to Carthage. There, instead, he developed a passion for literary study and, on the death of his father, became a teacher of rhetoric.

In his famous *Confessions*, written long afterwards, he bitterly deplores the sinfulness of his youth. He recounts with horror such early misdeeds as stealing food from his parents' cellar, cheating at boyish games, and weeping over tragic scenes in Vergil! He dwells with loathing on his love of the theater, his "damnable and vainglorious" pride in rhetorical skill and profane wisdom. He describes his lustful character and tells how he formed an irregular union with a woman who shared his life for a dozen years and bore him a son. But worst of all, he declares, was his abandonment of Christianity for Manichæism.[13] This step, it would appear from his story, was due to his intellectual curiosity; he was possessed by a craving for certitude—for a religion which his mind could grasp. The Christian scriptures repelled him because of their literary form; the Old Testament seemed obscure and somewhat barbarous, the New Testament rather childish. The Manichæans, on the contrary, promised him complete knowl-

---

[13] See above, p. 42.

edge. This sect, as we have seen, enjoyed great prestige during the fourth century; its devotees at Rome were praised by Jerome for an austerity of life superior to that of most Christians. Yet Augustine found in it only disillusionment. The Manichæan elect, he decided, were not always so pure as they were supposed to be, and even the greatest of the Manichæan bishops could give no positive answers to his questions.

About this time Augustine opened a private school in Rome, but he had not been there long when he heard that a teacher of rhetoric was needed at Milan. Entering the competition, he secured the appointment. And with this improvement in his material fortunes, he put away the mother of his son and betrothed himself to a young girl of wealth. The result, however, was merely to aggravate his spiritual conflict. Thanks to Latin translations, he had been able to read the works of the Neo-platonists[14] and through them he was finally enabled to reject the dualism of the Manichæans. Inevitably, too, he came under the influence of the great Ambrose, from whose sermons he discovered that the Old Testament was to be understood through symbolic interpretation and that the true meaning of the New Testament was in harmony with Platonism. In Paul, especially, Augustine found a kindred spirit. The great apostle, likewise, had suffered from the domination of the world and the flesh, had been oppressed by a sense of ineradicable sin, had failed to discover a cure in erudition.

His conversion (386)

Thus Augustine was prepared for the final impulse. A compatriot, surprised at his friend's interest in Pauline Christianity, was led to tell the story of St. Anthony: how the latter had been converted through a text of Scripture and how his example was being followed not only in Egypt but also in Gaul and Italy. Augustine, who had never heard of monasticism, was deeply impressed. Here were uneducated men gaining the peace which he, with all his learning, had sought in vain. Retreating into his garden, he threw himself under a tree and gave way to a passion of tears. And in the midst of his emotional crisis he heard the voice of a neighbor's child singing, as if in some game: "Take up and read! Take up and read!" To Augustine it seemed a message from heaven. Going back to the house and opening the book of Paul's epistles, he saw this passage:[15]

Not in rioting and drunkenness, not in chambering and wantonness, not in strife and envying; but put ye on the Lord Jesus Christ, and make not provision for the flesh, to fulfil the lusts thereof.

Augustine had received his answer. Abandoning his profession, together with his contemplated marriage, he received baptism and thenceforth devoted himself to the service of the church. On the death of his mother,

---

[14] See above, p. 36.
[15] *Romans,* xiii, 13-14.

who had lived to rejoice at her son's conversion, he returned to Thagaste, where he made his family home into a monastery. Here he spent a number of years, writing the first of a long series of books against the enemies of the Christian faith. It was not until 391, while visiting the bishop of Hippo, that he was persuaded to accept ordination. Becoming the bishop's assistant, he eventually succeeded to the episcopal office and held it for the remainder of his life. He died in 430 during the siege of Hippo by the Vandals—on the eve of disasters that were to begin the destruction of Roman culture in Africa.

His works   Augustine's fame depends, not upon his career as a bishop, but rather upon his intellectual dominance over succeeding generations. The essence of this dominance lay in the fact that he perfectly expressed what was to be the attitude of mediæval scholarship—rationalism subordinated to mystic faith. He left his mark on virtually every great problem that has remained to vex the theologian: especially on such subjects as the origin of evil, predestination, divine grace, human will, and the nature of salvation. From time to time in the following pages we shall have to turn back to Augustinian doctrine; for the present it must suffice to give a brief résumé of the *Civitas Dei*. This work has enjoyed high renown ever since it was first published, and is generally regarded as Augustine's masterpiece. In the eyes of the modern reader it suffers from two main defects: having been composed by a very busy man, it is rambling and repetitious; furthermore, it is written in the verbose and turgid style dear to the African rhetorician. Nevertheless, its underlying plan is of epic grandeur and, in spite of much argument which seems puerile to the historian of today, it is throughout inspired by a deep and impressive sincerity.

To refute the current allegation that the sack of Rome in 410 was due to the desertion of the ancient gods, Augustine begins with a sketch of Rome and its religion. He endeavors to show that the pagan deities had never brought their adherents any real benefits, and that the recent troubles of the empire were no more than what the Romans deserved for their sins. This part of the book, it must be admitted, could hardly have seemed very convincing except to one who already shared the author's ardent beliefs. Beginning with the eleventh book, however, Augustine comes to a subject more congenial to his talent. After all, the fortune of persons and the fate of empires are but episodes in the scheme of divine providence. Of more fundamental significance than the history of Rome is the history of humanity, but that cannot be understood apart from the design of the Creator. The City of Man is imperfect and temporary; the City of God is perfect and everlasting. So in magnificent perspective Augustine depicts God and the angels, Satan and the demons, the creation of the world, the fall of Adam and its consequences for mankind, human history under the Old Dispensation, the coming of Christ and the nature of His redemption, the church and the sacraments, the last judgment, the end of the world, and the perpetual triumph of God's City.

With a few bold strokes Augustine thus sketched a stupendous picture, embracing all that men knew or could hope to know. There were numerous pagans willing to dispute his statements, but none able to captivate men's imagination with a work of equal splendor. Many centuries were to elapse before the appearance of any Christian scholar competent to fill in the details of his outline.

CHAPTER V

The Empire in the Sixth Century

1. JUSTINIAN AND THE ROMAN WORLD

The contrast between the east and the west

The collapse of the Roman Empire under the successors of Theodosius has been sketched in a previous chapter. By the opening of the sixth century imperial rule throughout the western provinces was only a memory. Britain had long since been abandoned to the heathen Saxons and Angles or to those Celtic tribes which could manage to defend themselves against the invaders. To all practical intents Italy had been turned into an Ostrogothic kingdom, Spain into a Visigothic kingdom, and northern Africa into a Vandal kingdom. Before his death in 511 the unscrupulous Clovis had brought a large part of Gaul under Frankish control, and his aggressive policy was continued by his sons. The latter, though frequently embroiled in murderous wars with one another, co-operated well enough to complete a number of fresh conquests. Having subjugated the Thuringians in central Germany, they took advantage of Theodoric's death and the consequent weakening of his state to extend their dominion over Burgundy and Provence, as well as the lands of the Alamans and Bavarians on the upper Danube (see Map IV). What, in the meantime, had been the fortune of the eastern Mediterranean world?

Anyone who studies Roman history can scarcely fail to be impressed by the fact that one half of the empire was able to survive while the other half fell in ruin. The whole administrative system, civil and military, was the same in both regions, and it was a Latin, not a Greek, creation. Why should it perish in the land where it was native and persist in the land where it was foreign? To some extent this strange result was due to mere accident. The eastern emperors of the fifth century were remarkable neither for wisdom nor for energy. It was only their good fortune that, sooner or later, the principal barbarian hordes were attracted to the western provinces,

78

and that no serious offensive was launched by their enemies in Asia. Nevertheless, the divergent fate of east and west suggests that we are dealing with something more fundamental than what we call luck. The empire in the east displayed a really astonishing vitality, surviving the Theodosian dynasty for a thousand years. During this entire period its life was the city of Constantinople, which still maintained the imperial tradition after its outlying territory had all been lost. The new capital, obviously, was not only a position of great strength but also a source of great wealth.

Even before the end of the fifth century the economic condition of the eastern empire seems definitely to have improved. Zeno's successor Anastasius (491-518) was able to repeal several of the more oppressive measures that had characterized the earlier fiscal administration, and yet to leave a treasury well stocked with gold. At the same time he considerably strengthened the Syrian and Libyan frontiers by the erection of new fortresses and, to improve the defenses of Constantinople, built long walls to connect the Black Sea with the Sea of Marmora (see Map III). Thereby Anastasius revealed a wise mistrust of the Danube barrier, for it was constantly threatened by one or another of the barbarian peoples established along it. East of the Bavarians, in what is now Hungary, were two Germanic nations, the Lombards and the Gepids. Between the latter and the sea the north bank of the river was occupied by various tribes of Slavs, Huns, and Bulgars.[1] And still farther to the east the Pontic steppe had recently been seized by a horde of Asiatic nomads who called themselves Avars.

The eastern empire and its enemies

As yet the emperor could hardly perceive a terrible foe in the Avar herdsmen, but he was well aware of a growing menace from Persia. This powerful state had emerged in the third century, when a local Iranian prince overthrew the Parthians and extended his sovereignty from the Roman frontier on the west to the Indian frontier on the east. To a large degree the Persian revolution was inspired by the traditions of the ancient kingdom which, after long dominating Greece, had fallen before Alexander the Great. The Sassanids, the rulers of the new dynasty, were devoted to the extirpation of Hellenism throughout central Asia—a cause that was rendered doubly sacred by the support of the *magi*, the priests of the Zoroastrian cult.[2] The Persian language (Pahlavi) was revived for all official usage and acquired fresh glory through literary composition in both prose and verse. Persian artists and craftsmen, likewise developing non-Greek forms, produced a wealth of beautiful objects which, through religious or commercial channels, had widespread influence even within the imperial provinces.

[1] The Bulgars, as is shown by their name, had earlier lived near the Volga River; they seem to have been a portion of the people vaguely called Hunnic.

[2] See above, p. 37.

Hostility between Rome and Persia was inevitable from the first and was much aggravated in the fourth century as one power became Christian and the other, consequently, anti-Christian. Then came the weakening of the empire under the successors of Theodosius, and it was well for them that the Persians were diverted from Syrian conquest by nomadic inroads and internal dissension. But such good fortune could not be expected to last forever. Eventually the Romans would have to meet a determined attack from beyond the Euphrates and it behooved them to be prepared. Anastasius, as we have seen, adopted a sound policy of military defense combined with strict economy. If his example had been followed by later emperors, the fate of their country might have been altogether different.

Justin and Justinian (518-65)
The death in 518 of Anastasius without heirs brought on the usual mist of intrigue. When it had cleared away, the successful candidate for the throne was found to be Justin, the commander of the palace guard. He was by birth an Illyrian peasant who, like so many of his compatriots, had enlisted in the imperial army and had there risen from one high honor to another. Now, at the age of sixty-six or thereabouts, he was crowned emperor and, we are told, was still illiterate! Justin, however, had an able lieutenant in his nephew and adopted son Justinian, whom he had brought from his native village to be educated in the capital. By this time Justinian was about thirty-five and had already proved his intelligence and political shrewdness. Under his aged uncle he acquired the rank of *patricius* and master of troops; finally, having become the dominant power in the state, he was designated as co-emperor. Thus, since Justinian lived to the ripe old age of eighty-three, he actually governed the Roman world for about half a century.

To contemporaries Justinian's character was a matter of violent controversy, and so it has remained. Not a few of our perplexities in this connection are due to the historian Procopius. He was a well-educated lawyer who for a time held a staff appointment in one of Justinian's armies, and who apparently continued to be in close touch with politics at Constantinople. He produced three important works: the *History of the Wars*, a judicious account of Justinian's great campaigns, in which he is sparing of both praise and blame; the *Secret History*, a supplement to the first, in which he depicts the emperor as a devil incarnate; and finally the *Book of Edifices*, a description of the imperial buildings, in which Justinian's deeds are lauded without stint or scruple. These estimates defy reconciliation; and when we turn to official documents, we encounter the usual trouble of distinguishing the ruler's own ideas from those of his subordinates. As a whole, however, Justinian's reign was clearly dominated by a magnificent ambition of reconstituting the Roman Empire. Since he was an Illyrian, his native speech was Latin, and under him Latin remained the language of law and administration. Whatever else may be deduced from his acts, Justinian obviously considered himself a Roman and dreamed of restoring imperial rule in the west. In some ways he was a great man, in others a very foolish one. Much of his success, perhaps, he owed to his dauntless and talented wife Theodora.

That famous lady, according to the *Secret History*, was the daughter of an animal-trainer at the circus, an actress of singular beauty and depravity, who had already lived with various men before she met the future emperor. For these scandals of her early life we are entirely dependent on Procopius and his malicious gossip may well be taken with extreme caution. Yet Theodora does appear to have been a girl of low birth and dubious reputation, with whom Justinian became infatuated long before he entered upon his glorious career. That, as heir to the throne, he insisted on making her his lawful wife is wholly to his credit; and that, as emperor and empress, they set a shining example of mutual fidelity was admitted by their bitterest enemies. Until her death in 548 Theodora enjoyed unrivaled ascendancy at court; through her husband's indulgence she even found it possible to intervene in affairs of state. Having lands and revenues to manage as she pleased, she was assured of economic independence—a position that enabled her to maintain extraordinary freedom of action. Many persons complained of her passion for display, of her devouring ambition and capricious favoritism. In general, however, it is now agreed that she well deserved the official equality of rank and power which was conferred on her by the emperor.

The empress Theodora

On one occasion, as we are told by Procopius, Theodora's courage alone prevented Justinian's reign from coming to an untimely end. This was during the famous revolt of 532. The affair began as a tumult in the hippodrome, which was often the scene of riots between political and religious factions. But on the present occasion the disturbance went much further. Widespread economic troubles had filled the capital with desperate men from the provinces, and the court had its usual complement of malcontents and would-be usurpers. For three days mobs ran wild through the city, a large part of which was destroyed by fire. A rival emperor was proclaimed and Justinian was besieged in his palace. Utterly dismayed, he was about to accept the advice of his ministers and attempt escape by sea, when Theodora threw aside convention and spoke her mind to the council. It was impossible, she said, to avoid death at some time. For one who had worn a crown was not exile a worse prospect? Flight was easy; Cæsar might go when he chose. As for herself, she hoped never to see the day when she would no longer be greeted as empress. She held to the old saying, that the purple is a good winding-sheet! So the emperor and his generals took heart. New measures were adopted, the rising was put down, and Justinian was saved to perform great deeds.

Briefly stated, Justinian's military policy was to maintain the defensive in the east and wage an offensive in the west. On two occasions war broke out with Persia; but the emperor did his best to minimize the conflict and ultimately was glad to buy peace in Asia at the cost of an alleged subsidy for the protection of Roman territory. This was a distinctly unsatisfactory settlement which invited grave trouble for the future. In the Balkans, too, signs of approaching danger were at the time unheeded. From across the Danube the scourge of nomad raids was virtually continuous; for as the best troops were diverted elsewhere, that frontier was left in a chronically weakened state. Elaborate fortifications, treaties with barbarian *fœderati*, and payment of blackmail were together no more than a makeshift protection. Justinian's eyes were fixed on the western provinces, and to conquer them he had to neglect what he already possessed. When we consider the meager resources at his disposal his success appears truly marvelous.

The entire armed strength of the empire under Justinian has been estimated at 120,000 men; but the force dispatched on a single campaign rarely numbered more than 25,000 and was frequently less. The troops were of course mercenaries, commonly recruited from among the wilder peoples of the imperial borderlands. Whatever loyalty they had was reserved for individual commanders. All too often the government found them both rapacious and treacherous. Yet the imperial army, such as it was, could not be dispensed with and from the military point of view proved very effective. For offense the chief reliance was now placed on the so-called *cataphracti*—heavy cavalry equipped with bow and arrows, as well as with sword and lance, and protected by defensive armor of iron. The use of these troops was originally learned from the Parthians and was made possible by a breed of great horses which is said to have been developed in the rich grasslands of Mesopotamia. Whatever the origin of the breed, its importation into the empire served to revolutionize European warfare. Justinian's *cataphracti*, it was found, could easily ride through any larger host of the kind then raised by the barbarian kings. And the lesson thus taught eventually led, as we shall see, to the feudalization of the western armies.

The imperial cause, furthermore, was greatly aided by the disunion and incompetence of the western rulers. In Italy the heir to Theodoric's crown was a young boy for whom his mother acted as regent. In Gaul the sons of Clovis were busily engaged in fighting one another. And in spite of their earlier fame, neither the Visigoths in Spain nor the Vandals in Africa were now formidable. Broken by the Franks, the former had for many years owed their security to an Ostrogothic protectorate. The Vandals, sadly decayed since the time of their invasion, lacked even the prospect of outside assistance. Among the lost territories, Africa thus offered a good opportunity for reconquest and would in turn constitute an excellent base for further operations. All Justinian needed was a pretext for intervention, and this was supplied in 531 when appeals came to him against a usurping king. As soon as the Persian war had been ended and the insurrection of 532 put down, Belisarius, a general who had distinguished himself in both affairs, was placed in command of an expedition to Africa. He received a force of only about 16,000 men and it was supported by a very dubious navy. But the Vandal king stupidly diverted his fleet and permitted the army of Belisarius to disembark without opposition. Once on land, the Romans proved invincible. In less than six months the proud kingdom of Gaiseric had been wiped out and the Vandal nation thenceforth disappeared from the pages of history.

Justinian at once proclaimed the re-establishment in Africa of the Roman provincial administration. His decree was premature, for the defeat of the Vandals was merely the signal for a widespread revolt of the Moors, the Berber population of the desert borders who wanted no foreign domination of any kind. So the pacification of Africa was delayed for over a dozen years, and even then the Roman position remained precarious. In the meantime Justinian had turned to his second great project, the recovery of Italy. Once more an excuse for Roman conquest was opportunely provided—this time by the murder of the Ostrogothic regent. While one imperial force advanced through Dalmatia, another under the command of Belisarius occupied Sicily. Thence, in 536, he invaded Italy and took Rome without a battle. The Goths, however, proved their warlike temper by deposing the usurper and electing another king, under whom they held out until 540. Justinian, thinking that the war had at last been ended, recalled Belisarius; and again he misjudged the strength of the opposition. The Goths rallied under the heroic Totila, who regained virtually all Italy and, having built a fleet, captured Sicily, Sardinia, and Corsica. Belisarius reappeared on the scene, but with an inadequate army; for war had again broken out with Persia and additional troops were needed in Africa. Finally Belisarius was superseded by Narses, another talented general, and he, thanks to powerful reinforcements, gained a decisive victory. After desperate fighting, Totila was slain in 552 and in the next year Narses destroyed the last remnants of the Gothic host.

For a time it seemed as if Justinian might be able to win a third great triumph in Spain, where a civil war between two rival kings led to imperial intervention in 554. Eventually, however, the Visigoths united against the invaders, who were able to secure only a portion of the southeastern coast (see Map IV). It, together with the Balearic Islands, was organized as a Spanish province, and Justinian could boast that the Mediterranean was once more a Roman lake. Yet the total success of his imperial revival, brilliant as it was, should not be exaggerated. The territory regained in

The re-conquest of Italy (535-53)

The final result

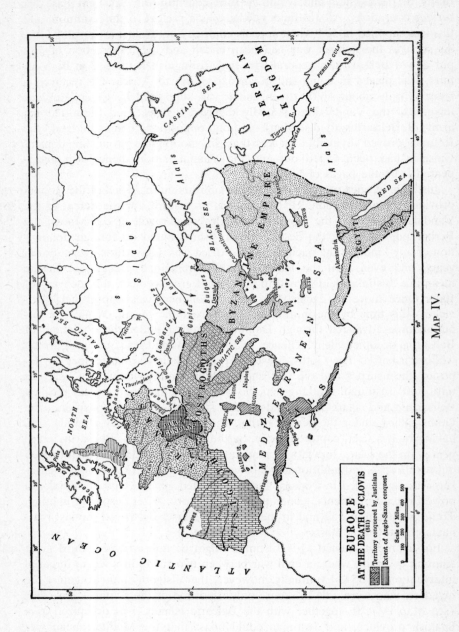

EUROPE
AT THE DEATH OF CLOVIS
(511)

Territory conquered by Justinian
Extent of Anglo-Saxon conquest

Scale of Miles
0   100   200   300   400   500

MAP IV.

MANHATTAN DRAFTING CO.,INC.,N.Y.

Africa did not extend all the way to the straits. The Visigoths still held most of Spain, as well as Septimania. Provence, which had belonged to the Ostrogothic kingdom, now fell into the hands of the Franks who, in spite of temporary alliances with the emperor, continued to act precisely as they pleased. The Roman dominions included the islands of the Mediterranean, the peninsula of Italy, and the Dalmatian coast, but not the old provinces of Rhætia, Noricum, and Pannonia, which were now in the possession of Alamans, Bavarians, Lombards, and other barbarians. And even within this limited area the reconstituted empire of Justinian had no real vitality. That, far from ruling the Mediterranean world, it was unable to defend either the Danube or the Euphrates was soon to be amply demonstrated. Although we may admire the energy and determination displayed by Justinian in his devotion to an ancient ideal, the fact remains that he squandered precious resources on a lost cause. His project of political reunification was hopeless of real accomplishment. The cost of his adventure was the exhaustion of his original empire.

Justinian, being one of the world's greatest legislators, can hardly be accused of wanton misgovernment. Nevertheless, the mounting cost of his grandiose wars meant the continuance of extortionate taxes and official spoliation. To millions of his subjects the splendor of his reign was no cause for rejoicing. And although the Roman reoccupation may have produced some benefits in Africa, it brought nothing short of ruin to his other great conquest. The city of Rome, which had survived pillage by Goth and Vandal, was virtually destroyed by the frightful wars of the sixth century. Through five successive sieges the once glorious capital was reduced to a mass of wreckage. Under Justinian its time-honored privileges—notably the free distribution of grain—were not restored; the result was depopulation and increasing misery. Senate and consuls alike disappeared, and the only remaining municipal officials came to be papal subordinates. Nor was Rome the only one of the ancient cities to suffer. Henceforth urban civilization throughout the peninsula rapidly declined, leaving society to be dominated by the agrarian aristocracy of the countryside. This, in all truth, was the end of classic Italy.

Justinian's ecclesiastical policy was even less successful. His aim, of course, was complete uniformity—the inclusion of all Roman subjects within one church dominated by himself. This naturally implied the rigorous suppression of pagans and heretics, to which end the emperor not only confirmed the edicts of his predecessors but also removed from the teaching profession all persons tainted with what he called Hellenism. The schools of Athens, with their illustrious history running back to the fourth century B.C., were closed; at Constantinople and elsewhere the staffs of instructors were thoroughly purged of all suspects. Although most Jews continued to enjoy a half-hearted toleration, they were excluded from all

Ecclesiastical affairs

offices of state—as were likewise all persons who could not prove their entire orthodoxy. Heretics were deprived of civil rights and subjected to severe penalties. Manichæism[3] was punished with death.

In these matters the opposition to the imperial administration was hardly strong enough to occasion serious trouble; but in the field of theological controversy[4] Justinian encountered a problem that defied all his attempts at solution. Arianism, as we have seen, had been uprooted in the empire only to spread throughout the Germanic world beyond the frontier. In much the same way Nestorianism, an exaggeration of the views originally set forth by Nestorius, found a refuge in Persia, whence it was extended across Asia by zealous missionaries and has persisted down to the present. The monophysite heresy proved even more stubborn because the imperial government had never been able to adopt a consistent policy with regard to it. An attempted compromise by Zeno had only made matters worse by producing a formal schism[5] between Rome and Constantinople, which had continued under Anastasius. Justin, immediately on his accession, ended the schism by reaffirming the canons[6] of Chalcedon and for a while Justinian maintained the same attitude—one that well agreed with his political ambitions in Italy. Theodora, on the contrary, sympathized with the monophysites and used her influence to relax the official persecution. So the emperor swayed first one way and then the other.

Conflict with the pope

Ultimately Justinian's decision was dictated by his military success. As soon as his armies had occupied Rome, he proclaimed a theological ultimatum and sought to impose it on all parties. After one pope had been deposed, his successor was taken to Constantinople and there compelled, in some measure, to accept the imperial dictum. A general council summoned to meet in Justinian's presence also submitted. The emperor felt that he had won a complete victory; yet he had only aggravated the old dispute. The monophysites, instead of agreeing to the official program, were encouraged to establish a separate church, which still continues today.[7] And in the west the sole effect of Justinian's despotism was to assure the permanent antagonism of the papacy and thereby to weaken the imperial hold on Italy. The logical reply to the reign of Justinian was the pontificate of Gregory the Great.

[3] See above, p. 42.
[4] See above, pp. 63-64.
[5] The principal weapon used by bishops to enforce their decrees was excommunication, i.e., exclusion from the Christian community and its sacraments. When two bishops denied each other's authority by mutual excommunication, the result was a schism.

[6] As used in this connection, a canon is a rule of law, a legal decision. For other meanings of the word, see the Index.

[7] Commonly known as the Jacobite church after its principal organizer, Jacob Baradæus, bishop of Edessa in the sixth century.

MAP V.

2. THE EMPIRE UNDER JUSTINIAN'S SUCCESSORS

The
Lombard
invasion
of Italy

The three emperors who succeeded Justinian in the later sixth century remained loyal to his glorious example. Yet they had to abandon all thought of offensive war; even to defend their inherited dominions proved an impossible task. Although they managed to hold Africa, because no formidable enemy appeared on that flank, the Visigoths reduced the imperial province in Spain to a few seaports, and most of Italy was taken by the Lombards. The latter had enjoyed a privileged status under Justinian, being commissioned as *fœderati* to defend the frontier against their neighbors and hired in large numbers for the Italian campaigns. Now, on the contrary, the Roman government shifted its favor to the Gepids and in retaliation the Lombards sought an alliance with the Avars. The result was not only the annihilation of the Gepid nation but also the flight of the Lombards. To escape their terrible allies, they deserted the Danube provinces and invaded Italy. The story of the Lombard conquest is a famous one. With its romantic plot and gory details, it has been told and retold in countless books—and without mention of the fact that it is drawn largely from the pages of Paul the Deacon, who wrote over two hundred years later.[8] In the present connection we may pass over all but a few outstanding events.

About 568 the Lombard king, Alboin, led his people across the Alps to seize the valley of the Po, which has since been called Lombardy. Neither Alboin nor his immediate successors gained much further renown. Even when the Lombards chose to have a king, they allowed him only restricted powers. And he had slight if any control over the chieftains who advanced into the south and there established a number of petty states. As a consequence, the Lombard kingdom was a mere sham. Lombardy itself was dominated by local counts, each administering an old *civitas*, while in Tuscany and the other outlying territories the royal authority amounted to still less. A glance at the accompanying map (V) will show that the empire, thanks to its command of the sea, was able to keep all the more important coasts. These possessions, however, were badly isolated from one another, and the imperial government found it increasingly difficult to hold them. Italy thus lapsed into what it was to be for many hundreds of years—a patchwork of little principalities.

The
Italian
duchies

Such principalities in Italy, as in the neighboring countries, were often called duchies—a term that demands a few words of explanation. Justinian, immediately after his first defeat of the Ostrogoths, proclaimed the restoration of the regular imperial system, which involved a sharp distinction between civil and military government. Then the continuance of the war induced him to confer unlimited powers on Narses as commander-in-

[8] See below, p. 148.

chief, with subordinate generals (*duces*) in charge of the provinces into which the peninsula was divided; and this arrangement persisted after his death. Since the exarch (i.e., governor general) maintained headquarters at Ravenna, that city, together with the surrounding territory, was known as the exarchate. An ordinary district, being ruled by a *dux* (or duke), was known as a *ducatus* (or duchy). So, for example, there was a duchy of Venetia, a duchy of Naples, and a duchy of Rome. Various other duchies —notably those of Benevento and Spoleto—were conquered by Lombard chieftains who thenceforth styled themselves dukes and preserved what they could of the Roman administration. But under the changed conditions all political uniformity disappeared and the title of duke, like that of count, frequently came to designate no more than some sort of local honor.

While the Lombards were overrunning Italy, the Avars established them- **Advance** selves in the old provinces of Dacia and Pannonia, whence they spread **of the** terror into all the neighboring lands. Before the end of the sixth century **Avars and** their able and ruthless khan, Baian, had built up a vast tributary empire **Slavs** that reached from the Black Sea to the Baltic. Like Attila's Huns, the Avars constituted a relatively small class of professional raiders who lived through merciless exploitation of other peoples. It was especially the Slavs who, by tens of thousands, were now driven into battle with the enemies of their masters or placed as servile colonists in territories which the latter had devastated. Within twenty years after Justinian's death hordes of Avars and Slavs had repeatedly crossed the Roman frontier to extend their ravages throughout Macedonia and Thrace. And since the imperial government was again engaged in a prolonged war with the Persians, it merely sought to buy off the northern barbarians with continuous payments of tribute. This was the situation until Maurice, Justinian's third successor, induced the Persians to sign a treaty of peace and, having transferred most of his army to Europe, launched an offensive against the Avars.

For a time Maurice was very successful; by 602 his forces had regained **The im-** the line of the Danube and advanced beyond it. Then the emperor, in spite **perial** of the fact that he had earlier had serious trouble with the army, gave **crisis:** orders that it should spend the winter on the frontier instead of returning **Phocas and** to the capital. This command was the signal for another mutiny. The soldiers **Heraclius** marched on Constantinople, overturned the government, and, after killing Maurice, proclaimed one of their own number, a certain Phocas. The result was the near-destruction of the empire; for the usurper failed to secure general recognition and was quite unable to defend even the neighboring provinces. While the Avars and Slavs occupied the interior of the Balkan peninsula, the Persians began the systematic conquest of Armenia and Syria. As on many later occasions, however, a period of degradation served to introduce a glorious revival of the Roman power.

In 610 an expedition prepared by the governor of Africa and entrusted to his son Heraclius arrived before the walls of Constantinople. No fighting was necessary. Phocas was deposed and slain by his own ministers. And before nightfall on the same day Heraclius had been raised to the vacant throne. This was indeed a triumph for the youthful liberator; yet for a dozen years he had to watch the continuous advance of his enemies on all sides. The barbarians roamed at will throughout the territory below the Danube and penetrated far into the classic lands of Greece. In 617 even the long walls of Anastasius fell to the Avar khan as the result of a surprise attack during pretended negotiations for peace; and although the city itself was stoutly defended, its wealthy suburbs were looted and burned. Meanwhile the Persians had reduced the greatest strongholds of Syria, including Damascus, Antioch, and Jerusalem. Thence they proceeded to invade Asia Minor and Egypt. By 619 they had taken Chalcedon, just across the strait from the capital, and had laid siege to Alexandria. The situation was one that called for desperate measures and Heraclius did not shrink from them. Buying off the Avars at their own price, he gained a short respite in which to devote his scanty resources to operations against the Persians. The very magnitude of the imperial calamities helped his cause. Since the most famous relic of Christendom, the Holy Cross of Jerusalem,[9] had been carried off by the invaders, the war for its recovery took on the aspect of a crusade. The emperor, vowing to gain either victory or death, prepared himself by religious exercises to assume personal command of the expedition. The churches set an example to all patriotic citizens by donating their sacred vessels to be made into coin for hiring troops.

The defeat of Persia (622-28)   Finally, in the spring of 622, Heraclius transported his little army to the Asiatic shore and, with the utmost audacity, struck directly at Armenia. By this move he obtained not only a good recruiting ground among sympathetic Christians but also a strategic base from which to threaten Persia. Thus outflanked, the Persian forces in Asia Minor rapidly withdrew and the emperor was free, if he chose, to attempt the relief of Syria and Egypt. During the next three years, however, he stubbornly refused to abandon his projected offensive and cleverly maintained his central position by preventing the junction of the various armies that were sent to dislodge him. Even when, in 626, a Persian army again appeared in Chalcedon while the perfidious Avars encircled Constantinople from the European side, Heraclius still held to his original plan. His decision was entirely justified; for the Roman control of the sea saved the capital from a major assault by either enemy and, after the Avars had withdrawn from the siege, the Persians could do no better than follow suit. At last Heraclius had found the

---

[9] According to a widely accepted tradition, St. Helena, the mother of Constantine, discovered at Jerusalem the cross on which Christ had been crucified. Although portions of the cross were sent to Rome and Constantinople, most of it remained at Jerusalem. It was this relic that was recovered by Heraclius.

opportunity for his cherished offensive. Driving south from Armenia in 627, he reached the Tigris at Nineveh and there won a great battle just in time to glorify his celebration of the Christmas festival. Chosroës, the Persian king, fled to Ctesiphon; but Heraclius, after coming within a few miles of the city, would not risk an attack. While the mountain passes were still clear of snow, he made good his retreat to the base from which he had earlier advanced.

No further campaigns were required. In the spring of 628 Heraclius received the glad news that Chosroës had been overthrown by a palace revolution and that the new king was willing to sign a treaty of peace. By the terms of the settlement thus made, the Persians evacuated all their conquests, re-established the frontier as it had existed under Maurice, and restored the Holy Cross to Christian possession. When, therefore, Heraclius returned to the capital in 629, the pæans of thanksgiving with which the city resounded were entirely justified. Justinian, because his western offensives—under charge of talented subordinates—brought him sensational renown, has gone down in history as the last of the great Roman sovereigns. Should not, rather, that honor be awarded to Heraclius? Engaged in a heroic struggle against desperate odds, he won amazing victories through sheer force of personal leadership. And although he finally met defeat, it was such as neither he nor anyone else could possibly foresee. Who could have dreamed that, within a mere decade, his magnificent reconquest would be permanently erased by an outpouring of tribesmen from the wild Arabian desert?

3. Byzantine Culture

Before the end of the seventh century, as will be seen in the next chapter, the Arabs had taken the imperial provinces of Syria, Egypt, and Africa, and had gained entire control of the southern Mediterranean. But this was merely the culmination of a decline that was already profound. For all his military genius, Heraclius could not restore the Roman dominion in Italy; nor could he roll back the barbarian tide from the Balkans. Throughout the interior of the peninsula the advance of the Avars and Slavs produced no less than an ethnic revolution, the effect of which may easily be perceived on the present-day map of Europe. In particular, the Latin civilization of Illyria, Justinian's homeland, was permanently destroyed. What was left to the emperor was actually a Greek kingdom deprived of all but a modicum of Roman character. Accordingly it has come to be known in historical writing as the Byzantine Empire—an apt designation, for the well-spring of its life was the city originally called Byzantium.

The term "Byzantine"

Whatever judgment may be passed on Justinian's foreign policy, there can be no doubt of his greatness as a legislator. His codification of the Roman law ranks among the world's finest achievements in the realm of

Justinian's legislation

statesmanship; for his compilation has been in continuous use ever since it was first promulgated. The empire over which he ruled perished long ago; yet his *Corpus* lives on in many of our modern states—not only in those of continental Europe and their colonies, but also in Scotland, Quebec, Louisiana, and the republics of Latin America. Later we shall see how the mediæval universities contributed to this result; for the moment our task is to see how Justinian's work came to be carried out. Through a process that has already been briefly examined,[10] the Roman courts had been provided with two great bodies of law: the constitutions of the emperors and the writings of the jurists. The former had from time to time been gathered into collections, of which the most recent was the Theodosian Code; but these collections had never been combined and were badly out of date. So far as jurisprudence was concerned, although the judges were now permitted to cite only the classical authorities of the earlier centuries, there was a huge library of such authorities. The ordinary magistrate of the sixth century could not be expected to do much with the original sources of the Roman law. Even if the pertinent manuscripts were available, how many Greeks of that day would be able to read them? So Justinian's decision to provide an official condensation of the entire law was an eminently practical one.

The Corpus Iuris Civilis   Almost immediately after his accession Justinian appointed Tribonian and other distinguished lawyers as a commission to collect and edit the imperial constitutions. The project was completed in less than two years by the publication of the *Code*. This, as revised some years later, included 4652 enactments—partly by Justinian, partly by his predecessors—now stated in the form that was to be binding upon the courts. Eventually, as the emperor had continued to legislate on all sorts of matters, it was found convenient to add a supplement called the *Novels*, i.e., new constitutions. Meanwhile the commission had been enlarged and set upon the infinitely harder task of codifying the works of the jurists. As a preliminary, the emperor rendered decisions on fifty disputed points and the experts were then commanded to summarize the whole of Roman jurisprudence in fifty books. On each subject in turn they were to set down the best opinions and, whenever possible, to preserve the language of the original. How many manuscripts the commissioners examined is not known, but their final compilation actually cited 1544 separate works by thirty-eight authors. The result of this enormous labor, known as the *Digest* or *Pandects*, was promulgated in 533 as an imperial act of legislation; for the jurists thenceforth had to be quoted from the official version. The preparation of the *Digest*, with the accompanying settlement of ancient controversies, led first to the revision of the *Code* and then to the production of the *Institutes*,

[10] See above, pp. 11-12.

a textbook of elementary principles arranged according to an analytical plan.

The *Code*, the *Digest*, and the *Institutes* (the *Novels* were an unofficial appendix) made up the *Corpus Iuris Civilis*—a collection that should not be referred to as the *Code*. The latter, as we have seen, was merely part of the *Corpus*, and one of less importance than the *Digest*. The *Code* resembled a modern book of revised statutes; however interesting it may be to the historian, such a work is soon outmoded. The *Digest*, on the contrary, was a systematic exposition of fundamentals and can never become obsolete as long as Roman law remains a living system. For the same reason the *Institutes* must continue to serve as an introduction to that subject wherever it may be taught. From the lawyer's point of view it is therefore the two latter works that have always been of pre-eminent value. Historical scholars naturally prefer originals to any sort of compilation; but we may be sure that, were it not for the *Digest*, the writings of the jurists would have largely perished. For all learning was then tending to disappear in the west, and only Greek learning was to preserve any vitality in the east.

By the time of Justinian, indeed, Latin was almost a dead language at Constantinople. The emperor's own *Novels* were issued in Greek, and before the end of the sixth century his great law-books were commonly used in Greek translation. Many Latin words and phrases—the ghost of a splendid tradition—lingered on in the official usage of the Byzantine government and the Byzantine army; but eventually they all lost their meaning or were absorbed into Greek. In its spoken form that language had come to reflect the cosmopolitanism of the capital, being intermixed with Roman, oriental, and barbarian elements. Even the vernacular of the educated was no longer classic in vocabulary, syntax, or pronunciation. Nevertheless, it remained so close to ancient Greek that the latter could be maintained inviolate for all artistic literature. Accordingly, when the Byzantine gentleman addressed his employees, he used one form; while conversing at home, he used another; if he attempted refined composition, he had to employ still a third. Under such circumstances literary education could hardly be other than static. The boy of good family continued to study grammar and rhetoric as they had been studied for centuries. He learned Homer and other poets by heart and gained an intimate knowledge of Herodotus, Thucydides, and the great orators—a pagan tradition that the eastern church was never able to break down.

This system had the obvious merit of preserving and honoring some of the greatest works that have ever been written. Its fault was that, by ignoring the spirit of the classics and maintaining an absolute devotion to old forms, originality was discouraged. The multitude of authors remained content with imitations, commentaries, and anthologies. Verses written in the

Byzantine education

traditional meters based on quantity lacked the vigor of the new Christian poetry that followed the popular pronunciation, with stressed syllables and rhyme. Prose works that attempted to be literary were generally inferior to those dealing with more practical matters, such as technical essays on civil and military administration. A relatively high standard was kept in biography and in historical memoirs. The ancient skill in philosophical discussion to some extent survived among the theologians. But scientific research all but disappeared; of the later Greek scholars there is not one who deserves mention as a worthy successor of Galen and Ptolemy. Many other phases of Byzantine culture will be discussed in later chapters. The present one must close with some appreciation of the glorious arts that may also be associated with the reign of Justinian.

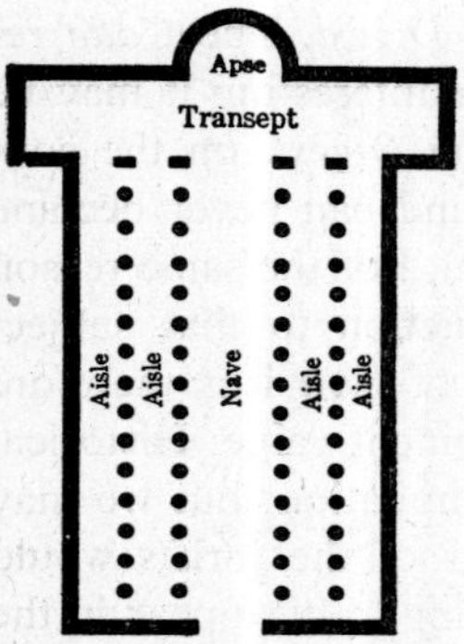

FIG. 7.　Ground Plan of a Basilican Church.

Byzantine architecture

Very remarkably, Byzantine architecture owed almost nothing to the Greeks, being a development of arch-construction combined with a decorative system that was essentially Christian. For their models the architects of Constantinople looked to Syria rather than to Italy; so the extent to which their style may be called an outgrowth of the Roman is a matter of argument. By the fifth century, in any case, the principle of the semicircular arch was well understood in both east and west. Such an arch of masonry, if placed on adequate piers, will hold up a portion of wall twice as wide as the arch is high. A single arch may be employed to provide a door, a window, or some other aperture; a series of arches may be raised to support an aqueduct, a bridge, or a more elaborate structure. Prolonged on a straight line, the semicircular arch becomes a semicylinder, or

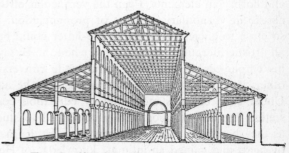

FIG. 8.　Section of a Basilican Church.

what is called a barrel-vault; extended in a circle, as if rotated on its axis, it becomes a dome. And either design may be used as a roof—the former to cover an oblong area, the latter a round area.

Basilican and domed churches

Although both domed and vaulted structures had been put up by the emperors in Italy, the Christians of that region generally adopted for their churches the simpler plan of the basilica. Extensively used by the Romans for public meetings, the basilica was a plain rectangular building divided lengthwise by rows of columns into a nave and aisles (see Figure 7). Illumination was provided by a clerestory—the section over the nave, elevated above the rest and set with windows (see Figure 8). The principal entrance was normally at one end of the nave; the other end was frequently rounded to form an apse, where, on a raised platform, the Romans placed the chair of the presiding officer. For that, however, the Christians substituted their altar and, when constructing a new basilica, oriented it so that the apsidal end would be towards the east. To north and south, furthermore, they often added a transept, thus bringing the whole into the shape of a cross. While the walls of the basilica might easily be made of stone or brick, the roof, in order to be held on its fragile supports, had to be of timber. A church of this kind was neither fireproof nor very substantial; but it had the great advantage of a well-lighted interior, which naturally invited gorgeous decoration.

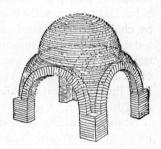

FIG. 9.   Dome on Pendentives.

Among the finest of all Christian basilicas are those erected by Theodoric and Justinian at Ravenna (see Plate I). The scheme of ornamentation will be described below; it should be remarked at this point, however, that in all such Byzantine work the Greek entablature has finally disappeared. The arches now spring directly from the supporting columns and the latter, to suit their altered function, are topped by capitals of a new type. Likewise at Ravenna are a number of buildings in which a dome constitutes the central element—notably the beautiful church of San Vitale. That design for an ecclesiastical structure, unlike the basilica, seems to have been an eastern importation, largely developed under Syrian influence. To place a dome over a circular, or even an octagonal, area was comparatively simple. The difficult problem was to construct a dome that would elegantly cover a square aperture, such as occurred in a church built on a cruciform plan. In Syria this problem had been crudely solved by building up the four corners of the square to produce an octagon. It was left for the Byzantine architects to invent a truly artistic solution—the dome on pendentives.

The accompanying diagram (Figure 9) shows that the first step is to design a dome touching the corners of the square to be covered and to trim it perpendicularly where it extends beyond the sides of the square. The next step is to cut off the top of this preliminary dome and over the circle thus provided to construct the final dome, which will then rest on four spherical triangles, or pendentives. It was fitting that so great a structural achievement should have been originally accomplished in the mag-

The Church of Santa Sophia

nificent church of Santa Sophia (see Plate II), erected by Justinian to replace an older edifice that had been burned during the revolt of 532. After the Turkish conquest of 1453 parts of it were removed and other parts, notably four minarets, were added in order that it might serve as a Mohammedan mosque.[11] But the central portion, rebuilt after an earthquake in 558, yet stands as it was lyrically described by Procopius nearly 1400 years ago—eloquent testimony to the solidity of its construction and to the excellence of its design. Justinian's great church is, indeed, one of the world's marvels. The central dome rises 180 feet above the pavement and, together with the two half-domes built against it, covers an area that is over 100 feet wide and some 250 feet long. The dome, as already noted, is borne on pendentives; and they rest on four great piers, each of which is backed by a heavily buttressed arch. Since the dome is not held together by chains or other steel supports, it does not tower into the air like one of today, and for that reason is often found disappointing. Besides, the materials of the exterior are rather mean—plain brickwork with a surfacing of plaster or lead. But this is characteristic of the Byzantine style, which paid little attention to external effect while demanding interiors of unparalleled brilliance.

Byzantine sculpture and mosaic

Sculpture, except for the adornment of capitals and altars, was little used by Byzantine architects; and in such places carving was usually restricted to plants, birds, and geometrical designs that clearly show a Persian influence. On the other hand, the walls, arches, vaults, and domes were turned into a blaze of color by covering the lower surfaces with variegated marbles and the upper ones with mosaic. Especially in this latter work the artists of Constantinople have never been surpassed. Placing bits of tinted glass edgewise to catch the light, they created pictures of a highly conventionalized but remarkably beautiful type. Human figures, animals, birds, trees, flowers, and other symbolic objects stand in sharp relief against a solid background, usually gold. The drawing is at best mediocre. The bodies of men and women are badly proportioned; their features have little individuality; their attitudes are stiff and ungraceful. Everything is represented on a flat plane and in a few simple colors. Yet this very lack of attempted subtlety or realism contributes to the success of Byzantine mosaic. Its total effect is one of barbaric splendor, combined with a religious appeal that is the more direct because the art is primitive. The men who produced these masterpieces had plainly lost all reverence for the decadent classicism of the previous age. Their inspiration came rather from the Christian faith and the eastern lands where it had first developed.

Two examples may be seen in the accompanying pictures (Plate I). The lovely apse of Sant' Apollinare in Classe (rather indistinct here) bears at the top the medallion of Christ, flanked by the four beasts of the Apoca-

[11] See below, pp. 172-74.

lypse.[12] Two lines of sheep, representing Christian souls, proceed upward from right and left through a flower-bedecked meadow, representing paradise. At the bottom stands St. Apollinaris between two other lines of sheep. In the mosaic of San Vitale the central panel shows, at the left, Abraham and Sarah providing the three angels (*Genesis*, xviii) with cakes of meal and a roasted calf; at the right, Abraham about to sacrifice Isaac (*Genesis*, xxii)—two scenes that Christians regarded as symbolic of the eucharist. Above on the one side is Jeremiah with a scroll, on the other side Moses receiving the Law on Mt. Sinai. In the center two angels support a cross with lamps hung from the arms. And these are only details in a magnificent interior that includes the famous mosaics of Justinian and Theodora surrounded by their court, as well as some of the most beautifully carved capitals in the world.

[12] Since this is a theme that runs throughout Christian art, it may be explained in some detail. Round about the throne of God (as described in *Revelation,* iv. 6-8) were four winged beasts, shaped respectively like a man, a lion, a calf, and an eagle. These, it was held, typified the four evangelists because they opened their gospels in the followings ways: St. Matthew with the descent of Christ according to the flesh; St. Mark with "the voice of one crying in the wilderness"; St. Luke with the sacrifice of Zacharias; St. John with Divinity itself (as the eagle, by repute, was the only bird that could look the sun in the face). Furthermore, as Christ had taken on human form, the man symbolized the Incarnation; the calf, being the sacrificial beast, the Passion; the lion, being alleged to restore his cubs to life by roaring at them, the Resurrection; and the eagle, flying into the sun, the Ascension.

CHAPTER VI

The Rise of Islam

1. ARABIA AND THE ARABS

The Semitic peoples

Like the central Asiatic plateau, Arabia has served as a vast reservoir of nomadic tribes. It is a roughly quadrangular peninsula, which to the north abuts on the rich and populous lands of Mesopotamia and Syria (see Map VI). Time and again these countries have been swept by great migrations from the south. Such, it is generally held, was the common origin of the peoples known as Semitic: Assyrians, Chaldæans, Hebrews, Phœnicians, Aramæans, and others. But their invasions took place in very ancient times. Until the seventh century neither Greeks nor Romans encountered anything more serious than petty raiding from the direction of the Arabian desert. To contemporaries, therefore, the Arab conquests seemed quite as unprecedented as the Mohammedan faith, and the entire upheaval was considered essentially religious. Modern scholars find it hard to believe that any degree of mere fanaticism could have accomplished so great a revolution in so short a time. They suggest, rather, that it can be explained only by taking into account the social and economic conditions of the invaded provinces, as well as of Arabia. On the side of the Roman Empire, certainly, Hellenism had long been weakening under pressure of an oriental reaction, which was now to be championed and turned to enormous profit by the hosts of Islam. How these hosts came to be constituted is the problem that immediately concerns us.

The Bedouin Arabs

The interior of the Arabian peninsula remains today much as it has been throughout recorded history. It is the home of the Bedouins (dwellers in the desert) who yet live as—to judge from the stories in the Old Testament—they were living in the time of Moses. The Bedouin, being a true nomad, depends for existence upon his animals, which depend in turn upon the pasturage of the desert. The autumn rains normally produce a scanty vegetation, sufficient for sheep and goats if they are kept constantly on the move. During the winter, accordingly, they are driven south; then, in advance of the summer drought, they are turned north, to eat their way back to the point from which they started a year before. The original and essential beast of burden among the Arabs is the camel; but their horses, bred for speed and endurance, have been famous since Roman times. Very naturally, the Bedouins have always maintained such institutions as are demanded by the nomadic life—especially the patriarchal system. Family groups, each under the absolute rule of its chief man, are united to form a tribe headed by a sheik. The latter holds authority over a strip of territory within which his people wander back and forth. It is part of his office to lead his young men on profitable expeditions against his neighbors. Caravan-raiding has been the special delight of the Bedouin for thousands of years. He has no use for centralized government and resists all interference with his time-honored habits. Thus he has been and thus, we may feel sure, he will be as long as his desert homeland persists.

Under such conditions the typical Bedouin has come to possess a splendid physique; he tends to be slender and graceful, with piercing black eyes and regular, often handsome, features. In youth the women, too, are likely to be attractive, though under the domestic labor to which they are doomed their beauty soon fades. In bearing, the Arab sheik is the personification of dignity, combined with a certain wild freedom that has ever endeared him to romantic authors. His courtesy and hospitality are proverbial, and according to his own peculiar standards—which exclude neither professional robbery nor bloody feud—he is strictly honorable. Among the Bedouins the average of intelligence is high. Though illiterate, they are far from ignorant. They can recite from memory the genealogies not merely of their great men but also of their great horses throughout a surprising length of time. They have always been passionately fond of poetry, story-telling, and discussion. And in new environments they have proved themselves among the most adaptable of peoples—extraordinarily quick to learn by observation and to apply the information thus acquired.

Nomadic society tends to follow a fixed routine of existence for an indefinite period; but this routine is one that depends on static conditions—a limited supply of food and a limited population. If the former unduly decreases or if the latter unduly increases, the balance of life is upset. When, for example, climatic change brings persisting drought to a region that has earlier supplied regular pasturage, thousands of tribesmen are immediately faced with starvation. To secure other territory, they have to drive out the present holders; and such a disturbance, once started, may have repercussions in far-distant lands. Occurrences of this sort have been common in the history of nomadic peoples and help us to understand the case of Arabia in the seventh century. It has been argued with considerable

The Arabs in the seventh century

plausibility that the gradual desiccation of the interior was mainly responsible for the outpouring of its inhabitants. In the light of what actually happened, at any rate, we must believe that the country was overpopulated; that, with the sudden appearance of an opportunity for migration and conquest, hordes of land-hungry adventurers were ready to grasp it.

In the seventh century the overwhelming majority of the Arabian population was nomadic; yet in certain localities there were tribes that had long been used to a settled mode of life. Beside the infrequent streams agricultural communities had grown up while along the coasts, both on the east and on the west, sea trade had developed a number of small towns, from which caravan routes led to the greater markets of Syria and Persia. In ancient times the peninsula of Sinai had been widely known as a source of copper and turquoise; and there, apparently, had been developed the system of writing from which we derive our alphabet. The southwest corner of Arabia, Yemen, had likewise been the seat of an advanced culture. In this region a people called Sabæans (whence the Biblical queen of Sheba) had built up a flourishing kingdom that exported large quantities of frankincense, myrrh, and spices for consumption in the Mediterranean countries. Early in the Christian era, however, the Sabæan kingdom was destroyed by invaders from Ethiopia, and the more important centers of Arabian civilization were thenceforth the new states that had arisen in the north.

Arabia
Petræa
and the
Hejaz

Trajan, having extended the Roman dominion over the peninsula of Sinai and the adjoining lands of the Nabatæans, organized the province of Arabia Petræa, named after its rockhewn capital of Petra. Under imperial patronage the neighboring tribes were then enrolled as allies against the nomads, and Persia, to defend the territory of Mesopotamia, followed the same policy. So, in the sixth century there were two Arab kingdoms guarding the desert frontier, one as a Roman and the other as a Persian protectorate. By the opening of the next century both buffer states had been destroyed through the jealousy of the great monarchies which, being engaged in a bitter struggle with each other, ignored a potential danger from the south. Yet, at the time, what menace could be seen in Arabia? Throughout the entire peninsula neither prince nor people could boast an authority that was more than local. The memory of man did not run to an age when the Arabs had ever united in a common cause. What could be more incredible than that such a union would be brought about by a visionary camel-driver?

The region called the Hejaz, lying between Yemen and Arabia Petræa, naturally included the caravan route that joined those two lands. To its coast, furthermore, came vessels from Africa and India, bearing precious goods for transhipment. The chief port for such traffic was Jidda, inland from which about fifty miles was the little town of Mecca, the center of a flourishing trade with the desert Arabs and an important station on the road to Syria. Some two hundred miles to the north was Yathrib (later

Medina), a settlement principally devoted to the raising of dates. Mecca was not only the more important commercially but also the holier. It contained a square temple known as the Kaaba (i.e., the cube), which housed the statutes of various local deities and sacred black stone—presumably a meteorite, for it was said to have fallen from heaven. To visit this shrine and to attend a sort of fair in the neighborhood, crowds of pilgrims annually came from far and wide. So Mecca, together with the tribe of the Kuraish which furnished its ruling families, was known to Arabs everywhere.

Concerning religious and intellectual conditions in early Arabia we have only meager information. From time immemorial the Bedouins had accorded high honor to the bards who traced the histories of the great tribes, celebrated glorious battles, or delivered mysterious oracles about future events. Famous poems of this kind, being committed to memory and recited generation after generation, formed a stock of song and fiction that was common to virtually the entire people. But it remained unwritten, for the use of letters was restricted to the extreme south and to the frontier territories of the north. Although a peculiar alphabet developed by the Sabæans had been anciently carried into Ethiopia, where it still persists, it never enjoyed more than a local influence in Arabia. What we know as literary Arabic—with its rich vocabulary and imaginative force—was essentially the vernacular of the northern Bedouins, written in characters borrowed from the Aramæans. By the time of Christ Aramaic had come to be generally spoken by the Semitic population of Mesopotamia and Syria. So it was quite natural that the Aramaic alphabet should be adopted by the Nabatæans of the Roman province for writing their own language and should thence be introduced into the Hejaz through the influence of trade. Further development of Arabic literature had to await the preaching of a new faith by Mohammed. *Early writings and beliefs of the Arabs*

Until then the religious beliefs of most Bedouins seem to have been extremely primitive. They kept up a rather perfunctory worship of various local gods and goddesses, such as those honored at Mecca; they recognized many sacred rocks, trees, wells, and the like; and they had a lively respect for the evil spirits (*jinn*) that were said to cause dust storms and other calamities in the desert. Along the northern frontier, however, there had been a considerable infiltration of foreign religions. On the side of Persia Zoroastrianism had obtained a considerable following; on that of Syria Judaism and Christianity had come to be accepted by a good many Arabs, notably those of Arabia Petræa and the Hejaz. These facts, such as they are, must serve to introduce the story of Islam's illustrious prophet.

2. Mohammed and Mohammedanism

Mohammed was born at Mecca about the year 570. His family, though belonging to the tribe of Kuraish, was not wealthy, and as a boy of nine or ten he was left an orphan. Thus coming under the care of an uncle, *Early life and conversion*

Mohammed spent his youth in comparative poverty—a period of which we know nothing except that he became thoroughly familiar with contemporary methods of trade. Of formal education he could have had little; that he ever learned to write Arabic has been denied, but is not improbable. In his travels with caravans, however, Mohammed unquestionably picked up a great deal of miscellaneous information. As a trader, he would have the opportunity of meeting men from different lands; as an intelligent Arab, he would store in his memory much of what they told him. And since there were many Arabic-speaking Jews and Christians, such a smattering of their doctrines as he later displayed would not be hard to obtain. We may be positive that he never read their Scriptures.

By the age of about twenty-four Mohammed had so far perfected his professional training that he was employed as commercial agent by a wealthy widow of Mecca named Khadija. And after he had successfully led a caravan to Syria on her behalf, he became the lady's husband—her third. Mohammed was of course much the younger of the two, but the marriage was a happy one; and it was during his life with Khadija that he began his career as a religious reformer. Being now a man of substance and leisure, he could devote himself to the problems of faith and conduct which must first have attracted his attention long before. The traditional polytheism of the Arabs, he felt, was wrong; there was only one God (Allah), the creator of all things, in whose sight man must live righteously in order to win salvation on the awful day of judgment that momentarily impended. When the last trump sounded, the good would be raised to the joys of paradise, while the bad would be cast into the flames of hell.

To Jews and Christians these ideas would seem very familiar; they must, in fact, have been somehow derived from such teachers. Mohammed insisted that his God was the God of the Jews and of the Christians—the God testified to by the prophets, including Moses, Abraham, Noah, and Jesus. For Jesus, he said, though miraculously born of the Virgin Mary, was not truly divine. In his eyes, Christian doctrine was incompatible with strict monotheism and he would have none of it. On the whole, therefore, his inspiration was essentially Hebraic. Christianity he regarded as at most a variety of Judaism. And even as the prophets of old had received direct commissions from the Almighty, might not he, Mohammed, be made the intermediary for a new dispensation from on high?

The prophet of Allah

It was not until Mohammed was over forty, and had spent much time in prayer and fasting, that he was rewarded by visions which convinced him of his prophetic mission. From the angel Gabriel, as he told his wife and a few intimate friends, came the messages that were eventually to found a new religion for Arabia and the world. There can be no question of his sincerity. Even if his sayings were often tinged with practical or perhaps opportunist considerations, we should no more impugn his honesty than that of his Hebrew predecessors, who had also employed common sense while acting as the spokesmen of God. The subconscious mind, as we know from the modern study of psychology, can perform marvels—especially in the case of a man like Mohammed, nervously high-strung, extraordinarily sensitive, and subject to periodic attacks of hysteria which he and others considered manifest evidence of supernatural powers. Yet, whether or not we call his visions hallucinations, the fact remains that they were real to him and to his followers; being so, they revolutionized the course of events on three continents. The historical importance of a religion is not that it is true, but that people believe it so.

At first Mohammed had little success with his preaching. While his wife Khadija and his cousin Ali embraced the new faith from the outset, most of his relatives, including the uncle who had brought him up, held aloof. Among the other early converts the only prominent man was Abu Bakr, who was to remain Mohammed's closest friend and adviser. Later he gained another important recruit in a young man named Omar, eventually to prove himself one of the world's great statesmen. The majority of the Kuraish, however, bitterly opposed the upstart prophet, who denounced the traditional worship to which they were attached by business interest as well as by sentiment. They ridiculed Mohammed as a crazy poet. His teachings, they said, were absurd. How could God restore them to life after they had turned to dust and dry bones? Why should they believe a simple fellow from among themselves, who ate like them and walked like them in the market? If he had a divine commission, let him show them an angel or work for them some evident miracle. To which Mohammed replied with eloquent stories about the persecution of the ancient prophets and with lurid descriptions of the hell that yawned for unbelievers.

Finally, after his position at Mecca had been further weakened by the death of his wife in 619, followed by that of his uncle, Mohammed was attracted to a more sympathetic environment. At Yathrib there was a considerable colony of Jews, or Judaized Arabs, at least some of whom were willing to recognize Mohammed as their promised Messiah. There was, furthermore, a long-standing feud between rival tribes of the neighborhood which had come to be found inconvenient for all parties. The upshot was that the men of Yathrib made a solemn treaty with Mohammed, swearing to accept whatever peace he might dictate and to protect him and his followers as members of their own families. So, in 622, the prophet and his little band of followers left Mecca, breaking all connection with their own groups of kindred. This was the famous Hegira[1] or Emigration,

The Hegira (622)

---

[1] Arabic *Hijra*. The preferable pronunciation is with the accent on the first syllable and with all vowels short.

from which Mohammedans reckon their years. And it was a noteworthy event, for it marked the definite organization of the new religion.

The formal
regulation
of Islam

Yathrib was renamed Medina (*Madinat-an-Nabi*, City of the Prophet), and from there Mohammed continued the promulgation of his divine messages, now turned from short exhortations in a highly poetic vein to detailed edicts on social and political problems, as well as on matters of faith and worship. The Mohammedan religion formally appears as Islam, meaning submission to God. One who has made his submission is a Moslem. His confession of faith is extremely simple: "There is no God but Allah, and Mohammed is His prophet." After ceremonial ablution with water or with sand, he should pray at certain fixed hours of the day— tradition says five times—and these prayers are accompanied by a mild discipline of bodily postures resembling athletic exercises. Service in the mosque is merely common prayer under the guidance of a leader, for there has never been a Mohammedan priesthood. At first the faithful prayed with their faces towards Jerusalem; subsequently, when Mohammed found that most Jews rejected his teaching, he substituted Mecca. To that holy place the Moslem should make a pilgrimage at least once during his life. He should, furthermore, give alms for charitable and pious ends, and he should fast from sunrise to sunset throughout the sacred month of Ramadan.

These were and are the major requirements of Islam, to which were added from time to time a large number of moral precepts—rather modifications of existing custom than innovations. To a limited degree polygamy and slavery were both retained. The prophet himself, after the death of Khadija, took many wives, often making such alliances for the sake of political advantage. Yet in various ways he sought to ameliorate the condition both of slaves and of women. Marriage customs were greatly improved. Sexual promiscuity, which earlier had been common, was severely punished. The primitive system of the blood-feud, by which the family avenged wrongs done to its members, was restricted by enforcing the acceptance of compensation when that was rightfully offered.[2] The Arabs were already acquainted with taboos in connection with food and drink, and Mohammed wisely refrained from adding any very rigorous prohibitions. Moslems should abstain from the flesh of all animals slaughtered in the name of any god except Allah, as well as from pork and from wine. But the latter restrictions, it should be noted, could work no great hardship on the Bedouins. As the mark of a national cult, the new discipline was eminently sensible in its moderation.

The Koran

With respect to all these matters our primary source of information is the Koran (*Quran*, Recitation), a collection of Mohammed's sayings, which in its present form dates from a period shortly after the prophet's

[2] Cf. the Germanic custom, above, pp. 58-59.

death. Most of its contents, however, had been written down earlier—either by Mohammed himself or by others—and much of it had been committed to memory by the devout. The authenticity of its substance is thus unquestionable, and allowance need be made only for revision of its wording and rearrangement of its parts. The latter consideration is of little importance; for the compilers merely placed the 114 chapters—with the exception of an opening prayer—in decreasing order of their length. The Koran is therefore so devoid of logical coherence that to read and appreciate it as a whole is extremely difficult. Each fragment must be taken as it was originally uttered—as a separate message delivered on a particular occasion.

Thus understood, the Koran is magnificent. To the student of Moslem law and institutions the later revelations are the more instructive; but as literature the earlier ones are infinitely superior. Most of them, being very brief, are to be found towards the end of the book. In form they resemble modernistic verse, being made up of irregular lines without definite meter or rhyme pattern, but with rhythmic cadences and combinations of syllables based on resemblances of sound. Although Mohammed considered the term an insult, he really was a poet and a very great one. To turn the Koran into matter-of-fact prose is to spoil it; much of its beauty is inevitably destroyed by any kind of translation. Yet those of us unfortunate enough to be ignorant of Arabic may gain some inkling of the original by a version in a familiar language.

This is the opening prayer (ch. i):

Typical chapters

> Praise be to Allah, Lord of the worlds,
> Beneficent and merciful,
> King of the day of judgment!
> Thee do we serve, and of Thee do we beg aid.
> Guide us in the right way—
> The way of them who are pleasing in Thy sight,
> Not of them who bear Thy wrath; not of them who go astray.

Other chapters are strongly reminiscent of the Psalms, but with touches peculiar to Arabia; for example (ch. lxxxvii):

> Praise the name of thy Lord, the Most High,
> Who created and designed all things,
> Who preordained them and directs them;
> Who makes the grass to grow in the pastures,
> And then burns it brown like straw. . . .
> Happy is he who, during his growth,
> Remembers the name of his Lord in prayer.
> But ye prefer the life of this world,
> Though that to come is better, and is everlasting.
> For this, verily, was in the books of old,
> The books of Abraham and Moses.

On one occasion, we are told, Mohammed for several days had failed to receive any revelation and on that account was being ridiculed by his enemies. Then God spoke to him as follows (ch. xciii):

> By the hours of the morning,
> And by those of the still night—
> Thy Lord has not forsaken thee, nor yet does hate thee.
> Verily the future shall be kinder to thee than is the present;
> The Lord will give thee wherewith thou shalt be pleased.
> Did he not find thee an orphan and give thee shelter?
> Did he not find thee wandering and give thee guidance?
> Did he not find thee needy and give thee riches?
> Therefore oppress not the orphan,
> Nor drive the beggar away,
> But proclaim the goodness of the Lord.

The majestic opening of this chapter—in the form of a solemn oath—is characteristic of many others. Among them the one following is especially fine (ch. lxxvii):

> By the winds one after another sent—
> By the storm-winds that rage,
> By those that bring new life to the verdure of earth,
> By those that serve for winnowing,
> By those that come as a reminder,
> Whether to approve or warn—
> Verily that will befall which has been promised.
> When, therefore, the stars are extinguished,
> When the sky is rent asunder,
> When the mountains are brushed away,
> When for the messengers their time has been fulfilled—
> What is the day for which is this fulfilment?
> The Day of Reckoning!

Heaven and hell

The Last Judgment is an ever-recurring theme (chs. l-lviii, liv-lvi, lxix, lxxvi-xcii, c-ci, etc.). On that awful day men shall rise from their graves like swarming locusts and then, according to how their balance may be weighted by good or evil, shall be parted to the right and to the left. "The people of the left hand," the prophet declares, shall go down to hell, which is a place of scorching wind and scalding water under a pall of black smoke. Heaven, on the contrary, is a cool garden, watered by gushing springs and shaded by thornless trees whose plentiful fruit hangs within easy reach. There shall dwell "the people of the right hand," reclining on silken couches, eating choice viands, and quaffing a divine beverage that causes neither drunkenness nor headache. They shall be waited on by glorious immortal youths and shall be wed to specially created houris—beautiful damsels with wide-set eyes like dusky pearls!

To the modern reader these descriptions of rewards and punishments in the hereafter must seem rather childishly realistic. But for that very reason did they not hold a greater appeal to a primitive people? The audience to which Mohammed addressed himself could hardly have appreciated a doctrine based on philosophical abstraction. Like all successful reformers, he had to teach new ideals in a familiar language. The gorgeous imagery of the Koran was such as even the illiterate Bedouins delighted in. And its religious ideas were so lofty that they could offset, in the eyes of the sophisticated, a possible crudity of presentation. After all, the essence of Mohammed's preaching was not belief in hell-fire and heavenly bliss but man's submission to God, to be shown by repentance and a virtuous life.

As a religion, Islam was founded during the prophet's ministry at Mecca. His later life was devoted to the establishment of an organization to assure the dominance of the new faith; and since there was no truly Arabian state, his system was of necessity semi-political. At Medina Mohammed was confronted by many problems. He had to prescribe details of worship and everyday morality for his followers. He became involved in conflicts with Jews and other local inhabitants who, refusing to recognize his prophetic mission, stubbornly opposed his authority. Also to be considered was the project of converting the Bedouins of the interior. All these matters depended on the outcome of the feud with Mecca. Since the Hegira the band of Moslems had of course ceased to owe any loyalty to the tribe of Kuraish, and they now, with the constant support of revelations from heaven, began raiding the caravans of their erstwhile kindred. This policy led to greater hostilities, during which Mohammed gained his first victory in 624. At Badr, near the Red Sea, his troops won a pitched battle against a force that outnumbered them three to one. Here, said the Moslems, was the miracle for which the Meccans had been clamoring; without the help of God's angels, who appeared in the field beside the prophet, he could never have prevailed against the hostile army.

In the desultory fighting that occupied the next few years the Moslems sometimes won and sometimes lost. Yet on the whole their cause steadily advanced. The antagonistic Jews were driven from Medina and their lands were confiscated by the faithful. More booty flowed in from successful raids against non-believers. Then, in 627, Mohammed gained his second victory. An army of several thousand men, recruited by the Kuraish from among their Bedouin allies, laid siege to Medina but were repulsed through Mohammed's employment of a trench as a line of defense—a trick he is said to have learned from a Persian slave. However this may be, his enemies gave up all thought of a further offensive and agreed to a ten-year truce. Mohammed thus became free to make the first Moslem pilgrimage to Mecca, fulfilling an obligation which he had declared essential to the new faith. The occasion, very naturally, served to advertise the prophet's increasing fame, and several prominent men of the Kuraish—among them

Mohammed's leadership

the great warriors Khalid and Amr ibn al-As—announced their conversion.
The final triumph came only a year later, when the failure of the truce led
to a renewal of hostilities. Mohammed, now possessed of an overwhelming
force, was allowed to occupy Mecca almost without striking a blow, and
the first campaign in the Holy War of Islam was brought to a close.

Moham-
med's final
victory
(630) and
death
(632)

The victor used his power wisely. The Kaaba was formally purified by
casting out the idols which it had long housed. But the temple itself was
preserved, and with it the black stone—an action justified by a special
revelation. The Meccan cult, the prophet announced, had originally been
founded by Abraham; his modern successor was merely restoring its
pristine character. Thus, consciously or unconsciously, Mohammed made
the revolution easy for the Kuraish to accept. As a matter of fact, they
soon found that, by guarding Islam's holiest shrine, they stood to gain
infinitely more than they had ever thought to lose. And with that ultimate
testimony to the might of Allah, all resistance crumbled. Although
Mohammed's death in 632 came as a frightful calamity to the mass of his
converts, his work was done. Within ten years after leaving Mecca as a
fugitive he had returned as a conqueror. His fame had spread throughout
the length and breadth of Arabia; and while as yet all the Bedouin tribes
had by no means submitted to his dominion, the war that he had proclaimed against the foes of Islam was to bring an amazing series of triumphs
such as his wildest dreams could never have foretold.

3. The Caliphate and the Arab Empire

Abu Bakr
and Omar
(632-44)

The first problem raised by the unexpected death of Mohammed was
how to perpetuate the organization he had founded. On this point, strangely
enough, the prophet had announced no revelation; yet it was one that
could hardly have escaped consideration by his relatives and associates. In
spite of his many weddings, Mohammed was survived by only one child,
Fatima, the daughter of Khadija. She was married to Ali, the prophet's
cousin, and by him had two sons. If the headship of the Moslems should
pass like that of an ordinary family, Ali would be the logical candidate
for the honor; but he was more remarkable for piety than for ability. In
preference to him, Mohammed's confidence had been given to Abu Bakr,
one of the earliest converts to Islam and the father of Mohammed's
favorite wife, the young and spirited Aïsha. So it was Abu Bakr whom an
informal assembly of the faithful hailed as caliph (successor of the prophet).
And whatever hostility was still nourished by Ali's legitimist faction soon
collapsed before the wonderful success of the newly established government.

The uni-
fication
of Arabia

Only two years remained to the aged Abu Bakr, but his work was carried
to a glorious conclusion by his talented friend and counselor Omar. Their
primary concern was the prosecution of the Holy War. This, it should be

emphasized, was properly directed against idolaters alone; for the Koran (ch. ix) commanded that they be slain unless they accepted the true faith, whereas the "people of the Book" (i.e., Jews and Christians) were to be subjected and made to pay tribute. Mohammed's authority, in spite of legendary exaggeration, had scarcely reached beyond the region of the Hejaz, and at the news of his death even those Bedouins who had already been subjected tended to throw off allegiance to Medina. This reaction was immediately checked by the energy of Abu Bakr. Under command of Khalid, the little army of Islam won battle after battle against the tribes of central Arabia; so that within hardly more than a year the caliph could shift operations from the desert to the adjoining regions, thus resuming a project already contemplated by Mohammed. As he had perceived, nothing would so quickly stimulate adhesion to the sacred cause as profitable raids against a common foe. Accordingly, while offensives were still being pushed in the southern peninsula, Abu Bakr sent various bands of volunteers into Syria and Mesopotamia.

The time was well chosen. Persia, since the great defeat of some five years earlier, had fallen into a state of helplessness. The deposition of Chosroës II[3] had been followed by a prolonged civil war, and the ultimate recognition of his grandson, Yezdegerd, had brought only a superficial restoration of the monarchy. Nor were conditions much better in the Byzantine Empire. Heraclius seemed exhausted by his heroic campaigns against Persia. His provinces were groaning under a terrific burden of taxation, and to economic grievances were added those occasioned by the imperial policy of religious despotism. Outside the Hellenized population of the great cities the government had few loyal supporters. The inhabitants of the countryside, exploited for a thousand years by the Greek aristocracy, would fight no desperate battles in its behalf. The Semitic peasantry of Syria, like that of Mesopotamia, would inevitably feel more akin to Arabs than to Byzantines or Persians. And the desert tribes along the border, although they might be Christian or Zoroastrian in faith, would be only too willing to join expeditions that promised unlimited plunder.

Moslem raids and the battle of the Yarmuk (636)

The possibilities of aggressive war on the part of the Moslems were clearly demonstrated by Khalid's campaign of 634. After a first success at Hira on the Euphrates, which paid him well to get rid of him, he advanced into Syria, where Arab raiders were being threatened by a superior Byzantine force. Combining speed with good generalship, Khalid drove past Palmyra and Damascus, effected a junction with his compatriots, and defeated the imperial army. At this moment Abu Bakr was succeeded by Omar who, appreciating the opportunity that lay before him, began the systematic conquest of the Roman provinces. In 635 Khalid, with the help of allies inside the walls, took the city of Damascus. But in the meantime

---

[3] See above, p. 91.

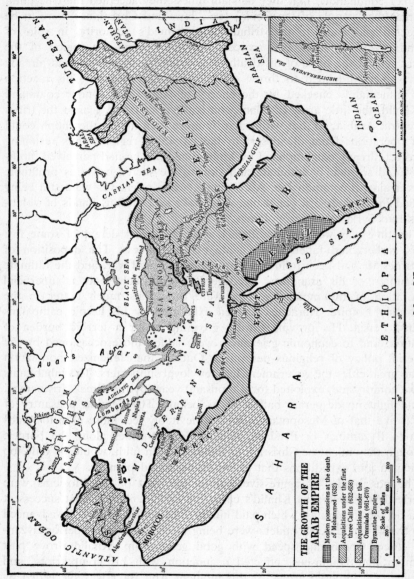

THE GROWTH OF THE
ARAB EMPIRE

Moslem possessions at the death
of Mohammed (632)

Acquisitions under the first
three Califs (632-658)

Acquisitions under the
Ommiads (661-670)

Byzantine Empire

Scale of Miles
0   200   400   600   800

MAP VI.

Heraclius had collected a greater army, and in the spring of 636 it fell upon Khalid's little troop, which had been pushed a hundred miles or so to the north of Damascus. Again showing rare generalship, he made no effort to hold his recent conquests and rapidly fell back on the Yarmuk, a westward-flowing tributary of the Jordan that would, if necessary, afford a sure means of escape into the desert (see Map VI, p. 110). That necessity, however, did not arise. Khalid's retreat had allowed him to call up needed reinforcements, while his opponents had been seriously weakened by the rivalry of their generals and the desertion of their Arab allies. After weeks of skirmishing with the elusive foe, the Byzantine army was trapped between two converging defiles and there annihilated in August, 636.

The battle of the Yarmuk assured the Arabs unmolested possession of **Conquest** Syria. Henceforth they had merely to consolidate their positions and to **of Syria** organize a permanent government. Under the able direction of Omar **and Persia** these tasks were quickly accomplished. The surrender of Damascus, Aleppo, and Antioch sealed the fate of Palestine, the conquest of which was completed by the taking of Jerusalem in 638 and of Cæsarea in 640. As long as the outcome in Syria remained doubtful, Omar launched no major campaign in Mesopotamia. Then, after the great victory on the Yarmuk, he sent a relatively small force against the Persians to avenge their defeat of a marauding expedition some years earlier. The result must have come as a surprise to both parties. Yezdegerd's best army was crushed in a single battle, and the whole of Iraq (i.e., the lower valley of the Tigris-Euphrates), together with the capital city of Ctesiphon, fell into the hands of the Arabs. The next step was to connect Iraq and Syria by reducing Mosul, which was done in 641. For a time the Persians succeeded in holding the line of the mountains to the east, but within another year that too had been broken, and all serious resistance came to an end throughout the kingdom. Yezdegerd, now a fugitive beyond the Caspian, is said to have been slain by one of his own satraps in 651. By that time, in any case, the ancient state of Persia had been obliterated and a new age had begun for central Asia.

Meanwhile Omar had opened a third major offensive. This was against **Conquest** Egypt, where local conditions once more proved an enormous advantage to **of Egypt** the invaders. The province was suffering not only from the usual evils of overtaxation and maladministration but also—even more than Syria— from religious discord. For a long time the population had been sharply divided into two parts: the Hellenized inhabitants of the cities and the native Egyptian peasants, or Copts. The former, since they constituted the ruling aristocracy, tended to obey the emperor and accept his dictates in religion. The latter, on the contrary, were fervently monophysite,[4] and the tyranny of the patriarch installed at Alexandria by Heraclius served merely

[4] See above, p. 86.

to intensify their opposition to the government. It was therefore a propitious moment for the Moslem army which now crossed the isthmus under the command of Amr ibn al-As, who had proved his ability during the campaigns in Syria. In 640 he broke through a defending body of Byzantine troops and captured Babylon (later Cairo) on the Nile. The sympathy of the Copts, the personal ambitions of the patriarch, and the death of Heraclius (641) all conspired to make the subjection of the province ridiculously easy. Even Alexandria surrendered before the end of 642, and in the next year Amr extended his occupation to the adjoining district of Barca.

The Arab migration and the spread of Islam

From every point of view these Moslem campaigns are among the most astonishing in history. To contemporaries it must have seemed incredible that mere Bedouin tribesmen, who had never before engaged in military operations on a large scale and who possessed no siege engines of any kind, could take Syria and Egypt from the Romans and destroy the Persian monarchy in little more than a dozen years. The feebleness of both ancient states, it is true, was largely responsible for their dramatic collapse; yet the achievement of the Arabs should not on that account be minimized. Their military superiority was due not only to the greater mobility of their light cavalry but also to the intelligence of their commanders and to the high morale of their troops—the characteristic verve of the Bedouin intensified by religious exaltation. Their campaigns, furthermore, by no means ended with bloodshed and looting. By tens of thousands the Arabs poured into the conquered lands, and this migration permanently altered their social, religious, and cultural complexion.

While the shifting of the Arabian population naturally resulted in a great expansion of Islam, other factors contributed to the same end. Large numbers of Zoroastrians, Jews, and Christians were eventually converted to the new faith. Its creed and discipline, as we have seen, were extremely simple; to accept them must have seemed to many, if not an actual religious advance, a mere change of ritualistic forms. And the practical considerations were most alluring. The Moslems were the lords of creation, the rest of mankind their tributaries. By joining that blessed group, many a poor Bedouin had attained riches and honor. What was to prevent a non-Arab from sharing the same good fortune? The notion that Mohammedanism was a religion of the sword, forced upon the masses by bloodthirsty fanatics, is based upon a false reading of history. The Moslem conquest was essentially political; its leaders deprecated unnecessary slaughter of unbelievers, or even their compulsory conversion, because they were to be the financial support of the state. As a matter of fact, the acceptance of Islam by too many subjects became a source of great embarrassment to the ruling class. But to understand the significance of that problem, we must examine the later fortunes of the caliphate.

In 644 the triumphant presidency of Omar was brought to an untimely
end by an obscure assassin. Before he died, however, the caliph named an
electoral commission of six men, authorized to select one of their own
number to succeed him. The choice fell upon Othman, a member of a
prominent Meccan family known as the Ommiads (more properly
Umayyad, descended from Umayya). Othman proved a much easier master
than Omar, and for that very reason a poorer statesman. Before long the
new caliph's weakness, together with his policy of filling the greater offices
with his own relatives, led to widespread discontent. As the great wars of
conquest came to a close, the flow of captured treasure naturally dwindled,
while the revenue from taxation was reduced by an increase in the number
of true believers who could claim exemption. The government, being yet
a sort of makeshift, lacked a sound financial basis. Far from inaugurating
the necessary reforms, Othman was unable to preserve order. Finally, in
655, an insurrection at Medina resulted in his murder.

The immediate consequence of this affair was a reaction against the
caliphate as originally established, and the man to gain by it was of course
Ali. As the son-in-law of the prophet, he was the logical chief of the
legitimist party—those who protested that the headship of Islam could
rightfully be held only by a member of Mohammed's own family and that,
accordingly, the first three caliphs were usurpers. Proclaimed at Medina
after the death of Othman, Ali found his principal support in Iraq and
Persia; so he removed his capital to Kufa on the Euphrates. Syria, on the
other hand, remained under the Ommiad Muawiya, whom Omar had
appointed to the governorship at Damascus. An able and energetic man,
Muawiya at once took up the cause of the martyred Othman and succeeded in forming an alliance with Amr, the master of Egypt. These two
carried all before them. In 660 Muawiya was hailed as caliph at Jerusalem,
and with the assassination of Ali in the following year the legitimist cause
collapsed.

Under Muawiya the caliphate may be said to have passed from the republican to the monarchical stage. As Medina had now ceased to be the
true center of the Arab dominion, and as Syria continued to be the foundation of the caliph's power, the capital of Islam was transferred to Damascus.
This change, in more ways than one, marked the substitution of Roman
for Arabian government. Hitherto the caliphate had been essentially a
personal leadership of the faithful; henceforth it was to be more of a territorial sovereignty. The caliph thus came to surround himself with professional ministers chosen solely with a view to their political usefulness—
among them many Christians. He now headed an elaborate system of
administration largely borrowed from the Byzantine Empire. And he succeeded in placing his state on a dynastic basis. At Muawiya's death in 680
his son secured the throne in spite of opposition from Arabia and Iraq.

A legitimist rising was suppressed, Ali's two sons were killed, and for the next seventy years the caliphate remained a possession of the Ommiad house.

Control
of the
Mediter-
ranean

The period of disorder that ensued upon the death of Omar naturally interrupted the advance of Moslem conquest; then, with the recognition of the Ommiad caliphate, the offensive was triumphantly resumed on all fronts. As governor of Syria, Muawiya had earlier turned his energies to the construction of a fleet, and in this project had been ably seconded by Amr in Egypt. The final result was the establishment of a Moslem naval supremacy on the Mediterranean that lasted for the better part of five centuries. In 649 the Arabs took Cyprus, and from this base they directed plundering expeditions against Rhodes, Crete, the Ægean Islands, and the coasts of Asia Minor. In 655 a Byzantine fleet, personally commanded by the emperor, was utterly destroyed in a naval engagement that proved as decisive as the battle of the Yarmuk. It not only isolated the imperial possessions to the west but also exposed Constantinople to direct attack by sea. While the caliph's armies advanced through Armenia and Asia Minor to converge on Chalcedon, his fleet tried to force an entrance into the Bosphorus and so to assure the fall of the great city. But the defenders, while abandoning their outlying possessions, were always able to muster enough strength to save their capital, and after the death of Muawiya the Moslems temporarily relaxed their efforts in this direction. To the south, too, the Byzantine fortune distinctly improved; so that, by the end of the seventh century, the Arabs were once more being held along the line of the Taurus Mountains. The next great triumph of Islam was to be won in Africa.

Conquest
of
northern
Africa

From Barca the Moslems had of course raided the imperial provinces to the west, but they did not attempt the systematic conquest of these lands until Muawiya had obtained the caliphate. They then occupied Libya, established a military base at Kairawan, and began the reduction of the old Carthaginian territory. The Byzantines, having lost control of the sea, were from the first powerless to defend their African possessions. The Moors, on the other hand, proved to be formidable antagonists. In the previous century they had almost undone Justinian's conquest of the Vandal kingdom. Since that time, through the constant arrival of fresh recruits from the borderlands, their hold on the countryside had steadily tightened. And as the Arabs, underestimating the independent spirit of the natives, maintained their usual attitude of magnificent pride, the Moors rose in revolt and drove them out of the whole region west of Barca.

During the wise caliphate of Abd-al-Malik (685-705), however, the lost territory was slowly but solidly reoccupied. The new commanders, with great success, combined force and diplomacy to win over the Moors. A last naval expedition from Constantinople ended in complete failure.

Carthage surrendered and the entire southern coast of the Mediterranean fell into the hands of the Moslems. Many years were of course required for the conquest of the mountainous interior, but in the meantime thousands of Moors found a fresh outlet for their untamed energy by espousing the cause of Islam. Thanks to their religious and warlike fervor, the African governor Musa eventually secured the armies with which to undertake an invasion of Europe.

Concerning the later history of the Visigoths there is little of interest to record. By the opening of the seventh century they had retaken the Mediterranean shore from the Byzantines. But this success was due rather to the weakness of the enemy than to the strength of the Visigothic kingdom, the annals of which become a wearisome recital of conspiracies and insurrections. To a prince seeking an adventure wherewith to occupy his restless subjects Spain appeared to be a promising field. So, in 711, Musa authorized one of his lieutenants, a certain Tariq, to lead a force of Moors across the strait. Skirting the rock that still bears his name (Jabal Tariq, or Gibraltar), he landed at Algeciras and thence proceeded towards Cadiz. Roderick, doomed to be the last king of the Visigoths, tried to drive back the invaders and suffered a crushing defeat. Before the end of the summer Tariq was in the royal capital of Toledo. What had begun as a mere plundering expedition thus turned into another momentous victory for Islam. Musa soon arrived with a larger army and the Visigothic state went the way of Persia. Within seven years the Moslems had reached Septimania beyond the Pyrenees; within another seven they were raiding the plains of central Gaul. *Conquest of Spain*

In the east, likewise, the hosts of Islam continued to advance. While completing the reorganization of Persia, the Arabs—thanks to the zealous recruits whom they found among the Iranians—pushed their raids far beyond its frontiers into the lands of the Turks, Chinese, Afghans, Thibetans, and Hindus. There, as usual, marauding served as a preparation for conquest. By the second quarter of the eighth century the domains of the caliph had come to include the valleys of the Indus and the Oxus, with advanced posts as far east as Turkestan. In Asia Minor, however, the Byzantine power, which had earlier seemed on the point of utter collapse, revived sufficiently to hold a frontier extending from Adana on the Mediterranean to Trebizond on the Black Sea. And out of the warfare in this Anatolian country emerged a general named Leo, who secured the imperial crown in 717—just in time to organize the defense of the capital against another great attack of the Moslems by land and sea. Again the issue turned on the holding of the Bosphorus; and when, after twelve months of bitter fighting, the caliph's fleet had been driven off, his armies abandoned the campaign. *Advance in Asia*

The Arab Empire of the eighth century, thus reaching from the Atlantic Ocean to the Himalayas, was the ultimate product of raids undertaken by the nomads of Arabia. When they came into the territories of their powerful neighbors, they brought with them no political institutions beyond those of their ancient tribal system, and no political ambition beyond that of collecting tribute. But they were not mere despoilers like the Huns. On taking over the administration of the conquered lands, they carefully preserved anything that might be turned to their own advantage. The provincial organization of Romans or Persians they left intact, merely substituting Arabs for natives in the topmost offices. Subordinates, as long as they proved loyal to their new masters, remained unmolested. Accordingly, the only persons to suffer complete ruin were the members of the old official aristocracy. To lesser men the Moslem conquest was no great calamity. Their burdens could hardly be greater than those already borne, and by the easy process of accepting Islam they could themselves enter the favored class in the state.

Many thousands quickly grasped the advantages offered by the new faith, and throughout the centuries down to the present their descendants have largely remained Mohammedan. Legally they at first became Arabs as well as Moslems, for converts had to be adopted into Arab tribes and receive Arab names. But eventually, as the nomads dropped the primitive customs of the desert and mixed with the native population, maintenance of the old distinctions became impossible. The religion, language, and to some extent the traits of the conquerors came to be shared by the inhabitants of a vast region; and although the latter were not Arabs like the Bedouins who had remained in the homeland, their culture may properly be called Arabic. The Romans of the principate were by no means all descended from citizens of the city-state on the Tiber; what is known as Latin culture was largely Hellenic by origin. Even if the Arabs borrowed much from Greeks, Romans, Persians, Hindus, and Chinese, the civilization which they developed truly reflected their own genius and ranks as one of the greatest in history.

Fuller discussion of this subject must be postponed until a later chapter; for the moment we shall deal only with the earlier caliphate, which came to an end in 750. Although the Ommiads were able to extend their dominions both to the east and to the west, it soon proved impossible to support the state from the profits of war and conquest. Consequently, the ancient freedom of true believers from all tribute was gradually restricted to an exemption from personal taxes, and lands were assessed without regard to the holders. Yet, while the Ommiads thus broadened the liability for taxation, they maintained the old tradition that the original Arabs constituted a ruling aristocracy. Political authority and social eminence remained virtual monopolies of a few families from Mecca and Medina—a policy which, coming more and more into conflict with the Moslem population, produced increasing discontent.

As was to be expected, the opposition came to a head in Persia, where a deep antagonism to Syrian domination outlived the monarchy from which it was inherited. There the prejudices of the Iranians coincided with the ambitions of the Arab tribes who had momentarily enjoyed great prestige during the caliphate of Ali. And there the legitimists, who declared the descendants of Ali to be the only true caliphs, naturally maintained their headquarters. From time to time they had launched futile risings against the Ommiads. Now that the latter had come into general disrepute, they allied with the supporters of the Abbasid house—descended from Abbas, the uncle of Mohammed—and very foolishly; for it was the Abbasid claimant who, in 750, carried out a successful insurrection and thereby gained the caliphate. The Ommiads, except for one fugitive who made good his escape to Spain,[5] were massacred and the capital of the Arab Empire was again moved eastward, eventually to be placed in the new city of Bagdad on the Tigris. This, we shall see, was a momentous event in the history of Christendom, as well as of Islam.

[5] See below. p. 137.

CHAPTER VII

The Papacy and the Barbarian West

1. GREGORY THE GREAT

The Franks and their neighbors   By the close of the sixth century, as has been noted,[1] the Franks had come to hold a prominent position in the western world, and this prominence tended to be enhanced by the evil fortunes of their greater rivals. The states of the Vandals and the Ostrogoths had been destroyed by Justinian. That of the Visigoths, it is true, persisted for over another hundred years; but long before it fell to the Moslems it had become thoroughly decadent. Of the other Germanic peoples on the continent only one was to play a leading part on Roman soil—i.e., the Lombards whose invasion of Italy brought them into close contact with the papacy and with the Franks. The Gepids had been crushed by the Avars. The Bavarians, Alamans, and Thuringians had recognized Frankish overlordship. The Saxons and Frisians still remained heathen, like the Scandinavians to the north and the Anglo-Saxons in Britain.

Few traces of Latin civilization could now be detected in the old Roman province of Britain. The Germanic invaders had occupied the whole agricultural plain of the southeast and partitioned it into many small kingdoms: Northumbria, East Anglia, Mercia, and Kent, together with the states of the East, Middle, South, and West Saxons (Essex, Middlesex, Sussex, and Wessex). Northern Britain was the scene of constant warfare between the more ancient population of Picts and various bands of Scots who had come over from Ireland. In the extreme west the Britons, whom the Anglo-Saxons knew as Welsh (*wealh*, foreign), held the mountainous promontories of Cornwall, Wales, and Strathclyde (see Map VII). But many other Britons had fled across the Channel to the Armorican peninsula, where they established the Celtic speech and customs that have

[1] Above, p. 78.

persisted down to the present. Brittany, as the region has since been called, thus came to be sharply distinguished from, and wholly independent of, the Frankish lands to the east.

The Merovingian kingdom, as shown on a map, has an imposing appearance, but its grandeur should not be exaggerated. What little strength it possessed in the early sixth century quickly faded in the subsequent years. The decline began when the last surviving son of Clovis divided the king-

Decay of the Frankish kingdom

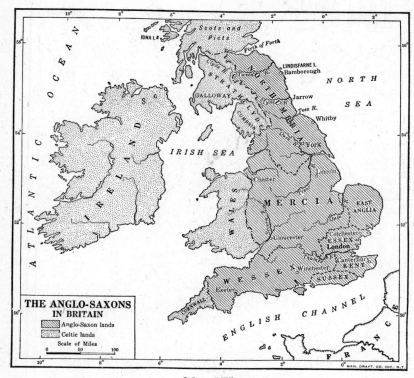

MAP VII.

dom among his four sons. Two of them, led by their wives, became involved in a bloody feud, which was perpetuated under their children and grandchildren. During this barbarous war the two royal courts, one at Metz and the other at Soissons, became the centers of two autonomous states, Austrasia and Neustria (see Map VIII). Even after the Neustrian ruler had exterminated the rival dynasty, Austrasia maintained its separate identity under the domination of the local aristocracy. Burgundy and Aquitaine had long been virtually independent. On the Danube the Bavarians threw off the overlordship of the Franks, and in Thuringia their

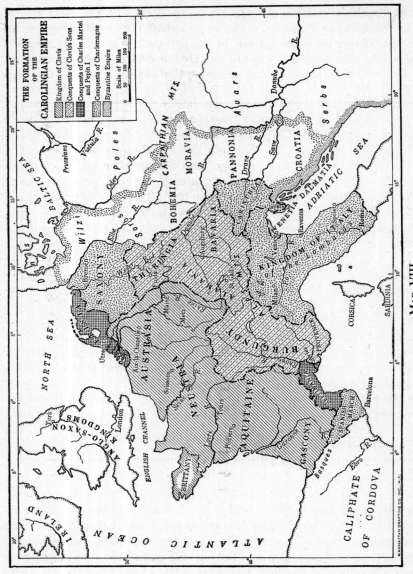

THE FORMATION
OF THE
CAROLINGIAN EMPIRE

Kingdom of Clovis
Conquests of Clovis's Sons
Conquests of Charles Martel
and Pepin I
Conquests of Charlemagne
Byzantine Empire

Scale of Miles
0   50   100   150   200

MAP VIII.

control was at most a doubtful quantity. Meanwhile, too, the kingship had become a mere sham. Dagobert (d. 639) was the last of the Merovingians who amounted to anything. Thenceforth the house of Clovis degenerated into a series of inconsequential puppets controlled by their ministers.

The contemporary development of the papacy was of infinitely greater significance. Halfway in point of time between Justinian and Mohammed the see of St. Peter was held by the eminent statesman and teacher, Pope Gregory I. He was born about the year 540 of a noble and wealthy Roman family, one that had long been distinguished in both church and state. Of his youth little is known except that he received a good education in Latin grammar and rhetoric, while remaining entirely ignorant of Greek. As he grew to manhood, he witnessed the last phase of the Gothic war, the closing years of Justinian's reign, and the invasion of Italy by the Lombards. During this time Gregory apparently worked through the lower grades of a political career at Rome; for by 573 he had become prefect, the highest of the municipal officials. But within a year or so he resigned his honors, gave his fortune to charity, converted his home into a monastery, and there became one of the brothers, presumably under the rule that had recently been drawn up by the famous St. Benedict. *Gregory's early career*

It was about 578 that Gregory was called from his monastic retreat to be ordained deacon at Rome, and not long afterwards he was sent as papal ambassador to Constantinople. The period was one of critical importance for the papacy. The popes had by no means found the Byzantine conquest an unmixed blessing; under Justinian they had enjoyed less toleration than under the Arian Ostrogoths. Even after the death of that willful emperor they remained in an uncomfortable position. To submit to eastern opinion and modify the canons of Chalcedon[2] was to lose the support of the west; to refuse to do so was to invite imperial persecution. Nevertheless, for a pope unwilling to renounce moral grandeur the way was clear. What could he do but follow the tradition of Leo the Great? And as it turned out, this decision was made easier by the Lombard invasion. Although the Lombards were heretics as well as uncivilized barbarians, they constituted an effective counterpoise to the ambitions of the emperor. The logic of the situation inevitably suggested that the papacy, to assure its necessary independence, should play off one potential enemy against the other.

Whether or not Gregory appreciated this truth when he went to Constantinople, he did so after a residence there of about seven years. Officially, his mission—to secure imperial aid against the Lombards—was a complete failure. The emperor Maurice, preoccupied with wars against the Avars and the Persians, could or would do nothing for Italy. That country, Gregory discovered, must work out its own salvation—a conviction that he brought back with him to Rome and ultimately made the cornerstone *Gregory as pope (590-604)*

[2] See above, p. 64.

of the papal policy. For a while, however, he again retired to his monastery, this time as abbot. Then, on the death of the pope in 590, Gregory was raised to the vacant see. His reluctance to assume authority was not the conventional modesty of the bishop elect, for he always regarded the years of his abbacy as the happiest of his life. Yet, if ever a man was fitted by birth, training, and capacity for the office which he acquired, it was Gregory. During the fourteen years of his pontificate the nobility of his ideals, combined with his rare practical wisdom, brought the Petrine supremacy from the realm of theory to that of actuality. With him the papacy may be said to have definitely become a world power.

While Gregory consistently maintained an attitude of deep respect towards the emperor, this did not prevent his following a policy that at times verged on insubordination. By an edict of Justinian the bishops throughout Italy had been associated with imperial officials in the work of local administration. Then, as the Lombard advance cut off Rome from the exarchate, the pope became *de facto* ruler of his capital. Gregory, with or without special authorization, assumed responsibility for the defense of the city. Indeed, he went so far as to negotiate a truce with the Lombard king and to advise the emperor that it should at once be made the basis of a permanent settlement. For such action he was severely reprimanded by Maurice in what Gregory considered an insulting letter. His reply, to say the least, was frank. He virtually accused the emperor of negligence in the handling of Italian affairs, and the government, with characteristic feebleness, took no action against him. Finally, after a more capable exarch had been sent to Ravenna, Gregory's policy was officially adopted. In 599 general peace was signed with the Lombards, recognizing them as the lawful rulers of the lands which they had so long occupied.

Enforcement of the papal supremacy

In his dealings with the prelates of the east Gregory could do little more than reiterate a claim to sole headship for the see of St. Peter. In the west, on the contrary, his superiority was not merely asserted but actually enforced. Throughout Italy the papal authority was generally recognized, both within and without the Lombard territory. In Africa, likewise, Gregory's supervision of all major ecclesiastical affairs was constant and efficient. Nor was there any question of the Petrine supremacy in Gaul. The trouble there was to preserve even a semblance of Christian unity and discipline when the Frankish kings, plunged in murderous feuds, appointed and controlled the local clergy to suit their own selfish interests. It was largely in vain that Gregory preached reform of public and private morals to the Merovingians and their bishops; yet it was not without consequence that the cause of idealism was identified in the minds of the more intelligent Franks with that of papal intervention. And in Spain, meanwhile, Gregory won a great triumph through the conversion to the orthodox faith of

Recared, king of the Visigoths—an event followed by the general submission of his subjects to the papacy.

From these labors of Gregory the Roman Church acquired the international character which it was thenceforth to maintain. Being actually independent of such transitory factors as imperial residence and political favoritism, it could logically assert a universal authority transcending all temporal arrangements. The practical Gregory, however, saw that to preserve this happy status the papacy must have a sound economic basis. Scattered throughout Italy and other provinces lay the estates that constituted the patrimony of St. Peter—chiefly lands donated to the Roman Church by pious benefactors. Under Gregory the administration of this property was brought to a new state of efficiency. Although some of it was leased to tenant farmers, most of it was worked directly by the church through local stewards, nearly always clergymen appointed by the pope. Gregory's correspondence reveals the care with which he looked after each source of income, whether fields, domestic animals, or peasant cultivators. His attention to detail is nothing short of amazing. While engaged in multifarious projects of world-wide interest, he still found time to issue instructions to his agents concerning everything they were supposed to do —from supervising agricultural routine to reporting on the conduct of parish priests. *The patrimony of St. Peter*

These were great accomplishments; but a greater one, as the history of Europe amply proves, was Gregory's extension of papal influence to the British Isles. How Christianity, together with monasticism of the Egyptian type, was carried into Ireland by St. Patrick has been seen in an earlier chapter. The result, as the Irish became more isolated from the continent, was the development of a peculiar ecclesiastical government, in which the clan was the unit and the priests were also monks. The majority of the people, it is to be feared, remained as wild as before; yet many of the new converts adopted Christianity with such zeal that within a hundred years the Irish monasteries had acquired great renown for their religious austerity, pious learning, and missionary activity. From the sixth to the eighth century, in fact, the scholars of Ireland led all western Europe, having a remarkable knowledge of Greek as well as Latin literature, and producing illuminated manuscripts that still rank as artistic masterpieces. Meanwhile Irish missionaries, headed by St. Columba (d. 597), had revived Christianity among the Celtic tribes of Britain and introduced it to many of the Picts and to at least some of the Anglo-Saxon peoples. *The Irish monks and their missions*

From the British Isles the Irish monks were naturally led to Brittany, where they learned that much good work could be done throughout the Merovingian dominions. Thus it came about that the illustrious St. Columban, an Irish disciple of St. Columba, devoted himself to the preaching of Christianity among the more barbarous inhabitants of Gaul. He attracted many followers and for them established several monasteries, of which the most famous was Luxeuil in Burgundy. Having been driven from Gaul by the hostility of the Merovingian rulers, Columban spent a number of years in the country of the Alamans, where a great monastery came to bear the name of his disciple, St. Gall. But eventually he was induced to seek a quiet refuge in Italy. At Bobbio, on the slopes of the Apennines, he founded the last of his monasteries and there died in 615. By that time many religious communities had come to accept his rule, which naturally embodied such features of Irish monasticism as have already been noted—an extremely austere discipline combined with remarkable freedom for the individual monk. These hermit priests, as long as they shared the zeal of fresh converts, maintained a high standard of Christian life. But would so lax an organization be practical under all conditions? And how could it be reconciled with the established government of the western church? Although the Irish monks were to have lasting influence upon the development of European culture, their monastic system inevitably yielded to that of St. Benedict.

Gregory's monastic policy

The victory of the Benedictines was primarily due to the support of Pope Gregory. He had begun his ecclesiastical career as a monk and had spent several years as abbot. Though later called to serve the church in the world, he remained an ardent champion of monasticism and devoted much care to the founding of new religious communities and the reform of old ones. As is proved by his numerous letters on the subject, his monastic ideal was that of St. Benedict. Gregory held that a monk should stay in his monastery unless specially authorized to leave; only under such conditions could he share the work of the secular clergy. And if a priest wished to take the monastic vows, he should surrender his parish and submit to the discipline required of all brothers. The two callings, for the good of both, must be kept distinct. Accordingly, while the pope applauded the Christian zeal of the Irish, he disapproved their form of government. His dispatch of Roman missionaries to Britain was a decisive event not only for the Anglo-Saxons but for the entire western world. Bede, the great English scholar of the eighth century,[3] tells how Gregory, before he became pope, saw some Northumbrian boys in the slave market at Rome and so became fired with the ambition to Christianize their country. Whatever may be thought of that popular legend, there can be no question of Gregory's interest in the conversion of the Anglo-Saxons.

The British mission

The opportunity for papal action arose towards the close of the sixth century when Æthelberht, king of Kent and overlord of various other states, married a Christian princess of the Merovingian house. It was stipulated that she might bring with her a Frankish bishop, but the man whom she chose lacked the talent for missionary endeavor and the pope decided that

[3] See below, p. 131.

the time was ripe for his intervention. In 596, accordingly, he sent to Britain a group of Benedictine monks headed by Augustine, from Gregory's own monastery in Rome. Within the next year they arrived at Canterbury, the old Roman city that now served as Æthelberht's capital. The king was converted and Kent became the first of the Anglo-Saxon states to accept Christianity as its official faith. Thence the Gospel was carried to the neighboring kingdoms, though many years were to pass before all of them accepted it. Meanwhile a tentative organization of the British church had been promulgated by the pope. His original plan was to divide Britain between two metropolitans, one at London and the other at York. London, however, proved inhospitable and so Augustine was installed as archbishop at Canterbury. Gregory's correspondence in this connection remains a monument of political wisdom. Augustine is advised to convert heathen temples into Christian churches rather than to destroy them and, whenever possible, to adapt heathen practices to the celebration of Christian festivals. "For," declares Gregory, "he who would ascend a height must mount, not by leaps, but step by step."

2. THE DARK AGE OF LATIN LEARNING

The term "Dark Age" has been much abused. For reasons that will later be evident, it is by no means applicable to the mediæval period as a whole. Even when it is employed to designate the centuries that immediately followed the barbarian invasions, it must be understood as being restricted to the Latin world and as having a relative significance for that. The darkness there was never absolute, for at no time was the light of culture entirely extinguished. By concentrating attention on forms and traditions it is of course possible to obtain an impression of wonderful continuity from ancient to mediæval times. But this is to gain a false perspective of history. If, rather, we contrast the actual conditions of the seventh century with those of the second, we are obviously confronted with the result of a great catastrophe—the almost total collapse of an ancient civilization. Especially if we take prevalent ignorance as our criterion of darkness, we have to admit that, at least in the west, there was a Dark Age and it was very dark indeed. *Latin letters in the sixth century*

The outstanding Latin writer of the later sixth century was Gregory of Tours. He was born in 538 at Clermont, the chief city of Auvergne. His family was an eminent one, for it had long enjoyed senatorial rank as well as high honor in the church. In preparation for an ecclesiastical career Gregory received the best education then available in Gaul. At the age of twenty-five he was ordained deacon and shortly afterwards went to Tours, where one of his kinsmen was bishop and where he hoped the shrine of St. Martin would provide a cure for his ill health. Finally, in 573, he was himself raised to the bishopric of Tours—an office which he filled with great distinction until his death in 594. As a prominent ecclesiastic and a *Gregory of Tours (538-94)* man of exceptional ability, Gregory could hardly escape playing a considerable part in Merovingian politics. Yet he consistently refused to become the servitor of any king or queen and gave his true devotion to the church alone. It was in this interest, assuredly, that he composed his famous books.

The History of the Franks

At first, Gregory tells us, he was loath to undertake literary endeavors because he realized the inferiority of his Latin. Never having been able to master the subject of grammar, he could be sure neither of genders nor of cases. And as a rhetorician he was at most a "stolid ox." He nevertheless found encouragement in the thought that, even because his writing was crude, it would be understood by all readers; that he could best serve God by not trying to be other than he was. So Gregory chose to lead a useful life rather than to bury himself—as many a cultured gentleman had done—in the dead world of tradition. For the honesty and enthusiasm with which he carried out his project we are all extremely grateful. His most famous work, *The History of the Franks,* begins with the creation of man and ends with the year 591. The first few books, being copied from standard accounts, have little if any value. But those dealing with the early Franks, since we no longer have the authorities that he used, constitute the best of our pertinent sources; and those relating the events of his own lifetime are altogether priceless. It is to them that we are indebted for a vivid picture of social and political degradation under the later Merovingians—an amazing recital of bloodshed and infamy that must be read to be appreciated.

Furthermore, Gregory's account of his own career splendidly illustrates the decay of learning among the aristocracy, the brutality of the life to which its members had become accustomed, and the dominance of their minds by mystic religion. His confession of grammatical ignorance is amply borne out by his writings. A glossary to his work shows that he put almost any case after a preposition; that he often confused masculine, feminine, and neuter endings; and that he paid little attention to the agreement of subject and verb, or of noun and adjective. He was equally naïve in argument. After telling how Clovis gained power by treachery and assassination, *The History of the Franks* attributes his success to the fact that he walked before the Lord "with an upright heart and did what was pleasing in His sight." For Gregory, obviously, the acceptance of the orthodox faith served to excuse a good deal of irregularity in other respects. And he was inclined to see in any event, whether great or trivial, the direct intervention of God or Satan. With regard to the efficacy of holy relics his faith was boundless. Scorning the medicine of physicians, he relied on the miraculous power of St. Martin to cure every ailment. A drink mixed with dust from the local shrine he found a sovereign remedy for pain in the stomach. Licking the rail in front of the tomb healed a sore tongue. His throat, being rubbed with the cloth that hung there, was relieved of a troublesome fishbone. An object placed within that sacred environment acquired the virtue of allaying fevers, driving out devils, and performing other marvels. But in these matters, of course, Gregory merely shared the common convictions of his age.

Before Gregory of Tours died, the see of Rome had already come into the possession of the remarkable pope Gregory. The latter, in addition to being the greatest statesman of his time, was one of the world's most influential writers—beyond all doubt the most popular of the illustrious Four Doctors.[4] Although a distinctly learned man, Gregory cared nothing for mere erudition; it were better, he said, for the foolishly wise to learn the "wise foolishness of God." And he roundly denounced those who devoted themselves to the perfection of a rhetorical style. He was proud of the fact that his own books were written simply; for they, like his acts, were inspired by practical considerations. He composed them for the average reader of his day, and—as it happened—of centuries to come. Throughout the Dark Age all students might admire the genius of St. Augustine, but few of them could really grasp his meaning. Everybody who could understand Latin could understand Gregory.

One of the pope's most widely read books was that entitled *Pastoral Care* —a manual on the character and duties of the bishop, which he wrote shortly after being elected pope. The episcopacy, says Gregory, entails grave responsibility. The bishop must be a trained man, but with his learning he must possess true spirituality, despising all pleasures of the flesh and all goods of this world. Especially to be shunned is the man who seeks ecclesiastical preferment through sheer ambition, or the man whose apparent wisdom is the cloak of pride and vice. The bishop is the pastor of the flock, who must teach by example as well as by words; the physician of souls, who must himself enjoy the health he would impart to others. To be a successful leader, he above all should have a deep understanding of human nature, so that he may be able to distinguish one kind of people from another and to vary his instructions accordingly. Gregory then enumerates no less than thirty-six distinctions of that sort and devotes a chapter to suitable admonitions for each pair of opposites: such as men and women, masters and servants, the rich and the poor, the joyful and the sad, the learned and the ignorant, the sick and the well, the impudent and the bashful, the gluttonous and the abstinent. This is the meat of the book—practical advice from a practical man who was himself a very great bishop.

In preaching, as in the other episcopal duties, Gregory provided a model for all later generations. His sermons, published as *Homilies*, were enormously popular, being simple discourses on texts of Scripture to explain the truths of Christianity. Devoid of all florid rhetoric, they presented plain lessons for the benefit of plain people. In them Gregory admirably dis-

Marginal notes: Writings of Gregory the Great — Pastoral Care — Homilies and Dialogues

[4] See above, p. 72.

played his talent for direct and forceful statement, which—despite the pseudo-classic tradition—was and is the best form of eloquence. And to drive home a moral his favorite device was the pious anecdote, the story of saint or sinner drawn from the homely experience of his listeners. The same plan was further developed by Gregory in his famous *Dialogues*. As the name implies, the author expounds his subject by means of conversation with a friend—one Peter, who combines extraordinary curiosity with a rather slow wit, and so is made to represent the audience for whom the volume is compiled. By means of this slender continuity Gregory relates a series of tales about holy men and women, thus illustrating man's constant exposure to the wiles of Satan and the absolute need of reliance on God.

The entire second book of the *Dialogues* is devoted to St. Benedict of Nursia and constitutes, as noted above, the earliest biography of that illustrious monk. But to the student of history the great interest of the compilation as a whole arises from the fact that it so clearly reflects the religious beliefs of the age. Everybody then expected and constantly discovered miraculous events in everyday life. Gregory, being inclined to explain almost any occurrence as the result of divine or satanic influence, relates a profusion of marvels. He tells of streams that changed their beds at saintly command; of birds, beasts, and serpents that fulfilled commissions given them by holy men; of demons who appeared on all sorts of occasions and in all sorts of guises; of apparitions, prophecies, ecstatic visions, and raisings from the dead, as well as supernatural cures, inventions, and deeds of all kinds. The catalogue of diabolic pranks and priestly remedies is full and varied—well deserving the attention of anyone interested in the history of ideas.

Moralia   Much Christian doctrine, obviously, is woven into the *Dialogues*; but Gregory's principal work in the realm of theology is that called the *Moralia*, a commentary on the book of Job. Although his method of exposition was by no means new, its possibilities were now more clearly shown than ever before. In the *Moralia*, for example, we find logically developed the allegorical system of interpretation that was to characterize biblical study throughout the Middle Ages. To Gregory the entire Old Testament contained a hidden prophecy of the New Testament. The books of the Hebrews, to be sure, were valuable for their literal message; yet they were infinitely more valuable for the mystic revelation that underlay the superficial meaning of the words. To understand the former was a comparatively simple task; to understand the latter was the test of true wisdom. And this wisdom, it should be noted, was not something the individual could secure through his unaided faculties; without the sacred tradition of the church he could never hope to discover the truth.

This principle, of course, was the basis of Gregory's Christianity. However violent the controversy that may yet rage over the precise origin of various mediæval doctrines and usages, everyone must admit that, at least in large part, they go back to Gregory the Great, and that he did no more than restate the established beliefs of his day. Most of his theology he took from the massive works of St. Augustine; other ideas, which his own writings emphasized for the first time, he evidently got from oral tradition— a procedure which must seem eminently logical and right to one who accepts that tradition as itself inspired. Gregory's works thus contain definite statements regarding the powers of angels and demons, the efficacy of prayer to the saints, the sacrificial nature of the eucharist, and the purification in purgatory of those who fail to perform adequate penance in this life. Such definition of popular faith serves to illustrate an important phase of Gregory's mentality. Whether or not we believe what he believed, we must recognize the commanding genius of a man who could be great, not only as a monk and a bishop, but also as a statesman, an administrator, and a writer.

The magnificent success of Pope Gregory as an author was due to his talent for explaining large subjects in simple language; men used his popularizations of theology, as far as possible, in preference to older and more difficult books. The same tendency was clearly marked in all fields; for a long time, in fact, the decline of scholarship had stimulated the production of manuals and epitomes, which in turn were likely to be combined into still briefer texts. Thus the body of actual knowledge among the learned suffered a continuous loss of substance and men were confirmed in the pernicious habit of accepting statements merely because they had been often repeated. Among the post-classical writers whose works were constantly cited as authoritative were, in addition to the fathers of the church, Donatus, Priscian, Capella, Boëthius, and Orosius. Of these men four have already received a brief notice,[5] the fifth, a mediocre pupil of St. Augustine, enjoyed the distinction of having composed the most popular book on ancient history during the early Middle Ages. As a supplement to his master's *Civitas Dei*, Orosius developed the thesis that the distress of the later Roman world really marked an improvement in human affairs. To prove that ancient times had not been happy, he picked all the worst calamities from the classics and combined them in one horrific narrative. The result was not accurate history, but it was easy reading and it had an edifying moral —hence its great vogue in the schools. *(margin: Other writers)*

With the Vandal invasion Roman Africa lost its intellectual pre-eminence, and Justinian's reconquest brought it no revival of Latin scholarship. In Spain, on the other hand, the church preserved a relatively superior culture, the chief exponent of which was Isidore, bishop of Seville from about 600 to 636. As if to celebrate Pope Gregory's conversion of the Visigoths, Isidore produced a series of books that made his name synonymous with *(margin: Isidore of Seville)*

[5] Above, p. 71.

contemporary learning. He was a prolific writer, dealing after a fashion with theology, history, literature, and the sciences. Finally, towards the close of his life, he composed a summary of his teachings and published it under the title of *Etymologies*. The book had an immense success, for it served as a manual of universal knowledge throughout the next five centuries. From Isidore's *Etymologies*, accordingly, we may gain a more complete picture of what constituted wisdom in the Dark Age than from any other one volume. The key to the compilation is provided by its title. Isidore believed that the essence of a thing was contained in its name: by discovering the derivation and significance of the latter, one could better remember and understand the former. So his compendium is resolved into a series of definitions, based often enough on fanciful etymology. The following examples will at least serve to illustrate his approach to a variety of subjects.[6]

Night (*nox*) is so called from injuring (*a nocendo*), because it injures (*noceat*) the eyes. It has the light of the moon and the stars so that it may not be unadorned and that it may console all who work by night; also that the light may be adequately tempered for those creatures that cannot stand sunshine. . . .

Man (*homo*) is so called because he was made of earth (*ex humo*), as is told in Genesis. . . . The liver (*iecur*) has its name because there is resident the fire (*ignis*) which flies up into the brain. Thence it is spread to the eyes and the other senses and members and by its heat it changes into blood the liquid that it has drawn from food, and this blood it supplies to the several members to feed and nourish them. . . . The spleen (*splen*) is so called from corresponding to (*a supplemento*) the liver on the opposite side, so there may be no vacuum. And certain men say that it was also made on account of laughter. For by the spleen we laugh, by the bile we become angry, by the heart we gain wisdom, and by the liver we love. . . .

The ant (*formica*) is so called because it carries morsels (*ferat micas*) of grain. For it looks forward to the future and in summer makes ready food to be eaten in the winter. At the harvest, too, it picks out wheat and refuses to touch barley. After a rain it always puts out the grain to dry. It is said that in Ethiopia there are ants shaped like dogs, which dig up golden sand with their feet and watch it to see that no one carries it off; and those that do take it the ants pursue and kill.

The author's information, to be sure, was sometimes a little better than is displayed in these passages; but that was because he sometimes copied from more reliable sources. In no case can we attribute much critical insight to Isidore himself, for he merely compiled a scrapbook from earlier writings. Often he adopted statements that were flatly contradictory, and occasionally he seems to have quite misunderstood what he repeated. Even the plan of the book was in large part borrowed from Cassiodorus, Theodoric's famous secretary, who had spent the last years of his life in a monastery and had there written a sketch of ecclesiastical education. Following Cassiodorus, Isidore first described the seven liberal arts (grammar,

---

[6] *Etymologies*, v, 21; xi, 1; xii, 3.

rhetoric, dialectic, arithmetic, geometry, astronomy, and music) and then passed on to a review of medicine, law, theology, the natural sciences, and other great subjects—all covered in the same desultory fashion. The contrast between the book's pretensions and its actual substance is ridiculous; yet the author, we should remember, was doing what he could to enlighten a desperately ignorant world.

For a better standard of intellectual achievement we must turn from the **Bede** continent to the British Isles, where by the eighth century the learning of the Irish monks, as well as their missionary zeal, was being taken over by the Anglo-Saxons.[7] The foremost scholar of the age was Bede, a Northumbrian who spent the greater part of his life in the monastery of Jarrow, dying there in 735. It was presumably through the tradition of the Irish schools that Bede had so remarkable a knowledge of Greek and Latin letters, but with it he combined a devotion to the papal ideals that was characteristic of the Anglo-Saxon monks. His erudition was wholly subordinated to the practical ends of Christian education. Even an unconscious delight in literature as an æsthetic study is never revealed in his many writings, which were in the main commentaries on Scripture, useful compilations, and textbooks. His essay on chronology deserves special mention because it was largely responsible for our system of dating in the years of the Christian era.

Bede's most famous work, however, has always been his *Ecclesiastical History of the English*. It is by far the best history written in western Europe between the seventh and twelfth centuries, not merely because of the author's excellent Latin but because of his superior intelligence and thorough honesty. Most remarkably, Bede nearly always cites the sources of his information: documents preserved in local archives, written accounts drawn up for his especial use, or traditions learned by interviewing venerable persons. He often quotes letters and charters in full; when the tale is only a matter of hearsay, he frankly says so. We should not, of course, expect Bede to be skeptical concerning the universal beliefs of his time. His books are filled with reports of miracles, many of them given on his own authority. He avows that a snake will die as soon as it is brought into the air of Ireland; that a tincture made of scrapings from Irish manuscripts is a known antidote for snake-bite. He tells how the sudden recovery of a sick horse after eating grass in a certain place proved that it was where a Northumbrian king had been martyred; and how a great hole was dug as people removed the dirt for the sake of its curative properties. And there is much else of the same sort. Yet, if all the writers of that age had been as scrupulous as Bede, how much better our knowledge of it would be!

[7] For further details about the spread of Christianity among the Anglo-Saxons, see the following section.

3. The Revival of the Frankish Monarchy

The rise of the Caro-lingians

The death of Dagobert in 639 seemed to extinguish the last spark of Merovingian worth. His descendants ceased to play any part in the world of affairs; they became *rois fainéants*—kings in name only, who spent their lives in seclusion and were hardly seen by their subjects except when, like long-haired dolls, they were drawn in their regal ox-carts from one estate to another. Accordingly, while the members of the one family still bore the crown, all real authority in any of their kingdoms was exercised by the chief of the royal household (*maior domus*), inaccurately known to historians as the mayor of the palace. In Austrasia, for example, it was a certain great landlord named Pepin who, by gaining control of the king's finances, became the head of his government and the commander of his army. And Pepin's successors were able to make the all-important office hereditary in their house—that which, after its most distinguished representative, was to be styled Carolingian.

In 687 Pepin II, grandson of Pepin I, crushed the Neustrian mayor in battle and made himself supreme in both regions. This proved to be the beginning of a new era in Frankish history, for it brought under one strong ruler the two main fragments of the old Merovingian dominion, and Pepin's unification became permanent through the remarkable achievements of his son Charles. The latter, by a series of vigorous campaigns into Burgundy, Aquitaine, and the Germanic lands to the east, enforced his authority on all sides and so re-established the Frankish kingdom as it had been under the sons of Clovis. But while he was thus engaged, a more formidable enemy appeared to the south—the Moorish conquerors of Spain, who from their base in Septimania now extended their raids into central Gaul. Taking the field in 732 with an army composed in part of heavy-armed cavalry,[8] Charles met and defeated the invaders in a great battle between Poitiers and Tours. His victory, since it coincided with the weakening of the caliphate at Damascus, gave a decisive check to the Moslem advance. And Charles thereby obtained not only his surname of Martel (the Hammer) but also the acclaim of the western world as the champion of Christendom. It was to him, consequently, that the pope naturally turned for much-needed aid.

The disturbing factor in the Italian situation was the rejuvenation of the Lombard monarchy by an energetic king named Liutprand. Having subdued the duchies of Spoleto and Benevento, he now proceeded, on the north, to attack the exarchate of Ravenna and, on the south, to threaten the city of Rome. No effective support could at any time be expected from the Byzantine emperor, and at this particular moment he was embroiled in a violent controversy with the western church over the iconoclastic pro-

[8] See below, p. 140.

gram.[9] To the pope it must have seemed utterly absurd that he, the actual ruler of the Roman duchy, should be the subject of a distant and incompetent prince with whom he had forbidden all good Christians to have any dealings. The Frankish mayor, on the other hand, had proved himself a heroic and loyal son of the church—a true king lacking only the regal crown. The logic of events demanded that the two outstanding powers of the west should ally for their great mutual advantage. Charles Martel, as it happened, was unwilling to embark on an Italian adventure and, as the Lombard state relapsed into temporary inactivity, matters continued to drift until the office of mayor had been inherited by Pepin III, son of Charles.

The crisis came in 751, when another ambitious king of the Lombards, Aistulf, actually took the city of Ravenna. Almost at once an embassy from Pepin asked the pope a momentous question with regard to the Merovingian kingship, and returned with the answer that the man who had the actual power better deserved the crown than the one who had not. Accordingly, a great assembly of the Franks elected and solemnly proclaimed Pepin as their king. The last of the Merovingian puppets was sent to a monastery, and the house of Clovis ended in oblivion. Three years later, when Aistulf threatened to conquer the duchy of Rome, Pope Stephen II crossed the Alps into Gaul and, adopting the ritual of the ancient Hebrews, anointed Pepin king of the Franks and *patricius* of the Romans. The latter title, vague as it was, seemed to imply that the Frankish king was to hold lawful authority at Rome, was in some measure to be the successor of such imperial representatives as Odoacer and Theodoric. But if the office was more than an empty honor, what right had the pope to award it? Although the language displayed a certain respect for tradition, the act was as revolutionary as Pepin's assumption of the crown.

Whatever the theory in the minds of contemporaries, the sequel proved that the papal recognition was no mere gesture. Pepin twice invaded Italy and twice defeated Aistulf. Having finally taken the exarchate away from him, Pepin formally bestowed it on the pope. By this famous donation he created the Papal States of history—an irregular territory extending across the peninsula from Rome on the west to Ravenna on the east. Otherwise he made no change in the map of Italy. Aistulf retained his Lombard kingdom which, on his death, was secured by Desiderius, duke of Tuscany. Pepin was thus able to devote the remainder of his life to projects nearer home. Following up a campaign that he had earlier launched, he took Septimania from the Moors and so established his frontier along the Pyrenees. About the same time, furthermore, he succeeded in bringing the Frisians under his dominion. And since the latter advance was made possible by the

Pepin, king of the Franks (751-68)

---

[9] See below, pp. 159-60.

collaboration of famous missionaries from Britain, it might be well to review the progress of Christianity in that island.

The Council of Whitby (664)

The final victory of the Roman Church among the Anglo-Saxons did not come until sixty years after the death of Gregory the Great. His missionaries, on extending their activities beyond the frontiers of Kent, encountered not only the hostility of heathen rulers but also the rivalry of the Irish monks. Eventually, however, the Northumbrian king Oswy forced the acceptance of his overlordship, and with it of Christianity, throughout the Midlands. Then, in 664, he summoned a council at Whitby to decide between the claims of the Romans and the Irish. The latter were distinguished by many peculiarities. Instead of using the round tonsure that was now customary, the Celtic monks shaved the front of the head from ear to ear; and they fixed the date of Easter by a computation that had elsewhere been abandoned. These practices, of course, were mere symbols of independence. The major issue was whether the church in Britain should or should not be organized under papal discipline. After considerable argument, the council voted in favor of Rome. The Irish thereupon withdrew from the Anglo-Saxon country, which soon came to be divided into dioceses and placed under the control of two archbishops, one at Canterbury and one at York.

St. Boniface (680-754)

The decision at Whitby also had important consequences on the other side of the Channel. As the Irish influence in the British Isles continued to yield to the Roman, it became impossible for Columban's foundations on the continent to maintain a separate custom. By the end of the seventh century the Benedictine system had definitely gained supremacy in the Latin world, and Anglo-Saxon monks, devoting themselves to the papal service, had superseded the Irish as leaders of missionary enterprise among the Germans of central Europe. About 690 Willibrord, a Northumbrian educated in Ireland, undertook the task of converting the Frisians who inhabited the estuary of the Rhine. He was so successful that some five years later he was consecrated bishop of Utrecht under the name of Clemens. Then, shortly before his death, he was joined by one Winfrid, a West Saxon monk. But Winfrid's stay in Frisia was brief. Having—under the name of Boniface—secured direct authorization from the pope, he transferred his activities to the Austrasian border, where he soon reported thousands of converts among the Thuringians and other Germanic peoples.

Hitherto all effort towards Christianizing these districts had been sporadic. Irish monks and other volunteers had founded monasteries and local churches without the slightest supervision on the part of any central authority, for the chaotic conditions that prevailed throughout the Merovingian dominions had prevented decisive action by the monarchy. Now, with the effective backing of the Carolingian house as well as of the papacy, Boniface was able to create a unified ecclesiastical system for this entire East Frankish territory. Older monasteries were reformed and new ones established on all sides—chief among them the illustrious Fulda. Bavaria and Thuringia, together with the adjacent country, were divided into bishoprics under the jurisdiction of an archbishop at Mainz, eventually Boniface himself. Yet, as an old man of seventy-four, Boniface still longed for a fresh world to conquer. Resigning his see, he resumed his missionary career among the Frisians and was there slain by heathen pirates in 754. As Augustine had begun a new epoch for Britain, so Boniface, a product of the earlier mission, began a new epoch for Germany. A century and a half of religious history serves as a commentary on the statesmanship of Pope Gregory the Great.

CHAPTER VIII

The Carolingian Empire

1. CHARLEMAGNE AND HIS GOVERNMENT

Italian and German conquests Pepin, third mayor and first king of the name, died in 768, leaving his dominions to be shared by two sons. But with the early death of one the entire inheritance fell to the other, whom the world knows as Charles the Great or Charlemagne. The new king, as soon as he had secured undisputed possession of the throne, proved his military genius by the energy and effectiveness with which he advanced the great projects of his father and grandfather. The first of these projects was the subjection of the Lombards, whose king, Desiderius, the pope accused of seeking to undo Pepin's settlement. In one campaign Charlemagne ended that danger. Occupying northern Italy, he deposed Desiderius and himself assumed the crown of the Lombards (774). Then, without attempting the reduction of the southern Italian provinces, he turned his attention to the conquest and Christianization of the Saxons, the fierce Germanic people who inhabited the country north of Thuringia and east of the Rhine. The task was a difficult one, completed only after a general uprising had been cruelly suppressed. Thereafter, in spite of sporadic insurrection, Saxony constituted an integral part of the Frankish kingdom.

To supplement his conquest of northern Germany, Charlemagne next led an army down the Danube and ousted the Bavarian duke, who had been conducting himself very much as an independent prince. And from the position thus gained Charlemagne proceeded to deal with the Avars. Two hundred years earlier they had built up a considerable empire that extended far into the Balkans. Now, however, their power was so far decayed that the victorious Franks were able to take even the great Rings, the central camps where the Avars had piled the accumulated booty of a thousand raids. Towards the close of the eighth century, therefore, Charlemagne could draw his eastern boundary from the Baltic to the head of the Adriatic. All along the frontier lay a series of territories with a special military organization. These marches, or marks, included, to the south of the Danube, Croatia and Pannonia; to the north of it, Moravia and Bohemia, mainly inhabited by the Czechs; and, to the east of the Saale and Elbe, the lands of various other Slavic peoples. Against the Danes, similarly, a march was created in the region that was later to become known as Holstein (see Map VIII).

At the beginning of his reign Charlemagne seems to have been convinced that he might easily conquer Spain. On the fall of the Ommiad caliphate at Damascus Abd-al-Rahman, last survivor of the ill-fated dynasty, made good his escape to Cordova. There, from 756 on, he ruled as emir, successfully defying the authority of the Abbasid caliph, who therefore urged the Frankish king to dethrone the usurper. But an expedition of Charlemagne in 778 utterly failed, and on the return journey his army was ambushed by the Christian Basques in the pass of Roncevaux—an incident that was to inspire a glorious epic of the feudal age. To Charlemagne it probably served merely as a warning not to pursue fantastic projects beyond the Pyrenees. Thenceforth he adopted a defensive policy towards the Moors and sought to acquire only enough territory for the organization of a frontier district. The result, after the capture of Barcelona, was the establishment of the Spanish March, which remained an outpost of northern influence for many centuries to come. The Spanish March

Meanwhile a matter of surpassing interest had diverted men's thoughts from such paltry events as the taking of a Spanish fortress. This was nothing less than the revival of the imperial office in the west, to explain which entails a brief review of the preliminaries. To his father's titles, king of the Franks and *patricius* of the Romans, Charlemagne had added a third by acquiring the crown of the Lombards. But the Lombard kingdom included neither Rome nor Ravenna; when Charlemagne acted as sovereign in those regions, it was presumably by virtue of his Roman patriciate. Whatever the theory may have been, he exercised a very real authority over the Papal States; so, when serious trouble broke out in Rome, he was called upon to settle it. In 800 Pope Leo III was driven from the city by a violent insurrection. Taking refuge with Charlemagne, he appealed for reinstatement, while the opposing faction, to justify its revolt, filed a series of grave charges against the fugitive. Charlemagne accordingly proceeded to Rome and there held a great council of clergy and laity, which eventually decided that the pope should clear himself by swearing his innocence on the Gospels. This he did on December 23 and was forthwith recognized as the lawful holder of the papal insignia. The imperial coronation (800)

Two days later Leo presided over the Christmas festival in St. Peter's church. After saying mass, and while Charlemagne was praying at the altar, the pope placed a diadem on his head and the assembled throng shouted: "To Charles Augustus, crowned of God, great and pacific emperor of the Romans, life and victory!" Are we to believe, as we are told by the official annalists, that the ceremony took Charlemagne entirely by surprise and that he was actually displeased at the high honor so unexpectedly thrust upon him? The statement is incredible. The stage was too carefully set for the affair to have been other than premeditated. The tradition of an indestructible Roman Empire still charmed the minds of men, including that of Charlemagne himself. The west had had no resident emperor since 476; now, as the reward of the Frankish might, one was again installed. The assumption of the imperial title was the logical climax of Charlemagne's whole career. He must have willed it.

Byzantine recognition   In strict theory, of course, Leo had no more right to bestow the crown than Charlemagne to assume it; but a pope had earlier given a Frankish king the title of *patricius* and it was now superseded by the title of emperor. The revolution had been so gradually brought about that the final step was natural enough. Although the Byzantine court might register a protest, it would hardly trouble anyone in the Latin world, for at that moment the holder of the purple in the east was the notorious Irene.[1] Besides, the acquiescence of Constantinople might ultimately be purchased. To that end Charlemagne devoted earnest efforts, and just before his death he was assured that, in return for the cession of Dalmatia and Venetia, his newly acquired rank would be recognized by the Byzantine emperor. Yet, after the formalities had been concluded, Charlemagne was still essentially the warrior Frank—speaking his native German, wearing the barbarian costume, and delighting in the traditional sports of his people. And when we more closely examine his state, we find it as slightly Roman as his personal character.

The royal authority   Indeed, so far as government was concerned, the Carolingian Empire was merely an enlarged Frankish kingdom, for Charlemagne ruled Lombardy in much the same fashion as his other dominions. Like his Merovingian predecessors, he had three principal functions: to command the army, to administer justice, and to protect the church. He was not supposed to be absolute. He neither claimed nor exercised arbitrary control over the ancient laws of his people. His nearest approach to imperial legislation in the Roman sense was the establishment of judicial reforms and other extraordinary measures with the counsel and consent of his great men. In such cases, however, we generally hear of Charlemagne's decisions, not from formal edicts, but from capitularies, sets of instructions to the royal officials. Occasionally a capitulary would be restricted to a single subject— the administration of the royal estates, the improvement of education, the organization of the Saxon territory, or the like. More often it would embody

[1] See below, p. 160.

a haphazard group of enactments dealing indiscriminately with church and state, and with both the public and the private affairs of the emperor.

Immediately under Charlemagne was the royal household, an institution derived, through adaptation by the Merovingians, from the court of Diocletian. Charlemagne's household included the chamberlain, who acted as governor of the palace and of the royal treasure; the seneschal, who managed the king's food and in some degree supervised the estates that produced it; the butler, who had charge of the royal cellar and vineyards; and the marshal or constable, who through control of the stable had obtained high command in the army. Another important officer of the household was the chaplain, the superior of the priests who administered the sacraments to the king and his family, and of the clerks who wrote his letters and drew up his legal documents. It was not till considerably later that the writing-office (*scriptorium*) acquired a separate head called the chancellor.

Officers of the household

As in Merovingian times, the all-important agents of the central government throughout the provinces were the counts, appointed by the king to act during his pleasure. Each normally combined judicial, military, financial, and other executive functions within a small district, frequently an old Roman *civitas*. But along the frontiers wider regions were assigned to counts of the border, styled marquises (German *markgraf*, margrave) or dukes, each of whom was apt to have authority over a number of ordinary counts. All such officials, in the absence of a trained civil service, were merely Frankish noblemen, who in addition to grants of land customarily received a share of the revenues they collected. To keep an effective check upon the counts was therefore the king's great difficulty. Charlemagne met it principally through personal activity, for he was continually moving about at the head of his troops. With the same end in view, he also revived a practice which had formed part of the Roman system, but which had lapsed under the Merovingians. According to a famous capitulary of 802, distinguished laymen and ecclesiastics were to be sent out (*missi*) as inspectors. They were to superintend the entire government of both church and state, listening to all complaints, investigating the facts through sworn witnesses, and reporting back to the emperor. They were, indeed, to see that everybody, in or out of office, did what he ought to do—a noble ideal which, it is to be feared, even the best of *missi* could not wholly live up to.

Counts and *missi*

As noted in a previous chapter,[2] justice had long since tended to become a matter of local usage. All that Charlemagne could do was to introduce, by means of capitularies, a number of minor improvements in the established procedure. In the Carolingian courts, as earlier, judicial routine was attended to by a select group of doomsmen called *scabini* (French *échevins*). It was these judgment-finders who had to determine what law

Law and justice

[2] Above, pp. 56-57.

should be enforced in a particular case. Throughout most of the Italian kingdom, for example, official recognition was given to the enactments of the Lombard kings—rather detailed codes that provide valuable information concerning the primitive customs of the Germanic invaders. Similar compilations for the Bavarians, Alamans, Saxons, Frisians, and others were promulgated by the Carolingian government; but even under Charlemagne the older Frankish lands continued to enjoy their time-honored systems with only slight amendment. Accordingly, a man's residence in Aquitaine, Burgundy, or Neustria would normally subject him to the law of the Visigoths, the Burgundians, or the Salian Franks. His actual descent had ceased to have any significance whatsoever.

Military service

In connection with military obligations, too, the earlier distinction between Romans and non-Romans had completely disappeared. The royal government had come to regard all able-bodied men as Franks, who could be called for service whenever it might be needed. But by the time of Charlemagne far-reaching modifications of the primitive system were being rapidly introduced. Each person, in proportion to his means, was required to possess certain weapons and defensive armor. And since the obligation of serving at one's own cost for a period of three months was burdensome, the emperor restricted it to men owning particular amounts of land— amounts that varied according to the distance from the scene of war. For this purpose, therefore, estates came to be assessed in a rude unit known as the manse or hide—the land presumed requisite for the support of a single family. Great landlords were made responsible for one soldier from every so many hides (manses). Small men were grouped together so that their joint contributions would suport one of them on the campaign.

For the procuring of mounted troops similar arrangements were even more essential. The emperor might, of course, require certain properties to furnish horses instead of men; but to obtain a force of expert cavalry something better was demanded than casual levies made through the counts. This truth had long been appreciated. Charles Martel and Pepin, needing a stronger army and lacking funds for hiring cavalry, solved the difficulty, we are told, at the expense of the church. To their most reliable followers they gave ecclesiastical lands as life estates, or benefices, and in return specified service with horses and arms. Presumably such military benefices had already been created out of property belonging to the king; at any rate it became increasingly common, in the second half of the eighth century, for all great men thus to provide contingents of trained horsemen. Charlemagne deliberately encouraged the practice, providing that in time of war armed retainers might follow the standard of the lord whom they served. This development of feudal tenure, as will be more thoroughly explained below, had prime significance for the future of Europe.

In financial organization, likewise, the monarchy remained funda- **Taxation**
mentally as it had been in the earlier age. The two great political concerns
of the royal administration, justice and military defense, were largely taken
care of through gratuitous service on the part of the individual subject. In
the same way the maintenance of public works, the housing and provision-
ing of royal agents, and the transportation of men and materials were secured
by direct requisition. An endless plague of such exactions had, in fact,
continued to afflict the countryside since the days of the Roman Empire.
Nor was there any interruption in the levy of indirect taxes, now called
thelonea, tolls. On the other hand, the ancient system of taxes on land and
persons had so far decayed that only indistinct vestiges of them henceforth
appear in the records. Charlemagne invented no new imposts to take their
places. Tribute might be paid by various subject peoples, but the nearest
approach to a general tax throughout the empire was the practice of taking
contributions, styled gifts (*dona*), from the great men when they attended
the formal assemblies. That they in turn recouped themselves by requiring
similar offerings from their followers is extremely probable. Finance, like
military service, was tending to become a matter of seignorial arrangement
—that is to say, a matter brought under the control of the lordly class in
society.

The bulk of Charlemagne's income, plainly, was got from his own estates, **The royal**
for he was the greatest landowner in the kingdom. This side of the **estates**
emperor's activity is known to us in intimate detail from his famous
capitulary concerning his villas, which contains minute instructions as to
how they should be managed. Each villa was placed under a steward
called *maior* or *villicus*, responsible to a superior official who acted as
superintendent for a considerable number of such properties. The steward
saw to the cultivation of the estate and had the produce carried to central
barns, where the superintendent kept it for the disposal of the emperor.
Each steward, according to the capitulary, was to make out an annual
statement, describing the sources of income under his care and listing everything that was produced: grain, hay, fruits, nuts, vegetables, wine, beer,
vinegar, oil, flax, hemp, honey, wool, hides, horns, tallow, meat, lumber,
firewood, domestic animals and fowls, eggs, dairy products, game, fish,
and all manufactures. He was to keep account of all the tenants and their
respective obligations; to see that there were skilled artisans for the production of all necessary articles; to make an inventory of all buildings,
tools, and furnishings; and to attend to a dozen other matters as well. And
from extant reports made by the emperor's agents we may see that his
regulations in this connection were actually enforced.

Charlemagne, regarding himself as the anointed of God and the successor **Ecclesi-**
of Theodosius, constantly asserted a general power of supervision over **astical**
the church. He very plainly held that Rome was under his supreme **affairs**

jurisdiction, and that the pope should exercise no more than the autonomy befitting so distinguished a prelate. The pope, on his side, seemed to acquiesce in the imperial leadership, having good reason for personal gratitude and apprehending no threat of an immediate dictatorship. So Charlemagne's capitularies regularly included measures affecting both clergy and laity. Even when problems of a purely ecclesiastical nature arose, it was through his initiative and under his presidency that action was taken by the bishops in council. They, in fact, were quite submissive to his desires, for episcopal elections were under his control. And by nominating candidates to be chosen by the monastic chapters he virtually appointed abbots also. Both groups of prelates, it should be noted, had come to hold extensive temporal power by grant of the emperor or his predecessors. Even under the Merovingians great ecclesiastics had often received charters of immunity, by virtue of which each beneficiary was assured that within a specified territory he should be immune from the authority of the count and should there exercise the regalian rights himself. Originally, perhaps, he was obliged to make an equivalent return to the king; but eventually the effect of an immunity was to give the immunist the profits of justice, tolls, military service, and other dues that normally would have accrued to the state. By the ninth century all important prelates had thus become actual princes, sharing the king's sovereign rights and equaling the counts in official dignity.

2. SOCIETY AND CULTURE

The decay of commerce   Turning now to the question of social organization in the Carolingian Empire, we encounter a number of highly controversial problems. The view here maintained is that western Europe suffered a progressive decline from the third century onward. This decline was not primarily the result of the barbarian invasions, but was undoubtedly stimulated by them. In both Gaul and Italy conditions were much worse in the sixth and seventh centuries than they had been in the fifth. Meanwhile the widening separation between east and west had removed from the latter the major part of its shipping industry and sea trade. And by the eighth century the encroaching power of the Arabs had definitely broken most of the ancient routes across the Mediterranean. With Africa, Spain, and Septimania in the hands of the Moslems, and with Italy torn by chronic warfare, the lands to the northwest of the Alps were further isolated. Charlemagne's state was entirely a construction of the mainland; for he left Dalmatia, Venetia, and southern Italy to Byzantine control and had little success against the Moors of Spain. However brilliant the Carolingian Empire may have superficially appeared, it brought no economic improvement of any significance.

Commercial decay was thus unchecked, with the consequence that society became more and more thoroughly agrarian. By the ninth century the overwhelming mass of the population lived through agriculture and so fell into two main classes: the few, who constituted the aristocracy of land-lords, and the many, who constituted the servile or semi-free peasantry. Such a society had no conspicuous place for a town-dwelling class of traders. Small industry, of course, continued, for people had to have manu-factured articles; but production was localized on the great estate. As described in Charlemagne's capitularies, artisans were attached to the villa and subordinated to its agrarian routine. Ordinary trade shrank to petty dealings in a neighborhood market, which, being held on a single day in the week, attracted no resident population of professional merchants. It is significant also that the money coined under the Carolingians was at most silver pennies; and since the privilege was widely distributed, each little region came to have its own currency—a situation that bespeaks small transactions on the part of people who were chronically poor. From the east, it is true, bands of wandering merchants, generally called Syrians, still penetrated into the remote provinces of the west. All the evidence, however, tends to show that they were relatively few in number and that on their infrequent visits they brought articles of luxury that could be afforded only by the very wealthy. Commerce of this kind is of practically no importance in building up the economic resources of any country.

As will be shown in the next chapter, Moslem Africa and Spain remained in close touch with Egypt and Syria, and so developed a brilliant culture that was wholly foreign to the lands across the Pyrenees. Some of the Italian ports, too, never lost contact with the great metropolis of Con-stantinople; and while the Franks fought for control of the interior, the city of Venice, under Byzantine protection, arose on the lagoons of the upper Adriatic. The Carolingian Empire witnessed no such development. Although Gaul was dotted with places which were called *civitates* and which still bore their Latin names, that fact by no means proves the per-sistence of a truly urban civilization. Many of the cities in the western Roman Empire had never been more than centers of administration and defense, and in the succeeding period that character became the rule. From archæological investigation it is clear that even a great metropolis like Cologne or London had lost all but a few of its inhabitants long before the time of Charlemagne. Counts and bishops, to be sure, often used Roman cities for their capitals, but the persons whom they attracted were principally soldiers, clerks, and serving-men, supported like their masters by the labor of peasants on adjoining estates. Economically, these cities were not centers of production. Socially, they had no peculiarity to mark them off from the countryside. Politically, they lacked every vestige of true municipal organization.

The Caro-lingian Cities

Growth
of the
manorial
system

So far as rural life was concerned, there can be no doubt that the Roman villa persisted under the barbarian conquerors. The model for the Carolingian manor was the great estate of the later empire. There we encounter the division of the arable between the proprietor and the tenants, so that each of the latter had his own plot in return for rents and labor owed to the former. The cultivators included slaves (*servi*) as well as the theoretical freemen called *coloni*. But all of them had come to be settled in much the same way, and through imperial legislation the *coloni* were as firmly attached to the estate as if they had been slaves. By the fifth century the mass of the agricultural population in the west had already become an economically dependent peasantry. And as the greater landlords rapidly acquired grants of immunity, the dependence of the peasantry tended to become also political. These agrarian arrangements were in general left unchanged by the barbarians, who merely took over a share of the existing estates and allowed them to be cultivated as before. Even the distinction between the invaders and the native Romans soon vanished. By the time of Charlemagne there was a single agrarian aristocracy, throughout Gaul usually speaking a Latin dialect, but in dress, habits, and disposition remaining predominantly barbarian. Beneath the ruling class a variety of Roman dependents, poorer German settlers, captives in war, and other subjected persons had been fused into the villein class of the Middle Ages. Many, perhaps most, of the peasants were legally free; yet they were economically unfree, being reduced to the position of *coloni*. The *servus*, too, had become what we know as a serf; and to designate the rightless bondman a new word was introduced—*esclave* or slave, derived from the tribal name of the unfortunates then being sold in the markets of the west.[3]

Benefices
and
precariæ

Along with the development of manorialism—the economic subjection of the masses to the greater landlords—the records of the Frankish kingdom reveal a striking growth of dependent tenure on the part of landlords themselves. During the troubled centuries that followed the collapse of the western empire, the lot of the small proprietor became increasingly hard. Often, to secure protection or other advantage, he would give his land to a church and receive it back as a benefice, a life estate to be held in return for a nominal payment. Sometimes an ecclesiastic or a layman would, on his own initiative, grant such an estate in order to have valuable service performed by the recipient. And very much the same result would ensue when a man requested land to live on and obtained it by virtue of a similar agreement. In the latter case the holding was technically called a *precaria*, because it was received in answer to formal prayer (*preces*); but it was also a benefice, because it was alleged to be a boon (*beneficium*) conferred by the donor.

The names are a matter of secondary interest. The really important

[3] See above, p. 46.

point is that, whatever the preliminaries, a certain property while owned by one man was actually possessed by another. Under Roman law a "precarious" tenure had been one enjoyed during the pleasure of a grantor. As developed under Frankish law, however, the *precaria* or benefice became a form of legal possession—whether for a term of years, for one life, for several lives, or for an indefinite period. Here we find an important element in the growth of the institutions called feudal. But what was eventually to become known as a fief (*feudum*) was only a special kind of benefice—one held by a vassal in return for military service. To understand feudal development, therefore, we must turn our attention to the earlier history of vassalage.

According to many famous scholars, the mediæval relationship of the vassal to his lord (French *seigneur*, Latin *senior*) was derived from that of the Roman client (*cliens*) to his patron (*patronus* or *senior*). The weakness of the argument is that, for all the persistence of a few vague Latin words, the two institutions were utterly unlike. The vassalage of the feudal age was essentially honorable and military.[4] The clientage of Rome, on the contrary, was merely a form of economic dependence; on helping to swell some wealthy man's escort, the poor man received donations of money, food, and clothing. It would thus appear more reasonable to find the origin of vassalage in the Germanic *comitatus* described by Tacitus.[5] In so far as the aristocracy of the eighth and following centuries was primarily warlike, it must have been descended from the warrior class of the conquering barbarians. Through appeal to an ancient tradition of that class, the Carolingians attempted to strengthen their dubious authority in an overgrown kingdom. Important offices in church and state were now increasingly given to royal vassals; soon it became the rule that only they should hold such offices. Thanks to endowment with rich benefices, royal vassals supplied the king with an enlarged force of expert cavalry. And as the royal vassal came to have important political functions, so he came to enjoy high political privilege. In particular, his military benefice brought him official immunity—the delegation of certain governmental powers within a restricted territory.

Vassalage and the Carolingian policy

Further discussion of these social and political developments must be postponed for a later chapter so that we may now take up another prominent feature of the Carolingian policy—the revival of learning on the continent. Very significantly, when Charlemagne sought to improve education within his kingdom, his inspiration came not from the Mediterranean lands but from the British Isles. Italy, since the days of Gregory the Great, had been the victim of increasing anarchy. Spain had been conquered by the Moslems. It was only among the Irish and the Anglo-Saxons

Education of the Dark Age

---

[4] See below, pp. 181, 213-16.
[5] See above, p. 48.

that the tradition of Latin scholarship still flourished. And it was those peoples who had sent to Gaul such eminent missionaries as St. Columban and St. Boniface. The latter, we should remember, was a contemporary of Bede and had himself been a teacher before he began his greater career of organizing the church in Germany. The reform of the Frankish clergy, though warmly supported by Charlemagne and his predecessors, was primarily the work of such men as Boniface. To understand what the so-called Carolingian Renaissance amounted to, we must briefly review the educational system of the Dark Age.

The period following the calamitous fifth century was characterized by an ignorance that far exceeded the range of academic instruction. Whether we examine archæological or literary remains, the conclusion is the same: there had been an appalling degradation of culture. It was not merely the study of the classics but the ability to read and write that was threatened with extinction. The spoken Latin, even of the upper classes, had drifted so far from literary Latin that a knowledge of the former was a hindrance rather than a help in formal composition—witness especially the honest Gregory of Tours. As yet no one dreamed of writing in the crude vernacular, though such polished languages as French, Provençal, Italian, and Spanish were eventually to develop from it. And, to judge from the works of the comparatively learned, the quality of education had rapidly deteriorated. The depth was reached in later Merovingian Gaul, where the king's official documents prove that his clerks were ignorant of the simplest grammatical rules, and where the best handwriting had degenerated into a grotesque scrawl. Under such conditions the preservation of ancient learning depended mainly on ecclesiastics.

Monastic schools

The attitude of the church fathers towards scholarly pursuits has already been well illustrated in the views of Ambrose, Jerome, Augustine, and Gregory. All four were fundamentally mystic in that they insisted on the primary need of faith and to it subordinated the rational faculties. Their intellectual labors, though often profound, were consecrated to pious ends: to refute pagans and heretics, to expound the truths of revelation, and in all practical ways to advance the cause of Christianity. A passionate delight in literature or learning for its own sake they were inclined to regard as sinful. The opinions held by the great monastic leaders were apparently much the same, but the varieties of religious discipline that they advocated permitted considerable divergence in practice. The Irish monks, commonly acting as priests among the people, had especial need of education; and since Greek was no stranger to them than Latin, they developed extraordinary zeal in the study of both languages. Many of them, in fact, came to have a deep regard for the classics, which they copied and recopied with loving care. Yet their conscious purpose was solely the promotion of the true faith.

Benedictine monasticism seems to have given somewhat less encouragement to scholarship during these early centuries. Although the subject is hardly referred to in the rule, Benedict obviously took for granted a certain amount of study and clerical work. The monastery had to have missals for the routine of divine service and books to be read aloud at mealtime or privately read by those brothers who were literate. To provide for such needs, younger monks received appropriate instruction, which boys from the outside might occasionally be permitted to share. Nevertheless, the Benedictine monastery was not primarily an educational institution; the religious life that it enjoined was essentially worship alternating with manual labor. Furthermore, through the Benedictine insistence on the separation of the regular from the secular clergy, the monastery lost whatever functions it had earlier had in the training of priests. It became an isolated community subject to the benevolent despotism of its abbot. If he chanced to have scholarly tastes, his house might become famous for its learning; but such a development was exceptional. In this early time the average monastic school was a small group of brothers studying penmanship and Latin composition; the average monastic library was a press containing perhaps a score of books, mainly religious in nature.[6]

Degradation of the secular clergy The secular clergy was thus left responsible for the work of the church in the world. To carry on this work effectively, priests had to have some education. If it could not be obtained in monasteries, the bishops would have to provide it. Although cathedral schools eventually became prominent in ecclesiastical organization, such institutions remained very obscure in the pre-Carolingian period. And we may be sure that, at least in Gaul, the priesthood of that time was generally debased. Too frequently even the bishops were worldly and ignorant, spending their lives in family feud, political intrigue, warfare, hunting, and other favorite pursuits of the semi-barbarous noblemen. Those exceptional priests who were competent to act as intellectual leaders found their energies so absorbed by the Christianization of new countries, or the attempted reform of old ones, that much scholarly endeavor was beyond them. It is not remarkable that, as we have seen, the seventh and eighth centuries were a singularly unproductive age in literature and learning. Authors worth mentioning in the history of European thought were exceedingly few, and such as there were had a mental outlook that to us seems childlike. If they were the great teachers, what should we think of their pupils?

The Carolingian reform It was to improving such conditions that Charlemagne, as is shown by his letters and capitularies, came to devote much of his attention. Under his father, Pepin, a number of teachers had already been attached to the imperial court for the instruction of young nobles. From this nucleus Charlemagne now developed his famous palace school, bringing over the

[6] See Plate XII, Monastic Library.

Northumbrian Alcuin to superintend it. As the director of the cathedral school at York, which had been founded by a pupil of Bede, Alcuin represented a noble tradition, and in every way he was eminently fitted to carry out Charlemagne's plan. To Aix-la-Chapelle, the king's favorite residence, he attracted teachers from all sides: English, Irish, Italians, and Spaniards, as well as Franks from Gaul and Germany. Within this early generation there were few noteworthy authors; yet they, by imparting to their students an enthusiasm for learning, inspired the production of many influential books in the next century. On men from this group Charlemagne conferred great abbeys and bishoprics, entrusting to them the task of organizing local schools, collecting libraries, reproducing ancient texts, standardizing the services of the church, and improving the quality of ecclesiastical music. Such projects, backed by the amazing energy of the king himself, rapidly stimulated the cultural advance that is often known as the Carolingian Renaissance. The description is somewhat exaggerated. What was actually done was to make more general a system of education that already existed in isolated communities, particularly those of the British Isles.

Alcuin   Although in minor respects some of the Carolingian scholars may have surpassed Bede, on the average they were distinctly inferior. Alcuin's own books were not at all remarkable, consisting chiefly of dialogues on the liberal arts and of commentaries on the Scriptures. In both respects his work was continued with great success by his pupil, Rabanus Maurus, who rose to be abbot of Fulda (d. 856). The more popular writings of Rabanus included a universal encyclopædia, which was only a revision of Isidore's *Etymologies*; a long essay on the education of the clergy, which was largely a compilation of extracts from the church fathers; and many volumes of biblical interpretation, which of course used the allegorical approach. These products, on the whole, were characteristic of Carolingian scholarship, which but rarely wandered into the more dangerous fields of original speculation. A profound thinker was out of place in the ninth century; it was the very mediocrity of Rabanus that assured his renown.

Einhard   Among the other writers at the Frankish court two of the better known were historians: one who ended and one who began his career during the reign of Charlemagne. Paul the Deacon, a monk of Monte Cassino, spent only a few years in the north; then, returning to Italy, he devoted the rest of his life to composing a *History of the Lombards*. The book has enjoyed great popularity because it is filled with a variety of engaging legends; but, for that same reason, it is not a very trustworthy source, and the author unfortunately did not live to describe the age of which he had direct knowledge. In every way a finer scholar was Einhard, a young Frank who came from Fulda to complete his education in the palace school. There he gained the friendship of Prince Louis and, after the latter had inherited the throne, continued to enjoy high favor at the imperial court. Einhard thus was able to pursue a literary career without becoming either priest or monk, and while a mere layman to write the most remarkable biography of the early Middle Ages. Being steeped in the Latin classics, he consciously set out, as a second Suetonius, to describe the deeds of another Cæsar, the late emperor Charlemagne. This is a fact of great significance in appraising Einhard's work; for, as he constantly borrowed language from his model, his statements cannot always be taken literally. The *Life of Charlemagne*, nevertheless, is a brilliant piece of literature and parts of it have great historical worth. In particular, the graphic picture of the aged emperor is unforgettable and should be read by everyone interested in the Carolingian age.

Einhard, it is clear, prized literary study as something beyond an element of practical education. He felt that, within limits, admiration of the classics was not incompatible with Christian character, and prominent clergymen occasionally shared his attitude. For instance, Lupus, abbot of Ferrières, devoted much more time to pagan letters than to theology. At the same time many other students are known to have attempted imitations of classic authors. To modern eyes the most noteworthy of them was John the Scot, an Irishman who came to Gaul about the middle of the ninth century and who seems never to have secured ecclesiastical preferment. His knowledge of Greek was so excellent that he even tried his hand at verses in that language. But his truly significant accomplishment was a book called *On the Division of Nature*—a reconciliation of Neoplatonism and Christianity, which few if any of his contemporaries could have understood. John the Scot was the only man of the period whose mentality approached that of the great church fathers, and he had no immediate heirs. As a matter of fact, the age was one in which original investigation could hardly flourish, and an uncritical devotion to the ideals of ancient authors could lead only to affectation. The really significant issue was the advancement of such practical education as had been advocated by Gregory the Great.

Other scholars

In theory the instruction given by the Carolingian schools, whether attached to monastery or cathedral, was based on the traditional scheme of the seven liberal arts. They were divided into two groups: the *trivium*, consisting of grammar, rhetoric, and dialectic; and the *quadrivium*, consisting of arithmetic, geometry, astronomy, and music. What of all this did the student actually get? In the first place, he would learn to read and write Latin—in itself no mean accomplishment, for Einhard tells us that even the great emperor never learned the art. Having gained a knowledge of elementary Latin, the youth could proceed with the popular textbooks of Donatus, Boëthius, Isidore, Bede, Alcuin, and Rabanus. Besides, if he were to perfect his style, the leading masters agreed that he should have at least selections from the pagan classics. And the more zealous learner

The seven liberal arts

would not stop with a mere understanding of grammatical construction; according to the ancient tradition, the first of the liberal arts included most of what we should call the study of literature. This, however, was a secondary consideration, pursuit of which depended on the talents and sympathies of the instructor.

In rhetoric and dialectic ordinary education was restricted to the reading of standard treatises by Alcuin and his predecessors. Classical rhetoric had lost all meaning except as it might be adapted to the needs of the Christian preacher. To be effective, however, he now had to speak in the vernacular, and he would probably find the homilies of Gregory the Great more useful than theoretical discussions of the ancient art. Dialectic, too, had slight practical importance in the Carolingian age; and even if curiosity impelled a student to exhaust all his authorities, he could not progress very far. After working back to Boëthius, he could read in translation Porphyry's *Isagoge* and the elementary logic of Aristotle. Of Plato nothing beyond a portion of one dialogue was available in Latin. All the rest of Greek philosophy and science, aside from scattering quotations, remained unknown in the west.

The learning imparted under the head of the *quadrivium* had therefore become negligible. Neither the Romans nor the Greeks before them had been able to do much with arithmetic, because they had continued to use letters as numerals and without specific values based on position—a system under which addition and subtraction remain formidable operations, while multiplication and division are almost impossible. Now that even Euclid's geometry was lacking in the western libraries, the Carolingian scholar could not be expected to be very proficient in advanced mathematics. On the theoretic side he had only such essays as those of Boëthius, Isidore, and Bede; on the practical side he was interested in nothing more abstruse than determining the date of Easter. Music had been included in the *quadrivium* through the Greek discovery of the mathematical ratios underlying the musical scale; but the notion of music as a liberal art was now little more than a vague tradition, and the actual technique of playing instruments or of singing was hardly a subject of academic instruction.

Development of handwriting

Accordingly, aside from fundamental training in grammar, the education offered by the Carolingian school was very superficial, consisting of little more than definitions and catchphrases. Compared with the contemporary learning of the Moslem world, that of the Latin west was puerile. Yet, if it had not been for the enthusiasm of Charlemagne and his helpers, our irreparable losses of ancient literature would have been immensely greater, for many a classic has come down to us through a single manuscript written in some Frankish monastery. To the obscure scholars of the eighth and ninth centuries our modern culture is also indebted for the system of letters in which this book is printed—a remarkable development of which only the first stage may be considered here. For all formal writing the Romans had originally employed the square letters known to us as capitals, but in the later centuries a more rounded hand gained popularity because it was easier to use. Meanwhile, as the break-down of oriental commerce took papyrus out of the western market and compelled the use of parchment, the factor of economy became increasingly potent. To get more words on a page, the scribe had to use smaller letters and squeeze them closer together. Some, to preserve their distinctive shapes, were extended above the line, some below. The ultimate result was the form of writing called minuscule—little letters, with capitals inserted for emphasis—as distinguished from majuscule, which consisted only of large letters.

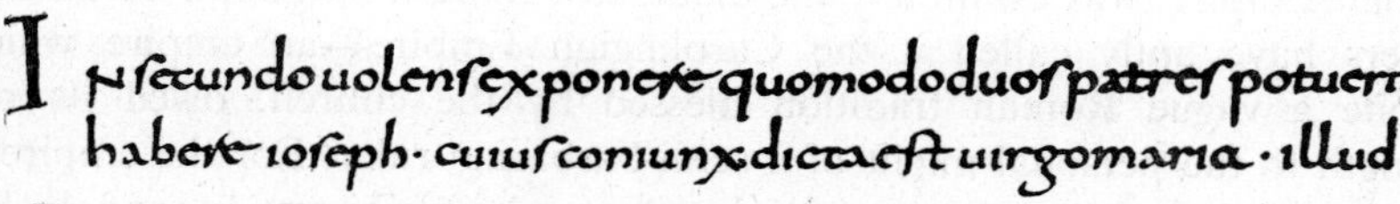

FIG. 10.   Example of Carolingian Minuscule. In secundo uolens exponere quomodo duos patres potuerit habere ioseph. cuius coniunx dicta est uirgo maria. illud . . .

The precise way in which this evolution came about is a highly technical and somewhat controversial subject. Here it need only be remarked that by the eighth century there were several well-defined minuscule hands: the Irish, from which was derived the Anglo-Saxon; the so-called Visigothic, which had been devised in Spain; and the Beneventan, which was employed in southern Italy. Through the migrations of scholars and the interchange of manuscripts, all these hands became known in Gaul, where the Carolingian revival of learning produced a growing demand for handsomely and legibly written books. Through this demand was eventually developed the Carolingian minuscule, characterized by the rounded form of its letters and its general distinctness and simplicity (see Figure 10). Written in this beautiful hand and illuminated in color—the method of decoration perfected by the Irish monks—a manuscript became a treasure of art as well as of erudition. It was no wonder that, indirectly, the books of the ninth century later became the models followed by the printers of Italy, from which our most popular type has been inherited. **Narrow scope of the Carolingian revival**

Outside the narrow field of Latin education there was no Carolingian Renaissance. Vernacular literature as yet did not exist, except in the form of heroic tales chanted by wandering minstrels. Einhard tells us that Charlemagne had these "ancient barbarian poems" put into writing; none of them, unhappily, has survived, and we may only guess that they were somewhat like the sagas preserved from a later age. So far as the fine arts were concerned, we have only one Carolingian monument of any importance. Einhard says that Charlemagne constructed at Aix-la-Chapelle "an extremely beautiful basilica," adorned with gold, silver, and bronze. And since the materials could not be procured elsewhere, he had them brought from Rome and Ravenna. The emperor's church is still preserved as a chapel within the cathedral of Aix-la-Chapelle. It is, as Einhard implies, built in the Byzantine style; but it is not imposing, being only a domed octagon some forty-seven feet across. Was not this pathetic little imitation of Roman grandeur somewhat typical of Charlemagne's whole imperial structure?

3. THE RUIN OF THE CAROLINGIAN SYSTEM

Weakness of the Carolingian Empire

We have already seen that Charlemagne's state, though officially styled Roman Empire, was essentially the enlarged Frankish kingdom. So modern writers have aptly called it the Carolingian Empire—an empire which, despite a vague Roman tradition blessed by the church, owed its real strength to the personal might of a semi-barbarian ruler. For the empire of Charlemagne had no truly imperial system of administration and lacked the economic resources on which one could be based. There was as little solidarity among the dominions of the emperor as there had been among those of his Merovingian predecessors, and the common bond of religion was devoid of political significance. How long would such a hasty agglomeration of disparate lands and peoples hold together when it passed to a prince who, being no military genius, could not enforce his authority by a continuous series of campaigns? Or could even a Charlemagne successfully defend so broad a territory if it were assailed on all fronts by formidable antagonists?

Charlemagne's successors

As a matter of fact, Louis, who fell heir to the entire empire in 814, was far from being another Charlemagne. Excellently educated and sincerely devoted to the ideals of the church, the new emperor deserved his nickname of "the Pious." In personal morality he was, moreover, a distinct improvement over his father. But he was neither a general nor a statesman, and before long the political situation had got completely out of hand. To aggravate the trouble caused by local insurrection and foreign invasion, a bitter conflict arose among the emperor's own sons, and it was still raging when he died in 840. By that time the rivals had been reduced to three. Lothair, the eldest, was king of Italy and emperor. Against him, to check his assertion of supreme authority, were arrayed Louis the German, king of the East Franks, and Charles the Bald, king of the west Franks—an alliance that produced the famous Strasbourg Oaths. A contemporary tells us how Louis first swore unfailing loyalty to Charles, using the *lingua romana* (i.e., Romance, French) so that his brother's retainers could understand him; and how Charles followed, using the *lingua teudesca* (i.e., *Deutsch*, German). Besides, he reports the forms that were then employed,

and from them we gain valuable information concerning the two languages
in the ninth century.

More important from the political point of view was the final settlement
forced upon Lothair in 843. This was the Peace of Verdun, which extended
the kingdom of Charles to an irregular line running along the Scheldt and
the upper Moselle to the valley of the Rhone, and which brought the kingdom of Louis to the Rhine, excluding Frisia on the north. Lothair was thus
left with the kingdom of Italy, plus Provence, Burgundy, Alsace, the west-

MAP IX.

ern Rhinelands and the Low Countries (see Map IX). The fact that such
a straggling territory, devoid of all cohesion, was thought a fit portion for
the eldest son proves the absence of foresight in the treaty. And whatever
solidarity was possessed by the other sections was purely accidental, for
nationalism played no part in the politics of the ninth century. Nevertheless, the Peace of Verdun was to have permanent results. It marked the
first stage in the dissolution of the Carolingian Empire. While Lothair's
middle strip was soon broken into half a dozen fragments, the kingdoms to
the west and east maintained at least a superficial integrity, becoming
known respectively as France and Germany. But before their later fortunes
can be sketched, something must be seen of the peoples who were then
threatening their frontiers.

Although Scandinavian freebooters had occasionally appeared in earlier
times, it was not until the ninth century that their raids became a source

of terror throughout the Christian northwest. The fundamental cause of the outpouring was undoubtedly overpopulation. Besides, the advancing authority of various local kings tended to drive adventurous spirits abroad, and the defenseless condition of the neighboring countries, quickly advertised by the success of preliminary expeditions, encouraged a growing stream of marauders. For the character and activities of these northerners we are dependent on the accounts of Christian chroniclers, supplemented by archæological evidence and the Icelandic sagas.[7] But the latter, being written at a much later time, give traditional stories in poetic form and must be used with great caution. What we actually know about the primitive Scandinavians in their old homeland is slight; the main facts can be very briefly stated.

In the first place, it should be remembered that Denmark, Norway, and Sweden are political units which hardly existed in Carolingian times. Although it may be convenient to speak of Danes, Norwegians, and Swedes as invading southern lands in the ninth century, those names should be understood as merely indicating the vague regions from which three groups of invaders came. Commonly they called themselves Vikings, meaning creekmen or men of the *fiords*. Being still heathen, they showed no mercy to Christian churches or clergymen. It was, indeed, the wealth of the monasteries and cathedrals that chiefly attracted them; for their primary object was loot. But they also took delight in sheer devastation. Often they put entire settlements to the torch and slaughtered the inhabitants with a cold fury that spread universal horror. In such respects they closely resembled the original Anglo-Saxons who had terrorized the shores of Roman Britain.

So far as institutions were concerned, the Vikings could contribute little that was new to the semi-barbarous society of the west; their customs were very much the same as had earlier been common to all the Germans. The *comitatus* described by Tacitus reappears in the wandering band of warriors led by the Scandinavian *jarl*. In the material arts of civilization, as in matters of education and morals, the Vikings were learners rather than teachers. Only in one respect they were manifestly superior to the peoples they despoiled: they were beyond doubt the greatest sailors of western Europe. In open boats, propelled by oars or small sails, they not only skirted the coasts of Europe from the Baltic to the Mediterranean but constantly made long voyages into the stormy Atlantic, where days had to be spent beyond the sight of land.

Viking raids and conquests

As the Scandinavian peoples spread across the seas, geographic position naturally dictated the directions they normally took. The Swedes, facing east, were attracted to the southern shore of the Baltic and thence through the interior by the river routes that led to the Black Sea. Along these routes

[7] See below, p. 212.

slaves and furs had long been carried by Avars and other Asiatics to be sold to the Moslem traders of the Caucasus or the Christian traders of Constantinople. Now that the Avar power had been broken, the northerners encountered no serious opposition; lured by opportunities for brigandage, they eventually established themselves on the Dnieper and extended their raids to the ports of the Black Sea. So, by the end of the ninth century, they had gained the attention of Byzantine writers, who called them Russians (*Rhos*) or Varangians. From these beginnings, as will be seen in a following chapter, a great empire was to be developed in eastern Europe.

To the west, meanwhile, the Norwegians and Danes had been led to attack the British Isles and the Atlantic shores of the continent. Long before the close of the eighth century Viking raiders had begun to make annual visits to Ireland and Britain, and within the next hundred years both islands had been ravaged from end to end. Everywhere the great religious houses, ancient centers of Irish and Anglo-Saxon learning, were looted and burned. The kingdoms of Northumbria, East Anglia, and Mercia were practically wiped out. The cathedral cities of southern Britain were repeatedly taken; even London was sacked. On the continent it was the same story. Beginning with inroads in Frisia, the Northmen, as they were generally known to the Franks, gradually pushed their fleets along the coasts to Aquitaine and Spain. In 859 a great expedition actually rounded Gibraltar and plundered the Mediterranean shore as far east as Italy. Nor did the inland districts escape. Sailing up the larger rivers, the Vikings often captured a walled city or built a fortified camp; thence, by means of horses taken from the unfortunate inhabitants, they rode across country, spreading desolation far and wide. From such practices it was only a step to effect permanent conquests. Sometimes, as in eastern Ireland, the native population was subjected and forced to supply the conquerors with food; sometimes, as in what the Anglo-Saxons called the Danelaw and in what the Franks called Normandy, colonists were brought from the homeland to occupy the devastated regions. The political significance of these settlements will be considered below.

One important cause of the Viking successes on the continent was assuredly the lack of Carolingian defense by sea, and this same lack permitted a continuous scourge of Moslem raids along the Mediterranean shores. All danger of Moorish incursions across the Pyrenees, it is true, had been ended by the campaigns of Pepin and Charlemagne; but the independent emirs of Tunis[8] soon launched an active maritime offensive and continued it throughout the ninth century. While Sicily was being systematically conquered, other Moslem forces ravaged Sardinia and Corsica, terrorized the coasts of Provence and Italy, and even preyed on the commerce of the

Moslem raids and conquests

[8] See below, p. 165.

Adriatic. About the time that the sons of Louis the Pious were swearing the Peace of Verdun, the Moslems took Messina and made it a base for further operations on the mainland. In 846 the great church of St. Peter outside the walls of Rome was looted and burned; and not long afterwards the monastery of Monte Cassino suffered the same fate. As late as the tenth century it was still problematical whether the Italian peninsula would remain a Christian possession.

The Hungarian invasion To increase the misery of the Carolingian lands, another horde of Asiatic nomads now appeared on the eastern frontier. Because of their affinity to the ancient Huns these invaders came to be generally known as Hungarians, but they have always called themselves Magyars. Like their predecessors, they were apparently forced to migrate by some sort of disturbance in the homeland and they came by the same route, over the grasslands of the Pontic steppe. Crossing the Dniester in the closing years of the ninth century, they advanced into the plain between the Carpathians and the Danube. There the remnants of the Avars quickly became amalgamated with the newcomers, so that ever since then the territory has been known as Hungary. According to all contemporary descriptions, the invaders were of the primitive nomad type—savage horsemen, repulsive in appearance, rapacious and pitiless. While the Frankish lands of the west were still suffering from the inroads of the Vikings, those of the east were devastated by the Hungarians. Unchecked by the feeble defenses of the empire, they drove through Bavaria, Venetia, and Lombardy. In the following years they turned north, desolating Thuringia, Saxony, and the Rhine valley. Some of their bands even penetrated as far west as Burgundy.

Degradation of the empire From the mere recital of these tragic events it should be evident that the glory of the Carolingian Empire did not long survive its founder. Conditions were bad under Louis the Pious; under his sons they became infinitely worse. Although the royal brothers indulged in fine talk about imperial unity and Christian co-operation, their acts continuously belied their words. While their subjects were being slaughtered by heathen marauders and Moslem pirates, they presented a most unedifying example of selfishness, cruelty, and bad faith. It was only during intervals between dynastic quarrels that their attention was given to the defense of the country, and then their efforts were singularly ineffective. Their reigns merely prepared for the general disintegration that followed. Lothair's middle kingdom was the first to disappear, for he divided it among his three sons (see Table I). None of them is worth mentioning except Lothair II, after whom his nondescript territory was called *Lotharii Regnum*, Lotharingia or Lorraine. By the last quarter of the ninth century all three of these sons were dead and their lands were being fought over by their relatives and by local usurpers. By that time, too, the Vikings were beginning to turn from mere plundering to systematic conquest. As the disorder increased, the empire was momentarily reunited under Charles the Fat, a son of Louis the German; but in the face of a new invasion he quickly proved his incompetence and so was dethroned in 887.

The deposition of Charles the Fat marked the end of Charlemagne's empire. Despite the titles held by later kings, it was thenceforth as dead as the empire of Constantine. Nor did the old dynasty long survive. In the eastern kingdom the throne was given to Arnulf, an illegitimate member of the house, because he had the reputation of being an energetic fighter, and he intervened in Italy long enough to be crowned emperor. He was succeeded, however, by a mere child, with whose death in 911 the line came to an end. In the western kingdom the events of 887 led the magnates to proclaim the valiant Odo, count of Paris; and his descendants, after a hundred years of rivalry with the later Carolingians, finally gained undisputed possession of the throne as the Capetian dynasty. While France and Germany thus became independent states under elected kings, the old middle kingdom utterly vanished. The northern end, Lorraine, for a short time was held by the French king; then it was taken from him by the German. To the south lay the two petty kingdoms of Burgundy and Provence, and beyond the Alps the theoretical kingdom of the Lombards or Italy—the scene of a murderous warfare that defies narration. The imperial title, disgraced by the local princes who last held it, eventually went begging.

Since, according to the Carolingian ideal, church and state were but two phases of one administration, it was inevitable that both should be affected by the calamities of the ninth century. Down to the time of Charles the Bald learning and literature continued to flourish at the Frankish courts. Then, as all central authority collapsed and the principal seats of education were destroyed by barbarian or Moslem invaders, the little that remained of Latin culture was threatened with extinction. At the same time the papacy, after a brief period of splendid leadership, sank so low as to forfeit any claim to the respect of Christendom. Nicholas I (858-67), the ablest man to hold the see of St. Peter in many generations, asserted his rights in three important respects: by compelling Lothair II of Lorraine to take back a wife whom he had unlawfully repudiated, by enforcing direct papal jurisdiction over the Gallic bishops in the face of opposition from the powerful archbishop of Reims, and by excommunicating the Byzantine emperor for arbitrarily deposing the patriarch of Constantinople.[9] But Nicholas died prematurely, and his successors had the misfortune of becoming immersed in local politics and so of losing their spiritual headship of Europe. By the tenth century the popes had actually been reduced to the rank of ignoble puppets controlled by vicious Roman nobles and their equally vicious women.

The age thus seemed to be one of complete ruin. Yet, obscurely, forces

Degradation of the papacy

[9] See below, p. 161.

of regeneration were at work. From the welter of armed conflict, massacre, and desolation that marked the close of the ninth century were to emerge new political units, characterized by regard for necessity rather than for tradition. These political units were the relatively small fragments into which the empire and its component kingdoms had broken. As a rule, they lacked the appearance of sovereignty, being styled duchies, marquisates, or the like; but they had the great merit of military efficiency. And among them the strongest were what we recognize as feudal states—a term that demands fuller discussion in a separate chapter.

CHAPTER IX

The Greek and Moslem Worlds

1. The Byzantine Empire and Its Cultural Influence

How the once glorious Roman Empire was reduced to the fragment **Leo III** that historians call the Byzantine Empire has been explained in previous **(717-40)** chapters. At the opening of the eighth century it was as yet questionable whether even this fragment of the empire could survive the Moslem attack. That it did survive was largely due to the ability of a general named Leo. Having waged a number of victorious campaigns in Anatolia, he was raised to the imperial throne in 717—just in time to organize the defense of the capital against a last great assault by the caliph's fleet. Again, after months of bitter fighting, the Bosphorus was successfully held, and the opportune weakening of the Ommiad state ended the danger of a renewed offensive. Leo consequently was left in possession, not only of the remaining territory in Europe, but also of Asia Minor as far as a line extending from the Taurus Mountains to the Armenian Highlands (see Map VI). And the respite now gained in the Moslem war was turned to good advantage by a thorough reform of the administration, both civil and military.

Leo's religious policy was not so fortunate. During his early life in southern Asia Minor he had become well acquainted with Mohammedanism, as well as with various Christian sects that condemned many beliefs and practices of the orthodox—especially what they termed the pagan ceremonial of the established church. While sympathizing neither with heretic nor with Moslem, the emperor seems to have been convinced that both were right in at least one respect: the customary use of images and pictures in Christian worship was hardly better than idolatry. In 725, accordingly, he officially denounced it and launched a violent campaign of iconoclasm (image-breaking). Though zealously supported by many of the educated, the decree was

159

intensely unpopular with the mass of the people. Riots broke out both in
Greece and in Italy. For opposing the imperial will the aged patriarch of
Constantinople was ousted from office, but in Rome no such action was
possible. From the beginning the pope gave vigorous support to the traditional cause and eventually pronounced excommunication against all who
accepted the iconoclastic program. East and west thus came once more into
religious conflict, which intermittently continued until the use of images
was formally restored by imperial edict in 843.

**Origin
of the
Mace-
donian
dynasty**

Meanwhile, with the passing of the Moslem danger, the Byzantine government had fallen into a chronic state of incompetence. The history of the
capital becomes a wearisome recital of palace intrigue, more and more
dominated by refined but vicious women. Such was the regent Irene, who
had her own son blinded and deposed in order that she might reign as
empress (797-802)—and so, as we have seen, to justify the coronation
of Charlemagne. After Irene had been dethroned by one insurrection, a
series of others kept the empire in constant turmoil. And for a long time
no improvement was visible in the character of the sovereigns. Its low ebb
may be said to have been reached with Michael III (842-67) who, from
one of his minor vices, was popularly called "the Drunkard." Being passionately fond of chariot-racing, he singled out for his especial favor a
Macedonian horse-trainer named Basil. From the office of chief equerry
Basil eventually rose to be co-emperor; and when Michael gave signs of
transferring his affections, Basil secured undisputed title to the crown by
having him murdered. Thus, strangely enough, was founded the remarkable Macedonian dynasty, under which the Byzantine Empire enjoyed a
last interval of glory.

**The Serbs
and the
Bulgars**

Political decadence, however, did not prevent a noteworthy extension
of Byzantine influence among the barbarians to the north. For lack of records, the early history of the Slavic and other peoples who occupied the
interior of the Balkan peninsula in the seventh and eighth centuries remains
very obscure. Presumably it was the decline of the Avars, culminating in
their utter defeat by Charlemagne, that began a new era for such nations as
the Bulgars and Serbs. The latter—together with the Croats, who were included within the boundary of the Carolingian Empire—are classified as
Jugo-Slavs (i.e., South Slavs). In the ninth century they were still divided
into various tribes and, because of their disunion, were generally dominated
by their more powerful neighbors. The Bulgars, on the other hand, were
by origin Asiatic nomads[1] who, after settling to the south of the Danube,
had intermingled with the Slavs and to some extent adopted their language.
Now, under independent khans, the Bulgars became a formidable power.
In 814, having overrun most of Thrace, they appeared before the walls of
Constantinople itself. Their siege failed, but the ensuing peace gave them

[1] See above, p. 79.

all Byzantine territory to a line running just north of Adrianople. By this time, furthermore, the Bulgars had conquered a large part of Macedonia and had subjugated the Serbian princes, thus bringing the Bulgarian frontier to the Carolingian march on the upper Adriatic and to the Byzantine province along the Dalmatian coast (see Map VIII).

This was the situation when two Christian brothers of Slavic descent— **Sts. Cyril** eventually known as Cyril and Methodius—undertook a great missionary **and Meth-** enterprise among their heathen compatriots. Having been educated at **odius** Constantinople and ordained as priests, they decided, about 862, to preach the Gospel among the Slavs of Moravia. But in that country, we are told, they encountered the opposition of Germans devoted to the Roman Church and therefore transferred their activities to the Balkan peninsula. So it came about that Cyril, in order to translate the Christian scriptures and liturgy into the vernacular of the South Slavs, invented a modified Greek alphabet—one which, with considerable changes, has remained in use throughout eastern Europe. The first victory of the Cyrillic alphabet[2] came with the conversion of the Serbs, the second when Boris I of Bulgaria (852-907) accepted Christianity for himself and his people. Since the khan's action was determined by a peace signed with the Byzantine emperor, the Bulgars were of course subjected to the patriarch of Constantinople; and in their case the official adoption of the new faith involved that of the Slavic language for both civil and ecclesiastical purposes. It was left for Simeon, son of Boris I, to assume the title of Tsar (i.e., Cæsar) and so, after a fashion, to proclaim a Bulgarian Empire.

During this time, as we have seen, the Byzantine throne came into the **Disputes** possession of the Macedonian Basil I. Despite its bloodstained inauguration, **between** his reign (867-86) was not unsuccessful. He actively pushed a much-needed **the Greek** reform of the finances, issued some admirable law-books to supplement **and Roman** Justinian's compilation of three centuries earlier, and called a general coun- **churches** cil to re-establish peace in the church. An earlier schism between Rome and Constantinople had been ended by an imperial decree restoring the use of images in Christian worship. Nevertheless, the Greek east continued to be embroiled with the Latin west in a series of other ecclesiastical disputes. The popes had now come to recognize the Frankish emperor as their official protector and to date their acts according to the year of his reign. Moreover, the able Nicholas I had refused to recognize as patriarch of Constantinople the distinguished Photius[3] because he owed his preferment to the imperial deposition of his predecessor, and had objected to the extension of his authority into Bulgaria. Photius had replied by formally condemning a number of Roman usages—such as eating eggs in Lent, using unleavened bread in the mass, shaving the faces of priests, and saying that the Holy

---

[2] The original Cyrillic alphabet is probably the one now known as Glagolitic.
[3] See above, p. 157; below, p. 223.

Spirit proceeded from the Father and the Son (*filioque*). Such trivial differences obviously disguised the really fundamental issue: whether the Byzantine Empire should or should not accept the Petrine supremacy. It was not until 898—after the death of Basil I and Photius, and while the papacy was suffering complete degradation—that a form of settlement was once more agreed to by the two churches. How this agreement merely served to introduce a final schism will be seen in a later chapter.

The later Macedonians

Basil's son and grandson were men of scholarly tastes, who not only encouraged learning on the part of others but themselves produced noteworthy books, mainly dealing with phases of administration. With respect to private morals, however, the record of the Macedonian emperors is far from edifying; ultimately, indeed, it becomes quite fantastic. In the later tenth century the Byzantine court was dominated by the empress Theophano who, it was said, acquired that rank by helping her husband to murder his father; she then poisoned this husband in order to win a second one, who through her connivance was assassinated by his nephew; but the latter, ungratefully, sent her to a convent and married her daughter. Whatever may be made of all this scandal—and it is significant that everyone then took such stories for granted—Theophano's second husband was the general Nicephorus Phocas, who had gained renown by taking Crete from the Moslems and fighting successful campaigns in Asia. As emperor he continued his triumphant offensive, completing the conquest of Cilicia, Cyprus, and a portion of northern Syria, including Antioch and Aleppo. Momentarily it seemed as if the Roman state, outliving the empire of the caliphs, might yet revive the glories of Heraclius. But John Tzimisces, the nephew and successor of Nicephorus, was diverted northward by the increasing troubles of the Bulgarian tsar.

Bulgarian and Russian relations

Simeon, the first to bear that title, had died in 927 and his heirs had been unable to maintain the integrity of their newly proclaimed empire. While, on the western frontier, the Serbs re-established their independence by a successful rebellion, the Russians crossed the Danube, captured the Bulgarian capital, and demanded the payment of tribute by the Byzantine Empire. These Russians, as noted above, were by origin Swedish Vikings who had gained control of the trade routes between the Baltic and the Black Sea. By the tenth century their scattered bands had come to be more or less united under the rule of a prince at Kiev, who also enjoyed a wide dominion over the nomads of the steppe and the Slavic tribes of the interior. From the Dnieper the Russians, at the head of mixed armies, extended their plundering on the one hand to the shores of the Caspian and on the other to the Balkan kingdoms. Down to the middle of the tenth century the princes of Kiev bore Scandinavian names, after that Slavic. For example, it was Igor who led an attack on Constantinople between 941 and 945. His wife and successor was Olga; but their son was called Svyatoslav and his son was the famous Vladimir, whose occupation of Bulgaria led to Byzantine intervention.

The campaign of John Tzimisces ended with a signal victory. The Russians were driven beyond the Danube and forced to make peace. Although the Bulgarian tsar was allowed to keep the western part of his alleged empire, the eastern part was turned into a Byzantine province. The Bulgarian war was continued by John's successor, Basil II. After putting down an insurrection in eastern Bulgaria, he turned upon the western kingdom and reduced it also. By an amazing recovery the imperial border was thus brought back to the Danube. And in the meantime Basil had established friendly relations with the Russian prince Vladimir, whose dominions had been extended from the frontiers of Poland to the Black Sea. According to the peace now sworn, commercial advantages were assured to both states, while the emperor, for his personal protection, obtained the famous Varangian guard, which continued to serve at Constantinople for well over a century. More important, Vladimir agreed to accept Christianity for himself and his people—a promise which he faithfully carried out. Thereby the Russians were brought within the pale of civilized nations, like the Bulgarians adopting ecclesiastical rule from Constantinople and all that implied: especially the use of the Cyrillic alphabet and the abiding influence of Byzantium upon Russian arts and institutions.

So far as the empire itself was concerned, the political successes of the Macedonian house were naturally accompanied by a noteworthy revival of culture. Great zeal was displayed by numerous scholars—particularly by Photius (tenth century) and Michael Psellus (eleventh century)—in collecting and studying Greek manuscripts. It is, in fact, to the interest of these men that we are indebted for the preservation of much ancient learning. If the Byzantine Empire, despite the calamities of the seventh and eighth centuries, had not maintained the old standard of classic education, how great would have been our loss! Yet, in point of originality, it must be admitted that the later Greek writings were generally deficient. Historical memoirs of considerable merit continued to be produced. As already remarked, technical essays on civil and military administration were composed even by the emperors. And there was no lack of hymns, sermons, or theological tracts. The literary revival of the tenth century, however, was chiefly characterized by condensations of earlier works and by encyclopædias based on excerpts from them. Likewise in architecture and the decorative arts, although a number of handsome monuments were raised, they made little if any modification of the forms established during the reign of Justinian.

The literary influence of the Byzantines in western Europe remained very slight until the fourteenth and fifteenth centuries. During the earlier period Italians and Franks to some extent accepted Byzantine inspiration for their

Revival of culture

architecture and allied arts; but on the whole, as will be seen, they tended to prefer their own original developments. The greater contributions of the mediæval Greeks to the Latins were probably military and commercial. In such matters, assuredly, the barbarians of the west had much to learn from the east. Especially after the reforms of Leo III, the Byzantine Empire was able to maintain a highly efficient army, navy, and civil service—and all this by virtue of a cash economy which, we may be sure, depended on mercantile prosperity. At Constantinople, as well as in various provincial towns, trade and industry flourished to such a degree that the government, for all its recurrent ineptitude and corruption, found existence comparatively easy. Through lack of study, unfortunately, our information concerning the material civilization of the Byzantine Empire, and in particular its customary organization of business, remains very unsatisfactory. Accordingly, before we attempt to draw any further conclusions in that respect, we should examine the contemporary life of the Moslem world.

2. The Literature and Learning of Islam

The Arab Empire under the Abbasids

Just before the coronation of Pepin as king of the Franks the Ommiads were supplanted in the caliphate by the Abbasids. The second of the new line was al-Mansur (754-75), who built the city of Bagdad on the Tigris to serve as his capital. His grandson was the famous Harun al-Rashid (786-809), and the latter was succeeded, after a short interval, by al-Mamun (813-33). With these gorgeous princes the Abbasid caliphate reached its height of power—and so became even more foreign to the ideals of Abu-Bakr and Omar. The last vestiges of its old simplicity had now disappeared. The ruler of Islam was no longer an Arab chieftain who lived on terms of equality with his nomad followers, but an oriental despot of mixed blood who treated all men as his subjects, whether or not they belonged to the great families of Mecca and Medina. Although the Abbasid caliphs emphasized the religious character of their office, their conduct was inspired by the traditions of the Persian monarchy rather than by the precepts of the Koran. It is chiefly as magnificent builders, as patrons of secular learning, as lovers of wine, women, and song, that they are celebrated in the pages of history.

Politically, the Abbasid revolution produced a rapid weakening of the Arab Empire. Devout Mohammedans found the new caliphs quite as worldly as their Ommiad predecessors. In the eyes of legitimists, who continued to support the house of Ali, they were equally usurpers. And in so far as the Bagdad government favored the Iranians, it antagonized the Syrians and other western peoples. The result was that, in some fashion, the outlying provinces soon gained autonomy. Spain, as we have seen, came under the absolute control of an Ommiad emir, later styled caliph, at Cordova. In 788 another rebel, claiming descent from Fatima and Ali, secured dominion over Morocco, where the succeeding emir established a new capital for himself at Fez. Early in the next century the emir of Kairawan made Tunisia into a virtually independent state, and later a Turkish adventurer obtained a similar position in Egypt and Syria. Meanwhile, to the east, various powerful governors had successfully adopted the same policy. By the end of the ninth century, accordingly, the caliph's rule was actually restricted to the central portion of his theoretical empire, and even there he lived in constant fear of his own ministers and generals. He kept himself in magnificent seclusion, guarded by Turkish mercenaries, while to maintain authority in his palace he developed a capricious terrorism that has seldom been equaled. Such a despot, known to few outside his harem and his household of slaves and eunuchs, utterly lacked the heroic character of the early caliphs. His headship of the faith remained little more than a legal form; all semblance of religious unity was lost among the "two and seventy jarring sects" of the *Rubaiyat*.

Nevertheless, the world of Islam continued to be distinguished by a common civilization. From the Oxus and the Himalayas to the Sahara and the Pyrenees, society and culture remained very much the same. Despite the endless quarrels of Mohammedan theologians, all recognized the sanctity of the Koran and obeyed the injunction that it be used in the original—a fact that maintained the supremacy of Arabic throughout all Moslem territories. No-one could there be thought educated unless he knew the vernacular of the Prophet. And that flexible language soon proved itself as well adapted to the technicalities of philosophy and science as to the subtleties of the more traditional literature. By the eighth century, of course, relatively few persons outside Arabia were of pure Arab descent, and by no means all the subjects of Moslem princes were themselves Moslems. On every side Hindus, Parsees, Jews, and Christians learned Arabic for the sake of commercial, social, or legal advantage, and so became able to combine lessons from a dozen scattered countries. Largely through men of this sort Abbasid culture developed the cosmopolitan richness and variety that characterized it for many generations.

Poets had flourished in Arabia long before Mohammed's time; and although he was not favorable to the profession, it continued to enjoy great honor. As the Arabs spread over the world and increasingly adopted city life, the older forms naturally became obsolete and popular demand shifted from conventional accounts of tribal warfare to matters of personal experience—that is to say, towards lyric themes. Yet the old passion for storytelling lived on; tales from every land were reworked and put into prose. This was the origin of the collection known as the *Thousand and One Nights*, which in some measure reflects the early Abbasid age. For a long time historiography continued to be a closely related form of literature; for the older writers restricted their interest to the deeds of heroic

Arabic language and literature

persons and introduced every alleged fact by enumerating a chain of nar-
rators to link the present reporter with an original eyewitness. But gradually, somewhat influenced by Persian and Jewish example, Arab historians
undertook the composition of general annals that began with the creation
of the world and presented a chronological record of subsequent happenings. The most distinguished of these annalists was al-Tabari (838-923).
Eventually, however, his fame was eclipsed by that of al-Masudi who,
towards the middle of the tenth century, wrote a comprehensive history in
thirty volumes, arranged topically and based on his own investigations
during the course of extensive travel.

Theology and juris-prudence   In both theology and jurisprudence, of course, the prime authority of
Islam is the Koran; but like other legal and religious compilations it must
be continuously applied and interpreted in order to meet the changing
needs of various societies. Having no ordained clergy, Mohammedans have
never had anything that Christians would recognize as a church. So, throughout Moslem countries, the divine revelations embodied in the Koran have
come to be supplemented by a considerable body of tradition. During the
eighth and ninth centuries many scholars devoted their lives to recording
such deeds and opinions of the Prophet as could be attested by his companions and followers. The result was the acceptance by the orthodox of
the six books called the *sunnah*. And these, in turn, served as the basis of
elaborate commentaries, justifying no less than four systems of interpretation. Some one of these systems has come to be adopted by all Moslem
peoples except those of the *shiah*—the Persians and others who have stubbornly refused to recognize the historical caliphate or any of its works, and
who hold that a rightful supplement to the Koran may be promulgated
only by some particular descendant of Ali and Fatima.

Transla-tions from the Greek   Aside from the Koran and a stock of vernacular poetry, the Arab conquerors of the seventh century brought with them hardly anything that
could be called either literary or scholarly. The rudiments of their science
and philosophy, as of their arts, had to be taken from the lands which they
invaded. There, especially in the cities of Syria and Egypt, they found great
schools with a tradition of study running back to the golden age of Athens.
Great libraries were stored with books embodying the accumulated wisdom
of a thousand years. The Arabs, it should be noted, carried out no wanton
destruction. Only a foolish story of a much later time alleges that Amr, the
ruler of Egypt, heated the Alexandrian baths by throwing precious volumes
into the furnaces. But such libraries as still existed in the occupied provinces
were filled with Greek works, which—like the writings of Hebrews, Persians, Chinese, and Hindus—remained generally closed to the inquiring
Moslem until they could be translated into Arabic.

     Although the Ommiad caliphate had witnessed significant beginnings
in this direction, it was only with the development of a cosmopolitan civ-

ilization under the Abbasids that conditions became favorable for the introduction of Hellenistic learning on a large scale. The needed intermediaries were readily found. Since the time of Justinian various groups of Christians, particularly Nestorians and Jacobites,[4] had extended their missionary efforts into central Asia, and through their agency a number of Greek works had already been put into Persian and Aramaic. Besides, there were numerous Hellenized Jews who had been led to acquire a thorough knowledge of Arabic. Thanks to the patronage of the caliphs, the work of translation was rapidly accomplished. Begun under al-Mansur, it was continued under al-Rashid and greatly developed under al-Mamun, who organized a regular school for the study of Greek science and philosophy. The leader in this activity was a Nestorian Christian named Hunayn ibn-Ishaq (d. 877), a skilled physician and a prolific writer. Hunayn and his pupils translated Galen, Hippocrates, parts of Aristotle, and many other books, including Plato's *Republic*. Ransacking the cities of Egypt and Syria for manuscripts, they formed at Bagdad one of the greatest libraries in the world. Meanwhile other translators had turned their attention to such classics as Euclid and Ptolemy. By the end of the ninth century practically the whole body of Greek writings on medicine and mathematics, together with all of Aristotle and some of the Neoplatonists, had been made available to Moslem students. And through more obscure channels they had likewise obtained very useful information from Persian, Hindu, and Chinese sources.

Having accumulated this formidable mass of learning, the scholars of Islam—unlike their Byzantine contemporaries—were by no means satisfied with perusal and admiration of the old. Instead, they carried out an original advance in thought that can best be appreciated by examining particular fields of investigation. Hunayn was famous not only as a translator but also as the author of works based on his own experience as a practicing physician. Among his books we thus find, alongside commentaries on the classics of medicine, a compendium of the subject as a whole and a remarkable essay on diseases of the eye. Al-Razi, who belonged to the next generation, similarly combined much theoretical writing with a very active participation in the medical activity of his day. He is said to have composed well over a hundred books—among them an encyclopædia that was to enjoy widespread use in Latin Europe and the first scientific treatise on smallpox. As director of the state hospital at Bagdad, al-Razi was intimately connected with all the medical projects of the Abbasid caliphate: the establishment of definite courses in pharmacy for men who sold drugs to the public, the extension of charitable treatment among the poorer classes by endowing a regular staff of physicians, and eventually the licensing of all persons who engaged in medical practice.

Two other scientists of the ninth century may be singled out for particu-

Ninth-century scholars [marginal note]

---

[4] See above, p. 86.

lar attention, al-Kindi and al-Khwarizmi. The former has the distinction of being called the first Arab philosopher. He was, at any rate, the first Arab to make an extensive study of Aristotle and so to become interested in the reconciliation of Greek thought with Moslem theology—a project that was to occupy his successors for many generations. Al-Kindi was a sort of universal scholar, writing not merely on logic and metaphysics but also on meteorology, optics, and music. The reputation he came to enjoy may be judged from the fact that, rightly or wrongly, 265 books are attributed to him. No such imposing list of works bears the name of al-Khwarizmi (d. c. 850). Yet he was to have momentous influence on European science; for he produced the first known exposition of our everyday arithmetic and the treatise through which the subject of algebra came to have that designation, as well as various books on trigonometry, astronomy, and geography. The connection between al-Khwarizmi and modern mathematics must be left for treatment in a later chapter; that between him and ancient mathematics should be more fully explained at this point.

Arabic mathematics

Thanks to the translations by Hunayn and his school, the Arabs became acquainted with the great work of Ptolemy, which they called *al-Majisti*—later made into *Almagest*. From it they obtained not only the theoretical science of trigonometry but also the basis for all their geographical and astronomical studies. Geometry, together with a few algebraic processes, they learned from Euclid and other Greek writers. On the contrary, the nine numerical symbols that we know as Arabic were derived from India, apparently in connection with certain Hindu works on astronomy that were translated before the end of the eighth century. In themselves, these nine symbols have no especial significance; for any series of marks, arbitrarily agreed on, will do as well. It is the zero that allows our numerals to be arranged in columns and so, under a decimal system, to represent tens, hundreds, thousands, and the like. To explain the origin of modern arithmetic, we must therefore explain the origin of the zero.

The Greeks and Romans, using letters for numerals and having no zero, had been forced, like other ancient peoples, to make their larger computations on some sort of abacus—an instrument with counters set in grooves or strung on wires. With an abacus addition and subtraction are easy, multiplication is not difficult, and division is at least possible. But the Greek or Roman, after working his problem, had to write his answer in numerals that by no means corresponded to the columns of his abacus. The Hindu, with his nine symbols, was not much better off; for how would he represent a vacant column on the abacus? Precisely who first thought of inventing a symbol to stand for such a vacant column we do not know.[5] But it was al-

---

[5] It has been recently stated that the zero appears on monuments of Indo-China dating from the seventh century. This would perhaps indicate that the Chinese were the inventors of the symbol rather than the Hindus or the Arabs.

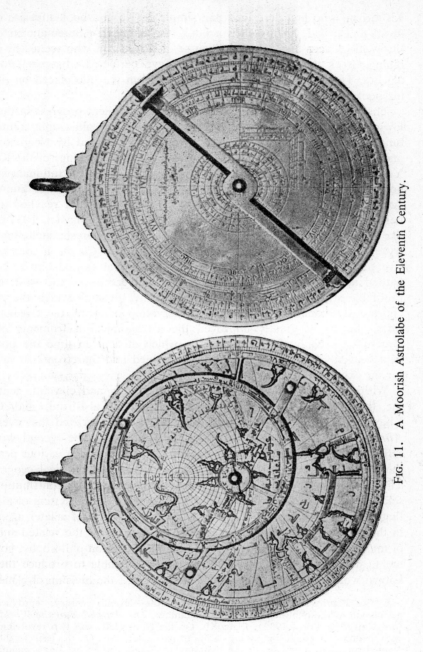

FIG. 11. A Moorish Astrolabe of the Eleventh Century.

Khwarizmi who first described that simple device in a book that has come down to us; and, having such a book, the harassed mathematician could throw his abacus away. It was likewise al-Khwarizmi who seems, by combining Greek and Hindu elements, to have perfected what we know as algebra. The name, at any rate, is derived from the title placed on one of his books.

Later development   Thus established, Arabic scholarship made excellent progress in the following centuries. Under the successors of al-Kindi philosophy remained fundamentally Aristotelian, though somewhat influenced by Neoplatonism and, in more orthodox circles, subordinated to the teachings of the Koran. Yet the Moslem schools produced many distinguished rationalists, the greatest of whom was assuredly ibn-Rushd of Cordova, better known as Averroës (d. 1198). Medicine continued to flourish and reached a new height of excellence in the work of ibn-Sina, or Avicenna (d. 1037). He, like al-Kindi, was an encyclopædic writer of broad interests, including poetry, religion, and mathematics. It was, however, his *Canon*, a comprehensive summary of medical theory and practice, that caused him to be regarded as the peer of Galen in the later universities of the west. Much profitable study was also given to astronomy, through which the Arabs enormously extended the tables of observation made by the Greeks. Besides, the Arabs greatly improved the astronomical instruments of the Greeks—especially the astrolabe,[6] by which at a given time the position of a heavenly body can be readily determined and therefrom the latitude for an explorer or a navigator.

Within the field of astronomy during the tenth and eleventh centuries the three outstanding scholars were al-Battani, al-Biruni, and Omar Khayyám. The first, by means of original research, proved that even the *Almagest* should be amended in certain particulars. The second wrote a series of books to describe the measurement of time among various peoples, the earth's rotation on its axis, and many aspects of physical geography. The third, though best loved as a poet, made noteworthy contributions to science, including an improved calendar and a developed system of algebra that to some extent anticipated the analytical geometry of a later age. And in the meantime a distinct advance had been made in the related subjects of music and optics. In addition to numerous essays on philosophy, government, and mathematics, al-Farabi (d. 950) was able to produce the first known work on the measurement of music—i.e., the division of a melodic

---

[6] See Figure 11: a Moorish astrolabe of the eleventh century, reproduced by permission of the publishers from R. T. Gunther, *The Astrolabes of the World* (Oxford University Press, 1932), Plate XL. On the front (left) are two revolving disks with pointers for establishing the location of particular stars. On the back (right) is a pivoted rule that, by means of the right-angled design, can be used as a quadrant to measure heights and depths or, by means of provided peep-holes, to find the altitude of the sun or other celestial body.

composition into equal intervals of time, or measures. The contemporary al-Haytham (Latinized as Alhazen) was another prolific author. While holding the post of chief astronomer to the Egyptian emir, he carried out experiments that disproved the Greek theories with regard to eyesight and led to a better explanation of such phenomena as light, color, reflection, magnification, and refraction. Finally we should note that, beginning with al-Razi, the physicians and other scholars of Islam continuously devoted their energies to the science of chemistry (i.e., alchemy)[7] and that, for all their misapplied efforts, they attained many results of lasting worth.

To our minds, of course, the Arabs perpetuated and further developed many absurd ideas. Their alchemists spent much time in the vain search for a medium by which to transmute metals, or for an elixir of life. Despite their original work in medicine, they held to the physiology of Galen.[8] Their astronomy was never divorced from the Ptolemaic system, according to which the earth is the center of the universe and is surrounded by the spheres of the seven planets and by that of the fixed stars. Many also accepted the ancient lore of the Persians and Egyptians concerning the influence exerted by the heavenly bodies on the destinies of men. Yet, whatever its shortcomings, the science of the Arabs was infinitely superior to that of the Latin west and in certain respects marked an advance over that of the ancient Greeks. It may be added that the casting of a horoscope then, as for centuries to come, seemed no more mysterious than the prediction of an eclipse. If the sun could affect the growth of crops and the moon could control the movement of the tides, why could not Mars govern the course of a war, or Venus that of a love affair? And before we condemn alchemy as sheer foolishness, we should remember that to the Arabs the true elements were the earth, air, fire, and water of Aristotle; and that even the elements of the modern chemist are now being transmuted.

General features of Arabic science

3. MATERIAL CIVILIZATION IN THE EAST

The subject here presented for discussion should be understood as being limited by a dominant interest in the history of western Europe. However valuable a study of eastern civilization may be for its own sake, our attention must be concentrated upon the influence of eastern civilization within the Latin world. Even as thus defined, the problem is not at all easy. Most historians have concerned themselves with the political and ecclesiastical developments reported by chroniclers and have been satisfied with the vaguest of generalizations regarding the life of ordinary people. As a consequence, we can ask a dozen questions about actual conditions in the Byzantine or the Arab Empire for every single answer that we may hope

Urban life and commerce

[7] Alchemy (Arabic *al-kimiya*) is the original word; later scholars, to distinguish themselves from the mediæval alchemists, invented the term chemistry.

[8] See above, p. 16.

to obtain. And when we suddenly discover an important novelty in Latin Europe, we often have no idea as to whether it was owed to Greek or Moslem, or as to how it was introduced. In the following pages, accordingly, we can merely glance at some of the more prominent features that distinguished eastern from western culture in the tenth century, and leave to experts the task of determining the origin of these features and their particular significance in oriental history.

It has been noted above that the effective organization of the Byzantine state depended on the continued prosperity of Constantinople and other Greek cities. It is likewise evident that the establishment of the Arab Empire was made possible by the wise economic policy of the early caliphs as well as by their military genius. The Moslem conquest by no means ruined the cities of Syria, Egypt, and Africa. Their connections with Greece and Italy, it is true, were largely destroyed; but to make up for that severance they were now brought into much closer contact with Persia and the far east. The caravan trade of central Asia naturally fell into the hands of the Arabs, who had long been expert in such business. They brought precious things from China and the Indies direct to the Syrian ports. On the north they had access to the Black Sea and, through the nomads of the steppe, dealt largely in the furs and slaves of eastern Europe. From Egypt they penetrated into Ethiopia, and from the Sahara into the gold-bearing country about the Niger. By sea their ships linked the coasts of India, Persia, Arabia, and Africa as far south as Madagascar. Much of this traffic converged on Egypt, where Alexandria and Cairo gained enormous wealth through the transhipment of exports to the west. The Mediterranean, except for the Adriatic and the Ægean, became virtually a domain of the Moslems; from the mountains of Asia Minor to those of Spain the shores of the mainland were all theirs. In the ninth century one or another of the nearby emirs secured the Balearic Islands, Sicily, Malta, and Crete. A hundred years later it was still doubtful whether Italy could be successfully defended by the Christians.

Moslem architecture

The Moslem dominions, though now divided among rival princes, were thus characterized by a commercial and industrial activity that certainly approached, and perhaps surpassed, the standard of the Græco-Roman world. An important factor in that activity was, of course, the linguistic unity of Islam, and it stimulated the interchange not only of goods but also of ideas. The result was one of the finest cultural achievements known to history. As we have seen, the Arab scholars took from both east and west certain bodies of traditional learning, which they developed in many original ways. Their splendid art was much the same kind of product. So far as architecture was concerned, the nomads of Arabia had literally nothing of their own. It was not until they had occupied Syria and Persia that they could learn the first principles of monumental construction in stone. Then, however, the caliphs were soon led to the erection of new structures for the use of their followers, and so to the creation of an architectural style that may properly be called Moslem.

The characteristic building of Islam has always been the mosque, which is essentially a place where persons may congregate at fixed hours for the divine worship prescribed by the Koran. The first mosque was that established by Mohammed at Medina—principally a courtyard which was attached to his own residence and which was partially covered by a wooden roof. Later, as the Arabs spread into the neighboring regions, they naturally came to use the existing basilicas and temples, either Roman or Persian, for the same purpose. And eventually the Ommiad caliphs, seeking to rival the Christian churches of Syria, undertook the construction of glorious

Round   Pointed   Horseshoe   Cusped   Flamboyant

FIG. 12.   Arches.

new buildings in their principal cities. The earliest of these was the Dome of the Rock at Jerusalem, which was put up by Byzantine workmen in the last decade of the seventh century. The dome itself is of timber and metal set on an octagon of masonry and all is gorgeously decorated with mosaic. A greater monument of architecture is the mosque of Damascus, erected early in the next century (see Plate II). Here, for the first time, we encounter a mosque that was designed to be not merely a place of worship but also a center of political and educational activity. Internally, it is an aisled structure occupying one portion of an ancient temple. Externally, the two stories are marked by a double arcade, and the whole is dominated by a series of minarets, slender towers from which the muezzin calls the faithful to prayer. A series of remarkable mosaics on the adjoining walls have now again been uncovered after being whitewashed by some puritanical sultan.

None of the magnificent buildings erected by the Abbasids at Bagdad survived the Mongol conquest of the thirteenth century. So our knowledge of the later Moslem architecture is largely restricted to the monuments of the emirs in Egypt, northern Africa, and Spain. Among their mosques those of Cairo and Cordova are outstanding. The latter, now transformed into a Christian church, is distinguished by no less than 1293 columns, mainly of antique origin, and by extremely rich adornment. In Spain, likewise, are to be seen the most splendid of all the palaces constructed by Moslem rulers: the Alcazar at Seville and the Alhambra at Granada, both dating from the period after 1200. Throughout the architecture of Moorish Spain and Africa, as of Moslem countries generally, the horse-shoe arch remains very prominent—especially in the bulbous cupolas that, together with the loftier minarets, give a characteristic skyline to so many of the great mosques. Sometimes, for the sake of variety, the arches are pointed or cusped (see Figure 12).

Decorative arts

The precise relationship of the various features mentioned above to earlier work in Syria and Mesopotamia need not detain us. Nor are we particularly interested in whether the Moslems derived their systems of ornamentation directly from Persia or through a Byzantine medium. Suffice it to say that in many spheres of decorative art they attained great perfection. Their sculptors and painters, it is true, continued to suffer from one serious disadvantage. An early Mohammedan tradition was held to forbid the representation of either men or animals, and the rule was strictly enforced at least in religious edifices. But by way of compensation the Moslem artists developed astonishing skill in other forms of creative work. Largely inspired by Persian models, they made charming patterns of flowers and leaves, both naturalistic and conventionalized. They turned calligraphy—such as the mere inscribing of verses from the Koran—into a truly fine art. And by combining geometric figures they produced the intricate and graceful designs that are still called arabesques. These schemes of decoration were lavishly applied to the later Moslem buildings through a variety of techniques: notably mosaic, carved stone, paneled wood, colored stucco, and glazed tile.

However splendid the craftsmanship of the Byzantine Empire, it was matched in all but religious iconography by that of Islam. Long before the Crusades the Moslems had come to lead the Mediterranean world in the production of articles that were both useful and beautiful. For example, in the manufacture of all luxurious fabrics—whether of linen, silk, wool, or cotton—they have never been surpassed. The carpets, rugs, tapestries, brocades, and embroideries of Persia and the neighboring lands remain the despair of modern artisans. The influence of the Arab textile industry upon later Europe is still attested by the derivation of damask from Damascus, muslin from Mosul, and fustian from al-Fustat, a suburb of Cairo. Cotton and satin are words imported into English from Arabic; as are scarlet, crimson, saffron, and lilac—the names of colors that were usually associated with particular stuffs from the orient. The Moslem superiority in metal-working, glass-making, the carving of crystal and ivory, the decoration of leather, and every branch of ceramics was equally pronounced. All Europe thus came to prize the tempered sword blades of Toledo, the sumptuous leather goods of Morocco, the luster ware (pottery with a metallic glaze) of Egypt, and the damascened armor of Syria (i.e., steel inlaid with gold and silver by a process perfected at Damascus).

Closely related to these artistic developments were the improved techniques which the Arabs came to employ in other fields of industry. Paper-
making, and with it the earliest forms of block-printing, they seem to have
learned from the Chinese and to have brought into the Mediterranean
world before the twelfth century. Greek fire, on the other hand, is said to
have been a Syrian invention that was kept as a military secret by the
Byzantine emperors of the seventh and following centuries. Little is really
known about it except that it was a variable compound based on
naphtha. Squirted onto water and then ignited, it proved a deadly weapon
in naval warfare. Or, in an earthenware container provided with a sort of
fuse, it could be hurled by a catapult over a castle wall and counted on
to produce dangerous conflagration. Eventually the Arabs, having somehow
discovered the secret, were able to turn the Greek fire against their Christian antagonists. And in the meantime, either from the Persians or from
the Byzantines, they had acquired an excellent knowledge of siegecraft,
including the use of such military engines as had been perfected by the
Romans. That the Ommiad caliphs built a navy and so gained control of the
southern Mediterranean has been noted in a previous chapter. For this
achievement, obviously, they depended merely on galleys and other war
vessels constructed after Byzantine models. But it was presumably the
Arabs who, by virtue of their oriental contacts, later taught the mariners
of the west two invaluable lessons. One was how to rig a ship with tri-
angular, or lateen,[9] sails and so to make possible its being tacked against
the wind. The other was how to steer a course with the help of a magnetic
compass[10]—the device that first permitted safe navigation when beyond
sight of land.

Among the other inventions which the Arabs probably brought westward were the windmill, first mentioned by al-Masudi in the tenth century,
and the spinning-wheel, said to have originated in India or China. Experts
on agriculture remind us that the Moors of Spain introduced an improved
system of irrigation for the sake of raising such new crops as rice, indigo,
sugar, oranges, and lemons. The last three of these products, it may be
remarked, bear names derived from Arabic; as do spinach, artichoke, and
various other vegetables. It is obviously to the traders of Islam that we are
indebted for the importation of such things into Europe. And it is to them,
as well as to the scientists, that we are indebted for the many Arabic works
on geography—the great authorities of the learned world until the Por-

[9] Although the word lateen is supposed to be a derivative of "Latin," neither
the Greeks nor the Romans were familiar with rigging other than square—see
above, p. 24.

[10] The earliest literary references to the compass, either in Christian or in
Moslem writings, date from the twelfth century. But the instrument was obviously
older than that, and we should naturally suppose, until proof to the contrary is forthcoming, that the invention was eastern rather than western.

tuguese explorations of the fifteenth century. In general, too, a practical consideration inspired the Arabic encyclopædias on plants, animals, stones, metals, and the like; for these books were valued not only by the scholar but also by the physician, the artisan, and even the farmer.

Conclusion   Throughout the Dark Age in the west the Byzantine Empire remained a strongly organized and highly cultured state. Its influence throughout mediæval Europe should never be ignored—especially, as we shall see, in the realm of military tactics. We have, furthermore, every reason to suppose that the Venetians owed much of their skill in shipbuilding and in all phases of maritime enterprise to their intimate association with Constantinople; and the Venetians became the instructors of the other Italians. Yet, with regard to most aspects of material civilization, as of intellectual activity, the Latins will be found to have borrowed from the Moslems rather than from the Byzantines.

CHAPTER X

The Development of Feudalism

1. BEGINNINGS OF POLITICAL RECONSTRUCTION

By the opening of the tenth century not only Charlemagne's empire but also the three kingdoms of his grandsons had practically disappeared, being resolved into such fragments as could be politically managed. In Germany the change was to some extent legalized when, on the death of the last Carolingian in 911, the magnates raised one of their own number to the vacant throne. If Conrad of Franconia, the new king, had ever thought of governing the entire kingdom, he soon abandoned the idea and recognized as his actual equals the three great dukes of Saxony, Suabia (earlier Alamania), and Bavaria (see Map X). He could, indeed, do nothing else; for the kingdom was paralyzed by the Hungarian raids and the dukes had generally risen to power through revolutionary movements inspired by local patriotism. Nor was the situation greatly modified under Conrad's successor, Henry the Fowler (919-36), whose activities as king merely continued what he had begun as duke of Saxony. It was to defend the valleys of the Elbe and Weser that he constructed his famous *burgen*— fortified camps to serve as centers of military and civil administration. And it was on the Unstrut, a tributary of the Elbe, that he won his great victory over the Hungarians in 933. Even the conquest of Lorraine, which had earlier been seized by the French king, was accomplished with little or no co-operation from the other dukes, whom Henry left to enjoy virtually sovereign powers in their own territories. How Otto, Henry's illustrious son, was led to reverse this policy, and how the reversal affected the destinies of his country, will be seen in a following chapter.

In France, meanwhile, the disintegration had been carried even further. Charles the Bald, with a view to checking the ravages of the Vikings, had established three great marches in the northern part of his kingdom:

Germany: Origin of the Saxon dynasty

177

**France:
Origin
of the
Capetian
dynasty**
Burgundy—which should not be confused with the kingdom of Burgundy, or Arles—under one of the local counts; Flanders under an adventurer called Baldwin Iron-Arm; and Neustria, the region between the Seine and Loire valleys, under a similar adventurer, Robert the Strong. And Robert's son Odo, count of Paris, was chosen king by the western magnates when Charles the Fat was deposed in 887.[1] Odo's title, however, was bitterly contested by the descendants of Charles the Bald; and it was only after a hundred years of rivalry, and the extinction of the direct Carolingian line, that the Parisian house secured undisputed claim to the throne. Hugh Capet, great-grandson of Robert the Strong (see Table II), was elected in 987 and thenceforth the ruling dynasty came to be named for him, Capetian.

**Feudal
states of
the north**
By that time northern France had been divided into the feudal states that were to dominate its history for over two centuries. The duchy of Burgundy was held by a branch of the royal family; but these Capetian dukes, obtaining neither riches nor power from their backward country, remained comparatively obscure. Flanders, on the contrary, grew into a strong principality, as the descendants of Baldwin Iron-Arm acquired additional fiefs on both sides of the French frontier, and as the revival of commerce brought increasing wealth and population to the new Flemish towns. Brittany had no such good fortune. Though generally styled one of the French duchies, it was a wild region which had scarcely formed part of the Frankish kingdom and which continued to be the scene of barbarous warfare over the ducal title. Adjoining Brittany on the Channel lay the territory conquered and largely resettled by the Vikings in the previous century—since 911 formally recognized as a fief held of the French crown by the duke of the Northmen or Normans. Since then Normandy had become an integral part of France; for the inhabitants, converted to Christianity, had quickly adapted themselves to their environment and made its customs and language their own.

**The
Capetian
domain**
What was known after 987 as the royal domain was by origin the march of Neustria, but of the splendid principality held by Hugh Capet's ancestors little was left when he finally obtained the crown (see Map X). The strong Norman duchy had shut him off from the sea by including the lower Seine valley, together with the city of Rouen. And to east and west he was now hemmed in by the lands of powerful vassals who had taken advantage of the previous rivalry to make themselves all but independent. Thus the count of Troyes, by accumulating a mass of little fiefs, had built up the great county of Champagne, while on the other side of the king's territory two ambitious viscounts had created the rival counties of Blois and Anjou. Hugh Capet, therefore, had little more than the Île de France—a narrow strip extending north to Laon and south to Orleans, with its center at

[1] See above, p. 157.

Paris. The kingdom of Charles the Bald was only a tradition, for below the Loire the king had even less authority than he had above it.

The south of France, indeed, was a country entirely foreign to the north—one having its own language, Provençal, and enjoying its own customs, which in many respects were Roman rather than Germanic. The great barons of the north regularly attended the royal court and provided whatever slight service they owed in addition. But the princes of the south recognized the Capetian solely by dating their acts according to the year of his reign. Foremost among these southern states was the duchy of Aquitaine, which from the tenth century on was held by the counts of Poitiers. Earlier a Carolingian sub-kingdom, it reached from the Loire to the Garonne and from the Bay of Biscay to the Rhone, and because of its very size was not always thoroughly controlled by the duke. Between the Garonne and the Pyrenees the Gascons were governed by their own duke until, in the later eleventh century, Gascony was absorbed into Aquitaine. Finally, on the Mediterranean, lay the two important principalities held by the counts of Toulouse and Barcelona, respectively the old Septimania and the old Spanish March.

Feudal states of the south

As remarked above, the British Isles were still devoid of political unity when the Viking inroads began. Ireland was the scene of chronic warfare among its rival clans, and similar conditions prevailed throughout the west and north of Britain, where Welsh, Scots, and Picts had long been fighting one another as well as the Germanic invaders from the east. Although the kings of Northumbria, Mercia, and Wessex had in turn gained a vague lordship over their neighbors, there had been no real consolidation of the Anglo-Saxon states. Under such conditions the Danes, as all Vikings were called in Britain, found it comparatively simple to conquer the little kingdoms of the eastern coast. When, in 871, Alfred came to the throne of Wessex, it seemed very doubtful whether his heritage could be saved from a like fate. But Alfred proved to be a man of remarkable ability and determination. Adopting the Danes' own tactics, he organized a system of defense based on a continuous series of fortified camps or boroughs,[2] and at the same time he built a fleet to co-operate with a mobile army in the field. After many reverses he won a decisive victory. The Danish king of East Anglia signed peace, accepting Christianity for himself and his followers and recognizing as Alfred's all lands to the southwest of a line drawn between Chester and the mouth of the Thames (see Map IX). The West Saxon kingdom was thus enlarged in two directions: on the south it had incorporated such older states as Kent and Sussex, and on the north about half of Mercia.

Formation of the kingdom of England

During the early tenth century Alfred's successors, Edward and Æthelstan, carried out a triumphant offensive in the Danelaw, the lands

---

[2] Cf. the *burgen* of Saxony and Flanders, above, p. 177; below, p. 238.

ruled by a number of Danish chieftains. As the West Saxons gradually occupied this territory, they reorganized it by establishing administrative districts centered in boroughs—an arrangement that is still reflected by the map of the midland counties; for these boroughs and surrounding shires were henceforth to serve as permanent units of civil and military government. All the old English territory thus came to be united under the West Saxon dynasty, and the resulting kingdom, so much broader and stronger than the original Wessex, received the name of England. It did not, of course, include the whole of Britain. Wales and Strathclyde remained entirely independent under various Celtic princes; while to the north the Scots and Picts combined against the Danes to form the state that has since been known as Scotland.

The Danish conquest of England

Until the last quarter of the tenth century England continued to enjoy prosperity and peace. Then the accession of Æthelred, whom contemporaries called "the Redeless" because he never knew what ought to be done, brought a revival of old troubles. The kingdom, though nominally subjected to a single administration, had never been really unified. In particular the northern shires, being largely populated by descendants of Danish raiders and colonists, remained quite distinct from the rest of the country. In response to local demand, the Saxon kings found it necessary to recognize as their lieutenants a good many Danish earls; and the latter, constantly striving for greater autonomy, secured useful allies among their friends and relatives in Scandinavia. By this time the kingdoms of Denmark, Norway, and Sweden had already emerged, and within another generation all three had been Christianized. But the time-honored habits of the Vikings still persisted. Thousands of the more adventurous crossed the stormy Atlantic to Iceland, and from that new home extended their voyages to the shores of Greenland and, about the year 1000, to those of North America. Other thousands, meanwhile, had continued to live as freebooters, preying on commerce and ravaging defenseless coasts—such as those of England.

The incompetent Æthelred, by levying taxes in order to pay blackmail to the marauders, finally encouraged the Danish king Sweyn (Svein) to invade England with a larger force. And this adventure led to his conquest of the kingdom; for Æthelred, after a feeble resistance, took refuge with his father-in-law, the duke of Normandy. How the Normans thus came to be interested in English affairs, and with momentous consequences for all Europe, will be seen when we have examined the contemporary development of feudalism on the continent.

2. FEUDAL INSTITUTIONS

To introduce the present discussion it should be remarked that only one peculiar combination of customs can properly be described as feudal—

the one developed in the older parts of the Frankish kingdom and thence
spread far and wide throughout mediæval Europe. Whether the customs
of other peoples in other ages may be called feudal by analogy is a somewhat dubious matter which may here be passed over. We are concerned
merely with the original feudalism. That term, of course, implies some
kind of system built upon fiefs (*feuda*); but the latter, as already noted in
a foregoing chapter, presupposed the personal relationship known as
vassalage. There could always be vassals who, like the "companions"
depicted by Tacitus, had not been endowed with fiefs; there could never
be a fief without a vassal to hold it. The truth of this statement will become
apparent as we more closely examine particular feudal institutions.

Of prime importance was the Frankish ceremony of homage, which can
certainly be traced back to early Carolingian times and was probably older.
Through Christian influence it had come to be associated with an oath
of fealty, sworn on the Gospels or on holy relics. Such an oath, however,
was often prescribed for all subjects of a ruler and did not in itself create
the bond of vassalage. To become a vassal a man had to perform homage.
Coming before A, the prospective lord, B knelt, placed his two hands
between those of A, and acknowledged himself A's man (French *homme*).
A then raised B to his feet and kissed him, thereby accepting his homage
and recognizing him as vassal. Thenceforth the pair were supposed to be
bound by a permanent tie of mutual loyalty and support—a relationship
portrayed by the feudal epics as to the highest degree sacred and honorable.[3] In real life, unfortunately, the relationship was not so ideal. Lords
and vassals often quarreled over their respective rights, exchanged de-
fiances, and engaged in bitter warfare. As will be seen from the study of
actual cases, the effectiveness of vassalage depended on a number of
variable factors, notably the character and political ambitions of the persons
concerned.

In this connection it must always be remembered that vassalage and
lordship are relative terms. Since all vassals might themselves be the lords
of other men, neither term designated an exclusive group. To be a vassal
was by no means disgraceful. On the contrary, vassalage was the equivalent
of gentility; for by ancient tradition the vassal was a member of the warrior class. Besides, by the eleventh century, it had become exceptional for
vassals to live in their lord's household; instead they had normally received
lands on which to set up their own domestic establishments and in return
for which they had agreed to give special services. As a fief-holder, the
vassal possessed, not merely a certain acreage, but organized estates that
included peasant cultivators free and unfree. And over the local population
he exercised political as well as economic control, assessing a variety of
public dues and charges, raising fortifications, and administering justice.

[3] See below, pp. 213-16.

In other words, the vassal belonged to the agrarian aristocracy, the governing class in the feudal state.

In many cases the privilege thus enjoyed by a feudal lord could be justified by a grant of immunity or other delegation of authority by the king. Frequently, however, the lord's title rested on nothing more than sheer usurpation; for the later Carolingian age was one in which men followed[4]

> The good old rule, . . . the simple plan,
> That they should take who have the power
> And they should keep who can.

By the end of the tenth century, as we have seen, the French king had lost all effective control over his realm as a whole. His principal officials— usually styled dukes, marquises, or counts—had come to hold what amounted to hereditary sub-kingdoms. And often enough their authority was contested by a number of their own vassals, both ecclesiastic and lay. To make hard and fast generalizations about such arrangements is impossible; they were the result, not of systematic planning, but of circumstance. Each territory had its own custom, which must be individually studied to be understood.

Inheritance of fiefs

Yet, despite all local variation, the common political character of fiefs gave rise to certain common principles. One was primogeniture. Land could be easily divided. An office could not be, and the fief was a sort of office even when it was not styled a dukedom, a marquisate, or the like. The furnishing of troops was itself a state service, the value of which depended on a personal responsibility. So feudal law, unlike Roman and Germanic law, came to require that a fief should pass in its entirety to the eldest son. This principle involves what is commonly known as the inheritance of fiefs, also an established custom by the end of the tenth century. What was actually inherited, however, was the right to obtain the fief on certain conditions. Vassalage was not hereditary. The son had no legal title to his father's fief until he had performed homage for it, and he was not permitted to do that until he had reached man's estate. A girl, since she was no warrior, could be neither a vassal nor a fief-holder. It was only in default of male heirs, and after she had been married to a proper vassal, that a daughter could legally inherit a fief. Meanwhile it remained in the lord's hands and technically ceased to be a fief at all.

Feudal tenures

Wherever fief-holding had not degenerated into a mere fiction, it was held to imply a contract between the two parties. Along with his fief the vassal received from his lord a guarantee of protection and justice; in return he owed the lord various forms of service and assistance. Very commonly the fief bore a specific obligation for mounted soldiers, or

[4] Wordsworth, *Rob Roy's Grave.*

knights[5]—in which case the vassal was said to hold by knight service. Occasionally he was bound to furnish arms or other objects of value, or to perform some duty at court; such tenures are usually classified as serjeanty. By a sort of legal fiction, a church might obtain a fief to be held by free alms—to owe no service except prayer for the donor's soul or the souls of his ancestors. But this tenure was not always enjoyed by ecclesiastics. Most bishops and abbots held at least part of their lands by knight service and—through a special compromise that exempted them from personal service—supplied their quotas by granting fiefs to vassals. In any case, the obligation resting on the fief was not supposed to be indefinite. Service, as a rule, could be demanded no more than once a year and, when troops were provided, only for a fixed term—in northern France forty days.

Whatever the nature of his tenure, the vassal regularly owed suite to the lord's court; that is to say, he had to attend the lord whenever summoned. At irregular intervals great assemblies would be held for ceremonial purposes, and on these occasions the lord would submit to his men for their approval projects of general interest to his territory. Such times would also be appropriate for celebrating a son's knighthood or a daughter's marriage. Often, however, the court would be held for the sake of administering justice, in which connection the vassal, if not appearing as defendant or plaintiff, would be called as a judge. For the feudal court, though presided over by the lord, was legally the body of suitors themselves, who rendered decisions according to recognized custom. The vassal, therefore, claimed the right to judgment by his peers, his social equals. Even when he came to trial, he kept his gentleman's weapons, appealing to a decision by judicial combat. The two parties, after God had been solemnly invoked to defend the right, fought it out and the victor was held to be justified in his contention. *Suite to court*

The vassal, furthermore, owed hospitality to his lord. This was a very expensive obligation when the latter came with a large retinue and made a protracted stay; so the exaction of entertainment was frequently limited by written charter or commuted into a money payment. Besides, if the lord incurred some extraordinary expense, the vassal was usually liable for a contribution called aid. The occasions varied from region to region; in northern France an aid was commonly due when the lord knighted a son, celebrated the wedding of a daughter, or was captured and held to ransom. In case the lord was a clergyman, the installation of a successor or the necessity of a trip to Rome provided a good excuse for seeking pecuniary assistance. The general rule always held good, however, that the vassal was not subject to arbitrary taxation; if subsidies were wanted for purposes other than those recognized by custom, or if service was needed in addition *Hospitality and aid*

[5] See the following discussion of chivalry.

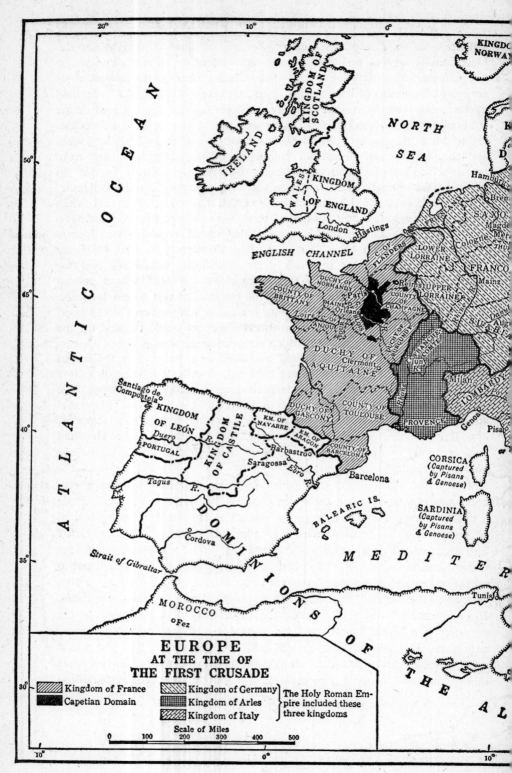

ATLANTIC OCEAN

NORTH SEA

ENGLISH CHANNEL

MEDITER

THE

AL

KINGDOM OF NORWAY

KINGDOM OF SCOTLAND

IRELAND

WALES

KINGDOM OF ENGLAND

London Hastings

FRIESLAND

SAXO
Magde
Mer
Cologne
THU

FRANCO

Hamburg
Bren

C. OF FLANDERS

LOWER LORRAINE

UPPER LORRAINE

DUCHY OF NORMANDY

COUNTY OF BRITTANY

MAINE

Paris

Orleans

COUNTY OF CHAMPAGNE

Mainz

Loire

ANJOU

Loire

DUCHY OF BURGUNDY

SWABIA

Dan
Aug

R.

DUCHY OF AQUITAINE

Clermont

FRANCE K.

Cluny

Milan

LOMBARDY

Santiago de Compostela

KINGDOM OF LEÓN

Duero

PORTUGAL

R.

KINGDOM OF CASTILE

DUCHY OF GASCONY

KM. OF NAVARRE

KM. OF ARAGON

Barbastro

COUNTY OF TOULOUSE

PROVENCE

Genoa

Pisa

Saragossa

Ebro R.

COUNTY OF BARCELONA

Barcelona

CORSICA
(Captured by Pisans & Genoese)

Tagus R.

DOMINIONS

BALEARIC IS.

SARDINIA
(Captured by Pisans & Genoese)

Córdova

Strait of Gibraltar

OF

MOROCCO

Fez

Tunis

THE

EUROPE
AT THE TIME OF
THE FIRST CRUSADE

Kingdom of France
Capetian Domain
Kingdom of Germany
Kingdom of Arles
Kingdom of Italy

The Holy Roman Empire included these three kingdoms

Scale of Miles

0   100   200   300   400   500

MAP X

to what was definitely owed, the lord had to ask his men for a voluntary grant.

Feudal incidents

More profitable than the aids were those perquisites of the lord that we know as feudal incidents. Relief was a sum paid by an heir on securing possession of a fief. Wardship was exercised by a lord over an heir who was under age, and it included the right to the income from the fief during such minority. Marriage, in the technical sense, was the lord's power of approving the husband chosen by the heiress to a fief—a privilege that commonly led to the selection of the highest bidder in a sort of private auction. Escheat was the return of a fief to the lord's possession when a vassal died without heirs. Forfeiture was the penalty for felony—the confiscation of the fief should a vassal refuse to perform his owed service. But the penalty was easier to declare than to enforce. A rebellious vassal could always justify his action by alleging default on the part of the lord, and the issue would be left for determination by force of arms. Finally it should be noted that, since none of the ordinary incidents could be expected from ecclesiastical fiefs, the lord by way of compensation generally took over the lands of a dead prelate and treated them as his own until a successor was installed.

Subin-feudation

The services and incidental revenues just enumerated were received by any feudal lord from lands granted as fiefs to vassals. What remained in his own possession was called his demesne (less technically, domain), and from it he received the manorial income that will be described in the following chapter. Each vassal could in turn give fiefs to vassals of his own and so provide for part of the service required by the lord. But, to support himself and his family, he would have to keep at least some of his lands in demesne. The profit in fief-holding, we may say, arose only from the surplus of demesne income over and above the cost of the owed service. From these facts it should be apparent that a particular village could be included within any number of fiefs, being held of one another by any number of vassals. Eventually, however, it would be directly managed as demesne of some landlord. Below the feudal hierarchy and supporting it by their labor were always the peasants.

Chivalry

The gulf between the two classes was hard to cross. A man of low birth, though not actually unfree, could rarely become a fief-holder. Through the service of a prince—by acting as administrative agents of some sort— even serfs occasionally gained wealth and power; yet in the eyes of the gentry they never lost their base blood, and it was long before the origin of their families could be forgotten. And to keep the peasant youth from the military class, there was not merely the handicap of social prejudice but also the professional training required by the code of chivalry. This term (derived from the French *chevalier*, horseman) refers to the set of customs that were generally held to regulate knighthood. During the early feudal age the boy of noble birth, unless destined for a clerical career, was not expected to have an education in letters. Since his profession was to be that of a warrior, his training was essentially military. While still a child, he began his lessons in riding and in the use of weapons. His graduation from this rude school was the attainment of knightly rank, but first he had to pass through two preliminary grades. Commonly he would serve in some feudal court as a *valet* (i.e., a little vassal) or *damoiseau* (little lord), while learning how to conduct himself in polite society and continuing his martial exercises. Later, in his early teens, the youth would rise to be a knight's assistant or squire (French *écuyer*, shield-bearer). Eventually he would be allowed to ride to battle with his elders and, after proving his fitness, would be knighted—usually by the lord at whose court he had been brought up, though the honor could be conferred by any knight. In the final ceremony of *adoubement*, when the candidate was formally invested with the arms and armor of a mature man, we may clearly see the perpetuation of an ancient custom described by Tacitus.[6]

Fig. 13. Duke William Knights Earl Harold. (From Bayeux Tapestry.)

Primitive chivalry was therefore non-Christian, and originally it had no feminine implications. It was simply the standard of conduct adopted by members of the warrior class to govern their relations with one another. The knight should be brave to the point of foolhardiness. He should fight according to certain accepted rules, scorning tricks and strategy as savoring of cowardice. He should be loyal to his friends. He should keep his plighted word. He should treat a conquered foe with gallantry. Yet, although the gentleman was chivalrous towards social equals and their womenfolk, he felt no such obligation towards the baseborn. In this respect, as in all, his attitude was intensely aristocratic. The fact that in contemporary records *miles* (Latin for soldier) always refers to the mounted warrior, the *chevalier*, summarizes a whole chapter in the military history of Europe. But why were the Franks left to develop what we know as feudal cavalry and so to revolutionize warfare throughout the western states?

[6] See above p. 48; and for *adoubement,* Figure 13. This drawing, like Figures 15 and 16, is reproduced from C. Stephenson's *Mediæval Feudalism* by permission of the Cornell University Press.

Originally the Franks, like the Anglo-Saxons as late as 1066,[7] had merely ridden to the battlefield, where they dismounted and fought on foot; their horses were too small for any other use. The development of the feudal army was presumably made possible by the introduction of the thoroughbred charger or *destrier*,[8] whose size and strength permitted the heavy-armed warrior to fight on horseback. The subject remains very obscure through lack of investigation. Yet, since neither the Romans, the Gauls, the Germans, the Moors, nor the later invaders of western Europe had other than light cavalry, it seems necessary to conclude that the knightly array of the Carolingians was somehow derived from the *cataphracti* of the Byzantine Empire.[9] In whatever fashion the great war-horse may have been brought to Gaul, the importation was of prime significance. According to an English doom of the tenth century, a horse was already worth as much as four oxen; but the Carolingian sources prove that, as early as the first half of the eighth century, the equipment of a Frankish warrior—including horse, shirt of mail, leggings, helmet, shield, lance, sword, and sheath—was valued at over twenty-two oxen. The aristocratic basis of chivalry is thus no mystery. The average peasant, whose movable wealth fell far short of a plow-team,[10] could no more hope to be a knight than to wear the papal tiara.

These facts help us to understand the character of feudal warfare. The obligation for knight service was heavy; one knight would include not merely the warrior himself but also a supply of expensive arms and armor, a change of horses, perhaps a squire and his mount, a number of grooms or other servants, and finally enough food to maintain all these men and animals for the specified period. Through feudal tenure the ruler of a mediæval state obtained a whole army with a minimum outlay of cash, but even among the knights who led the attack discipline was slight. Each gentleman considered himself the ally rather than the subordinate of the commander. Fighting for the lord did not at all prevent a vassal's fighting for himself; except through the acquisition of booty and captives, he stood to make nothing from the campaign. Pitched battles were infrequent; when one occurred, it resolved itself into a series of individual affrays—of charges and countercharges with lances atilt, followed by hand-to-hand combat with sword and axe. There would be a magnificent display of knightly prowess, and little generalship. Although one side might gain much in honor and plunder and prisoners, the opposing force would largely escape, to fight again on some more fortunate day.

[7] See below, p. 194.

[8] Latin *dextrarius*; so called, it is said, because the right hand was used to lead the horse.

[9] See above, p. 82.

[10] See below, p. 200.

Feudal warfare, as a matter of fact, was normally restricted to skirmish- **The**
ing between roving bands and to devastating the enemy's territory. During **feudal**
most of the time the efforts of the combatants would be concentrated in **castle**
and about castles. In the ninth century the castle, or *burg*, had been primarily a center of refuge from the invading Northmen; now, at least in
France, it had become a specialized form of stronghold adapted to the
needs of a feudal chieftain and his garrison of professional warriors. This

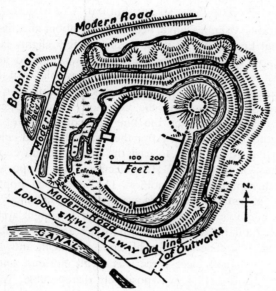

Fig. 14. Plan of a Motte-and-Bailey Castle:
Berkhampstead. The motte is the circular elevation at the upper right, the bailey the larger enclosure in the center. Both, it will be noted, were
protected by a double system of moats. (Taken
from E. S. Armitage, *Early Norman Castles of the
British Isles,* John Murray, London, 1912, Fig. 9.)

form, after its two essential parts, is called the motte-and-bailey castle
(see Figure 14). The bailey was a courtyard surrounded by a moat, an
earthen embankment, and a palisade of tree-trunks—or a series of such
fortifications. Friends gained admittance by means of a gate and a draw-
bridge that could be let down for their special benefit. Enclosing houses,
stables, and other necessary buildings, the bailey constituted the outer
defense of the castle. The motte was its more inaccessible portion—a hill or
an artificial mound protected by a separate line of entrenchments and
surmounted by a wooden tower called a donjon or keep.

A fortress of this primitive type, among a population that had forgotten Roman siegecraft, could offer stout resistance to attack, but was especially vulnerable to fire. In the twelfth century, therefore, castles generally came to be reconstructed in massive stonework. Such improvements, together with many other details concerning the life of the feudal nobility, will be discussed in the following chapters. For the moment we must turn to the actual application of feudalism in certain states of the eleventh century.

3. THE SPREAD OF FEUDAL CUSTOM

The early Capetians Although sizable volumes have been written about the first four Capetians, our actual knowledge of them is surprisingly slight. Hugh Capet is chiefly remarkable for the fact that a dynasty was named after him. Yet all he did was to have his son crowned during his own lifetime, thus setting a precedent that was followed by his successors for the next two centuries. Throughout that time the ceremony remained essentially the same. On the day appointed by the king the coronation of his heir took place in the cathedral of Reims. After the archbishop had celebrated mass, he formally explained his right to cast the first vote and chose the prince as his candidate for the throne. His "election" was supported in turn by each of the other prelates and nobles. The assembled populace shouted approval. And at last the new king was solemnly installed by conferring upon him the symbols of regal office, though he might not be anointed with consecrated oil till after the death of his father. In this way Hugh Capet was peacefully succeeded by his son, grandson, and great-grandson (see Table II). None of these three was at all glorious, and the third of them, Philip I (1060–1108), was positively disreputable. Who could then have predicted that the Capetian name would soon become illustrious through a great revival of the monarchy?

In the eleventh century, obviously, there was no chance of the king's enforcing his authority throughout his theoretical kingdom. His problem was rather to save what was left of his hereditary principality. Even within the Île de France there were various petty *seigneuries* over which he had little if any control. Equally troublesome were the *châtelains* who, though supposed to be mere keepers of the king's castles, generally defied their lord and lived by rapine. Other agents styled *prévôts* might be empowered to administer the king's estates, hold his local courts, and collect his revenues. But very often they had come to claim their office by hereditary title and to appropriate all or most of the royal income. The position of the early Capetians would have been desperate indeed if it had not been for the support which they received from a number of wealthy ecclesiastics. In or near the Île de France the great bishoprics and abbeys still remained subject to the royal patronage. Such bishops and abbots, being appointees and vassals of the king, furnished him with much regular entertainment, as well as with troops and supplies when he was threatened by serious insurrection. Yet, except in the matter of traditional honor, the king was no match for any one of his more powerful barons.

For example, let us take the count of Flanders who, in some fashion or another, had long since acquired regalian rights throughout his territory. Legally, these rights constituted a fief which he held of the French crown; actually, he was himself the ruler of a miniature kingdom. Within Flanders he was the supreme military commander, raising armies, requisitioning labor and materials, and building castles for its defense. In time of need he could exact the services not merely of the knights owed by his vassals but, by proclaiming the *arrière ban*, of all able-bodied men. It was the count who named the prelates of Flanders, protected their churches, and in return enjoyed a number of valuable perquisites. He coined money, regulated commerce, and levied various taxes. As guardian of the general peace, he maintained the principle that, while ordinary cases might be determined in feudal courts, his justice was paramount. To enforce his powers the count relied on subordinates called *vicomtes* or *châtelains*, each of whom had charge of an important castle together with a surrounding district. And although the *châtelains* normally held their offices by feudal tenure, the count was able to keep them, like the rest of his vassals, under effective control. {.marginnote Flanders}

Various other principalities in northern France were to some extent organized like Flanders, though it was by no means usual for them to attain the same degree of political stability. Blois and Champagne, after brief union under a strong count, again fell apart and somewhat weakened. Anjou, meanwhile, had been brought to a high stage of military efficiency by the redoubtable Fulk Nerra and Geoffrey Martel (987-1060)—the first princes who are known to have constructed castles with stone keeps. Then, however, the county came to be distracted by civil wars until, as we shall see, Geoffrey Plantagenet (1129-51) launched the Angevin dynasty upon a new and splendid career. This was the environment that assuredly had much to do with the early development of Normandy. Since the duchy had only been established in 911, and then for the benefit of a newly converted Viking, its feudal constitution must have been modeled on those of the neighboring states, especially Flanders. In the eleventh century, when we begin to obtain reliable information on the subject, the Norman duke and the Flemish count are found in possession of very much the same powers. But it will be easier to comment on the Norman system of government in connection with Duke William's conquest of England. {.marginnote Normandy and the Normans}

If at this time we look for a sharp distinction between the Normans and their neighbors, we fail to find it. By the eleventh century the culture and institutions of Normandy were thoroughly French. Scandinavian traits have been detected in the icy hardness of the Norman and in his passion for combat under distant skies. Yet the Norman temper was hardly different from that of the feudal nobility in general; and it should be remembered that the more famous Norman armies were largely recruited from Flanders, Picardy, Anjou, Brittany, and other adjacent regions. The Normans were merely the greatest of many great adventurers produced by eleventh-century France. In every warlike expedition of the French the Normans were always prominent; and wherever they went they displayed an uncanny faculty for seizing political opportunity and turning it, often by unscrupulous means, to their own advantage. Such was to be the reputation of the Normans on the great crusade of 1095, as on many another campaign—in Italy, in Spain, and in the British Isles.

The Hauteville family in Italy

The chaotic conditions that had come to prevail in Italy by the opening of the tenth century have already been briefly noted. A hundred years later the situation remained unchanged, except that the German king now bore the imperial title and occasionally led an army across the Alps.[11] But even his pretended sovereignty did not embrace the lower peninsula. There a series of petty nobles, some of them theoretic deputies of the Byzantine emperor, engaged in a never-ending war of siege and skirmish, varied by attacks of Moslem raiders and revolutionary outbursts on the part of dissatisfied subjects. Opportunities for mercenary service and loot were therefore abundant, and among the adventurers drawn to this congenial environment were the inevitable bands of Normans—particularly a group of brothers named Hauteville. Their father, a lesser baron of Normandy, had been blessed with no less than twelve sons: five by his first wife and seven by his second. Being devoid of prospects at home, the younger boys, like hundreds of their compatriots, took to the road in search of fortune, and eventually most of them appeared in Italy.

By the middle of the eleventh century three of the brothers Hauteville—William Iron-Arm, Humphrey, and Drogo—had won great fame as warriors, and under their leadership an army of French knights had found it more profitable to fight for themselves than for others. Seizing castles in the mountains of the interior, they rapidly developed haphazard brigandage into organized conquest. William was the first elected count of these freelances; later his place was taken by his half-brother Robert Guiscard (the Sly), who by sheer native force and cleverness completed the reduction of the southern peninsula. Meanwhile the bitter conflict of the papacy and the empire had reached a crisis; and this, for reasons that will be explained below,[12] brought Guiscard the legal recognition that he might otherwise have sought in vain. In 1059, after surviving many anathemas, the ex-brigand was accepted by the pope as a vassal and formally proclaimed as duke of Apulia and Calabria. To Roger, Guiscard's brother, the pope furthermore entrusted the conquest of Sicily, which was officially blessed as a

[11] See below, pp. 218-19.
[12] See below, pp. 223-24.

holy war against the infidel. Messina was taken by the Christians in 1061, Palermo in 1072. And although the Moslems still held out in other parts of the island, it was only a matter of time until they were forced to surrender. Thus were laid the foundations of a splendid Norman state that was soon to become the marvel of the Latin world.

Another theater of constant warfare was the Spanish peninsula, where the Ommiad caliphate of Cordova, after reaching its height of splendor in the early tenth century, was now broken into a number of independent emirates. This situation naturally provided the opportunity for a Christian offensive, which might have gained headway somewhat earlier if the Christians, too, had not suffered from disunion. At the eastern end of the Pyrenees the old march of Charlemagne had become the autonomous county of Barcelona. To the west the Basque mountaineers, combating all invaders with equal enthusiasm, had successfully defended themselves against both Frank and Moslem and thus made possible the emergence of two little kingdoms, Aragon and Navarre. In the mountains of Asturias, meanwhile, other Christians had similarly maintained their independence, and so formed the nucleus of a Galician state that grew into the kingdom of León, extending south to the Douro River. And a frontier region on the east, named for the castles built to defend it, became the kingdom of Castile. In the eleventh century León and Castile, which for a while were united under one king, both extended rapidly (see Map X). Navarre, after reaching the Ebro, found the way blocked by Aragon, which in turn was barred by the emirate of Saragossa. Finally a great Christian victory at Barbastro in 1065 opened the way for the annexation of the lower Ebro valley in the next century.

These conquests could hardly have been made by the little Spanish kingdoms had they been dependent solely on their own resources. From the beginning of their offensive, however, they had drawn an endless supply of recruits from the French principalities to the north. In the eleventh century the illustrious monastery of Cluny,[13] and later the papacy, gave active support to the holy cause of fighting the Moslem, issuing widespread appeals for enlistment and holding forth the promise of great spiritual benefits to any who should die on so sacred an undertaking. As would be expected, a host of volunteers came from the nearby lands of Gascony, Toulouse, and Aquitaine; but men of the northern baronies also crossed the Pyrenees in large numbers. And many of these adventurers won fine Spanish fiefs at the expense of the infidel. Eventually the royal house of Portugal was to trace its descent from a Burgundian knight who secured a border county along with the hand of a León princess.

Meanwhile, as the result of his father's conquest, Canute (Knut) of Denmark had acquired the crown of England on the death of Æthelred in 1016.

The
Spanish
kingdoms
and the
French
in Spain

---

[13] See below, p. 222.

England under Canute

His reign proved that, instead of a pirate, the English had a pious and statesmanlike king. Later conquests extended his dominion over Norway, part of Sweden, and the Viking settlements on the southern shore of the Baltic. Yet from the outset Canute's main concern was England. Anticipating the danger of Norman intervention, he shrewdly offered marriage to Æthelred's widow, Emma of Normandy; so that lady left her son Edward on the continent and returned to England as queen for the second time. To avoid trouble with the Scottish king, Canute ceded to him the territory of Lothian—all of Northumbria between the Tweed and the Firth of Forth. This treaty had two important results: it established the southeastern boundary of Scotland, to remain to our own day, and it brought the Scottish court into an English-speaking country. In England Canute honestly maintained established custom by reissuing the dooms of his Saxon predecessors. His only important innovation had to do with defense. It was apparently at this time that the Danegeld, which had first been levied by Æthelred to buy off the Danish raiders, was turned into a regular tax for the support of his house-carls, mercenary guards who fought either on land or on sea.

The Norman Conquest (1066)

If England had continued to be a Scandinavian dependency, its history would have been vastly different. But Canute's incipient empire fell apart after his death, and in 1042 the English crown was given to Edward the Confessor, son of Æthelred and Emma. Edward was therefore half Norman in blood, and since the troubled days of his infancy he had lived in Normandy. Returning to his native land, he brought with him a considerable group of Norman companions, and for a time they dominated English politics. Later it was Godwin, a Saxon nobleman, who gained the ascendancy; his daughter Edith was married to Edward and, when the latter died in 1066, her brother Harold was proclaimed king. Thereupon the Norman cause was taken up by Duke William who, declaring that Harold had sworn to support his claim to the English throne, at once prepared an expedition to cross the Channel. The final episode in this complicated story was the battle of Hastings, where William's knights broke the shield-wall of the English infantry and where Harold himself was numbered among the slain.

The Conqueror, though still under forty, was a statesman and warrior of long experience; for his father's premature death had brought him to the ducal throne at an early age. As a mere youth he had established firm control over the Norman state by crushing a baronial revolt. Since then he had engaged in successful war with the Bretons and Angevins, and had won a marriage alliance with the powerful house of Flanders. He was, we read in the *Anglo-Saxon Chronicle*, "a very wise and a great man," but "stern and wrathful"; "mild to those good men who loved God," but "severe beyond measure to those who withstood his will." Throughout England he maintained a firm peace, to the great benefit of all and especially to that of the king; for he was always "sharp-sighted to his own interest." He endowed many noble monasteries and built many strong castles. He also set apart wide forests as hunting preserves and enacted cruel laws against those who took game without license; for "he loved the tall stags as if he were their father." "The rich complained and the poor murmured, but he was so sturdy that he recked naught of them; they must will all that the king willed if they would live or keep their lands."

Such in fact was the Conqueror, as is well attested by the records of his own government. Having assumed the English crown and speedily put down local resistance, he proceeded to reorganize the kingdom after the model of his Norman duchy, that is to say, on a feudal basis. In Anglo-Saxon England the institution of personal lordship had long been familiar and lands had often been granted in return for miscellaneous services; but, for lack of heavy-armed cavalry, there had been no development of feudal tenure proper. William now proclaimed the rule that every bit of English soil was by ultimate title his—either held in his own hands or held of him as part of some fief. This, of course, did not mean that all landholders were dispossessed. The peasant cultivators generally kept what they had, as did most of the ecclesiastics whose places, until they had been vacated by death, were not taken by Frenchmen. It was only the lay aristocracy that immediately lost its estates to the victors of Hastings. For William at once rewarded each of his important followers with a fief, prescribing the service to be rendered and leaving the recipient to provide for his own retainers by subinfeudation. Indeed, all the feudal arrangements described in the preceding section were now suddenly, as the result of the Conquest, imposed on England, to govern for centuries its political and social constitution. *Introduction of feudal tenure*

Before 1066 the king's advisory council had been a loosely organized group of clergy and nobles called the *witan* (wise men). This body was henceforth supplanted by the *curia regis*, the king's feudal court, which included his barons (i.e., tenants-in-chief), or those of them whom he chose to summon. Here justice was administered and other matters were decided according to the feudal custom of Normandy. The king naturally continued to levy the Danegeld and the indirect taxes that had already been established in England; and to them he now added the feudal aids and incidents. From his vassals he also obtained a mounted army, the superiority of which had been amply demonstrated at Hastings. Each baron, when he received his fief from the Conqueror, was made liable for a certain number of knights, usually five or a multiple of that figure. The total force thus raised seems not to have exceeded 5000; if the king wanted more troops, he had to hire them. But in case of necessity he had the power, justified by both Norman and English precedent, of demanding service from all able-bodied men.

For administrative purposes the Anglo-Saxon kings had divided England into shires, and these into hundreds. Over each shire the king, or *Local government* the earl who represented him in many parts of the kingdom, named a sheriff to enforce the law in all fiscal, military, and judicial matters. In particular the sheriff presided over the shire court, an infrequent assembly of the greater landholders for the trial of exceptional cases. Routine business was attended to in the hundred court, which met every month under the presidency of the hundredman, a deputy of the sheriff. Besides, as we have seen, the country was dotted with royal strongholds called boroughs —old Roman cities and fortified camps, together with newer structures put up during the Danish wars. This entire system of shires, hundreds, and boroughs[14] was preserved by the Conqueror, but was now subordinated to a military and political organization that was essentially feudal.

In the first place, the Normans covered the land with castles of the motte-and-bailey type. Many of these castles were erected by barons as a normal means of protecting their fiefs. Others were peculiarly royal in that they were built by the king and put in charge of his officials, usually styled constables. The Anglo-Saxon earl, whom the French knew as a count, lost all governmental authority except along the frontier, where a number of such great barons were endowed with most regalian rights. The ordinary shire, henceforth also called a county, was administered by a royal sheriff, whom the French knew as a viscount. And the latter designation was an apt one, for the English sheriff now came to resemble the Norman *vicomte*. Continuing the functions of his Saxon predecessor, he also acted as constable of the king's principal castle in the shire. Moreover, he was always an important baron and his office, though not legally part of his fief, often passed to his son. Much of the law which he helped to enforce was the ancient custom of England; yet this came to be very considerably modified through the influence of feudalism and the establishment by the king of new measures for the maintenance of the peace. While, for example, compurgation and ordeal[15] remained the normal methods of trial for common people, members of the knightly class insisted on trial by combat.

Political signifi- cance of feudalism
Many historians have repeated the assertion that feudalism was virtually the equivalent of political disintegration, being incompatible with an efficient central government. The statement is misleading. It is true that the feudal age coincided with the decay of the Carolingian Empire and of the greater kingdoms that took its place; but the cause of that decay was not feudalism. Nor can feudalism be blamed for the fact that the French king was too weak to enforce his rights even in his own domain. The great lack of the early Capetians was a well-integrated principality—one that was supplied by Louis VI, whose reign will be discussed below. Feudalism, it must be admitted, worked very effectively in many small states of that time.

From what has been seen about feudal institutions above, it should be

[14] On the later English boroughs see below, Chapter XIII.
[15] See above, pp. 57-58.

remembered that fief-holding presupposed vassalage and that vassalage was always a personal relationship. If the vassal failed to receive adequate support from his lord, he was justified in renouncing his faith (defiance) and in doing what he could to maintain his position. Under such conditions, as dictated by experience in the tenth and eleventh centuries, he had to be relatively close to his lord. Effective states, therefore, had to be small. The rulers of those states—e.g., Flanders, Anjou, Normandy, and England after 1066—found the system of feudal tenures the best means of governing their territories; for in that way alone could they provide for their administrative, judicial, and military needs. And their governments, as will be explained later, were to establish a foundation for all the great constitutional developments of western Europe.

CHAPTER XI

Agrarian and Military Society

1. THE MANORIAL SYSTEM

The Manor   The political significance of feudalism has been discussed in the preceding chapter. Here we are concerned with its economic significance, or —to be more precise—with the economic conditions it presupposed. For feudalism proper was not a stage in economic evolution; rather it was a peculiar form of military organization developed by the Carolingian rulers. Since the basis of the state was then agrarian society, fiefs normally consisted of the rural properties which we call manors. Yet it is important to remember that, at the opening of the eleventh century, the manorial system was practically universal throughout western Europe, while feudalism was not. A manor remained exactly the same, whether or not it was held by a vassal in return for feudal service.

The manor[1] may be defined as an agricultural estate possessed by a lord —an entire village, part of one, or a group of scattered homesteads. In other words, without regard to local peculiarities of agrarian practice, the manor was a unit of seignorial exploitation. It thus resembled the villa of the later Roman Empire. But the authority of the mediæval lord, thanks to the lavish dispersal of royal privilege, had generally come to be political as well as economic. Through long usage, rights that we should distinguish as public and private had been inextricably confused, and it made no difference to the men of that age whether particular institutions were five hundred or only two hundred years old. The manorial system flourished on all sides because under it, and under it alone, the mass of the people found the possibility of livelihood. The lord owed his dominant position not so much to his own rapacious greed as to the defenseless condition of the

[1] The Norman Conquest brought the word to England: Old French *manoir*, from the Latin *manere*, to dwell.

countryside and the vital needs of the inhabitants. Manorial organization was a simple administrative machine that ran on and on with a minimum of supervision; yet that minimum was essential and only a lord, we may well imagine, could supply it.

Although many scholars have believed that the manor somehow grew out of a free village community, in which the inhabitants worked only for themselves, positive evidence to warrant such a conclusion has never been forthcoming. It is true that the manor often appears as a village community, whose members had approximately equal holdings and performed approximately equal services. But did this equality result from the democratic arrangements of a primitive age or from seignorial control? We may only be sure that the latter definitely appears in our earliest sources. For instance, let us examine a typical entry in a famous survey drawn up for the abbot of Saint-Germain in the early ninth century. At A, one of the abbot's villas, he is said to have a demesne manse,[2] including a house and the usual out-buildings. There is so much arable land, which can be sown with so many measures of grain; so much vineyard, from which so many measures of wine are obtained; so much meadow, on which so much hay can be cut; and so much woodland, in which so many swine can be fed. Besides he has a church with the customary appurtenances. X, a *colonus* of Saint-Germain, and his wife, having so many children, hold a manse that contains so much arable, so much vineyard, and so much meadow. He pays such-and-such rents in kind. And he owes so much week-work, together with additional carrying service and manual labor as may be demanded. Then follow reports on the heads of other peasant families—*coloni, lidi* (freedmen), *servi* (serfs), or *ingenuiles* (wholly free)—and each, in spite of minor variation, is said to bear the same obligations.

In this manorial record, as in countless others, the striking feature is the rough equalization of the agrarian units held by the tenants on the estate. Whether technically free or servile, every peasant household was expected to live according to a fixed routine, sharing the common responsibilities of the village and so receiving a due allotment of land. Under such conditions it did not matter how many persons really occupied a particular manse or which of them performed the service that was owed from it. The important consideration was that the routine had to be maintained; otherwise all would suffer, the villagers as well as the lord. For it was only through certain forms of co-operation that men could subsist. Although lack of early sources prevents our knowing exactly when and how the manorial system originated, we can hardly doubt that it was the product of political and economic necessity.

The chief purpose of the manor was of course agriculture, concerning

The manorial community

---

[2] I.e., an agrarian property held in his own hands; see immediately below, and above, p. 144.

Agri-
culture

which absolute generalization is impossible. Customs varied according to the climate, the soil, and the aptitudes of the people. Statements applicable to a fertile plain will not hold good for a mountainous region or a country of marsh and dune. No one method of tillage could be successful in vineyards, orchards, and corn-fields. Throughout western Europe, however, the staple crop was wheat, for the raising of which plowing is essential. In Italy, southern France, and other regions where the soil was relatively light, the Roman plow[3] was generally retained. But for tilling the grasslands of Germany, northern France, and most of Britain men preferred the wheeled plow. The available draft animals, because of poor breeding and undernourishment, were at best puny. So we hear that, for the heavier plow, the standard team consisted of eight oxen—though all eight might not actually be used at the same time. Such a plow and such a team the average peasant did not possess. And although the lord might be well supplied with tools and animals, he had neither gangs of slaves to work the land nor adequate cash for hiring labor. He had to depend on the service of rustic tenants, who in turn depended on him for protection.

The open-
field
system

Manorial organization in western Europe thus seems to have been dictated by the necessities of life; yet it would be wrong to suppose that such organization held to an invariable pattern. Different geographical conditions naturally led to different agricultural practices, as has been noted in connection with plowing. The subject is too complicated to be discussed here in any detail. We need only remark two major results. In what may be called Type I of manorial organization, the agrarian settlement was made up of isolated homesteads, each possessed by a peasant family that cultivated separate fields and paid customary rents to the lord of the manor, rather than laboring on lands retained for his particular benefit. In Type II, the classic manor of historical textbooks, we find a more intricate plan. Here, especially, the use of the wheeled plow made it advantageous for peasants to cultivate the fields strip by strip and to co-operate in so doing. Accordingly they lived in compact villages and pooled their resources. Each household contributed its share to a common fund by providing a certain amount of labor together with certain tools, animals, or materials; and it followed that each should have an equal share of the produce. If any member of the community had all his land in one place, the quality of his harvest would vary with the fertility of his individual holding. So it was usual to equalize the allotments by scattering them over all sections of the arable. And since the portions were not fenced, the arrangement is known as the open-field system. The open field was divided into what the English called shots, subdivided into acre strips.[4] Each of the latter was terminated

---

[3] See Plate XII (Plowing) and above, p. 22.
[4] Such an agrarian plan is illustrated by countless maps of mediæval villages and can still be detected, thanks especially to aerial photography. See Plate XIV (East

by headlands, on which the team could be brought about. The length of such a strip was a furlong (i.e., furrow-long), its width four rods or perches (i.e., long sticks for urging the oxen); and these measures remain in common use throughout English-speaking countries.[5]

It will be noted that the basis of the open-field system was co-operation, not communism. Although the crop on a whole field would be sown, cultivated, and harvested by the villagers working together, in the end each received only what was raised on his own acres. Even the so-called rights of common were units of property attached to the individual holdings. The member of the community was entitled to pasture a certain number of beasts on whatever fields were not at the moment bearing crops and on whatever waste the manor included. He might also have a share of meadow, which was carefully set aside as the only source of hay; for neither grass crops nor vegetables were grown on the arable. In the adjoining woods he could gather a limited quantity of brush, twigs, and fallen timber, whether for fuel or for building purposes. And, usually on payment of a fee, he could put his pigs there, to feed on roots and mast. In addition, of course, the peasant had a house of his own, together with a small plot of land surrounding it. Here he could have a vegetable garden, keep a few geese or chickens, and set up a hive of bees. Such as they were, his animals, his cart, and his other chattels belonged to him personally. And there is no reason to suppose that the mediæval peasant was any worse off than his Roman predecessor. We find, indeed, considerable evidence to the contrary.

As already remarked, the Romans had been well aware of the fact that land is quickly exhausted by the continuous planting of grain. They had also known that such exhaustion could be prevented by the application of various fertilizers, or by growing and plowing under certain crops. But to more scientific methods ordinary Roman practice had preferred the two-field system of cultivation, under which one half of the land was planted while the other half lay fallow. During the Middle Ages this same plan remained in use throughout southern Europe as well as various regions to the north, especially those which were relatively barren. In all the richer plains of Gaul, Britain, and Germany, however, men early came to adopt the three-field system. Under it a third of the land rested every year; of the remainder half was planted in the autumn and half in the spring—a

Two- and three-field cultivation

Newton), here presented by permission of the British Air Ministry. Note how the ancient furrows run through fences erected as the result of modern enclosure, and without regard to the shocks of harvested grain shown as dots in the photograph. Also note how, from the east, the sea continues to encroach upon the old village.

[5] According to the standard of today, 1 rod = 5½ yards; 40 rods = 1 furlong; 4 rods × 1 furlong = 1 acre (4840 square yards). But in the Middle Ages there was no standardization of these measures. The acre was merely a piece of land that, according to tradition, could be plowed by one team in one day. And our yard, it should be added, is the cloth yard of later mediæval commerce.

procedure that can succeed only where summers are comparatively cool and moist. This improved system of cultivation, together with the use of the wheeled plow, largely explains the prosperity of northwestern Europe during the agrarian age. Among other mediæval contributions to agricultural technique—the date of which often remains problematical—may be mentioned the more general employment of the toothed harrow, the invention of the flail and the wheelbarrow, and the introduction of a horse-collar that made possible the gradual substitution of that animal for the ox in plowing.

The lord and his peasants

A traveler through the country in the feudal age would have no difficulty in perceiving the subjection of the agricultural village to seignorial control, for the settlement would be dominated by the manor house. Sometimes it might be used by the lord as a dwelling; more usually it merely served as administrative headquarters under the charge of a resident steward or reeve. Surrounding it, in any case, was the lord's close, containing gardens, fruit trees, beehives, barns, stables, and other outbuildings. Here was stored the produce from the estate, together with the usual wagons and agricultural implements. The lord generally had his own meadow; but his arable, very often, consisted of acre-strips scattered among those of his tenants. And like them he would pasture his beasts on the common. All labor required to maintain the lord's particular property—known as the manorial demesne or inland—was left to be done by the peasants. They cultivated the lord's arable along with their own, harvested the crops, threshed out the grain, and disposed of it according to instructions. To see that all rightful obligations were performed, so that the estate would show the normal profit, was the responsibility of the steward, assisted by subordinates chosen from among the peasants. The steward also held the manorial court for the settlement of disputes, the trial of persons accused of petty offenses, and the general enforcement of the lord's authority. In all such matters law was held to be, not the will of the lord or of his steward, but the custom of the manor as stated by the best men of the locality.

The fact that the entire feudal class was supported, directly or indirectly, by the peasants should not be taken to imply that in general the latter were cruelly treated. During wartime, of course, the people of the countryside were the first to suffer from the enemy's attack, and there were always barons who acted like brigands towards the defenseless tenants of others. But a lord would naturally be considerate of his own men, for without them his lands would be worthless. The peasant's life, however bad it may seem in comparison with modern conditions, was reasonably secure. Under the lord's protection he was assured at least of subsistence; even serfdom was infinitely better than the constant fear of death by violence or starvation. And many, perhaps most, peasants were not of servile status. Except in England after the Norman Conquest, serfdom and villeinage were not exactly synonymous. The serf was by origin the Roman *servus,* the bodily property of a master. The villein (*villanus*), on the contrary, was simply the ordinary villager who, no matter what his obligations were, legally remained like the Roman *colonus* a freeman. Actually all lived under much the same régime. The serf could not be sold apart from the estate to which he belonged, and either law or economic necessity made the free peasant also a mere appurtenance to the soil he cultivated.

The obligations of a peasant community cannot, therefore, be rigorously classified according to the status of the persons liable. About all that can be affirmed is that the baser tenants were generally responsible for unrestricted service, whereas the freer tenants were not. But the only sure test of such arrangements was local custom, which was hardly the same in any two places. The variety of rents, for example, was endless. Although each peasant owed the lord definite payments, the time when they were due might be any season of the year, and the specified amounts might be anything produced on the manor. Virtually every peasant was also obliged to perform labor service, or *corvée,* for it was only through such labor that the lord's inland was taken care of. Here again, however, there was wide variation. Lowest in the scale were the men said to be *corvéable à merci,* bound to do whatever might be commanded at any time. The average villein owed rather a number of days each week, together with extra days for sowing and harvest, and a fortunate few might be free of all *corvées* except such boonworks on special occasions. While ordinary *corvées* had to do with agriculture, others were more political in character. So the burden of repairing roads, bridges, and castles naturally fell on the peasants. It was they who cut the timber, dug the moats, hauled the supplies, and made themselves generally useful on military campaigns. *Labor services*

How the peasant spent his time is accordingly no mystery; for it must be remembered that, when he was not toiling for the lord, he had his own household to support. In this enterprise he had the assistance of his wife, sons, and daughters, all of whom customarily labored in the fields. And since the service owed the lord consisted of certain units due from the peasant's land as a whole, it could be performed by any able-bodied man. We frequently hear of poor villeins who had no arable in the village, but only huts and gardens. These cotters, as they were often called, could always be obtained when extra help was needed, for it was only by doing odd jobs that they could pick up a living. Exceptional in another way were the skilled craftsmen who might be placed at specialized tasks instead of ordinary labor. One villein, for example, would maintain a smithy for the repair of iron tools and another would have charge of the local mill. And along with the smiths and the millers—whose name is yet legion—there might also be peasants who in some degree served as masons, carpenters, leather-workers, and the like. Such an artisan still lived primarily by cultivating his own lands; he followed his trade as a sort of *corvée* and paid his rent in articles of manufacture. Even the parish priest held a share of the arable, while devoting most of his time to the saving of souls.

Whether legally free or unfree, the peasant and his family constituted valuable assets within the estate. If a son entered the church, he was lost to the manor; so it was everywhere the rule that such a step could not be taken until the lord's permission had been obtained, and that might not be gratuitous. For the same reason a daughter could not be wedded outside the manor without the payment to the lord of a sum known in French as *formariage*, in English as merchet. On the peasant's death his land passed as a matter of course to his children, but the lord generally claimed the chattels or the best beast as a token payment styled heriot or *mainmorte*. Occasionally we also find villeins contributing a yearly head tax (*chevage*) in recognition of their personal subordination. And the whole rural community was usually liable for tallage or *taille*—a more or less informal contribution that was taken sometimes annually, sometimes only when there was special need. In this way, if in no other, the villein could be prevented from accumulating undue wealth.

Within the manor the lord also enjoyed certain customary monopolies. Game and fish could be taken only by his permission, and poaching was severely punished. The villein was usually allowed to gather fallen branches in the woods, but the lord's license was required for the cutting of green timber. Sometimes the lord had his own mint, and he normally held control of local trade. This was exercised by issuing regulations known as bans, the proceeds from which were called *banalités*. He thus established official weights and measures and enforced their use in the market, levying customary tolls on articles displayed for sale. Commonly he had the only lawful wine-press, mill, and bake-oven. And for the service that the peasant was forced to accept he had to contribute a percentage of his wine, flour, or bread. In this same category may be included the lord's income from the manorial court—the fees collected from parties to suits and the fines assessed for violations of law. Justice in the feudal age was highly regarded as a source of profit, and all too often, especially when enforced over other people's tenants, was the pretext for sheer extortion.

The items enumerated in this section, when combined, will be seen to constitute the manorial income that the baron received from his demesne. His feudal income was what he obtained from infeudated estates; but that, as may easily be seen, was ultimately derived from some vassal's manorial income. Eventually every obligation of a superior, whether layman or ecclesiastic, was passed down the scale to the peasant at the bottom. To appreciate this truth is to understand the structure of feudal society, and accordingly to perceive how the development of new economic resources, by changing the fundamentals of human existence, would tend to revolutionize both church and state.

2. Life in Castle and Village

Our best source for the ideas and customs of the feudal nobility is the French epic poetry that will be discussed in the following section. But in many respects an even more vivid picture of the knight and his contemporaries is provided by the famous Bayeux Tapestry, an embroidery made as a decoration for the nave of the cathedral in that city and still preserved in the local museum. It is a strip of linen twenty inches wide and over 230 feet long, with scenes worked in colored worsted to describe the Norman conquest of England. Although the story thus told is interesting as a partisan tradition, the great historical value of the tapestry lies in its realistic presentation of eleventh-century life. This unique work, probably completed before 1100, allows us to be positive with regard to many odd details of military activity, of domestic habits, and, above all, of costume.

The Bayeux Tapestry

As here shown, men of all classes commonly wore tunic and hose: the former a loosefitting jacket belted at the waist, the latter a sort of tights pulled on over the legs.[6] For warmth or ceremony the man might also put on a mantle, which was fastened at the throat or over the right shoulder to leave the sword-arm free. He cut his hair short and commonly shaved his face. Women were dressed in robes of extreme simplicity, extending from the chin to the ground. They usually bound their hair with fillets and either let it hang free or caught it up under a coif. For outdoor wear both sexes used cloaks with attached hoods that could be brought over the head in bad weather. Even the wealthy wore plain clothes, merely substituting finer stuffs for the ordinary homespun and perhaps trimming them with fur. It was thus left for the clergy to preserve the regular use of a toga-like costume.

Civil costume

Fig. 15. Earl Harold in Mantle, Tunic, and Hose. (From the Bayeux Tapestry.)

[6] See Figure 15, and cf. the Roman and Germanic costumes described above, pp. 19, 47.

FIG. 16. Duke William at the Battle of Hastings. (From the Bayeux Tapestry.)

Only to please the pope, Einhard tells us, would Charlemagne ever submit to Roman dress. And his attitude was maintained by the princes of the later Middle Ages, who refused to wear long robes except on extraordinary occasions. In the Bayeux Tapestry the English king and the Norman duke thus appear when sitting in state—the former with a crown, an orb, and a scepter; the latter with a mace.

Defensive armor in this early period was not elaborate. The knight's **Arms and** lower legs were generally unprotected, except by strips of cloth or leather **armor** wound like modern puttees from the knee to the shoe-tops. Over the upper body he wore a hauberk, a shirt of link mail or one made by sewing metal rings on a leather foundation. The hauberk was slashed at the bottom to facilitate riding on horseback and was apparently fitted with a sort of hood that covered the back of the neck and provided a lining for the helmet. The latter was a conical iron cap with a narrow extension in front to serve as a nose-guard. On the left arm, by means of attached thongs, he bore a kite-shaped shield about four feet long. Presumably constructed of a metal facing on a wooden base, it might be painted with a fanciful design, though regular coats of arms hardly appeared before the twelfth century. For offense the knight's weapons were principally a cross-hilted sword slung on a belt at the left side, and a lance some eight feet long, which was hurled or held couched by the right hand.[7] In the Bayeux Tapestry only the English are shown using battle-axes; but it would appear from other sources that the French often used them too.

The Bayeux Tapestry gives us an equally fine portrayal of the great **Horses** horses which the invaders brought with them across the Channel.[8] Here **and castles** for almost the first time we obtain actual pictures not merely of feudal cavalry in the large but of such details as saddles, stirrups, bridles, and other harness—even the shoes on the horses' feet and the spurs on the knights' heels. Besides, we may see how Norman troops foraged the English countryside and how the meat they collected was broiled and served on spits to the leaders of the host. We learn that the Norman boats resembled those of the Vikings and were equipped with masts that could be raised or lowered. Other scenes depict the castles of Bayeux, Dol, Dinan, and Rennes, as well as the building of one at Hastings. The drawing, to be sure, leaves much to be desired; yet we can easily distinguish the moats, drawbridges, palisades, and keeps. And we may be sure that such fortifications were built of wood, for the attackers are shown using fire against them.

Castles, in addition to being fortresses, were the usual residences of feudal princes and their wealthier vassals. While the lower portion of the keep

[7] See Figures 13 and 16. The latter shows that even the primitive helmet so far concealed the features of the wearer that he had to raise it in order to prove his identity.

[8] See Figure 16 and above, p. 188.

would include the wells, storerooms, and military positions necessary for withstanding a siege, and while the roof might be devoted to the hurling of missiles and to other warlike purposes, the intermediate stories would constitute the living quarters of the lord and his family. Here would be found a great hall, a chapel, and a number of separate chambers. Cooking would normally be done in outside kitchens and the food would be brought up by servants. But in time of peace every nobleman spent a good part of the year traveling about from one rural estate to another. On any of the better ones he would be likely to have a comfortable manor house, built of timber or stone and perhaps surrounded by a moat to keep off marauders. In such a place he might have sufficient utensils and furniture to accommodate his household for a protracted stay; more likely he would have to bring an additional supply with him—wagonloads of it if he were one of the truly great whose progress was marked by a cavalcade of ministers and retainers. And there were, of course, numberless gentlemen who, possessing no castles, had manor houses as permanent homes.

In any case the center of the nobleman's domestic life would be the great hall, which according to modern standards was picturesque rather than luxurious. Heat would be supplied by open fires, the smoke from which—in the absence of chimneys—found its way out past the grimy rafters overhead. As windows were then unglazed, the weather had to be kept out by means of shutters. The walls would be hung with arms, banners, and trophies of the chase. The floor might be of hard-trodden earth covered with straw or rushes, where the ever-present dogs made themselves at home. Light would be furnished by candles. Here the lord sat in state to receive homage or to confer with his vassals in solemn court. Here was spread the festive board, with the company seated on benches in order of rank. Here of an evening took place whatever entertainment the age afforded—such as tales of heroic deeds chanted by wandering minstrels.[9] And here, after the lord and his family had retired to their chambers, would be laid the straw pallets of those who could not be accommodated elsewhere.

In the matter of food and drink the men of the early Middle Ages naturally followed the precedents established by their Roman and barbarian ancestors.[10] Then, as now, Europe was gustatively divided into two main sections: that of wine and oil and that of beer and butter. Throughout the grape-raising countries wine remained the standard drink, but in the northwest its place, except in wealthy homes, was taken by beer. The quantities of either that were then consumed by the average person were such as to stagger the imagination of the modern tippler; and temperance was equally unknown in eating. In addition to the ordinary beef, mutton, and pork, the feudal gentleman was fond of game—often a deer or a boar roasted

[9] See below, p. 279.
[10] See above, pp. 18, 47.

whole—accompanied by secondary dishes of fowl, pasties, vegetables, and fruit. On fast days, when the meats were supposed to disappear, the platters were well filled with fish and eggs. Bread and cheese were of course staples. Sweets, on the contrary, were rare because the sole available sweetening was honey, and imported spices, such as pepper, were found only on the tables of the great. So far as cooking was concerned, we are led to believe that quantity, rather than quality, was the principal consideration. And what we know as table manners were quite unknown. The man supplied his own knife and with it served himself and perhaps his lady; after that it was catch-as-catch-can. The appetite of the hunter and the fighter raged unchecked by an etiquette of delicacy.

The position of women during the early Middle Ages seems to have **Woman's** been one of complete subordination. It was not until later that feminine **place** influence came to be celebrated even by romantic poets.[11] Although we have every reason to suppose that love was important in society long before it became a fashionable theme in literature, marriage within the aristocracy was regularly dictated by dynastic and financial interest. The first obligation of the wife was to bring the inheritance of a fief, or at any rate a handsome marriage portion; the second was to bear at least one son. And if she were unfortunate enough to fail in the latter duty, a complaisant bishop was usually at hand to declare the wedding invalid. Upon the wife, furthermore, devolved the care of the house and the management of the servants. She was not expected to be literate; it was enough that she should know how to spin, weave, and sew. Occasionally we hear of some extraordinary lady who, on the death of her husband, continued his work by playing a dominant role in politics and war. Normally, however, the feudal age accepted the maxim that woman's place is in the home.

Indeed, since a woman could not be a knight, what greater honor could **Tourna-** she expect than to be the wife of one and the mother of several more? Ex- **ments** cept within the church, which constituted a world apart, there was but one honorable career—that of the professional warrior. And to such a person peace meant virtual unemployment. So, to break the monotony of routine practice with sword and lance, men invented the tournament. The contests familiarized by romantic fiction were mere pageants, involving a maximum of display and a minimum of bloodshed. The primitive tournament, on the contrary, was a real battle, in spite of the fact that it was pre-arranged and might be elaborately staged. On the appointed day two groups of knights, often the champions of rival houses or territories, would meet in some convenient field. There, according to a few established rules, they would proceed to fight until one or the other was adjudged victorious. This was the tournament proper; combats between pairs of knights—and they became increasingly popular—were called jousts. In either case the game was

[11] See below, pp. 285-86.

hardly less dangerous than actual war, and hardly less profitable. Although the contestant risked both life and limb, he stood to win rich booty as well as honor; for he was entitled to the horse and arms of a vanquished opponent, or to such ransom as he agreed to accept instead.

Hunting and other amusements

Next to fighting, the feudal gentleman loved hunting—riding down stags, boars, and other large game with dogs. So every prince maintained wide preserves in which he and his retainers enjoyed a monopoly of the chase. There too—and this was a recreation in which the ladies frequently joined —many days were spent in hawking. The taking of herons, pigeons, waterfowl, rabbits, and other small game by means of trained hawks, while the attendant company galloped across the country, was a sport that had long been known in the orient and had thence spread into the Roman provinces. The passionate devotion of the aristocracy to these pursuits is attested by countless writings of the Middle Ages: whether chronicles, popular tales, or governmental records. To the rulers of western Europe their stables, kennels, and eyries were important departments of state. On all sides Norwegian hawks and trained hunting-dogs ranked along with chargers and palfreys as gifts worthy of a king.

When condemned to remain indoors, the feudal gentleman, like his barbarian ancestors, spent a large part of his time in feasting, drinking, and gambling. His favorite games were dice, which in some form or another had been known to the ancient Germans; tables, apparently a variety of backgammon derived from the Romans; and, after the crusade of 1095, chess.[12] Sharing the illiteracy of his class, the ordinary noble could have had no great interest in books or, aside from the elements of practical religion, in the learning of priests and monks. The superintendence of his estates demanded little effort on his part. Agrarian management, since it involved merely the enforcement of an established routine, could well be left to subordinates. Even the clerk who kept the lord's accounts had only to know how to write and how to add or subtract simple numbers. These facts help us to understand why feudal society developed on a manorial basis and how greatly it was disturbed when that basis came to be changed.

Living conditions of the peasantry

With regard to the domestic arrangements of the peasantry our information is much poorer. We know that the villein's house could hardly have been more than a miserable hut, commonly made of wattle plastered with clay and covered with a roof of thatch. His clothes would be of the coarsest: tunic and hose of rough homespun or leather, and perhaps wooden clogs for his feet. His furniture would probably consist of a rude table, a bench or two, and bags of straw laid on the floor to serve as beds. His principal food would be black bread, supplemented by dairy produce, eggs, and such ordinary vegetables as cabbage, turnips, peas, and beans. Occasionally he might enjoy a fowl; normally he could not afford meat. Game

[12] See below, p. 316, n.

and fish he would be forbidden to take. Sheep, cows, and oxen would be too precious for slaughtering, except when the approach of winter and the lack of fodder made it imperative—and then the cost of salt would lead to insufficient curing. He would have, however, a plentiful supply of home-brewed ale or, in favorable regions, a very ordinary wine. He undoubtedly lived in what to us would seem unbearable filth; but in such respects even members of the aristocracy had by no means developed a modern delicacy.

We should, of course, like to know about the peasant's thoughts and feelings—what he believed, enjoyed, dreaded, and hoped. These things we shall never know; he could not express himself in writing, and as yet he had no spokesmen within the educated class. As usual, we must pass over the unrecorded lives of the many and be grateful for what little information we have about the few.

3. THE FEUDAL EPIC

The development of vernacular literatures in western Europe and their relation to the contemporary Latin of the church is a subject that will be somewhat fully discussed below. But one phase of that development—the *chanson de geste* and its antecedents—is so intimately connected with life in the feudal age that it may be drawn from its context to provide a conclusion for the present chapter. *Anglo-Saxon literature*

For reasons already explained, the first of the Germanic languages to be used for secular writings was Anglo-Saxon.[13] In the earlier period, from the seventh to the ninth century, the more significant productions, aside from the dooms, were poems. The later period, the tenth and eleventh centuries, was distinguished rather by Anglo-Saxon prose. For example, the *Anglo-Saxon Chronicle*, begun during the reign of Alfred, dramatically sketches his conflict with the Danes and, continued by many hands, reports the events of the following years until well after the Norman Conquest. Alfred, being greatly concerned with the restoration of learning among the English, also dictated or inspired various translations from the Latin, including Anglo-Saxon versions of well-known books by Orosius, Boëthius, and Gregory the Great. Interesting as these works may be, they are not, artistically, in a class with the great Anglo-Saxon poems. Among the latter are many remarkable compositions: hymns, adaptations from the Bible, and biographies of saints; warlike songs, of which the finest are those celebrating the battles of Brunanburh and Maldon; and a number of strangely beautiful lyrics in a minor key, such as *The Seafarer* and *The Wanderer*. But the most famous Anglo-Saxon poem is *Beowulf*—a heroic tale of weird adventure in which, despite the author's Christianity, the central theme is plainly heathen. The material of *Beowulf* thus appears to have been largely drawn from sagas, traditional stories of the Germans.

[13] See above, p. 55.

In German itself only fragments remain of what must once have been a rich literature. The *Nibelungenlied*, familiarized by Wagnerian opera, was written in Austria about the year 1200 and is imbued with the romantic chivalry then fashionable. Beneath the embellishment, however, may readily be detected an ancient legend about a magic treasure guarded by a dragon—the same legend that, remarkably enough, appears as the *Volsungasaga* in the Icelandic collection known as the *Edda*. Evidently the Norse, on finding new homes beyond the sea, had there preserved the popular literature of Scandinavia in isolation from continental influence. The Icelandic sagas, when put into writing in the twelfth and thirteenth centuries, thus retained much of their primitive character. Some of them, like the *Volsun-*

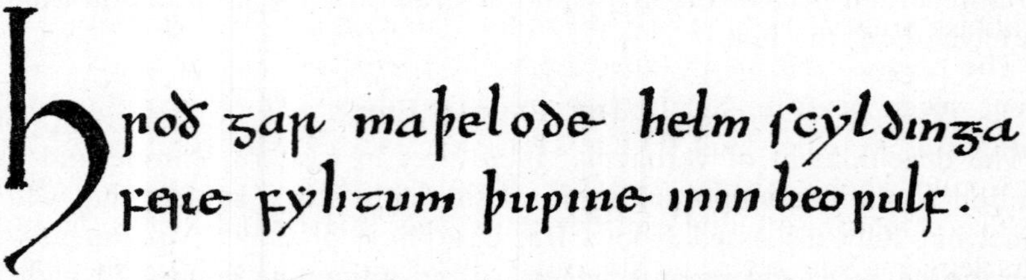

FIG. 17.   Lines 456-457 from the *Beowulf* Manuscript of *c.* 1000. Hroðgar maþelode helm scyldinga fere fyhtum þuwine min beowulf (Hrothgar, helm of the Scyldings, cried "On with the fight my dear Beowulf!").

gasaga, are wholly legendary; some, on the other hand, glorify the adventures of actual persons—as, for example, the finding of Vineland the Good by Leif Ericsson.[14] In either case the sagas provide us with much valuable information concerning the earlier age, though the task of separating the original elements from the accretions of later centuries is one that demands the attention of an expert.

From such pieces as survive we may at least be sure that the primitive saga was chanted to the accompaniment of a harp. The thoughts and feelings of the individual author are of no especial significance. Interest is concentrated on the tale itself, which is dramatic, idealized, and intensely serious. Poetry of this sort is called epic and is recognized as characteristic of a particular stage in cultural development. But the Icelandic sagas and the Anglo-Saxon *Beowulf*, however fine, remained apart from the main current of western civilization. The more typical epics of mediæval Europe are the *chansons de geste*—as the name literally implies, songs of great deeds. Whatever the influence upon them of ancient Frankish sagas, none of which are extant, the *chansons de geste* appear to be unified compositions of the eleventh and twelfth centuries rather than popular tales that gradually took form. They are written in French and, while borrowing

[14] See above, p. 180.

names and episodes from Carolingian times, they faithfully reflect the society and thought of feudal France.

The *Song of Roland* is not only the earliest and best of the *chansons de geste* but one of the finest poems in all literature. The author seems to have been a Norman clerk named Turold, who wrote under the immediate inspiration of the Spanish wars in the later eleventh century. The meter of the poem, like its language, is simple. There is no rhyme, but instead a rude assonance, by which the final syllables throughout a group of lines have the same vowel sound.[15] The story is that of Roland, count of the Breton march, who, according to Einhard, fell in the pass of Roncevaux when the rear-guard of Charlemagne's army was attacked by the Basques. But in the epic poem the antagonists become Moslems instigated by a Frankish traitor; Roland becomes the champion of Christendom.

The *chanson* begins by introducing Charlemagne who, we are told, has spent seven years in Spain and has subdued the entire peninsula except Saragossa. Marsile, king of that city, "who serves Mohammed and prays to Apollo," holds a council of war. There it is decided to send an embassy to the emperor, offering rich presents and treacherous terms of peace. Charlemagne, on receiving this offer, takes a seat under a pine tree and summons his barons for advice. They are very distrustful of Marsile, and Count Roland, the emperor's nephew, voices their sentiment in urging further war. Ganelon, however, persuades Charles to accept and the question then arises as to who shall make the perilous journey with the answer. The emperor refuses to allow either Roland or his friend Oliver to go, but agrees to send Ganelon. The latter, furious with jealousy, swears revenge on Roland. Thus it comes about that Ganelon turns traitor and joins Marsile in an attack on the Frankish rear-guard, left under command of Roland.

The Song of Roland

Charlemagne and his host have advanced out of Spain. Roland, with a picked force of twenty thousand knights, remains behind in the pass of Roncevaux. Oliver, full of foreboding, climbs a hill and so perceives the Saracen army preparing for attack. It is a magnificent sight.

Roland and Oliver

> Fair shines the sun, the day is bright and clear,
> Light burns again from all their polished gear.
> A thousand horns they sound, more proud to seem;
> Great is the noise, the Franks its echo hear.
> Says Oliver: "Companion, I believe,
> Sarrazins now in battle must we meet."
> Answers Rollanz: "God grant us then the fee!
> For our King's sake well must we quit us here;

[15] The following quotations are from *The Song of Roland,* translated by Scott-Moncrieff (Chapman & Hall, Ltd.; London, 1920), and are used by permission of the publishers. The translator has very happily reproduced the meter and, to some extent, the assonance of the original. Whenever necessary, the English words must receive an archaic pronunciation to suit the rhythm.

> Man for his lord should suffer great disease,
> Most bitter cold endure, and burning heat,
> His hair and skin should offer up at need.
> Now must we each lay on most hardily,
> So evil song ne'er sung of us shall be."

"Roland is gallant; Oliver is wise." Oliver urges Roland to sound his horn, by a miraculous blast to summon Charles to the rescue. But Roland refuses all entreaty and prepares for combat, thinking only of glorious battle and of the bright blood that shall soon paint his beloved sword, Durendal. If he is to die, he hopes only that the man who gets it may be able to say that it belonged to a "noble vassal."

Turpin

Up rides the archbishop Turpin and preaches the Franks a sermon, brief and to the point:

> "My lords barons, Charles left us here for this;
> He is our King, well may we die for him:
> To Christendom good service offering.
> Battle you'll have, you all are bound to it,
> For with your eyes you see the Sarrazins.
> Pray for God's grace, confessing Him your sins!
> For your soul's health, I'll absolution give;
> So, though you die, blest martyrs shall you live,
> Thrones you shall win in the great Paradis."

> The Franks arise, and stand upon their feet;
> They're well absolved, and from their sins made clean,
> And the Archbishop has signed them with God's seal.

So Roland now leads his troops to battle, galloping on Veilantif, his good horse. Proud and brave he goes, brandishing his sword and turning against the sky the point of his lance, from which streams a white pennon. Fringes beat his hands as he rides, noble of body, with face clear and smiling. And what does he say to his companions? "Lords, before night great and rich booty shall be ours!"

The battle

The battle is joined—a series of combats, man to man, lance against shield. After fifteen strokes, Roland's lance breaks and he draws Durendal. Striking the first-comer, one Chernuble, he cuts through helmet, man, saddle, and horse, slicing the spine "without striking a joint."

> The count Rollanz, he canters through the field,
> Holds Durendal, he well can thrust and wield,
> Right great damage he's done the Sarrazines,
> You'd seen them, one on other, dead in heaps,
> Through all that place their blood was flowing clear!
> In blood his arms were and his hauberk steeped,
> And bloodied o'er, shoulder and neck, his steed.

The fight becomes fiercer. Both Frank and Saracen strike marvelous blows, but the mightiest strikers are Roland, Oliver, and Turpin.

> The Franks strike on; their hearts are good and stout.
> Pagans are slain, a thousandfold, in crowds,
> Left of five score are not two thousands now.
> Says the Archbishop: "Our men are very proud,
> No man on earth has more nor better found.
> In Chronicles of Franks is written down,
> What vassalage he had, our Emperour."

The archbishop has a splendid horse, taken from a Danish king whom he had slain. He has a magnificent sword, equaled apparently only by his right arm. He rides against Abisme and cuts right through the Saracen's magic shield.

> So Turpin strikes, spares him not anyway;
> After that blow, he's worth no penny wage;
> The carcass he's sliced, rib from rib away,
> So flings him down dead in an empty place.
> Then say the Franks: "He has great vassalage,
> With the Archbishop, surely the Cross is safe."

The Franks, however, are sorely outnumbered. Before long very few **The end** will be left. So Roland, still unscathed by the enemy, sounds his horn—a mighty blast that starts the blood from his lips and cracks his temple. Charlemagne, distant thirty leagues, hears, summons his troops, and turns back. Too late! By the time the Saracens, hearing the approach of reinforcements, have fled, all the Franks are doomed. Oliver has died, breathing a last prayer for his emperor, France, and "above all men Roland, his companion." The archbishop is able only to pronounce a last blessing over the slain nobles laid before him by Roland. The latter, weakened by loss of blood, faints on finding the body of Oliver, and Turpin dies in the effort to bring him water.

Roland, thus left with an army of corpses, feels death approaching. Rather than have his sword Durendal, with all the sacred relics in the hilt, fall into pagan hands, he tries to break it but cannot. As his strength fails, he throws himself under a pine, his face towards the enemy.

> His right-hand glove, to God he offers it;
> Saint Gabriel from's hand hath taken it.
> Over his arm his head bows down and slips,
> He joins his hands: and so is life finish'd.
> God sent him down His angel cherubin,
> And Saint Michael, we worship in peril;
> And by their side Saint Gabriel alit;
> So the count's soul they bare to Paradis.

More battles ensue—battles of revenge, in which the Franks decimate the Saracens and complete their conquest. Then comes the journey homeward. At the imperial palace in Aix-la-Chapelle Charlemagne is confronted by Aude the fair, betrothed of Roland. He tells her not to grieve; that she

may have instead his own son Louis. Aude replies that without Roland
life is not worth living, and she falls dead at the emperor's feet. Ganelon,
after his guilt has been determined through trial by combat, is executed.
Charlemagne lies down to sleep, but St. Gabriel appears to him in a vision
and tells him of more Christians to be rescued from pagan oppression.

> "God!" said the king: "My life is hard indeed!"
> Tears filled his eyes, he tore his snowy beard.

Epic chivalry

This is the *Song of Roland*, the fame of which was spread by French
knights from Ireland to Jerusalem. Wherever feudal ideals came to triumph,
there men thrilled at the bitter fight at Roncevaux. Reading the *chanson*
today, we can understand, if we cannot share, their emotions; for through
the song we plainly know the singer and his audience. In the background
of the poem are Charlemagne, a majestic but shadowy figure; France, his
empire, with a geography of the vaguest; and the weary ceaseless war
against the infidel. The real theme, however, is vassalage, epitomized in
the person of Count Roland. Charles is not merely king and champion of
the faith; he is Roland's lord. To Charles, Roland is unswervingly loyal,
yet his loyalty is not disinterested. Fighting for his lord, Roland also fights
for himself—for conquest, loot, glory, and sheer delight. It is on his reck-
less valor, not the wisdom of Oliver, that the story turns. Like a true
knight, he is straightforward; the schemers of the piece are rogues. Ruthless to his foes, Roland is tender to his friends. Nearest his heart stands
his devoted companion-in-arms, Oliver; and next in his affections come his
war-horse and his sword. Of love for woman there is no word. His *fiancée*
dies at the news of his death; that is all. Roland's virtues are those of the
battlefield. Even the religion of the *chanson* is warlike: magic relics help
to make a sword invincible; the Cross is safest with a blood-smeared archbishop; a soldier on God's side is assured of salvation; warrior saints bear
Roland's soul to paradise.

To conclude that the French of the eleventh century thought no thought
not contained in this one poem would of course be erroneous. Most men
at that time probably loved their wives and sweethearts, took delight in
humble joys, lived ordinary lives, and missed heroic deaths. Vassals were
not always loyal to their lords, nor lords to their vassals. Yet, although
men could not be Rolands, they could dream of being so. The glorious
count could have been the paragon of none but the fiercely warlike and
naïvely religious aristocracy that spent itself on the crusade.

CHAPTER XII

The Empire, the Papacy, and the Crusade

1. THE HOLY ROMAN EMPIRE

Historians of an older generation told a very pretty story about the **The** opening of the eleventh century. From the *Apocalypse*, they said, men **legend of** had learned to expect the end of the world in the year 1000. So, with the **the year** imagined approach of the Last Judgment, Europe was swept by a wave of **1000** piety. The fateful year arrived and the world did not come to an end, but the cause of reform had gained a momentum that could not be checked. The result was a great age of ecclesiastical ascendancy—one marked by the triumph of the papacy over the empire, the glorious crusade, and the consequent advance of civilization. The finest achievements of the later Middle Ages could thus be ascribed to a misplaced confidence in the word of Scripture. Unhappily for the student, this neat explanation of a complicated development must now be classified among the legends of historiography. Investigation has shown that people who wrote towards the close of the tenth century expressed no dread of the year 1000; that, indeed, there was no reason why they should have had any such dread, for the mystic prophecy in the *Apocalypse* had never referred to that particular year.[1] Nevertheless, the events just mentioned did occur. And although we have no easy formula to fall back on, we must try to obtain some understanding of them.

Up to a certain point the kingdoms of France and Germany developed **Otto the** along parallel lines. In each all real power tended to fall into the hands of **Great** local princes; in each the Carolingian dynasty was supplanted by kings **(936-73)**

---

[1] The "thousand years" of the *Apocalypse*, xx, 1-7, can hardly be reckoned from the birth of Christ.

217

elected from among those princes; and in each a princely house finally obtained a semi-hereditary claim to the throne. If the descendants of Henry the Fowler had continued his policy, they would have remained, like the early Capetians, actual rulers of a principality with the kingship held as a sort of honorary title. But Henry's son, who came to be known as Otto the Great, was not satisfied with such a role. Leaving Saxony to be administered by subordinates, he turned to the enforcement of his authority throughout Germany as a whole. The inevitable result was a far-reaching insurrection. The dukes of Lorraine, Franconia, Suabia, and Bavaria, though willing to accept Otto's election and even to act as household officials at his coronation, would brook no interference with their local affairs. And in this attitude they were supported by many of the higher clergy. Fortunately for the king, the risings did not all occur at once; he was able to crush them in detail and, reasserting the Carolingian tradition, to appoint new dukes, generally members of his own family.

The plan was a complete failure, for even a royal son or son-in-law found it easier to champion local sentiment than to oppose it, and a fresh insurrectionary movement awaited only a favorable opportunity. It was provided by the king's ambitious projects abroad. Before 952 Otto had gained three noteworthy successes outside Germany. He had defeated the Czechs of Bohemia, now organized as a Christian state, and compelled their king to accept his overlordship. He had forced similar recognition from the youthful king of Arles and so extended his sovereignty westward to the Rhone. Finally, to complete his title to the old middle kingdom of Lothair, he had crossed the Alps, married the widow of one Italian king, and exacted the submission of another. From this adventure he was recalled by a German rebellion, combined with a renewed Hungarian offensive. Despite the apparent odds, Otto was able to reassert his mastery. Having crushed the rebels, he won a crowning triumph over the Hungarians on the Lech in 955—a decisive victory, for it ended the last great Magyar invasion of Germany.

The imperial crown

By 961 all was again quiet; with the frontiers secure and the duchies temporarily in loyal hands, Otto was free to resume his Italian enterprise. On the invitation of Pope John XII, one of the notorious profligates who disgraced the Roman see at this unhappy time, Otto crossed the Alps with a formidable army, occupied Lombardy, and assumed the Italian crown. In the next year he was crowned emperor by the pope—and what historians know as the Holy Roman Empire had come into existence (see Map X). Then, as the pope came to repent his hasty action, Otto took Rome by storm, had John deposed, and procured the election of his own secretary. Momentarily he even thought to conquer the rest of the peninsula, but abandoned the project in favor of a treaty with the Byzantine emperor. Thereby he secured the hand of a Greek princess for his eldest son, together with the promise of the southern Italian duchies as her marriage portion. The remaining years of his life the king devoted primarily to ecclesiastical reform and, thanks to his control of the papacy, he eventually obtained the erection of a new archbishopric at Magdeburg, with jurisdiction over the Slavic marches to the east. Dying in 973, he left a magnificent heritage to his son, Otto II, who had already been crowned emperor as well as king.

To understand the policy of Otto the Great is to understand that of his successors for over two hundred years. Thenceforth, generation after generation, the kings of Germany were to try to rival Charlemagne, but few of them were to equal the success of Otto. Glorious as it was, his example proved the bane of German politics. Under its talented ruling house Saxony might have been made the nucleus of a powerful state with infinite possibilities of expansion to the east—or perhaps to the north, for as yet there were no Scandinavian kingdoms of any strength. Otto, however, chose to abandon Saxony and to attempt the government of Germany through personal control of the dukes, while he pursued imperial ambitions in Burgundy and Italy. For the sake of a pseudo-Roman grandeur, too many of the men who followed Otto on the throne forgot to be German. Striving for an empire, they failed to secure even a duchy. *The successors of Otto the Great*

With these remarks to serve as an introduction, the next century of German history can be passed over in brief outline. Otto II ruled for only ten years (973-83). He put down several revolts, fought the Bohemians, and died in the midst of a futile campaign to enforce his claim to the southern duchies of Italy. His son Otto III (983-1002) lived only to be twenty-two. Brought up under the tutelage of his Greek mother, he spent all his time in Italy, where, surrounded by officials with Byzantine titles, he indulged in imperial play-acting while his kingdoms relapsed into anarchy. His one noteworthy act was the installation of Gerbert, his illustrious teacher, as Pope Silvester II.[2] Since Otto III died without direct heirs, the magnates proclaimed Henry II, a grandson of Otto I's brother (see Table IV). Although his reign was not spectacular, he somewhat restored the credit of the monarchy by devoting most of his time to the defense of Germany, which was now threatened by a new Slavic attack under the command of the Polish king. The latter, finally, was forced to submit and like the Bohemian king to recognize German overlordship.

With the death of Henry II in 1024 the house of Saxony, by descent on the male side, came to an end; but the German electors, remaining loyal to the dynastic principle, chose a Franconian noble named Conrad, the great-grandson of Otto I's daughter. So the new line of kings, known as the Salian or Franconian house, was merely the old under another name. There was no innovation either in theory or in practice. Conrad put down several revolts, spent a year in Italy, secured the imperial crown, fought the Slavs, and reasserted German overlordship in Poland and Bohemia. *The Franconian kings (1024-1125)*

[2] For Gerbert's contribution to European scholarship see below, pp. 256-59.

The outstanding event of his reign was the acquisition of a third royal crown, when the last king of Arles died without heirs in 1032. Seven years later Conrad's dominions passed to his son Henry III who, happily, enjoyed a rather uneventful reign (1039-56). Aside from a minor war in Lorraine, his empire remained generally peaceful, and externally it had no dangerous enemies. German influence, already dominant in Poland and Bohemia, was now extended over Hungary, which had recently emerged as a Christian kingdom. Altogether, Henry III held a magnificent pre-eminence in Europe; the speciousness of his imperial glory was not to be proved until it was inherited by his less fortunate son.

Theories of church and state
Meanwhile a subject of the greatest importance had again been brought to the attention of Christian princes—the relations, theoretical and actual, of church and state. So far as theory was concerned, an impressive mass of writing had already accumulated, and in the following years it was to be raised to mountainous proportions. Yet the fundamental arguments always remained the same and can be very briefly stated. The imperialist school continued to be fascinated by the tradition of Charlemagne, which was the tradition of the Roman Empire. The ecclesiastical system advocated by Otto I and his successors was substantially that of Justinian, Theodosius, and Constantine: the church, though permitted to decide matters of doctrine and to establish its own discipline, was a department of state. Like other departments, it was under the supreme control of the emperor, who held himself directly responsible to God. The ministers of the church, no less than lay officials, were imperial subjects; for men should "render unto Cæsar the things which are Cæsar's." As a matter of history, this was an excellent thesis. The question was: Could it be applied to the Europe of the eleventh century? The imperialist doctrine ignored the fact that the Christian world was no longer an empire except in imagination. It was to become increasingly doubtful whether the emperor could enforce any real authority even in those regions where his nominal sovereignty was recognized. An academic discussion might well appeal to memories of Roman majesty. But how could such an appeal bring inspiration or security to western Europe?

To refute the imperialist claims, the champions of the papacy might very properly emphasize the demands of practical religion. As an international organization, the church could not be subject to any state, whether or not the latter styled itself an empire. The papacy owed its existence as a world power to its independence of any western Cæsar. It was the dominance of the Byzantine government that had constantly brought the patriarchs of Constantinople into conflict with the popes. Furthermore, the great fathers of the church, notably St. Augustine, had written eloquent books to prove that all political institutions were the consequence of Adam's sin. If man had remained in his pristine innocence, there would be no evil in the world. And without evil there would be no need of governors, armies, police, courts, and penal laws. The state, therefore, was an ephemeral thing, necessary but not divine like the church. The latter was the immediate representative of God on earth. It held the sole power among men of distinguishing good from evil. And whatever authority Christ had conferred on His church could be lawfully exercised by its supreme head, the bishop of Rome. Must not, accordingly, the pope be recognized as the final arbiter of human affairs?

The logic of the papal argument was hard to escape, once its premises had been admitted. In the eleventh century, however, the church needed vastly more than logic—as will be seen from a sketch of its reinvigoration.

2. The Restoration of the Papal Authority

Since the collapse of Charlemagne's empire there had been no general reform of ecclesiastical institutions. Occasionally a wise ruler, like Alfred in England or Otto I in Germany, had been able to bring about a noteworthy improvement; but throughout the greater part of Europe conditions had grown worse rather than better. Bishops, when they were not actually vicious, were commonly submerged in secular affairs; and in this respect even the popes set a bad example. Besides, ecclesiastical properties and offices had often been turned into fiefs, to be secured by the methods that were everywhere in vogue among laymen. On all sides parishes, bishoprics, abbacies, and other preferments were solicited from patrons by means of suitable presents. And the successful candidate naturally recouped himself from his subordinates. Bishops charged priests for ordination; the priests took fees from the people for the administration of the sacraments. The rule of celibacy for clergymen in the Roman Church above the grade of subdeacon was everywhere relaxed. Priests and bishops were frequently married, and so came to endow their children with estates that were supposed to maintain religious service. The church, like the Carolingian kingdoms, was threatened with dispersion among a host of feudal dynasties.

The feudalization of the church

Inevitably, too, there had been a sad deterioration of monastic life. We have seen how Charlemagne, while virtually appointing all abbots in his dominions, strove to preserve a high standard of religious discipline and so to improve Frankish civilization. Yet in any particular case the emperor's wish was probably less important than the character of the abbot and the relative wealth of the monastery. In a richly endowed house, whose needs were supplied by peasants on outlying estates, the monk's vow of individual poverty, as well as the manual labor prescribed by his rule, had no economic significance. Often enough the brothers lived in comparative luxury. Their buildings—usually arranged about an arcaded cloister (see Plate XI)—would normally be of stone and would include, together with kitchens and storerooms, a dormitory, where they slept; a refectory, where they ate; a chapter house, where they met to discuss matters of common interest; and a church, where they celebrated the routine offices. Their abbot might well be more interested in politics or warfare than in the principles of St. Benedict. He might, indeed, be a mere layman who owed his position to royal patronage. Later, with the degradation of the church generally, conditions in the monasteries tended to go from bad to worse—until religious ideals were actually threatened with extinction.

The Cluniac reform

In the tenth century most persons seem to have taken the feudalization of the church quite for granted. Only a few purists denounced the marriage of priests as concubinage on the ground that they could not be lawfully wedded, and the buying of ecclesiastical preferment as simony—i.e., the sin of Simon Magus who had offered money for the gift of the Holy Spirit.[3] Such agitation, as we should expect, first gained significant headway in the cloister. Long before the allegedly mystic year 1000 various religious establishments had become famous as centers of zeal for a Christian revival, but only one of them was to achieve European prominence. This was the monastery of Cluny, founded with papal confirmation by the duke of Aquitaine in 910. According to the terms of its establishment, that famous abbey was to be strictly governed under the rule of St. Benedict; the monks were to choose whom they pleased as abbot without the intervention of any person; and the abbot thus elected was to be independent of all ecclesiastical authorities except the pope. The original Benedictine system had all too often resulted in domination by some local magnate and in the decadence of religious life. Now, as the new community acquired wide renown for purity and zeal, many ancient monasteries became affiliated with it under priors named by the abbot of Cluny. The resulting group of houses, known as the Congregation of Cluny, eventually numbered over three hundred and exerted great influence throughout western Europe—principally by means of preaching and political agitation, for the Cluniac monks paid little or no attention to scholarship.

Henry III (1039-56)

Worthy as it was, however, the cause of reform could have slight success without the backing of temporal authority, and most princes were reluctant to abandon established custom. The first noteworthy convert to the new religious movement was the emperor Henry III. On his accession in 1039 he immediately undertook to remove all taint of simony from his court and to enforce the rule that no son of a priest could hold any honor under the crown. But Henry III never dreamed of relinquishing his control of ecclesiastical affairs. Like Charlemagne, he regarded the church as a department of the royal government, and by his official acts he soon demonstrated that in this respect no distinction would be made between Germany and Italy. Crossing the Alps in 1046, Henry was confronted by the unusual spectacle of three rivals claiming to be pope at the same time. This

[3] *Acts,* viii, 18.

scandal he summarily ended by having all three deposed in assemblies of the clergy. Then he procured the election of a German successor, and on the death of the latter he virtually appointed three other popes. Of them the second was Leo IX, whose pontificate marked the resumption by the papacy of spiritual leadership in Europe.

In the first place, Leo personally launched a vigorous campaign to root out simony and clerical marriage, holding councils for that purpose in Italy, France, and Germany. And while he was thus engaged in traveling about the country, he actively sought to restore the papal influence over the great prelates and temporal princes of the west. Meanwhile the Norman conquests in southern Italy had given rise to fresh unpleasantness with the Byzantine government. At first Leo thought to advance his interests at Constantinople by joining forces with the emperor. But the Normans had no difficulty in defeating both the imperial and the papal armies. Then, while the pope's attitude was still in doubt, the headstrong Michael Cerularius, patriarch of Constantinople, precipitated a religious crisis. Reviving an ancient quarrel,[4] he denounced all the peculiar usages of the Latins and closed all churches in his capital where they were in force. Leo accordingly had no choice. Shortly before his death in 1054 he signed a peace with the Normans and excommunicated the patriarch. The latter, taking advantage of the vacancy at Rome, induced the weak emperor to reverse his policy and agree to the acts of a synod that formally condemned all followers of the Roman discipline. The schism between east and west, thus renewed in 1054, has remained unhealed down to the present and has had many evil consequences. The blame, no doubt, will always be differently assessed by persons of different faiths, but in any case little of it can justly fall on Leo IX.

Leo IX and the Greek schism

The pontificate of Leo is also important for the rise of a remarkable Italian with a German name, Hildebrand, who became archdeacon under Nicholas II (1058-61). As the pope's chief assistant, Hildebrand is generally credited with two significant measures which were then enacted. One was the formal alliance with the Normans in southern Italy, recognizing Guiscard's conquests as a papal fief, blessing his brother's expedition against the Moslems of Sicily, and assuring the pope of their armed support in case of a German attack upon Rome. The other was the famous electoral decree of the same year, 1059, which vested the control of papal elections in the cardinal clergy of Rome.[5] The new plan was merely the adaptation of a custom that was already widespread—having a bishop elected by the cathedral chapter, the clergy attached to the service of the bishop's church. But at Rome the change was especially momentous in that the initiative

Gregory VII and Henry IV

---

[4] See above, p. 161.
[5] The cardinal bishops, priests, and deacons are by definition those who are closest to the hinge (*cardo*) of Christendom, i.e., Rome.

in papal elections was given to the cardinal bishops, while the emperor was left with no function beyond that of confirming an accomplished act.

The election of the Italian Nicholas II in 1058 had gone uncontested by the imperial court because Henry III had died two years earlier, leaving an infant son to succeed as Henry IV. During the minority Germany was administered by a regent—first the queen mother and then the archbishop of Cologne, who kidnaped the young king to secure control of the government. Again in 1061 an Italian was proclaimed as Pope Alexander II, and under him Hildebrand continued to guide the papal policy, deciding among other important matters to bless the Norman duke's conquest of England as a means of ousting a rebellious archbishop of Canterbury. Finally, in 1073, Hildebrand himself was raised to the papal throne with the tumultuous acclaim of the Roman populace, and his accession as Gregory VII was promptly recognized by Henry IV. This action on the part of the king was due neither to weakness nor to a conciliatory temper. Henry was to prove himself a man of exceptional ability, inclined rather to violence than to moderation. At the moment, however, he was fully occupied with a dangerous revolt in Saxony. It was not until later, after he had crushed the Saxon rebels, that he revealed his true attitude towards the papal administration.

Gregory is described by contemporaries as a small man with a weak voice. But his physique was no measure of his greatness. Though never called to lead armies or remake the map of Europe, he possessed the qualities of a born commander and statesman. And the fact that his life was devoted to a lofty ideal gave him a moral grandeur that has been commonly wanting in generals and world-rulers. There can be as little question of his sincerity as of his experience. When Gregory said that through him one might hear the voice of St. Peter, he expressed a profound conviction. To him, as to St. Augustine, the problem of church and state resolved itself into a matter of right and wrong; the power that could absolve from sin must be superior to any other. A comparatively unlearned man, he based his policy on a few simple principles, to which he remained unswervingly loyal. He wisely abstained from counsels of perfection. Like the first Gregory, he realized that the most glorious advance had to be made step by step and that there was no easy formula for succeeding with all kinds of people. Whatever may have been said against him by his enemies, he had no fanatical desire for controversy. His relations with William I[6] of England prove that he was quite willing to come to terms with a strong king who would keep faith with him. His conflict with Henry IV arose, not from an attachment to abstract theory, but from a very definite issue that could not be avoided. When confronted by such an issue, Gregory thought clearly and acted decisively.

[6] See below, p. 317.

During the early years of his pontificate Gregory continued to give his The con- chief attention to the campaign against simony and clerical marriage. In flict over this he was stubbornly opposed by many bishops in Germany and Lom- lay in- bardy who had been appointed through the influence of the king. Even vestiture those who were not hostile to the proposed reforms obstructed the pope's efforts to enforce his direct authority. As Henry, plunged in political troubles and anxious to be crowned emperor, still maintained a submissive attitude, Gregory proceeded to suspend a number of German bishops for disobedience. Then, in 1075, he struck at what he considered another root of evil by prohibiting lay investiture. Although rulers might keep some influence over ecclesiastical elections, no successful candidate could be legally installed in office except by an ecclesiastic. But Henry was now gaining the upper hand in Saxony and displayed no eagerness to enforce the papal decree. Gregory, therefore, sent him a warning letter, threatening him with excommunication unless he at once proved his good faith by actively supporting the cause of reform. Dazzled by his Saxon triumph, Henry retorted by inspiring his bishops, early in 1076, to denounce the pope as a usurper and declare him unfit to occupy the Roman see. A royal letter to the same effect called Gregory a "false monk" and bade him come down from the apostolic throne which he had secured through violence and "be damned through all the ages."

Gregory's answer to this challenge could not be a matter of doubt. Every king, being human, was subject to the discipline of the church for his sins. Nearly seven hundred years earlier Ambrose of Milan had enforced that lesson against the magnificent emperor Theodosius. Henry had been warned to repent and to correct his ways. He had not only refused to do so but had attacked the divine authority of the Roman bishop. So Gregory, in language of admirable simplicity, declared Henry excommunicate and deprived of his regal power; his subjects, released from their oaths of fealty, were to elect another in his place. The very boldness of the pro- nouncement caused a tremendous sensation. Yet, if it had not been based on shrewd political calculation, it would have been no more than a heroic gesture. As it was, Gregory proved that he had clearly appraised the situ- ation in Germany. The princes, already aroused by the threat of royal absolutism, welcomed the pope's authorization of revolt. Meeting in the autumn of 1076, they declared Henry deposed unless he could secure absolution within a year and, being unable to agree on a rival candidate, postponed further action until they could reassemble under the presidency of the pope.

By the end of 1076 Henry thus found his victory of the previous year Canossa entirely undone. Virtually the whole nobility of the kingdom had turned (1077) against him; even the bishops, frightened by the consequences of their rash pronouncement, had hastened to make submission at Rome. There was only one escape for the king; to prevent the union of his enemies, he had to swallow his pride and come to terms with the pope. Accordingly, in the last days of December, Henry set out on his humiliating journey. Gregory, in the meantime, had started for Germany; but, hearing that Henry had already crossed the Alps, he fell back to Canossa, a Tuscan castle belonging to one of his staunch supporters. There the king appeared in January, 1077—barefooted and garbed in coarse wool. Gregory, as he tells us in his own letter, kept Henry waiting for three days; perhaps he was reluctant to abandon the dictatorship of German affairs. As a priest of the church, however, he had to receive the penitent and grant him absolution. This famous episode was hailed then, and has since been regarded, as a great moral triumph for the church. It proclaimed to the world that the papacy, within the lifetime of one man, had been rescued from its long decadence and raised to a new height of renown. Captivating the imagination of Europe, the incident seemed to usher in a new and glorious age of Christian idealism.

The triumph of Gregory's ideals

Otherwise the victory lay with Henry, who had now gained time to rebuild his fortunes. Although the rebels went ahead with their plans and set up a rival king, Henry was once more in control of Germany by 1080. Again he broke with Gregory and, leading an army into Italy, took Rome, where he installed an antipope who crowned him emperor (1084). Faced by a renewed threat from Germany, Gregory was compelled to seek aid from his unscrupulous Norman vassals. In 1080 Robert Guiscard had received papal consent, not only to enlarge his fief by annexing various disputed territories, but also to invade the Balkan peninsula. Thereupon the great adventurer, with the able support of his son Bohemund, launched a drive which he hoped would carry him to the Byzantine throne. After taking Corfu and Durazzo, however, he had to abandon the campaign in order to check the advance of Henry IV. This the Normans did very effectively, and for good measure subjected the city of Rome to three days' pillage. When they left, Gregory in fear of reprisals, went with them—to die at Salerno in 1085. His last days were spent in bitter despondency. At the end he is reported to have exclaimed: "I have loved righteousness and hated iniquity; therefore I die in exile."

Nevertheless, the cause for which he lived and died had suffered no lasting defeat. Henry's attempt to dominate Italy served only to weaken his hold on Germany, where insurrection followed insurrection and his own son eventually turned against him. Long before his death in the midst of this wretched struggle the papacy had regained complete independence. And the ideals of Gregory VII, maintained by his successors, carried the Roman see to a new height of renown in the glorious Age of the Crusades.

3. The First Crusade

Towards the close of the eleventh century a number of factors com- *The Turk-*
bined to produce the great movement known as the crusade. Two of these *ish advance*
factors have already been examined: the growth in France of a feudal *and the*
aristocracy that tended to swarm into the surrounding regions and the *Byzantine*
emergence of a reformed papacy that ardently laid claim to the moral *appeal*
leadership of Europe. A third, the great commercial revival that brought
to old cities a new population eager for mercantile expansion, will be
separately treated in the next chapter. A fourth, the rise of a Turkish power
at the expense of the Byzantine Empire, must now receive attention. On
many occasions the Byzantine state had shown remarkable ability to
recover from apparent ruin—as under Heraclius, under Leo III, and, more
recently, under the Macedonian house. At the death of Basil II (1025) the
imperial dominions had been extended to include Bulgaria on the north
and Antioch on the south. Then ensued another relapse. The Macedonian
line came to an end when the second of Basil's daughters died unmarried
in 1056. Thereafter the usual palace intrigues brought to the throne a
series of very ordinary, if not incompetent, rulers. It was under them that
Venice became entirely independent, that their other Italian provinces
were lost to the Normans, and that the patriarch of Constantinople forced
an open breach with the papacy. To cap the climax, the Byzantine
possessions in Asia were now endangered by a fresh Moslem offensive.

The source of the danger was not the caliphate, which had long been
helpless, but the Seljuk Turks—one of the many nomadic tribes that,
adopting Mohammedanism, had entered the military service of Moslem
princes in Khorasan (see Map VI). By 1038 Togrul Beg, grandson of
Seljuk, had established himself as autonomous sultan of Nishapur, and
in another seventeen years he had taken Bagdad, rescued the caliph from
a local chieftain, and substituted his own control. Inheriting his father's
office in 1063, Alp Arslan (Brave Lion) completed the subjection of Persia
and Armenia. And when the emperor Romanus IV rashly brought up his
army to drive out the invaders, Alp Arslan annihilated it at Manzikert
(1071). The result of this one battle was not only the loss by the Byzantine
Empire of all Asia Minor, except a few places on the coast, but also the
destruction of its military power. Anatolia, which for hundreds of years
had supplied the government with the best of its generals and civil servants,
was now resettled by wild tribesmen from central Asia, and down to the
present it has remained solidly Turkish. Alp Arslan, however, did not long
survive his great victory. Dying in the next year, he was succeeded by
Malik Shah (1072-92), under whom the Seljuk power reached its height.
While Asia Minor was organized as the sultanate of Roum (i.e., Rome),
a new Turkish offensive was launched against Syria, the conquest of which

was completed by 1080. So it came about that the successors of Romanus at Constantinople, unable to recover what they had lost or perhaps to defend what they still possessed, appealed to the pope for the aid of Latin Christendom.

The papal policy

The appeal was well calculated to awaken interest at Rome, for the papacy had already been led to champion a variety of warlike enterprises in the west. A great offensive against the Moors was still being waged by the Christian princes of Spain, and the church had aided enlistment for that holy cause by an offer of special indulgence—the promise to the recruit that whatever penance he had accumulated would be wholly or largely remitted. Under a similar blessing the conquest of Sicily was being pushed to completion by Count Roger and his Normans. Moreover, the predecessors of Gregory VII had backed Duke William against a schismatic king of England, and Robert Guiscard against the schismatic Greeks of southern Italy. Gregory himself had gone so far as to approve Guiscard's project for the reduction of the Byzantine Empire. Meanwhile a significant part in many of these conflicts had come to be taken by the greater Italian cities. The Venetians, in return for commercial advantages, gave valuable assistance to the Normans in Sicily. The Genoese and Pisans, despairing of any effective action by king or emperor, combined their fleets against the Moslem pirates who had so long dominated the neighboring waters. Having taken the island of Sardinia, they extended their offensive operations along the coasts of Spain and Africa. Finally, in 1087, they compelled the emir of Tunis to grant them favorable terms by seizing his principal port—a victory that may be said to have definitely ended the Moslem control of the western Mediterranean.

Urban II and his project

Active intervention in Byzantine affairs was, of course, never possible for Gregory VII. And his immediate successor was an elderly friend who survived him by only a few months. Then, in 1088, the cardinals chose a younger and an abler man, the famous Urban II. The new pope was a noble of Champagne who had resigned a knightly career to become a monk at Cluny. There his talents had quickly distinguished him and he had been deputed for service at Rome. Having long been Gregory's trusted assistant, he accepted the papal office as a solemn obligation to carry out the ideals of his departed master. Everything, by a striking reversal of fortune, now seemed to contribute to the same end. In the face of constant distraction from Germany, the aging Henry IV abandoned all effort to control Italy. The death of Robert Guiscard, shortly following that of Gregory, had brought confusion to the duchy of Apulia; for the recognized heir, a brother of Bohemund, turned out to be incompetent. Since 1081 the Byzantine throne had been occupied by Alexius Comnenus, a cultured man of the world and a highly successful intriguer rather than a soldier or a statesman. Thanks to the weakening of the Norman power, he was able to recover his lost positions on the Macedonian coast, but he was powerless to drive the Turks from Asia Minor. It was under such circumstances that Alexius, thinking to secure a force of mercenary adventurers, besought the aid of the pope and the western princes.

This was Urban's opportunity, and the use he made of it proved him to be a worthy disciple of Gregory VII. Instead of an ordinary campaign to be waged by the Greek emperor for the reconquest of his Asiatic provinces, Urban dreamed of a magnificent Latin enterprise organized and controlled by the papacy—a great Christian offensive that should absorb and surpass the lesser offensives already begun. If successful, such an undertaking might restore to Alexius some of his lost territories; that was a minor consideration. The main object was to unite all Christendom in a war to recover the Holy Land, thus ending the schism with the Greeks as well as the local conflicts that had so long distracted Europe. In this last respect Urban's plan was no more revolutionary than in others. For over a century the clergy, especially in France, had been engaged in a rather fruitless effort to check the excesses of feudal warfare. Despoilers of churches and ravagers of the poor were placed under a solemn curse, and sworn associations of nobles were set up to enforce the decree. More recently this so-called Peace of God had been supplemented by the Truce of God, a similar organization to assure peaceful week-ends by prohibiting all fighting between Thursday evening and Monday morning. If combined and amplified under papal leadership, would not all such movements be infinitely more effective and so bring about a general pacification dictated by the church?

The Council of Clermont (1095)

It was apparently in the summer of 1095 that Urban and his counselors decided on the action that was dramatically taken before the end of the year. Having ended a triumphal progress through northern Italy, he crossed the Alps into France, where he spent many weeks investigating local conditions. Finally, in November, he held a council at Clermont, the chief city of Auvergne, to which the clergy and nobility streamed from all directions. There Urban, a Frenchman speaking in the vernacular to a French audience, delivered his epoch-making appeal. The Turks, he reminded his hearers, had but recently, after almost destroying the Byzantine Empire, seized the holy places in Palestine. What a noble work it would be to rescue the Lord's sepulcher from their foul hands! And who should assume this most sacred obligation if not the Franks—a people long distinguished for purity of faith, and a people famed beyond all others for prowess in arms? Here, crowded in by sea and mountain, they inhabited a country that hardly produced enough food to support them; there, on the contrary, lay the Promised Land of Israel, "flowing with milk and honey." Let them cease from their murderous wars and dissensions. Let them rather join in one blessed enterprise, to wrest from the infidel the lands defiled by his presence, knowing that God would grant them not merely a rich earthly reward but also imperishable glory in the kingdom of heaven. So Urban concluded, and the entire assemblage, we are told, shouted as with one voice, "*Dieu le veut*—God wills it!"

How shrewdly Urban had calculated his chance of success was proved by the event. Thanks to the pope's untiring efforts, thousands soon vowed adherence to the sacred cause. Each of them, as prescribed by the church, marked his new status by sewing on his garments a cross made of cloth. Thus the volunteer became known as a *croisé*, and his expedition as a *croisade*, or crusade. Every crusader, together with his family and all his possessions, was brought under the protection of the pope and, by a plenary indulgence, he was assured of immediate entrance into paradise if he died in the course of the war. To heighten the general enthusiasm there now appeared many unofficial preachers, of whom the most famous was Peter the Hermit. Under their fervent exhortation, indeed, the crusading movement tended to get out of control. Crowds of ill-armed persons, without adequate funds or competent leadership, started on a mad pilgrimage to the Holy Land. Their march across the Balkan peninsula was attended by many disorders, and of those who reached Constantinople the majority, on rashly advancing into Asia Minor, were killed by the Turks. The few survivors who reached Palestine did so by awaiting the principal host.

The commanders of the host were all French, being actual barons of France or the relatives and associates of such persons. This, as Urban had clearly realized, was quite inevitable if his project was to succeed. The most famous exploits of the previous years had been carried out by French armies, and little co-operation could be expected from Henry IV and his German followers. In the absence of Philip I,[7] whose notorious life had led to a renewal of his excommunication at Clermont, the Capetian house was represented by his brother Hugh, count of Vermandois. William II of England,[8] being occupied with domestic problems, was quite willing to leave any distant expedition to his brother Robert, duke of Normandy, and his brother-in-law Stephen, count of Blois. None of these three crusaders, it soon appeared, was equal in ability to Robert, count of Flanders, the son of a renowned adventurer who had already made the pilgrimage to Jerusalem. And the neighboring house of Boulogne contributed no less than three important chiefs: Eustace, Godfrey, and Baldwin, of whom the second had been appointed by Henry IV to the undesirable duchy of Lower Lorraine.[9] An imposing contingent from southern France was headed by Raymond, count of Toulouse, who enjoyed

[7] See above, p. 190.
[8] See below, p. 315.
[9] See below, p. 318.

a great reputation on account of his piety, wealth, and experience in the Spanish wars. Nevertheless, the best general among the Christian forces was unquestionably Bohemund, son of Robert Guiscard. Having seen action in Italy, Sicily, and Greece, he was familiar with the peoples of those countries and, to some extent, with their languages. Since Guiscard's duchy had been inherited by a brother of Bohemund, he had no great expectations at home and was naturally attracted by the crusade as a fresh opportunity for eastern conquest. With him went another Hauteville soldier of fortune, his nephew Tancred.

From the list of the foremost crusaders the character of their followers may readily be imagined. On the whole, the Christian host of 1096 was much like those which had earlier fought in Spain, England, and southern Italy. It differed mainly in the fact that, instead of being enlisted for the service of a secular prince, it was mustered under the supreme command of the papacy. Previously the church had blessed various enterprises launched by other authorities; now it was directing a vast campaign of its own. This in itself was eloquent testimony to the might of the organization headed by Urban II. Yet the men who were to put his plan into execution remained distinct individuals. Among them there might be a few idealists who found their chief inspiration in mystic religion. And the multitude of knights, being quite sincere in their faith, could easily be induced under momentary enthusiasm to forget all worldly motives. It is more than coincidence, however, that the principal gainers from the crusade were to be hard-headed adventurers like the Norman Bohemund and shrewd merchants like the shipowners of Genoa and Pisa. Such men the papacy might for a time be able to use, but could it really dominate them?

That question had not yet been raised when the various sections of the crusading host started east in the autumn of 1096. Arrangements had already been made that all groups should converge on Constantinople, where the emperor Alexius had promised to furnish money, provisions, and additional troops. Godfrey of Lorraine, together with various French contingents, followed the route down the Danube that had been used by the earlier bands of irregulars; Raymond of Toulouse, after passing the Alps into Lombardy, proceeded along the Dalmatian coast until he struck the main highway from Durazzo through Macedonia. The same highway was chosen by the rest of the leaders, but to reach it they sailed from the Norman ports in southern Italy. There were many delays and various open conflicts between Greeks and Latins before all had assembled at the rendezvous. In particular, a violent altercation broke out between Alexius and the chiefs whom he sought to enroll for his service. He would not provide for their further progress until all did homage to him for whatever lands they might conquer, and to this demand a good many objected. Nevertheless, all finally agreed to some sort of oath; so, in the spring of

The March on Constantinople (1096)

1097, the Christian army crossed into Asia to deliver its first attack on the Moslems.

Eastward advance (1097)

Mediæval chroniclers, who have been followed by various modern writers, exuberantly reckoned the crusaders by hundreds of thousands. Such numbers, if our estimate is restricted to knights, must be divided by ten. Although to our eyes an army of twenty to thirty thousand is not impressive, it was tremendous for the eleventh century. And it could hardly be matched by the local Turkish emirs; for all Moslem unity in Asia had again vanished after the death of Malik Shah. The Christians, therefore, had a good prospect of success if they could hold together; but it soon appeared that they were by no means united in their counsels. The mutual distrust of the Greeks and Latins was nearly equaled by that of the southern and northern French, and it was only for brief moments that the bitter rivalries of so many feudal chieftains could be submerged by religious enthusiasm. In June, 1097, Nicæa fell and was immediately given to the emperor. Then, while the latter diverted his forces to conquer the Ægean coast, the crusaders struck bravely across the interior of Anatolia. Despite the unaccustomed heat and a grave shortage of food, they maintained their advance, routing the Turks at Dorylæum in July and by September crossing the Taurus Mountains into Cilicia.

Capture of Antioch (1098)

Here, on the very border of the Promised Land, the host began to disintegrate. While Tancred, nephew of Bohemund, entered Tarsus, Baldwin of Boulogne invaded the upper Euphrates valley, where he eventually secured Edessa. The rest of the crusaders spent the winter before the walls of Antioch, vainly awaiting the support of Alexius who had foolishly turned back with a group of deserters from the Christian camp. It was the arrival of an Italian fleet with supplies and siege engines that ended the crusaders' plight in the spring of 1098. Antioch was now closely invested and on June 3, thanks to the generalship and diplomacy of Bohemund, it surrendered—five days before a large relieving force was brought up by the emir of Mosul. But Bohemund again distinguished himself by leading a counterattack that drove off the besieging Turks (June 28). This battle was decisive in many ways. In the first place, it produced an open breach between the Latins and the Greeks. Bohemund, defying the emperor who had abandoned the crusaders in their hour of need, obtained definite title to the principality of Antioch. Because of the Roman-Greek schism, the pope found no occasion for intervening on behalf of the discredited Alexius. And since the ships of Genoa and Pisa had now established direct contact with Syria, Constantinople no longer dominated communications with the west. The crusade thus became an independent Latin venture, the course of which was left to be determined by the generals in the field.

The battle also precipitated a bitter quarrel between Bohemund and Raymond of Toulouse. who had himself been eager to rule at Antioch and who now, in the face of the northern French party, espoused the cause of

Sant' Apollinare in Classe (Ravenna), Interior

San Vitale (Ravenna), Mosaics

PLATE I.
(See pp. 95, 97)

Santa Sophia (Constantinople)

Great Mosque (Damascus)

The Colosseum (Rome)

Pont du Gard (Nîmes)

PLATE II.
(See pp. 14, 96, 173)

Saint-Sernin (Toulouse)

Abbey of Laach

Cathedral of Pisa

Sant' Ambrogio (Milan)

PLATE III.
(See pp. 293-94)

Sant' Ambrogio (Milan), Interior

Abbey of Vézelai, Interior

PLATE IV.

(See pp. 293, 297)

Saint-Trophime (Arles), Main Portal

Laon Cathedral, Interior

PLATE V.

(See pp. 294, 299)

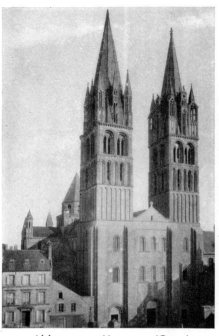

Abbaye-aux-Hommes (Caen)

Durham Cathedral

Notre-Dame (Paris)

Amiens Cathedral

PLATE VI.
(See pp. 295, 299, 461 n.)

Lincoln Cathedral

Salisbury Cathedral

PLATE VII.
(See pp. 300-01)

Notre-Dame (Paris), Chevet

Reims Cathedral, North Side

PLATE VIII.

(See p. 299)

Photo Clarence Ward

Amiens Cathedral, Interior

Photo Brown Bros.

Westminster Abbey, Interior

PLATE IX.
(See pp. 301 n., 299-300)

Abbey of Vézelai, Portal

Chartres Cathedral, Main Portal

PLATE X.
(See pp. 294, 301)

Virgin of the Salutation (Reims)

Vintage Capital (Reims)

Mont-Saint-Michel, Cloister

PLATE XI.

(See p. 302)

Weights and Measures

Pl...

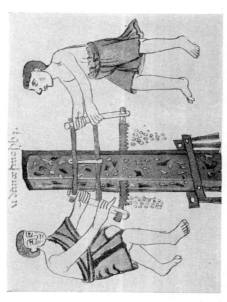

Marble-Working

Monastic Library

PLATE XII. Monte Cassino Miniatures of 1023
(See pp. 22, 147, 200, 303 n.)

Masonry Construction

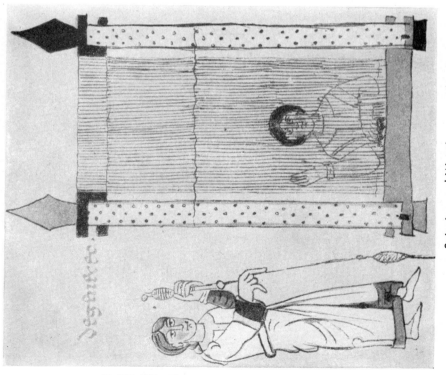

Spinning and Weaving

PLATE XIII. Monte Cassino Miniatures of 1023
(See pp. 23, 303 n.)

PLATE XIV.
(See pp. 200 n., 243 n.)

Portchester Castle

Kidwelly Castle

PLATE XV.
(See p. 443)

PLATE XVI.
(See p. 443)

Cloth Hall (Bruges)

Braun et Cie.

York Minster

PLATE XVII.
(See p. 461)

Van Eyck, "The Man with the Pink"

Illumination from the Duke of Berry's "Book of Hours"

PLATE XVIII.
(See p. 462)

Giotto, "The Descent from the Cross"

Masaccio, "The Tribute Money"

PLATE XIX.
(See p. 464)

PLATE XX.
(See p. 463)

Alexius. Besides, the southern French attributed the victory, not to the The
generalship of Bohemund, but to the power of a sacred relic—the lance affair
which had pierced the side of the crucified Christ and which, as the result of the
of a vision, had recently been discovered by Peter Bartholomew, a follower Holy Lance
of Raymond. The Normans, of course, scoffed at this alleged miracle,
intimating that their rivals had simply uncovered what they had already

MAP XI.

buried. Even after the host had resumed its march on Jerusalem, dissension
still raged. At last, during a halt on the coast, Peter Bartholomew agreed
to undergo ordeal by fire to prove the truth of his statements. Clad only
in a shirt and bearing the Holy Lance, he actually walked into a heap of
fiercely blazing olive branches and emerged on the other side. Twelve days
later he died, in consequence, said his friends, of excited handling by the
crowd; in consequence, said his enemies, of natural burning by the fire.
So the dispute continued as before—a remarkable commentary on the
mixture of religion and politics that characterized the whole crusade.

In spite of all distractions, however, the Christian host eventually found itself encamped before Jerusalem. Now all was again harmony. And now, thanks to the co-operation of the Italian cities, there was a plentiful supply of materials and trained men for conducting a siege. On July 15, less than six weeks after the enraptured crusaders had first sighted the Holy City, its walls were stormed. One week later Godfrey of Lorraine, whose forces had led the final assault and who had remained somewhat aloof from the previous wrangling, was proclaimed Defender of the Holy Sepulcher. And on August 12 the success of his rule was assured by his victory at Ascalon over a formidable Egyptian army. Strangely enough, the man who had launched the great enterprise survived but did not live to celebrate its triumphant conclusion. Urban II died at Rome on July 29, just before the glad news arrived that Jerusalem had fallen.

The success of the crusade had, of course, enormous repercussion throughout Europe. All Christendom rang with the deeds of the heroes who had participated, and for many generations their example remained a potent influence upon the chivalry of the west. But, above all, the victory was logically reflected in the exaltation of the power that had conceived the undertaking. It was more than coincidence that the mediæval papacy attained its height during the Age of the Crusades. Deepening knowledge of mediæval civilization has, to be sure, made it impossible to regard all the major developments of the twelfth century as effects of the crusade. Yet in itself it was a very wonderful event, and one that richly illustrates the thoughts and habits of contemporary Europe. Leaving the ultimate significance of the crusade for treatment in subsequent chapters, we may simply note here that its immediate result in the east was the organization of four Latin states. Extending from north to south, they were the county of Edessa, originally held by Baldwin of Boulogne; the principality of Antioch, which passed from Bohemund to Tancred; the county of Tripolis, finally created as a sop for Raymond of Toulouse; and the kingdom of Jerusalem, which carried with it a theoretical superiority over the other three (see Map XI).

Throughout these states the feudalism of contemporary France, modified to suit local conditions, was established as the governing principle of military and political organization—to the conquerors a very practical system such as had already been introduced in England, southern Italy, and northern Spain.[10] Godfrey of Lorraine, as we have seen, inaugurated Latin rule at Jerusalem, though without the royal title. It was his brother Baldwin who, on moving from Edessa, was formally crowned as king on Christmas Day, 1100. For the first time since the decay of ancient Rome, Europe had successfully carried out a great offensive against Asia.

[10] See above, pp. 192-97.

CHAPTER XIII

The Growth of the Towns

1. THE REVIVAL OF COMMERCE

Of the many centuries that had elapsed since the disruption of the Roman Empire, the eleventh was the first to witness positive signs of economic recovery in western Europe. There was then, for one thing, a noteworthy increase of population. Armies of younger sons made possible the great feudal expeditions into Britain, Spain, Sicily, and Palestine that have been described in previous chapters. At the same time we hear of a greatly enhanced commercial activity, of new trading settlements along highways and water routes, of projects to expand the cultivated area by draining swamps and clearing forests, and of the rural colonization that accompanied such projects. In the later Roman period a vicious cycle of impoverishment and depopulation had brought ruin to whole provinces of the empire. Now the reverse process brought renewed prosperity. The cause was assuredly no increase in human fecundity. It was not that the men of the eleventh century had more offspring, but that more of their offspring were permitted to survive and have offspring of their own. More jobs made it possible for more people to live, and the needs of these people led in turn to the appearance of still more jobs.

As usual when economic phenomena are concerned, it is hard to say precisely what was cause and what was result. We may, however, be reasonably certain of a few relationships: that the increase of agricultural production was necessitated by the growth of new trading centers, where the population was dependent on imported food; and that, of course, these centers arose to meet the demands of reviving commerce. We may also find significance in the fact that the tenth century was a period of political stabilization—marked by the emergence of new and efficient states, the absorption of the Vikings and Hungarians into the European system, and

235

the organization of French society on a feudal basis. But the problem of how and why the Dark Age was succeeded by the marvelous Age of the Crusades is too complex to be taken up in an introductory sketch. The interaction of economic, political, and cultural developments must be left for later discussion, our present attention given to preliminary questions regarding trade routes, mercantile colonization, and the rise of the class known as bourgeois.

The Latin world and its neighbors

In the first place, it should be remembered that we are dealing primarily with the Latin world—the countries dominated by the Roman Church, which were mainly Italy, France, the British Isles, Scandinavia, Germany, and the adjacent borderlands. To the east lay the Greek world, consisting of the Byzantine Empire together with the Slavic states under its cultural influence: principally Serbia, Bulgaria, and Russia. To the south was the great Moslem world, which at its height included Spain, most of the Mediterranean islands, Roman Africa, Egypt, Syria, and other vast territories in Asia. The Moslems were thus able, when they chose, to prevent all direct contact between Christian Europe and the far east, to force all trade between those regions to pass through their hands. And their control of Spain and Morocco broke the Latin world into two reaches of seacoast joined only by overland communications: a southern area on the Mediterranean and a northern area extending from the Bay of Biscay to the Baltic.

Trade routes: The Mediterranean

The center of the southern area was of course Italy, from which in the days of Roman prosperity lines of traffic had crossed the sea in all directions. But for many centuries regular trade had ceased to flow along most of the ancient routes—interrupted, as it was, by the piracy of barbarian peoples, by the political separation of east and west, and finally by the Moslem conquests. In this respect Charlemagne's pseudo-empire, being essentially a creation of the mainland, had brought no improvement; and its collapse in the ninth century, together with the continued decline of the Byzantine power, had encouraged a fresh series of Moslem offensives. Under such conditions Italian shipping had all but disappeared. The one notable exception was provided by Venice, the new commercial city that arose on Byzantine soil at the head of the Adriatic. Then, in the first half of the eleventh century, a holy war against the Moslem on the sea was launched by the Genoese and Pisans, who thus gained rich trading advantages in Corsica, Sardinia, Sicily, and Africa. And with the crusade the Italian merchants found themselves in position to reopen direct communications with Syria, carrying eastward the armies of pilgrims with their horses and necessary supplies, and bringing westward cargoes of oriental products.

Roads and rivers

This revival of the old sea routes linking Europe, Asia, and Africa inevitably brought new life to the land and river routes that ran north from Italy. The great Roman highways, which had originally been built to join the capital with the provinces, included two coast roads: one from Genoa to Marseilles and Spain, the other from Aquileia to Trieste and Dalmatia. Between them extended fanwise two sets of roads across the Alps: those crossing by the western passes to the valley of the Rhone and those crossing by the eastern passes to the upper valleys of the Rhine and Danube. Thence other paved highways paralleled the military frontiers and led through Gaul to the ports of the Atlantic and the North Sea. But, whenever possible, the mediæval merchant preferred to travel by water, restricting his overland carrying to short journeys between rivers. So the Garonne, Loire, Seine, Somme, Scheldt, Meuse, and Rhine provided important routes to the west and northwest; the Ems, Weser, Saale, and Elbe to the north (see Map XII).

In ancient times the waters of the Atlantic had been slightly used for **The** commerce. The only northern sea route that the Romans had found in- **northern** dispensable was the one crossing the Channel to Britain. But by the eleventh **seas** century enormous changes had been made in the political map of Europe. Beyond the Rhine what had been a wilderness inhabited by savage tribes had now been brought within the pale of Christendom, as had much of the Slavic borderland, northern Britain, Ireland, and parts of Scandinavia. In the ninth century the Vikings had appeared on the continent as pillagers and destroyers; during the next two hundred years they had been absorbed into older states or had founded new and vigorous states of their own, while their fleets had been diverted from piracy to peaceful trade. Thus the waterways of the Viking freebooters now served as commercial links connecting the lands bordering on the Baltic and the North Sea. And through the mediation of the Russians, who controlled the so-called Varangian route from the Dnieper to the Gulf of Finland, the northern region was brought into economic contact with the Black Sea and the Caspian, and so with the Arab and Byzantine Empires.

In the history of Europe the commercial prominence of Italy was no **Flanders** new phenomenon. The unprecedented development was rather that which now took place in the northwest. A glance at the map will show how Flanders served as the focal point for the great routes of the eleventh century. Goods brought by land and water through central France, down the Rhine, westward from the Baltic, or eastward from the British Isles, all easily converged on the little marquisate founded in the ninth century by Baldwin Iron-Arm. In Roman times that district had been largely uninhabited, being held merely as a military frontier. Now, on the contrary, it rapidly became a great center of population and wealth, a source of enormous power for its fortunate rulers, and on that account the object of wars and political intrigues that have continued down to our own day. Of secondary economic importance in the northwest region were Picardy, Normandy, the middle Rhine valley, the Île de France, and England. Central France remained backward, but the French Mediterranean coast, advantageously situated between Spain and Italy, tended to share the prosperity of the latter two countries.

Trade and towns

The connection between these developments and the revival of urban life in western Europe is obvious. On all sides towns and trade grew up together. No important trade route could exist apart from towns, and every great town arose on a trade route. This connection serves to explain many important facts. The outstanding features of urban life, which were to have profound influence on the culture of Latin Christendom, were very new in the Age of the Crusades. By the close of the twelfth century scores of communities in western Europe were enjoying extensive liberties, sometimes including rights of self-government. Two hundred years earlier such privileged communities had not existed. What amounted to a social revolution had been produced by economic advance during the intervening period. Some writers, it is true, have traced the municipal institutions of the Middle Ages back to Roman tradition or to the primitive customs of the Germans; but careful analysis of the problem indicates that they have been misled by treacherous words.

The transformation of old cities and *burgen*

We have already seen that the "cities" of the Carolingian Empire could have been little more than military and administrative centers. And the fortifications erected by kings and princes in the ninth and tenth centuries were hardly towns in our sense of the word. Whether situated in France, Germany, or England, and whether called *château, burg,* or borough, such a fortress had few if any urban features. Even when a walled area included an official market, the latter was by itself insufficient to support a mercantile population of any considerable size. Some trade, of course, persisted all through the Dark Age, but the professional merchant and the free artisan remained very exceptional. By the twelfth century the situation had been radically changed. Thenceforth, through the influence of revived commerce, cities tended to become truly urban centers. At the same time "borough" (*burg, bourg*) acquired the meaning of a privileged town, the citizen of which was known as a burgess, burgher, or bourgeois. That these words all came to denote a townsman, rather than the defender of a fort, resulted from the transformation of the place where he lived. Although most of the pertinent evidence is contained in charters and other documentary sources, much valuable information in this connection has been obtained through the study of local topography. By examining the traces of early fortifications and other archæological remains, we may often find out when and how a particular town developed.

Types of urban growth

The Roman city of Cologne, for example, was a walled rectangle of approximately 239 acres, in one corner of which only a small remnant of the ancient population continued to live throughout the period that followed the barbarian invasions. By the opening of the eleventh century, however,

a new settlement of merchants had appeared on the bank of the Rhine outside the wall. Within another hundred years three additional suburbs had
been fortified, and finally, in 1180, a new wall was erected to enclose an
area of about three times that of the original city (see Figure 18). Scores
of other communities can be proved to have grown in much the same way.
Along routes that had earlier been used by the Romans it was natural that
the new settlements should be formed in or about the old cities or camps

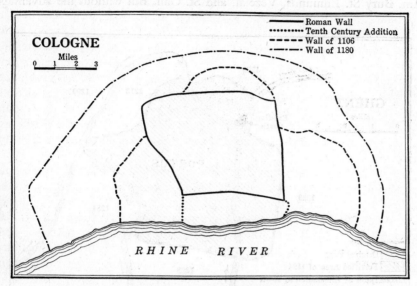

FIG. 18.   The Expansion of Mediæval Cologne.

of the Romans. In more recently organized states, where no such positions
existed, the settlers were attracted to other centers, usually the castles of the
local prince. Particularly fine examples of such development can be seen
in the great towns of Flanders: Ghent, Bruges, Arras, Ypres, Saint-Omer,
and others. What is still called the Vieux-Bourg (Old Burg) at Ghent was
the primitive fortress of the count—a triangle of about twenty-five acres at
the intersection of two rivers. But the town of Ghent grew from the New
Burg or Port—a trading quarter that by the eleventh century had appeared
across the river to the south. When surrounded by a wall in 1194, it had
already come to include over two hundred acres, and this was only the beginning of a rapid expansion that, with occasional interruption, has continued down to the present (see Figure 19).

Throughout France and Italy most mediæval towns will be found, like
Cologne, to have developed on the sites of old Roman cities, and a similar
origin can of course be attributed to a number of English towns: London,

York, Lincoln, Canterbury, Exeter, Winchester, and others. Beyond the Rhine, however, most of the German towns developed, like Ghent, in conjunction with an earlier *burg,* as is often testified by their names (Magdeburg, Merseburg, Quedlinburg, etc.). And the early history of many English boroughs—e.g., Bristol, Nottingham, Oxford, and Norwich—also resembled that of the Flemish towns. Occasionally a fortified cathedral or abbey served as the nucleus of an extensive urban settlement—as at Durham, Bury St. Edmunds, Vézelai, and St. Gall. But without the advantage

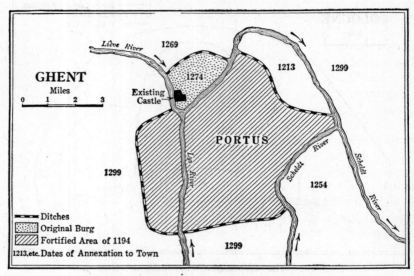

FIG. 19.   The Expansion of Mediæval Ghent.

of a good commercial location, neither church nor castle nor Roman fortress could ever become more than it had been in the previous age. Towns grew up in mediæval Europe precisely as they have grown up in modern America, through the operation of natural forces that no-one could entirely foresee or control. Although kings and princes frequently tried to create towns by deliberate planning, it was only rarely that their experiments produced urban communities of the first rank. The majority of the new foundations (*villes neuves*) remained comparatively small.

The town as a mercantile settlement   By whatever process the result was attained, the typical town of the later Middle Ages appears to have been essentially a mercantile settlement —a colony of persons engaged in commerce and allied activities. Only a restricted number of the inhabitants would be merchants in our sense of the word. The mass of the townsmen would be rather artisans and laborers. Many, in fact, would still be employed in agriculture, for the increase of

the population inevitably stimulated the production of food and raw materials in the immediate neighborhood. And since transportation by land
depended largely on domestic animals, wide pastures remained a vital
necessity. In spite of its rural features, however, the town was economically
very distinct from the simple village. The town had a continuous market,
where an increasing number of persons made a living through buying and
selling at a profit. There a man could earn enough for himself and his family
through his craft alone, and so become entirely independent of any manorial organization. In the smaller towns, which served chiefly as distribution centers for agricultural produce, a limited number of manufacturers
could exist merely by supplying the local residents with articles of daily use
—such as clothing, leather goods, tools, and food. Occasionally some community, becoming famous for the excellence of its work, would export manufactures to far-distant lands and accordingly develop industry on a much
larger scale.

Pre-eminent among such communities came to be the cities of Italy and **Sea trade**
Flanders, but their original prosperity depended mainly on their location **and ships**
with regard to the great trade routes by sea and land. Business always
flourished where cargoes had to be unloaded for transhipment, and in this
respect seaports or places towards the mouths of rivers tended to have the
advantage. For example, we find among the outstanding mediæval towns
Venice, Pisa, Genoa, Marseilles, Bordeaux, Rouen, Ghent, Liége, Cologne,
Bremen, Hamburg, London, York, and Bristol. And it should be noted that
important towns like Arras, Bruges, and Lübeck, which the modern maps
show apart from navigable water, were situated on streams readily ascended
by mediæval ships. Much trading continued to be carried on in long fast
boats propelled by oar. Such were the galleys of the Mediterranean, as well
as the Viking ships of the north, and they were all of very shallow draft.
For bulky cargoes slow round-built sailing-ships were preferable, but even
these remained comparatively small in northern waters. The largest were
those constructed by the Genoese and Venetians for use on the crusades—
with two or even three decks, and with raised "castles" at bow and stern
to accommodate noble passengers. By the thirteenth century such vessels
were sometimes a hundred feet in length, with a beam of nearly half that
amount.

During the earlier period we have very scanty information concerning **Gilds**
the life and habits of merchants on land. The roads, we know, were so bad
that wagons were of little use and goods had to be carried on pack animals.
Many regions, furthermore, were infested by robbers, and every feudal
boundary was made the excuse for collection of tolls. Under these conditions merchants came to travel in bands, accompanied by escorts of armed
men. And since journeys of this sort entailed careful planning and a considerable outlay of money, they naturally led to the organization of merchant

unions called gilds or hanses. Such associations are first definitely heard of
in the twelfth century, when princes came to guarantee their liberties in
formal charters. By that time, however, many gilds were already old and
held valuable privileges in widely separated countries. At London, for instance, the Flemings, the men of Cologne, and the men of Rouen were enjoying special rights long before the Norman Conquest.

Fairs

Another prominent feature of reviving commerce in twelfth-century
Europe was the fair. The rural market, normally held once a week for the
exchange of local products, played no part in the distribution of articles
imported from abroad. The men who engaged in that business needed larger
gatherings attended by merchants from all the neighboring towns. Religious
festivals might provide occasions that could be turned to profitable advantage by merchants; but as a rule the fair owed its formal establishment
to a territorial prince, who guaranteed special protection to all persons
coming to a certain place at a certain time every year. Annual fairs, each
lasting for several days, were eventually organized in series; so that the
great traders arranged their trips in order to attend as many as possible.
Thus they disposed of merchandise in large quantities, while small dealers
obtained stocks for resale or for use in manufacture, and the lord of the
fair got a handsome revenue from stallage, the fees charged for displaying
goods in stalls.

Articles of trade

With regard to the articles distributed, nothing more than a brief indication can be attempted here. A large proportion of the finer manufactures
still came from the Moslem countries of Spain, Africa, and Asia—especially
silks, rugs, and other luxurious fabrics; damascened arms and armor; and
artistic products in the precious metals, ivory, earthenware, and other materials. The demand for oriental spices, drugs, dyes, perfumes, and gems
was constant, and was greatly stimulated by the crusades. Many of our common words, by their derivation from the Arabic or Persian, show that they
originally denoted imports from the east:[1] e.g., sugar, syrup, cotton, satin,
damask, muslin, crimson, scarlet, azure, lilac, spinach, artichoke, orange,
lemon, apricot, camphor, and saffron. By the twelfth century, however, the
Moslem cities were coming to be rivaled by those of Italy. Venice, in particular, soon became famous for glass-making, metal-working, and other
skilled crafts. By that time, too, the woolen cloth of Flanders was finding a
ready market throughout Europe. Other regions of the north and west exported principally food and raw materials. There was a flourishing trade in
salt, which was obtained either from mines or from marshes on the seacoast.
Iron was in great demand. Stone and wood were scarce in some countries.
French merchants carried wine to England and returned with wool and
hides. The Germans from the Baltic brought oriental goods that had been
transported across Russia, as well as furs, lumber, naval stores, and amber.
It was in connection with this sort of trade that the towns developed in

[1] See above, p. 174.

the twelfth century. Even the greatest of them were still commercial rather than industrial—and they would not seem very great to us. In those days a city of twenty-five thousand was relatively huge. Yet even the ordinary town, of from five to ten thousand, was an island of privilege sharply contrasted with the surrounding country.

2. ELEMENTARY BOURGEOIS LIBERTIES

Many European writers, especially those devoted to legal study, have attempted to show that the towns of their own respective countries were based upon some sort of national trait or custom. Such a notion is unquestionably wrong. The differences that existed among mediæval towns were due, not to national or racial peculiarities, but to historical circumstance and environment. Despite political and linguistic variations, the urban institutions of the Middle Ages were fundamentally the same throughout wide regions. It is quite possible, for example, to consider the liberties of townsmen in northwestern Europe as a single subject. On the other hand, it would be hazardous to extend such generalization into the Mediterranean region. The Greek and Moslem cities belonged to worlds that were altogether foreign to the Carolingian lands. Some parts of Italy had never lost contact with the Byzantine Empire. In spite of other differences, northern and southern Spain remained economically akin. And the southernmost provinces of France were in many ways more closely related to Italy and Spain than to the Capetian domain.

In the following pages a more comprehensive picture of urban development may be obtained by examining each of these countries separately; as a preliminary, it will be simpler to restrict attention to the northwest. And within that region it will be convenient to begin, not with the big towns, but with the little ones. The former, having developed rapidly in the eleventh century, needed no written guarantees of elementary privileges in the twelfth, when such grants became usual. Their charters were commonly restricted to the definition of exceptional or newly acquired rights. For a detailed account of fundamental bourgeois liberties we must rather turn to a *ville neuve*. Such a town was a deliberately planned foundation. Inspired by the example of old and prosperous communities, some prince would seek to establish a similar source of revenue within his own territory. With the advice and financial support of business men, he would select a good site, lay out a market-place with streets leading into it, put up a church and other structures, and then offer inducements to prospective settlers by means of a solemn charter.[2]

A document of this sort would naturally emphasize the advantages that

The new towns of north-western Europe

[2] See Plate XIV: an aerial photograph of Friedeberg (in Brandenburg), which is typical of countless *villes neuves* founded along the east German frontier during the thirteenth century (see below, Chapter XXIV). Note how the lines of existing streets testify to the existence of a circular plan for the original town, together with two later extensions of the surrounding wall.

Freiburg-
im-
Breisgau

townsmen everywhere insisted on. Indeed, if we compare the hundreds of foundation charters that have been preserved, they are found to bear a strong family resemblance. By analyzing several of the earlier grants, we may gain an introduction to all. The first successful experiment in urban colonization to be carried out by a German prince was that of Conrad, duke of Zähringen;[3] for as the result of his efforts the town of Freiburg-im-Breisgau celebrated the eighth-hundredth anniversary of its foundation in 1920. It was on waste land adjoining his castle that Conrad created a new town, having called together and organized under oath, says his charter, distinguished traders from the neighboring regions. Each settler was provided with a plot measuring fifty by a hundred feet, for which he was to pay a fixed annual rent of one *solidus*.[4] This land he should hold by hereditary right, with the privilege of freely selling it or bequeathing it by will. The community was to be governed only by the custom of trading towns, especially that of Cologne. The inhabitants were to be exempt from all forced entertainment, from all arbitrary exactions, and from all tolls throughout the duke's possessions.

Chiefly because of its location—on the main road running through the Black Forest from the Rhine to the Danube—Freiburg prospered from the first, and its liberties, originally taken from Cologne, were in turn given to many other new towns in southern Germany, notably Colmar and Bern. To the east, likewise, a number of similar foundations were made in the course of the twelfth century, of which the most influential were Munich and Lübeck.[5] Indeed, a prominent feature of the German advance into the Slavic country was the continuous establishment of trading settlements modeled after those that had already appeared to the westward. This development, however, hardly reached significant proportions before the thirteenth century, and in the meantime urban colonization had rapidly progressed in France. The first of the Capetians to take an active part in such matters was Louis VI (1108-37),[6] who not only intervened on behalf of the bourgeoisie in many of the episcopal cities, but himself founded the famous liberties of Lorris.

Lorris

This little town, situated in the vineyard country of the upper Loire valley, was evidently designed by the king to serve as a center for the wine trade in that portion of his domain. Every man who came there to live was assured by the king's charter of a house and lot at a rent of only six *deniers* a year. If he resided without challenge for a year and a day, he was thenceforth free and could not be claimed by a previous master. He was to be

---

[3] See below, p. 318.

[4] The *solidus* (*sou* or shilling) was a weight of silver pennies (*denarii* or *deniers*); often, as in England, a twentieth of a pound. See above, p. 30.

[5] Both founded by Henry the Lion: see below, p. 332.

[6] See below, pp. 310-11.

quit of tallage and forced exactions; of all military service, except for one day within the immediate vicinity; and of all *corvée* aside from stated obligations. Whenever he pleased, he could sell his possessions and go elsewhere. He could not be brought to trial outside the town, and in it only according to certain specified rules of procedure. Fines and punishments were strictly limited. No-one should be molested while coming to or going from the market of Lorris unless he had committed an offense on that same day. Tolls were restricted as to amount and as to mode of collection. The king forbade that anyone should take food or materials from the townsmen without just remuneration. Nor should anyone be entitled to credit unless it was freely extended. Even the king and queen were to pay their bills inside two weeks.

The liberties of Lorris proved enormously popular. Extended by various Montkings to many other small towns in the royal domain, these liberties were auban also taken by numerous barons as a model for their foundations. So, within the next two centuries, the one set of customs came to be enjoyed by scores of communities in Champagne and Burgundy, as well as in the Île de France. And Lorris was but one of the many towns whose charters were widely copied throughout northern France. In the south, too, new settlements of the same sort were common under the name of *bastides*. Perhaps the most successful of them was that established in 1144 by Alfonse, count of Toulouse. As the consequence of a feud between the abbot of Saint-Théodard and the residents of a *bourg* adjoining his monastery, Alfonse offered the townsmen a new site on territory of his own. To guarantee their future security, he issued a formal charter containing the promise of building-lots at fixed rents, restriction of tolls, exemption from forced hospitality, prohibition of various exactions, and other familiar provisions. The tenor of the whole charter shows that it was a business arrangement; and it assuredly worked to the benefit of both parties, for the count's little colony became illustrious under the name of Montauban.

Thanks to the matchless records of the Conqueror's government, we can Newcastle-trace the establishment of privileged trading communities in England to upon-Tyne about the year 1066. From a little Norman *bourg* called Breteuil some of the invading barons borrowed a set of "laws" which they granted to new settlements along the Welsh frontier; and from there the same customs were carried into Ireland. Meanwhile Henry I (1100-35)[7] had been instrumental in founding a number of towns—among them Verneuil in Normandy and Newcastle in England. The latter, named after the new castle overlooking the river Tyne, received from Henry a group of liberties that were to have wide influence. If a peasant came to Newcastle and completed the lawful residence of a year and a day, no lord had any further claim on him. The burgesses were entirely exempt from manorial or servile obligations.

[7] See below, p. 316.

They could sell or bequeath their lands and were free to come and go as they pleased. Within the borough, as well as a certain district outside it, they enjoyed a monopoly of all trading. These liberties of Newcastle were extended to many other towns, both in northern England and in Scotland, where they were adopted by the king as his official standard of urban privilege.

Bourgeois liberties: Free status

Such charters as we have briefly examined present only the minimum demands of the townsman in the twelfth century. But these demands clearly reveal his great superiority over the peasant. First of all, the bourgeois enjoyed free status. No matter what his origin, the man who lived in a town unchallenged for a year and a day secured complete liberty. The town air, it was said, made him free. To be more exact, it was his residence on privileged soil that broke any ties of personal or manorial subjection to an outside lord. In legal theory the town was a sort of territorial immunity, created by a holder of political authority. It is, therefore, a mistake to explain the mediæval town as a servile community that gradually or suddenly became emancipated. And the principle thus enforced was merely the expression of a social fact: the mercantile pursuits of the inhabitants were incompatible with villeinage. Men would not come to a place as merchants or laborers unless they could have unhampered control of their bodies and of whatever they might acquire.

Burgage tenure

The personal freedom of the bourgeois tended to carry with it exemption from all the typically servile or manorial obligations. Rents were usually small, being set at a nominal figure to attract settlers. Other services were defined in advance and were owed, as a rule, by the entire community, rather than by individuals. A member of the community thus held his land on extremely advantageous terms. He could freely sell or lease any part of it, and keep the proceeds. He could even dispose of it by will; for bourgeois land, unlike the acres of the villein or the fief of the noble, was not bound by inflexible rules of inheritance. This free tenure, peculiar to the bourgeois class, is known by various names in various countries, but is familiar in English law as burgage. That it, rather than any other mediæval tenure, anticipated what we know as ownership of real property is obvious.

Special justice

Another almost universal feature of early municipal charters was the promise to the men of the town that they should not be tried outside it. The reason was that the bourgeois community enjoyed a peculiar law, and to secure its benefits the member had to be exempted from courts where justice was administered according to feudal or manorial custom. Townsmen naturally objected to procedure devised for knights or peasants; they demanded forms of action by which debts could be collected, contracts could be enforced, and property rights in land and chattels could be safeguarded. These advantages were obtained in the town court because there the judgment-finders were bourgeois. Although the presiding magistrates might be appointed by the ruler, the court itself was made up of prominent citizens who were familiar with the established custom of the locality. Each of the older communities had its own law, and a pre-existing system of this sort was usually proclaimed as the standard whenever a new town was founded. Thus Freiburg-im-Breisgau followed the law of Cologne, and dozens of other places later received that of Freiburg.

The chief mercantile privilege of the bourgeois was his right to sell freely in the town market. Anyone from the outside, even the citizen of a nearby town, was a foreigner against whom the municipal tolls served as a protective tariff. Frequently it was provided that certain articles could there be manufactured or sold only by members of the local community, that they had the first right to buy certain kinds of imports, or that all merchants coming within a certain region had to display their goods in the town. All these and many other regulations would have to be administered by men familiar with the details of business—in other words, by such a group as decided the law. Often the leading townsmen were combined in a gild having charge of all buying and selling; in that case the men who controlled the court were likely also to be the governors of the gild. In any case the community had to have some sort of mercantile organization, and by easy transition this might develop into formal self-government. Mercantile privileges

What the townsman chiefly wanted, however, was not political authority but legal and economic freedom—the opportunity to make a living where and as he pleased, without being subject to the arbitrary control of a manorial lord. On his side, the prince who founded the town was swayed by equally practical motives. He had learned from experience that trading communities could not be managed like agrarian estates. He was willing to renounce all the rights objected to by bourgeois populations. He was willing even to rent lands at a nominal figure, abandoning to the men who took them the chance of profit on future sales. Yet his action was by no means altruistic. He hoped to make a fortune out of the revenue that would later accrue to him if the settlement flourished. The greater and more prosperous the town, the more he could expect by way of tolls, profits of justice, and other incidentals. Wealthy communities were always glad to pay well for new privileges or for the confirmation of old ones. And by politic negotiation handsome subsidies might be secured from townsmen who appreciated the worth of a benevolent patron. The interests of the lord

The case of Lorris, noted above, introduces another important question in the history of western Europe: how the growth of towns immediately affected the rural districts that surrounded them. Although the men who came to enjoy the liberties of Lorris might be officially called *burgenses* (bourgeois), they often seem to have been engaged in agricultural pursuits. The same generalization applies even more strongly to hundreds of little communities in Lorraine and eastern France through the extension Reaction upon the countryside

MAP XII

TOWNS OF
WESTERN EUROPE
IN THE
THIRTEENTH CENTURY

Scale of Miles

0   50   100 150 200

of a charter originally granted by the archbishop of Reims to Beaumont-en-Argonne (1182). But the inspiration of his charter came from one earlier secured by the city of Laon and various groups of neighboring villagers.[8] Why should peasants thus be permitted to share the status that we call bourgeois?

The answer may apparently be discerned in the fact that the rapid expansion of urban populations enormously increased the demand for grain, wine, and other agrarian products, and so revolutionized old manorial practices by creating a cash market. Inevitably, therefore, the inhabitants of regions adjoining the greater towns demanded and obtained a freedom resembling that of the townsmen. A very early example of such progress is found in Flanders, where the tenth-century counts launched a magnificent project for reclaiming the coastal marshes. Through the construction of dikes and tidal gates, a wide strip of fertile land was brought under cultivation within a year or so. And to make the cultivation possible, settlers called *hospites* (French *hôtes*) were attracted by promising them what amounted to elementary bourgeois liberties. They were exempted from all forced labor and from all arbitrary exactions; so, by meeting fixed obligations known in advance, they were assured of whatever profits they could earn. How the precedents thus set contributed to the development of capitalistic enterprise, and eventually fomented social unrest, will be seen in later chapters.

3. THE COMMUNES

Venice

Sharply distinguished from the great majority of towns, which enjoyed merely the elementary bourgeois liberties, were the few that had at least some measure of autonomy—the group generally known as communes. Such great towns first developed in Italy, and there, strangely enough, the city to assume leadership had been unknown to antiquity. While the older urban centers of the west were threatened with extinction, Venice took form and prospered. Until the time of Justinian the low-lying region of Venetia had been thinly populated. Thenceforth, however, its marshes came to afford refuge to thousands of immigrants fleeing from the disorders of the inland regions. To gain a living in such an environment, the newcomers naturally turned to the established industry of salt-making and to coastwise trade. Then, as the Lombards took Ravenna, the settlements along the Venetian shore found their unbroken connection with Constantinople of enormous advantage in commerce. And their pre-eminence on the Adriatic was definitely assured when Charlemagne abandoned the duchy to the Byzantine emperor. Within the next hundred years an increasing population gathered at the Rialto, the lagoon that experience proved to be the

[8] They even had the right to elect their own local officials and were legally described as "communes." See the following section of this chapter.

most favorably situated—and the illustrious city of Venice, as poets have sung, was born of the sea.

Being built on islands and a shore cut by numerous streams, Venice from the outset used waterways for streets. On the west the city was isolated from the mainland by a great expanse of swamp that made it virtually immune from military attack; to seaward lines of sandbars constituted a naval barrier of even greater strength. Although in theory part of the Byzantine Empire, by the opening of the eleventh century the city was actually a republic, holding dominion over a considerable portion of the coast. The duke of Venetia had now become the doge of Venice—no longer an appointed official, but an elected magistrate who ruled by the advice and consent of the local aristocracy. In every respect Venice henceforth acted as a sovereign state; it coined money, signed treaties, and waged war. Venetian fleets assumed an active offensive against the Dalmatian pirates, the Moslems of Sicily, and various rival communities on the Adriatic. When, later in the eleventh century, the Venetians joined the Byzantine emperor against the Normans,[9] it was as allies rather than subjects and in return for the valuable privilege of free trade throughout the imperial lands, including the city of Constantinople itself.

Following the lead of Venice, though without the advantage of a Byzantine connection, Genoa and Pisa rose to great prosperity in the course of the eleventh century. While the sea belonged to the Moslems, these cities had remained obscure. Then, as the Moslem power weakened, they launched a Christian offensive in the western Mediterranean. By 1095 they had come to dominate the coast from Sicily to Barcelona, together with the islands of Corsica and Sardinia, and they had extorted special privileges from the emirs of northern Africa. How their fleets made possible the success of the First Crusade has been seen in the preceding chapter. Their reward was the allotment of trading quarters in the towns of the Syrian coast and a series of economic concessions from the rulers of the newly organized Latin states. Meanwhile Genoa and Pisa had tended, like Venice, to become autonomous republics. Before the end of the eleventh century both cities appear as communes, governed by groups of elected magistrates styled consuls. *Genoa and Pisa*

During that same time, or within the next few years, extensive rights of self-government were secured by a host of other towns in northern Italy—such as Siena, Florence, Lucca, Milan, Pavia, Brescia, and Bologna. Each of these municipalities had, of course, its own history, influenced by peculiarities of local custom and the varying attitude of persons in authority. In general, however, the commune arose as a sworn association of citizens—both noble and plebeian—for the maintenance and extension of their liberties. Though occasionally it might be formed with the consent and support of the existing government, it was more frequently a revolutionary organiza- *The Lombard and Tuscan communes*

[9] See above, p. 228.

tion that achieved its ends by means of insurrection. When, as was generally the case in Lombardy, the city had been legally subordinated to the bishop, the outbreak was primarily directed against his power. But the commune might also be employed as an effective weapon against a lay prince. Whatever the preliminaries, the ultimate result was the establishment of a *de facto* republic based on a league of citizens sworn to advance their common interests by persuasion, boycott, or force of arms. In the absence of an efficient monarchy, northern Italy thus tended to become a mosaic of city-states; for each commune sought to assure its lines of communication by annexing a considerable district outside the walled area.

It should also be noted that, consciously or not, these city-states held to the classic tradition of an urban nobility. The aristocratic families of Venetia identified themselves with the rising city of Venice. They lived in it, ruled it, and, through investment in ships and commercial enterprise, prospered with it. Similar customs prevailed among the Lombard and Tuscan communes, which always attracted a good proportion of the local gentry. There business and politics were generally controlled by a few great families who engaged in bitter feuds with one another and raised the fortress-like palaces that still dominate many an Italian street. In Spain and southern France, likewise, it was not unusual for the nobility to prefer urban residences or even to take part in municipal affairs. But in northern France and the adjacent regions the nobility was essentially an agrarian class. Living in the country, the feudal baron despised the town-dweller as an inferior, and his chivalrous prejudice may yet be detected in the implications of our word bourgeois.

Northern communes: Flanders Italy was long to be characterized by the complete sovereignty of its city-states; elsewhere the extent of urban self-government depended on the sympathies and powers of local princes. By 1100, as already remarked, flourishing towns had grown up about various *burgen* in Flanders, especially at Ghent, Bruges, Arras, Ypres, and Saint-Omer. And since the counts generally favored the ambitions of the bourgeoisie, each of these towns obtained the right to elect its own *échevins*[10]—magistrates who, under the superior authority of the count, had charge of the municipal administration. Each, furthermore, seems to have had a gild merchant, which included all local traders and so held monopolistic control of local business. For electing officers and regulating such matters as tolls, rights of sale or purchase, and standards of manufacture, the members had regular meetings in their gild-hall. Frequently, too, this building served as headquarters of the municipal government—a natural arrangement, for the same men would be in control of both organizations. The gildsmen, however, did not always spend the evening in serious debate—as we learn from a remarkable Saint-Omer document of about 1100. Every so often the gild held a wine-drinking,

[10] See above, pp. 139-40.

from which no brother could absent himself without good excuse. When he came into the hall, he had to leave at the door not merely his arms but likewise his wooden shoes—lest they be used as weapons. And a tariff of penalties was applied to offenses that disturbed the drinking, including blows with the fist, with a stone, or with a loaf of bread!

In contradistinction to the Flemish communes, those of Picardy very **Picardy** generally rose to power through violence. That region was sprinkled with many old Roman cities, which earlier had been little more than fortified centers of administration under the resident bishops. By the opening of the twelfth century, however, most of these cities had attracted a considerable population of merchants and artisans, who commonly occupied separate quarters beyond the ancient walls. And as the bishops, or other lords, refused to meet the demands of their bourgeois, the latter rose in revolt, forming sworn associations much like those of Lombardy. The first such revolutionary commune in the north was that of Cambrai in 1077. Although this rising was put down, a later insurrection was more successful. The townsmen then forced the bishop to grant them a communal charter, which was quashed only when, in 1107, the emperor intervened on the side of the church. Many more years passed and much more trouble ensued before the city obtained definite recognition of its liberties. Meanwhile the example set by Cambrai had been widely followed throughout the neighboring lands to the south. One after another, rebellions broke out in Saint-Quentin, Amiens, Laon, and Beauvais. Some failed and some succeeded, but sooner or later these towns and many others secured recognition as communes under elected magistrates.

In many cases the troubles of the northern cities were ended through the intervention of Louis VI, who restored order by arranging some sort of compromise. On the whole, his policy clearly favored the bourgeoisie; for his settlements tended to break the effective government of the cities by the bishops and to substitute that of the citizens under his own superior control. Eventually, after the revolutionary phase had passed, the Picard communes came to be organized quite like those of Flanders—normally under a board of elected officials called *jurés*.[11] Every resident was bound by oath to obey his magistrates and to lend aid to the enforcement of their judgments. Any townsman who refused to do so was declared a public enemy and subjected to the penalty of having his house torn down. Or should a noble of the countryside deny justice to a member of the commune and defy its authority, the citizens would be assembled in the market-place by the ringing of a great bell and all would march forth to take vengeance on the common foe. Such provisions as these are usual in the communal charters, and they show how, in the feudal society of the early twelfth cen-

[11] I.e., "men sworn" to carry out the decisions of the commune.

tury, the individual bourgeois was helpless without an armed union to support him.

Normandy and England

In Normandy we have clear evidence that the merchants of Rouen had been organized in a powerful gild even before the duke's conquest of England. From Henry I the city apparently received at least some political rights, but it is only at a later time that we definitely learn of a communal administration headed by a group of elected *jurés*. In his island kingdom Henry also gave a remarkable charter to London—the first known grant of formal self-government to an English town. In this respect, as in all others, the rest of the boroughs lagged far behind the metropolis. Until the closing years of the twelfth century most of them enjoyed only the elementary liberties of free status, burgage tenure, and the like. Almost every English borough had its gild merchant, through which the burgesses might to some degree control their local affairs. In this connection, too, mention should be made of the Cinque Ports. As the name implies, there were originally five (Hastings, Sandwich, Dover, Romney, and Hythe), but later the number was increased. According to a custom dating from the reign of Edward the Confessor, each of them was bound to furnish the king a certain number of ships for fifteen days' service annually, and in return enjoyed freedom from toll throughout England, together with other privileges. Under the Normans the Cinque Ports gained even more extensive liberties, and eventually all became self-governing. From this unique confederation, directed by the constable of Dover Castle, the king secured a regular navy throughout the Middle Ages.

Germany

In twelfth-century Germany the most advanced town both economically and politically was Cologne, where, by way of exception, municipal development seems to have continued without serious opposition from the local bishop. Before 1100 the city had a flourishing gild merchant, and within the next fifty years a communal organization under elected magistrates took form. The other cities of the Rhine valley became self-governing only in the following century. The same statement will apply to the leading towns of the Danube, headed by Ratisbon, and of eastern Germany, where the foremost urban center was Magdeburg. As yet the only great town of Holland was Utrecht, and on the Meuse Liége was hardly rivaled by Namur and Verdun. Most of Lorraine, in fact, remained comparatively backward, as did the central region of the Burgundies, Champagne, and Auvergne. The towns on the upper Seine and Loire—even Paris and Orleans—were of second rank as late as 1200. Brittany had no towns of any considerable size. Along the Bay of Biscay, however, La Rochelle, Bordeaux, and Bayonne were becoming important for sea trade, especially in wine.

Southern France and Spain

Throughout Toulouse and Provence, meanwhile, the revival of commerce in the western Mediterranean naturally brought new life to such Roman cities as Marseilles, Arles, Nîmes, Montpellier, and Carcassonne.

By the middle of the twelfth century at least a dozen of these towns had peaceably obtained extensive liberties from their respective lords, usually lay nobles. Following the example of the Italian cities, they installed magistrates with the title of consuls, and in other respects many of them resembled the southern rather than the northern communes. In Spain, too, municipal organization tended to be of the Italian type. It is true that many small trading settlements grew up under the protecting walls of castles, and some of them became prosperous enough to receive formal charters resembling those given to northern towns. But the Spanish nobles, like those of Italy, continued by preference to live in the great cities which, on account of the constant warfare against the Moors, remained especially important as military centers. Of those in Christian hands before 1200 the only one to attain prominence in European commerce was Barcelona.

The preceding pages have, of course, merely introduced a very large and complex subject. In the history of the mediæval town the twelfth century was the formative period. Further details concerning urban life and institutions must be left for a subsequent chapter. Meanwhile it should be noted that in all the great states of Europe the bourgeoisie came to exert a powerful influence on constitutional development and on political affairs generally. This influence will be apparent as we review the history of the French, English, German, and Italian kingdoms.

CHAPTER XIV

The Development of University Education

1. FROM GERBERT TO ABELARD

The Carolingian tradition

The Carolingian reform of education had a number of important results. It widely extended the organization of ecclesiastical schools, it introduced a new and beautiful form of handwriting, and it led indirectly to the preservation of many ancient books. When, in the dismal period that ensued, so many churches were destroyed and so many clergymen were slain, scholarship threatened to perish with them. Yet the old traditions were maintained in at least some localities. Otto I in Germany and Alfred in England did much to restore learning throughout their kingdoms, and similar efforts on the part of French princes were not without influence. Later, with the general improvement of economic and political conditions, a greatly increased demand for education brought the remarkable intellectual advance that characterized the eleventh and following centuries. The schools of course continued to be of two sorts, monastic and episcopal; but it was only the latter that retained any great prestige. The Cluniac reform, being essentially religious, stimulated no fresh interest in scholarly pursuits, and after the year 1000 most ancient abbeys ceased to be prominent as educational centers. The foremost teachers and students were attracted, rather, to the famous cathedral schools—such as Reims, Laon, Paris, Chartres, Tours, Cologne, Liége, and Utrecht.

Gerbert (d. 1003)

Meanwhile very few men had been able to devote their time to scholarship, and among those who somehow managed to keep alive the traditions of the Carolingian schools almost none produced anything original. The intellectual history of the Latin world between 850 and 1050 is, indeed, distinguished by only one great name—that of Gerbert, who died as Pope

Urania   Astronomia   Ptolomeus

FIG. 20. Armillary Sphere. (Frontispiece to Johannes de Sacro Bosco, *De Sphæra*, 1498.)

Silvester II in 1003. Little is known of his early life apart from the fact that he was born in Aquitaine and, after studying grammar at the monastery of Aurillac, visited the county of Barcelona, where he became very proficient in mathematics. Later, for the sake of training in dialectic, he attended the cathedral school of Reims and there became a famous master. When teaching the *trivium*, we are told, he introduced his students not merely to the standard textbooks but also to the great poets and prose writers of Rome. And his numerous letters show him to have been an ardent collector of books, building what for that age was a fine library of the classics. Yet to us, as to his contemporaries, Gerbert's most remarkable work was in the field of the *quadrivium*. He demonstrated the mathematical basis of music by means of vibrating strings, and for instructing his students in astronomy and arithmetic he used a number of inventions which then seemed utterly marvelous.

Astronomy and mathematics

According to his pupil Richer, Gerbert constructed two spheres. One was solid and on it he marked the poles, the horizon, various other imaginary circles, and both the northern and the southern constellations. The second was an armillary sphere—i.e., one made of concentric metal bands like bracelets, each representing a planetary orbit, with a ball for the earth in the center and on the outside a belt carrying the signs of the zodiac (see Figure 20). Gerbert's abacus was even more wonderful; for with it, Richer says, he could solve problems involving numbers so large that they could hardly be expressed in words. It had twenty-seven columns, in which he distributed counters made of horn and inscribed with nine symbols—variations, as we know, of the nine Arabic numerals. Since neither the abacus nor the Ptolemaic system had been expounded by the Latin authors commonly used in the schools of the west, it is clear that Gerbert must have obtained most of his mathematical learning in Spain, and the fact that he was familiar with the nine Arabic numerals shows that his information was derived from an Arabic source. Apparently, however, it came through some indirect channel; Gerbert knew neither Greek nor Arabic, and he made no use of the zero, with which educated Moslems had been familiar for over a hundred years.[1]

Whether Gerbert also introduced the astrolabe[2] to Latin Europe remains a matter of controversy. Certain it is that, after returning to France, he wrote to a friend in Catalonia for the translation of an Arabic work on the subject and that, before 1050, his name had been attached to a so-called *Geometry* which told how the instrument could be used for measuring the depth of a well, calculating the height of a mountain, and acquiring other information of the same kind. Before long the astrolabe was in common use by Mediterranean navigators, as it remained until the time of Columbus. For lack of scientific books on the *quadrivium*, Gerbert presumably had

---

[1] See above, pp. 168-70.
[2] See above, Figure 11.

to rely on such mechanical devices as he had been able to pick up on his travels. But would not the interest he aroused in his students tend to lead them, in a more favorable environment, to demand Latin versions of the Greek and Arabic classics that explained the theories on which such devices were based?

A Frenchman and a teacher in a great cathedral school of France, **Gerbert's** Gerbert stood at the forefront of the educational revival that was to cul- **influence** minate in the University of Paris. By examining his scholarly interests, we are introduced to those of many succeeding generations. In the field of mathematics Gerbert's influence was profound. He inspired a whole series of writings on the abacus, some of which had distinctly practical importance.[3] Within the fields of astronomy and geography, as just suggested, he seems to have awakened the curiosity that brought about a new era for those sciences in western Europe. From Gerbert, too, many pupils acquired a lasting enthusiasm for grammar—chief among them Fulbert, under whom the cathedral school of Chartres became the center of literary study in Latin Christendom. Dialectic, another topic emphasized by Gerbert, likewise flourished because his pupils fascinated their pupils with a problem left unsolved by their standard textbooks.

Porphyry's *Isagoge*, being merely an introductory essay, refers to the **Dialectical** subject of universals as one of great importance, but does not go on to **argument** explain it. Nor was it thoroughly treated by the works of Aristotle then available in Latin.[4] The scholars of the eleventh century were therefore led to answer for themselves such questions as arose concerning the existence of universals and particulars. For example, can we recognize an individual thing as an apple without first having an idea of apple in general? Is then our knowledge of this universal, apple, derived from our knowledge of particular apples, or vice versa? Can the former exist apart from the latter? If so where does it exist? And is it a thing (*res*)? Although the traditional dialectic of the schoolmen was Aristotelian, their philosophic attitude, under the influence of St. Augustine, remained Neoplatonic. So the orthodox generally held that all knowledge is based on divine ideas implanted in the human reason by the Creator; and certain doctors, without very careful definition, came to affirm that universals are *res*—the dialectical position called "realist." On the contrary, a well-known teacher named Roscellinus boldly advanced the "nominalist" thesis: that universals are not *res* but *nomina* (names), which are no more than *voces* (sounds). The more conservative schoolmen, ably led by Anselm, abbot of Bec and later archbishop of Canterbury, at once denounced the view of Roscellinus as heretical, being directly opposed to the revealed truths of religion. And Anselm's opinion was confirmed by a council at Soissons in

[3] See below, p. 316.
[4] See above, p. 71.

1092, which compelled Roscellinus to retract at least some of his statements before he was allowed to continue teaching.

At this point the discussion was taken up by a young Breton of noble birth, who had been christened Peter and who had somewhere gained the nickname of Abelard (Abailardus). In a famous autobiography[5] he tells us how, enamored of dialectic, he had abandoned his inheritance together with a knightly career to become "an emulator of the Peripatetics." As such, he wandered from school to school in search of the best instruction and so, inevitably, came to Paris, where William of Champeaux had won renown by defending the realist position. Attacking the master's thesis, Abelard refuted it with such effectiveness that he was encouraged to set up school for himself in the outskirts of the city. Then the hostility of the ecclesiastical authorities compelled him to resume his travels, and he decided to study theology under the learned doctor, Anselm of Laon.[6] But that old fogy, says Abelard, proved to be remarkable only for his fluency. "When he lighted a fire, he filled his house with smoke, instead of lighting it with the blaze." Having expressed his disgust, Abelard was challenged by his fellow students to do better. He agreed to expound any book of the Bible they might choose, and they gave him the prophet Ezekiel. What had begun in jest ended in earnest; he astounded and delighted the throng by lecturing on the Scriptures direct in preference to using a standard commentary. Thereupon the authorities again intervened and the upstart teacher was summarily expelled from Laon. This, of course, is Abelard's own account, and he was never one to hide his light under a bushel. Yet we may be sure that Abelard had real talent and that it eventually gained recognition; for by 1115 he had secured official appointment in the cathedral school of Paris, which William of Champeaux had recently deserted to become bishop of Châlons.

At Paris, as we learn from many independent sources, Abelard won prodigious success, attracting students in unprecedented numbers by the keenness of his intellect and the charm of his exposition. At Paris, too, occurred the love idyll with Héloïse that so quickly turned into tragedy. The immortal story should be read in the letters of the two unfortunates themselves; here it is possible to mention only one or two points of outstanding interest. Abelard's account of the affair, it should be remembered, was composed long afterwards when he was a monk, embittered by affliction and writing to justify himself in the eyes of pious enemies. It is hard to imagine him as a "ravening wolf" that deliberately pounced on a "tender lamb." We should rather imagine that, however wise in dialectic, he was foolish in love, and that it came upon him quite naturally. Héloïse, the niece of a clergyman attached to the cathedral, was a girl in her teens,

---

[5] The *Historia Calamitatum*; see immediately below.
[6] Not to be confused with Anselm, archbishop of Canterbury.

famed for extraordinary learning was well as for exceptional beauty. Since Abelard had taken only minor orders, he was still free to marry; yet, if he did so, he would have to forgo an ecclesiastical career. On that account Héloïse at first refused to be more than his mistress; then, after a son had been born to them, she unwillingly agreed to marriage and they became man and wife. Thinking solely of her husband, she tried to keep the wedding a secret and so brought about a series of misunderstandings with her uncle. The latter, to revenge an imagined wrong, contrived a brutal assault on Abelard, mutilating him in such a way as would not only ruin his life with Héloïse but also prevent his becoming a priest. The proud master thus took monastic vows and induced Héloïse to follow his example.

From now on Abelard's life was indeed unhappy. No matter where he went, he encountered trouble. He returned to teaching, only to have his book on theology condemned by those who, he declared, were unable to understand it. For a time he lived as a hermit, but even in the wilderness he was sought out by students from Paris who prevailed upon him to resume his lectures. By the labor of his pupils his straw hut was turned into a commodious house of stone and timber, which in gratitude he named the Paraclete (Comforter). Reviving fame then brought renewed threats of persecution. He accepted the headship of an abbey in Brittany and there, in the midst of brutal ignorance, became more miserable than ever. Thus he was led to write the *Historia Calamitatum* (The History of My Calamities), which is in the form of a letter to a friend to make the latter forget his own lesser misfortunes. Presumably this was only a literary device; for Abelard's work was obviously one of self-justification and on that account obtained wide publicity.

Héloïse in the meantime had become abbess over a little community of nuns established in the abandoned Paraclete. Since taking the veil when hardly twenty she had received no word from the man who had once been her husband. Now, finally, it was a copy of the *Historia Calamitatum* that came into her hands, and we may well imagine how she would be affected by such probing into old wounds. Breaking the silence of long years, and with it all monastic convention, she wrote: "To her master, nay father, to her husband, nay brother; his handmaid, nay daughter; his spouse, nay sister; to Abelard Héloïse." It is a piteous letter. She offers him sympathy in his afflictions, but reminds him that she too has been plunged in grief. Her unbounded love for him is known to all and she, at least, cannot regard that love coldly and bewail it as a sin. She still thinks of him as he was— famous, handsome, brilliant; a great scholar, yet more wonderful to her as a singer of love-songs. Although she may not see him, may he not write to her? He alone can give her solace. Abelard's answer is such as might be expected from a father confessor. He offers her spiritual consolation and

Letters of Abelard and Héloïse

asks that she and her sisters pray for him. When he is dead, he hopes that he may be buried at the Paraclete.

To this Héloïse replies in fierce revolt against the cruelty of her fate. How can he speak of dying? The very thought is death to her. She has only one joy in life: to know that he is yet alive. There is no use in pretending. She is racked by memories. The torment of longing will not leave her even during the solemnity of divine service. She despairs of cure, knowing that, miserable hypocrite, she has no hope of heaven.[7]

But in the whole period of my life (God wot) I have ever feared to offend thee rather than God; I seek to please thee rather than Him. Thy command brought me, not the love of God, to the habit of religion. See how unhappy a life I must lead, more wretched than all others, if I endure these things here in vain, having no hope of reward in the future. For a long time thou, like many others, hast been deceived by my simulation, so as to mistake hypocrisy for religion; and thus, strongly commending thyself to our prayers, what I expect from thee thou demandest from me. Do not, I beseech thee, presume so highly of me, nor cease by praying to assist me. Do not deem me healed, nor withdraw the grace of thy medicine. Do not believe me to be not in want, nor delay to succor my necessity. Do not think this strength, lest I fall before thou hold up the falling.

Héloïse was to have no such support. Another letter from Abelard convinced her that she would have to resign herself to fate, however unkind. So her final request was merely for professional advice—a disquisition on the origin of nuns and a modification of the Benedictine rule for the guidance of her community. These Abelard sent and their correspondence ended. Shortly afterwards he somehow obtained release from his abbacy and again set up a school in a suburb of Paris. The result was his condemnation for heresy in a provincial council dominated by Bernard of Clairvaux.[8] Appealing to Rome, Abelard was taken ill on the way to plead his cause before the pope and died at Cluny (1142). His body, as he had desired, was brought to Héloïse for burial—and she, we may hope, at last found the spiritual peace of which she had once despaired.

Works of Abelard

Abelard was unquestionably one of the greatest figures in the intellectual history of Europe. To the study of dialectic—as appears from his recently printed works on that subject—he made a contribution of fundamental importance. The question then at issue could be resolved into this: What does logic deal with? By denying that it deals with things (*res*), Abelard placed himself squarely in the nominalist camp. But, said he, a distinction must be made between *vox* and *sermo*—between the sound of a word and its meaning. The latter is the true universal, for the sound is only a par-

---

[7] This quotation, as well as the lesser ones preceding, are taken from Scott-Moncrieff, *The Letters of Abelard and Heloise*, by permission of, and special arrangement with, Alfred A. Knopf, Inc., authorized publishers.

[8] See below, p. 264.

ticular. To that extent Roscellinus had been mistaken, and to that extent Abelard was willing to accept a compromise. Thus the way was cleared for understanding logic as the study of concepts—a conclusion which few would now care to dispute, and which prepared the schools of that day for the more advanced logic of Aristotle, then about to appear in translation. Besides, it was Abelard who really introduced the academic world to systematic theology. During the previous centuries there had, of course, been extensive writing on theological subjects, but no attempt had been made to combine and analyze the results. This fact Abelard made eminently clear by publishing his little book called *Sic et Non* (Yes and No).

The book must have seemed rather scandalous to many of Abelard's contemporaries, for in it he lists 158 questions about such matters as faith and reason, the Persons of the Trinity, the angels, Adam and Eve, human nature, sin, and the sacraments. For example, we find (1) Whether or not faith is to be supported by reason; (9) Whether or not God is a substance; (48) Whether or not good angels and saints who enjoy the sight of God know all things; (58) Whether or not Adam was saved; (88) Whether or not, after the resurrection, Christ showed to doubting persons scars rather than wounds; (135) Whether or not marriage is a good thing; (147) Whether or not Cain was damned; (157) Whether or not it is permitted to slay men. After each question Abelard quotes appropriate extracts—from the Old and New Testaments, Jerome, Ambrose, Augustine, Gregory the Great, Isidore of Seville, Bede, and other authors, as well as from the decrees of councils and the letters of the popes. His object—and there is no reason to question his sincerity—is stated in the prologue: he desires to stimulate inquiry, the key to wisdom. These opinions (*sententiæ*), he says, have been collected because they are to some extent contradictory. The contradiction can be explained in various ways and sometimes can be reconciled. Sometimes, however, it cannot be; then the best authority must be taken. In any case the student must work out the problem for himself, and he must first realize that a doubt exists as to the proper answer. "For by doubting we come to inquiry, and by inquiring we perceive the truth."

2. SCHOLASTICISM AND THE NEW LEARNING

Abelard was by no means—as his nineteenth-century admirers liked to believe—a freethinker. He never disputed the authority of the church or the truths defined by it as a matter of sacred tradition. He merely insisted that, to supplement revelation, one could rightfully employ the reason with which man had been endowed by the Creator. In support of this opinion he could cite the greatest doctors of Christendom. He could, in fact, argue that anybody who denied it was himself open to prosecution as a heretic; for how could a Christian hold that Christianity was contrary to reason? It was only when scholars allowed their academic discussions to question

Abelard's influence

the established beliefs of the church that they encountered serious trouble. Roscellinus, as we have seen, was disciplined for advancing a logical argument that, his opponents declared, was contrary to a Christian dogma. Earlier a well-known teacher of dialectic named Berengar of Tours had been condemned by a provincial council for denying that the bread and wine in the sacrament of the eucharist were substantially changed into flesh and blood.[9] But he had been mildly treated by Gregory VII, who permitted him, after signing a rather vague retraction, to live in peaceful retirement.

St. Bernard (d. 1153)

So far as Abelard was concerned, the local judgments against him were never upheld at Rome, and within another hundred years the soundness of his position had been attested by the whole development of scholastic education. In Abelard's own day, however, the new trend in academic thought was bitterly opposed by many influential ecclesiastics; and they found an eloquent spokesman in Bernard of Clairvaux. The latter was a man of noble birth who had left the world to enter the monastery of Cîteaux, a community founded by an Englishman, Stephen Harding, and pledged to the literal observance of the Benedictine rule. At Cîteaux Bernard had quickly proved his talent for spiritual leadership, with the result that he had been named as abbot of a daughter house at Clairvaux. Thereafter Bernard came to have extraordinary influence throughout Latin Europe. It was, indeed, primarily a tribute to him that the Cistercian order enrolled 343 abbeys before his death in 1153. Bernard was pre-eminently a monk, and a very conservative one. Like the order to which he belonged, he was devoted to a primitive austerity of Christian conduct. The greatest preacher in the west, he fiercely denounced the growing luxury of the age —its wicked delight in magnificent architecture, orchestral music, secular literature, and rationalistic study. To Bernard such a man as Abelard, who scorned the faith of his ancestors for the sake of academic vanity, was a grave menace to Christian society.

Hugh of St. Victor (d. 1141)

Through his sermons, hymns, and books of devotion, as well as through the example of his saintly life, Bernard has never ceased to be a force in Christendom. Yet, in so far as he opposed the intellectual and æsthetic advance of the age, he fought a losing battle; for the universities and cathedrals of the thirteenth century must always be ranked among the chief glories of the mediæval church. Religious feeling was to be stifled neither by scholastic learning nor by Gothic art. When we come to examine the latter, we shall see that it was thoroughly imbued with mystic symbolism—a factor that had long influenced other forms of Christian expression. It was through allegorical interpretation that the church fathers had read the Old Testament as a foreshadowing of the New. If the Hebrew and Christian traditions could be thus reconciled, might not the same

---

[9] The dogma of transubstantiation was first promulgated by Innocent III in his Lateran Council of 1215; see below, p. 337.

method be successfully applied to other discrepancies between authorities? Such, at least, was the thesis presented by a second of Abelard's critics, Hugh of St. Victor. The meaning of things, said Hugh, can never be revealed by dialectical quibbling. As we must look beyond the literal sense of Scripture to discover the truth, so in the study of nature we must take each object as having a transcendental value with respect to the divine plan. Properly, the philosopher is he who, by the aid of revelation, can apprehend more than the superficial—can perceive in the most ordinary phenomena the symmetry of God's universe. Elaborated by other writers, Hugh's argument had far-reaching influence on the thought of later generations.

Meanwhile the craze for dialectic had brought sarcastic comment from an entirely different quarter—from those scholars who carried on the tradition of the earlier grammarians. Of the many eager youths who now entered upon the ancient *trivium* some would inevitably be inspired, as Einhard had been, by enthusiasm for literature. All the Latin authors that we know were then available, and at least the greatest of them had been continuously read and praised. In the twelfth century the most famous center of classical study was the cathedral school of Chartres, which found its most ardent champion in John of Salisbury. From his native England John went in 1136 to France, where in one place or another he studied for nearly a dozen years. His lively account of the schools in Paris, Chartres, and other cities, and of the great teachers whom he there encountered, is our best source for the educational habits of the twelfth century. John heard all the great masters, including Abelard, but consistently refused to be the disciple of any. He preferred to do his own reading and to make his own interpretations. To his mind, wisdom lay in a broad understanding of many subjects, rather than in narrow devotion to a single one. In particular, he decried the exaggeration of dialectic. Although that study might be useful in so far as it furthered others, it was in itself "bloodless and barren," incapable of quickening "the soul to yield fruit of philosophy." Nevertheless, for all his wit and erudition, he was defending a lost cause. The ideals of the triumphant scholasticism were not to be determined by John of Salisbury. *(John of Salisbury (d. 1180))*

Taken in its widest sense, scholasticism was merely the system of education that characterized the early universities, and it was one that bore the unmistakable marks of Abelard's influence. The illustrious Peter Lombard, for instance, was one of Abelard's actual pupils. Before Peter's election as bishop of Paris in 1159, he like his master had made a collection of theological *sententiæ*, though he added careful arguments to reconcile the differences of opinion or, when reconciliation was impossible, to decide where the weight of authority lay. For example (in Book II, ch. xxii), Peter takes up the question: Who committed the greater sin, Adam or *(Peter Lombard's Sentences)*

Eve? He quotes St. Augustine and Hugh of St. Victor to the effect that the woman sinned more in that she wished to usurp equality with God. This view, indeed, seems to be opposed by St. Augustine's remark in another connection, that both were proud and so sinned alike. But, in Peter's opinion, the apparent difference may be avoided by deciding that, while "each was the equal of the other in the sin of excusing their wrongdoing, and also of eating of the forbidden tree, they were unequal—the woman being much the greater sinner—in that she thought and wished to be like God." By similar logic he refutes a statement by Isidore of Seville—to agree with those who hold that "sin entered the world through a woman." Peter Lombard's book was enormously successful, for it became a standard text in the schools and has remained in use down to the present.

Gratian's Decretum   The theology of Abelard, which thus became a prominent subject in the scholastic curriculum, was characterized by two outstanding features. In the first place, it was deductive, being essentially the development of general principles taken from authoritative sources. Secondly, it was practical, in that it came to be the required preparation for high office in the church. Both features also characterized the contemporary study of law. For a thousand years the church had been accumulating a mass of legal rules, or canons, in the form of biblical precepts, papal decretals, acts of councils, decisions of courts, and opinions of learned men. But little had as yet been done with the material beyond the making of incomplete collections. Now, about 1148, an Italian monk named Gratian published his monumental *Concordance of Discordant Canons*. The *Decretum*, as Gratian's book was popularly called, is precisely the same kind of work as Peter Lombard's *Sentences*, being at once a code of laws and an exposition of their principles. It is analytically arranged according to hundreds of separate problems, under each of which the pertinent canons are quoted and a logical solution is proposed for the settlement of disputed points.

Thus the twenty-third cause in the second part of the *Decretum* sets forth these facts. The clergy and people of a certain region lapse into heresy, which they try to force upon the Catholic population of the surrounding territory. Thereupon the bishops in that territory, at the behest of the papacy, gather troops and launch war against the heretics. After many of the latter have been killed, imprisoned, or deprived of their goods, the remainder submit and are again joined to the true church. Here involved, says Gratian, are no less than eight questions: Is it a sin to fight? What kind of war is justifiable for Christians? Should injuries to one's fellows be repulsed by arms? Should feuds be prosecuted? Should judges order the slaying of convicted persons? Should bad men be compelled to become good? Should heretics be despoiled of their belongings? Should clergymen under any conditions bear arms themselves? In considering this last question—to take only one example—Gratian cites the Gospels, certain papal letters, the decisions of various councils, and many other authorities. After weighing the arguments pro and con, he decides that, although clergymen may properly authorize a war against an enemy of God, they should not themselves engage in fighting.

Gratian's work elicited a library of weighty commentaries and supplementary collections. And though unofficial in origin, it was eventually placed at the beginning of the great papal compilation entitled *Corpus Iuris Canonici*. The choice of a name reminiscent of Justinian's *Corpus Iuris Civilis* was, of course, no accident; for the systematic study of the canon law was directly influenced by that of the Roman law. The latter as a customary system had never gone out of use in Italy and southern Gaul, but the little instruction that had continued to be necessary in no way depended on the *Corpus* of Justinian. The all-important *Digest,* in particular, remained virtually unknown in the west until, towards the close of the eleventh century, its discovery led to the revival of jurisprudence in the Italian schools. After an obscure early development this study came to be especially prominent at Bologna. There, following the method first rendered famous by Irnerius, generations of glossators, as they were called, lectured on the *Digest*, expounding it by dialectical argument and illustrating difficult points through citation of the *Code*. And there the same method was applied to ecclesiastical jurisprudence when that came into existence. Accordingly, as the ensuing age became more and more legalistic, a host of young men, trained in one or both of the two laws, were able to enter upon profitable careers in church or state. *The revival of jurisprudence*

For the study of law and theology practically all the needed sources were available in Latin, but other fields were not so well provided. In response to scholarly demand, therefore, an extensive work of translation from Greek and Arabic was begun and rapidly advanced in the course of the twelfth century. At one time it was usual to attribute this sudden activity to the influence of the crusades. It is now evident, however, that the average crusader was as little interested in books as had been the average Venetian merchant. Almost none of the translating was done in Syria, and comparatively little of it at Constantinople. The more important centers of the work were Spain and Sicily;[10] and although the latter country included a number of men who had a thorough knowledge of Greek, most of the popular translations were made from Arabic texts. The translators came from many lands, as is indicated by their names: Adelard of Bath, Robert of Chester, Rudolf of Bruges, Hermann of Carinthia, Gerard of Cremona, John of Seville, and the like. Among them, by 1150, they had translated the geometry of Euclid, together with the trigonometry, algebra, and arithmetic of al-Khwarizmi—from whom the last-mentioned subject *Translations from Greek and Arabic*

[10] See below, pp. 322-23.

came to be called algorism.[11] By that time, too, the more advanced logical essays of Aristotle had appeared in Latin, to take their place as the New Logic in the prescribed dialectic of the schools. And by the end of the century western scholars were also supplied with Latin versions of Ptolemy, Galen, Hippocrates, and other Greek authors, as well as scores of books by al-Farabi, al-Haytham, ibn-Sina (Avicenna), and other Arabs. The philosophical and scientific writings of Aristotle were, for the most part, translated early in the thirteenth century, together with a mass of Arabic commentary, especially that of ibn-Rushd (Averroës).

The scholarly interests of the Latin world are clearly revealed in this list of outstanding textbooks. By the close of the twelfth century the schools of France, Italy, and the neighboring countries had adopted a course of instruction that emphasized logic, mathematics, and general science as a preparation for professional training in theology, law, and medicine. The curriculum thus defined kept grammar as an elementary study, through which the youth obtained merely the ability to write and speak correct Latin. And since the Latin that he had to use was a rapidly growing and highly technical language, he was normally unwilling to spend much time on the niceties of classical style. So the study of literature as an end in itself tended more and more to be disregarded. The masterpieces of Greek prose and poetry remained unknown; even some of the Latin authors were almost wholly neglected. The result was the scholastic education of the thirteenth century—a system that will be more fully described in later chapters. Our present task must rather be to examine the contemporary development of the universities.

3. THE BEGINNINGS OF THE UNIVERSITIES

Original
nature
of the
university

The rapid expansion of advanced study during the twelfth century naturally implied a huge increase in the number of teachers and pupils. Being attracted to certain great centers of instruction, they tended, like merchants or artisans, to become self-governing and eventually to gain legal recognition. Such an educational unit is what we know as a university, but the word acquired that meaning by a very gradual process. At first the Latin *universitas* was merely one of several vague terms that could be applied to any association of people. All men teaching or studying in a particular place might be so referred to, or the same designation might be applied to a separate union of masters or of students. In other words, the university was at first a gild, or perhaps a combination of gilds. No specific dates can be assigned to the emergence of the oldest universities; they gradually took form in the course of the twelfth century. A second group

---

[11] The book of al-Khwarizmi (above, p. 168), when translated, bore the title *Algoritmi de Numero Indorum,* the first word of which was taken to be the subject rather than the name of the author.

arose through migration—when for some reason a number of masters and students came to establish themselves in a new center. Finally, when the models had been perfected, it became usual for princes, lay or ecclesiastical, to found universities by formal charter.

For a long time after the year 1100 no-one could have predicted which **Bologna** of many schools would eventually dominate western education. By 1200, however, the issue was settled: the mother universities of Europe were to be Bologna and Paris. At Bologna the great attraction was the teaching of civil and canon law by the successors of Irnerius. These masters seem from an early time to have formed gilds, there styled colleges, for the regulation of their common affairs, particularly the qualifications demanded for admission to their own ranks. The students, having already completed a course in arts and being of mature age, were left to shift for themselves. And they, in the absence of all control by cathedral school or royal government, proceeded to organize gilds of their own, which they called universities. Before the end of the twelfth century two such universities had come into existence at Bologna: the cismontane, including the Italian "nations," and the transmontane, including those from beyond the Alps. But the two acted together through groups of deputies, each headed by a rector, and so came to be thought of as one. The completed organization was first used to force concessions from the municipal authorities—to secure, by threat of migration, a schedule of fair rents and prices. Then the students turned on the masters, who of course were dependent on them for fees. It was provided that each master should give a certain number of lectures and cover a certain amount of work in a certain way. He had to agree to supervision by student inspectors, who fined him if he did not begin on time and quit on time, or if he left town without permission. Even on the occasion of his wedding he was allowed to have only one day off.

Thus at Bologna, while the masters' colleges retained the granting of **Paris** degrees, they were definitely subordinated to the students' university. At Paris, on the other hand, it was the masters' gilds, or faculties, that from the outset controlled the students. Most of the latter, having come for work in arts, were boys in their teens, for whom their teachers would naturally be held responsible. In the time of Abelard such matters of discipline were still regulated by the chancellor, the head of the cathedral school. But by the close of the twelfth century his authority had become merely nominal. The crowds attracted to the study of dialectic and allied subjects had quickly spread beyond the cloister of Notre-Dame and across the Petit-Pont to the left bank of the Seine, which—from the scholarly language there spoken—became known as the Latin Quarter. Under these changing conditions the academic population came to demand extensive rights of self-government and, as was usual in university towns, had frequent altercations with the civil authorities. One such affair in 1200 led to important consequences. Having intervened in a student riot, the Parisian police were clumsy enough to kill certain high-born Germans. In protest, all the masters suspended teaching and threatened to leave the city unless the king gave immediate redress. Philip Augustus[12] acted promptly to prevent so calamitous an event, throwing his *prévot* into jail and issuing a charter that confirmed the exemption of his *scholares* at Paris from all but ecclesiastical jurisdiction.

Having secured formal recognition of their clerical immunity, the Parisian masters proceeded with equal determination to assert their independence of the episcopal authority. And at least some of their established customs were confirmed in 1215 by a legate of Pope Innocent III,[13] who had himself studied at Paris. According to the statutes thus made, a master of arts had to be at least twenty-one years of age and to have completed six years of academic work; but to teach theology he had to be at least thirty-five, with many additional years spent in that study. The master had to maintain a decent exterior and wear a dark-colored gown reaching to his heels. A student had to be enrolled under a particular master, who would be responsible for him and have the right to discipline him. Both students and masters were permitted to form associations to defend their rights and to aid one another in charitable enterprises. Through the development of this principle the University of Paris took definite form in the course of the next hundred years. The faculty of arts, subdivided into four nations, gained the supremacy by sheer force of numbers; so that its rector became the acknowledged superior of the deans elected by the other faculties—those of theology, law, and medicine—and accordingly the head of the university. The chancellor, to be sure, still held the right of issuing the final license to teach, but he could do little more than accept candidates recommended by the faculties.

Younger universities Although the universities of Paris and Bologna used much the same method of teaching, they continued to emphasize different studies. At Bologna jurisprudence always dominated and very little attention was given to arts or theology. For those subjects the student went by preference to Paris, where canon law was of secondary importance and civil law was not taught at all. In the twelfth century we hear vaguely of a university at Salerno which was renowned for instruction in medicine, but in the next century leadership in that field passed to the newer universities of Padua, formed in 1222 as an offshoot of Bologna; Naples, founded outright by the emperor Frederick II in 1224;[14] and Montpellier, gradually developed under the joint patronage of the pope and the local princes. About the same time another distinguished university emerged at Orleans,

[12] See below, p. 330.
[13] See below, p. 333.
[14] See below, p. 360.

and it quickly became the foremost center of legal study outside Italy. Oxford University seems to have originated towards the close of the twelfth century through the settlement of certain masters who had earlier been at Paris. Cambridge, the second English university, began through a migration from Oxford in the thirteenth century. The first Spanish university to be permanently successful was established at Salamanca by the king of León about 1220. Germany had no university until the fourteenth century, when such institutions were set up at Prague, Vienna, Erfurt, Heidelberg, and Cologne. By that time universities had likewise arisen in Angers, Toulouse, Pavia, Florence, Lisbon, Cracow, Buda, and a score of other places.

For all these younger institutions the two older ones continued to serve as models—Paris generally throughout the north and west of Europe, Bologna generally throughout the south. It should not be imagined, however, that the two academic organizations were really very different. The students at Bologna, with few exceptions, had already completed the arts course before coming there to study law. The dominant element in the University of Paris was the faculty of arts, consisting mainly of young men who, having spent six years of preparation, were teaching arts while they continued as students of theology, law, or medicine. In other words, the ruling groups of both universities were masters of arts engaged in work for advanced degrees. Such a degree could be awarded only by the proper gild, whether styled faculty or college; for the degree signified admission to the gild. *Doctor, professor*, and *magister* were synonymous terms; all of them meant "teacher." So LL.D. (*Legum Doctor*), M.D. (*Medicinæ Doctor*), and S.T.P. (*Sanctæ Theologiæ Professor*) were the titles of men competent to teach respectively civil and canon law, medicine, and theology. These degrees we still recognize as professional; but the degree of A.M. was by origin equally professional, marking the person formally admitted to the gild of arts teachers. Even the baccalaureate fitted into the same plan of professional advancement. The grade of bachelor— it was not really a degree at first and was not prized for its own sake— entitled the youth, after four years of competent study, to give preliminary instruction in elementary subjects.

As in the ordinary gild, the man who had passed the required tests was formally invested with the insignia of his profession—in this case the cap and gown peculiar to his chosen field. The final ceremony was his inception or commencement—his beginning of professional activity. No legal hindrance then remained to prevent his entering upon actual instruction; all he needed was a vacant room over a tavern and enough student fees to make his lectures worth the giving. It was only later, when endowed chairs had been set up by rival municipalities or by wealthy patrons, that the new graduate was confronted by the unhappy distinction between a degree

Degrees and graduation

and a faculty appointment. But in the meantime other splendid opportunities had arisen. Lucrative positions in church and state were opened
to trained theologians, canonists, and jurists. It became possible to earn
a good livelihood by practicing law or medicine. And for any of these
learned professions the fundamental requirement was the doctorate—the
certified fitness of a man to teach the subject.

Student life
Numerous sources provide us with detailed information concerning
student life during this early age of the universities. To judge from contemporary sermons, the typical student was a prodigal roisterer who
respected neither God nor man—such a fellow, indeed, as often plays the
hero's role in the *fabliaux*.[15] And the verdict of the preachers and story-
tellers is to some extent borne out by the writings of the students themselves, as well as by the records of the courts. Yet, allowing for the laxer
standards of the time, we may well believe that conditions then were
very much as they are now: the average student was law-abiding and
conscientious, although his wilder brethren were always the more conspicuous. Of routine matters—such as disputations in the classroom,
dinners to celebrate graduation, and the hazing administered to the unfortunate freshman or *bejaunus* (*bec jaune*, yellow beak)—we have many
descriptions. Manuals for student use provide Latin words and phrases for
everything that could be thought of, and incidentally illustrate daily life
in the university community. Even more remarkable are the letters exchanged by students and parents. Well adorned with rhetorical flourishes
and appropriate quotations from Scripture, the models kept by professional
letterwriters were inspired by very practical motives. Almost invariably
the student asks for money and is chiefly interested in a good excuse for
being short of cash. Sometimes the father replies simply and generously.
More often he takes occasion to deliver a lecture on the evils of sloth and
extravagance.

Residential colleges
Among the youths who sought an education there were at all times
hundreds of boys from poverty-stricken homes, for the church offered the
baseborn the surest means of advancement. And it is greatly to the credit
of the mediæval university that it recognized scholarship without regard
to social distinction; many a peasant's son rose to fame as master and
author. Yet, at the beginning, such a student found life desperately hard.
His chief trouble was the question of lodgings. Wealthy students and
masters maintained separate quarters; the rank and file clubbed together
in co-operative houses; the poorest starved in garrets and cellars. The
foundation of the mendicant orders[16] brought aid to a good many youths;
but those who did not want to be friars remained at a disadvantage.
So, about 1258, Robert de Sorbon endowed a hall at Paris for sixteen

[15] See below, p. 287.
[16] See below, pp. 349-51.

deserving seculars, candidates for the degree in theology—a noteworthy event in the history of culture, for it marked the beginning of the famous Sorbonne,[17] oldest of residential colleges. Similar establishments at Paris soon came to house the bulk of the university population, both masters and students; and from there the practice spread far and wide, attaining great popularity especially in England.

Meanwhile the development of the educational system that is technically called scholastic had raised problems of serious concern to the organized church. Before they can be understood, however, attention must be shifted to other prominent features of mediæval civilization.

[17] After the theological faculty had come to reside in the Sorbonne, the name was generally applied to that faculty.

CHAPTER XV

Developments in Literature

1. MEDIÆVAL LATIN

The church and vernacular literature

It was once usual to explain the sudden perfection of vernacular literature in the twelfth century as the final stage of a slow evolution out of folk-tales, folk-songs, folk-plays, and the like. But since none of the supposed primitive forms have ever been found, scholars now prefer a less fanciful explanation: that the prototypes of the vernacular masterpieces should rather be sought in the Latin literature of the church. For hundreds of years there had been virtually no educated persons outside the clergy; and the clergy, it should be remembered, were by no means all priests or monks. Most clerks were men who had taken minor orders, to become students in the schools or—as the word came to imply—secretaries and accountants. When employed, they frequently served in baronial households; when unemployed, they lived by their wits. As a class they were remarkable neither for piety nor for virtue; many of them, in fact, were notorious rascals. Yet, because they were not responsible holders of churchly office, they were the more likely to give free play to whatever talents they might have for original composition.

Latin prose

The language normally used for all official or formal writing was Latin, which, though not classical in either vocabulary or syntax, was an admirable medium of expression. The days when even the better-educated had been unable to write correctly were long past. In the twelfth century the Latin of the schoolmen, according to contemporary standards, was entirely grammatical. And how could it remain a living language unless it met the demands of changing environment? A glance at the appendix of a modern dictionary will show how rapidly English has admitted new words and invented new meanings for old ones. In precisely the same way

274

mediæval Latin was adapted to the needs of government officials, business men, lawyers, physicians, theologians, scientists, and other experts, as well as to less technical use by preachers, chroniclers, biographers, story-tellers, and the like. The great bulk of this literature was intensely prac-tical; yet all of it was not on that account lacking in beauty. From the æsthetic point of view, the greatest prose of the age is to be found in the liturgy of the church—rhythmic Latin chanted to the accompaniment of gorgeous ceremonial. A similar majestic quality pervades many of the documents issuing from the chanceries of great ecclesiastics. A papal bull, for instance, has a sonorous timbre that to the trained ear is very charac-teristic.

In Latin, as in Greek, the best mediæval poetry did not follow classic **Latin** models, but used the system with which we are familiar—rhyme and a **poetry** meter based on accent. Monks, priests, and schoolmen turned out an enormous quantity of such poems on religious themes; and although most of it was distinctly mediocre, occasional pieces have remained justly famous. In particular, the great Latin hymns of the twelfth and thirteenth centuries rank among the world's artistic masterpieces. Equally remark-able, yet wholly different, are the lyrics known as Goliardic, the authors of which appear to have been principally students, the wandering clerks who were not displeased at being called sons of Goliath (i.e., Philistines). This poetry, written in the Latin of the schools, is on the whole delightfully fresh and gay. It has the wit and irreverence of youth, together with a sensuous outlook on life that ascetics would consider sheer paganism. To some extent—especially by frequent mention of Venus, Cupid, Pan, Bacchus, and the like—it reveals the influence of classical study. Its chief inspiration, however, must surely be found in the joys and griefs of the poets themselves. They needed no instruction from antiquity to learn that in the spring the sky is very blue, the grass is very green, and love is very sweet. Why have so many writers made out that mediæval people were fundamentally unlike us?

Many of the Goliardic poems are no more than frivolous jingles, like **Goliardic** the begging song immortalized by John Addington Symonds:[1] **verse**

> I, a wandering scholar lad,
>   Born for toil and sadness,
> Oftentimes am driven by
>   Poverty to madness.
>
> Literature and knowledge I
>   Fain would still be earning,
> Were it not that want of pelf
>   Makes me cease from learning.

[1] In his book of translations entitled *Wine, Women, and Song.*

These torn clothes that cover me
    Are too thin and rotten;
Oft I have to suffer cold,
    By the warmth forgotten.

Scarce I can attend at church,
    Sing God's praises duly;
Mass and vespers both I miss,
    Though I love them truly.

Oh, thou pride of [Normandy],[2]
    By thy worth I pray thee,
Give the suppliant help in need;
    Heaven will sure repay thee.

Originality was as precious then as it is now. For the dozens of lyrics that celebrate love in the springtime there is only one that shifts the scene to the early winter:[3]

Down from the branches fall the leaves,
A wanness comes on all the trees,
    The summer's done;
And into his last house in heaven
    Now goes the sun.

Sharp frost destroys the tender sprays,
Birds are a-cold in these short days.
    The nightingale
Is grieving that the fire of heaven
    Is now grown pale.

The swollen river rushes on
Past meadows whence the green has gone,
    The golden sun
Has fled our world. Snow falls by day,
    The nights are numb.

About me all the world is stark
And I am burning; in my heart
    There is a fire,
A living flame in me, the maid
    Of my desire.

With this work of grace and beauty we may compare another which, from its first line, is called *Dum Diane Vitrea*:

[2] Left blank in the manuscript, so that the singer could insert any appropriate name.
[3] Translation by Helen J. Waddell, *Medieval Latin Lyrics* (Constable & Co., Ltd.: London, 1929). This selection and the two following are used by permission of the publishers.

When Diana lighteth
Late her crystal lamp,
Her pale glory kindleth
From her brother's fire,
Little straying west winds
Wander over heaven,
Moonlight falleth,
And recalleth,
With a sound of lute-strings shaken,
Hearts that have denied his reign
To love again.
Hesperus, the evening star,
To all things that mortal are,
Grants the dew of sleep. . . .

Very different, but very fine in their own way, are a number of drinking **The** songs. And closely akin to the latter is that masterpiece of the twelfth **Archpoet** century, *The Confession of Golias*, by one who was justly styled the Archpoet:

Seething over inwardly,
    With fierce indignation,
In my bitterness of soul,
    Hear my declaration.
I am of one element,
    Levity my matter,
Like enough a withered leaf
    For the winds to scatter. . . .

Down the broad way do I go,
    Young and unregretting;
Wrap me in my vices up,
    Virtue all forgetting. . . .

He has been accused of being a devotee of Venus. He admits it. So what then?

Yet a second charge they bring:
    I'm forever gaming.
Yea, and never have I scorned,
    Stripped me to my shaming. . . .

Look again upon your list.
    Is the tavern on it?
Yea, and never have I scorned,
    Never shall I scorn it.
Till the holy angels come,
    And my eyes discern them,
Singing for the dying soul
    Requiem æternam.

For on this my heart is set:
  When the hour is nigh me,
Let me in the tavern die,
  With a tankard by me;
While the angels, looking down,
  Joyously sing o'er me,
Deus sit propitius
  Huic potatori.

This is very nearly François Villon[4] in the twelfth century—a gay jesting with dishonor and death.

Lyrics such as these spread all over Europe and are found, interspersed among hymns of devotion, in manuscripts of many countries. Here also stand parody and satire of a more scandalous kind: a mock creed, a burlesqued service of the eucharist, and the *Gospel according to Marks of Silver*. The last is a bitter parable of a poor man who seeks charity at the papal court, but is told:

"Friend, thy poverty perish with thee! Get thee behind me, Satan, because thou knowest not the wisdom of cash. Amen and amen! I say unto thee, thou shalt not enter into the joy of thy Lord until thou hast given the uttermost farthing."

Even after he has sold his clothes, he cannot gain admittance and is cast into outer darkness. Then comes to Rome a certain clerk guilty of homicide but rich. He tips the usher and the chamberlain and the cardinals.

Then the lord pope, hearing that his cardinals and ministers had received many gifts from the clerk, fell sick, even unto death. But the rich man sent him an elixir of gold and silver, and straightway he was healed. Then the lord pope called unto him his cardinals and ministers and said unto them: "Brethren, beware lest ye be seduced by vain words. For lo! I give unto you an example, that even as I grab, so also shall ye grab."

The preceding excerpts will at least show how dangerous it is to generalize about the "mediæval mind." As soon as we look beyond certain conventional writings, there is no uniformity of sentiment. That all persons of the twelfth century were struck from the same mold is one of many legends invented by imaginative historians. This truth will be even more apparent when we turn to vernacular literature.

2. THE VERNACULAR LYRIC AND MEDIÆVAL MUSIC

In a previous chapter we have seen something about the early French epic and the more primitive sagas in Germanic languages. At one time it was the common opinion that such poems were gradual accretions, which in the course of centuries had grown around cores of historical fact. Now, on the contrary, it is realized that no work of art could ever have been formed in this way; that we owe *Beowulf* and the *Song of Roland*, like

---

[4] See below, pp. 476-79.

the *Divine Comedy* and *Paradise Lost*, to individual authors. Thus understood, the *chansons de geste* become more intelligible; for they can be interpreted as true products of the feudal age, deriving from the past no more than a few familiar names. The vogue for the *chansons de geste*, spread by French knights into all the surrounding countries, lasted for many generations; so hundreds of such pieces came to be written and combined in regular cycles dealing with characters at Charlemagne's court or the members of various legendary dynasties. And there can be no doubt that the writers were for the most part clerks.

From the facts already cited it should be clear that the ranks of the mediæval clergy included men with a talent for writing either prose or poetry. We may, indeed, suspect that the same persons would often produce songs both sacred and profane. Abelard was a hymn-writer as well as a dialectician, and he tells us himself that his poems in praise of Héloïse were widely sung in France. Héloïse adds that he was skilled not only as a poet but also as a composer of music. Although, unfortunately, his lyrics have not come down to us, the Goliardic verse enables us to guess their general character. Presumably, they were in Latin. Yet, if he had wanted to, could he not have used his native Romance? Others were then beginning to do so—with the result that, within another hundred years, vernacular literature had gained a lasting triumph. This, surely, would have been impossible had not the church, directly or indirectly, supplied the preliminary training.

Although the later *chansons de geste* sometimes introduced unconventional elements, they usually remained loyal to the epic tradition. Great epic is long, sonorous, and dramatic—an impersonal recital that is suited to rhythmic chanting. Great lyric, on the other hand, is brief, simple, and passionate—a little poem that can be sung to a lilting tune. In all ages the typical lyric has been the love-song, and that is at its best when it is most spontaneous. As may be seen from the examples quoted above, the Goliardi produced some exquisite lyrics in their rhymed Latin; but it became evident during the twelfth century that pre-eminence in this field of composition was to be won by the vernacular. The standards of modern lyric poetry were even then being set by the troubadours[5] of southern France. The *chansons de geste* were sung by *jongleurs* (literally jugglers)—wandering minstrels who also acted as popular entertainers at markets and fairs. In general they were men of low birth, whereas most troubadours were gentlemen—nobles who prized their skill in poetry and music as highly as their chivalrous reputation.

The first known troubadour was none other than William IX, duke of Aquitaine and grandfather of the Eleanor who was to be successively queen

The troubadours

---

[5] Provençal *troubadour,* French *trouvère*—a finder or a composer.

of France and queen of England.[6] From his pen we have eleven lyrics—love-songs that vary from the delicate to quite the opposite. But the fact that his verse was sometimes libertine did not prevent his having sincere religious convictions, as is shown by his famous poem on departing for the Holy Land:[7]

> Since now I have a mind to sing,
> I'll make a song of that which saddens me,
> That no more in Poitou or Limousin
> Shall I love's servant be.

While he is away, what will happen to his fair *seigneurie* of Poitiers, and to his son, who is young and weak? He prays his neighbors to forgive him for any wrongs he may have done them, and he offers the same prayer to Jesus, "both in Romance and in Latin."

> Of prowess and of joy I had my part
> But now of them my heart hath ta'en surcease.
> And now I go away to find that One
> Beside whom every sinner findeth peace.
> All that which I have loved I leave behind,
> The pride and all the pomp of chivalry.
> Since it so pleases God, I am resigned;
> I pray Him have me of His company.

There was, however, no necessity that a troubadour should be of aristocratic birth, as is proved by the careers of Marcabrun, a foundling, and of Bernard de Ventadour, the son of a servant in the local castle. Bernard, according to legend, long enjoyed the favor of the viscount, but was finally driven from Ventadour because he had a fatal attraction for the viscountess. At any rate, he left his native land to serve first the English queen, Eleanor of Aquitaine, and later the count of Toulouse. Of his poems, which were very famous throughout Europe, at least forty-five have survived. They are virtually all love-songs, celebrating with remarkable delicacy and grace a number of ladies—each of them disguised by a pet-name, so that we have no idea who they really were. To show the simplicity of his verse, one stanza may be quoted in the original:

> Quan la douss' aura venta
> Deves vostre pais,
> Vejaire m'es qu'eu senta
> Un ven de paradis,
> Per amor de la genta
> Vas cui eu sui aclis,

[6] She was married first to Louis VII of France and then to Henry II of England; see below, pp. 312-14.

[7] Helen J. Waddell, *The Wandering Scholars* (Constable & Co., Ltd.: London, 1927), p. 116. This selection and the one given below are used by permission of the publishers.

> En cui ai mes m'ententa,
> E mon coratge assis;
> Quar de totas partis
> Per leis, tan m'atalenta.

A fairly literal translation, preserving the meter if not the rhyme, runs as follows:

> When blow the gentle breezes
> From out your countryside,
> They breathe upon my senses
> As winds from paradise;
> Through love of the fair lady
> Towards whom I fondly lean,
> On whom my thoughts are centered,
> For whom my passions burn:
> To her I pledge myself
> Alone, so she has charmed me.

The true beauty of the Provençal lyric, however, can be more fully appreciated from a free translation, such as Helen Waddell's exquisite version of Jaufré Rudel.[8] Of the poet almost nothing is known, except that he was a baron of Limousin who went on the Second Crusade.[9] And before he left, he wrote this enigmatic poem, celebrating a dream lady in a far-off land, whom his heart longed for, but whom his reason told him he should never meet. **Jaufré Rudel**

> When the days lengthen in the month of May,
> Well pleased am I to hear the birds
>   Sing far away.
> And when from that place I am gone,
> I hang my head and make dull moan,
> Since she my heart is set upon
>   Is far away.
>
> So far, that song of birds, flower o' the thorn,
> Please me no more than winter morn,
>   With ice and sleet.
> Ah, would I were a pilgrim over sea,
> With staff and scrip and cloak to cover me,
> That some day I might kneel me on one knee
>   Before her feet.
>
> Most sad, most joyous shall I go away,
> Let me have seen her for a single day,
>   My love afar.
> I shall not see her, for her land and mine
> Are sundered, and their ways are hard to find,
> So many ways, and I shall lose my way,
>   So wills it God.

[8] Helen J. Waddell, *The Wandering Scholars,* p. 205.
[9] See below, p. 325.

Yet I shall know no other love but hers,
And if not hers, no other love at all.
    She hath surpassed all.
So fair is she, so noble, I would be
A captive with the hosts of paynimrie
In a far land, if so be upon me
    Her eyes might fall.

God, who hath made all things in earth that are,
That made my love, and set her thus afar,
    Grant me this grace,
That I may some day come within a room,
Or in some garden gloom
    Look on her face.

It will not be, for at my birth they said
That one had set this doom upon my head,
    —God curse him among men!—
That I should love, and not till I be dead,
    Be loved again.

The problem of origins

Altogether, poems are extant from some four hundred troubadours of the twelfth and thirteenth centuries, and we know the names of many others whose works have perished. No attempt can here be made to discuss this mass of literature, except by way of setting down a few conclusions as to its general nature and influence. The original language of the vernacular lyric, though called Provençal, was actually the dialect of Limousin, and the fact that it was not the native tongue of William IX shows that conventional standards for this kind of composition had already been established before his day. William, obviously, adopted a recognized literary form, the origin of which we are left to guess. It was not at all classical, and there is no evidence that it had been gradually evolved out of folk-songs. The more probable supposition is that the preliminary experimentation had been carried out by clerks familiar with poetical expression in Latin. There is also the possibility of an Arab tradition obscurely received from the Moors who had long ruled the province of Septimania. In the twelfth century, at any rate, an increasing number of southern French gentlemen devoted themselves to the writing of lyrics, which they set to music and sang to the accompaniment of a guitar.[10]

Courtoisie in the north

From southern France the new fashion spread to all the neighboring lands. Long before 1200, troubadours had come to enjoy the patronage of the Spanish princes, of the Sicilian king, and of other lords to the north. In this respect the marriage of Eleanor of Aquitaine first to Louis VII and then to Henry II began a new epoch in the history of their kingdoms. Ber-

[10] The word is merely a form of "cither." The instrument, being played with a bow, was a forerunner of the violin and was introduced into Europe by the Arabs; see below, p. 284.

nard de Ventadour was only one of many lyric poets who sang at the Angevin court. Bertran de Born, a turbulent baron of Périgord, gained renown throughout Europe for amorous as well as political intrigues, and both of these interests are reflected in his verse. He was the devoted friend of Henry II's eldest son; and when the young king suddenly died, Bertran wrote a lament that stands among the finest works of the century. Later he became a follower of Henry's second son, Richard Lion-Heart, who was himself a troubadour though hardly one of genius. With such encouragement, it is not strange that the poetic urge came to be felt by dozens of feudal nobles whose grandfathers had rarely been able to read or write.

As late as the thirteenth century the poets of southern Europe, even in Spain and Italy, continued to write in Provençal; but by that time the northern *trouvères* had generally adopted the French of their own countryside. Although their verse is occasionally attractive, most of it lacks the spontaneity of that composed earlier. For example, when Conon de Béthune, on departing for the crusade of 1201, pens a love-song to his lady, we feel that he is merely doing the fashionable thing. "My body," he says, "may go to serve our Savior; yet my heart remains wholly in her keeping."[11] Had the first crusaders gone "sighing to Syria" or thought that each must "act chivalrously to secure at once paradise and honor and love of his lady"? By this time, in truth, aristocratic literature had entered a world of make-believe. It had come to be dominated by *courtoisie*—a code of courtly love that subordinated the old masculine chivalry to the glorification of women. Courtly love was defined as a kind of sentimental vassalage. The knight must have a lady to serve; the lady must have a knight to do her service. And if the two were kept apart by a geographic barrier, by social inequality, or by marriage to other persons, the situation was all the more favorable to lyric effusion.

In the poetry of *courtoisie*, accordingly, we can never be sure where actuality ends and artistic imagination begins; for it is a poor poet who cannot invent mysterious lady-loves and affecting scenes. Under such influences lyric verse tended to become more and more stereotyped. A number of conventional forms had been established even before the close of the twelfth century. We find, for instance, the *alba* or dawn-song, in which two lovers are warned that the night is past but protest the incredible news—"it is not day; the lark has lied to us." The *pastourelle* explains how the knightly singer meets a lovely shepherdess, how he praises her, and how she inevitably succumbs to his charm. The spinning-song is a form of ballad wherein the lonely maid or the unhappy wife, over her monotonous work, sighs for the man of her heart. Ultimately, when any such type of verse was chosen, it not only had to follow a certain theme but also had to include a certain

[11] See the complete translation in C. C. Abbott, *Early Mediæval French Lyrics*, p. 105.

number of lines, each with a certain number of syllables and a certain rhyme. Later chapters will show how these conventions long dominated poetic composition in France, as well as in the adjoining countries.

Mediæval music

The history of the mediæval lyric is further complicated by the fact that it was intimately related to mediæval music, which is a very technical and somewhat controversial subject. Here again an alleged influence of folk-songs has been emphasized by various authors to account for the remarkable innovations of the Middle Ages. But again, for sheer lack of direct evidence, that opinion has come to be generally rejected in favor of one that finds the decisive factor in ecclesiastical practice. From primitive times the church had declared official what is known as plain chant—a system under which certain limited scales are used in certain prescribed ways. Only the notes indicated by the white keys on the piano are sounded, and

Fig. 21.   Example of Musical Notation, Twelfth Century.

they vary in length only as may be demanded by the rhythm of Latin prose. All voices sing the same part in unison, and without instrumental accompaniment. Ultimately derived from the choral music of the Greeks,[12] plain chant was consecrated by use in the Roman Church and, through papal regulation, became universal in western Europe. Though often called Gregorian, it was not invented by Gregory the Great; he merely gave it, as part of the accepted ritual, the prestige of his support. Naturally, therefore, the sole method of musical notation that was known to Latin writers of the earlier Middle Ages was one originally devised to represent plain chant.[13]

Meanwhile, for less formal music, many instruments remained in common use: various kinds of harps, lyres, cithers, pipes, trumpets, and horns, as well as the organ that had been known to the Greeks and Romans. The Germanic sagas and the French *chansons de geste*, we know, were chanted to the accompaniment of a lyre or harp which, like that of antiquity, was struck by the fingers. The troubadour's guitar, on the contrary, was played with a bow—a technique that was assuredly introduced into Europe by the

[12] See above, p. 16.
[13] See Figure 21; taken from Pierre Aubry, *Les plus anciens monuments de la musique française* (Paris, 1905), Plate IV. In the same work those interested will find a literal transcription of this *chanson de croisade*.

Arabs. In all probability the latter also influenced the musical and poetic composition of southern France, though it is hard to say precisely where their influence lay. One source of our trouble is the use of the current ecclesiastical notation in the earliest manuscripts of the troubadours' lyrics; for the experts sadly disagree when they come to reproduce the original tunes. Presumably the determining factor was the rhythm of the spoken language, which was well known to the troubadours but is not so well known to us. The improvement that made written music intelligible to readers of all generations was the division of the composition into uniform measures, within each of which the length of every note was clearly indicated.

The formal measurement of music was not expounded by Latin writers until the thirteenth century, and they must have been familiar with the translations of al-Farabi and other Arabic authors.[14] The scholarly works of the later age, however, were evidently prepared for by the writings of various Carolingian ecclesiastics on the contemporary practice of polyphonic singing and playing. The first arrangement of music in parts—for example, with tenor and bass—seems to have been inspired by a practical consideration: since voices in a monastic choir would naturally vary in pitch, some men would be allowed to sing above the melody and some below it. Such usage would gradually lead to experimentation in harmonious effects, like those obtained by striking chords on a harp or by combining instruments of different sorts to form an orchestra. During the ninth and following centuries, at any rate, a number of books were written to explain how pleasing results could best be obtained through the union of vocal or instrumental passages. And since the elaboration of harmony made it vitally important that the various parts should begin, continue, and end on time, the measuring of music—according to a plan already described by the Arabs—eventually followed. Whatever may be made of this argument, our modern music can be said to have definitely emerged in the course of the thirteenth century.

Polyphonic composition

3. THE ROMANCE AND OTHER LITERARY FORMS

Although *chansons de geste* continued to be written throughout the twelfth century, a different sort of long poem, inspired by the *courtoisie* of the troubadours, gained increasing popularity. This literary form, composed in rhymed couplets to be read rather than chanted, became known as the romance. The subject matter is what will still be recognized as romantic: beautiful damsels, gallant knights, cruel husbands, sinister magicians, benevolent fairies, talking animals, mysterious forests, enchanted palaces, perilous quests, and the like. Love is always prominent and the exotic element is strong. The authors, finding no romantic charm in the old-fashioned epics, borrowed from antiquity themes concerning Alexander the Great, Æneas,

The romance

14 See above, p. 170.

and the siege of Troy. Yet, no matter when the scene was laid, the characters were made to act and talk like lords and ladies of feudal France. The famous cycle of King Arthur, mythical leader of the fifth-century Britons, began in much the same way. Some of the Arthurian material may have come into France by way of Brittany, but most of it seems rather to have been derived from Norman writers in England. Of the latter the most influential was Geoffrey of Monmouth (d. 1154), whose Latin *History of the Britons*, a combination of legend and sheer fancy, became a mine of treasure for poets and story-tellers.

Marie de France
Among the first to dip into the *matière de Bretagne* was Marie de France, of whom nothing is known except that she was an educated Frenchwoman at the court of King Henry II and Queen Eleanor. From Marie's pen we have about a dozen romances or, as she called them, lays. They include stories of a knight who changes himself into a falcon in order to visit his lady-love (*Yonec*), of a fairy princess who carries off her lover to Avalon (*Lanval*), of a werewolf (*Le Bisclavet*), and of various episodes in the Arthurian legend. Very characteristic is the lay of Gugemar. He, Marie tells us, was a baron of King Arthur and had but one fault, that he remained untouched by love—and so, of course, brought upon himself dire trouble. One day, while hunting in the forest, he wounds a marvelous white doe. But the arrow, glancing back, strikes him in the thigh. Then the doe speaks to him and tells him that he can never be healed except through the love of a dolorous lady. Mounting his horse, Gugemar rides to the sea, where he finds a ship with a bed waiting for him. He goes to sleep and a magic wind wafts the ship to the shore of a garden, beside which a beautiful lady is imprisoned in a tower by a cruel husband. She finds the knight, nurses him back to health, and for a while enjoys his love. Then he is discovered by the husband and sent away on the ship by which he arrived. Other adventures follow and eventually, after long separation, the lovers are reunited. The husband is slain and the two henceforth live happily.

Chrétien de Troyes
Like Marie de France, Chrétien de Troyes in the later twelfth century took old materials and rewrote them to suit the *courtoisie* of the fashionable world. But by his time society was more sophisticated. Ovid's *Art of Love* and similar compositions in the vernacular were enjoying a great vogue. So, when Chrétien retold an ancient tale, he adorned his pages with elaborate pictures of beauty and chivalry in luxurious surroundings and with eminently polite conversations; and he constantly emphasized the psychology of love. Each of his romances is, in fact, a sort of problem play. For instance, his *Lancelot* turns on the conflict between a knight's honor and his love for a lady. In *Érec et Énide* the plot concerns the tests that one lover may properly demand of the other. These and other stories of the same type, after delighting the countless generations that have intervened, may still be read in the verse or prose of all European nations, and may even be

heard in the form of grand opera from the stage of a metropolitan theater. There is, nevertheless, a limit to the enjoyment that one can receive from such literature. Sooner or later the world of make-believe, with its people who never could have lived and its events that never could have happened, grows tiresome. And after one has read a certain number of conventional lyrics, the charms of *belle Yolanz*, *belle Aiglentine*, and *belle Amelot* begin to pall. One longs for a point of view other than that of the fine gentleman with a fatal attraction for both queens and peasant girls.

Such a reaction in the thirteenth century helped to popularize the *fa-* bliaux—stories composed in rhymed verse and, to judge from the subject matter, intended for the marketplace rather than the baronial hall. Being written for the sole purpose of provoking a laugh, they ignore all chivalrous prejudice. Members of the nobility rarely appear and, when they do, are treated as ordinary persons. And since peasants are considered too stupid to be interesting, it is the bourgeois class that receives the chief attention. The typical merchant is rich, but in all matters apart from his business apt to be a fool. The hero is generally the wandering clerk, a clever rascal who makes the most of any opportunity, whether for love, for gain, or for sheer amusement. When one of these fellows arrives, the sensible burgher locks up his valuables—also his wife and daughter; for, according to the *fabliaux*, women are never to be trusted. However beautiful and intelligent, they are devoid of morals. Equally unprincipled are priests and monks, who excel only in hypocrisy and amply deserve the grief that always befalls them. These, of course, are stock characters—such as today win laughs in the films and comic strips. It is not to be supposed that bourgeois audiences of the thirteenth century actually believed that there were no virtuous women or honest clergymen. The spice of the jest lay in depicting the opposite of what would be found in pious or romantic literature.

Although some of the *fabliaux* are cribbed from the Latin classics and in others the wit does not rise above the level of plain smut, a good many are both funny and original. A fair example of elementary humor is found in the tale of Brunain. A villein and his wife go to pray at Notre-Dame and there they hear a sermon by the priest, who tells them that all should give liberally to God and so receive a double reward. At home the villein and his wife talk over the matter and decide to give the priest their cow, Brunain. They do so and the priest, after blessing them, puts Brunain out to graze along with his own cow. But during the night Brunain becomes homesick, breaks down the fence, and escapes, bringing the priest's cow along with her. So in the morning the villein and his wife discover that they have indeed received a double reward, and give fervent thanks to God for an evident miracle.

The story of the Poor Peddler is a little more subtle. Arriving in a certain region with his horse and pack, he is unable to pay for fodder at the

The fabliaux (margin note)

inn. But he hears from a local merchant that nearby is the pasture of a nobleman who is known to be very generous. The peddler takes this suggestion, solemnly entrusting his animal to the care of the nobleman and to Almighty God. Then in the course of the night a wolf breaks into the pasture and kills the horse. What to do? In desperation the peddler goes to the nobleman and tells him what has happened. "All right," says the latter, "here are thirty sous for the half of the horse that was entrusted to me; the other thirty you will have to collect from God." So the peddler starts down the road on foot; and before he has gone far, he meets a monk. "Whose man are you?" he asks the worthy brother. "I am a man of God," is the response. "Aha!" exclaims the peddler; "you're just the fellow I'm looking for." Whereupon he makes off with the monk's clothes for the thirty sous still owed him.

The Romance of Reynard

Applied to the romance, satirical humor of the same kind produced the very popular cycle of Reynard the fox. Fables about animals, notably those of Æsop, had been widely read since ancient times and there seems also to have been a body of Germanic folk-tales about a fox (Reynard), a bear (Bruin), a wolf (Isengrim), a cat (Tybert), and the like. Yet it was unquestionably French clerks who first worked these various materials into a series of mock romances which remain among the best-loved works of the Middle Ages. Reynard and his peers are vassals of King Noble, the lion, who is very grand but who is quite powerless to control his state. His barons are engaged in endless feuds and Reynard, in particular, is a professional robber. This unprincipled rascal plays cruel tricks on Isengrim and Tybert, eats the favorite wife of Chantecleer (the cock), lies his way out of trials before the royal court, and keeps the reader's sympathy throughout. His fame is still attested by the fact that in modern French any fox is still *un renard*, instead of *un voupil* (from the Latin *vulpes*).

Aucassin et Nicolette

Inevitably, too, the realistic touch came to be applied to the more conventional romance and the result, among lesser pieces, was the immortal story of *Aucassin et Nicolette*. Although the author's name is unknown, he lived in the early thirteenth century and was a great artist. To be appreciated, the romance itself should be read; here can be mentioned only two or three points of especial interest. In the first place, the form is very original, being part prose and part verse—both clever, and blended in such a way as to enhance the charm of each. Secondly, the substance, though superficially conventional, is frequently turned in a very unconventional way. Aucassin is told by his father that he may not marry Nicolette, who was originally a slave girl, and that if he does not give her up he will go to hell. Aucassin replies that he does not mind; all the best people go there and he prefers their company. Later we hear of a miracle, but such a miracle as never appeared on the ecclesiastical stage. A pilgrim, lying sick in bed, is suddenly healed by the sight of Nicolette, who chances to pass that way with her kirtle and smock held high.

In such passages the quiet irony of the author is obvious; he never takes even his leading characters quite seriously. But once, when we least expect it, we obtain a brief glimpse of real tragedy. Aucassin, searching for Nicolette with tears running down his face, meets a villein who asks him why he weeps. Loath to tell the truth, Aucassin lamely answers that he has lost his dog. Then the villein turns on him and cries him shame, that he should weep over such a trifle. As for himself, he has cause to grieve. "Wherefore so?" asks Aucassin.[15]

"Sir, I will tell thee. I was hireling to a rich villein, and drove his plough; four oxen had he. But three days since came on me great misadventure, whereby I lost the best of my oxen, Roger, the best of my team. Him go I seeking, and have neither eaten nor drunken these three days; nor may I go to the town, lest they cast me into prison, seeing that I have not wherewithal to pay. Out of all the wealth of the world I have no more than ye see on my body. A poor mother bare me, that had no more but one wretched bed; this have they taken from under her, and she lies in the very straw. This ails me more than mine own case, for wealth comes and goes; if now I have lost, another tide I will gain, and will pay for mine ox whenas I may; never for that will I weep. But you weep for a stinking hound. Foul fall whoso thinks well of thee!"

So Aucassin tells him that he is a good comforter and gives him money to pay for his ox—but the writer was thinking of more than an episode in a sentimental story.

Meanwhile romantic literature had also come to be affected by a very different influence. This was allegory, the form of mystic interpretation extensively used by the schoolmen. If a Christian meaning could be found in the Hebrew Bible or in the works of pagan antiquity, why could not one be read into the tales of King Arthur and the Round Table? So the ancient materials were again reworked to produce a new cycle of prose romances— the famous series that is built round the quest for the Holy Grail. About the same time Guillaume de Lorris set another literary fashion with his allegorical *Romance of the Rose*.[16] Here the Rose typifies the Lady sought by the Lover, who is aided or impeded by Idleness, Danger, Evil-Tongue, Fear, Shame, Fair-Welcome, Reason, and the like. His device, being quickly adopted by a host of other writers, proved especially popular in dramatic representations—the morality plays that for hundreds of years delighted audiences with more or less realistic impersonations of the virtues and vices.

Allegories

For the beginnings of the mediæval drama we must, of course, look to an earlier age, when on special occasions the liturgy of the church was enlarged by the insertion of added features. At Easter, for example, the choir might present the story of the Resurrection, or at Christmas that of the

Growth of the drama

[15] From the translation by Andrew Lang.
[16] For the additions by Jean de Meun, see below, pp. 389-91.

Nativity. From merely singing the sacred story, the participants came to act it out, with appropriate costumes and stage effects. Thus arose the religious plays called mysteries, the themes of which were taken not only from the Bible but also from the lives of popular saints—a practice that allowed the introduction of many a homely touch drawn from real life. At first the mystery, being a supplement to the regular service, was presented inside the church and in Latin. Later the performance was often transferred to the porch or to a stage erected beyond it. And since the object of the play was to instruct the people, it might to good advantage be put in the vernacular. A very early example of such composition is the *Mystère d'Adam*, written in the twelfth century. The parts were of course taken by clergymen, and for their benefit the stage directions are in Latin; but the dialogue is in French verse, amazingly spirited and with a touch of subtle wit that is wholly delightful.

As the scene opens, Adam is working at one end of the stage, while Satan approaches Eve and says that he wants to talk to her. She promises discretion, for which Satan compliments her. Adam, he thinks, is distinctly her inferior. A little hard, admits Eve. "Though he be harder than hell (*plus dure que n'est emfers*), he shall be made soft," promises Satan; for he really should take better care of his wife.

You are fresher than the rose and whiter than crystal, or snow that falls on ice in the vale. The Creator did not mate you well: you are too tender and he is too rough. Nevertheless, you are wiser than he. That's why I have done well to speak with you.

With such diabolic flattery the main theme is introduced. The fruit which God has allowed them is no good, but that which He has denied them has marvelous virtue. In it is the secret of life and of power, the knowledge of both good and evil. "How does it taste?" asks poor Eve. "Celestial. . . ." "Is that the fruit?" "Yes, look at it." And so the story proceeds to its familiar end—a very human little play, as may be seen from even these brief excerpts. Although the ecclesiastical drama might become more elaborate, it could hardly be more effective.

German literature   The southern French set the fashion in lyric; the northern French in all other forms of poetic composition, as well as in prose—with Villehardouin's memoirs of the Fourth Crusade and Joinville's life of St. Louis.[17] Anglo-Saxon had virtually disappeared as a literary language after the Norman Conquest of England. And although the old Germanic traditions were yet maintained in far-off Iceland, they had been generally abandoned on the continent. From the twelfth century on, German writers devoted a good part of their time to translating and adapting the poetry of France. Much of their work, being mere imitation, was naturally inferior; but by the thir-

[17] See below, pp. 339, 367.

teenth century certain German developments of the Arthurian cycle—especially the *Tristan* of Gottfried von Strassburg and the *Parzifal* of Wolfram von Eschenbach—had attained striking originality. And the ranks of the local troubadours, or *Minnesänger*, had come to include at least one great lyric poet, Walther von der Vogelweide. Born of a noble family in the Austrian Tyrol, Walther began his literary career at Vienna; subsequently, as a professional poet, he wandered from court to court, finally to be rewarded with a small fief from the emperor Frederick II. Walther's later poetry thus tended to be of the bread-and-butter variety, and to suffer from overly intricate meters and rhyme patterns. His finest lyrics are those of his youth—simple love-songs like the famous *Unter den Linden*.

In contemporary Spain and Italy the literary models were likewise French and Provençal, and most poets, when they came to use their own vernacular, were satisfied with copies and adaptations. Yet the great Spanish epic of the Cid, a semi-legendary character of the earlier wars, began to take form in the twelfth century—with the *Poema del Cid*, of which only a fragment remains. We have no Italian epic or lyric for another hundred years, and nothing of either sort especially remarkable before Dante, whose glorious career will be sketched in a later chapter.

Spanish and Italian literature

CHAPTER XVI

Developments in the Structural and Decorative Arts

1. ROMANESQUE ART

Development of Romanesque

In eastern Europe the sixth and following centuries witnessed the perfection of the architectural style known as Byzantine, which, with modifications, came to be widely used throughout Moslem countries. In parts of Italy, too, Byzantine influence remained strong—especially at Venice, where as late as the eleventh century the church of St. Mark was modeled after that of the Holy Apostles at Constantinople. Yet, despite a few borrowings of this sort, the separation of the Latin and Greek worlds was no less decisive in art than in other phases of civilization. When, with the economic recovery of western Europe, the local prelates were able to undertake new and monumental structures, they generally preferred what they considered the true Roman tradition and designed their churches on a basilican plan.[1] As we have seen, the early Christian basilicas at Ravenna and elsewhere had timber roofs, whose light weight permitted the retention of a clerestory supported on slender columns and liberally supplied with windows. But such roofs often caught fire and burned—to the irreparable damage of whatever the church might contain. So architects came to be greatly concerned with the problem of how to place stone vaults over the entire building, and out of their experience in this connection were evolved the structural systems known as Romanesque and Gothic.

For vaulting a rectangular area the Romans had employed two devices. The simpler was the barrel-vault—a half-cylinder of masonry, the weight of which was equally distributed along the supporting walls. In the other case the area was divided into squares, and over each of these bays, as they

[1] See above, pp. 94-95.

are called, two barrel-vaults were made to intersect at right angles (see Figure 22). The weight of such a cross-vault was concentrated at the four corners (A, B, C, D), which were joined by four semicircular arches (AB, BC, CD, DA) and by two groins (AC, BD). In the basilican church the aisles could readily be cross-vaulted; for the thrust of the arches towards the nave could be counteracted by the weight of heavy clerestory walls resting on sturdier columns, while that towards the outside could be met by placing buttresses, thick fins of masonry, against the exterior walls. The more difficult task was to vault the nave. Transverse lines from column to column would divide it into oblong rather than square bays. How could half-cylinders of different diameters be made to intersect on the same plane? And how could the clerestory walls be buttressed over the aisle roofs? So builders rarely attempted to cross-vault a nave. Instead they raised a barrel-vault, and its mass tended to doom both clerestory and colonnade. Since the walls on which the vault rested had to be of uniform thickness, they could not be pierced for windows of any useful size; and to support such walls mere columns had to be replaced by enormous piers.

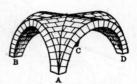

FIG. 22.   Cross-Vault.

The Romanesque church with a vaulted nave consequently has a low gloomy interior, characterized by massive stonework, extensive flat surfaces, and strongly marked horizontal lines. These principles necessarily hold good whether the building was put up in Italy, Germany, France, Spain, or England, although minor differences of style could be produced by varying the arrangement of the essential parts or the decoration of the exterior. Scores of examples could be given, but space permits mention of only a few. The cathedral of Pisa, dedicated in 1118, is justly renowned for its leaning bell-tower, its arcaded façade, and its sumptuous interior, adorned with varicolored marbles. Structurally, however, it is somewhat primitive. Only the aisles are cross-vaulted; the nave is covered by a timber roof, which permits the retention of a windowed clerestory and of antique columns to support it (see Plate III). The contemporary buildings of Lombardy, less elegant in form and materials, are better illustrations of Romanesque construction. Among them the most interesting is the church of Sant' Ambrogio at Milan, the rebuilding of which was begun in the eleventh century. Here the nave is divided into five bays, each corresponding to two in the aisles and so obtaining a square outline. Three of the bays are cross-vaulted, with heavy diagonal ribs set along the groins; one is barrel-vaulted; and one is topped by a low octagonal tower to admit light over the altar. Without such illumination the interior would be very dark, for a continuous gabled roof covers the church and there is no clerestory at all (see Plates III and IV).

Since the greater Romanesque churches of Germany, like the cathedral

Italian Romanesque

of Pisa, were originally built with timber roofs over their naves, they have little to offer by way of innovation in vaulting. Their chief originality lies in their general design. Often they were planned with a western as well as an eastern apse and with the main entrance, consequently, on one side. Sometimes they have two transepts. In any case the ends of the church are commonly marked by groups of three towers, as in the famous abbey of Laach (see Plate III). French Romanesque, on the contrary, held to the

tradition of a single transept and a single apse, with a place thus reserved for a western façade —one of the glorious features in all the Gothic cathedrals of France. Furthermore, the French architects came as a rule to enlarge the apse by adding a number of concentric chapels, so perfecting what is known as the *chevet*. An early example of the completed design is to be seen in the monumental church of Saint-Sernin at Toulouse.[2] But even here, it should be noted, the covering of the nave with a barrel-vault reduced the clerestory windows to a row of mere portholes.

Indeed, the normal system of Romanesque construction throughout Lombardy, Provence, southern France, and Spain called for cross-vaults over the aisles and a barrel-vault over the nave. In the churches of Saint-Trophime at Arles and of Notre-Dame at Clermont-Ferrand, for instance, the nave is covered by solid masonry shaped on the outside to form a gabled roof and on the inside a barrel-vault—an enormous weight

FIG. 23. Section of Notre-Dame (Clermont).

borne on thick walls buttressed over the aisles by quadrant vaults, quarter-cylinders of stone that leave no room for clerestory windows (see Figure 23). The interior of such a building is inevitably dark; its beauty is one of strength and majestic proportion. By way of compensation, therefore, the exterior was often handsomely decorated. Thus the church of Saint-Trophime has an especially fine cloister and a magnificent portal, on which elaborate carvings are happily combined with plain surfaces (see Plate V). Compared with this sculpture, which clearly suggests classic inspiration, that of Vézelai, a Burgundian abbey begun in the later eleventh century, seems barbarous (see Plate X). Yet, for all its crudeness, the sculpture of Vézelai has extraordinary vigor—an original quality that marks the emergence of a new art rather than a reminiscence of the past.

[2] See Plate III. The tower and steeple over the crossing are later additions.

Owing to the development that will be explained in the following section, little Romanesque construction survives in northern France. For additional examples of the style we must pass through the Capetian domain to Normandy, the rulers of which proved themselves as ardently devoted to building as to warfare. In their tremendous structures—plain to the point of grimness, but magnificently strong and admirably proportioned—the Norman character is vividly reflected. Such are two great abbeys founded at Caen by William the Conqueror and his wife Matilda, the Abbaye-aux-Hommes and the Abbaye-aux-Dames. Each of them apparently was at first provided with a wooden roof over the nave, which was later replaced by a masonry vault of advanced design. In both cases, too, the exterior has been much altered by additions made in the twelfth and thirteenth centuries. The primitive Romanesque must be looked for below the steeples and decorated upper stories. If attention is centered on that portion, the characteristic Norman façade will stand out prominently—the gabled end of the nave, with round-arched doors and windows flanked by massive square towers almost devoid of ornamentation (see Plate VI).

Norman and English Romanesque

In their Sicilian kingdom the Normans quite naturally made use of the architectural forms that had already appeared there. Such great buildings as the palatine chapel at Palermo and the cathedral of Monreale are a combination of the Romanesque, Byzantine, and Moslem styles. In the England of 1066, on the contrary, there was no architecture to rival that of Normandy; for the Saxons had never been great builders. On taking over the country, the Normans systematically razed the older cathedrals and abbeys and at once began new structures of unprecedented grandeur, thus turning much confiscated wealth into thank-offerings to God. Few of the major churches erected between 1066 and 1100 have retained their original design; yet, in spite of all subsequent changes, England contains a good deal of Romanesque. The finest monument of the sort is unquestionably Durham Cathedral, with its commanding position inside a loop of the River Wear (see Plate VI). Begun in 1093, the exterior of the church was virtually completed in the first quarter of the twelfth century. Only the central tower is of a later design; the two western towers are typically Norman and rank among the world's architectural triumphs. The beautiful cathedral of Norwich may likewise be classified as Norman, although it received a number of additions in the fifteenth century. And in many other churches various features reveal an eleventh-century origin. The Norman work is everywhere characterized by its massiveness—enormous columns, piers, and arches, decorated with simple geometrical patterns. Only rarely did the Norman artists attempt human figures, and then their results were not at all happy. They were masons rather than sculptors.

Symbolic sculpture

Reverting to the church of Saint-Trophime at Arles, we may note that the portal is surmounted by a representation of Christ and the four beasts of the Apocalypse.[3] Symbolism of the same kind continued to pervade much of the later sculpture. To understand the carvings on any mediæval cathedral, we have to be familiar with the conventions of early Christian art. Thus, a plain nimbus marks a saint; one with a superimposed cross denotes God. Wavy lines are water; curved lines with zigzags between them are the sky. A stalk with a few leaves is a tree or a forest. A battlemented tower is a city; if an angel peers from the top, it is heaven. Doll-like figures in the fold of a benevolent-looking man's robe are souls reposing in Abraham's bosom—i.e., enjoying the state of blessedness. Hell is represented by a monster's yawning mouth into which devils with pitchforks cast the souls

FIG. 24.   The Basilisk and the Adder on Amiens Cathedral. (From
E. Mâle, *L'art religieux du XIIIe siècle en France*.)

of the damned. The apostles and many of the saints are regularly pictured in such a way that they may be easily recognized. Holy men frequently stand on symbolic objects or persons, such as the kings who persecuted them.

An especially famous example is provided by the later cathedral of Amiens. Below the statue of Christ that adorns the main portal the mediæval sculptor sought to illustrate the biblical text: "Thou shalt tread upon the adder and the basilisk; the lion and the dragon shalt thou trample under foot."[4] Accordingly, under the feet of Christ he placed a lion and a dragon, symbolizing the Antichrist and Satan, and still lower on the shaft two other beasts. The first, half cock and half serpent, is the basilisk or cockatrice— a fabled monster that could kill by a glance, and so typified death. The second is a sort of long-legged dragon which holds one ear to the ground and stops the other with the end of his tail. This is the legendary adder, which was said to follow such a plan in order to avoid being charmed by singing, and so to typify the willfulness of the sinner (see Figure 24). Altogether, the composition may be taken as a sermon in stone: the Savior, at the entrance to His church, proclaims His victory, in spite of all diabolic agency, over sin and death.

[3] See above, p. 97, n.
[4] This is the reading of the Vulgate: *Psalms*, xc, 13.

2. GOTHIC ART

Among the problems confronting the builder of Romanesque churches, **Development of Gothic** the most troublesome was that of vaulting the nave. In the cathedral of Sant' Ambrogio at Milan, as we have seen, the nave was successfully cross-vaulted only by eliminating the clerestory. In the abbey of Vézelai, on the other hand, a bold designer tried the experiment of cross-vaulting the nave and at the same time raising a comparatively high clerestory (see Plate IV). The result was a well-lighted interior, but a fatally weak structure. Since the transverse arches were not buttressed on the outside, the vault would have collapsed had it not been saved by the later invention of the flying buttress. Frequently, in the case of a barrel-vaulted nave, continuous support had been provided along the sides by quadrant vaults placed over the aisles (see Figure 23). When cross-vaulting was similarly employed, such a quadrant vault would logically be reduced to a series of curved buttresses set against the points that needed support. But these points, if a high clerestory were erected, would be set far above the aisle roofs. No matter—some adventurous builder, ignoring tradition, brought the buttresses out from their concealment

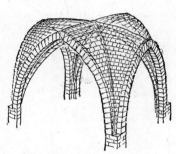

FIG. 25.   Gothic Vault.

and made them "fly" through the air to meet any thrust from the interior arches. And his device made possible the architecture misnamed Gothic.[5]

Two other prerequisites for this development were the pointed arch and **The rib-and-panel vault** the ribbed vault. Neither was new in the twelfth century. The Arabs, long before, had used pointed arches for the sake of variety in decoration, and in a number of Romanesque churches barrel-vaults had been designed with a pointed section to reduce the outward thrust on the walls (see Figure 23). The great architectural advance came with the adoption of the unconventional form in order to simplify cross-vaulting. As noted above, trouble had been experienced in putting a cross-vault over an oblong area. Half-cylinders of different diameters could not be made to intersect without resorting to clumsy expedients. But eventually the fact came to be realized that, if the half-cylinders were pointed, the task could be accomplished easily and elegantly; for the height of a pointed arch can be varied without changing its breadth. Meanwhile, from at least as early a time as the planning of Sant' Ambrogio at Milan, diagonal ribs had sometimes been set along the groins of a cross-vault. And experience proved that, under such conditions,

[5] It had, of course, no connection with the Goths. As the result of the fifteenth-century reaction against the mediæval styles, the term Gothic came to be used as a synonym for barbarous; see below, p. 462.

lighter stone could be used to cover the intervening spaces. Thus the weight of the vault would be reduced and a considerable saving made in the cost of materials. The next step was to turn these ribs into pointed arches and make them intersect at the geometrical center of the bay, whatever its shape might be. Finally, without regard to the traditional surfaces, thin slabs of stone could be arched from one rib to the next (see Figure 25).

The Gothic skeleton

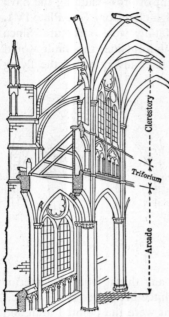

FIG. 26.   Skeleton of Amiens Cathedral.

The Romanesque building, no matter what its decorative pattern, had continued to be a series of walls holding up a roof. The perfected Gothic building, on the contrary, was a towering framework of slender masonry piers and arches supported from the outside by flying buttresses. So far as stability was concerned, it needed no walls, even after the vaults had been completed and slanting timber roofs had been placed over them to keep off the weather. When architects came to appreciate this truth, they enlarged the windows of aisle, clerestory, and apse, so that glass filled virtually the entire space from one pier to the next. The interior was thus flooded with light; the massive columns, the heavy arches, the extensive wall-spaces that had characterized the Romanesque style disappeared. The three horizontal stages of the nave—arcade, triforium, and clerestory—were still indicated by delicate moldings, but their height was enormously increased and all structural members received soaring outlines that rose from the pavement to the crown of the vault (see Figure 26).

Famous Gothic churches

The development sketched above can be traced step by step in the churches of northern France, where the growth of material prosperity in the towns, coinciding with a great religious and educational revival, made possible the erection of finer monuments by the secular, as well as the regular, clergy. Especially in and about the Capetian domain the cities vied with one another in putting up more and more splendid churches. Under such impetus ecclesiastical architecture made rapid progress—so very rapid, indeed, that one part of a new structure would become antiquated before the rest could be completed and the plans would be changed as the work continued. While, for example, round arches were preserved in the façade of Suger's abbey church at Saint-Denis, pointed-arch construction ruled throughout the interior—and within a hundred years his additions had been largely replaced by others. So, too, many cathedrals dating from the middle of the twelfth century display a transitional stage of architecture. One may thus see in the cathedral of Laon (Plate V) a perfected system of Gothic vaulting combined with a typically Romanesque colonnade. Cylindrical columns even appear in the nave of Notre-Dame at Paris, which was not begun till 1163. Yet, before the western end had been reached, someone had been inspired to design a column with four attached shafts (see Figure 27) —a form of pier that immediately came into general use, because it brought the structural lines of the vault down to the pavement itself.

Discrepancies of one sort or another are therefore characteristic of all the great French cathedrals. To appreciate the masterpieces of Gothic architecture, we must compare individual features rather than entire buildings. Among all the Gothic façades, that of Notre-Dame at Paris may be hailed as the loveliest, by virtue of its rather primitive simplicity, its graceful proportion, and its complete harmony (see Plate VI). That of Amiens is marred by its superstructure—an addition made long after the body of the church had been erected. That of Chartres combines Romanesque towers with one masonry spire of the twelfth century and another of the sixteenth. That of Reims, though symmetrical, is excessively ornate, reflecting the tendency of the

Fig. 27.   Section of the Gothic Pier.

later Gothic to degenerate into meaningless decoration. But the monumental plan of this cathedral deserves all the praise it has received (see Figure 28). The exterior of the nave, with its series of pinnacled buttresses, has great dignity and charm (see Plate VIII). And its double-aisled transept leads to a magnificent apse set with five semicircular chapels. The cathedral of Paris, too, is famous for its *chevet*—internally, a marvel of Gothic vaulting; externally, an intricate pattern that artists along the Seine never tire of sketching (see Plate VIII).

The beauty of a Gothic masterpiece, it should be noted, arises directly from its structural design, to which all decorative effects are rigorously subordinated. To give windows a fancy outline, to spread exuberant sculpture across a façade, or to cover a roof with spires and pinnacles is not and never has been to produce a Gothic building. Anyone who has imagined that the Gothic style implies a lavish display of ornament should study the interiors of such cathedrals as Chartres, Reims, and Amiens. There he will find, aside from the pictures in stained glass, only the simplest of designs. The capitals and an occasional molding are carved in unostentatious patterns, and a little delicate tracery may be added to set off the openings in the triforium and elsewhere. That is all, except for an almost incredible refinement of structural outlines. In the undecorated stonework of nave, transept, aisle, and apse, rather than in some accidental feature of the exterior, is to be

The Gothic interior

seen the acme of Gothic art (see Plate IX). And in mere point of size these buildings are impressive. The nave of Chartres reaches a total height of 106 feet, that of Reims 125 feet, and that of Amiens 141 feet. Only one Gothic structure is still loftier—the cathedral of Beauvais, which collapsed twice in the course of construction and was never finished.

The spread of Gothic to the south and east

Perfected in the Île de France, the Gothic style quickly spread to the adjoining provinces and by the close of the thirteenth century had come to exert an influence throughout the Latin world. The results on the whole were mediocre. In the southern regions pointed-arch construction was at best an imported fashion which never wholly displaced the older Romanesque and which rarely was well developed. To the Italians, in particular,

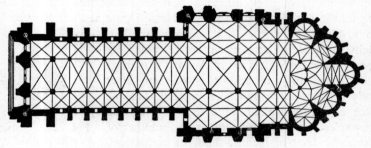

FIG. 28.   Ground Plan of Reims Cathedral.

Gothic was largely a system of decoration—one that too often degenerated into a riot of peaks and spikes and pointed openings. In Germany there was little Gothic construction before 1300, and what there was merely followed French models. In some cases, as at Worms, a rib-and-panel vault was placed over a purely Romanesque nave; in others a larger portion of the church was rebuilt in the perfected style. At Strasbourg a pleasing effect was obtained; but the pretentious cathedral of Cologne, which was not finished until the nineteenth century, is generally felt to lack refinement. For all its plainness, German Romanesque is artistically superior to the German adaptations of Gothic. From this point of view the more significant advance in architecture was made by the English.

English Gothic

In Britain the Romanesque architecture of the Normans was generally superseded before the close of the twelfth century by the form of Gothic that is locally known by the rather unfortunate term Early English. Its chief characteristic is the pointed arch, frequently introduced for decorative effect only. Of the churches actually based on pointed-arch construction an especially fine example is Lincoln Cathedral (see Plate VII), although the eastern towers were eventually masked by a screenlike façade, and many additions, notably the central tower, were made in the fifteenth century. Salisbury Cathedral, for the most part erected between 1220 and

1258, is perhaps the most symmetrical expression of the Early English ideal. But here, as in many of the English cathedrals, the relatively low vaults are supported by massive walls that render flying buttresses unnecessary—a system of construction that is modified Romanesque rather than Gothic (see Plate VII). Judged by the contemporary French standard, the purest English Gothic is to be found in Westminster Abbey, which is built on a complete framework of ribs and buttresses.[6]

French pre-eminence in mediæval architecture as a whole has often **Gothic** been disputed, for many critics continue to prefer a Romanesque or semi- **glass** Romanesque style to the logically perfected Gothic of the Île de France. In the decorative arts, however, French pre-eminence throughout the Age of the Crusades is unquestioned. For the best sculpture of the twelfth and thirteenth centuries we must turn to the cathedrals of Chartres, Reims, and Amiens. And the stained glass of these same churches remains the despair of the modern artist. One factor in the success of the mediæval craftsman was that he never treated a window as other than a flat translucent surface. Attempting neither realism nor perspective, he gained his effect by the simplest of means. His figures were outlined by the strips of lead in which the pieces of glass were set, and for this glass only solid colors were used, with details of face or costume indicated by a few pencil touches. The great rose-windows, placed to catch the rays of the setting sun, are geometrical designs of plain glass set in stone tracery. The principal windows of nave and aisle, on the other hand, commonly portray stories from the Bible or the lives of the saints. Here are to be found the most graphic examples of symbolic art—scenes from the Old and New Testaments to show the harmony of the Scriptures, animal fables to illustrate the life of Christ by mystic analogy, and the like.

Much the same generalization holds true of the major sculptures on a **Gothic** mediæval cathedral. They were placed there to teach lessons as well as to **sculpture** adorn the building. So, before we judge the work of the artist, we must remember what he was hired to do. It was the ecclesiastical authorities who dictated all the principal designs; and, as we have seen, many of the latter had to follow traditions already established in Romanesque and Byzantine usage—for example, the four beasts of the Apocalypse over the main portal of Chartres (see Plate X) or the Last Judgment to be found represented on many of the great churches. The art of such carvings, being conventional and symbolic, could never be made to portray actual people and actual things. The artist had somewhat greater latitude when statues were ordered. Yet even here he generally had to produce sculptures of sacred persons, of characters from biblical history, and of saints—to express a religious

[6] See Plate IX. The eastern end of the church is original Gothic of the thirteenth century; the western façade is a rather unfortunate addition designed by Wren and built in the eighteenth century.

ideal rather than to depict living people. The skill with which the Gothic statuary of the thirteenth century was made to observe these prerequisites, and at the same time to be intrinsically beautiful, is one of the world's artistic triumphs. It is an absurd legend that all mediæval art is stiff and lifeless.

The twelfth-century sculpture that adorns the façade of Chartres is, to be sure, distinctly primitive in certain respects. The statues beside the main portals are elongated like columns and resemble in their complete rigidity the forms of Byzantine mosaic; yet the faces are strongly individual and sometimes very handsome (see Plate X). This, we may say, is the sculpture of the transition. When we turn to the perfected Gothic style of the thirteenth century, we find that sculpture has lost its archaic stiffness and is characterized throughout by charming ease. The principal statues, still imbued with religious idealism, have become lifelike from head to foot. Famous Gothic masterpieces of this kind decorate the façade of Amiens, the porches of Chartres, and virtually the whole cathedral of Reims. Against the walls of that church, for example, stand the marvelous draped figures of Mary and Elizabeth, almost Athenian in their dignity and grace (see Plate XI). And the minor sculptures of Reims, compositions in which the artist was allowed to enjoy much greater freedom, are often very fine—especially the capitals carved with scenes from the French countryside (see Plate XI). This is naturalistic art of a high order. All that was necessary for its further development was to end its subordination to architecture, and such independence was actually brought about in the period that immediately followed.

3. INDUSTRIAL ARTS AND CRAFTS

Masonry construction

As we have already seen, the material civilization of the eastern world during the Middle Ages is almost impossible to describe because the attention of most scholars has been turned to political, religious, educational, or artistic developments. Study of the first three subjects mentioned is facilitated by the survival of pertinent writings; that of the fourth by the survival of numerous great monuments. The task of one interested in the routine of human existence is not so easy; for that was a matter generally ignored by the writers of books, and all but scattered fragments of man's ordinary handicraft has long since perished. The historian of western civilization is, of course, confronted by the same difficulties. In that connection we can ask infinitely more questions than can possibly be answered from the information now available. Here, accordingly, no more can be attempted than the statement of a few well-established facts, which may be taken to illustrate the need of further research in a neglected field.

From the foregoing section it should be plain that the structural arts of the twelfth and thirteenth centuries presupposed a high degree of skill on the part of anonymous artisans. Too many historians have fostered the belief that mediæval cathedrals arose through sheer popular enthusiasm. We may be perfectly certain that in the Middle Ages, as at present, great buildings of stone could be erected only by trained workmen under the direction of an expert designer; and that all these men, being hired for particular jobs, received wages. How well they worked may be judged from their achievements. What we do not know is precisely how they did anything, how they learned to do it, and how such learning was related to that of the ancient world. Between the third and eleventh centuries western Europe unquestionably experienced a grave deterioration of the structural arts. No architecture worthy of the name was then produced by any of the barbarian kings except—as in the case of Theodoric and Charlemagne[7]—through the employment of Byzantines. It was not until the ninth century that local rulers, under pressure of the Viking invasions, generally came to repair the ancient cities and camps of the Romans. And it was not until the twelfth century that masonry was commonly substituted for earth and wood in the newer fortifications of castles and towns.[8] For hundreds of years, obviously, such ordinary techniques as bricklaying and stonecutting were all but forgotten throughout the west; and they could not be relearned overnight. In this respect, as in others, the amazing improvement of the Latin world during the later Middle Ages was presumably due to Byzantine and Moslem influence.

Whichever of these two influences may be thought the more important, **The architect** there can be no doubt that the mediæval artisan of the west depended, in the main, on the simple tools and materials of the ancient Romans;[9] and that he did not learn his trade from books. His school was that of actual experience; whether or not he could read and write was a matter of indifference. The man whom we should call an architect, on the contrary, had to be proficient not only in the techniques of construction but also in the principles of mechanical engineering, which then as now included a good deal of theoretical science. Besides, he had to have a thorough knowledge of draftsmanship. To build a pigsty may be possible without first drawing it to scale; to build a masonry church or castle is a very different business. It is idle to suppose that anything of the sort would be authorized by a mediæval lord until satisfactory plans had been submitted by an expert; and the latter, though he might be styled a master-mason or an engineer, was essentially an architect. Since neither he nor anyone else then pub-

---

[7] See above, pp. 95, 151.

[8] See above, pp. 189, 238.

[9] See Plates XII-XIII: Weights and Measures, Marble-Working, Spinning and Weaving, Masonry Construction. The last of these miniatures, though intended by the monkish artist to illustrate the building of the tower of Babel, actually shows how a stone wall was put up in eleventh-century Italy. Note the construction of the scaffold, the hods filled with mortar, and the trowel used for spreading it.

lished books to celebrate his art, his fame in literature never approached that of the magnates who hired him. Yet, for his age, his talent might well approach that of a Leonardo da Vinci—as will be seen when we come to examine the sketchbook of Villard de Honnecourt.

All we have to do is to look at a great mediæval church, or even at the picture of one, to realize that the mere placing of the cut stones one upon another involved considerable skill in engineering. From the study of existing structures, together with the few hints left by mediæval writers, modern architects can fairly well imagine how the work was accomplished—by means of hoisting devices, scaffolds, wooden centering for the arches, and the like. Similar skill, it must be remembered, was constantly applied to the raising of secular buildings. The twelfth and thirteenth centuries witnessed the erection of tremendous castles, in which masonry construction made rapid progress. To the same age are attributed a number of remarkable bridges, as well as the oldest *hôtels de ville*, gildhouses, and belfries of the Flemish and Italian communes.[10] Nor should we overlook the work of municipal fortification which was then carried out. During the earlier period the towns had usually relied for defense upon old-fashioned ditches, embankments, and palisades; now they substituted masonry walls, built in accordance with the latest rules of military architecture. And in the meantime commerce had been greatly aided by the building of moles and docks, the dredging of harbors, and the digging of canals. To mention one example of municipal engineering, the burgesses of Bristol, with the support of the English king, excavated a new channel to connect the Frome and the Avon, thus reclaiming a large expanse of swamp and giving their city a maritime approach that has remained in use ever since.

It should be quite evident that the impressive development of military architecture during the twelfth and thirteenth centuries was the direct result of an improvement in siegecraft. This art, as we have seen, had been carried to a high degree of efficiency by the Romans but, like so much of their technical knowledge, had been largely forgotten by their barbarian successors in the west. What little we hear about the use of battering-rams, catapults, and the like in Carolingian times comes from sources of dubious worth and is contradicted by the fact that subsequent generations long continued to rely on primitive fortifications of earth and wood. By the second half of the eleventh century, however, the Italians—presumably through Byzantine or Moslem influence—had largely recovered the siegecraft of the Romans and had even, by application of its principles, invented a new hand-weapon in the crossbow. Then came the crusades, and in them the westerners learned many additional lessons. Within another hundred years, although they still considered Greek fire a mystery, they had gained an excellent understanding of military architecture and had come to use

[10] See below, p. 461.

an improved machine for the hurling of missiles. This was the *trébuchet*, which substituted counter-weights as the propelling agency in place of the twisted or stretched ropes of the Roman engines.[11]

Lack of space, if not of information, renders it impossible to add a comprehensive account of the minor arts and crafts that flourished among the western peoples during this same period. Here, at most, are some examples of such development, together with some pertinent queries and comments. Although the eleventh and following centuries witnessed the invention or improvement of various agricultural implements,[12] few metal tools were then used and most of them were distinctly primitive. Thus the spade continued to be made of wood, except for an attached cutting-edge of iron; and even the plow remained essentially an iron blade fastened to a wooden frame. The average smith would do no more than construct tools of this kind and shoe horses; he would remain a comparatively crude workman. The armorer, on the contrary, had to be a highly trained artisan. The standard equipment of the eleventh-century knight included sword, lance, shield, helmet, and hauberk.[13] Of these the last, in particular, was greatly improved during the following period. Thanks to the perfection of link mail, the hauberk was extended to protect the knight's chin, ears, and forearms; and he would wear gauntlets and leggings of the same material. How could the armorer supply his noble customers without understanding the production of steel? And for that, we should remember, there were no scientific formulas until quite recent times. The armorer, in other words, had to know from what ore he derived his iron, how it had been smelted, and how it must be wrought to produce the proper result. He had never heard that it should contain a certain percentage of carbon; the excellence of his sword-blades and shirts of mail depended solely on traditional processes developed within his craft. *Metal-working*

Prominent among other metal-workers were the pewterers, who made drinking-cups, plates, and the like from an alloy of tin and lead; also the gold- and silversmiths, who specialized in the manufacture of luxurious objects. The Germanic peoples, even before their invasion of the imperial provinces, had become familiar with the art of *cloisonné*. The enameled jewelry of the Scandinavians and Anglo-Saxons is very striking—the more beautiful to modern eyes because its barbaric design owed nothing to the conventional models of the Roman Empire. Yet there can be no doubt that in all the finer crafts—whether the material was wood, stone, metal, *Other techniques*

[11] To construct a *trébuchet*, a pole was pivoted towards the butt, to which heavy weights were attached. A sling fastened on the other end of the pole, when released from a catch, hurled a stone or other missile in a high arc. For the description by Villard de Honnecourt, see below. The origin of the engine is not known. Proof of its use by the Arabs comes from a later time.

[12] See above, p. 202.

[13] See above, p. 207.

ivory, glass, clay, leather, or cloth—the products of the eastern world were vastly superior to those of the western world at the time of the First Crusade. Much of the technical skill displayed by Italians and other Europeans in the thirteenth century, one feels, had somehow been obtained from Moslem or Byzantine craftsmen. It is an acknowledged fact that the Arabs brought the manufacture of paper from China to the shores of the Mediterranean. When other industrial arts come to be thoroughly studied, it will probably be discovered that for many of them we are indebted to the same intermediaries.

When we turn to mining, we should naturally suppose that Roman tradition was the determining factor. At one time or another the Romans had extracted considerable quantities of gold, silver, tin, lead, copper, and iron from the western provinces; and at least some of their mines, notably those in Gaul and Britain, continued to be worked under the barbarian kings. Obviously, too, a good knowledge of carpentry persisted throughout the Dark Age in the west, together with the ordinary techniques of agriculture and allied pursuits. Yet, even in such respects, we must take into account an important Arab influence that spread northward from Sicily and Spain. The Moslems undoubtedly introduced the Europeans to various new crops, as well as to improved methods of irrigation.[14] A similar origin may perhaps be found for the windmill. During the earlier Middle Ages water-driven wheels, though rare among the Romans, had come into widespread use throughout the west; and from the twelfth century on windmills became equally common in those regions where the streams provided insufficient power for the other sort of mill.

Pierre de Maricourt

An additional case in point is the interaction of Byzantine and Moslem influence upon the development of western navigation. Various facts that bear upon this problem have already been given, and others will be brought out when we come to discuss later mediæval commerce. For the moment we are concerned rather with the progress of technology and may therefore restrict our attention to the mariner's compass. The lodestone, or magnet,[15] had been well known to the ancient Greeks; but the use of a magnetized needle to guide a course by land or sea is first mentioned by writers of the twelfth century, both Arabic and Latin. Whoever may have originally discovered the basic principle, the earliest full description of what we know as a compass is contained in a letter written by a certain Pierre de Maricourt, or Petrus Peregrinus, in the year 1269. The author, not satisfied with the ordinary vague remarks, tells how, by actual experiment, to determine the poles of a magnet, how to test its uncanny ability to point towards the poles of the heavens, and finally how to suspend it on a pivot in such fashion that it will unfailingly indicate the quadrants

[14] See above, p. 175.
[15] So called because ore of this sort was first discovered in Magnesia.

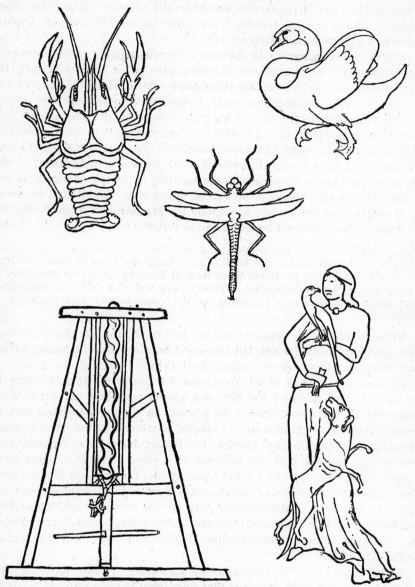

FIG. 29. Drawings by Villard de Honnecourt.

and intermediate degrees of a circle. Pierre de Maricourt, it should be remarked, was not an academic person; on the contrary, he was a military engineer who wrote his famous letter while helping Charles of Anjou[16] to besiege a fortress in southern Italy.

Villard de Honnecourt

Villard de Honnecourt was likewise a French engineer of the thirteenth century, though his specialty was architecture rather than siegecraft. He is known to us solely from his sketchbook which, as in the case of the Bayeux Tapestry, miraculous good fortune has preserved until today. Through information supplied by his own notes, we may be reasonably sure that Villard designed the cathedral of Cambrai; that, to obtain hints in this connection, he watched the construction of the great cathedrals at Laon, Chartres, and Reims; and that, about 1250, he was commissioned by the queen of Hungary to superintend the building of certain churches in her country. During the course of his career, at any rate, Villard kept an album of drawings, and this he left as a guide for persons who might follow his profession. Such persons he addresses as follows:

Villard de Honnecourt salutes you, and asks those occupied with the various kinds of work contained in this book to pray for his soul and to remember him; for in this book may be found great help in learning about the principles of masonry and of construction by carpentry. You will also find in it methods of portraiture and drawing, according to the requirements and teachings of geometry.

Villard's address to posterity was no idle boast, for his album contains precisely what he said it did. His free-hand drawings are of amazing variety and interest. Many are of architectural details—such as the towers of Laon, the rose-window of Chartres, and the *chevet* of Reims—which he to some extent adapted for his own churches. Alongside these stand numerous designs for statues or for pictures in windows, together with all sorts of decorative patterns to be executed in stone or wood. And in many cases, as his introduction implies, his figures have been reduced to a geometrical plan, so that one may see at a glance how they ought to be proportioned in order to fill a particular space. To drawings that accepted the traditional symbolism of the church Villard added a good number that reflected the trend of thirteenth-century art towards increased naturalism. Such clever sketches as the girl, parakeet, dog, swan, crawfish, and dragonfly in the accompanying illustration (Figure 29) must have been made from life.

Besides, to justify his introductory statement, Villard included page after page of technical drawings that admirably explain various problems of masonry and carpentry: how to determine the size of a column not wholly seen, how to find the center of a given area, how to estimate the height of a tower from the ground, how to prop up a leaning wall, how to

[16] See below, pp. 370-71.

construct a roof vaulted in wood, and the like. The author, obviously, had a good knowledge of geometry and surveying, as well as of the more usual craftsmanship. Nor was this the limit of his scientific attainments. He had apparently devoted much study to mechanical toys and engines. The one pictured here (Figure 29) is a screw turned by levers at the bottom and so made to hoist a heavy object suspended from a fitting over the screw. Among Villard's other designs may be seen a statue whose finger will point towards the sun throughout the day, a machine for cutting off the ends of piles under water, a saw-mill driven by water-power, and a *trébuchet* that will hurl great arrows.

Of all the sketchbooks kept by all the architects of the twelfth and thirteenth centuries one has come down to us; but it suffices to prove that art and engineering could be as intimately associated then as they are at present, and that neither could be wholly learned from ancient books. Indeed, the more one studies the progress of mediæval culture, the more one realizes that even in the age of Villard de Honnecourt and Pierre de Maricourt—which was also the age of Frederick II, Albertus Magnus, Roger Bacon, Francis of Assisi, and Jean de Meun[17]—direct observation of nature had vital significance for the æsthetic, religious, and intellectual life of Europe.

[17] See below, pp. 348-49, 353-54, 357-59, 364-65, 389-91.

CHAPTER XVII

The Latin World After the First Crusade

1. FRANCE AND THE BRITISH ISLES

The twelfth century

The twelfth century is almost exactly the period between the death of Urban II, the pope who launched the great crusade, and the election of Innocent III, the pope who enjoyed a virtual dictatorship throughout Latin Europe. Some of the triumphs won by the church during this period—especially those in the fields of art and learning—have been sketched in the preceding chapters. Our task in the next few chapters is to review the dynastic rivalries of the twelfth-century kings and emperors, to estimate the significance of their governmental policies, to see how all such activities were gradually drawn into the sphere of papal influence, and so to gain a better understanding of the problems that confronted the church in the thirteenth century.

Louis VI of France (1108-37)

For England as well as for France an event of prime importance was the rise of the Capetians. At the accession of Louis VI in 1108 the prospects of the French royal house seemed far from brilliant. Up to that point the successors of Hugh Capet (see Table II), as if content with great exploits on the part of their barons, had themselves accomplished little. Under Louis's father, Philip I, the prestige of the crown had, indeed, sunk lower than ever.[1] From the beginning the Capetian had enjoyed no real authority throughout the kingdom as a whole; his effective government had been restricted to his own domain, a long narrow territory devoid of seaports or natural frontiers. To make the situation worse, the king now lost control of his subordinates in the Île de France, the *prévôts* who collected his revenues and the *châtelains* who held his castles. In every direction lawless vassals made the roads unsafe for travel and terrorized the churches of which the king was supposed to be the patron. Obviously, before the

[1] See above, p. 190.

310

Capetian could hope to be a real king, he would have to make himself master of his own principality. To this undertaking Louis VI devoted his life.

Louis is described by contemporaries as tall and handsome—an athlete, passionately fond of riding and hunting, and a brave soldier. He was also a huge eater. In his later years he put on so much flesh that he gained the nickname of *le Gros*; but even as Louis the Fat he remained exceedingly active. His reign actually began before the death of his ignoble father; at eighteen he had already been knighted, associated in the royal office, and placed in command of military operations on the Norman frontier. As soon as the defenses on that side had been put in better condition, he turned to the unspectacular but highly important work of pacifying his domain. Year after year he assembled a small force and launched a campaign against some obstreperous official or robber baron. Gradually the royal cause triumphed. By 1120 Louis could move about in the Île de France without an army to cut a passage. His castles were in charge of loyal vassals. Revenue flowed steadily into his treasury. Peasants and traders joined the clergy in fervent thanks to God for a virtuous and able king.

In connection with this work Louis developed an active policy of stimulating economic projects. Like other progressive rulers of the day, he issued special charters to attract cultivators to his waste lands. The colonist, or *hôte*, who would settle in some particular region obtained a status very superior to that of the ordinary villein: he was exempt from all arbitrary exactions, being liable only for a small rent and strictly defined services. Somewhat wider liberties, as we have seen, were established by the king at Lorris, whence they were extended into many other small towns. To Paris and Orleans, as to most places under his immediate authority, he made no formal grants of self-government; but on ecclesiastical territory he helped to found numerous communes. The alliance between monarchy and bourgeoisie, which was to have such great importance in the constitutional development of France, was essentially the product of Louis VI's reign.

Except for his intervention on behalf of the communes, which was a **Suger** matter of recognizing the inevitable, Louis remained a staunch friend of **(d. 1151)** the church, and on that account enjoyed the support of many powerful ecclesiastics. Among the latter was Suger, abbot of Saint-Denis. He had been born a peasant but, like many youths of his class, had been permitted to enter a monastery. There he became famous for his learning and was appointed as instructor to Prince Louis. Through the friendship thus begun, and through his own extraordinary talents, he became the king's chief adviser and head of the greatest religious house in the neighborhood of Paris. With regard to his career Suger could therefore quote Psalm 113: "He raiseth up the poor out of the dust and lifteth the needy out of the

dunghill, that He may set him with princes." Suger continued to play a
prominent part in affairs of state until his death in 1151. From his letters
and other writings we obtain a vivid picture of contemporary politics, as
well as of his daily cares in the abbey of Saint-Denis. It was not the least
of his distinctions that he directed the construction of the first great church
to be planned throughout in the new Gothic style.[2]

The
French
princi-
palities
and the
English
succession Earlier we have had occasion to review the political subdivisions of
France in the eleventh century. Throughout the first half of the twelfth
century they remained essentially the same. Although Louis VI was able
to increase his power within his own domain, he was virtually helpless
when it came to changing the relations of the great fiefs to the crown. His
princely vassals acted very much as they pleased. When left to their own
devices, they ordinarily treated the king with due respect, and those in the
north occasionally appeared before him to do homage or to take part in
a solemn convocation of his feudal court. Yet even they seem never to
have paid him reliefs or aids, and such military service as they gave him
was quite nominal. In this connection Louis won his outstanding success
through no especial effort of his own. Until 1127 the duchy of Aquitaine
was held by the famous troubadour, William IX.[3] Being widely criticized
for his lack of crusading ardor, he finally led an expedition to the east, but
was badly defeated by the Turks in Asia Minor and returned home to
pursue the more congenial career of a romantic poet. On his death he was
succeeded by his son William X. And when the latter was stricken by
mortal illness in 1137, he expressed the desire that Eleanor, his daughter
and heiress, should be married to the son of Louis VI—a noteworthy
tribute to the enhanced prestige of the monarchy and, as will be seen, a
momentous decision in more ways than one.

By the middle of the twelfth century Catalonia had been united with
the kingdom of Aragon[4] and so, though nominally remaining part of
France, had actually broken away from it. The county of Toulouse had
passed to the heirs of Raymond IV, the distinguished crusader, and on
account of their interest in Tripolis had somewhat weakened. In the north
of France, meanwhile, the rivalries of the greater princes had tended to
be merged in a contest over the succession to the English throne, to understand which is impossible without some attention to feudal genealogy.
William the Conqueror died in 1087, leaving Normandy to his eldest son
Robert and England to his second son William Rufus (the Red). His
third son Henry as yet had nothing beyond a sum of cash (see Table III).
William II, unlike his elder brother, proved himself an able though unscrupulous ruler, and his reign, as will be seen, had a number of important

[2] See above, p. 298.
[3] See above, pp. 279-80.
[4] See below, p. 322.

results. An intermittent war between him and Robert of Normandy was interrupted by the latter's assumption of the cross in 1095. And before Robert had returned from the crusade, William was accidentally killed in 1100. The chief gainer by this misadventure was Henry, who had long been hoping for a favorable turn of events and who quickly seized the opportunity now presented. Taking possession of the royal treasury, he secured the support of the chief barons by pledging a reformed administration and within two days was crowned king of England. He, too, was soon led to take up arms against Robert of Normandy and, after winning a decisive victory in 1106, once more united the conqueror's possessions.

Louis VI, making the best of a situation which he could not control, received Henry I as his vassal for Normandy. But relations between the two continued to be strained, and before long they were embroiled in a war that lasted for the better part of twenty years. Throughout this struggle Henry maintained his position with complete success, securing recognition of his lordship over Brittany and extending his power over certain disputed territories on the Seine. Hitherto the French king had regularly depended on the count of Anjou for aid against the Normans, and Henry in reply had allied with Louis's bitter enemy, the count of Blois. In 1128, however, there was a surprising diplomatic reversal. Some years earlier Henry's two sons had been drowned as the result of a shipwreck in the British Channel; so the king was left with only a daughter, Matilda, whom his barons recognized as heiress of both Normandy and England. Then, to assure the lady powerful support, Henry gave her in marriage to his most dangerous enemy, the count of Anjou. The latter was now Geoffrey Plantagenet[5]—an able ruler, who, by ending a long civil war, had restored his county to the strength that it had enjoyed under his ancestors. In 1133 the aging Henry I was delighted with the news that he had a grandson who was named for him and who, it might be expected, would in time rule the combined states of England, Normandy, and Anjou.

Henry I of England (1100-35)

Nevertheless, when Henry died in 1135, most of his barons refused to carry out the settlement to which they had previously agreed. Recognition of the infant Henry seemed to them out of the question; as good Normans, they hated to submit to an Angevin and they did not like the idea of being governed by a woman. Accordingly, they shifted their support to Stephen of Blois, younger son of Count Stephen the crusader, and on his mother's side grandson of the Conqueror (see Table III). Although well-meaning and personally likable, Stephen quickly proved his incompetence as a ruler and so encouraged the Angevins to push their claim by means of armed invasion. In the resulting war, though Geoffrey and Matilda secured

[5] So called from the broom-flower he was accustomed to wear. It was his personal nickname and was not borne by his descendants. For Geoffrey's ancestors, see above, p. 191.

Normandy for their son Henry, they failed to oust Stephen from England. And it was during this conflict that Louis VI was succeeded by Louis VII, the son who had already been associated in the royal dignity and who, by a lucky marriage, had just acquired the magnificent inheritance of Aquitaine. All the new king had to do, apparently, was to make the most of his favorable opportunity, and the Capetian dynasty would gain a commanding position in western Europe.

Louis VII
of France
(1137-80)

Louis VII, however, utterly lacked the statesmanship of his father. For all his virtue and piety, he nearly ruined the Capetian cause by a series of grave political blunders. In the first place, he joined Conrad III of Germany in a futile crusade, and all that saved the royal government was the fact that he could turn it over to Suger, a trained minister of his father. Even Suger, however, could not prevent Louis from being shocked by the flirtatious habits of his wife, the granddaughter of a famous troubadour, and in 1152 Louis persuaded the ecclesiastical authorities to annul his marriage. Thereupon Eleanor at once accepted a match with the young Henry of Anjou, who thus added her duchy to the possessions already inherited from his father and mother. The king, having amiably permitted the union of Normandy, Anjou, and Aquitaine, still remained inactive when Henry took up arms against Stephen, won recognition as heir to the English throne, and gained it in 1154. The damage had then been done. It was merely an aggravation of the Capetian misfortunes that Henry later asserted his feudal lordship over Wales and Scotland, extended his dominion into Ireland, married a son to the heiress of Brittany, and built up powerful alliances in Germany, Spain, and Sicily.

The
British
Isles

Leaving the reign of Henry II to be taken up in the next chapter, we may close the present section with a rapid survey of conditions throughout the British Isles in the years immediately following the Norman Conquest. Although Scotland had been organized as a kingdom for well over a century, the Celtic tribal system continued to flourish there, as well as in Wales and Ireland. All three countries remained decidedly barbarous in comparison with contemporary England. In Britain the Norman barons who had been entrusted with the defense of the Welsh and Scottish frontiers engaged in constant warfare with the clansmen to the west and north. As a consequence, a wide strip of Wales was conquered and largely recolonized by French-speaking adventurers. Many Norman families like-wise settled in the lowlands of Scotland. But there they generally served as vassals of the Scottish king, who was strong enough to establish and hold a definite boundary against the English. This line, as finally accepted by William II, ran along the Cheviot Hills to connect the River Tweed with Solway Firth—and since that time it has never been shifted. The Irish, meanwhile, had been left very much to their own devices. Maintaining their ancient customs with the utmost vigor, they had absorbed a good part of the Danish population along the eastern coast and were now threatening even the old Viking strongholds of Dublin, Wexford, and Waterford. And in spite of the fact that their more famous monasteries had long since been destroyed, the Irish still held to their peculiar ecclesiastical system. It was only with the establishment of Henry II's dominion in Ireland that the whole island, at last following the example of Britain, came to be regularly incorporated in the Roman Church.

So far as England was concerned, we have seen that the Norman Conquest made it into a thoroughly feudalized state. Under William II the situation remained fundamentally the same. That king, by crushing an insurrection of discontented barons, stoutly maintained the authority left him by his father. Indeed, by pushing his rights to unprecedented extremes, he gained a reputation for tyrannical and extortionate government. In particular, the church complained that, when prelates died, William deliberately prolonged the vacancies for the sake of incidental revenue.[6] After the death of Lanfranc, archbishop of Canterbury under William I, we are told that the new king was induced by what he considered a mortal illness to appoint the learned Anselm; but that, when he recovered, he greatly repented his piety. On securing the crown, at any rate, Henry I saw fit to issue his famous Coronation Charter, promising to abolish the more unpopular features of his brother's government. Some of the articles were too vague to be of any practical value—as the one stating that only "just reliefs" should thenceforth be exacted from the heirs of royal vassals. Others made very specific pledges, but the king's own records prove that in such cases he often broke his word. For example, his assurance to the church that he would take nothing from its demesnes during a vacancy in abbacy or bishopric seems to have been utterly disregarded. Accordingly, Henry's charter was chiefly significant because it recognized the fact that feudal custom placed definite limits on the royal authority.

The government of England

Henry, of course, never thought to rule as a capricious despot; on the whole, he maintained the system established by his father and, like any statesman, tried to develop existing institutions to his own best advantage. In particular, his reign is noteworthy for the greater prominence of professional administrators and judges who, when dispatched on special missions, were called itinerant justices. Although the king might at any time summon a general assembly of all his barons, his ordinary government was superintended by a small group of them. Thanks to a contemporary document, we know that the great officials of the royal household were the chancellor, steward, butler, chamberlain, treasurer, and constable.[7] In lieu of salary, each of them would hold a valuable fief of the crown. But in addition he would be entitled to regular meals at the king's expense and

[6] See above, p. 186.
[7] Cf. the Carolingian household, above, p. 139.

to an allowance of bread, wine, and candles that of an evening he could take to his own apartment. The royal court was still migratory, following the king on his continuous journeying from his own castles or manors to those of his wealthy vassals. So wherever he went there went the ministers, clerks, and other assistants who made up his permanent council, or *curia*. As yet there was only one such body, which attended to all sorts of business. On one day it might discuss relations with the French king, on the next sit as a court of law, and on a third take up matters of finance.

The exchequer

In the last capacity the *curia* under Henry I became known as the exchequer because the table about which the members gathered was covered with a checkered cloth—i.e., one marked with a series of columns crossed by horizontal lines.[8] This so-called chess-board was a kind of abacus, designed to facilitate the work of addition and subtraction without recourse to the clumsy Roman numerals. By ancient custom the king's ordinary revenue in a shire was farmed out to the sheriff, so that he was responsible for a fixed annual payment. When, accordingly, the sheriff appeared before the court, the clerks arranged counters in the columns to represent the pounds, shillings, and pence that he owed. Then they subtracted, item by item, whatever cash he had paid into the treasury and whatever expenditures he had made on the king's order. Finally, after his account had been completed, the sum remaining on the table indicated what he still owed. Meanwhile other clerks had kept a written record of the transaction on sheets, or pipes, of parchment. These, when sewn together and rolled up, were known as a pipe roll. The oldest one extant is that of the year 1130, the sole survivor from the reign of Henry I. But from the time of his grandson, Henry II, the annual rolls, or their equivalents, have all been preserved.

The Norman inquest

Henry I's reign witnessed a number of other important developments, concerning which our information is somewhat scantier. As already remarked, his charter to London includes the first known concession of formal self-government to an English borough. He seems also to have improved the organization of the Cinque Ports and to have granted elementary liberties to various lesser towns, such as Newcastle-upon-Tyne.[9] Many of the fiscal and judicial reforms of Henry II were apparently inspired by precedents under Henry I. This was certainly true of the greater use that came to be made of the inquest, which was derived, somewhat obscurely, from Carolingian practice.[10] The essence of the inquest was that a question was put to a group of men selected because of their special knowledge and sworn to tell the truth. The group was called a jury (from *jurati*, sworn

---

[8] "Chess," "checker," and "exchequer" are all derived from the Arabic word for the famous game learned by the crusaders from the Arabs, who had learned it from the Persians.

[9] See above, pp. 245, 54.

[10] See above, p. 139.

men) and their return a verdict (from *veredictum*, a true statement). In 1086 William I had ordered a comprehensive survey by which the actual value of every manor in England was to be determined. In each hundred a jury, consisting of both English and French, gave answers to certain questions about local properties, and the testimony thus obtained was eventually combined in the famous *Domesday Book*, the greatest single record that had been produced in western Europe since the collapse of the Roman Empire. Similar procedure came to be more and more frequently used for judicial purposes, to culminate under Henry II in what we know as jury trial.

The conquest of 1066, having been blessed by the pope, naturally brought England into much closer agreement with Roman ecclesiastical practice. Episcopal sees were removed from country villages to more important urban centers; the primacy of the archbishop of Canterbury was definitely recognized; monasteries were generally reformed in harmony with the Cluniac ideals; a series of church courts entirely separate from those of the state was established. In all these matters William I acted in hearty co-operation with Archbishop Lanfranc and the pope. When, however, Gregory VII suggested that the king perform homage to him for England, he was met with blunt refusal. Besides, the Conqueror insisted on his right to appoint and invest prelates in the usual fashion. Gregory never brought the matter to an issue in England, but it was revived by Anselm after he had quarreled with William II, and it remained to trouble the administration of Henry I. Finally, in 1106, both parties agreed to a compromise. Although bishops and abbots were to be elected by the cathedral or monastic chapters, the election had to be held in the king's presence and to him the chosen prelate had to perform homage before receiving any fief held of the crown. Formal installation with the ring and the staff, the symbols of spiritual office, was to be subsequently carried out by a clergyman. So far as England was concerned, investiture was thenceforth a closed issue. And much the same compromise was eventually accepted in Germany—a conclusion that may logically serve to introduce a new section. *[Church and state]*

2. GERMANY, SCANDINAVIA, AND EASTERN EUROPE

In the eleventh century Germany was still essentially what it had been under Otto I—a rather loose union of various great duchies. The kings, it is true, had generally enforced their right to make and unmake dukes at pleasure, and had frequently sought to tighten their control over outlying territories by giving them to members of the royal house. But experience had proved that ties of blood were wholly inadequate to overcome the separatist tendencies of the local populations. Nor could the emperor, in the absence of an efficient civil service, really govern the entire kingdom *[The German duchies]* himself. Henry III, after dispensing with half of the dukedoms, eventually restored the old system, and with it the chronic evils that had long distracted the monarchy. So the reign of Henry IV ended as it had begun, in a turmoil of ducal insurrection, and the problem was left to be solved, if at all, by his successors. The only important change in the situation was that some of the original duchies had now been broken up and that the others, reduced in size, had been entrusted to new men who had somehow gained the royal favor. The details of this redistribution may not in themselves be deeply interesting; yet they must be studied by anyone who hopes to understand the history of twelfth-century Germany.

Otto I, as we have seen, had turned Saxony over to a subordinate, whose descendants continued to rule the country as hereditary dukes until the last of them was ousted and jailed by Henry IV. Then, towards the close of his reign, Henry bestowed the duchy on a local nobleman named Lothair of Supplinburg. Meanwhile, as the result of royal confiscation, two other great duchies had been acquired by comparatively obscure men: Suabia by Frederick of Hohenstaufen, husband of the king's daughter Agnes (see Table VI); Bavaria by a certain Welf (or Guelf), who succeeded in marrying his son to a daughter of Lothair, the Saxon duke (see Table V). Neither duchy, however, was by any means as extensive as it had once been. Part of the old Suabia had been allotted to the duke of Zähringen, while Bavaria had been reduced, first by the creation of a new duchy in Carinthia, and then by the separation of two frontier districts called the North Mark and the East Mark.[11] Normally, by this time, there was no duke of Franconia; and even when the title came to be revived, it brought no revival of the ancient duchy, which had actually been partitioned among such local princes as the archbishop of Mainz, the bishops of Worms and Speier, and the count palatine[12] of the Rhine. Lorraine also tended to disintegrate. For a while it was divided into the two duchies of Upper and Lower Lorraine. Subsequently, as the latter disappeared altogether, the name of Lorraine was restricted to the former, which ceased to have any political solidarity.

Feudalism in Germany   It was during this same time that feudal institutions came to be widely extended throughout Germany—sometimes encouraged, sometimes hindered, by the monarchy. The subject is a complicated one, and generalization is hazardous with regard to so large and diversified a country; yet a few elementary facts may be stated as fairly applicable to the whole. In the first place, we know that the German armies were not predominantly feudal before the twelfth century; until then the emperors largely relied

[11] Later famous as Austria (Österreich); under Hitler restored to its ancient name of Ostmark.

[12] The title was originally borne by a count attached to the royal palace; later it lost all such particular significance.

on infantry of the old-fashioned type. The reason, evidently, was the economic backwardness of the kingdom; for, as has been explained above, the introduction of heavy-armed cavalry was a very expensive business that necessitated an elaborate development of fief-holding. Therefore, so far as feudal tenure was concerned, Germany lagged behind France. Vassalage had long been a common institution in western Europe. According to Carolingian precedent, all the great officials of the king had to be royal vassals. As late as the eleventh century, however, their offices were regarded as quite separate from any fiefs they might hold, and the bulk of their estates might still be allodial property.[13]

The kings, as we have seen, successfully prevented the dukes from making their duchies into hereditary principalities like those of contemporary France—compact states in which all lay and clerical barons were ducal vassals. On the other hand, the kings tended to favor the establishment of hereditary tenures for the lesser men who held their honors of the dukes, and constantly made use of feudal relationships to strengthen their own authority over important persons in Germany as well as over the rulers of neighboring countries. Furthermore, the prevalent disorder under Henry IV led powerful men on all sides to raise castles, surround themselves with knights, and generally organize their territories on a feudal basis. The outcome ultimately depended on the prolonged conflict between the monarchy and the aristocracy. In Germany, as in other regions, feudal organization was a matter of practical politics. By the opening of the twelfth century the king had definitely undertaken to break up the old duchies. But could his authority be more effectively enforced over a horde of little princes than over a few great ones?

The unhappy life of Henry IV finally ended in 1106 during a cruel war with his only surviving son. The latter, as Henry V, then deserted his baronial allies and adopted his father's policy. Although he succeeded in obtaining the imperial crown, he won little honor either in Germany or in Italy. The only important event of his reign was the Concordat of Worms in 1122—a settlement of the investiture controversy in accord with the compromise already adopted in England. Three years later Henry V died without direct heirs and the question of the royal succession once more became acute. A similar situation had arisen in 1024 on the death of Henry II, the last of the Saxon house by male descent. At that time the magnates had supported the hereditary principle by at once recognizing Conrad II, who was descended from a daughter of Otto I (see Table IV). If the same rule were now to be applied, the crown would go to Frederick, duke of Suabia. In 1125, however, the prestige of the Franconian house was not sufficient to overcome the desire of the electors to assert their

Henry V and the election of 1125

[13] The allod, as distinguished from the fief, was property acquired in full ownership through gift, purchase, or inheritance.

independence of action. Deliberately passing over the grandson of Henry IV, they awarded the throne to Lothair, duke of Saxony, who had no drop of royal blood in his veins.

Guelf
vs.
Hohen-
staufen

The determining factor in this election was Lothair's alliance with the Guelfs, who as dukes of Bavaria were bitterly hostile to their Hohenstaufen neighbors in Suabia. And the Guelf victory began a civil conflict that continued intermittently for upward of a hundred years. Under Lothair the Hohenstaufen leaders revolted and were put down. Then, on Lothair's death, the electors disregarded his son-in-law, who combined the duchies of Bavaria and Saxony, to choose Conrad of Hohenstaufen. Thereupon the Guelfs took arms, and it was only after a prolonged war that Conrad found the opportunity of joining Louis VII of France on his mismanaged expedition to the Holy Land.[14] On the death of Conrad the electors gave the crown to his nephew Frederick, for the latter was half Guelf by descent and bore an excellent reputation. The new king, nicknamed Barbarossa by the Italians on account of his reddish beard, ranks among the greatest of mediæval Germans. Even those who disliked him as a matter of principle agreed that he was a worthy foe—a thoroughly imperial figure like Otto the Great or Charlemagne. It was, indeed, the tradition of those men that colored his whole career and, while lending a certain grandeur to his reign, ultimately proved its curse. The dramatic events of Barbarossa's life, however, must be left for consideration in the following chapter.

The Scan-
dinavian
kingdoms

Culturally, it may be said that Germany accepted the leadership of France and in turn led the peoples of the northern and eastern borderlands. The political history of Scandinavia during this period offers little of interest. The successors of Canute, king of Denmark and England, engaged in a long struggle with the rulers of Norway that proved generally indecisive. Neither country was able to conquer the other, or the kingdom of Sweden. Meanwhile Christianity had been definitely established in all three states, most recently by St. Olaf, king of Norway—and had thence been carried to the Norwegian colony of Iceland. At first the Scandinavian lands were ecclesiastically subordinated to the German archbishop of Hamburg; later, as a matter of course, they received a separate organization. Until the twelfth century social and political conditions throughout the north remained distinctly primitive—still, in the main, reminiscent of the age that had produced the Vikings. Thenceforth, however, institutions came to be radically altered through the introduction of feudalism and, eventually, of urban liberties borrowed from the German towns. The earliest legal records of the Scandinavian kingdoms date only from the thirteenth century; until then their constitutional development remains conjectural. And even the testimony of the Icelandic sagas,[15] however remarkable they

[14] See below, p. 325.
[15] See above, p. 212.

may be as works of literature, is very dubious in so far as it is applied to earlier times.

While the Scandinavian peoples who thus came under the influence of Germany were themselves Germanic, the people to the east of the Elbe were generally Slavic. There, in addition to many lesser tribes, lived the Pomeranians, Poles, Bohemians (or Czechs), and Moravians; all of whom, as well as the Russians, spoke Slavic languages. The Prussians and the Lithuanians, on the other hand, belonged to a different linguistic group— the one vaguely known as Baltic. And, like the Magyars of Hungary, the Esthonians and Finns of the eastern Baltic are classified as Ural-Altaic.[16] We have already seen that, by the end of the tenth century, the Russians had been brought under the jurisdiction of the Greek Church, but that it was the Roman Church which won Moravia, Bohemia, Poland, and the adjacent regions to the west. This extension of Christianity was accompanied by the extension of German dominance. In particular, Otto the Great had conquered and in some degree colonized the lands between the Elbe and the Oder, and had compelled the rulers of the Poles and the Czechs to recognize his lordship. Towards the end of the century, however, his work was largely undone by Boleslav, the first king of Poland.[17] An earlier kingdom of Moravia had been destroyed by the Magyars; so Boleslav was eventually able to subjugate that country, together with Bohemia, the German conquests to the north, and Pomerania. Boleslav's successors, to be sure, could not hold so wide a territory; yet they remained strong enough to oppose any effective expansion of the Germans to the east. Well into the twelfth century Poland, as an independent monarchy with its own ecclesiastical organization, constituted a solid buffer-state between Russia and the Holy Roman Empire. From the Slavic point of view, it was a great tragedy that Poland was then partitioned among a number of rival princes and so rendered powerless to prevent the decisive changes of the next two hundred years.

The decline of Poland naturally led, not only to the renewal of German activity throughout the Saxon marches, but also to the re-establishment of German lordship over Bohemia. It was now the Czechs who, with the support of the German kings, created a new state, of which Moravia was a mere province. The duke of Bohemia, though a Czech, became a vassal of the emperor and, as such, was promoted to the royal dignity by Henry IV[18] and later recognized as hereditary cupbearer in the imperial household. From the eleventh century on, German penetration in Bohemia was continuous—to result in the virtual annexation of the country to Germany. Meanwhile the Magyars of Hungary had abandoned their old life as pro-

The eastern borderlands of Germany

[16] See above, p. 44.
[17] See above, p. 219.
[18] Confirmed by Frederick Barbarossa and thereafter permanent.

fessional marauders to adopt the institutions of their more civilized neighbors. The hero of this transformation was the famous St. Stephen, who completed the Christianization of his people and, having become the vassal of Pope Silvester II, received from him the gift of a royal crown in the year 1000. Unlike Bohemia, Hungary thus escaped being made into a dependency of the Holy Roman Empire; and, unlike Poland, it remained vigorous enough in the subsequent period to block the Germans from all but restricted colonization along the lower Danube. The Hungarians, moreover, considerably strengthened their barrier in the twelfth century by acquiring Croatia—a position that gave them access to the Adriatic and, as we shall see, involved them in the troubled politics of Italy and the later crusades.

3. Spain, Italy, and Syria

The kingdoms of León, Aragon, and Portugal

Of the Christian states in Spain during the second half of the eleventh century the kingdom of León, which included Castile on the east and Portugal on the west, was by all odds the largest and strongest. It therefore made the greatest advance against the Moors, reaching the Tagus with the capture of Toledo in 1085 (see Map XV). Afterwards, through the introduction of fanatical recruits from Africa, the Moslem resistance stiffened and for many years the Christians did well to hold their previous conquests. It was not until 1118 that the fall of Saragossa permitted the kingdom of Aragon to annex the whole of the Ebro valley and so to shut off the county of Barcelona from expansion along the coast. But in 1150 the ruler of the latter state more than compensated himself by acquiring the crown of Aragon as the result of a fortunate marriage. Meanwhile the kingdom of León had been paralyzed by a series of wars over the succession to the throne, in the course of which the count of Portugal declared his independence by assuming the royal title. In 1143 the Roman Church accepted Portugal as a papal fief and finally, in 1179, accorded it the rank of a kingdom.

The kingdom of Sicily under Roger II

Some of the major developments in contemporary Italy have already been mentioned: especially the rise of Venice as a commercial power on the Adriatic, with potential rivals in Genoa and Pisa on the other side of the peninsula; the spread of communal revolution, through which Lombardy came to be dotted with *de facto* republics; and the vain efforts of the German kings to enforce their authority south of the Alps. In this last connection we have seen how the successors of Gregory VII carried the policy of that great pope to a triumphant outcome by vigorously withstanding imperial aggression and by uniting western Europe for the sake of the crusade. Both papal enterprises were strongly supported by the Normans of southern Italy. Although one of Guiscard's sons allowed the duchy of Apulia to lapse into anarchy, the other, Bohemund, established himself as prince of Antioch, while Roger, Guiscard's brother, completed the conquest of Sicily (see Table VI). Even after the death of the great count in 1101, his trained ministers effectively governed the island in the name of his infant son, Roger II. The latter, on attaining his majority, at once revealed the imperialistic trend of his ambition by launching a series of raids against the emir of Tunis. But that project was temporarily dropped when the death of his cousin without direct heirs brought him a possible claim to the duchy of Apulia. Roger acted promptly and decisively to force recognition throughout all Guiscard's dominions. By 1128 the pope had no choice but to accept his homage as duke, and two years later Roger took advantage of a disputed papal election to secure the title, King of Sicily.

The kingdom thus established was a most remarkable structure, for it combined the feudal custom of northern France with institutions drawn from various parts of the Mediterranean. Its rulers, who commonly spoke a French or Italian vernacular, kept their official records in three other languages: Latin, Greek, and Arabic. The polyglot population included Jews and Moslems together with Christians of both the Roman and the Greek communions—all living under their own laws and enjoying religious toleration. And loyal men of any faith were accepted for the king's civil service, as well as for his army and navy. In some respects Roger II's policy may be seen to have resembled that of the Norman kings in England: for example, in his assertion of exclusive control over warfare, in his enforcement of appeals from baronial courts, and in his appointment to ecclesiastical office. With regard to the towns Roger II of Sicily, like Henry I of England, was generous in grants of elementary bourgeois liberty, but chary in those of political autonomy. As soon as he had consolidated his position in Italy, he rescinded many charters issued during his earlier years and brought all communes under tight governmental supervision. In England a Norman dynasty built up a powerful administrative machine by combining native and foreign custom. In Sicily a similar combination produced even more noteworthy results because the king could draw upon the more advanced civilizations of the east.

From those civilizations, too, Roger II gained an appreciation of art and learning that set him apart from his feudal contemporaries. While Greek was virtually unknown in the schools of France and Germany, one of Roger's Frankish ministers, Henry Aristippus, was translating Plato into Latin, and one of his Arab ministers, al-Idrisi, was composing the best geographical study of the age.[19] At the Sicilian court minstrels and troubadours, who sang in Provençal or French, were rivaled by Moslem poets, who followed literary traditions old in the days of Mohammed. And the same mixture of cultures was reflected in Roger's palaces and

[19] See below, p. 449.

churches, which strangely but strikingly amalgamated the Byzantine, Arabic, and Romanesque styles.[20] It was under the same influence, we may suppose, that Roger developed his realistic diplomacy, preventing any dangerous combination of his numerous enemies and reigning with uninterrupted success for nearly half a century. By means of commercial treaties he gained the support of the great Italian cities and through them the command of the sea. He cleverly made use of the German peril to win concessions from the pope. By playing off the emperor in the east against the emperor in the west, he kept either from decisive action. He was thus able not only to retain possession of southern Italy but also to revive Guiscard's Byzantine project and seize the island of Corfu. Finally, he resumed the offensive in Africa and before his death in 1154 had occupied the coast from Tunisia to Tripoli.

The crusaders and their states in Syria

Roger II, it will be noted, displayed no enthusiasm for crusading in Syria, though conditions there had gone from bad to worse. Two factors had largely contributed to the victory of the original crusade: the success of the papacy in uniting the Christians of the west for the sake of a holy war and the failure of the Moslems to make common cause against them. During the twelfth century this situation tended to be reversed. While a new Turkish power gained control of both Syria and Egypt, the crusading zeal of the westerners threatened to disappear before the advance of political and commercial ambitions. Practical considerations had from the beginning dominated the action of those leaders who intended to settle permanently in Palestine. As rulers of conquered territories, they became rivals of one another as well as of their Moslem neighbors. The Italian merchants, having established themselves in the Syrian ports, thought more of economic advantage than of altruistic projects in the name of Christianity. And few of the resident Franks, as all crusaders were called in the east, had any deep affection for the newly arrived pilgrims, who denounced their tolerant ways as obstructing the sacred undertakings of the church.

Although the local princes of Syria were disposed to resent the fanaticism of the newcomers, maintenance of the Christian conquests would have been impossible without such recruits. Fortunately for all concerned, leadership in matters of defense came to be assumed by the great military orders, composed of knights who had bound themselves by monastic vows to the service of the Cross. The Knights of St. John, or Hospitallers, originated in the eleventh century as a band of men pledged to care for sick pilgrims. The Knights Templars, on the other hand, were founded about 1120 as a fighting organization, and shortly afterwards the Hospitallers adopted a similar constitution. Each group was governed by a grand master resident in the Holy Land, where the principal body of knights was stationed. But

[20] See above, p. 295.

subordinate officials were also established throughout western Europe, to enlist members and in every way to further crusading interests. Both orders received extensive privileges and accumulated valuable properties on all sides, and the Templars especially, by widespread banking operations,[21] became a power in the world of business. To hold the straggling possessions of the crusaders in Syria, however, more was demanded than occasional reinforcement by some hundreds of volunteers.

From the Moslem point of view, a favorable turn in the war began with the rise to power of one Zangi, governor of Mosul. Having gained control of Aleppo and various other places in northern Syria, he shocked all Christendom by overwhelming the county of Edessa in 1144. The result, after prolonged exhortation by the pope and the eloquent Bernard of Clairvaux,[22] was the major expedition that is known in history as the Second Crusade (1147-49). In spite of the fact that it was led by two kings, Louis VII of France and Conrad III of Germany, it was an utter failure. The Christian armies, separately defeated in Asia Minor, never reached the Holy Land, and the Moslems were thenceforth free to pursue their victorious advance. Zangi's work was ably continued by his son Nuredin (Nur-al-Din), who by occupying Damascus obtained control of all Syria behind the crusaders' little states. Not long afterwards he had the satisfaction of seeing the nephew of his best general become ruler of Egypt. This nephew was the illustrious Saladin (Sala-al-Din), revered by the Moslems as a saintly hero and hailed even by the Christians as a mighty warrior and an honorable antagonist. Saladin first became vizier to the Fatimid caliph of Egypt.[23] Then, on the death of the latter, he won the title of sultan by restoring Egyptian allegiance to the orthodox caliph at Bagdad. Finally, supplanting an incompetent son of Nuredin, he extended his authority over Mosul, Aleppo, and Damascus.

Under the inspiring leadership of Saladin, the Moslem cause in Asia regained somewhat of its old-time ardor. The Christians, outnumbered and divided among themselves, could offer little effective resistance. Jerusalem fell in 1187 and within another year nothing was left of the crusaders' conquests except three isolated positions: Tyre, Tripolis, and Antioch. How this desperate situation affected political relationships in Europe will be seen when we come to study the careers of the later popes and their rivals.

Saladin (d. 1193) and his conquest

[21] See below, pp. 435-36.

[22] See above, p. 224.

[23] Since the Egyptian ruler claimed descent from Ali and Fatima, he refused to recognize the caliph at Bagdad and assumed the title himself; see above, pp. 164-66.

CHAPTER XVIII

The Triumph of the Papacy

1. EUROPE IN THE LATER TWELFTH CENTURY

Henry II of England (1154-89)

Henry of Anjou, though only twenty-one when he acquired the English crown, was already a man of considerable experience. During the previous five years, as we have seen, he had obtained first Normandy, then Anjou, and finally, by marrying the divorced wife of Louis VII, Aquitaine. As befitted a prince of his generation, he was well educated; furthermore, being highly intelligent as well as ambitious, he took an active part in the work of government and was personally responsible for many of the enactments that bear his name. Henry, it should be remembered, was primarily a continental ruler, who could devote only a minor part of his time to his island kingdom. The fact that, among all the kings of England, none has left a greater impress on the institutions of that country is eloquent testimony to his genius. Like his Angevin father and grandfather, he was red-haired, freckle-faced, and bull-necked; and with these physical traits he combined a fiery temper for which all his associates had a lively respect. Henry's restless energy was also the cause of much comment. His courtiers complained that they scarcely had a chance to sleep; the king was always getting up early in order to go somewhere else. And wherever he went he had to be constantly employed—if not in fighting or hunting, in some matter of politics or administration. Even during mass he had to be supplied with writing materials to keep him from fidgeting.

Finance

The king's initial task in England was to restore the governmental system of Henry I, which had completely lapsed during the troubled reign of Stephen. Under Henry II the exchequer again met regularly and from its annual rolls, together with other official records, we get detailed information about the king's income. In the first place we find that, more and more frequently, he substituted a money payment called scutage for the owed knight

326

service of his barons. Although the latter were usually quite willing to accept the substitution, especially when the campaign was to be fought in France, the greater advantage accrued to the king. By taking cash and hiring troops, he could procure a force entirely subject to his command and so become less dependent on the feudal class. Likewise significant of economic and political transition was the royal tallage, a tax which was collected primarily from the boroughs and which increased so rapidly that it became the largest single item in the king's revenue. From the towns, too, came a variety of other profits, including good sums for the confirmation or extension of the local liberties. Henry II issued municipal charters by the score. It is true that the Londoners, because they had earlier opposed the Angevin succession, now lost their rights of self-government; but Henry confirmed communes in Rouen and other continental cities, and to the English boroughs generally he was very liberal with grants of the more ordinary bourgeois privileges.

Financial interest may also be said to have dominated Henry's judicial reforms. During earlier reigns members of the king's central court had occasionally been dispatched into the counties on special missions. Under Henry II the use of such itinerant justices became a regular part of the government. Every so often they held full meetings of the county courts, to which the local hundreds and boroughs were required to send representatives for purposes of taxation, police, and the like. More particularly, the itinerant justices were now empowered to hold inquests with a view to bringing notorious criminals to justice. Within each county, Henry commanded, twelve men from every hundred and four men from every vill should meet the itinerant justices and on oath present the names of all persons commonly suspected of being murderers, robbers, or similar violators of the king's peace. This was the origin of the grand (i.e., big) jury, which brings accusations (presentments or indictments) preliminary to criminal trials. Men thus accused continued to be tried by ordeal in the twelfth century, though the king showed his mistrust of the ancient procedure by exiling those of very bad reputation even when they had been cleared by the required test.

Judicial reforms

Under Henry II trial by jury was restricted to civil suits. In certain cases of disputed title to land the king provided that the matter should be laid before a jury of lawful men to be chosen from the neighborhood by the sheriff. For instance, if A possessed a particular property, X, and B claimed it by inheritance from his father, the following question would be put to the jury: Did B's father possess X on the day that he was alive and dead? And according to their verdict the land would or would not be awarded to B. As yet, it will be noted, even this petit (i.e., little) jury was a group of expert witnesses who rendered a verdict from their own knowledge, not from evidence produced in court. Many centuries were to pass before our familiar procedure was developed. As it was, however, Henry's trial jury was a great improvement over judicial combat; so his courts attracted an increasing host of suitors, and with them much incidental revenue. Eventually every freeholder, whether or not a tenant of the king, was allowed to buy a writ that through some technicality brought his case before a royal court. The feudal law of the baronial courts, together with the ancient custom of the Anglo-Saxon courts, thus came to be rapidly superseded by a body of royal law, known as the common law because it was common to the entire kingdom.

The civil service

In these respects it is evident that Henry, profiting by the growth of money economy in the later twelfth century, was gradually able to place his government in control of professional ministers. By the end of his reign barons of the traditional type had been generally supplanted by trained experts, not only in the king's central courts, but also throughout the local administration. Such experts, of course, were highly educated men; they might even have studied Roman or canon law at one of the rising universities. Yet, on the whole, their professional attainments were non-academic; for a thorough knowledge of English governmental practice could only be learned from actual experience. Two private works dealing with phases of that subject are very characteristic of the new age. One is the *Dialogue on the Exchequer* by Henry's treasurer, Richard Fitz-Nigel—a technical essay on the royal financial system. The other is the *Treatise on the Laws and Customs of the Kingdom of England* attributed to Henry's justiciar, Ranulf de Glanvill—the first of many famous writings on the English common law.

Ecclesiastical affairs

Despite local resistance on the part of a discontented few, Henry was loyally supported by most of the barons, who joined the clergy and the bourgeoisie in welcoming the restoration of an effective royal government. It was merely unfortunate circumstance that brought the king into conflict with Thomas Becket, archbishop of Canterbury, who before then had zealously served the king as chancellor. The cause of the altercation was an article dealing with criminous clerks in the Constitutions of Clarendon, an official document by which Henry sought to define the relations between church and state in England. The king was willing that the church should continue to decide such matters as perjury, the execution of wills, and the validity of marriages. He would even permit clergymen accused of murder, robbery, and the like to be tried in ecclesiastical courts. But he insisted that such persons, if convicted, should be handed over to him for punishment according to the ordinary law. Becket, denouncing this very sensible proposal,[1] spent many years in bitter controversy with the king. Then, after a supposed reconciliation had failed, certain courtiers took Henry's angry words too literally and slew the archbishop before his altar at Canterbury.

[1] Cf. trials for heresy, below, p. 351.

The result was the canonization of Becket as a martyr and the partial abandonment of the royal program. For centuries thereafter an English criminal
could go scot-free on the first offense by pleading "benefit of clergy" and
proving that he was clerk by reading one passage in the Bible. In all major

MAP XIII.

respects, however, the king's authority over the clergy remained undimin-
ished and was not seriously challenged for another generation.

During all these years, as already remarked, Henry's chief attention was
devoted to his continental dominions. The superintendence of affairs in
Normandy, Anjou, and Aquitaine was in itself no slight task. Besides, Henry
was deeply concerned with numerous other projects, including an ambitious
series of family alliances. His three daughters became the wives respectively
of the duke of Saxony, the king of Castile, and the king of Sicily; and at
least the first of the three matches had important consequences for Euro-

Conti-
nental and
British
projects

pean politics.[2] Meanwhile, by marrying his third son, Geoffrey, to the heiress of Brittany, that county was definitely brought within the Angevin sphere. Under such circumstances it is not surprising that Henry made no effort to assert more than a nominal lordship over the Scottish king or the Welsh princes, and that he delayed intervention in Ireland until it was forced on him. Finally, after various adventurers from the marches of Wales had actually seized a good part of that island, Henry saw fit to establish a royal justiciar at Dublin and to exact homage from the local chieftains, whether Irish or Norman.

Philip Augustus (1180-1223)

The excellence of Henry II's governmental machine was demonstrated by the fact that it ran efficiently under his successor. Richard I (1189-99) was a fine soldier who deserved his nickname of Lion-Heart (*Cœur de Lion*), but who left his kingdom to be ruled by ministers while he won renown on the crusade.[3] Meanwhile, in France, the Capetian throne had been inherited by Philip II, son of the inglorious Louis VII by a second wife. As a mere youth Philip displayed the wisdom that was to gain for him the surname of Augustus. Neither chivalrous nor especially pious, he was greatly inferior to Louis VII in traditional goodness; yet there can be no question as to which was the better king. Philip's crafty self-control and cold intelligence, though they brought him few warm friends, enabled him to redeem his father's mistakes and triumphantly to resume the policy of his grandfather. His first success was to make good his claim to the marriage portion of his wife, a daughter of the Flemish count, and so to acquire Artois together with the upper Somme valley (see Map XIII). So far as breaking the Angevin power was concerned, he could, while Henry II lived, merely hope for a future opportunity. And although Philip abandoned his crusade to plot against Richard, he won little glory until the sudden death of the latter brought the ignoble John to the English throne.

His conquests from John of England

Ever since his accession Philip Augustus had deliberately fomented quarrels within the Angevin house. Against Henry II he had supported Richard's demand for the duchy of Aquitaine; then, when Richard became king, he had transferred his affections to John. It was only logical that in 1199 Philip should warmly champion Arthur of Brittany, the youthful son of John's elder brother Geoffrey (see Table III). But John, as a mature man whose real character was still unknown, easily gained the support of the magnates and was recognized throughout Richard's dominions. So Philip perforce accepted his homage for Normandy, Anjou, and Aquitaine, and again adopted a policy of waiting. Two years later he was rewarded by a chance for decisive action. By carrying off a lady betrothed to one of his continental vassals, and by various other deeds, John inspired appeals to his feudal lord, the king of France. Such appeals he treated with scorn;

---

[2] See the following pages in this chapter.
[3] See below, p. 338.

accordingly Philip's court, on John's refusal to appear, adjudged him a felon and declared his fiefs forfeit to the crown. The amazing part of the story is what followed. John began the war by capturing and, as was generally believed, murdering his nephew Arthur of Brittany. Thereafter he lapsed into apathy and allowed Philip to take from him Normandy, Anjou, Poitou, and Auvergne (see Map XIII). It was not until 1205 that John bestirred himself to defend the remainder of Aquitaine, and it was then too late to save his ancestral fiefs to the north. Before we can understand the culmination of these events, however, we must examine contemporary developments in central Europe.

The crown of Germany, as we have seen, was acquired in 1152 by the remarkable Frederick Barbarossa, who in every way sought to be another Otto the Great. The quest for a pseudo-Roman glory inevitably led him to Italy, which remained a strange land to the German. Furthermore, by diverting his attention from his own country, Frederick played into the hand of Henry the Lion, duke of Saxony and Bavaria, who led the antimonarchical faction and, by marriage to a daughter of Henry II, was allied with the powerful house of Anjou. Frederick's first Italian expedition in 1154 brought him the imperial crown as a reward for helping Pope Hadrian IV against Arnold of Brescia[4] and the opportunity of proclaiming his regal authority in a great diet at Roncaglia. Four years later, after arranging a settlement with the Guelfs, he held a second diet at Roncaglia and there issued a series of grandiloquent constitutions, asserting his right to appoint officials, levy taxes, and administer supreme justice throughout his Italian kingdom. And when Milan headed an insurrection of the Lombard communes, he took the city after a protracted siege and destroyed it. Having come into violent controversy with the papacy, he now occupied Rome, drove out Alexander III, Hadrian's able successor, and installed an antipope.

Frederick I of Germany (1152-90)

Frederick's triumph, however, was only the beginning of a long war in the course of which the papal cause steadily advanced. By 1168 Alexander had regained his capital through the support of his Sicilian vassals, had found allies among the Guelfs in Germany, and had organized the great Lombard League, a defensive combination of virtually all the city-states of northern Italy. Milan was rebuilt and a new fortress, named Alessandria in honor of the pope, was constructed to offset the imperial position at Pavia. Frederick, though deserted by the Guelfs, accepted the challenge and again invaded Italy. But in 1176, after vainly besieging Alessandria, his army was overwhelmed at Legnano by the united forces of the league. Alexander's victory was complete, as Frederick promptly acknowledged by granting him formal recognition. Finally, by the Peace of Constance in 1183, the allied cities obtained the guarantee of what amounted to the *status quo* in

[4] See below, p. 345.

Italy, having merely to accept the reservation of certain theoretic rights on the part of the emperor.

The fall
of Henry
the Lion

In Germany, on the other hand, Frederick proved that he was still master; for by 1182 he had confiscated the duchies of Henry the Lion and forced him to crave the royal pardon on bended knee. The fall of the Guelf chieftain brought about a momentous change in the map of Germany. The historic duchies of Saxony and Bavaria were never reconstituted. Although a local margrave came to be styled duke of Saxony, his holdings were confined to the eastern border, and it was only a fragment of the old Bavaria that eventually passed with the ducal title to the house of Wittelsbach. Austria, recognized as a separate duchy, became increasingly prominent, as did Brandenburg, another frontier state. And between them the kingdom of Bohemia, though still ruled by a native dynasty, was more and more subjected to German influence. Meanwhile a great work of recolonization was carried out in the region to the east of the Elbe, which had been laid waste by the Poles in the previous century. Here, too, may be perceived the effect of commercial revival, for the Saxon princes—both the Guelfs and their local rivals—brought hundreds of Flemish and Westphalian peasants to drain and cultivate the marshy wastes along the Baltic. At the same time economic considerations led to the founding of many famous towns. For example, Henry the Lion created a flourishing center for the Bavarian salt trade at Munich, and in his other duchy he was largely responsible for the establishment of a mercantile settlement at Lübeck—a project that had a greater success than all the Italian expeditions of all the emperors combined!

Henry VI
and the
Sicilian
succession

For Frederick Barbarossa there are only two other events to chronicle. Profiting by the fact that the great Alexander III had only short-lived and mediocre successors, the emperor in 1184 had the satisfaction of marrying his son, already crowned as Henry VI, to Constance, daughter of Roger II and potential heiress of the Sicilian kingdom. Lastly, as a fitting close to his picturesque career, he took a splendid army to join Philip of France and Richard of England on the crusade. But he never reached the Holy Land, being drowned, as the result of an unexplained accident, in a little river of Cilicia. Thus, in 1190, Germany came under the sovereignty of Henry VI —a man of harsh and cruel disposition who nevertheless proved to be an efficient ruler and a shrewd diplomat. Besides, he had amazing luck. Through the complaisance of the aged pope, Celestine III, he not only secured the imperial crown but also, with the opportune death of Roger II's last grandson, made good his claim to the kingdom of Sicily. Following up this success, and the joyful news that his wife had presented him with a son, Henry launched plans for making the imperial office hereditary and for including in a greater crusade the capture of Constantinople and the reunion of the Roman world. His magnificent design was never to be put to actual trial. Stricken by fever in 1197, Henry died at the age of only thirty-two. And through one of the most dramatic reversals in history his reign introduced a new age of splendor, not for the empire, but for the papacy.

2. INNOCENT III

The death of Henry VI was shortly followed by that of the ninety-year-old Celestine; and the cardinals, realizing that the moment was critical, gave the vacant throne to a young and vigorous man with a known talent for practical affairs. They chose well; for Innocent III, as the new pope came to be styled, ranks among the greatest statesmen of Europe. During his earlier years Innocent had studied theology at Paris as well as canon law at Bologna; but he was more of a lawyer than a theologian. Thanks to his energy and ability, all phases of the papal administration were brought to a new height of efficiency. And in dealing with the temporal princes of Europe Innocent proved himself a politician and diplomat of superlative skill. Few kings or emperors have had his power of grasping the essentials in any situation and thus turning it to full advantage. Once he had made a mistake, Innocent was quick to realize the fact and to modify his strategy accordingly. As a clever opportunist, he earned the reputation of being decidedly unscrupulous. Yet his fundamental sincerity cannot be doubted; like Gregory VII, he envisioned a magnificent ideal—the ultimate dominance of all human relationships by the church. His failure quite to attain the moral grandeur of his sainted predecessor was in part the consequence of his amazing success. He was never called to be a martyr. *Accession and character*

To appreciate Innocent's diplomacy, we must give further attention to the dynastic rivalries that disturbed all Europe in the closing years of the twelfth century. The sudden death of Henry VI inevitably ruined his plan for a hereditary empire. The German electors, of course, would have none of it and refused to consider the three-year-old Frederick of Sicily as a candidate. The Hohenstaufen party, it is true, remained strong enough to declare the election of Henry VI's younger brother, Philip of Suabia; but this action was immediately challenged by the Guelfs and their friends, who proclaimed Otto, a son of Henry the Lion (see Tables V and VI). Since Otto's mother was a sister of Richard Lion-Heart who, on his way home from the crusade, had been imprisoned and held to ransom by Henry VI, the Guelfs were warmly supported by the Angevins. So Philip Augustus of France became the natural ally of the Hohenstaufen Philip of Suabia, and all the barons of the French borderlands took sides according as they did or did not favor the Capetian cause. Innocent, meanwhile, had promptly responded to an appeal from Constance of Sicily, who recognized him as the feudal lord and therefore the lawful guardian of her little son, the king. While successfully maintaining his right to sole wardship over the youthful Frederick, the pope took advantage of the anti-German reaction in Italy *European politics* to consolidate his position within the city of Rome, to enforce his authority throughout the rest of the Papal States, and in every way to weaken the imperial hold on the adjacent regions to the north.

Finally, with an impressive show of legality, Innocent proceeded to intervene in Germany. He acknowledged the right of the local princes to elect their own king; but, he reminded them, the imperial crown could be obtained only from the pope. In the case of a disputed election, when two rivals claimed the honor at once, he obviously had to examine their credentials. And the examination took considerable time, which Innocent used to good purpose for diplomatic negotiation. As was to be expected, he decided for Otto, after the latter had sworn to advance the ecclesiastical interest in many specific ways. While supporting Guelf against Hohenstaufen, it was only natural that Innocent should favor Angevin in preference to Capetian; and such a policy was encouraged by the fact that Philip Augustus, in defiance of the papal authority, had repudiated a first wife in order to marry a second. Even after he had been excommunicated and his lands had been placed under an interdict,[5] he remained obdurate until his great war with John of England made it imperative to conciliate the pope. So he grudgingly agreed to a retrial and eventually, on the death of his second wife, went through a form of reconciliation with the first.

Meanwhile, in spite of the papal decision, the civil war over the German succession dragged on year after year. It was only after Philip of Suabia had been murdered in 1208 that Otto definitely triumphed. Then, having received the imperial crown, he abruptly changed his policy and launched a vigorous campaign for the reduction of all Italy. Outraged by this display of ingratitude, Innocent placed Otto under the anathema of the church and in his stead urged the German princes to elect Frederick of Sicily. At the age of fourteen he had been installed as actual ruler of his hereditary kingdom and shortly afterwards married to an Aragonese princess. Now, in 1211, Frederick was formally proclaimed king of Germany by a diet of rebel princes and, with the active support of Philip Augustus, set out to dispose of his Guelf rival. Innocent, it should be noted, had broken not only with the emperor but also with the English king; hence the papal willingness to accept the half-hearted surrender of Philip Augustus in the matter of his divorce.

John's famous conflict with Innocent arose out of a disputed election to the archbishopric of Canterbury. In 1205, when that see became vacant, the right of filling it devolved on the cathedral chapter, there organized as a monastic body.[6] Without waiting for royal license, the canons chose one of their own number and sent him off to obtain the papal confirmation.

[5] The ecclesiastical interdict normally suspended all public worship and the administration of all but particular sacraments under certain conditions.

[6] See below, p. 344.

But news of the affair leaked out and the king forced a second election, in which his candidate was named, to be likewise dispatched to Rome. Innocent, after listening to representatives from the two sides, declared both elections invalid and finally prevailed on those of the chapter who were present to accept Stephen Langton, an able Englishman trained in the papal service. When notified of these proceedings, John furiously swore that he would never allow Langton in his kingdom and kept the archbishopric in his own hands. Consequently, in 1208, the pope placed England under an interdict and released John's subjects from their oaths of fealty. The king thereupon seized all the property of the church in England and so put himself in position, through the distribution of subsidies, to coerce the clergy into obeying him. For over five years the situation remained unchanged—during which time, as was later admitted, John obtained more than £100,000 in ecclesiastical revenue; and that was only a fraction of what the church actually lost.

Perhaps, if the king had not been personally unpopular, he could have withstood the pope indefinitely. He headed a powerful government and, as long as he had plenty of cash, could easily hire troops to do his bidding. But John's despotic ways had come to be generally hated, and under the official encouragement of the papacy an uprising of the discontented baronage was only too likely. Besides, the rebels would have the valuable assistance of Philip Augustus, whose victorious war on the continent could now be extended into a sort of crusade against England. Though indifferent to religious penalties, John had good reason to fear a French invasion. So, when the Capetian forces were ready to sail in 1213, he suddenly announced his submission to the papal terms. He agreed to recognize Langton, to restore all ecclesiastical property, to compensate the church for damage it had sustained, and to do whatever else was necessary to secure absolution. He was willing even to hold England as a papal fief, performing homage to Innocent's legate and promising, in recognition of his vassalage, the annual payment of a thousand marks.

John's submission (1213)

Down to this point the pope's diplomatic position had been eminently logical. At first he had supported Guelf and Angevin against Hohenstaufen and Capetian; then, by his reversal of 1208-10 he had swung round to the side of the latter pair. John's action in 1213, however, resulted in a situation to tax the ingenuity of even a master-statesman like Innocent III. He had, of course, to accept John's deliberately planned submission and to forbid the pending French expedition. Yet John continued to subsidize Otto in Germany and Philip refused to abandon his plans for the conquest of England. How could the pope be the ally of John against Philip while remaining the ally of Philip and Frederick against Otto? Actually he could do little more than wait until, in 1214, the French king crushed the forces of the Angevin-Guelf coalition at Bouvines. That battle ruined not only

The battle of Bouvines and its consequences

John's dream of recovering his lost fiefs but also the cause of Otto in Germany. Within a year the unfortunate Guelf was virtually a fugitive on his ancestral estates in Saxony, where he continued to maintain a losing defense until his death in 1218.

No sooner had Innocent been relieved of one dilemma than he was confronted by another. John's crushing defeat at Bouvines was the signal for the outburst of a long-smoldering insurrection in England. Baronage, clergy, and the city of London made common cause against the hated master whom, momentarily, they found unprepared. To gain time, John granted their demands in the famous Magna Carta of 1215,[7] meanwhile appealing to his feudal lord for support. Innocent at once absolved him from his oath, ordered the rebels to lay down their arms, and, when they refused to do so, placed them under excommunication. Still they would not yield. So, by strange fortune, the pope now found arrayed against him all his staunch supporters of a few years before, including Stephen Langton, his own nominee for the see of Canterbury. Nor was Philip Augustus more obedient. In direct opposition to the papal command, he sent to England his son, the later Louis VIII, who was admitted to London and recognized as king by the baronial party. Then, at the critical moment, John's death in October, 1216, removed the chief cause of unrest and the insurrection collapsed —just too late for Innocent to know that the papal cause had again triumphed, for the great pope had himself died in July.

The papal monarchy   Leaving the further results of Philip's victory at Bouvines for consideration in a later chapter, we may now attempt to appraise the political accomplishment of the papacy at the death of Innocent III in 1216. Apparently, at least, he had been on the verge of establishing a Roman theocracy by combining the spiritual with the temporal headship of the Christian world. Long before his time the Roman Church, in so many ways the true heir of the Roman Empire, had come to be recognized as an absolute monarchy. For the Latin world constituted a single ecclesiastical unit, within which the pope was sovereign—held supreme authority in all matters, legislative, executive, or judicial. His actual administration, naturally, was entrusted to a host of subordinates. Chief among them were the cardinals, whom he frequently summoned to meet with him in consistory, a sort of cabinet to which he customarily submitted important questions for discussion. Besides, he appointed the ministers who acted as his judges, secretaries, financial experts, and the like, and who together made up his great central *curia*. To enforce his decisions, he dispatched on all sides special emissaries called legates, with powers superior to those of any local prelate. Normally, of course, each diocese was governed by its own bishop under the supervision of the metropolitan, and from time to time the bishops of a whole province, or of a larger region, would meet in council to legislate

[7] See below, pp. 369-70.

on matters of general concern. Their acts, however, could always be set aside by papal edict, for the ruling of any ordinary court of canon law could be reversed at Rome. And, as had now come to be generally acknowledged, even a more comprehensive assembly of the church could only give advice to the chief pontiff.

During the twelfth century three of Innocent's predecessors had called Lateran Councils as a means of rallying Christendom in support of their major policies. Adopting the same plan, Innocent provided a fitting culmination to the dramatic events of the previous seventeen years. His Lateran Council of 1215 was attended by over twelve hundred bishops, abbots, and priors, as well as by a host of other delegates, both clerical and lay. The states thus represented included not merely those of western and central Europe but also those erected by the crusaders in Syria and the Balkan peninsula.[8] This was the greatest assembly of Christian prelates that had been held for more than seven centuries. And unlike the Councils of Nicæa, Constantinople, and Chalcedon, the Lateran Council of 1215 was a creation of the papacy. Innocent summoned it, presided over it, and controlled it. The seventy canons formulated by the council were really the work of the pope—a final synthesis of decisions made and promulgated on his sole authority. They dealt with a wide range of subjects: such as heresy and its punishment,[9] the sacramental system and the clergy, the improvement of ecclesiastical government and discipline, the relations of church and state, and the revival of the crusade. Although various matters of faith and practice were here defined for the first time, the decrees of 1215 were essentially a restatement or reapplication of established principles. Even the papal monarchy, for all its added prestige under Innocent III, was nothing new in theory.

Innocent implicitly accepted the traditions of his office—the infallibility of the church, the apostolic succession, and the Petrine supremacy—as set forth by the great doctors of the fifth and sixth centuries. Thus believing himself the holder of a divine commission, he sought to enforce the papal authority by whatever means he could find. The extent of his success has in part been seen. As ruler of the Papal States, protector of the Lombard League, and guardian of the Sicilian kingdom, he dominated the Italian peninsula. In Germany he had helped to depose two kings and to install others. John of England, threatened by French invasion and baronial revolt, had agreed to hold his kingdom as a papal fief. The kings of Poland, Hungary, Portugal, Aragon, and Denmark had also acknowledged themselves vassals of the pope. Yet, the more closely we examine these victories of Innocent, the more dubious their worth appears. His triumph over the Holy Roman Empire, for example, resulted in the coronation of Frederick

*The
Lateran
Council
of 1215*

*The
question
of a
papal
theocracy*

[8] See below, pp. 341-42.
[9] See below, p. 351.

II, which proved to be no blessing for his successors. The papal lordship over isolated states like Portugal was rendered advantageous by local conditions that were subject to change at any moment. The vassalage of the English king was a mere by-product of the Angevin-Capetian war and led to very embarrassing consequences, from which it was sheer luck that the papacy emerged with flying colors. Additional evidence to the same effect is provided by the contemporary history of the crusade.

3. THE THIRD AND FOURTH CRUSADES

Failure of the Third Crusade

By 1187, when Jerusalem fell to Saladin,[10] the crusade had ceased to be a feudal enterprise inspired and guided by the papacy. It now seemed that any great European offensive would have to be a campaign undertaken by the jealous and preoccupied kings of Germany, France, and England. These kings, having allowed affairs in the east to reach a desperate stage, finally joined in a magnificent but ill-concerted expedition (1189-92). Frederick Barbarossa's host was exhausted by fighting its way through Asia Minor even before the emperor's death ended all hope of its accomplishing anything significant. Richard Lion-Heart of England and Philip Augustus of France, when they at last arrived, failed to co-operate in any way. The former, it is true, delivered the final blow in the recapture of Acre and won a number of victories against Saladin in the field. Yet, when a three-year truce was signed in the autumn of 1192, the Christians had to be satisfied with a guarantee of free access to the Holy City under toleration of its Moslem rulers—a concession that might well have been gained without bloodshed. So far as its avowed purpose was concerned, the Third Crusade was a failure.

The close of the twelfth century brought no important change in the eastern situation. Saladin died in 1193, leaving to his brother the combined territories of Egypt and Syria, except for a strip of coast where the Christians maintained a precarious hold. In Europe, meanwhile, the rivalry of the French and English kings had culminated in active warfare. Henry VI momentarily united the kingdoms of Germany, Arles, Italy, and Sicily, but died before he could launch an imperial crusade to the east. Then, as all Europe was drawn into the furious struggle of Guelf against Hohenstaufen and of Angevin against Capetian, Innocent III came to the papal throne. No ecclesiastical statesman could allow the sacred cause of the Holy Sepulcher to be forgotten by Latin Christendom, and the very fact that all the great kings were engaged in fighting one another provided an opportunity for reviving the crusade as a papal undertaking. So Innocent, while trying to dictate terms of peace to the warring princes, fervently exhorted all Christians to renew their devotion to the ideals of Urban II.

[10] See above, p. 325.

As a consequence, a group of French knights, headed by the counts of Champagne and Flanders, took the cross in 1199. Their project received the enthusiastic support of Innocent and by 1201 had advanced far enough to warrant the making of final arrangements. Since the expedition was to go by sea, certain of the crusaders were delegated to contract with the Venetians for the necessary food and transportation. Among them was Geoffroy de Villehardouin, who has left us a vivid description of the events that ensued. Aside from what he says of himself—and it is restricted to matter-of-fact references in the third person—little is known of him. Being marshal of Champagne, Villehardouin was from the outset a prominent member of the crusading host and, having lived through famous adventures, dictated a record of them in his own vernacular. His book, therefore, is doubly remarkable—as the first great monument of French prose and as an eye-witness account of the amazing Fourth Crusade. Villehardouin seems to have been entirely honest, but somewhat naïve. The story, as he tells it, is incredibly simple; we cannot, as he apparently did, ignore the motives that constantly governed the principal actors in his drama. The significance of these remarks will be evident with the unfolding of the tale.

The Fourth Crusade: Ville-hardouin

The Venetians, says Villehardouin, finally made the following proposal to him and his associates. They would transport the army and provide it with supplies for nine months at the rate of two marks per man and four marks per horse. And "for the love of God" they would add fifty armed galleys—on condition that they should receive one-half of all conquests and of all booty to be won by sea or by land. These terms were accepted by the crusaders and sworn to by both parties. But when the host assembled at Venice in the summer of 1202, it was discovered that less than half the required sum had been collected. Even after the wealthier barons had made additional contributions, 34,000 marks were still lacking. The Venetians thereupon made another proposal. They would forgive the debt if the host would help them to regain the city of Zara, which had recently been taken by the king of Hungary. The crusaders, in default of an alternative, agreed; and, as if by miracle, a wave of enthusiasm swept all Venice. The blind doge, Henry Dandolo, had a cross sewn on the front of his hat, while a multitude of citizens took the pilgrim's vow along with him. The decision thus made was held to even in defiance of specific commands from Innocent, who pointed out that the king of Hungary was not only an orthodox Christian but also a vassal of the Roman see. Europe thus came to witness the interesting spectacle of a crusade launched by men under papal excommunication; for in November, 1202, the host crossed the Adriatic and took Zara after a five-day siege.

Capture of Zara (1202)

This, according to Villehardouin, was the beginning of a marvelous adventure. We must concur in his opinion, for most of the pilgrims were to see neither Egypt nor the Holy Land; instead they were to capture the city

The Byzantine project

of Constantinople and partition the Byzantine Empire. Yet we cannot, with Villehardouin, accept the result as sheer accident; it was too logical a fulfillment of ambitions that were already old in the days of Urban II. Following the example of Robert Guiscard, Roger II of Sicily and Henry VI of Germany had both contemplated offensives against the moribund empire in the east. The Hohenstaufen glory had now faded and the kingdom of Sicily was in the hands of the pope; but another western power was willing and anxious to have the Greek world brought under Latin domination. This was the republic of Venice. For the better part of two centuries the erstwhile province of the Byzantine Empire had been steadily advancing at its expense. From the emperor's need of support against the Normans the Venetians had secured a commercial pre-eminence at Constantinople which they threatened to extend into an economic dictatorship. Byzantine resistance to such a design had merely stiffened the determination of the Venetians to protect their interests in whatever way they could. And recent happenings could not fail to suggest the possibility of armed intervention. In 1185 one Isaac Angelus had gained the Byzantine throne by means of an insurrection, only to be deposed and imprisoned by his brother some ten years later. As a result of these disorders and the utter incompetence of the government, the empire had once more lapsed into anarchy. While the Serbs and Bulgars, reasserting their independence, overran Thrace and Macedonia, the Turks again pushed forward in Asia Minor. Under such circumstances the Venetians might indeed welcome the proposal now made by Alexius, son of the unfortunate Isaac.

Capture of Constantinople (1203-04)   Even before the host sailed from Venice, Alexius had been in touch with some of its leaders and had presumably been listened to with a good deal of interest. Now, at any rate, the crusaders were told that, if they would come to the rescue of Isaac, he would do wonderful things for them. He not only would restore the east to communion with the Roman Church but would also assure the conquest of Egypt and Syria by enormous grants of men, money, and supplies. The offer of Alexius led to a division of the host. A minority of the pilgrims insisted on going straight to the Holy Land, where they accomplished little. But the great majority, headed by the Venetians and the French princes, agreed to undertake the Byzantine adventure. So, again in defiance of the pope, the host set sail for Constantinople in the spring of 1203. Having taken Corfu and various Ægean islands on the way, the crusaders appeared before the imperial city in June. Then ensued the dramatic events so graphically described by Villehardouin. In July the crusaders broke into the harbor and stormed the sea-walls. The usurping emperor fled and Isaac was restored. Unfortunately for the Latin cause, however, Isaac died while Greek insurgents slew his son, proclaimed a new emperor, and compelled the invaders to take refuge on the Venetian ships. At the opening of the year 1204 the host thus had the choice of abandoning the whole enterprise or of taking Constantinople for the second time. They chose the latter alternative and, following one repulse, scaled the walls on April 12. Thereafter all opposition collapsed.

Before delivering their attack, the crusaders had signed an agreement as to what should be done if they succeeded. Of all the booty, half should go to the Venetians and half to the French. Each of the two parties, furthermore, should name six men, and these twelve should elect an emperor. Whoever was thus chosen should have a quarter of the conquered territory;

Estab-lishment of the Latin Empire

MAP XIV.

the remaining three-quarters should be equally divided between the French and the Venetians. Now that the victory had been won, this arrangement was carried out. Baldwin, count of Flanders, was elected emperor and installed with due Byzantine pomp. The other leaders of the host, including Ville-hardouin,[11] were rewarded with fiefs on the mainland. All the important islands, together with the shores of the Peloponnesus, Gallipoli, and a large section of the capital, were assigned to Venice—enough to assure the re-

[11] It should be noted that the chronicler's nephew, also named Geoffroy de Villehardouin, eventually established in the Peloponnesus the principality of Morea, which outlived the Latin Empire as well as the kingdom of Jerusalem and all its component parts. How he and his associated barons thus created an efficient state, governed according to the feudal custom of contemporary France, is graphically shown by the so-called assizes of Romania, originally drawn up in the thirteenth century.

public a commercial monopoly throughout the empire (see Map XIV).
To the men engaged in this astonishing adventure the triumph was so immense, and so rich in unforeseen consequences, that they naturally postponed any advance against the Turks. Innocent, very characteristically, now
hailed the unexpected success of the outlawed enterprise as an evident
miracle to permit the reunion of the Roman and Greek Churches. But the
crusade, he insisted, must not be abandoned. It was only after years of futile
remonstrance that he realized the hopelessness of gaining any action from
Constantinople and so, in his Lateran Council of 1215, proclaimed the
launching of a new expedition to redeem the Holy Sepulcher.

The papal theocracy in actuality   Nothing better illustrates the limitation of the papal theocracy than this
Fourth Crusade, which turned out to be no crusade at all. In the east as in
the west Innocent's political victories were due, not to the general acceptance of his theocratic ideal, but to his extraordinary skill in diplomacy,
aided by a very fortunate turn of events over which he had no real control.
The design of a world-wide Christian commonwealth was doomed to failure by two principal facts: that succeeding popes could not all be men of
Innocent's peculiar genius and that the rivalries of European politics were
as little compatible with Christian idealism then as they are today. Merely
to superintend the legal and financial administration of the papal monarchy
was a tremendous responsibility. How, in addition, could any pope think of
acting as a sort of moral dictator in all national and international affairs,
disciplining temporal rulers for their misdeeds in public as well as in private
life? If, in the changing life of the thirteenth century, the papacy chose to
devote its chief attention to government and diplomacy, would it not gravely
endanger its spiritual leadership?

CHAPTER XIX

Heresy, the Friars, and the Universities

1. THE PROBLEM OF ECCLESIASTICAL REFORM

To sketch the achievements of the twelfth and thirteenth centuries in arts and letters is to pay constant tribute to the influence of the church, which for the better part of a thousand years had been the dominant institution of the Latin world. It should always be remembered, however, that the church controlled much which it could not create. The armies and fleets that made possible the capture of Jerusalem were not in themselves clerical. The fact that a boy learned to read and write in an ecclesiastical school was no assurance that he would produce ecclesiastical books. A cathedral was designed by architects and built by skilled workmen, not by the bishop who ordered its construction. And the money with which he bought materials and hired labor was amassed principally through contributions by the faithful. In other words, man power and talent and wealth were devoted to the service of the church because of its inspiring hold on the minds of the people. This hold it could not afford to risk for the sake of outworn prejudices or grandiose ambitions.

At the opening of the thirteenth century the church was faced with a number of grave problems. As remarked in the preceding chapter, the papacy was pledged to a tradition of political intervention and dictation that, to be even moderately successful, required an Innocent III in the Roman see. Could the magnificent dream of Christian unification, however promising in the days of Urban II, be actually realized a hundred years later? All subsequent experience with the crusades had proved that, from the papal point of view, times had sadly changed. Economically, the western states were already emerging from the feudal age. On all sides ambitious princes were developing stronger governments, with ministers trained for professional service and with revenues drawn from the mount-

The church and the world of the thirteenth century

343

ing wealth of the towns. Could the church, as was vitally necessary for its continued strength, maintain the loyalty of the bourgeois class? Ecclesiastical organization had been perfected to meet the demands of an agrarian society; urban populations, rapidly growing outside that organization and living a life utterly foreign to its traditions, had found themselves misunderstood and neglected. Now, within such bourgeois environments, the universities were taking form. How could the church effectively govern the new associations of unruly masters and students? And how could it secure the reconciliation of the new learning—mainly the work of pagans and Moslems—with the sacred principles of Christianity?

Monasticism

For many hundreds of years the church had been legally established throughout the European world as an institution to which, normally, all persons were born subject.[1] Under such conditions its ordinary services had necessarily been molded to suit the capacities and needs of the masses, while to those who demanded a more rigorous discipline it had offered the monastic life. This compromise, at least in the west, had been eminently successful. There had been no serious outbreak of heresy in any of the Latin states; and although the morals of the secular clergy had at times deteriorated, improvement had always been effected by some reformation emanating from the cloister. It was not until the twelfth century that religious discontent reached a dangerous stage in spite of all that could be accomplished by traditional methods. The age was assuredly not one of monastic decay. Scores of ancient Benedictine houses, both within and without the Cluniac Congregation, continued to flourish. The Cistercian Order, asserting a return to the original ideals of St. Benedict, attracted a host of recruits. Many others were led to join the Carthusians[2] who, reverting to the pre-Benedictine system, insisted that true holiness could be found only in a community of hermits devoted to extremes of asceticism. Meanwhile a large number of cathedral chapters and other groups of secular clerks had come to adopt a rule attributed to the sainted bishop of Hippo, and therefore styled Augustinian, or Austin, canons. Besides, the crusading orders of Templars and Hospitallers now attained great renown.

Anticlerical agitation

The crucial point seems to have been that none of these organizations, however beneficial in other respects, appreciably influenced the relation of the church to the mass of the people. Neither the revival of monastic purity nor the liberation of bishops from secular control could obscure the fact that the higher clergy were more interested in politics, law, and finance than in the fate of the common man. He was poor and they were rich: that to most critics was the all-important consideration. And anyone

---

[1] See above, pp. 65, 222, 264.
[2] So called from the monastery of La Grande Chartreuse, established in 1084 on a mountain in eastern France.

who could read had only to open the Gospels to find a cogent argument. The contrast between the life of the apostles and that of their contemporary successors was only too apparent. So countless writers of the twelfth century came to denouce the rulers of the church for chronic avarice and hypocrisy —in which evils, they said, a potent example was set by the Roman *curia*. It is very significant that the leaders of this attack were almost invariably townsmen, who had perhaps acquired the technical status of clerks but were not incumbents of ecclesiastical office.

One current of criticism runs through the *fabliaux* and other bourgeois writings, to culminate in a series of great satirical works that will be examined in a later chapter. Like the Goliardic literature, however, these compositions hardly go beyond coarse jesting and irreverent burlesque; they attack the corruption of the church rather than the church itself. The same can be said of the preachers who berated the upper clergy as politicians and money-getters, exhorting them to return to the pure simplicity of apostolic times. For example, Arnold of Brescia, an eloquent theologian who had studied at Paris, gained a large following in the Italian cities by advocating the abolition or restriction of clerical property. Arrested by Frederick Barbarossa at the request of the pope in 1154, Arnold was hanged by the Roman authorities as a rebel—not, it should be noted, as a heretic; for heresy involved the rejection in whole or in part of the orthodox Christian faith. Since no bishop could pretend to be other than human, to accuse even the pope of deadly sin was not heretical; though it might be dangerous if the accuser lived at Rome.

Peter Waldo (Pierre Valdo), a well-to-do merchant of Lyons, also rose to fame through popular agitation against the worldliness of the clergy. It was about 1170 that he, inspired by the precepts of the Gospel, devoted all his wealth to charity and organized a group of Poor Men to engage in work among the people. Although the original project was approved by Pope Alexander III, Waldo soon embroiled himself with the local clergy. He and his Poor Men were accused of unauthorized preaching in the course of which, by means of a Provençal translation, they interpreted the Bible to suit themselves. So in 1179 the pope ordered Waldo to submit to episcopal authority, and he replied that he must obey God rather than man. Finally, in 1184, the Waldensians were excommunicated and driven from Lyons. As a proscribed sect, they quickly developed heretical doctrines, reviving the Donatist assertion that the validity of a sacrament depended on the character of the minister[3] and establishing their own forms of worship without an ordained clergy at all. Like the later Protestants, they tended to discard all dogma and practice that were not specifically mentioned in the New Testament. Their missionary zeal was impressive. Spreading into southern France, Spain, Italy, and the Rhine-

The Waldensians

---

[3] See above, pp. 62-63.

lands, they merged with various other groups of ecclesiastical rebels, such as the converts recently made by Arnold of Brescia.

**The Albi-
gensians**
It was not, however, the Waldensians whom the rulers of the church most detested; rather it was a totally different sect, the members of which called themselves Cathari (i.e., the Pure). Apparently originating in the Byzantine Empire through a combination of earlier heresies, Catharism was brought by traders to the growing towns of Italy and southern France, where by the time of Innocent III its supporters were generally known as Albigensians, from the city of Albi in the county of Toulouse. Their success was due in large measure to popular dissatisfaction with the established church. It was the especial boast of the Albigensians that, without a richly endowed clergy, they attained a higher standard of morals than was dreamed of by orthodox Christians. Besides, their doctrines had certain practical advantages. Like the ancient Manichæans,[4] they maintained two disciplines: one for the ordinary man and one for the perfected. The latter was pledged to rigid asceticism, including celibacy and a vegetarian diet. The former had only to revere his betters until, at the last moment, he might be fully initiated and so die in purity. Anyone who thus ended his life was assured of paradise. The soul of the impure man was doomed to inhabit a lower animal; for, according to the Albigensians, there was neither a hell nor a purgatory. In the absence of a strong central authority, their theology varied somewhat from congregation to congregation; but in general it was based on a sharp dualism of spirit and matter, light and darkness, good and evil.

By the close of the twelfth century the Albigensian heresy had attained such proportions in southern France that the ordinary agencies of the church were powerless to combat it. Most of the local clergy were suspect, and the efforts of papal investigators and missionaries broke down before the indifference or hostility of the local princes. The latter, indeed, could hardly be other than friendly to a religion cherished by a large proportion of their subjects, including most wealthy townsmen. And a semi-pagan nobleman might himself find the double standard of Catharism very agreeable, in that it offered a comparatively easy road to salvation. Innocent III, as usual, acted circumspectly in this matter; but in 1208 the murder of his legate at the court of Raymond VI, count of Toulouse, precipitated a crisis. Declaring Raymond excommunicate and unworthy of holding his county, Innocent offered the lands and goods of his heretical subjects to any Christian warriors who would enlist in the sacred cause.

**The Albi-
gensian
Crusade**
Philip Augustus, being preoccupied with his great project for the conquest of England and being extremely cautious about fighting wars for another's advantage, abstained from all personal activity in this Albigensian Crusade. He did, however, give his vassals permission to join it, merely

---

[4] See above, p. 42,

stipulating that no final disposition of conquered territory could be made without his consent. Accordingly, in 1209, a host of northern volunteers under ecclesiastical leadership proceeded to invade the county of Toulouse. Since by that time Count Raymond had made formal submission to the pope, the crusaders turned their attention to his recalcitrant vassals. The viscount of Béziers was the first to suffer. Amid shocking scenes of rapine and massacre his cities were taken and his lands devastated. The conquered fief was then awarded to Simon de Montfort, a rather obscure baron of the Île de France. Earlier he had taken part in the Fourth Crusade, but had left the host after the capture of Zara and had gone to Syria. Now, by virtue of a ruthless determination and a remarkable genius for military command, he quickly became the master of Languedoc. Raymond, under pressure of constant aggression, again broke with the church and was again excommunicated. By 1211 a fresh army was advancing to complete the conquest of the county when its defense was undertaken by Peter II, king of Aragon. Although he was a staunch Catholic, his orthodoxy did not prevent him from objecting to northern intervention in southern affairs.

The result was merely to assure the triumph of Simon de Montfort, who overwhelmed the allied forces at Muret in 1213. Peter was killed, his coalition was scattered, and Raymond was forced to make unconditional surrender to the pope. For some time Innocent had been trying to check the political ambitions of his crusaders. He had again asked the French king to take charge of the expedition; but Philip still held aloof, agreeing only to send Prince Louis into southern France for a brief visit. Now, after Muret, the only solution was to install Simon de Montfort as count of Toulouse; and when Raymond VI abdicated in favor of his son, the latter obtained a mere fragment of the original principality, hardly more than a small imperial fief to the east of the Rhone. This was the situation until Simon's death in 1218, when Raymond VII easily regained his patrimony. Simon's heir, finding himself powerless, resigned all claims into the hands of the king. Accordingly, just before Philip died in 1223, he had the satisfaction of seeing the whole Albigensian adventure turned to the enormous advantage of the monarchy.

Immediately on securing the crown, Louis VIII assumed command of **Louis VIII** a new crusade proclaimed by Pope Honorius III[5] to oust the restored **(1223-26)** count of Toulouse. The king drove an excellent bargain: at the expense of the church he could now conquer a very desirable province and keep it for himself. Besides, he had ecclesiastical authorization for encroaching on imperial territory beyond the Rhone. Proceeding down that river in 1226, Louis took Avignon by storm and made a triumphal progress through southern Languedoc, where he received the submission of Béziers,

[5] See below, p. 360.

Narbonne, Carcassonne, and other famous cities. Then, as Toulouse itself was about to fall, he was stricken by disease and died before he could return to his own country. How these events formed a prelude to the significant reign of Louis IX will be seen in the next chapter.

2. THE MENDICANT ORDERS AND THE INQUISITION

Francis of Assisi (d. 1226)

Between heresy and sainthood the gulf is normally thought of as wide and deep. Yet Peter Waldo and Francis of Assisi began their public careers in almost identical fashion. The boy whom his companions knew as Francesco apparently owed his name to the fact that his father was a cloth merchant constantly engaged in journeys to and from the great fairs of France. Thence, at any rate, came the romantic literature that was to have a continuing influence upon the life of the future saint. For many years, however, Francis was distinguished as a leader of fashion rather than of religion—a gilded youth of luxurious tastes and fastidious ways. Disliking his father's business, he became a soldier. He was captured during a local war and while in prison experienced a severe illness. Then, on his return home, a series of incidents revealed a change in his character. Instead of avoiding lepers, he gave them personal care. He renounced his wealth and dressed as a hermit. In the belief that, while praying, he had received a divine command to "repair my house, which is everywhere falling into ruins," he began, with a few other volunteers, to rebuild various ruined churches in the neighborhood of Assisi.

The friars and their mission

The true purport of the divine command did not become clear to Francis until he chanced to hear the reading of Christ's commission to the apostles:[6]

And as ye go, preach, saying The Kingdom of Heaven is at hand. Heal the sick, cleanse the lepers, raise the dead, cast out devils: freely ye have received, freely give. Provide neither gold nor silver nor brass in your purses, nor scrip for your journey, neither two coats nor yet staves: for the workman is worthy of his meat.

This message Francis took literally. Henceforth he devoted himself to absolute poverty, traveling barefoot from place to place and living by charity, while he preached the Gospel and ministered to the sick and needy. Soon he was joined by a small band of followers—the nucleus of what quickly became a world-wide organization, for the success of the movement was immediate. Especially in the towns, where the church had lamentably failed in its mission among the people, the Franciscans caused a sensation. Here were men who, by example as well as by words, revived the simple faith which Jesus had inspired in His disciples.

Francis called himself and his followers the Friars Minor, that is to say, the Lesser Brothers. It was indeed as a kindly brother that he treated all men, including the meanest outcasts of society. He loved the animals, the

[6] *Matthew*, x, 7-10.

birds, and the bees; he had a sympathetic tribute even for "brother worm." In nature, like the contemporary poets and sculptors, he found a keen delight; yet to Francis, as to Hugh of St. Victor, all created things served mainly to proclaim the glory of God. And in gratitude Francis wrote hymns of praise, employing not the language of formal worship but the Italian vernacular. One of these hymns, fortunately, has come down to us. In it he thanks the good Lord for brother sun, who lights the day; for sister moon and the stars, who shine at night; for brother wind and sister water and brother fire, so gay and strong; for mother earth, who sustains us by her fruits; and, lastly, for sister death. To say that Francis was the troubadour of Christianity is no mere figure of speech. He would sometimes, we are told, hold a stick over his left arm like a viol and, with another for a bow, pretend to play on it, all the while singing a joyous French song about the Lord.

This was the spirit of the Franciscan revival in the freshness of its youth and enthusiasm, and it brought to the masses a Christianity such as they never could have learned from a princely bishop or a monkish recluse. But how the new movement could be brought into harmony with the existing system of ecclesiastical government was a difficult problem. Happily for the church, it was at that moment headed by a great statesman. Innocent III, appreciating the opportunity that confronted him, was careful to guide, rather than to antagonize, the reforming energy of the friars. They at once received papal authorization to maintain their desired poverty, not merely as individuals but as a group, and to preach repentance. Besides, these new missionaries, having no fixed habitations, were removed from the territorial jurisdiction of ordinary bishops and placed under the direct authority of the pope—an innovation whose significance the saintly Francis, in all probability, never realized. Nor was he personally responsible for the elaborate constitution that now came to be drawn up for the Franciscan Order. Under papal control administrative provinces were created, with a hierarchy of officials extending upward to a minister general, elected by a great central chapter that met every three years. Within an amazingly short time the Franciscan organization had been extended throughout the Latin world. The friars proper were those men who had taken the prescribed vows after completing a year's novitiate. The Second Order included women who, following the example of a wealthy heiress named Clara, were authorized by the pope to live according to a modified Franciscan discipline. The Third Order, or Tertiaries, were laymen who, while pursuing ordinary occupations, were affiliated with the charitable and other activities of the friars. In spite of many troubles, some of which will be discussed below, all three orders have persisted down to the present.

Innocent III, in the meantime, had likewise blessed the Dominican organization. The man whose name was thus to be perpetuated was a

The Franciscan Order

Castilian, about a dozen years older than Francis of Assisi. While the latter was still a gay youth, Dominic completed a ten-year course in arts and theology. Having been drawn into controversy with the Albigensians of Toulouse, he became convinced that no headway would be made against them until their leaders were matched in zeal and austerity by Catholic missionaries. So, with a few companions, Dominic devoted himself to a life of poverty and preaching among the heretics. In 1215 his enterprise was sanctioned by the pope and shortly afterwards, as it came to be widely extended, the Dominicans adopted a constitution modeled after that of the Franciscans, but with a more fully developed system of representative government. The two bodies were also distinguished in other ways. The Dominicans, being by origin a learned order, frankly substituted intellectual pursuits for the manual labor of monastic tradition and gave more attention to foreign missions than to charitable work at home. Consequently, although there were Dominican nuns and even Dominican tertiaries, enrollment in these groups was relatively slight.

By the middle of the thirteenth century noteworthy success had thus been won by two great orders of mendicants (literally beggars): the Franciscans or Friars Minor, popularly called the Gray Friars, and the Dominicans or Friars Preachers, popularly called the Black Friars. Practical necessity, it is true, had already produced a modification of their primitive discipline. Houses and churches, which could not be owned by the friars, were readily provided for their use by wealthy patrons. Local groups even came, through trusteeships or other legal devices, to enjoy the revenues from permanent endowments and so to be actually far removed from apostolic poverty. Nevertheless, the work of the friars continued to be primarily in the world; they were not bound to remain within monastic walls, nor within a single district except as ordered by their superiors. Through papal authorization they gained the power not only of preaching but also of hearing confessions and granting absolution. And despite the complaints of the parish clergy, the friars proved so popular that their influence steadily increased for many years. The papacy had good reason to encourage the mendicant orders; for it thereby obtained an army of preachers, scholars, and charitable workers who, among them, solved the greatest problems confronting the church. Thanks mainly to the Franciscans, the spiritual needs of the masses could be better satisfied. Thanks mainly to the Dominicans, heretics could be more effectively refuted and the new learning of the schools brought into agreement with the traditional ideals of Christian education.

The friars' contributions to scholarship will be described in the following section; here it will be convenient to see how they were associated with the beginnings of the Inquisition. At the time of Innocent III there was, of course, no thought of tolerating heresy, which had been a crime at civil law for over eight hundred years.[7] But the Christian states of the west had never agreed on a suitable penalty and the church itself could inflict no punishment involving death or mutilation. Prosecution for heresy was still governed by the ordinary rules of the canon law: trials to be held in open court, the defendant to be confronted by his accusers, only certain kinds of evidence to be admitted, and the like. Such procedure, though adequate when heretics were almost unheard of, completely broke down when they filled the countryside. Accordingly it was decreed by various ecclesiastical asemblies, including the Lateran Council of 1215, that the bishops, through their own efforts and through the appointment of special investigators, should strive to detect all persons suspected of heresy and bring them to justice. At the same time civil governments were induced to stiffen their laws in defense of the orthodox faith. Innocent III pointed out that heresy was really treason to God, implying that so hideous a crime deserved a worse punishment than the betrayal of a temporal prince. As a consequence, death by burning came to be prescribed for heretics in most states before the end of the thirteenth century.

Meanwhile the popes had developed special tribunals to complete the work of the Albigensian Crusade. In this connection, Dominicans had already been employed as agents and investigators under the local bishops. Then, in 1233, Gregory IX[8] gave the friars independent authority to hear and determine cases of heresy in southern France, with the right to call upon the bishops for all necessary co-operation. Thus inaugurated, the system was rapidly extended until nearly all regions of Latin Christendom were allotted to one or the other of the mendicant orders as the judicial agents of the Roman see. The new papal courts were entirely removed from the restrictions of the canon law. Their procedure was inquisitorial in that the judges themselves sought out and prosecuted suspects. Trials were held in secret. The defendant was not faced by his accusers and was not permitted to have an advocate. In theory, torture could only be applied once and any confession thereby obtained had to be verified by the accused while under no compulsion. In practice, the inquisitors eventually set the law at naught by "continuing" the first torture until the desired confession was secured. For incurring suspicion of heresy, or for in any way aiding heretics, various degrees of penance were imposed. The heretic who confessed and recanted might be subjected at most to imprisonment for life. On the contrary, one who remained obdurate, or who relapsed into his previous error, was "relinquished to the secular arm" for punishment under the civil law. And although this was done with the request that he escape "the effusion of blood and the peril of death," everybody expected the normal penalty of burning to be carried out.

The Papal Inquisition

[7] See above, pp. 62-63.
[8] See above, pp. 85-86.

In extenuation of such practices it can at least be said that the primary object of the inquisitors was to win converts rather than to produce victims and that, until the later years of the mediæval period, judicial persecution was only occasional. Furthermore, the church ought not to be blamed for the faults of the entire age. All criminals then received what we should regard as inhuman treatment. Secular princes were no more tolerant than the clergy, while armies and mobs proved that they were even less merciful than the law.

3. The Progress of Scholasticism

Thir-teenth-century education

Scholasticism is now likely to be regarded as devoid of practical sense— an intricate and obscure quibbling over matters of no importance. Yet the proper meaning of the term is merely the educational system of the mediæval schools, and that was not sheer foolishness. In the thirteenth century, at any rate, the universities were extremely vigorous institutions that had recently developed in response to professional needs for advanced instruction. The subjects which thus came to be taught were principally logic, mathematics, Aristotelian philosophy and science, medicine, Roman law, canon law, and theology. This, compared with anything that had ever been offered in the earlier Latin schools, was an impressive curriculum. The works on which it was based, though many of them were translations from Greek or Arabic, were the best that the age afforded. And the scholastic method, with its emphasis on argumentation in the classroom, demanded analytical thought—an intellectual discipline that one may hope will never be outmoded. Thirteenth-century education, of course, had its shortcomings. On the one hand it tended to neglect the study of literature as a form of artistic expression or as a means of understanding the historic past; on the other hand it underestimated the importance of contemporary developments in non-academic fields and the necessity of using fresh human experience to correct the time-honored statements of classic authors.

Leonard of Pisa

Nevertheless, when we consider the enormous mass of the learning that had suddenly been made available to Latin scholars, we may readily understand why their primary task was assimilation of the old, rather than discovery of the new. Besides, it is now coming to be realized that in many respects they were by no means satisfied with traditional lore; that the thirteenth century witnessed a good deal of original research and experimentation. Leonard of Pisa, for instance, has been hailed by all subsequent generations as a great innovator in mathematical science. His *Book of the Abacus* and his essay *On the Practice of Geometry* (1202-30) not only combined the results of his Arabic and Latin predecessors but added many contributions of his own: including a remarkably complete exposition of practical arithmetic, new solutions for various trigonometrical problems, and a thorough description of quadratic and other algebraic equations.

Logic was then, as it remained until very recent times, essentially Aristotelian. Roman law, though primarily derived from Justinian's *Corpus*, was progressively developed to meet the demands of contemporary Europe; and canon law, as will be noted below, was enormously extended by the thirteenth-century popes. With regard to medicine our information remains unsatisfactory. It is certainly a mistake to suppose that dissection was prohibited to all physicians of that age; for most of them, being laymen, were not bound by the canonical injunction against the shedding of blood. If we were better informed concerning their practice, we should probably find that it anticipated much that has been attributed to later times. The other subjects of instruction can be more adequately discussed in connection with the writings of the friars.

In all university centers the Dominicans, as a matter of supreme interest to their order, maintained houses with resident masters, to whom the best of the pupils educated in their local schools were sent for advanced training. And the Franciscans, despite their founder's deprecation of book-learning, followed suit; so that, by the second half of the thirteenth century, they had enrolled a number of distinguished men both at Paris and at Oxford. This invasion of the universities by the mendicants had important results. Eventually, as we have seen, it led to the establishment of residential colleges for the benefit of secular scholars. Furthermore, the resistance of the Parisian faculties to foreign domination—whether by the religious orders or by the papacy—helped to bring about their close union and assure their rights of self-government. From the standpoint of the universal church, however, the all-important result was the work now undertaken by the friars to determine the standards of orthodox scholarship. Earlier popes, perceiving especial danger in Aristotle's philosophy and the Arabic commentaries upon it, had tried to exclude the obnoxious books from the curriculum. But as students everywhere insisted on reading the whole of Aristotle, later popes adopted the wise policy of encouraging its reconciliation with Christian dogma—a task for which the Dominicans, and to a lesser degree the Franciscans, were admirably fitted.

The first of the Parisian masters to attempt a *summa* (i.e., a compendium of knowledge) was the English Franciscan, Alexander of Hales (d. 1245). His effort was continued by the French Dominican, Vincent of Beauvais, who produced an enormous book of 9885 chapters called *Speculum Maius* (The Greater Mirror). In its three parts—the mirrors of nature, of doctrine, and of history—it covers the whole expanse of contemporary study, but is more remarkable for its comprehensive plan than for the quality of its thought. As a philosopher and as a scientist, Vincent was far surpassed by Albertus Magnus (Albert the Great). The latter was by origin a Suabian, who joined the Dominican Order at an early age, rose to be a teacher in various German schools, received his doctorate at Paris, and,

The Summists: Albertus Magnus

after a distinguished career there and elsewhere, died in 1280. Albert was the most learned man of his generation. His monumental books—thirty-eight quarto volumes in the last printed edition—deal with virtually all the subjects then taught in the universities, with noteworthy sections devoted to science and Aristotelian philosophy interpreted in the light of Christianity.

His interest in natural science

Albert's acceptance as an orthodox theologian is sufficiently attested by his enrollment among the saints of the church. Should it be considered remarkable that he was also an outstanding biologist for his age? Merely to repeat the titles of Albert's volumes is to prove him a disciple of Aristotle, and the substance of his chapters reveals the same influence even more clearly. Yet Albert was no mere copyist or commentator. Time and again he presents the opinion of Aristotle only to remark that it does not agree with what he has himself observed. Although in the course of his ambitious works Albert repeats a good deal of traditional nonsense, his customary attitude is by no means one of credulity. Compared with Isidore of Seville, the great master of the Carolingian schools, he is a very radical critic. Particularly refreshing are his remarks about the fauna of his native land: such as his descriptions of bees, ants, and spiders; his careful lists of birds, interspersed with refutations of the popular story-tellers; his acute remarks concerning whales, fish, eels, and turtles; and his catalogue of four-footed beasts, many of them unnoticed by Aristotle.

To cite a well-known example, here is what Albert says about shepherd dogs:[9]

The dogs . . . that follow sheep for the sake of guarding them differ in size, but all are habitually trained to run down wolves. The female, especially, is distinguished in this chase. I have seen one of them teach her young to pursue a wolf by running ahead of them to incite them on their course. When the wolf threatened to escape, she would hold it until the young dogs had caught up; then she would let it go again. And if the wolf bit the young dogs, she would not immediately come to their aid; for she wanted them to be provoked against the wolf. These dogs vary in size, some being very large, bigger and stronger than wolves, and some being smaller. All belonging to this breed, however, are larger and fiercer than other dogs.

Thomas Aquinas

To many it has seemed that Albert's most significant work was, after all, the training of his famous pupil, Thomas Aquinas. Thomas owed his surname to the fact that he was born near the Italian town of Aquino, being the son of the local count. He was apparently a precocious youth; for he was still in his teens when, after spending six years at the university of Naples, he entered the Dominican Order. Thereupon, as a promising theologian, he was sent to study under the illustrious Albert, first at Cologne and then at Paris. Even before he acquired the doctorate in 1257, Thomas

[9] *De Animalibus,* bk. viii, tract. i, ch. i.

had won renown in teaching and writing; and to these pursuits he devoted the rest of his brief life, dying prematurely in 1274. Although Thomas fully shared his master's enthusiasm for Aristotle, he was somewhat less of a scientist and somewhat more of a theologian. His *Summa Theologiæ*, whether or not we agree with his conclusions, must be recognized as an intellectual achievement of the first magnitude. The author's purpose is to expound and reconcile the truths of reason and the truths of revelation. The latter he finds in the authoritative precepts of the church; the former he accepts as best set forth in the philosophy of Aristotle. The two must agree, for truth is truth; we cannot hold one conviction on rationalist principles and the opposite on faith. Indeed, as long as the believer in traditional Christianity is unwilling to abandon all reliance on reason, he must arrive at some such compromise as that of the sainted Dominican.

Here, of course, it is quite impossible to sketch Thomas's theological system either in whole or in part. Some attempt may be made, however, to illustrate the scholastic method as he employed it—to show that to one generally familiar with the subject-matter his reasoning, like that of Peter Lombard, is simple and straightforward. After discussing God and the Creation, his *Summa* takes up the character of the divine government and under it the capacities of the angels, good and bad. Question 114 deals with the assaults of the demons and is subdivided into five points of inquiry, of which the fourth considers whether, to lead men astray, demons can work real miracles. In support of the negative Thomas states three objections, quoting the New Testament and St. Augustine; but to each of the three he appends a reply based on other citations of the same authorities. His conclusion is that,[10]

His views on miracles and magic

if we take a miracle in the strict sense, the demons cannot work miracles nor can any creature, but God alone: since in the strict sense a miracle is something done outside the order of the entire created nature, under which every power of a creature is contained. But sometimes a miracle may be taken in a wide sense, for whatever exceeds the human power and experience. And thus demons can work miracles, that is, things which rouse man's astonishment, by reason of their being beyond his power and outside his sphere of knowledge.

In this connection, remarks Thomas, it should be noted that, although the marvelous works of demons are not true miracles, they may be very real—as when Pharaoh's magicians, through diabolic agency, produced actual frogs and serpents.[11] This they were able to do because, within nature, frogs and serpents are sometimes brought forth by putrefying matter.[12] Yet Satan himself is powerless to change the natural order; he

[10] The translation is that by the Fathers of the English Dominican Diocese (London, 1922).

[11] *Exodus,* vii-viii.

[12] Belief in the spontaneous generation of worms and other forms of life was common even among educated men until the nineteenth century.

cannot, like God, transform a man into a beast or restore the dead to life. "If at times something of this sort seems to be effected by the operation of demons, it is not real but a mere semblance of reality." For demons are clever deceivers. They can either, by influencing a man's faculties, make him imagine he sees what he really does not see or, by forming shapes out of air,[13] therein clothe themselves, as well as corporeal things, and thus impose upon the human senses. Such opinions, as will be seen below, are of fundamental importance for anyone who tries to understand the witch-craft delusion of the later Middle Ages.

Robert Grosse-teste Since the triumph of Thomas Aquinas in the field of academic instruction was also a triumph for the papacy, it is not surprising that his *Summa* has now been officially recognized as the basis of theological education in all Roman Catholic schools. Yet there was no unanimity with regard to his doctrine in the Middle Ages. At Paris, the increasing power of the Dominicans was bitterly opposed by the other masters, who in this respect were quite as willing to quarrel with a pope as with anybody else. And the anti-Dominican cause obtained vigorous support from the Franciscans of Oxford. Inasmuch as the Dominican doctors became ardent Aristotelians, the Franciscan doctors eloquently defended the Platonic traditions of St. Augustine. The more radical of the Oxonians might even accuse the Parisians of neglecting important sciences for the sake of fruitless argumentation. At one time the justification of such an opinion was exclusively attributed to Roger Bacon. Now it is beginning to be understood that for his major ideas Bacon was indebted to his master Robert Grosseteste, an Englishman of low birth who rose through sheer ability to be chief lecturer to the Franciscans of Oxford, chancellor of the university, and finally bishop of Lincoln (1235-53).

Although Grosseteste thus became a prominent ecclesiastic, immersed in episcopal administration and deeply involved in English politics, he continued to devote much of his time to scholarship. A recent and dependable bibliography of his writings lists forty-four philosophical and scientific works, thirty-two religious essays of one sort or another, seventeen commentaries (chiefly on the Bible or on Aristotle), fourteen translations from the Greek, and various other books, including some remarkable allegories in Norman-French. Grosseteste, obviously, was not only a prolific but also a versatile author. His thorough knowledge of Greek was in itself no mean accomplishment for the thirteenth century, and it enabled him to offer sound criticism of many translations then in use. Equally impressive was Grosseteste's familiarity with Arabic science, in so far as it had then been made available in Latin. Among his own scientific writings are note-worthy treatises on mathematics, astronomy, chronology, and optics. His discussion of this last subject, to be sure, is largely based on Alhazen

[13] I.e., vapor, which is known sometimes to assume the form of an apparition.

(al-Haytham).[14] Yet, after repeating well-known facts about mirrors, he adds some interesting remarks about the new perspective glasses, which "make large objects that are near seem tiny and . . . make distant objects appear as large as we choose, so that it is possible to read the smallest letters at an incredible distance, or to count sand or grain or grass or any other minute objects."[15] From these and other statements it would appear that Grosseteste had himself experimented with lenses—a conclusion that is rendered the more probable by the fact that spectacles were certainly in use before the end of the same century.

It was these accomplishments and predilections that Robert Grosseteste passed on to his pupil, Roger Bacon, whose alleged martyrdom for the cause of science has brought him posthumous fame in the modern world. The known facts about Bacon are far less romantic. He, like his master, was an Englishman of obscure origin who came to Oxford in pursuit of education in the liberal arts. Having completed the required studies, he attained a mastership at Paris, where for a time he taught the ordinary subjects in the ordinary way. Later, about the middle of the thirteenth century, he seems to have become disgusted with what he was doing and, in order to gain leisure for original investigation and for learning the necessary languages, joined the Oxford Franciscans. With them, so far as we know, he spent the rest of his life, writing the books on which his reputation has since depended. There is no reason for supposing that he was ever persecuted on account of devotion to research. The story that he was condemned by the Franciscan order for teaching "suspected novelties" is derived from an inferior chronicle of the next century. Taken at its face value, the entry could hardly have referred to anything but theological irregularities, which are not to be found in any of Bacon's extant works; and there is not the slightest evidence that he was actually imprisoned. So why should we, with various imaginative authors, presume that he was compelled to hide his discoveries in the natural sciences by means of a cipher?

Roger Bacon

Bacon's most famous book was written in response to an urgent request from the pope himself. Clement IV,[16] before acceding to the papal throne, had spent some time in England and had there heard that Bacon was completing a great work on philosophy. This, in 1266, the pope asked the presumptive author to send to him. Bacon's *summa*, however, was still in the theoretical stage; so the best he could do was to furnish a prospectus, his *Opus Maius*, together with elaborate excuses for his failure to carry out his principal undertaking. Later he composed two supplements of the

His Opus Maius

[14] See above, p. 171.
[15] Translation adapted from L. Thorndike, *A History of Magic and Experimental Science*, II (New York, 1923), 441.
[16] See below, p. 371.

same kind; but the *summa* itself never appeared. Since Clement died in 1268, it remains doubtful whether he ever saw Bacon's efforts. The pope, in any case, could scarcely have ranked the English Franciscan with the great Dominican encyclopædists of Paris. To understand the *Opus Maius*, accordingly, we must take into account the circumstances that produced it. However interesting, it was merely the sketch of a *summa* that remained unwritten—a strongly partisan document in which Bacon consistently minimized the accomplishments of other scholars in order to glorify his own. When it is read in actual comparison with contemporary works, much of its alleged originality tends to vanish.

On the whole, Bacon's plan for the improvement of education was not revolutionary. Nor did he intend it to be; his object was merely to emphasize what he described as badly neglected fields. In his eyes the crown of all human learning continued to be theology, and he offered no objection either to the accepted principles of that subject or to the way in which it was then taught. Aristotle he revered as the greatest of philosophers, whose work constituted the basis of rational understanding. But Latin scholars, said Bacon, should not depend on corrupt translations of the original; they should learn Greek. To further this end he composed a Greek grammar and, for the advancement of biblical study, at least contemplated a similar work on Hebrew. While the Latins' ignorance of languages had caused them to suffer a great loss, Bacon added, their neglect of mathematics had been fatal to their pursuit of other sciences for which it constituted a prerequisite. Most students, furthermore, knew absolutely nothing about experimental science, without which reasoning was inconclusive. Such criticism, when divorced from its context, sounds better to a modern scientist than it really was. Anyone who reads the whole of the *Opus Maius* will realize that Bacon's language cannot bear the interpretation that has often been placed upon it.

Bacon's experimental science Mathematics Bacon considers the key not only to "natural" but also to "divine" philosophy; so with physics, optics, music, geography, and astronomy he combines the significance of mystic numbers for the elucidation of Scripture, and much else of the same sort. By "experimental science" Bacon seems first to mean knowledge based on "experience," then knowledge based on "experiment." Experience, he says, is of two kinds: that gained through the senses and that gained through the inner faculties by divine inspiration. To illustrate experiment, he begins with a lengthy discussion of the rainbow, largely derived from Grosseteste. Next he takes up the problem of how to prolong life, adding to good advice regarding diet and the care of the body the recommendation of an elixir compounded of gold, pearl, flower of sea-dew, ambergris, aloes, bone from a stag's heart, Tyrian snake, and Ethiopian dragon. Lastly—and this is his most interesting observation—he describes various marvels of what we should call applied science: explosives, magnets, burning-glasses, military engines, and the like. In the same connection, though in another work, Bacon gives his famous tribute to Pierre de Maricourt:[17]

He knows by experiment natural history, and physic and alchemy, and all things in the heavens and beneath them: indeed, he is shamed if any layman, or grandam, or soldier, or country bumpkin knows anything that he himself does not know. Wherefore he has inquired into all operations of metal-founding, and the working of gold and silver and other metals, and of all minerals; and he knows all things pertaining to the army and to arms and the chase; and he has examined all that relates to agriculture, the measurement of land, and earth-works; and he has even studied the experiments, devices, and incantations of witches and magicians, and likewise the illusions and tricks of all jugglers; so that nothing is hidden from him which he ought to know, and he knows how to reprobate all things false and magical.

Bacon himself was hardly more than a theorist. He had no profound knowledge of mathematics; and if he was familiar with the excellent work of such men as Leonard of Pisa, he gave no indication of the fact. He was manifestly unfair to Albertus Magnus, who was his superior in various fields, particularly in biology. From Grosseteste, the Arabic writers, and other sources Bacon had learned a good deal about mirrors, lenses, fire-works, and machines of one sort or another. There is, however, no evidence that he ever constructed a telescope, a compound microscope, or a gun. And his description of engines which he has seen or heard of are too vague to be of any great worth—like his reports concerning the mysteries of alchemy and astrology. Bacon, in other words, was not so different from his contemporaries as he tried to make out. In some respects he was less original than the scholars whom he criticized. From the modern point of view the most remarkable feature of his work was his appreciation of non-academic learning, especially the technical skill of engineers, architects, and craftsmen. Wonderfully enough, as Bacon seems to have realized, they were advancing in a new direction—one that, as will be more fully shown below, led straight to the scientific technology of today.

[17] See above, pp. 306-08. The following translation is from the essay of S. P. Thompson in the *Proceedings of the British Academy,* 1905-06, p. 380.

CHAPTER XX

Church and State After Innocent III

1. FREDERICK II

Relations
with the
papacy
The son of Henry VI was unquestionably a Hohenstaufen; yet few
mediæval kings were less German than Frederick II. He and his reign
are to be explained rather by the fact that, as the grandson of Roger II,
he fell heir to the Sicilian kingdom, and with it to the tastes and talents
of the Hauteville dynasty. Left an orphan at the age of four, Frederick was
brought up in his native land of Sicily under the wardship of Innocent III.
He never saw Germany until 1211, when he was elected king in opposition
to Otto IV. By that time he had been declared of age, had been married to
Constance of Aragon, and by her had a son, Henry (see Table VI). During his youth he had played a cautious game, remaining in all ways submissive to his papal guardian; but this docile exterior had come to conceal
a fully matured character. At eighteen Frederick II was a statesman who
had already determined his policies, a many-sided genius who was soon
to astonish the world.

To secure Innocent's support in Germany, Frederick had formally
repeated the broken promises of Otto and had sworn that, as soon as he
obtained the imperial crown, he would confer upon his infant son the
sovereignty of Sicily, to be held under papal wardship. Later, on Innocent's proclamation of a new and greater crusade, Frederick had taken the
cross. But in 1216 Innocent was succeeded by Honorius III, an elderly
and benevolent cleric who, though a good administrator, lacked all cleverness as a politician. Frederick, taking advantage of the favorable situation,
now postponed his crusade and, through grant of extraordinary privileges,
induced the German magnates to accept Prince Henry as king. By thus
abandoning Germany in order to concentrate attention upon Italy,
Frederick reversed the policy to which he had been solemnly pledged. In

1220, nevertheless, the amiable Honorius crowned him emperor, and it soon became apparent that the coronation had confronted the papacy with a very real danger. Frederick II's design was no such dream of Roman imperialism as had dazzled his predecessors. To create an actual kingdom of Italy, he had only to annex a few northern provinces to the magnificent state inherited from Roger II. Within six years, thanks to the pope's enthusiasm for the future crusade, the emperor was beginning to assert effective authority throughout the peninsula.

The first challenge to Frederick's ambition came with the installation of a new pope in 1227. Gregory IX was not only an eminent student of canon law but also a fiery champion of the papal tradition. Ecclesiastical penalties, he declared, would at once be imposed if the promised crusade were further postponed. Frederick, as it happened, now had a personal interest in the project, for he had recently taken as his second wife the heiress of the kingdom of Jerusalem. After he had actually embarked, however, he came down with a disease then prevalent among his troops and was forced to return for medical treatment. Thereupon he was promptly excommunicated by the pope and, remaining unrepentant, was still under the ban of the church when he again sailed for Palestine in 1228. On his arrival, Frederick continued his unorthodox behavior. Making skillful use of local jealousies among the descendants of Saladin, he secured by treaty what had been the despair of all Latin hosts for the past forty years. The Christians received possession of Jerusalem, as well as a strip of territory connecting it with Acre, merely in return for a guarantee that resident Moslems could freely worship in their two great mosques. Within a year after leaving Italy Frederick victoriously entered the Holy City and there assumed the royal crown—a remarkable crusade, which triumphed in the face of papal excommunication, and without a battle. *Frederick's crusade (1228-29)*

The success of Frederick's expedition failed to abate Gregory's hostility. While Christian rule was being restored at Jerusalem, the pope was absolving the emperor's subjects from their oaths of fealty and calling upon the faithful to invade and conquer the imperial dominions. It was not until 1230 that Frederick obtained absolution after agreeing to rather severe terms. The peace, though hailed as a great ecclesiastical victory, was only the prelude to another extension of Frederick's power. With his crusade officially blessed, the emperor now resumed his European projects where they had been dropped three years before. At this time, for example, he published the famous decrees that made his Sicilian kingdom into a sort of enlightened despotism. An insurrection in Germany caused him only momentary embarrassment; a graver threat was the revival of the Lombard League by the communes of northern Italy. But Frederick II was more fortunate than his grandfather Barbarossa had been. In 1237 it was the communal army that went down to crushing defeat at Cortenuova. The *Italian activities* inevitable result was a fresh crisis with the papacy. An exchange of violent recriminations was followed by open war, in which Gregory allied with the defeated league, and Frederick began the systematic reduction of the Papal States. The death of the pope brought no more than a lull in hostilities; for his successor, Innocent IV, renewed the conflict after a few years of apparent reconciliation. Finally, in the midst of further conspiracies and revolts, the great emperor suddenly died (1250).

Legisla-
tion and
tolera-
tion

Frederick's hope of creating an Italian kingdom thus remained unfulfilled; yet his reign should not, on that account, be considered a failure. Quite apart from his imperial ambitions, his achievements as king of Sicily were sufficient to rank him among the world's greatest statesmen. While Gregory IX was formulating the first official code of canon law, Frederick issued his famous *Liber Augustalis*, the finest secular code since the time of Justinian. It included 217 separate constitutions arranged in three books, to which a supplement of *novellæ* was eventually added. As a whole, the work was of course inspired by Roman example; much of it, in fact, was actually produced by the "civilians" of the royal court, notably Piero della Vigna. It was not, however, an academic disquisition, for its substance was drawn from the legislation of Frederick's Norman predecessors. He had merely to systematize practices that were already a century old and to define them in the formal language of jurisprudence. If he ruled Sicily as a despot, it was by virtue of the actual authority that he inherited, not because he was able to quote the *Digest*.

For every major feature of Frederick's government precedents had existed under Roger II[1]—for his administrative system, combining feudal tenures with institutions learned from the Greeks and the Arabs; for his monopoly of warfare and military fortification; for his method of detecting and trying criminals; even for his very effective diplomacy. Frederick's religious policy is especially interesting in the same connection. Like the earlier kings of Sicily, he encouraged Christians and non-Christians to live together in peace and harmony; but it would be a mistake to think that he therefore believed in religious toleration on principle. The Jews and the Moslems constituted national units within the state, each marked by a distinctive garb and assigned to a particular territory. Although anybody in either of these two groups could lawfully be converted to Christianity, the Christian had no choice. He had to remain scrupulously loyal to the church; if he did not, he was burned as a heretic. In this respect Frederick set a cruel example to the princes of Europe. The limited freedom of worship permitted under his régime resulted from practical necessity, not from beneficent theory.

It was, perhaps, in the economic sphere that the pre-eminence of Frederick's administration was most clearly marked—a feature that resulted from

[1] See above, pp. 322-24.

the emperor's use of Moslem precedents. As part of the governmental **Economic** reform which he carried out after 1220, he abolished all internal tolls **adminis-** throughout his hereditary kingdom and substituted a tariff[2] levied only on **tration** the frontiers of the state. There he established royal warehouses, to which both importers and exporters had to bring their goods; and there the king's tax had to be paid before anything could be transhipped or resold. By this system of customs duties, known as the *doana*,[3] Frederick not only secured a handsome revenue but also facilitated the laying of an embargo on whatever he pleased. This might be for the sake of war, of diplomatic advantage, or of private gain; for, besides being the greatest landed proprietor of the country, he was a keen business man, always willing to make a good profit by turning to advantage his public authority.

Frederick showed his understanding of economic questions in many other ways. He instituted a series of monthly fairs, each held in a different region. He negotiated commercial treaties with the Moslem princes of the African coast. He maintained state monopolies in salt, iron, tar, hemp, and silk, assuring his control of important industries and notably adding to his income. By experimentation on his own estates and by offering special inducements of various sorts, he sought to improve agriculture and the breeding of domestic animals. He was particularly active in introducing the date palm, indigo, sugar cane, cotton, and other oriental plants. His minting of gold *augustales* in 1231 set a useful example for the Italian republics.[4] He encouraged immigration, colonized waste lands, and founded a number of new towns. He was the first prince of Europe to call representatives of the bourgeoisie to meet with the barons and other important persons in his great central courts.[5]

Like his Norman predecessors, Frederick lived in a semi-oriental mag- **Personal** nificence that astonished and somewhat shocked his western contempo- **habits** raries. It was said that, after the fashion of a Moslem sultan, he maintained an extensive harem. The story, as repeated by Gregory IX, was undoubtedly exaggerated, though in such matters Frederick was quite frankly a libertine. Another accusation, that he bathed on Sunday, seems to have been well founded! Nor could it be denied that he treated Moslems with great consideration, both inside his dominions and elsewhere—which was one of the points emphasized by Gregory IX in condemning his crusade. Besides, Frederick was alleged to have made all sorts of scandalous remarks. The pope roundly charged him with being at heart a pagan, who feigned orthodoxy for political effect. It would indeed appear that, in spite of the emperor's stringent laws against heretics, these rumors had some basis in

[2] From the Arabic *tarif*.
[3] From the Arabic *diwan;* cf. the French *douane*.
[4] See below, p. 434.
[5] See below, pp. 383-84.

fact. Frederick was not a man of childlike faith. From his own writings, as well as from the testimony of his friends, we gain the distinct impression that he was an intellectual with an absorbing interest in the problems of philosophy and science.

One of the most famous sights in the Sicilian kingdom was the emperor's menagerie, which always accompanied his formal journeys from place to place. On such occasions the people crowded to see a collection of birds and beasts from distant lands: ostriches, parrots, monkeys, leopards, panthers, lions, camels, a giraffe, and lastly a great elephant bearing a howdah filled with Moslem troops. Before these wonders even visiting statesmen were awestruck. But Frederick's motive in keeping his menagerie was not simply to advertise his magnificence; he was sincerely interested in biology. The proof is to be seen in his book *On the Art of Hunting With Birds*.[6] He presents as certain only what he has learned by observation; for previous writings on the subject, he declares, are unreliable. Even Aristotle repeated too much hearsay. Frederick's book is in truth a marvel of accuracy and completeness. He does not restrict his attention to hawks, falcons, eagles, and other hunting birds, but precedes his more technical essay with a general sketch of ornithology; and from time to time he inserts information about animals, plants, geography, and much else. The original work, as well as a copy owned by Manfred, was profusely illustrated with pictures of birds, skillfully drawn and colored from life by artists under the emperor's personal direction.

Among the many experiments which Frederick reports, two may be briefly stated. Having heard that in Norway certain geese were alleged to be hatched from barnacles, he sent there for some of the latter, but found that they would not produce geese. So he concluded that the legend arose because men had failed to discover where the geese nested. He also tells that, wishing to learn how vultures detected the presence of food, he took such birds and covered their eyes. And since, under these conditions, they failed to notice meat placed close by, he decided that their acuteness was not in their sense of smell. Many other stories are told about this remarkable author-emperor, and some of them sound quite like him—such as the tale of his bringing up babies in silence, to determine what if any language they would naturally speak.[7] That experiment failed, we are told, because the children did not survive it. Another habit that made the emperor's curiosity a byword was his addressing of questionnaires to learned men in all countries. We hear, for example, that to certain Egyptian scholars he gave these among other problems: why an object appears bent

[6] The emperor's work antedated the *De Animalibus* of Albertus Magnus, where it is cited as authoritative (see above, pp. 353-54).

[7] If, as was commonly believed, Adam had been created with the ability to speak Hebrew, would not that ability be inherited by his descendants? Cf. Dante, below, pp. 394-95.

when plunged in water, why a star looks bigger when it is near the horizon, and what produces the semblance of spots before the eyes.

A similar list of Frederick's queries—concerning earth, heaven, hell, purgatory, the nature of the soul, salt and fresh water, hot springs, volcanoes, and winds—is reported by Michael Scot. The latter, a distinguished student of Aristotelian and Arabic science, served the imperial government as a sort of philosophic expert. He was even supposed to apply his knowledge of the stars to matters of state; for Frederick, like all princes of that day and of many days to come, was a firm believer in astrology. Connected in one way or another with the Sicilian court were many other scholars: Moslems and Jews as well as Christians. Leonard of Pisa,[8] though not a resident of Frederick's kingdom, enjoyed his friendship and dedicated to him the *Liber Abaci*. So far as academic education was concerned, the emperor recognized its importance but characteristically sought to make it a branch of his government. The University of Salerno, already in decline, became a mere department of state for the training of licensed physicians. And the University of Naples, Frederick's own foundation, was from the outset an official school whose chief purpose was to produce lawyers for the royal administration.

Patronage of scholarship and literature

Piero della Vigna has already been mentioned in connection with the *Liber Augustalis*. He was renowned both as a jurist and as a rhetorician, being considered the foremost stylist of the thirteenth century. What Michael Scot was to the scientific group at the imperial court Piero was to the men of letters. Frederick himself was no mean linguist; for, in addition to the vernaculars of Italy, France, and Germany, he knew Latin, Greek, and Arabic. His learned essay on birds was of course written in the language of the schools; but he also, troubadour-fashion, composed lyric verse. And although in most regions of the peninsula Provençal remained conventional for all romantic poetry, the king, Piero della Vigna, and their fellows preferred to use the Sicilian dialect. As Dante was soon to proclaim, Italian literature owed much to the patronage and leadership of Frederick II. Truly he earned the description of *stupor mundi*, "the amazement of the world."

2. FRANCE AND WESTERN EUROPE

Like the Norman conquest of England, the Capetian conquest of Normandy marked a significant turning-point in the history of the western monarchies. So far as England was concerned, John's defeat, though long considered a shame and a disgrace, eventually proved to be a distinct benefit. The island kingdom, instead of being merely the outlying possession of a continental prince, became a state regarded for its own sake. Norman barons, who hitherto had held lands on both sides of the Channel, now had

Results of John's loss of Normandy

[8] See above, pp. 352-53.

to choose which they would be, English vassals or French vassals. The Angevin house, to be sure, kept southern Aquitaine; but that land had always seemed foreign to the men of the north. The first step in the direction of an English nationality had perforce been taken. So far as France was concerned, Philip Augustus was now able to revolutionize the political situation. The king became actual ruler of his kingdom, many times more powerful than any one of his remaining vassals. As his domain was extended to include Picardy, Normandy, Anjou, Poitou, and Auvergne, he greatly improved the royal administrative system by adapting institutions already established in the annexed territories. And the heightened prestige of the Capetians throughout Europe was strikingly shown by a series of great events during the next hundred years. It is these developments that constitute the central theme of the present discussion.

Louis IX (1226-70)   The brief reign of Philip's son, Louis VIII, was remarkable only for the royal intervention in the Albigensian Crusade. As noted in the preceding chapter, Louis had invaded and in part conquered the county of Toulouse when he fell a victim to disease in 1226. It was fortunate that his widow, the able Blanche of Castile, was now proclaimed regent for her infant son Louis IX. She promptly defeated the hostile moves of various ambitious barons and extorted an advantageous treaty from Raymond of Toulouse. That portion of the county which had already been taken was to remain in the king's hands; the rest should pass with the hand of Raymond's daughter to one of the king's brothers. Accordingly, when Louis IX assumed control of the government, Capetian rule had actually been extended to the shore of the Mediterranean (see Map XIII). By this time, too, the great Angevin principality had been reduced to a mere fragment of the old Aquitaine, popularly called Guienne. Although Burgundy and Brittany remained virtually independent, neither was at all formidable. Flanders, since Baldwin IX had secured the crown of the Latin Empire,[9] had rapidly come under the dominance of the French court and was now on the verge of a paralyzing civil war. Blois and Champagne, once again separated, were held by peace-loving vassals. As the future was to show, the greater peril to the monarchy lay in the new practice of conferring feudal estates, or appanages, on members of the royal house (see Table II).

Being delivered from the necessity of constant war against jealous princes, Louis IX could devote his energies to whatever projects lay near his heart. It was thus possible for him to be a successful king of France and at the same time to lead a saintly life; for he was canonized by the church in 1297. As between these two phases of his career, it was of course the latter that especially impressed his contemporaries and inspired the justly famous memoirs of Jean, sire de Joinville. He, like Villehardouin, was a prominent nobleman of Champagne. He was never, he tells us, the

[9] See above, p. 341.

king's man; it was only as a friend and companion that he accompanied Louis on the ill-fated Egyptian expedition. Happily he survived it; likewise the king, the king's son, and the king's grandson. This last-named prince, Philip IV, was married to the countess of Champagne, and it was at her request that Joinville undertook to dictate his memoirs of St. Louis. The task was not completed till 1309—and the author still lived another ten years, to die at the fine old age of ninety-five.

The book which Joinville "caused to be written" must remain one of the world's classics as long as human character and moving incident continue to hold their charm for readers. The central figure, of course, is the saintly king, on whose Christian faith and conduct the author lovingly dwells. But the account he gives us is no sanctimonious eulogy; it is what he has remembered—no saint himself, but a plain knight and a man of the world who liked his wine straight, who refused to wash the feet of dirty beggars, and who avowed he would rather have committed thirty mortal sins than be a leper. He is so engagingly honest, so enthusiastic and yet so sensible, that he immediately wins our respect and affection. We decide that St. Louis must indeed have been a wonderful man to have inspired such a devoted follower as Jean de Joinville. Memoirs of Joinville

Louis, beyond doubt, was deeply and sincerely religious. All the acts of his reign testify to the fact that he was fundamentally a mystic whose first thought was of heaven. While governing his kingdom as a matter of duty, he always found time for prayer, meditation, and ascetic practices. He seems to have married and reared a family principally for reasons of state; Joinville, at any rate, tells us that for five years on end he never heard the king refer either to wife or to children. Even among his intimates, though always kind and gentle, Louis remained strangely detached—a man to be revered rather than loved. In all matters of belief he was exceedingly conventional. He warmly supported the activities of the Inquisition and helped to extend its authority throughout the kingdom. For unbelievers he had no more sympathy than for heretics. He once told Joinville that, while a learned doctor might profitably argue with Jews, the layman's refutation must be to run them through with the sword. Louis's crusade was launched as much the same kind of unreasoning gesture. The enterprise seems decidedly out of place in the thirteenth century; a grandson of Philip Augustus might well have realized that the reconquest of the Holy Land was a task beyond the resources of any European prince, no matter how brave or pious.

Louis, however, had learned nothing from the experience of his predecessors. Against the advice of his mother and all his ministers, he took the cross in 1244, when Jerusalem was recovered by the Moslems, and spent several years in preparing for his expedition. In 1248, with a pathetic ignorance of the Moslems and their world, he led a fine army across the sea. Crusades of Louis IX

The plan was one that had been vainly tried earlier—to regain Palestine by first securing Egypt. In the spring of 1249 the host took Damietta without opposition and then, after considerable delay, struck south across the delta towards Cairo. This was in itself a foolhardy effort and its failure was assured by the king's blunders, which Joinville takes no pains to conceal. Vanquished in battle and decimated by pestilence, the army turned back in 1250, only to be surrounded and captured by the enemy. So the crusade ended with the surrender of Damietta and the payment of an enormous ransom for the survivors.

Even after a four-year sojourn in Syria, the king's passion for holy pilgrimage remained unappeased. While attending to the needs of his king-dom and acting as general arbiter of European affairs, he still dreamed of another crusade. Finally, in a royal council of 1267, the expedition was formally announced—this time an attack upon Tunisia. In 1270 the fleet sailed for Africa, anchoring before the ancient city of Carthage at the worst season of the year. During most of his life the king had been a chronic invalid, and before embarking he was already too weak to sit on a horse. Now, as the inevitable pestilence seized the army, he was among the first of the victims. Joinville, who lived to thank God he had refused to join the campaign, stated his opinion thus frankly:

To my mind they committed mortal sin who encouraged him to go, for France had reached a condition when all the kingdom was at peace within itself and with its neighbors—and never again has it been so since he left it. . . . Weak as he was, if he had stayed in France, he might have lived long enough to do a great deal of good.

Govern-
ment of
Louis IX

A king whose heart was thus set on visionary crusades would naturally tend to follow a pacific policy in other respects. Louis, as we shall see, made no attempt to profit by the misfortunes of the Hohenstaufen dynasty; nor did he take advantage of a feeble administration in England to com-plete the conquest of the Angevin inheritance. Had he done so, he might have saved his country from the horrors of a long war; instead, he agreed to a treaty by which the English king was to obtain double his present fief, plus a considerable sum of money, in return for his abandonment of all claim to Normandy, Anjou, and Poitou. In the sphere of domestic govern-ment Louis's reign was less noteworthy for the establishment of new insti-tutions than for the development of old ones—and precisely what the king's personal influence was in such matters is somewhat conjectural. For both France and England it was an age of rapid legal and constitutional progress which was carried on by an army of trained civil servants with or without much royal supervision.

In both countries the great central organ of government was the king's feudal court, or *curia regis*. Normally it consisted of a few permanent ministers; but to grant aids, proclaim campaigns, or transact other extraordinary business, it might be expanded by a general summons to all royal vassals. Already filled with professional judges and administrators under Philip Augustus, this *curia* in thirteenth-century France tended to break into separate groups, each with a special function. So, under Louis IX, we find two subdivisions maintaining their own peculiar records: the *chambre des comptes*, which had charge of the king's revenues, and the *parlement*, his court of justice at Paris. In all such matters of central organization the French kings had much to learn from Norman-Angevin example. Thence too came many lessons in local administration. Under Philip Augustus and his successors districts within the royal domain were assigned to officials called bailiffs (*baillis*) in the north and seneschals (*sénéchaux*) in the south, who exercised very much the same powers as the English sheriffs. And to supervise the working of his government, Louis IX regularly sent out *enquêteurs,* royal agents like the itinerant justices of England, empowered to hear complaints and to hold investigations (*enquêtes*).

In England Henry II's governmental system had continued to run smoothly in spite of his sons' many distractions. It was, in fact, the efficiency of that system which enabled the unpopular John to act despotically and so to invite a general insurrection of the barons in 1215. Momentarily yielding, the king agreed to the baronial demands by issuing the famous *Magna Carta*, in which he promised to do many things and not to do many others. And although the pope declared the original charter null and void, it was reissued in modified form and repeatedly confirmed under succeeding kings. *Magna Carta* was not, as nineteenth-century scholars generally believed, a great monument of national liberty. Its concession of privileges to the "freemen of England" could not apply to the mass of the people, which was still thoroughly servile. Interpreted in the light of contemporary usage, the Great Charter will be found to contain little beyond provisions dictated by baronial interest. Most of the articles were conservative or perhaps reactionary. The barons wished, first of all, to define the rights of the king as feudal lord and so to prevent a number of unwarranted exactions. Furthermore, they sought to undo much of Henry II's reform by restoring to their own courts some of the cases that had been diverted to royal courts. A few articles deserve to be called progressive because in certain particulars they recognized the king's improvement of justice. But *Magna Carta* itself established virtually nothing that was new. Even by insisting that the king was below the law, it enunciated no revolutionary principle. There were many things that a feudal prince was not supposed to do; the difficulty was to prevent his doing them if he were powerful enough to defy the threat of insurrection. The problem was an old one and to it *Magna Carta* brought no solution. The final article of the original grant merely set up a baronial committee to hear complaints and

The English government and *Magna Carta*

to authorize war against the king if he failed to give redress; and even that was dropped in the reissues.

**Henry III
(1216-72)**

On his sudden death in 1216 John was succeeded by his nine-year-old son. Thus beginning with a minority, the long reign of Henry III was chiefly remarkable for the advance of culture, which has been sketched in the preceding chapters, and the growth of institutions, which can be more adequately discussed in the one following. Aside from continuous disputes over the confirmation and enforcement of *Magna Carta*, the history of England during these years was politically uneventful. As Henry gained maturity, his government became increasingly unpopular. The English barons accused him of favoring unworthy foreigners—especially southern Frenchmen like the relatives of his Provençal wife—and of being too submissive to his papal lord. The king, in fact, was not only a very pious man but also a very meek vassal, who allowed the successors of Innocent III to enjoy a greatly increased authority throughout the kingdom. By a form of nomination called provision the pope came to fill many local sees and parishes, often with Italians who regarded their appointments as mere sources of revenue and hired cheap substitutes to do all the work. For the sake of alleged crusades, moreover, the pope collected heavy subsidies from the English clergy. Meanwhile Henry increased his own demands for taxes, to be largely spent in waging unsuccessful campaigns against the French king and in maintaining an extravagant court.

In 1258 Henry was forced to accept a baronial plan of reform, but was later emboldened to rescind his concession. The result was an armed uprising headed, strangely enough, by a Frenchman who had once been denounced as a foreign favorite. Simon de Montfort, youngest son of the famous crusader,[10] had indeed come to England as an adventurer. There he had made good his claim to the earldom of Leicester and had so far won the royal friendship as to marry the king's sister. After a series of quarrels, however, he had joined the baronial opposition and was now placed in command of the insurrectionary forces. Though badly outmatched in point of numbers, he was able, through generalship worthy of his father, to win a brilliant victory. In 1264 Simon routed the royal army and captured the king. So for a little over a year he was master of England —an opportunity which he used for noteworthy experimentation with the royal government.[11] Then, in 1265, Simon was slain in battle with Edward, Henry's able son, who thenceforth took over the task of restoring the monarchy.

**Charles
of Anjou
in Italy**

The virtual collapse of the Angevin power under Henry III naturally enhanced the prestige of the Capetian Louis IX, and events in Italy after the death of Frederick II tended to serve the same end. The emperor's

[10] See above, p. 347.
[11] See below, p. 380.

eldest son, Henry, had failed to survive him; his second son, who for some years had reigned in Germany as Conrad IV, died in 1254. Thereupon the Sicilians, defying the papal authority, recognized Frederick's illegitimate son Manfred, a handsome youth with much of his father's brilliance and popularity. This was the situation when, in 1261, the Roman see was given to a Frenchman, Urban IV. He at once offered the crown of Sicily to Charles of Anjou, brother of Louis IX and already count of Provence by a lucky marriage. The negotiations were so long drawn out that Urban died before they were completed; but his successor Clement IV, being also French, saw the plan actually carried out. Charles, with the consent of his royal brother, accepted the Sicilian kingdom as a papal fief on such conditions as the pope chose to stipulate. To raise an army, Clement proclaimed a crusade against Manfred and authorized a special tax on the clergy. Consequently, by the end of 1265, Charles was in command of another host such as had been employed to crush the Albigensians, and with it he won a decisive battle in which Manfred himself was killed. The hope of retrieving the Hohenstaufen fortunes then fell to Conradin, the sixteen-year-old son of Conrad IV. It was a vain hope. The Angevin followed up his victory with slaughter and proscription. The last of the imperial breed was hunted down and executed as a traitor. The pope saw fit not to enter a plea of mercy.

Italy thus obtained a new master in Charles of Anjou, who quickly proved himself not only a good general but also a highly resourceful and ambitious statesman. Making the most of a vague papal commission and profiting by the Interregnum in Germany,[12] Charles proceeded to establish a sort of dictatorship in northern Italy. As the *de facto* heir of Frederick II, he then revived a number of other imperial projects: chiefly the conquest of Constantinople, where a Greek emperor was again installed;[13] the recovery of Jerusalem, which had once more fallen to the Moslems; and the extension of Sicilian control over Tunisia, Sardinia, and the adjacent waters. It was only natural that the successors of Clement IV should feel that his substitution of Angevin for Hohenstaufen was no unmixed blessing and should try to check their over-zealous vassal. In 1281, however, Charles removed that source of opposition by securing the election to the papal throne of another complaisant Frenchman, Martin IV. Everything now seemed propitious for the launching of a magnificent enterprise to the east, when all his dreams were shattered by a major catastrophe in the west— the Sicilian Vespers of 1282.

On Easter Monday, while the church-bells were ringing for the evening service, an anti-French insurrection began at Palermo. Thence it spread throughout the island, to end in a general massacre of all who had sup-

[12] See below, p. 373.
[13] See below, p. 427.

ported the Angevin cause. The disaster was irreparable; for it coincided with armed intervention from Aragon, a power which Charles had foolishly underestimated. As already remarked, a new era had begun for that little kingdom in 1150, when it was acquired through marriage by a count of Barcelona. Henceforth established on the sea, Aragon was pushed southward at the expense of the Moors, finally to include, under James the Conqueror (1213-76), the port of Valencia and the Balearic Islands (see Map XV). It was his son Peter III who now, being married to a daughter

MAP XV.

of Manfred, showed an interest in the kingdom of Sicily. At the very moment when the Sicilians rose in revolt, Peter happened—so he said— to be nearby with a fleet bound for Africa. Having landed at the request of the rebels, he agreed to be their king and to defend them against all aggression.

The immediate result of this affair was the proclamation by Martin IV of a crusade against Aragon. The prime mover in the enterprise was of course Charles of Anjou; but Philip III of France, who had succeeded Louis IX in 1270, was enlisted as commander of the expedition by the offer of the Aragonese crown to his younger brother. Whatever the hopes of the papal coalition, they quickly faded, and the year 1285 brought death to all the major participants: first to Charles of Anjou, then to Pope Martin, next to Philip of France, and finally to Peter of Aragon. Of the four the most picturesque figure was assuredly the Capetian adventurer.

His passing marked the end of the last serious attempt in the Middle Ages to bring Italy under one secular administration. Henceforth the peninsula was left to unceasing conflict among a horde of petty states. One of them was styled the kingdom of Sicily; but it no longer included the island of that name, which continued to form a separate kingdom under a branch of the Aragonese house. This was the origin of the famous Two Sicilies, which were marked on the political map of Europe until the nineteenth century. The fortunes of the other Italian states can be more conveniently examined in later chapters.

Superficially the popes seemed now to have gained the independence for which they had so long striven. The Hohenstaufen dynasty had been extirpated; the Holy Roman Empire had virtually ceased to exist; Italy had relapsed into chaos; even the proud kingdom of Sicily had been divided and ruined. This series of disasters to the imperial cause might indeed be taken to mark a signal triumph for the papacy, but its cost was heavy. Gregory VII's political defeat proved to be a great moral victory for the church; the political victories of his thirteenth-century successors were accompanied by a shocking decline in ecclesiastical prestige. It was not that the later popes were bad men; their average in personal integrity was extraordinarily high. The source of trouble lay rather in the traditions of their office—traditions which forced them to devote their best energies to the non-religious tasks of diplomacy, warfare, and finance. In a more primitive age the pope could play an active part in world politics and yet remain primarily a spiritual leader. That was now impossible. *The waning prestige of the papacy*

The test of a good politician is success. In their effort to be successful, the popes of the thirteenth century forgot that there are nobler ambitions— and they could not always succeed. The Roman Church, by identifying itself with the Angevin cause in Italy, suffered defeat along with it. The Sicilian Vespers were a disaster from which the papacy, as a secular power, never recovered. And the ensuing war of revenge against Aragon was even more calamitous, for it proclaimed the utter degradation of the crusading ideal. While papal threats and curses were being ignored by the disillusioned peoples of the west, the Moslems completed the reconquest of the Holy Land, taking Antioch in 1268 and Acre in 1291. Thereafter the great crusade was merely a glorious memory.

3. GERMANY AND EASTERN EUROPE

The later thirteenth century also witnessed the final disintegration of Germany. Even while Frederick II lived, his northern kingdom had been virtually abandoned to the local princes. With the disappearance of the Hohenstaufen dynasty, they for a time continued to rule the country without a king at all. And when they finally agreed to hold an election, they deliberately chose an obscure Alsatian landgrave named Rudolf of Habs- *Rudolf of Habsburg (1273-91)* burg. The new king very sensibly accepted conditions as he found them. He never went to Italy and even at home made no effort to revive the monarchical power. Instead he devoted his energy to improving the fortunes of his own family—a project in which he won remarkable success. Rudolf's opportunity arose when Ottokar, king of Bohemia, refused to recognize his accession or to attend his court. After the rebel's fiefs had been declared forfeit, Rudolf took the field against him and slew him in battle. Seizing Austria, Styria, Carinthia, and Carniola, which Ottokar had held of the German crown, Rudolf gave them to members of his own house. Thus was established a Habsburg dominion on the upper Danube that was to persist until 1918 (see Map XVIII).

Origin of the Swiss Confederation

Thenceforth the Holy Roman Empire, practically identified with Germany, remained a sort of theoretical union, symbolized by an elected king who had no real power beyond what he might enjoy as ruler of a hereditary principality. Under such conditions many local associations were established for the sake of common defense, but of them only two can be mentioned here. One was the Hansa, the great league of German towns, which will be discussed when we come to the subject of Baltic trade. The other was the Swiss Confederation founded in 1291 by the mountaineers of Uri, Schwyz, and Unterwalden, the so-called Forest Cantons that constituted a portion of the original Habsburg territory. To explain the origin of this confederation we do not have to imagine the persistence of primitive institutions in isolated valleys. As a matter of fact, the Swiss were not isolated; for their homes were situated on the highroad connecting the St. Gothard pass with the Rhine. From the Italian side had long come tales of victorious communes. To the north was Freiburg-im-Breisgau,[14] whose customs had been extended to Bern and other nearby towns. In demanding rights of self-government the Forest Cantons were merely following the example already set by rural communities in all the more advanced regions of Europe. When, in 1291, the Swiss took an oath to resist aggression and defend their rights, their object was to free themselves from the Habsburg rule. With the elevation of Rudolf to the German throne they had recently come to stand directly under the monarchy. Now that the king was dead, they sought to maintain that position—like the free cities of Germany, to hold their liberties immediately from the empire. And eventually, thanks to events that will be described in a later connection, they were able to attain their ambition.

Eastern European peoples

Turning our attention to eastern Europe, we find that by 1250 two major changes had been made in the political map. As a consequence of the Fourth Crusade, the Byzantine Empire had all but disappeared, while another great horde of Asiatic nomads—the Mongols or Tartars of Jenghis Khan and his successors—had destroyed the Russian state and subjected

[14] See above, p. 244.

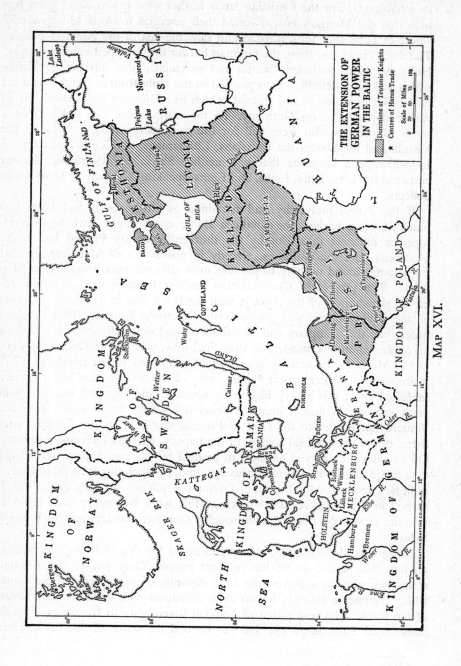

THE EXTENSION OF
GERMAN POWER
IN THE BALTIC

▨ Dominions of Teutonic Knights
★ Centres of Hansa Trade

Scale of Miles
0 20 50 75 100

MAP XVI.

its inhabitants. For the Christian lands farther west it was sheer good fortune that the Mongols now diverted their energies towards Mesopotamia, where in 1258 they took Bagdad and slew the last of the Abbasid caliphs. The three kingdoms along the German border thus escaped serious danger: Hungary, which included Croatia and so reached the Adriatic; Bohemia, which had been definitely incorporated in the Holy Roman Empire as a fief of the German crown; and Poland, which like Hungary had thrown off its earlier dependence on Germany. To the north along the Baltic lived a series of peoples who were still for the most part heathen: between the Vistula and the Dwina the Prussians, Lithuanians, and Letts, speaking an Indo-European language that was neither Slavic nor Germanic; farther eastward the Livs, Kurs, Esths, and Finns, speaking a variety of Ural-Altaic dialects.

The Teutonic Knights

If the Polish monarchy had remained as strong as it had been two hundred years earlier, the southern Baltic coast might have had an altogether different fate. But by the thirteenth century Poland had badly weakened, and the Germans, already in possession of Mecklenburg and Pomerania, found nothing to prevent their advance into Prussia (see Map XVI). The project of Christianizing another heathen land naturally received the support of the papacy, with the result that in 1230 the direction of the Prussian war was given to the Teutonic Knights. This religious order, like the Templars and Hospitallers, had originally been founded as an organization of crusaders in Palestine; now, with the victorious advance of the Moslems, its activity was gradually diverted to the north. In 1237 it absorbed a similar order, the Brothers of the Sword, that had been established by a missionary bishop in Livonia, and together the two won great success. Within a hundred years the whole Baltic coast from the Pomeranian border to the Gulf of Finland was held by the Knights, who there, under the nominal control of the papacy, exercised sovereign powers. On all sides they carved out fiefs to be held by German barons, settled the devastated areas with German peasants, and, co-operating with the Hansa,[15] built new towns for the benefit of German merchants. In spite of the Polish revival in the next century,[16] much of this work has never been undone. Prussia, especially, became a thoroughly German country, and so remains today.

Meanwhile the Russians, submerged under the tide of Mongol conquest, all but disappeared as an independent people. Only one of the Russian states was able to survive—the little republic of Novgorod, whose flourishing commerce brought it into close affiliation with the Hanseatic towns of the Baltic. The restoration of political sovereignty to Russia as a whole came much later, in an age that lies beyond the scope of this book. Here

[15] See below, pp. 446-48.
[16] See below, p. 426.

it can merely be noted that the nucleus of modern Russia was the principality of Moscow (Muscovy), whose rulers led a successful revolt against their Mongol lords towards the close of the fourteenth century and then, in the course of the next two hundred years, subjected all their Russian rivals. As had often happened in the past, it was the Slavs, rather than their conquerors, who throve and multiplied.

CHAPTER XXI

The Growth of Opposition to the Papacy

1. THE EMERGENCE OF CONSTITUTIONAL MONARCHY

Edward I (1272-1307)

Edward I, already an experienced man of thirty-five when he acquired the English crown, proved to be an admirable king, famous not only for his conquests and his legal enactments but also for his unstained private life. An ardent knight and a loyal son of the church, he allowed neither romantic chivalry nor exaggerated piety to outweigh the practical demands of his office. He made good use of his excellent education, especially in the fields of law and administration. His reputation for justice rivaled that of St. Louis. Throughout his life, despite a proud and ambitious temper, he strove to deserve the motto that was eventually carved on his tomb, *Pactum Serva* (Keep Troth). His enemies, and occasionally his subjects, found him a hard man; yet even his hardness, after the feeble rule of Henry III, might be accounted a political virtue. In many ways the reign of Edward I influenced the whole future of England.

Development of the common law

How the judicial reforms of Henry II inaugurated the English common law has been seen in an earlier connection. During the succeeding reigns, without regard to the fluctuations of foreign war, the system maintained a vigorous growth. Its basis was the series of writs[1] granted by the royal justices to persons who wished to have their suits tried in the king's court. And since new writs were devised at pleasure until the practice was checked under Edward I, the thirteenth century witnessed the rapid development of the common law. In this respect the prohibitions of *Magna Carta* were of no avail; what the judges might not do under one form they did under another. As a consequence, the royal courts rapidly secured a monopoly

[1] A writ is an order in writing issued by a court. Since the writs were originally in Latin, many of them are still known by their initial words in that language: e.g., *certiorari, mandamus, scire facias, subpœna, habeas corpus.*

378

of justice, with noteworthy exceptions. Ecclesiastical courts still enjoyed extensive powers, especially in cases of marriage, wills, perjury, and, to a limited degree, criminous clerks.[2] Manorial courts continued to deal with matters of villeinage, for servile tenures were not protected by the king's law. The boroughs and certain other localities remained under their own peculiar customs for many centuries to come. Furthermore, a large number of barons asserted the right to exercise criminal jurisdiction of an inferior sort; but such claims were rigidly investigated under Edward I and allowed to stand only as a specific delegation from the monarchy.

The thirteenth century was also the age when the jury system was extended in many ways not contemplated by Henry II. In cases regarding the tenure of land the question put to the jury was gradually changed, by means of various preliminary motions, from a matter of possession to one of legal title. And as juries came to be employed for settling these and other disputes over civil rights, the men who were impaneled, instead of rendering a verdict on the basis of their own knowledge, had to learn the facts from the testimony of witnesses in open court. Under the original plan criminals presented by a grand jury were sent to the ordeal. Then, in 1215, that method of trial was forbidden by Innocent III in his Lateran Council. The English government, being thoroughly obedient to the papacy, thus had to devise a substitute, and eventually the practice was adopted of leaving the accused man's guilt or innocence to a special jury of twelve. It was a long time, however, before jury trial came to be governed by such elaborate rules as are enforced today.

By the time of Edward I there had also been a significant evolution of the English courts; as in France, the *curia regis* had tended to subdivide into a number of distinct organizations. The first to take form was the exchequer, which kept the financial accounts of the kingdom and sat as a court of law for fiscal cases. In the thirteenth century it came to have a separate personnel under a chancellor of the exchequer, the official who is today an important member of the British cabinet. The second offshoot from the central *curia* was the court of common pleas, permanently set apart for the trial of cases between private citizens. Suits to which the king was a party normally followed his person until Edward I constituted another permanent court styled the king's bench. The three great courts of common law, thus fixed at Westminster, remained essentially unchanged until the nineteenth century. Below them were the circuit courts, held in the counties by regularly empowered justices on mission. And exceptional matters of all kinds could yet be taken to the king by means of petition— the procedure that later gave rise to the supplementary legal system called equity.

Even more significant for the history of England and of the world was

2 See above, pp. 328-29.

Parlia-
ment:
The house
of lords

the development of the assembly that became known as parliament. The word long retained its literal meaning—a talking or discussion, rather than a particular group of men. In thirteenth-century England it was especially applied to deliberations of the king's central *curia*. Established custom, as set forth in *Magna Carta*, required that for all scutages and extraordinary aids the king had to secure the consent of the baronage. And since the lesser barons were only too glad to avoid the expensive journey to court, parliaments came to include only the greater barons, lay and clerical— those who were summoned by individual letters. This group, later known as the house of lords, was therefore the original parliament, which then constituted, as it still constitutes, the supreme court of England. But for business other than judicial, parliaments also came to include deputies of the counties and boroughs. In particular, the mounting cost of the royal government necessitated more and more frequent demand for special subsidies—a regular system of taxation in place of the occasional aids, scutages, tallages, and the like of the previous century. Experience proved that the best results were obtained from a uniform levy on the personal property of all classes and that, to facilitate assessment, all classes should be asked to make a voluntary grant.

The house
of
commons

For a long time the kings had made increasing use of the counties and boroughs in connection with the levying of taxes and all sorts of administrative business. Through the itinerant justices and other commissioners constant negotiations had been kept up with both sets of communities. Such practices led by easy transition to the calling of representatives to meet with the king. Although occasional assemblies of deputies from the counties can be traced back to the early thirteenth century, Simon de Montfort[3] was the first, so far as we know, also to summon deputies from the boroughs. Edward probably had no need of a precedent set by a rebel earl, for arrangements of this sort were being adopted all over Europe. Nevertheless, he followed it. For his greater parliaments Edward assembled no less than three groups in addition to the barons: knights of the shires, elected in the county courts; burgesses, chosen in any way agreeable to the particular communities; and representatives of the lower clergy, both secular and regular. In his day none of these groups had a definitely constituted membership. By the middle of the fourteenth century, however, it became recognized practice for the king—dispensing with the representation of the lower clergy—to order the election of two knights in each county and of two burgesses in each borough. And since those quotas had been used by Edward for his parliament of 1295, the latter became known as the Model Parliament. Meanwhile, too, the knights of the shires and the burgesses had adopted the custom of sitting together;

[3] See above, p. 370.

so, being the deputies of the English communities, they were called the house of communes or, as we say, commons.

Edward, it is worth repeating, never thought of organizing a house of commons, and under him the powers of the local representatives remained vague. He had, in fact, no concept of legislation as distinct from the issuing of royal ordinances. Although various important enactments of his reign have always been referred to as statutes, the latter term as yet was not restricted to formal acts of parliament. In such matters, as in taxation, the practical Edward adopted any plan that seemed feasible, without regard for what future generations might turn into constitutional principles. His handling of a parliamentary crisis in 1297 is especially significant. After a long and bitter controversy, he finally promulgated his famous Confirmation of the Charters. Thereby he promised to observe *Magna Carta* as reissued by his father, abandoned his recent increase of duties on imports and exports, and agreed to take no aids or other taxes without the common consent of the kingdom, "saving to the crown those aids and taxes anciently accustomed." Precisely what the king gave up by this last article is hard to see; yet the moral victory lay with parliament. The really important consideration was that, by assuring the good will of all classes in the state, he could afford to drop old exactions that caused more trouble than they were worth. Parliamentary control of royal taxation, the basis of the later constitutional government, was already becoming an established fact.

Edward's parliamentary policy

Throughout his entire reign Edward's parliamentary policy was mainly governed by his warlike undertakings in Wales and Scotland. Long before his accession the mountainous peninsula between Bristol Channel and the Irish Sea had come to be divided into two main portions: the southeast under a series of Norman lords marchers and the northwest under a Welsh prince who acknowledged himself the vassal of the English king. In 1272 Llewellyn, prince of Wales, foolishly refused the accustomed homage and thus gave Edward a good excuse for marching against him. Finally, after Llewellyn had submitted and again rebelled, his country was incorporated with England and has so remained down to the present—leaving only a memory to be perpetuated by the title, Prince of Wales, that is borne by the king's eldest son. Another important consequence of the Welsh war was Edward's reform of the army. From experience in the field he learned how to supplement a force of knights with light-armed troops, especially infantry equipped with long-bows; and this military lesson, coinciding with his policy of weakening the nobility, led him to supersede the old feudal tenures by a system of voluntary enlistment and pay. The superiority of the army thus formed was soon demonstrated in Scotland.

The conquest of Wales

Although the English kings had earlier claimed a vague overlordship in the north of Britain, Edward was the first of them to exercise any real

The con-
quest and
loss of
Scotland
authority there. His opportunity arose from a disputed succession to the throne in 1290. Having been invited to arbitrate the affair, he awarded the crown to John Balliol. The new king, in accordance with a previous agreement, duly became Edward's vassal, but rebelled when his lord called on him for service in France. Thereupon Edward took his army north, deposed Balliol, and set up a government of his own. A Scottish insurrection under William Wallace led only to another English victory. Using his long-bows to prepare for a cavalry charge, Edward annihilated the Scottish array at Falkirk in 1298 and once more established his rule throughout Britain. The Scots, however, refused to submit. A new uprising was headed by Robert Bruce, who assumed the crown in 1307, just before Edward was succeeded by his incompetent son. Attempting to punish the Scottish rebels while ignoring the military lessons of his father, Edward II suffered crushing defeat at Bannockburn in 1314—a battle that established the independence of Scotland for the next three centuries.

Philip
IV of
France
(1285-1314)
Meanwhile, in 1285, the French throne had passed to Philip IV, whose handsome face won him the nickname of "the Fair." Little is known of his personality because he never inspired a biographer like Joinville. His official acts were always carried out by ministers, principally laymen trained in the new universities and devoted to the traditions of the civil law. Yet it would seem that Philip's government, in fact as well as in theory, was essentially his own—ambitious, mercenary, and unscrupulous. There can, at least, be no doubt that it had grave consequences both for France and Europe as a whole. One of his chief concerns was of course the relation to the crown of the ancient French principalities. Failing an opportunity to secure a great fief by escheat or forfeiture, the king inevitably sought to undermine the baron's power by extending direct control over his subjects. Languedoc, the old county of Toulouse, had now been wholly incorporated in the royal domain and Philip IV, by marrying the heiress of Champagne, had recently acquired that rich territory. Since Burgundy and Brittany were of secondary importance, the royal attention would naturally be concentrated on Guienne and Flanders.

Flanders
and
Guienne
Edward I, in lawful possession of Guienne, could be counted on to resist all French encroachment and to push his claim to the lands promised by Louis IX but never received. The count of Flanders was a much weaker antagonist. To all practical intents his state was a union of great self-governing cities, whose prosperity depended on the cloth industry and so upon the importation of wool from England. By threat of embargo the English king could normally force the count into alliance, although the Flemish aristocracy, fearing the urban populace, tended to be strongly pro-French. These issues are worth emphasizing because they lay at the root of the so-called Hundred Years' War that began in the next century. Edward I and Philip IV engaged in only brief hostilities, the former en-

couraging the count of Flanders to oppose French aggression, the latter supporting the rebel Scots under Wallace. When the two kings signed peace in 1298, each deserted his allies. Edward, as we have seen, thereupon conquered Scotland, while Philip conquered Flanders. But the mass of the Flemish population, consisting largely of artisans in the weaving trade and the economically allied peasants of the coastal strip,[4] refused to accept French domination. Having seized control of their localities, the popular militias met and defeated an invading French army at Courtrai in 1302—the first great victory of infantry over cavalry since the advent of the feudal age in Europe. Although Philip somewhat repaired his fortunes in later campaigns, he was soon persuaded to abandon his design of annexing Flanders and to restore the count; for in the meantime he had become embroiled in a much greater controversy with the pope. This affair will be discussed in the following section; for the moment something should rather be said of Philip's governmental policy.

The most striking contrast between the English and French states arose from the fact that, whereas the former had been conquered as a whole by its ruling house, the latter was built up piece by piece, as first one fief and then another was absorbed into the royal domain. Thus it came about that France had no common law and that, down to the Revolution of 1789, each province retained its own peculiar institutions. In England the king's military, judicial, and fiscal pre-eminence had been recognized for over two centuries; in France such powers had to be gradually revived. Philip's taxes and decrees had no validity in the great fiefs without the consent of the respective princes. Even within the territory that now constituted the royal domain there were scores of nobles and privileged communities that had to be separately dealt with, often at the cost of a stiff consideration. At one time or another the king, in addition to debasing the currency, tried almost every known expedient for raising money. He levied feudal aids, tallaged the towns, obtained special grants from the clergy and nobility, extorted loans and gifts, increased the customary tariffs, laid an impost on sales, and, in order to substitute cash equivalents, revived the Carolingian principle that every able-bodied subject owed him military service. But the collection of these taxes caused him serious trouble, sometimes leading to sanguinary riots. It was only towards the end of his reign that Philip learned the advantage of securing subsidies by the vote of representative assemblies called for that purpose. *Government of Philip IV*

Throughout western Europe it had long been the established custom that, except perhaps in special cases, a prince could tax his noble tenants only by their consent, and this was normally sought from them as a body when assembled in a great court. The clergy, as a matter of legal necessity, received the same treatment when it was asked for subsidies. By the later *The system of estates*

[4] See above, p. 250.

thirteenth century two orders or estates had thus appeared in the central assemblies convoked to facilitate taxation or to provide other political support. Meanwhile the towns, as privileged communities, had been consulted individually; had been visited by princely agents whenever they were required to pay an aid or otherwise co-operate with the administration. Eventually, however, it was found more convenient to consult them by means of deputies sent to a particular place. Through such procedure arose what was later to be called the Third Estate. The first authenticated meeting of estates for all France was in 1302,[5] when Philip IV summoned representatives of the towns, together with the barons and the clergy, to one great central court. But consultations with smaller groups had been held earlier, and the more normal procedure in fourteenth-century France was to call estates for separate districts, such as Normandy and Toulouse.

Despite all local variation of custom, constitutional development in France and England thus remained fundamentally the same. Earlier, as noted above, Frederick II had provided that representatives of the bourgeoisie should attend the councils held for his Sicilian kingdom. Within another generation the *cortes* of the Spanish kingdoms had likewise come to include deputies from the towns. And by the close of the century similar practice had come to prevail in the kingdom of Germany, as well as in many of its component states. How the influence of such assemblies grew in direct proportion to the fiscal needs of the rulers will be seen in the following chapters.

2. BONIFACE VIII AND THE AVIGNON PAPACY

Italy in the later thirteenth century

The ruin of the Hohenstaufen kingdom and the eventual collapse of the Angevin power left Italy to be fought over by a medley of local states for the next five hundred years. And the participants in these conflicts long continued to use the old names of Guelf and Ghibelline.[6] The latter, an Italian substitute for Hohenstaufen, had come to designate the party of the imperialists; the former to designate their opponents, the papalists. So the Angevins were Guelfs and the Aragonese were Ghibellines. Traditionally, Florence and Milan were Guelf, while Pisa and Pavia were Ghibelline. But the alignment was at most a matter of vague loyalty. Florence, for example, had no desire for a papal government and might be willing to fight either Milan or the Angevin king. Indeed, the traditional epithets soon lost all but a local significance, to be tossed back and forth in feuds of city against city and of faction against faction. At Florence a Ghibelline coalition, aided by Manfred, took the city in 1260. Then, six years later, the power of the Guelfs, under a new and more democratic constitution, was restored by Charles of Anjou. His death brought further changes in

[5] See below, p. 386.
[6] Said to be a corruption of Waiblingen, a family estate of the Hohenstaufen.

the government, accompanied by fierce contests between nobles and gilds-men, between the greater and the lesser gilds, and between rival groups of nobles—in all of which the popes played an active and not disinterested part. Such was the environment that influenced Dante Alighieri and, after him, so many other distinguished writers.

Largely on account of similar turmoil, it was now the general practice throughout Lombardy for a commune to be governed by a dictator. Some-times he was formally elected by the citizens; sometimes he installed him-self by force. Whatever the local circumstances, Italians were already becoming used to the despots who were to play a prominent part in their later history. To this fashion one northern city was never to submit; instead Venice became synonymous with political stability through the unbroken rule of a closed oligarchy. The final step in that direction was taken in 1298, when membership in the great council, and with it eligibility to governmental office, was made into a strictly hereditary privilege. Thenceforth political power at Venice remained the monopoly of certain great families, whose marriages and births were listed in an official register, the famous Golden Book. How the Fourth Crusade brought the Venetians a splendid maritime empire has already been seen. Much of it they retained, although the restoration of Greek rule at Constantinople in 1261 broke their control of the straits and readmitted the Genoese. The result, as will be explained below, was a commercial war that lasted for almost another hundred years.

In the meantime the failure of Martin IV's Sicilian policy had naturally produced an anti-French reaction among the cardinals, which eventually carried into power the energetic but unfortunate Boniface VIII. The latter, before his election, had long been prominent in the service of the Roman Church. He was unquestionably a man of considerable ability, especially in law and business administration. As papal legate in France he had gained the ill will of many influential persons and his election was con-sequently opposed by the French cardinals; but he received the votes of the principal Italian factions. Subsequently all sorts of scandalous charges were leveled against him, ranging from atheism to moral turpitude. There is no reason to take such accusations for more than the usual invective of fierce partisanship. Judged by his own words and acts, Boniface appears rather a misguided enthusiast than a monster of corruption. The ideals to which he gave his passionate devotion were those of his office, consecrated by centuries of tradition. The means he took to serve his ends differed in no essential from those of his predecessors. To a large degree he was the victim of circumstances, being made to suffer for the upholding of long-established principles. On the other hand, it must be admitted that Boniface was no statesman. He was utterly lacking in the tact demanded by his position. Having no real understanding of men, he failed to grasp the

Boniface VIII (1294-1303)

realities of any situation. With him violence of affirmation seemed always to take the place of intelligent thought.

Conflict
with
Philip IV

The first two years of Boniface's pontificate passed quietly. Then, by the bull *Clericis Laicos*,[7] he suddenly forbade all secular princes to levy any taxes on the clergy without papal authorization. This act, directed primarily against the subsidies which the kings of France and England were then raising for their war, was based on good ecclesiastical theory. Yet the event proved that the pope was in no position to enforce his prohibition. While Edward outlawed all who disobeyed him, Philip stopped the exportation of gold and silver from his dominions and so, indirectly, cut off a good portion of the papal revenue. Within a year Boniface had first modified and then rescinded his decree. Nor was this all. Reversing his previous attitude, he proceeded to treat the French government with the utmost consideration. The reason, obviously, lay in the "crusades" which he was then pressing on two sides. One he inherited from his predecessors—the vain effort to re-establish the Angevin authority throughout the kingdom of Sicily and to punish the house of Aragon for its presumptuous opposition. The other was a war of Boniface's own making—a feud with the Colonna family in Rome, which resented the pope's aggressive acts for the benefit of his relatives.

Having forced the Colonna chiefs to submit, Boniface in 1300 celebrated the opening of the new century with a great jubilee at Rome. Enormous throngs of pilgrims poured into his capital from all regions of Christendom, and this apparent evidence of universal ascendancy seems to have heightened his already exalted concept of the papal office. At least, he now acted as if he were in truth the dictator of Europe. Even while calling upon Charles of Valois, younger brother of Philip IV, to overturn a hostile government at Florence and reconquer Sicily, Boniface saw fit to bring on a second quarrel with the French king. Again the pope took his stand on solid legal ground—the defense of a bishop against arbitrary judgment in a lay court. But he wrecked all hope of a peaceable settlement by gratuitously issuing a bull that revived the claims of *Clericis Laicos* and by following that with another, *Asculta Fili* (Listen, My Son!), which the French could not fail to regard as an insult.

Philip's reply was to summon, in 1302, the great assembly of clergy, nobility, and bourgeoisie that is known in the history of France as the first meeting of the estates general. Although the king got from it the support he wanted, the effect was overbalanced, in the eyes of the pope, by the Flemish victory at Courtrai. So Boniface did not hesitate to continue his offensive with the bull *Unam Sanctam*. All must believe, it is there proclaimed, in one Holy Catholic Apostolic Church, outside which there is no

---

[7] The formal decrees of the popes are called bulls and are commonly known by the first few words of the Latin text.

salvation. This one true church has a single head, namely Christ, who is represented on earth by the bishop of Rome, the successor of St. Peter. The two swords spoken of in the Gospel are the spiritual power and the temporal power. Both belong to the church. "The former is to be used by the church, the latter for the church; the one by the hand of the priest, the other by the hand of kings and knights, but at the command and permission of the priest." "If the temporal power errs, it will be judged by the spiritual power, and if the lower spiritual power errs, it will be judged by its superior. If, on the other hand, the highest spiritual power errs, it cannot be judged by men, but by God alone." Whoever resists God's vicar resists God. "We therefore declare, say, and affirm that submission on the part of every man to the bishop of Rome is altogether necessary for his salvation."

The sequel to this pontifical utterance would have been ludicrous had it not been so tragic. While the French government was formally accusing the pope of the most shocking crimes and demanding his trial before a general council of the church, Nogaret, one of the king's ablest and most unscrupulous ministers, went to Italy and joined hands with certain vindictive members of the Colonna faction. Gathering a small army of Boniface's personal enemies, they broke into Anagni, where the pope happened to be, and arrested him. Then, in the face of growing hostility, they abandoned whatever project had at first been contemplated, and left Boniface to be escorted back to Rome by a group of his friends. The blow to the aged man's pride, however, was more than he could survive. Completely broken in spirit, he died one month after his release, in October, 1303. Such a disgraceful affair was in itself no moral victory for the French king. That Philip was able to turn it to his advantage is sufficient proof of the discredit into which the papacy had already fallen. *The incident of Anagni (1303)*

To succeed Boniface, an Italian of high character was at once installed, but his efforts at compromise were ended by his death in the following year. Then, after a protracted vacancy, the papal office was conferred on the archbishop of Bordeaux, who assumed the name of Clement V. If some had expected him, as a vassal of the English king, to be unfriendly to Philip, they were quickly disillusioned; for he quashed the decrees of Boniface that had offended the French king and gave full absolution to the persons who had attacked the pope at Anagni. Meanwhile, Clement, for one reason or another, had continually posponed his expected journey to Rome. He had first celebrated his coronation at Lyons and then summoned a council at Vienne in Dauphiné. Temporarily the papal residence was established at Avignon, a city belonging to the Angevin count of Provence, but practically surrounded by the papal territory of the Venaissin.[8] And *Clement V (1305-14)*

---

[8] It had earlier belonged to the count of Toulouse, but had fallen to the pope as the result of the Albigensian Crusade.

although Clement may have been honest enough in his declared intention of going to Rome, that project was virtually annulled by his appointment to the cardinal college of numerous Frenchmen. Whether partisans of Philip IV or not, they were agreed in disliking Italy. The momentary halt at Avignon lapsed into a continuous residence.

The affair of the Templars (1307-14)

One cause for the papal delay on or near French soil was the trial of the Templars, which dragged its scandalous course through the years between 1307 and the pope's death in 1314. That order, since the fall of Acre in 1291, had of necessity lost its crusading functions; yet through extensive banking operations[9] it continued to accumulate wealth. It was a secret organization, surrounded by much mystery. Its members lived in luxury and many of them were devoted to worldly interests. Earlier popes had suggested combination with the Hospitallers, who were still engaged in charitable work; but the Templars objected and so gave a certain color to the charges made against them. In 1307 Clement was prevailed on to authorize an investigation; and when Philip ordered the arrest of all Templars in France and placed Nogaret in charge of securing adequate confessions by the use of torture, the case was virtually decided in advance.

A tale of horrid deeds was drawn up by the royal commissioners, acting in collaboration with the Inquisition, and some scores of unfortunate victims were sent to the stake as relapsed heretics. Finally, after much hesitation, the pope removed the case from his council at Vienne and abolished the order. By the terms of the papal decree, the property of the Templars, except in the Spanish peninsula, was to go to the Hospitallers, but they found it difficult to enforce their rights. In France the cash of the condemned order had already been appropriated by the king, whose grasp on such assets never relaxed. Even the Templars' lands had been brought under royal occupation, and before they could be obtained by the beneficiaries the latter had to pay under the head of expenses what amounted to a good price. As a whole, the affair served, even in the eyes of contemporaries, to advertise the decadence of the papacy and the ruthless greed of the French monarchy.

The Avignon popes

Clement V was the first of six French popes who maintained their residence at Avignon. Life was indeed pleasanter on the Rhone than on the Tiber. Rome and the adjacent countryside had now fallen into a chronic state of disorder. Avignon, on the other hand, was a relatively tranquil spot immune from foreign invasion; and, after its purchase by the pope in 1348, it became papal territory. Meanwhile an older episcopal building had been converted into the great fortified palace that remains one of the most impressive monuments in southern France. There the popes lived in magnificent state, surrounded by their cardinals, each of whom had a princely establishment of his own. But the peace and com-

[9] See below, p. 435.

fort of Avignon were more than counterbalanced by the fact that, to remain there, a pope had to absent himself from his proper see. The very essence of his authority was the Roman episcopate; separation from the Petrine city, except in case of dire necessity, could be no less than a scandal in the eyes of the devout. Avignon, though not in France, was encircled by Capetian lands; and it was only too apparent that, beginning with Clement V, the popes were very careful not to displease the French king. To Europe at large the papacy thus appeared to have lost its independence—to be suffering what ecclesiastical historians came to call the Babylonian Captivity.

Personally, the Avignon popes were by no means inferior to most of their predecessors. They remained devoted to such traditional ideals as the promotion of peace among Christians, the organization of united resistance to Moslems, missionary work among the heathen, and the suppression of heresy. They were, however, more successful as jurists and administrators than as religious leaders. While the inspirational failure of the church was bewailed by a growing multitude of the faithful, the popes gave their principal attention to finance and administration. They established many reforms to increase the efficiency of their central government and improve its resources. Some of them were really distinguished jurists, who contributed important sections to the *Corpus Iuris Canonici*.[10] These labors, admirable as they were, could not make up for a lack of spiritual leadership. It was no new complaint that the papal court was mercenary and corrupt. The charge now gained added force from the unprecedented luxury of the pope's establishment at Avignon, the mounting cost of his government, and the multiplication of his demands for money. In these respects, of course, the papal monarchy was merely developing ambitions common to all the great states of the age. That was the trouble. If the papacy was not to be different from its secular rivals, it could hardly be immune from attack.

3. Popular Literature and Anti-Clerical Agitation

Under the conditions that had come to prevail by the early years of the fourteenth century it was only natural that Europe should be swept by a flood of anti-clerical writings which continued and amplified the attacks of satirists and reformers in the preceding period. On the side of vernacular literature the critical spirit of the *fabliaux*, if not their humor, reappeared in the *Romance of the Rose*, one of the most remarkable and influential books of the Middle Ages. Begun by Guillaume de Lorris as an allegory of courtly love,[11] the poem was completed in a very different vein by Jean de Meun. The latter was a well-educated man of bourgeois origin who,

Jean de Meun and the Romance of the Rose

[10] See above, p. 267.
[11] See above, p. 289.

presumably employed by Philip IV, came to live at Paris and died in 1305. Although perfectly familiar with the scholastic learning of the day, Jean was no theologian; and although he had read and reread all the Latin classics then available to students, his dominant interest lay in the contemporary world. Very significantly, he translated into French a number of Latin works: together with others, the letters of Abelard and Héloïse; Boëthius, *On the Consolation of Philosophy;* and the fourth-century treatise of Vegetius on warfare, which included a famous discussion of siegecraft. Why he decided to continue the unfinished poem of Guillaume de Lorris he does not tell us; we know merely that, beginning with 4220 lines in the original, he brought the total up to 21,780.

As resumed by Jean de Meun, the *Romance of the Rose* becomes a satire against the follies of mankind. The plot is wholly subordinated to the convictions of the author. By putting words into the mouths of his characters, Jean speaks his mind on every subject. Caring nothing for convention, he flays the great and respected of all classes. Neither birth nor authority nor wealth nor a reputation for holiness is sacred in his eyes; each must justify itself by something more than tradition. In the course of one passage or another he is able to ridicule many an honorable belief; yet his diatribe, we feel, gains momentum when he approaches two particular subjects. On women—and this in a romance!—he quotes Juvenal with relish and adds a bitter invective of his own. Also against the clergy, particularly the mendicant orders, he levels a damning indictment, accusing them of avarice, pride, sloth, and general worthlessness.

The clergy

Thus, as one of the Lover's advisers, the author introduces False-Seeming, who describes himself as follows:[12]

Sometimes I am a knight, sometimes a monk, sometimes a prelate, sometimes a canon; or perhaps a clerk or a priest. Sometimes I am a pupil, sometimes a master; sometimes a *châtelain,* sometimes a game-keeper. In other words I am of all professions. Sometimes I am a prince and sometimes a page; and I know by heart all languages. At one moment I am old and decrepit; at the next I have renewed my youth. I am Robert or Robin, Franciscan or Dominican. And for the sake of my companion, the lady Forced-Abstinence, who goes with me and solaces me, I assume many another disguise; as may please her, I do whatever she says. Thus I may appear in the robes of a woman; I am either dame or damsel, either *religieuse,* prioress, nun, abbess, sister, or novice. I go through all countries seeking all religions; but of religion itself I always leave the grain and take the straw. In order to fool people I need only the dress.

The favorite residence of False-Seeming, therefore, is among the clergy—especially among those who pretend to be poor but live in luxury, or among those new apostles of the church who prefer begging to honest work. In itself a robe means nothing. True saints are more likely to be found in the clothes of laymen than in the habits of religion.

[12] Lines 11,189-11,218.

Of the many other examples that could be given to illustrate this **Origin** astonishing romance two must suffice. The Friend, in the course of a long **of kings** disquisition on the madness of love, tells how society has degenerated since **and** the Golden Age.[13] At that time all men were equal and held everything in **princes** common. It was only later, when this primitive simplicity had succumbed to evil, that it became necessary to protect either persons or property. Then the people decided to find someone to defend them against male- factors and enforce justice. "They elected a big villein, the strongest and largest in body and bones that they could find, and they made him prince and lord." He swore that he would guard their homes if they would give him enough to live on. But eventually the people had to enlarge his powers, setting aside vast estates for his household and establishing taxes to sup- port his government. "This was the origin of kings and territorial princes." And it led to the growth of a wealthy class in the state—of men who, "through cupidity, appropriated what had earlier been as common as air and sunshine."

Even more interesting as a reflection of contemporary learning is the **Nature** tribute to Nature which is abruptly inserted towards the end of Jean's **and her** poem.[14] "Meanwhile Nature, meditating on things under the heavens, had **confes-** entered her workshop, where she gave all care to the creation of individuals **sion** who should perpetuate the species." For black-visaged Death pursues all, and none may escape. "Sweet merciful Nature, seeing that jealous Death comes with Corruption to destroy whatever they find in her workshop, hammers and forges without ceasing to replace her creatures in new gener- ations." Art, for all his marvelous works in divers materials, can make nothing that of itself will live, move, feel, and talk. Nature is infinitely more wonderful—so wonderful that no human talent can describe her. Jean has tried a hundred times, only to abandon the task as quite beyond his powers. The beauty of Nature is inexpressible. "For God . . . made her into a fountain, ever flowing and ever full from which all beauty is derived; but of which no man knows the depth or the breadth." This eloquent tribute serves to introduce Nature's confession—a sort of miniature en- cyclopædia, in which Jean reviews the wonders of the natural world. Here are merely some of the subjects there discussed: the creation of the earth, its elements, and its inhabitants; the heavens, the planets, and the influence of celestial bodies upon man; predestination, free will, and how they can be reconciled; meteorology, including floods, clouds, rainbows, shooting- stars, comets, eclipses, winds, hail, snow, and tides; mirrors, burning-glasses, and other optical phenomena; dreams, apparitions, and hallucinations; true nobility, as contrasted with that of birth; the value of learning and the chronic disloyalty of mankind to Nature.

[13] Lines 9603-9661.
[14] Lines 15,893-19,405.

Unlike Jean de Meun, Pierre Dubois was famous neither in his own day nor in those to come, until his work was discovered by nineteenth-century scholars and published as a mediæval curiosity. Dubois, a lawyer at the court of Philip IV, addressed to that king various Latin pamphlets, including one entitled *De Recuperatione Terræ Sanctæ* (Concerning the Recovery of the Holy Land). Its nominal theme, the revival of the crusade, merely provides an excuse for the author to air his opinions about the reformation of almost everything. Crusading enterprise, he declares, has been prevented by chronic dissensions among the princes of Europe, both lay and ecclesiastical. Nothing can be expected of the clergy; for they, as a consequence of their wealth, are sunk in general corruption. European wars can be ended only by force and there is only one prince strong enough to apply it, the king of France. Without waiting for further justification, Philip should undertake the project of uniting Christendom and, to secure the necessary funds, should confiscate all ecclesiastical property. Dubois then proceeds to show how such funds can be used for the improvement of many institutions. For example, education should be taken over by the state and extended to both sexes. It should also be made more practical by introducing the study of contemporary languages and of technical subjects like agriculture, engineering, and pharmacy. The surprising feature of this little book is its realistic point of view, which utterly disregards the ecclesiastical and imperial traditions of the past thousand years. Fantastic as its suggestions were, they reveal a world of actuality far removed from the world of theory that continued to fascinate Boniface VIII.

The ancient controversy between papacy and empire flared up again in the fourteenth century, but it remained largely a war of words. Clement V exchanged recriminations with the emperor Henry VII,[15] who invaded Italy and died there in 1313. The former was succeeded by John XXII, the latter by Louis of Bavaria; and they, too, indulged in violent altercation over prerogatives that neither could enforce. Altogether it was a thoroughly tiresome affair, which is worth mentioning only because it came to be involved with a more significant quarrel. By the close of the thirteenth century, as we have seen, the Franciscans had widely departed from their original ideals. Without holding actual title to property, they had generally come to live in houses and not infrequently to engage in other than charitable pursuits. The change of discipline was frankly recognized as necessary by the governing majority in the order; but a zealous minority, called the Spiritual Franciscans, fiercely resented all lax interpretation of the rule and insisted upon a life such as had been led by the saint's early disciples. Some went so far as to preach and write against the wealth of the clergy, thus allying with numerous radical groups that had waged a similar campaign for generations. Although Clement V commanded the

[15] See below, p. 420.

Spiritual Franciscans to obey their superiors, many refused to do so and instead formed a separate organization styled the Fraticelli. John XXII then made the situation worse by issuing various extreme pronouncements that antagonized the entire order. Although the majority of the Franciscans eventually submitted, their minister general and a number of his ablest associates took refuge with Louis of Bavaria.

Among these refugees was William of Ockham, the foremost scholar of Latin Christendom.[16] As a doctor of theology at Oxford, he had gained especial fame from a bold attack on the teachings of Aquinas. Now he devoted his dialectical skill to the writing of weighty volumes against John XXII in particular and against the papal claims in general. The pope, said Ockham, has no authority at all in temporal affairs; even in matters of faith his decision is not absolute, for against him there must always be an appeal to Scripture as interpreted by wise and honest men. Thus the Franciscans fell back upon the defense which had been raised by Peter Waldo a hundred and fifty years earlier, and which was to be raised in the future by a host of other dissenters. **William of Ockham (d. 1349)**

At the imperial court Ockham was joined by a great Parisian master, Marsiglio of Padua. As a feature of the campaign against John XXII, he wrote a remarkable book entitled *Defensor Pacis* (Defender of Peace). It is divided into two main parts, one dealing with the state and the other with the church. The first part is largely drawn from Aristotle's *Politics* and develops the familiar thesis that monarchy rests on a delegation of power from the people. The second part, on the other hand, is strikingly original—an ample justification of Marsiglio's lasting fame as a political theorist. Here he sets forth the idea that the church is really the body of believing Christians. Within that congregation clergymen have the power to determine purely ecclesiastical questions; but they have no power to assess temporal penalties, for God alone may punish violations of His law. Nor have clergymen any just title to worldly goods; their sole function is to save souls by preaching the Gospel and by administering the sacraments. The pope is merely the elected head of the clergy. His alleged plenitude of power is sheer usurpation. Sovereign authority within the church lies with the community of Christian citizens. A general council representing them not only can but must carry through a sweeping reform. Until that is done, there will be no lasting peace in the world. **Marsiglio of Padua (d. 1342)**

Thus formulated as a matter of academic discussion, the conciliar theory of ecclesiastical government was soon to become a practical issue of supreme interest to all Europe. Meanwhile, however, Italy had produced another famous man, whose work may well be examined before we continue the troubled history of the later mediæval church. The illustrious Dante Alighieri owed his literary career to the fact that, in the course of **Dante (1265-1321)**

[16] See below, pp. 465-66.

a municipal revolution encouraged by Boniface VIII, he was exiled from Florence in 1302. For nearly a score of years, as the son of a prominent lawyer, he had taken an active part in the politics of the republic and had been intimately associated with a number of talented artists and scholars. He had received a good education, presumably of the scholastic type then prevalent, and he had assuredly come under the influence of the vernacular poets. Some Italians, loyal to an ancient tradition, still wrote in Provençal; others, adopting a fashion set under Frederick II, preferred one of the native dialects. Dante, for reasons that he was subsequently to expound at length, followed the example of the latter group. Writing lyrics, he was naturally led to celebrate a beautiful lady whom he was compelled to adore from a distance; but his treatment of the familiar theme was distinctly original. The story is told in Dante's first book, the *Vita Nuova*—the New Life, to which he had been introduced by Beatrice. Actually, she was the wife of another Florentine gentleman and, according to Dante's own account, she had only spoken to him once, when he chanced to meet her on the street. Yet she had inspired the young poet to compose a series of mystic sonnets, which are included in the *Vita Nuova;* and, after her premature death in 1290, she had come to be his spiritual guide, leading him ever upward towards ultimate truth. Although Dante later took a wife and lived with her happily, it was not she whom he glorified in poetry but the idealized Beatrice.

The Convivio   At the close of the *Vita Nuova* we are told how, in a vision, Beatrice had inspired Dante to proceed with certain labors so that he might speak of her more worthily. Within half a dozen years after his exile, these labors led him to begin the *Convivio* (Banquet)—a curious mixture of verse and prose, of personal reminiscence and scholastic reasoning. Through the elaborate allegory of a spiritual feast the reader was to be introduced to universal knowledge but the work was left unfinished. It is interesting, first, because it reveals the author devoting himself to study in order to forget his bereavement. By reading Boëthius and Cicero, he had discovered that the lady Philosophy might govern his mature life even as the lady Beatrice had governed his youth. A second remarkable feature of the book is its use of the vernacular, which shows that Dante, a bourgeois and a layman like Jean de Meun, was interested in popularizing the learning of the schools. The Florentine poet, however, was contemplating a grander project than the *Romance of the Rose*, and to justify his preference for Italian he presented a lengthy argument.

De Vulgari Eloquentia   This subject, broached in the *Convivio*, was developed in a separate essay called *De Vulgari Eloquentia*—a defense of the vulgar tongue, put into Latin so that it would be read by the learned. At the outset Dante briefly considers the origin of human speech, accepting the orthodox view that men spoke Hebrew from the Creation until they incurred God's anger by attempting to build the tower of Babel. He passes rapidly over the ensuing confusion of tongues and so comes to the three related languages of *oïl* (French), *oc* (Provençal), and *si* (Italian). The first two of these, he says, have proved their fitness for literary composition. The last, on the other hand, has suffered from the fact that it is a jumble of fourteen dialects, each of which has grave defects. Having given examples to prove his point, Dante decides that literary Italian must be the speech that would prevail at the imperial court if only there were one in Italy. Such a courtly language, combining the best features of all the dialects and being common to the peninsula, is what he proposes to adopt for his own poetry. The invention of a fine-drawn theory to justify the use of what was essentially the speech of his native Florence is very characteristic of the author.

A similar disquisition is found in his *De Monarchia*, another Latin essay, dealing with the nature of the state. Dante, exiled from his beloved Florence through the political machinations of Boniface VIII, had no love for the papal pretension to sovereignty in both spiritual and temporal affairs. But his Ghibellinism was more than spite. He dreamed of Italy united and happy under a strong kingship, and to him the king could only be the emperor. So he applauded the vain attempt of Henry VII[17] to restore the monarchy and wrote a pamphlet in defense of what had long been a lost cause. The book repeats and amplifies a very old contention: that the empire, being itself a divine establishment, is quite independent of the papacy. And Dante's thesis is thoroughly conventional in that it accepts the traditional symbolism and seeks merely to pick flaws in the papalists' logic. They, he says, have insisted that, since the moon shines by reflected light, the state is inferior to the church. He does not think of denying that the sun and the moon respectively typify the church and the state; he alleges that the moon really has a light of her own and does not borrow everything from the sun. He reinterprets such famous texts as Boniface VIII had cited in his bull *Unam Sanctam*. And to clinch his argument he states that Christ would never have chosen to be born under the Roman Empire if it had not been the perfect form of government!

De Monarchia

Interesting as they are, these minor works are utterly dwarfed by the magnificent *Commedia*, which came to occupy Dante's later years. The *Divine Comedy*, as it is generally known, is unlike anything else that has ever been written. Though epic in scope and solemnity, it is by no means an impersonal narrative. In a way it is a tale of adventure, but the adventure is such as no man could really have and the hero is Dante himself, who relates in the first person what he has seen and heard. The author is thus permitted to express his own emotions whenever he pleases, giving to many passages an intensely lyric quality. The subject-matter of the poem is equally remarkable, for it deals with the entire universe—God and the

The *Divine Comedy*

[17] See below, p. 420.

world and all the creatures who have inhabited it. His literary device thus provides unlimited opportunity for criticism of contemporary society. In substance, therefore, the *Divine Comedy* is a sort of encyclopædia, like those of the schoolmen; yet in form it is a vernacular poem, combining and developing elements drawn from the epic, romantic, and lyric compositions of the preceding two centuries. The poet who could conceive such a work, perfect a language in which to express it, and then complete it with sustained artistry must always be recognized as a towering genius.

Hell and purgatory

To give any idea of the *Divine Comedy* as poetry is here out of the question. The meter and triple rhyme of the original have never been satisfactorily reproduced in English, and the theme is such that a few haphazard quotations are quite useless. Nor can any but a brief indication be made of the contents. The scene is laid in the year 1300. Dante, lost in a forest, is being attacked by certain symbolic beasts when he is rescued by Vergil, who explains that he has come at the request of Beatrice in paradise. He himself, as a virtuous pagan, has been condemned to limbo, a sort of neutral zone just inside hell, through which he offers to escort his fellow poet. The two descend by an underground passage. Hell is a hollow cone with its point reaching to the center of the spherical earth. It is divided into a series of nine circles, of which the topmost is limbo. There Dante sees Vergil's companions in exclusion from heaven: including Hector, Æneas, Cæsar, Lucretia, Aristotle, Plato, Orpheus, Cicero, Seneca, Euclid, Ptolemy, Avicenna, Averroës, and Saladin. The souls of the good Hebrews, he is told, have been removed to heaven. In the second circle are the lustful—among them Cleopatra, Helen of Troy, Achilles, and Tristan. And below it Dante passes through the circles of the gluttonous, the slothful, the avaricious, the violent, the false, and the traitorous, each group suffering worse punishment than the one above it. He encounters many Italian acquaintances and from them hears various prophecies. Among the simoniacs in the eighth circle he finds Pope Nicholas III[18] who momentarily mistakes him for Boniface VIII and who predicts that the latter will soon arrive and then be joined by Clement V.

Finally, after discovering Brutus, Cassius, and Judas Iscariot among the traitors at the bottom of the pit, Dante and his guide emerge by another passage to the hemisphere opposite that of the inhabited earth. Here is situated the mountain of purgatory, to which those who have died absolved by the church are ferried by angels. The mountain is the converse of hell, with nine ledges where the souls of the repentant are compelled to perform labors in proportion to the evil which they did while alive. In this region, too, Dante sees many famous characters and speaks to a number of recently arrived Italians. On the top of the mountain he enters the earthly paradise—the original garden of Eden—where he has a series of ecstatic

[18] The Italian predecessor of Martin IV.

visions and where Beatrice assumes charge of his further progress. She, looking into the sun like an eagle,[19] draws him up through the air to the encircling spheres of the seven planets. Each is visited in turn and Dante finds out many new facts, both astronomical and theological. Beatrice herself explains to him the cause of the spots on the moon, the nature of the angels, and the distribution of the blessed in paradise according to the principles of symbolic justice.

In the course of his tour Dante is also able to converse with many of **Paradise** the departed great. In the sphere of Mercury, among the souls of the active, he finds Justinian, who expounds the history of the Roman Empire. In that of the sun the spirits of the wise are identified for him by St. Thomas Aquinas—among them Albertus Magnus, Peter Lombard, Gratian, Orosius, Boëthius, Isidore of Seville, and Solomon. The great schoolman also sketches the history of the mendicant orders, bitterly commenting on their present decadence. In Mars, along with Charlemagne, Roland, and other soldiers of the Cross, Dante encounters his own crusading ancestor, who describes Florence in the good old days, foretells Dante's unjust exile, and assures him fame on account of the work which he shall publish. In Saturn St. Benedict discusses the foundation of his order and laments the fact that his rule has fallen into complete neglect. In the heaven of the fixed stars Dante is examined by St. Peter, who approves his faith and encourages him to speak boldly concerning the present degeneration of the papacy. Finally, in the Empyrean, the topmost heaven, Dante is permitted to have a brief glimpse of God, and the tale of his mystic adventure comes to an end.

Such a poem as the *Divine Comedy* utterly defies an attempt at brief **The qual-** appreciation. As is proved by the library of criticism which it has inspired, **ity of** there is not a canto in any of its three parts that does not demand profound **Dante's** study, both as a literal narrative and as an allegory. The sheer weight of **poetry** erudition implied in its composition is, to say the least, formidable. Yet Dante was anything but a pedant. Being a very great poet, he gave to his work a beauty of expression and a depth of feeling that remain unsurpassed in literature. Although we may dislike his crude descriptions of torments in hell and smile at his naïve catalogue of the saved and the damned, we cannot doubt his passionate sincerity. It is that which gives to his writing the force of a Hebrew prophecy. Dante was intensely religious and his religion, despite his attack on individual priests, was thoroughly orthodox. It was, in fact, the mediæval church that, through the teachings of the schoolmen, provided him with the materials for his book. And he was keenly interested in the contemporary world. This truth is shown by his popularization of science—the best that the age afforded—and by his devotion to his native tongue. From that day to this, literary Italian has remained essentially the language that he perfected.

[19] See above, p. 97, n.

CHAPTER XXII

France and England During the Hundred Years' War

1. THE BEGINNING OF THE WAR AND CHARLES V

The fundamental issue

What is popularly known as the Hundred Years' War was an intermittent conflict between the French and the English kings that lasted into the second half of the fifteenth century. Its outbreak is generally placed in 1337, when Edward III took up arms against Philip VI. But by indulging in hostilities with each other these two kings followed a precedent that was already two centuries old; for practically every king of England since the Norman Conquest had at some time fought a king of France. The underlying cause was always the same: the English king held of the French king certain great fiefs over which the latter consistently tried to gain control. In other words, the so-called Hundred Years' War was merely the continuation of an ancient struggle—one in which the French naturally had the military advantage, though they often failed to use it; and one which logically ended when the English had at last abandoned their continental possessions. If these facts are appreciated, much of the detail that popular accounts have rendered famous may be passed over as relatively insignificant. In the following sketch emphasis will be placed rather on those events which have an important bearing on social or constitutional development.

The Valois succession

First of all, a few words must be given to the matter of the royal succession. By the opening of the fourteenth century primogeniture had been recognized as governing the inheritance of both the English and the French crowns. In England inheritance had already been admitted on the female side of the house (see Table III); in France the question remained open until 1328, when the last son of Philip IV died without a male heir (see Table II). Thereupon Edward III of England, who had succeeded his incompetent father as the result of a baronial insurrection in 1327, laid claim to the throne as the son of Philip's daughter. But a council of French mag-

398

nates decided that, since regal power had already been refused to a woman, no woman could give such power to her son. Philip of Valois thus won the royal title, and Edward accepted the verdict, which thenceforth governed the law of France.[1] Even if the decision had gone the other way, the crown would eventually have passed, not to the English claimant, but to Charles of Navarre (see Table II).

As king, Philip of Valois became master of virtually all France with the exception of four principalities: Guienne, Brittany, Flanders, and Burgundy. These were important lands, but none of them appeared strong enough to withstand royal encroachment for any length of time. And outside his realm the king's prestige had never been so great. The pope was now a Frenchman residing at Avignon, where he was actually, if not legally, under Capetian protection. The house of Anjou, still enjoying the special favor of the papacy, ruled Provence, Naples, and Hungary.[2] That of Luxemburg, which was closely associated with the French court, had recently held the German throne and was now established in Bohemia.[3] The whole of the imperial borderland to the west of the Alps and the Rhine was under the cultural domination of France, as were also northern Spain and the British Isles. Philip VI, however, was a bad king. Incurably frivolous, he considered his government a mere source of funds with which to satisfy his taste for chivalrous display. Even the disastrous English war he seems to have regarded as a sort of entertainment, although it brought untold suffering to his people. His reign, indeed, was fortunate in but one respect; he was able to purchase the rights of the childless count of Vienne, popularly known as the Dauphin because of the dolphin in his coat of arms. Dauphiné, though nominally an imperial fief, was thus acquired by the king of France, who customarily bestowed the title of its ruler upon his eldest son.

Philip VI (1328-50)

Meanwhile Edward III had revealed himself a man somewhat like Philip VI—showy, sport-loving, dissolute, and lazy. Nevertheless, the English king had considerable native ability. He was not only a better diplomat than Philip but also a better general. This fact was demonstrated by his brilliant opening of the so-called Hundred Years' War. Excuses for the resumption of hostilities were not hard to find. The boundary of Guienne continued to be the cause of bitter dispute; Bruce, the Scottish king, whom the English sought to overturn, was actively supported by the French; and the Flemish question once more became acute.[4] No sooner had Philip secured the crown

Edward III and the Flemish question

---

[1] The principle of succession thus defined really had nothing to do with the ancient Salic Law (see above, pp. 55, 57); that tag was falsely attached by lawyers to justify an action already taken.

[2] Charles of Anjou acquired Provence by marriage, the Sicilian kingdom by grant of the pope (above, p. 371). Hungary, as a papal fief, was conferred on one of Charles's descendants by Boniface VIII.

[3] See below, p. 420.

[4] See above, pp. 382-83.

than he led an army north and set up what amounted to a royal administration in Flanders. The result was another insurrection, in which the burghers of various towns joined the peasants of the coastal strip. Although Philip eventually crushed the rising, popular resentment continued and had much to do with the later course of events.

Philip's domination of Flanders was naturally distasteful to Edward III, who proceeded to build up an anti-French coalition and then, in 1336, to lay an embargo on the export of wool. Consequently, as he seems to have calculated, came still another Flemish insurrection. It was led by a prominent cloth merchant of Bruges named Jacob van Artevelde; and as the other towns of Flanders quickly joined the revolt, he became virtual dictator of the county. Under his presidency the Flemings signed a commercial treaty with the English, and it was followed by a political alliance that recognized Edward III as the lawful sovereign of Flanders. Thereupon, in 1337, Edward reasserted his claim to the French throne, however worthless, and issued a formal defiance to his feudal lord.

The battle of Crécy (1346)

Philip replied by declaring Guienne forfeit to the crown and sending a fleet to hold the Channel. But Edward, thanks to his Flemish allies, gained a naval victory at Sluys in 1340 and thereafter was able to raid northern France with a small force every year. Then, in 1345, Artevelde was murdered and, to remedy the situation in Flanders, Edward landed in Normandy and marched north with an army of about ten thousand. At Crécy in the Somme valley he was overtaken by Philip with a force that outnumbered his two to one. The ensuing battle, nevertheless, was a brilliant victory for Edward, who turned to good advantage the tactical innovations of his grandfather. He dismounted his cavalry and grouped them in three battalions on the crest of a hill. On the flanks of each battalion he stationed archers equipped with the English long-bows. Philip's knights charged bravely time and again, but, faced by a deadly storm of arrows, could not reach the enemy position. And when at last the English men-at-arms swept down the hill, they carried all before them.

The battle of Poitiers (1356)

The immediate consequence was Edward's capture of Calais, which, recolonized by English merchants, he turned into a useful base for future operations and a commercial rival to the Flemish towns. Otherwise the war reverted to its previous routine of pillaging expeditions and local skirmishes. By the middle of the century the command of the English forces had passed to the king's eldest son, known as the Black Prince, while Philip VI had been succeeded by John. Like his father, the new French king was a gallant gentleman, fond of chivalrous display and courteous entertainment but utterly devoid of ability either as a statesman or as a general. After long delay, John in 1356 set out with his army to rescue Languedoc from the Black Prince. The English, again badly outnumbered, stood near Poitiers and, repeating the tactics of Crécy, won another victory of the same sort.

Some two thousand French knights fell on the field and an equal number were taken prisoner, including the king and his youngest son. This catastrophe brought France to the verge of ruin. While the king passed a pleasant captivity in England, the royal authority collapsed throughout his kingdom. Hostilities were suspended by a series of truces, and the mercenary companies, now generally employed by both sides, proceeded to live off the country. Before long hardly a French province had escaped devastation or the payment of heavy blackmail.

Meanwhile, too, the country had been visited by the great pestilence known as the Black Death. This, it is now recognized, was an epidemic of plague—a germ disease frequently carried by the fleas that infest small animals, especially rats. It is significant that the course of the Black Death can be traced along the routes followed by ships and, of course, by their rats. According to contemporary accounts, the pestilence came into Europe from the east, being brought from the Crimea to Italy in 1347. Thence, during the next two years, it spread into Germany, France, Spain, and England, eventually to ravage every part of the continent. In the absence of reliable statistics all estimates of its mortality are guesswork. Throughout the towns, where sanitation was worst, more than half of the inhabitants often died, and some rural villages were practically wiped out. But within a whole country we should hardly imagine that more than a quarter of the total population could have been killed—quite enough to constitute a major calamity. The effect on agrarian conditions has been much disputed, and something more will be said on the subject in a later chapter.[5] In the present connection the epidemic is mentioned chiefly because, by increasing the misery of the French people, it helped to produce the political crisis of 1357-58. *The Black Death*

The nominal ruler of France during this unhappy period was the dauphin Charles, as yet an inexperienced youth. Placed in a hopeless situation, he could do no more than yield to the leaders of the estates general. For over half a century it had been customary for the king to summon great assemblies of the clergy and nobility, together with deputies elected by the towns, in order to secure the grant of taxes, the authorization of military levies, or the approval of other extraordinary measures. Occasionally a single body had been called for the entire kingdom, as was first done by Philip IV in 1302 to gain support against Boniface VIII. But such meetings of estates general had been infrequent; the more usual practice had been to hold two assemblies, one for the north at Paris and one for the south at Toulouse. This was the plan followed in 1356, and the estates had already met when the disaster of Poitiers produced a sudden crisis. With the king and the aristocracy wholly discredited, the popular spokesmen at Paris—especially Étienne Marcel, head of the local gild merchant—were able to combine *The estates general and the Grande Ordonnance*

[5] See below, p. 442.

and carry through all the reforms that earlier estates had urged in vain.

The *Grande Ordonnance* of 1357, accepted by Charles in desperation, provided that the royal council should be filled with ministers nominated by the estates. The latter should meet regularly, whether called by the king or not; and when not in session, they were to be represented by a standing committee. No tax could be levied, no military force could be raised, no truce could be signed except by authorization of the estates. They were to appoint deputies (*élus*) to collect all subsidies that might be granted; also generals (*généraux*) to receive the money, pay the troops, and submit accounts for audit. This great enactment, if it had continued in force, would have made France, like contemporary England, a constitutional monarchy. But the increasing disorder throughout the country eventually allowed the patient dauphin to revive and even to enhance the royal authority. By 1358 the Parisians, led by Marcel, had set up what amounted to a revolutionary commune; and their example was being followed in other towns when the men of the adjacent countryside rose in the famous Jacquerie.[6]

The
Jacquerie
(1358)

The peasants, commonly known as Jacques, had from the first been the chief sufferers from the ravages of war and the chronic disorders that followed the collapse of the royal government. More recently the rural districts of northern France had been the scene of constant turmoil in which the troops of the French and English kings vied with companies of brigands in making the life of the people intolerable. The last straw was the appearance of bailiffs to collect the ransoms of various nobles captured at Poitiers. The local inhabitants, already accustomed to organizing for the sake of defense, then followed the example of Paris by defying all superiors and rising against the discredited aristocracy. Actually, the insurrection did not prove to be very formidable. It hardly extended beyond the valley of the Oise and there, despite the horrid tales of the chroniclers, resulted in little more than the pillaging of a few manor houses. But the threat of a social war temporarily induced all factions to make common cause against the rebels. Within a month an army of knights had cut to pieces the main force of the Jacques and mercilessly crushed all resistance in their villages. Meanwhile Marcel had been imprudently led to form an alliance with the insurgents and so to stimulate a sharp reaction at Paris. By the end of the year the bourgeois dictator had been slain and the dauphin had triumphantly regained his capital.

Charles V
(1364-80)

In 1360 peace was signed with the English, and John recovered his freedom on the promise to pay a huge ransom and to cede Guienne in full sovereignty to Edward III. John's spendthrift habits, however, prevented his meeting even the first payment; so, chivalrous to the end, he went back into captivity and there died (1364). At last Charles could wear the crown of which he had so long wielded the authority; and no prince ever deserved

[6] See below, p. 439.

the honor more than he. At the age of twenty-six he already merited the name by which he was to become known, Charles the Wise. In physique he was not impressive, having neither a handsome face nor a well-proportioned body. He was not a chivalrous warrior—for which his subjects should have been very grateful—but a statesman, patient, cautious, and hard-working. By these qualities, in combination with his virtue, piety, and general refinement, Charles V set a new standard for the French kingship. Under him it became apparent to even the humblest peasant that the well-being of the country depended on the monarchy, rather than on the estates. And with the support that now rallied to his cause Charles achieved a brilliant success.

To direct the English war, recommenced since the failure of John's peace, Charles found a talented collaborator in his constable, Bertrand du Guesclin. Together, he and the king reformed the French army by organizing it in permanent companies, pacified the countryside, improved the system of local fortification, and, by developing a sensible strategy of defensive warfare, gradually forced the English back. Meanwhile Charles also reconstituted the royal government. Earlier the estates had granted to John, as a means of paying his ransom, a considerable revenue for an indefinite period—excise taxes on salt, wines, liquors, and other merchandise, together with a direct tax on certain kinds of real property. Subsequently, when the estates objected to new imposts which Charles sought to levy, he agreed to drop them on condition that the old ones should be made permanent. And with the taxes the king took over the machinery of collection set up by the estates. Henceforth the *élus* and *généraux* were royal officials, and estates ceased to be called except for particular regions that had come to enjoy special liberties. The fiscal system that was to characterize the French monarchy until the Revolution of 1789 thus appears as the work of Charles V. In his day, at least, royal absolutism meant the re-establishment of order throughout a distracted country. Apparently, too, it meant the turning of defeat into victory; for at the king's death in 1380 the English possessions in France had been reduced to three patches of territory about Calais, Bordeaux, and Bayonne.

Quite unwittingly, in his desire to circumvent the English, Charles helped to build up a power that was soon to overshadow the Valois kingdom itself. Since the eleventh century the duchy of Burgundy had continued its obscure existence under a collateral branch of the Capetian house, which had also secured as an imperial fief the adjoining county of Burgundy, or Franche-Comté. Then, in 1361, the last of the old line died without heirs, leaving as heiress a young widow, Margaret of Flanders. Just at this time John of France had regained his freedom, and he at once took steps to provide for the succession to the two Burgundies. The duchy, as an escheat to the crown, he gave to Philip, the son who had shared his captivity abroad; and

The new Burgundian dynasty

he prevailed upon the friendly emperor, Charles IV,[7] to invest the prince with Franche-Comté also. The third prize to be disposed of was the widow Margaret, for she was heiress of Flanders. Momentarily the contest seemed won by Edward III, who succeeded in betrothing the lady to one of his sons. But Charles V, thanks to his influence at the papal court, was finally able to break off the match and to substitute his brother Philip. He could not know that what he considered a handsome diplomatic victory over the English would result in deadly peril for his own descendants.

2. THE DECLINE AND REVIVAL OF ENGLAND

Govern-ment of Edward III

Charles V's triumph, though mainly the result of his own intelligent effort, was aided by the contemporary weakening of England. Edward III, out-living the military glory of his youth, soon convinced everybody that he was quite unprincipled; that he cared for nothing but his own pleasure and so preferred a corrupt to an honest administration. As the Black Prince sickened and prematurely died, the efficiency of the English army inevitably suffered. And in the meantime popular dissatisfaction with the royal gov-ernment was reflected by the increasingly bitter protests of parliament. Such protests, combined with the constant need of money for the war in France, induced the ease-loving Edward to agree to numerous reforms. The king's promises, it is true, often proved worthless; yet, in one way or another, he helped to establish various precedents of great constitutional importance.

The English peerage

As remarked in the preceding chapter, it was under Edward III that parliament came to be definitely organized in two houses. The original parliament, with the abstention of the lesser barons from attendance, had become the house of lords—or of peers, to use the more technical name. These peers were either clerical or lay. The former group included bishops, abbots, and heads of military orders, all of whom continued to be sum-moned as barons even after the lower clergy had dropped out of parliament, to meet in a purely ecclesiastical assembly styled convocation.[8] The latter group consisted at first of the earls and other barons who, according to the prescription of *Magna Carta*, received personal letters of summons. In the fourteenth century, however, it became customary for the rank of earl or of baron to be created by royal patent, as well as that of duke or of mar-quis (above the earl) and that of viscount (below the earl). On the con-tinent nobility generally remained a matter of feudal tradition, whereby all descendants of the old fief-holding families were alike noble. In England, by virtue of the development sketched above, nobility was identified with peerage, and that was the equivalent of membership in the house of lords.

[7] See below, p. 420.
[8] Until the seventeenth century the clergy continued to vote subsidies to the crown in convocation.

Such is still the law of England. A peerage, whether old or new, is inherited according to the rule of primogeniture. The wife and children of a peer have only courtesy titles; even the eldest son is legally a commoner until the death of his father.

The house of commons, as we have seen, was an addition to the ancient parliament—one that came into existence as the burgesses and the knights of the shires were drawn by largely identical interests to hold joint deliberations. As yet no-one cared how the members were elected; they merely had to be lawful deputies of their respective communities, so that the latter would be bound by any action they might take, particularly the vote of taxes. For the commons, whatever their incidental usefulness to the monarchy, undoubtedly owed their recognition as a necessary part of the government to the fact that, without them, the king could hardly obtain his much-desired subsidies. Before the death of Edward III it was definitely established that no direct tax could be levied unless it had been formally granted by parliament; and that parliament, to be legally so termed, had to include not only a properly constituted house of lords but also a house of commons elected according to Edward I's model of 1295.[9] The feudal aids, scutage, and tallage now became obsolete. The normal tax was one called a tenth and a fifteenth—i.e., a tenth of personal property inside the boroughs and a fifteenth outside them. The law with regard to indirect taxes remained somewhat vague, though in practice the king restricted his claims to such fixed duties on exports and imports as had been granted by parliament. *The commons and taxation*

The precise definition of parliament also led to a sharp distinction between statute and ordinance. The former was a legal enactment of especial importance, promulgated by the king but incorporating the substance of parliamentary petitions to which he had given assent. The latter was a decree issued by the king in his privy council, the small body of household officials and other ministers whom he appointed and dismissed at pleasure. Exactly what might or might not be enacted by ordinance was a question on which king and parliament were by no means agreed. The principle that a statute could be amended only by statute was easier to declare than to apply, and judicial custom maintained its old importance. Thus parliament had insisted that the king should no longer change the common law by arbitrarily devising writs. To some extent, however, the royal judges accomplished the same end by using the old forms of action in a variety of new ways. And anyone who failed to obtain justice at common law could always appeal to the king's residuary power by means of a petition. As such petitions were customarily turned over to the chancellor, the chief judicial officer of the crown, he became head of a special court called chancery, which enforced a supplement to the ordinary law called equity. This distinction is yet recognized throughout the English-speaking world. If, for example, a *Statute law and equity*

[9] See above, p. 380.

plaintiff does not want damages or restitution of goods, the two remedies at common law, he must bring his suit at equity. Then, in case he wins, the court will grant him an injunction commanding the defendant, under severe penalty, either to do or not to do something in particular.

Richard II and the Revolt of 1381

The other constitutional issues that arose under Edward III can be more adequately discussed in connection with the reigns of his successors. When the old king died in 1377, the throne was inherited by Richard II, son of the Black Prince. Being only nine years of age, Richard could not be expected to carry out the reforms demanded by public opinion, and the same corrupt ministers remained in power. The result was even greater political discontent, which was aggravated by the economic troubles of the age.[10] The climax came when the royal government adopted a peculiarly stupid method of raising funds for the unpopular French war—a poll tax, which was supposed to be assessed on a sliding scale but was so administered that in the poorer districts the average inhabitant had to pay more than many of the rich in the others. An attempt to collect the tax in the spring of 1381 led to the outbreak of rioting, and within a short time the monarchy was faced by a serious insurrection. The two main centers of disturbance were Essex and Kent. In the former the insurgents were chiefly peasants, in the latter artisans and other townsmen. After local depredations had shown that there was little to fear, organized forces from the two regions advanced on London. Having been admitted by sympathizers within the walls, the rebels terrorized the city for two days and dispersed only on being assured by the young king that he personally would redress their grievances.

The Revolution of 1399

Richard II, however, quickly disillusioned his many friends. In quashing the charters of emancipation, which had been granted to the peasant insurrectionaries, and in ruthlessly suppressing all further risings he had the warm support of parliament. But he then proceeded to alienate that support by asserting despotic powers and seeking through force of arms and legal chicanery to remove all limitations on his authority. As a consequence the leaders of parliament in 1399 threw their support to Henry of Lancaster who, heading a baronial revolt, succeeded in capturing the king. Richard was finally deposed by parliament and the duke of Lancaster, as a grandson of Edward III, was proclaimed as King Henry IV. This Revolution of 1399 was momentous in more ways than one. It established the Lancastrian dynasty and in so doing passed over an elder branch of the royal house, whose claims were eventually acquired and reasserted by the duke of York (see Table III). The Lancastrians, since they could hardly justify their possession of the throne by hereditary right, sought ecclesiastical support by furthering the cause of orthodoxy.[11] And they naturally tended in every way to confirm the principles of parliamentary government that had been un-

[10] See below, pp. 437-39.
[11] See below, p. 419.

successfully challenged by Richard II. Many of these principles, surviving all subsequent reaction, have since remained fundamental to the English constitution.

Even before the death of Edward III the house of commons had been definitely organized under an elected president called the speaker. The latter, in his address to the king on the assembling of a new parliament, now came to state the traditional privileges of the commons. And in spite of considerable altercation over details, such privileges—including freedom to introduce petitions, freedom of debate, and freedom from arrest— were formally recognized by the Lancastrians. It was also established that the house of commons could review the elections of all members and declare invalid those in which certain rules had not been enforced. And by a famous statute of 1429 it was provided that, for electing the knights of the shires, only such persons should be entitled to vote as were possessed of a forty-shilling freehold—i.e., a feudal estate with an annual income of at least 40s. Parliamentary control of taxation was more positively confirmed, with the addition that any grant of subsidy must originate in the house of commons. Moneys thus obtained, furthermore, should be expended only as appropriated by parliament, which, to enforce its authority, had the right of auditing the royal accounts. By thus controlling the king's purse, the parliament was often able to dictate appointments to the privy council, matters of governmental policy, and the like. But another Lancastrian institution was of more permanent significance—what came to be known as bill procedure in parliament. Earlier the houses had presented vague petitions to the king; henceforth they couched their desires in the form of a statute and merely asked for the royal assent—the method of parliamentary legislation that has remained in use ever since.

Principles of parliamentary government

By such means, as well as by effectively suppressing a series of revolts, Henry IV was able in 1413 to leave his son a kingdom well satisfied with the new dynasty. The young man of twenty-five who then succeeded as Henry V, aside from the continuation of his father's general policy, had only one ambition—the achievement of military glory. The war that had languished for so many years should be revived; the just claims of the Angevins to their ancient holdings on the continent should be enforced, and thereby an added splendor given to the house of Lancaster. In this ambition Henry V was greatly encouraged by contemporary events in France. Charles V's son and heir, Charles VI, had proved to be thoroughly incompetent and, to make a bad situation worse, became intermittently insane. As the royal authority thus weakened, a bitter feud developed between two factions at court: one headed by the king's younger brother, Louis, duke of Orleans; the other by the king's uncle, Philip, duke of Burgundy (see Table VII). The latter, as we have seen, had been rewarded with the Burgundian duchy when it escheated to the crown in 1361; and to that

Outbreak of civil war in France

he had added not only Franche-Comté, a fief of the holy Roman Empire, but also Flanders, acquired through fortunate marriage to the heiress of the county. Thanks especially to this latter acquisition, the duke' of Burgundy had become a great and powerful prince, whose strategic position on the frontier led him to pursue an aggressive policy in both France and Germany. But Philip's ambition to control the French government was continually thwarted by Louis of Orleans, who preferred to use his high favor at court for his own advantage. So John the Fearless, inheriting the old quarrel along with the Burgundian territories, adopted the simple expedient of having the duke of Orleans assassinated in 1407. The immediate consequence was the outbreak of a murderous civil war that paralyzed France for a generation.

3. JEANNE D'ARC AND THE END OF THE WAR

Henry V and the battle of Agincourt (1415)

In 1415, hoping to repeat his great-grandfather's exploits of 1346, Henry V took an army of about 10,000 men across the Channel, landed on the coast of Normandy, and advanced northeast along the Somme. At the moment Paris, together with the insane king, was in the hands of the Orleanist faction, chiefly nobles of southern France under the count of Armagnac, father-in-law of the youthful duke. To the Armagnac government the bitter experience of the previous century was as nothing. With incredible folly a glittering array of knights proceeded to attack Henry V at Agincourt precisely as their ancestors had attacked Edward III at Crécy. The result was the same. The English repulsed and slaughtered a force that outnumbered them three to one. While Henry then completed the reduction of Normandy by taking Rouen, the Burgundians drove their discredited rivals from Paris and took over the royal administration. The fifteen-year-old dauphin Charles fled south with his Armagnac friends; Queen Isabelle, to maintain her position at court, came to terms with the victors. John of Burgundy now had the responsibility of meeting the English and so opened negotiations for peace with the Armagnacs. But in 1419, while arranging final terms with the dauphin, he was stabbed by a feudist who thought only of avenging Louis of Orleans.

The Peace of Troyes (1420)

The Burgundian reply was the Peace of Troyes signed in 1420 between Charles VI and Henry V. Actually, of course, the treaty was the work of Philip, the new duke of Burgundy, aided by the shameless queen. The dauphin was repudiated as being no lawful heir; on the death of Charles VI his throne should go to his "only true son," Henry of England, now married to the princess Catherine. But Henry was not to enjoy his triumph for long; before the end of 1422 both he and the unfortunate Charles VI were dead and the newborn child of Henry and Catherine was proclaimed king of both realms. Momentarily the change of sovereigns hardly affected the political situation. Two royal uncles, the dukes of Gloucester and Bedford, were installed as regents, and in France the latter proved himself an able soldier. Acting in co-operation with the Burgundians, his armies continued to advance, occupying the country north of the Loire and in 1428 laying siege to Orleans. The uncrowned Charles VII, who was recognized only in the southeast, remained sunk in apathy, apparently indifferent to the fate of his kingdom. Yet his cause was by no means hopeless. If only he would shake off the Armagnac tutelage and assert the powers inherent in his kingship, he would gain widespread sympathy. The English hold on Paris and the north could not survive the loss of Burgundian support and, in the face of a national awakening, Duke Philip might well abandon his allies in order to keep his fiefs. Through one of the most amazing episodes in history the king was to learn his proper role from an illiterate peasant girl.

For the early life of Jeanne d'Arc we have only one documentary source of any great value—the testimony that she herself gave at her trial in 1431. **Jeanne d'Arc and her mission** She had been born, she then declared, in the village of Domrémy on the Lorraine border, the daughter of one Jacques Darc[12] and his wife Isabelle. She was not sure of her age; she thought she was about nineteen—which would make the date of her birth about 1411. She had no book-learning, knowing "neither A nor B," but her mother had taught her to say her prayers, and also to spin and sew. In this domestic skill she took pride; she was no mere shepherdess, for at home she had never tended animals. To these simple facts concerning her early life a few others of more general significance may be added. She had grown up since infancy under the direct influence of the civil war. Domrémy, on the border of Lorraine, was included within a small corner of Champagne that remained continuously loyal to the Valois house. In 1429 it was still being held for Charles by a detachment of royal troops stationed at Vaucouleurs under a captain named Robert de Baudricourt. The villagers, however, had lived in constant dread of Burgundian conquest. On one occasion Jeanne had been sent into Lorraine, where she stayed for two weeks with a friend of the family. Under such circumstances, neither she nor other peasant girls of her age needed instruction as to the evils from which the country was suffering.

She was thirteen years old when she had a voice from God for her help and guidance; and the first time she was greatly frightened. That voice came towards noon on a summer's day, in her father's garden. . . . After she had heard the voice a third time, she knew it was the voice of an angel. . . . It told her to be good and to go to church often; also that she must go into France. . . . Two or three times a week the voice said that she must leave and go into France. . . . She must no longer stay where she was . . . ; she must raise the siege then being made of the city of Orleans. . . . She should go to the captain Robert de Baudricourt in the town of Vaucouleurs and he would provide her with an escort—though she protested that she was a poor girl who knew nothing of

[12] This was the original spelling of the name; it was later changed to d'Arc when the family was declared noble.

riding and fighting. . . . It was St. Michael whom she saw before her eyes;
and he was not alone, but came with a goodly company of angels from heaven.
. . . And when they left her she cried, she wished so that they had taken her
with them.

Thus Jeanne testified in 1431. Did she really hear the voices and see the
angels? On later occasions she frequently reported having talked with the
saints while persons beside her failed to see or hear anything extraordinary.

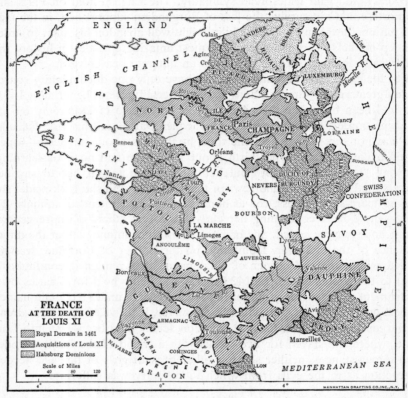

FRANCE
AT THE DEATH OF LOUIS XI

Royal Domain in 1461
Acquisitions of Louis XI
Habsburg Dominions

Scale of Miles
0   40   80   120

Map XVII.

The historian may therefore conclude that her experiences were purely
subjective, and beyond that he need not go. There is no good reason for
doubting the girl's honesty. Her messages must have been very real to her.
Otherwise, how could she have acted as she did?

**The re-
lief of
Orleans
(1429)**
Early in 1429 Jeanne went to Baudricourt who, being finally persuaded
of her sacred mission, gave her a suit of armor and an escort of six soldiers.
With them she made the long and perilous journey to the castle of Chinon
on the Loire, where Charles maintained his headquarters (see Map XVII).

Here, after being carefully examined, she convinced the suspicious king that she had been miraculously sent to aid him. So she obtained from him a force of troops and set out for Orleans, having first dictated a most remarkable letter to the English besiegers. The Maid has been commissioned by Almighty God, she declares, to rescue all the good towns of France.

She has come here, in God's name, to reclaim the blood royal. She is quite ready to make peace if you will come to terms with her; will abandon France and pay for whatever you have taken. You—archers, companions at arms, gentlemen, and others who are before the city of Orleans—in God's name go back to your own country; and if you do not, expect to hear news of the Maid who will shortly visit you to your very great damage. King of England, if you do not agree . . . , in whatever place I encounter your people in France, I will make them leave whether they will or no; and if they do not obey, I will have them all killed. I am sent here by God, the king of heaven, to drive you out of all France.

In advancing on Orleans, Jeanne displayed good sense by attacking the besiegers from the north, where they had as yet failed to erect fortifications. Otherwise she needed little generalship; for the French believed they were led by an angel from heaven and the English feared her as a devil from hell. Having driven the enemy in panic from the intervening territory, Jeanne brought Charles to Reims where, standing at his side, she saw him crowned. If Charles had now displayed any nobility of character, his success would have been even more brilliant. But he listened to the advice of jealous ministers and gave scant support to the Maid, who by no means regarded her mission as ended. While the king resumed his old life and signed a truce with the Burgundians, Jeanne continued the war. During a vain attack on Paris she was wounded; finally, in 1430, a brave sortie before the walls of Compiègne led to her capture by a Burgundian soldier. Charles, to his everlasting discredit, made no offer of ransom; the English were only too glad to do so.

The tragic sequel was inevitable. By that time the witchcraft delusion **Death of** had taken firm hold on the minds even of the educated.[13] In English eyes **the Maid** Jeanne was unquestionably a witch; the matter of her condemnation was merely a detail. At Rouen, in the spring of 1431, she was placed on trial before a special court of French clergy headed by the bishop of Beauvais, who had been driven from his diocese by the royal advance. He and his associates, of course, gave her no chance of acquittal. In spite of a courageous and witty defense, the court declared her guilty of heresy. At the reading of the accusation, Jeanne broke down and confessed her guilt; but later, after being sent back to jail, she reasserted her unflinching faith in her mission and denounced her confession as sheer cowardice. The court thus had the pleasure of sentencing her as a relapsed heretic. Given over to the secular government, she was burned in the public square of Rouen.

[13] See below, pp. 481-83.

The death of Jeanne d'Arc was hailed with delight by the English and their partisans; yet, by making their pitiful captive a martyr, they did not better their cause. Alive, the Maid had not proved invincible; dead, she became the inspiration of a patriotic cause. Although its progress was slow, the demand for a national monarchy eventually grew so strong as to overcome even the inertia of Charles VII. In 1435 he succeeded in buying a separate peace with Philip of Burgundy, and the ruin of the English cause in northern France was assured by the death of Bedford before the end of the same year. A series of truces permitted the king to re-establish the military and financial administration of his grandfather. And when hostilities were renewed about the middle of the century, the victorious march of the French could not be checked. Having regained Normandy, they invaded Guienne. Bordeaux fell in 1453 and the war was over. Now at last Charles decided that something ought to be done for Jeanne d'Arc; it should not stand on the record that so glorious a king had been saved by a witch. Accordingly, by papal authorization, the case was reopened at Rouen in 1456. The errors in the previous trial were blamed on the deceased bishop of Beauvais and, after a prolonged eulogy of the poor burned girl, the judgment was reversed—belated thanks for the winning of a crown and the reinvigoration of a kingdom.

However miserably the reign of Charles VII may have begun, it thus ended in triumph. Henceforth the royal absolutism was never to be effectively challenged until the Revolution of 1789. And throughout this entire period the essence of the monarchical power lay in the king's ability to levy taxes without formal grant by a central assembly. According to the fiscal system established by Charles and perfected by his famous son, Louis XI,[14] the royal taxes were of three principal kinds: the *taille*, a direct tax paid generally by the non-noble classes; the *aides*, indirect taxes on sales of various articles; and the *gabelle*, a tax on salt. The second and third were usually farmed out to syndicates which advanced the king definite sums for the privilege of making the collections. The first was normally apportioned among fiscal districts called *généralités* and *élections* after the *généraux* and *élus* who administered them. There was, however, no uniformity. In some regions, notably Normandy and Languedoc, the royal tax had to be voted and assessed by local assemblies. So the kingdom was said to include two kinds of provinces: the *pays d'états* and the *pays d'élection*. This distinction, together with the hundred others that affected the administration of law for particular persons, classes, and communities, remained to the very end characteristic of the Old Régime in France.

In England, meanwhile, events had pursued an opposite course. The Lancastrian dynasty, which had attained so glorious a height with the Peace of Troyes, ended amid the horrors of civil war and massacre. Henry VI

---

[14] See below, pp. 471-74.

grew up to be a virtuous man utterly devoid of political ability. Under more favorable circumstances the ruinous consequences of the king's incompetence might have been avoided through the employment of wise ministers. But he was surrounded by ambitious courtiers who thought only of their own private interests. Among them the more prominent figures were the king's relatives—a prolific tribe claiming descent, legitimate or illegitimate, from the children of Edward III, and intermarried with practically every baronial house of England. Under the feeble administration of Henry VI their feuds disturbed the entire country. The king, tainted by descent from Charles VI, became hopelessly insane and, as in France, this misfortune helped to precipitate a murderous conflict. The leader of the anti-Lancastrian party was Richard of York, heir of the boy whose rights had been passed over by parliament in 1399 (see Table III). In 1453, when the birth of a son to Henry VI precluded the possibility of a peaceful succession, York raised the standard of revolt.

Although the war which thus began never involved more than small bands of noblemen with their retainers, it was a very sanguinary affair. Being fought in a violently feudist spirit, it produced a relatively huge number of victims, either killed in battle or murdered in cold blood. Before it was over, the English aristocracy was very nearly exterminated. From the military point of view, its battles were insignificant, and their political results may be very briefly summarized. After winning several engagements, York was killed in 1460. But the cause of his son Edward was ably championed by the earl of Warwick, who in the next year drove Henry VI into exile and had the Yorkist prince crowned as Edward IV. Then, when the new king proved ungrateful, Warwick changed sides, forced Edward to seek refuge with the duke of Burgundy, and in 1470 reinstated Henry VI— an action that won him the name of the King-Maker. Again his triumph was short-lived, for in 1471 the Yorkists, with Burgundian aid, gained two decisive battles, during or after which Warwick, Henry VI, his son, and the other prominent Lancastrians were all slain. For the remainder of his life Edward IV reigned unmolested.

The duke of Burgundy to whom reference has just been made was Philip the Good, son and successor of the murdered John the Fearless. Philip was the most resplendent prince of western Europe. From his father he inherited Burgundy, Franche-Comté, Flanders, and Artois; from cousins, as the result of family alliances in Germany,[15] he inherited Luxemburg, Brabant, Holland, Zeeland, Friesland, and Hainaut. In addition he bought the county of Namur and installed various relatives in the bishoprics of Liége, Utrecht, and Cambrai. Under him, for the first time since the disruption of Charlemagne's empire, the region of the Netherlands was thus

Philip the Good of Burgundy (1419-67)

---

[15] One was with the house of Wittelsbach, another with that of Luxemburg; see below, pp. 420-21.

brought into political union (see Map XVIII). In 1435, as we have seen, Philip signed the Peace of Arras with Charles VII. By its terms the king promised to punish the murderers of Duke John and to found a monastery in his honor. Besides—and these were the more practical articles—Charles ceded to Philip various territories already in Burgundian occupation, together with the cities and castles of the Somme valley, which could be redeemed only by the payment of 400,000 gold crowns. Philip was freed from all feudal service and his lands were exempted from all royal taxes.

As the virtually independent ruler of an extensive and prosperous territory, the Burgundian duke lacked but two steps of attaining ultimate success. In the first place, he needed Alsace and Lorraine to combine in one well-rounded unit the Burgundies and the Netherlands; in the second place, he coveted the royal title. How these ambitions, together with the princely heritage, passed to Charles the Rash and governed his tragic career will be explained in the concluding chapter.

CHAPTER XXIII

The Decline of the Church

1. The Great Schism and the Spread of Heresy

The long-continued residence of the popes at Avignon was finally ended The
by Gregory XI, who, shortly after returning to Rome, died there in 1378. double
Of the sixteen cardinals who now had to choose a successor eleven were election
Frenchmen. Had they been voting at Avignon, their action would undoubtedly have been different; but in the midst of the wildly excited Roman
populace, and just before a mob broke into the Vatican, they named an
Italian who was crowned as Urban VI. Almost at once they repented their
action. So, encouraged by Charles V of France, they withdrew to Anagni,
where they declared the previous election void on account of intimidation
and elevated the bishop of Geneva as Clement VII. Thereupon Urban excommunicated all the old cardinals and replaced them with new ones.
Clement, establishing himself at Avignon, replied with anathemas of his
own, and the Great Schism had begun. On earlier occasions disputed elections had usually ended after a few years of quarreling, when one of the
contestants died or abdicated. Now, however, the opposing forces were so
evenly balanced that their conflict threatened to last indefinitely.

It has been held that the schism was based on sincere disagreement with
regard to the merits of a difficult case. Weighty arguments were indeed advanced on both sides of the dispute; yet the dominance of political factors
seems too obvious to be denied. The fundamental cause of trouble was
unquestionably the antagonism between the French cardinals and the Roman
populace—neither party conspicuous for its altruism. Italian opinion quite
naturally favored the latter, and it was no mere coincidence that the king
of France sympathized with the former. An assembly of the French clergy
gave Clement their allegiance and the University of Paris, under royal
pressure, grudgingly did so too. The English, of course, declared for Urban,

415

as did the continental states within their sphere of influence, such as Portugal and Flanders. For the same reason Scotland supported Clement, and so eventually did Navarre, Castile, and Aragon. Most of eastern, central, and northern Europe followed the emperor in pronouncing for the Roman pope. A number of German princes, however, asserted their independence by taking the opposite side.

Efforts to heal the schism

As the century drew to a close and all Europe seemed to be falling into chaos, it was natural that the leadership of the distracted church should be assumed by the University of Paris. Such action became the more necessary because the death of Urban VI had merely led to the installation of a successor at Rome, and because Clement VII could not be expected to live much longer. The university had never given him more than half-hearted support and the French people had found the maintenance of a separate papacy an expensive luxury. The passing of the original contestants might therefore provide a good opportunity for the healing of the schism. So the doctors of Paris now presented the royal government and the world at large with a definite program. The efforts of Christians should be directed, first, towards securing the abdication of both popes in favor of a single candidate; secondly, towards devising some other settlement through arbitration between the two; or, as a last resort, towards the calling of a general council with jurisdiction over the whole matter—a procedure that would virtually accept the radical theory advanced by Marsiglio of Padua.[1]

When Clement died in 1394, however, his cardinals were unwilling to permit a prolonged vacancy and elected a man pledged to abdicate whenever the occasion should arise—a Spanish prelate who took the name of Benedict XIII. Then ensued several years of diplomatic effort, in the course of which the university, the king of France, and various other princes vainly sought to obtain a joint abdication on the part of the popes. Benedict, especially, refused all co-operation. Ignoring his solemn promise, he displayed such obstinacy that he soon antagonized most of his partisans and inspired the archbishop of Reims to remark that Spain had always been famous for its mules! Coming to share the same conviction, the French government decided to use force as a supplement to moral suasion. In 1398, accordingly, it induced an ecclesiastical assembly to vote "subtraction of obedience" from the pope. This was a revolutionary act that could be justified only by arguing that the clergy of a particular state constituted an autonomous unit, a national church which could grant or withhold allegiance at pleasure. In other words, the so-called Gallican Liberties—a concept that was to gain increasing prominence during later centuries—owed their first definition to the collapse of the papal authority in France.

Whatever its importance as a legal precedent, the French act of 1398 soon lost all efficacy with the outbreak of civil war between the Armagnacs

---

[1] See above, p. 393.

and the Burgundians. Benedict, encouraged by the paralysis of the mon- **The**
archy, stubbornly maintained his position. Then in 1406 fresh hope arose. **Council**
A renewed vacancy at Rome resulted in the election of Gregory XII on **of Pisa**
condition that he would try to end the schism by holding a personal inter- **(1409)**
view with his rival. Indeed, both popes actually started out and, under
enormous pressure, were finally brought within sight of each other at Lucca.
But while one was on land the other was on the sea, and neither could be
persuaded to forsake his element! Disgusted by this farcical performance,
a majority of the cardinals from the two camps made common cause and,
defying papal commands, summoned a general council to meet at Pisa in
the following year, 1409. Although it lacked hearty approval in various
countries, the Council of Pisa immediately adopted drastic measures. Benedict and Gregory, after their refusal to appear for trial, were deposed from
office. Finally, as the result of an election held by all the rebel cardinals,
the Neapolitan John XXIII was installed. And since John was unable to
oust either Gregory or Benedict, there were now three popes instead of
two. The very fact that the situation was thus made worse, however, united
all western Christendom in support of a new and greater council, which
was summoned to Constance by John XXIII in co-operation with Sigismund, king of Germany.[2]

Even before the Great Schism dissatisfaction with the organized church **Fourteenth-**
had steadily increased and had shown itself in many ways. The Avignon **century**
popes, having become embroiled with the more radical Franciscans, natu- **mystics**
rally turned the machinery of the Inquisition against them as well as other
dissenters. But the growing disorder of the age prevented the enforcement
of decisive measures. As a result, the dissenters continued to win strength,
and some of their leaders, in the face of ineffectual threats, became out-and-
out heretics. A great number of the dissatisfied, on the other hand, refused
to break with the traditional system and sought consolation in various forms
of mystic faith. There were, for instance, many such persons associated
with the Spiritual Franciscans, either as actual friars or as lay brothers
pledged to an especially austere life. In the early fourteenth century two
German Dominicans, Eckehart and Tauler, had an important influence as
preachers of contemplative piety, and so helped to found the religious association of laymen called the Friends of God. Somewhat similar were the
Brothers of the Common Life, established in the Netherlands by Gerard
Groote. The New Devotion to which they were committed is eloquently
revealed by the well-known *Imitation of Christ*, traditionally ascribed to
Thomas à Kempis. The list of other mystics who gained fame by preaching
or writing could be extended indefinitely. But the greatest of them was unquestionably St. Catherine of Siena, a simple Italian girl whose ecstatic

[2] See below, p. 421.

visions led her to play an active part in the contemporary agitation for reform.

Anti-papal agitation in England

In England, where the French sympathies of the Avignon popes were hotly resented, the anti-papal movement gained rapid headway towards the middle of the fourteenth century. With the cordial support of the royal government, parliament forbade papal appointment to ecclesiastical office in England by the Statute of Provisors,[3] restricted the carrying of appeals to the papal court by the Statute of Præmunire, and finally denied all papal lordship over the realm on the ground that King John's homage to Innocent III had been illegal. Besides, an increasing number of politicians, authors, and preachers joined in denouncing the other abuses then being fostered by the papacy, especially the indiscriminate sale of indulgences. The theory of indulgence was itself based on good canonical authority. The church had long taught that a particularly holy act might be rewarded by a remission of penance, or of equivalent pains in purgatory.[4] In the case of a crusader such remission was complete, in that of a less meritorious person only partial. If, for example, anyone contributed towards the expense of a crusade or the raising of a sacred monument, the extent of his indulgence would vary according to the amount of his contribution. Through an easy transition the later popes thus came to raise funds for all sorts of projects by authorizing a special issue of indulgences. The recipient was never supposed to buy forgiveness of sin, whether past or future; but all too often the papal agents were unscrupulous enough to misrepresent their wares in order to augment their commissions.

John Wycliffe (d. 1384)

It was therefore no wonder that powerful men at the court of Edward III welcomed the learned essays of one John Wycliffe. Almost nothing is known of his early life. By 1360 he was a well-known master at Oxford and, as an ordained priest, was helping to maintain himself at the university by holding a parish in the country. Since he had previously been a student at Oxford, he must have come under the influence of such famous men as William of Ockham and Marsiglio of Padua.[5] At any rate, when Wycliffe himself came to publish books, they developed arguments that had long been familiar in the controversial writings of the Franciscans and others— as that the rightful authority of a ruler, lay or clerical, is in direct proportion to the reciprocal service that he performs for his subjects; and that, at least in some cases, a state may be justified in confiscating ecclesiastical property. Wycliffe's favor at court stood him in good stead when Pope Gregory XI condemned as erroneous eighteen of his opinions, affirming that they were reminiscent of those expressed by Marsiglio "of damned memory." For a time Wycliffe even kept his position at the university.

[3] See above, p. 370.
[4] See above, p. 230.
[5] See above, p. 393.

Then, as he became a confessed rebel against ecclesiastical authority, he lost the support of the conservative elements at Oxford and retired to his parish of Lutterworth, where he died in 1384. Although his books had been condemned, he had been immune from personal molestation.

Until his later years Wycliffe remained essentially a scholar. His more important works were all in Latin; and since they are filled with the fine-drawn distinctions of the schoolmen, it is often hard to determine his exact position. Some points, however, are certain. Wycliffe repudiated the papal headship as a corruption of the primitive church. Without excluding all miraculous quality from the celebration of the mass, he denied transubstantiation as it had been defined since the days of Innocent III. And after his writings had been formally declared heretical, he naturally tended to press his argument to increasingly radical conclusions. Like the Waldensians, he came to emphasize the saving power of Christ rather than priestly mediation, and to prefer the authority of Holy Scripture to that of the organized church. Through force of circumstance he at the same time shifted his appeal from men in power to the ordinary inhabitants of town and country, preaching in the vernacular, supervising an English translation of the Bible, and inspiring his disciples to adopt a life of poverty among the people.

Wycliffe's followers, who came to be known as Lollards, rapidly multiplied during the troubled years that closed the fourteenth century. That their attack upon various evils in the existing church was justified is proved by many contemporary writings. Wycliffe, as we shall see, was by no means alone in his denunciation of luxurious prelates, degenerate monks, hypocritical friars, dishonest peddlers of indulgences, and the like. Although he personally never turned his doctrines to justify political insurrection, some of his popular preachers may have done so. There were, we know, rebellious priests who encouraged the Great Revolt of 1381. In any case the Lollards hardly suffered from governmental interference until the opening of the fifteenth century. Then the Lancastrian Henry IV, anxious to obtain ecclesiastical recognition of his title to the throne, gave warm support to the orthodox cause. The punishment of heretics by burning, hitherto unknown in England, was now established by act of parliament; and after a rising of the Lollard gentry had been suppressed, the law was rigorously enforced against the remnants of the sect. Within another generation, at least the public avowal of Wycliffite doctrines had disappeared. *The Lollards*

Meanwhile these doctrines had become widely prevalent in Bohemia— a strange development that can only be explained by reviewing the history of Germany in the fourteenth century. Except as an honorary decoration, the German kingship was now chiefly valuable because it enabled the holder to enrich himself and his family by means of forfeited or escheated fiefs. It was in this way, as we have seen, that the Habsburgs first gained *Bohemia and Germany* prominence. It was in the same way that Henry of Luxemburg, elected in 1308 on account of his poverty, advanced the fortunes of his house; for he was lucky enough to place his son on the throne of Bohemia, which had recently become vacant through the failure of the old royal line.[6] Having thus established a new dynasty at Prague, Henry spent his remaining years in a foolish expedition to Italy. There, like so many of his predecessors, he secured the imperial crown, quarreled with the pope, fought useless battles, and died of malaria. He was succeeded, after a civil war, by Louis of Bavaria, who has already been mentioned as the patron of Ockham and Marsiglio. Louis also did very well by his house, that of Wittelsbach, which now acquired a series of fine inheritances, including the duchy of Carinthia, the margravate of Brandenburg, and the county of Holland. His unabashed greed, however, invited a rising of the princes, who in 1346 gave the crown to Charles of Bohemia, grandson of Henry VII (see Table VIII).

Charles IV (1346-78)

The reign of Charles IV in Germany was memorable, not only for his breaking of the Wittelsbach power, but also for his promulgation of the so-called Golden Bull of 1356, which confirmed and regulated the traditional procedure used in royal elections. It recognized seven electors: the archbishops of Mainz, Trier, and Cologne, together with the king of Bohemia, the count palatine of the Rhine, the duke of Saxony, and the margrave of Brandenburg. The electors were to assemble within a month after a king's death and, if at the end of thirty days they had failed to reach a decision, they were to be put on a diet of bread and water until they did so. By other articles, which guaranteed the vested interests of the great princes, Charles assured the persistence of the monarchy. Under his plan, it is worth noting, the papacy lost all opportunity of reviewing the action of the electors, and future kings were encouraged to assume the imperial title without coronation at Rome. The popes of course protested; but since the emperor no longer asserted any control over Italy, they had no valid cause of complaint.

John Hus

In Bohemia, meanwhile, Charles had given the Czechs an excellent government, based on a wise reform of their ancient institutions, and had there founded the illustrious University of Prague. Dying in 1378, he was succeeded on the thrones of Germany and Bohemia by his eldest son Wenceslas (Wenzel). National resentment against German encroachment in Bohemia had only been allayed by the statesmanlike Charles IV. Now, as Wenceslas became known as a boor and a drunkard, it flared up again. The fact that so many high positions in church and state were held by Germans was bitterly denounced by the Czechs, who therefore, as a matter of patriotism, supported any movement directed against the domination of their country by foreigners. The University of Prague, from which a large

[6] See above, pp. 321, 376.

number of German masters were forced to emigrate, naturally became a center of the nationalist organization. And among its leaders at the opening of the fifteenth century was John Hus, a young theologian attached as preacher to one of the local chapels. Already convinced that the church was suffering from many evils, he now became acquainted with the writings of Wycliffe. Since the marriage of Richard II to a daughter of Charles IV various Bohemians had studied at Oxford, including Jerome of Prague, who brought back with him certain of the famous Englishman's later works. Hus, while hesitating over Wycliffe's extreme conclusions on points of doctrine, accepted the Lollard reform in general and ardently devoted his energy to its furtherance. His views, taken up by a host of volunteers, quickly spread throughout the countryside, where the agitation grew more and more violent.

This was the situation in 1414. Wenceslas, deposed in Germany, had been succeeded by his younger brother Sigismund who, thanks to a marriage alliance, had already acquired the crown of Hungary. Bohemia, still ruled by the unpopular Wenceslas, had been thrown into turmoil by the preaching of Hus and his followers. Sigismund, as a supporter of Pope John XXIII, joined the latter in summoning the Council of Constance. What, confronted by so many other grave problems, would it do to restore religious peace in Bohemia?

2. THE COUNCILS OF CONSTANCE AND BASEL

Having met in the autumn of 1414, the new council at Constance did not formally organize until January of the next year. Normally in such assemblies only prelates had been permitted to vote. Now, on the proposal of the Parisian spokesmen, it was agreed to extend the privilege to all doctors of theology or of canon law, and furthermore to divide the council into four nations: Italian, French, German, and English.[7] The former measure assured the dominance of the reforming party; the latter prevented the exercise of undue influence by the Italian clergy, for they could be outvoted by the other nations. Chief among the persons displeased by this action was John XXIII, who had summoned the council in the expectation that it would support him against Gregory XII and Benedict XIII. On the contrary, since neither Sigismund nor the French leaders cared to take so unpopular a stand, he was treated as merely one of three rivals. In March, 1415, John therefore denounced the whole proceeding and left the city. His flight, instead of paralyzing the council, facilitated its program. Declaring its sovereign authority under the direct inspiration of God, it annulled all decrees that John might issue and menaced him with deposition if he did not at once submit. In May the threat was carried out and John, by that time a prisoner in the hands of Sigismund, formally accepted the

The end of the schism

---

[7] Later, on the arrival of the Spanish, they were recognized as a fifth nation.

judgment. Next Gregory, to avoid a less dignified fate, wisely decided to resign. There remained only the stubborn Benedict. Up to this point he had enjoyed the allegiance of Castile and Aragon, but before the end of the year they had deserted him. Still the aged Spaniard refused to abdicate; so, while he shut himself up in a castle and launched anathemas against a hostile world, he was condemned afresh and thenceforth ignored.

Trial and death of Hus (1415)

In the meantime the council had taken up the case of John Hus, who had come to Constance under Sigismund's letters of safe conduct. There he found few sympathizers. Even the extreme champions of conciliary supremacy had no desire to break the doctrinal traditions of the mediæval church; indeed, the very fact that they opposed the papal absolutism made them the more anxious to prove their orthodoxy in matters of faith. While a preliminary investigation was being held, Hus was seized and imprisoned. Sigismund protested, but was assured that a promise made to a heretic had no validity. In May, 1415, the council affirmed the earlier condemnation of Wycliffe by the English clergy, commanding his books to be burned and his bones to be cast out of consecrated soil. In June Hus was arraigned for trial. Although he insisted that he had not denied transubstantiation, he freely admitted that in many respects he believed Wycliffe to have been right. For saying that a king living in mortal sin was no king in God's sight, he was abandoned to his fate by Sigismund. The council thereupon drew up a list of thirty-nine articles taken from his writings and asked him to abjure them. With absolute bravery Hus refused until they could be proved contrary to Holy Scripture. Accordingly, he was adjudged an incorrigible heretic, handed over to the civil authorities, and burned (July 6, 1415). Jerome of Prague followed him to the stake in the next year.

The problem of reform

While demonstrating thorough conservatism as to Christian doctrine, the majority of the council continued to demand extensive reform in the sphere of ecclesiastical government. As to what should be done, however, there was no unanimity. The bishops, of course, wanted no reform of the episcopal system, and as soon as they proposed changes in the papal administration they encountered the bitter hostility of the cardinals. Even the question of future assemblies quickly became controversial. Should a general council have permanent functions in connection with routine matters, or should the exercise of its powers be restricted to emergencies? And in such emergencies precisely what might it do? The year 1416 saw little accomplishment at Constance, for the ecclesiastical disputes were aggravated by political dissension among the nations—especially the civil war in France and the English invasion of Normandy. So the church still remained without a recognized head.

The autumn of 1417 brought a crisis. One party had demanded the immediate election of a pope; another had insisted on the adoption of reforms as a necessary preliminary to such action. But everybody was tiring of the long delay and in October a compromise was effected: the articles already agreed to by the nations should be enacted as a basis for subsequent legislation and the election held at once. Six decrees were accordingly promulgated, the more important of which concerned the holding of general councils in the future. The first of these councils should be called in five years, the second seven years later, and thenceforth one every ten years, except that in case of schism a council should meet even without being summoned. The sixth decree enumerated eighteen points with regard to which the newly elected pope should establish reforms in consultation with the present council. All eighteen had to do with papal rights and practices: such as the pope's taxes and other revenues, his powers of appointment, appeals to his court, his granting of dispensations and indulgences, the constitution of his cardinal college, and the offenses for which he might be tried before a general council.

In the following month, after considerable dispute over procedure, **Election of** twenty-three cardinals met with thirty deputies of the five nations and by **Martin V** unanimous vote elected a pope. Their choice fell on one of Gregory XII's **(1417)** cardinals, a member of the great Colonna family, who took the name of Martin V. In personal character he was above reproach and his political skill was attested by the fact that he had made no violent enemies during the troubled years preceding. Being now the head of a reunited church, he inevitably took advantage of the council's growing fatigue to reassert the papal authority. One or two measures of no far-reaching consequence were proposed by him to the entire assembly and there adopted. At the same time, however, he began discussion with the separate nations, which eventually agreed to a series of minor concessions as in part satisfying their demands. Accordingly, in April, 1418, the pope was able to pronounce the dissolution of the council on the ground that there was no longer any need of it. Whether, if it had continued to sit for another year, anything further would have been accomplished may well be doubted. At any rate, the program of thorough reform that had occasioned so much talk seemed now to be forgotten, and people as of old turned for leadership to the all-powerful papacy.

Meanwhile the council's Bohemian policy had also proved an utter **The Hus-** failure. In the eyes of the Czechs John Hus was a national hero who had **site war** been grossly betrayed by Sigismund. Thus, when the latter laid claim to the throne of Bohemia on the death of Wenceslas in 1419, the whole country burst into revolt. Though united in the patriotic cause, the Hussites were sharply divided on the matter of religion. The moderates, or Calixtines, demanded four reforms: full liberty of preaching the Gospel, communion in both kinds,[8] restoration of the apostolic life by abolishing the temporal power of the church, and strict enforcement of the canons

[8] In the Roman mass the communicant received only the consecrated bread, not the wine. Those who demanded communion in both kinds were called Calixtines because they wished to receive also the cup (chalice, *calix*).

against mortal sin. This group included practically all the masters in the University of Prague, together with the majority of the upper bourgeoisie and the landed aristocracy. Among the lower classes of town and country, on the other hand, it was the more radical doctrines of Wycliffe that had secured a firm hold through the missionary efforts of popular preachers. Merging imperceptibly into older congregations of Waldensians, they rejected all beliefs and practices for which they found no direct justification in Scripture: especially adoration of the saints, monasticism, purgatory, indulgences, and the sacraments aside from baptism and the eucharist. Under such a régime the necessity of an ordained clergy tended to disappear; the priest became primarily a minister of the Gospel, leading a simple life in the midst of his flock and setting them an example of the strict morality which we know as Puritanical.

As was soon to be demonstrated, there was wide disagreement among the more radical Hussites, but the strongest of their associations was that of the Taborites, so called after a central village which they had renamed from the Bible. Although feeling was very bitter between them and the Calixtines, the two factions for the moment had no chance to fight each other. In 1420 Martin V proclaimed a crusade against the Bohemian heretics and the consequence was the enthusiastic union of the Czechs in national defense. The Catholic army was a nondescript aggregation of feudal levies and volunteers, directed by papal legates while Sigismund remained occupied with a Turkish war.[9] On their side the Czechs had solid popular support and a thorough knowledge of the country. Besides, in John Zizka, a lesser noble associated with the Taborite organization, they found a general of outstanding genius. He perfected a tactical system that ranks among the most effective of the Middle Ages. Heavy wagons mounted with cannon[10] were turned into movable bulwarks behind which he stationed his crudely armed infantry. Thanks to his skillful use of such primitive tanks and to the spirit of his troops, he was able to defeat three successive crusades (1420-22). Then followed a devastating civil war, in the course of which Zizka died. Yet the Czechs repulsed a fourth invading host in 1427; and despite the return of Sigismund and an attempted reform of the German army, a fifth expedition in 1431 met the same disastrous fate.

The Council of Basel and the Bohemian settlement

This series of events, a discredit to empire and papacy alike, produced a fresh crisis in the church. Following the decision made at Constance, Martin V had reluctantly summoned a general council at Pavia in 1423; but the few ecclesiastics who attended did little more than select Basel as the meeting-place of the next council. By 1431 conditions were very different. Martin, having authorized the council of that year, died before the

[9] See below, p. 429.
[10] See below, pp. 486-89.

delegates had actually assembled. His successor, Eugenius IV, appeared to have no interest except local politics, while all Christendom was alarmed by the Hussite triumph and its possible inspiration of outbreaks in other countries. The consequence was a great influx of clergy into Basel—especially of men determined on bold measures for the sake of rehabilitating the church. The new council, instead of dividing into nations, adopted a sort of committee system for preliminary discussion of measures. Then, on the recommendation of leaders just returned from the Bohemian war, it invited the moderate Hussites to send a deputation for the purpose of arranging an amicable settlement. The scandalized Eugenius thereupon pronounced the dissolution of the assembly, only to elicit the reply that no general council could be dissolved without its own consent. Eventually, after the pope had been driven from Rome by a coalition of his enemies, he again recognized the council, which proceeded to sign a compact with the Calixtines. Although on three of their four articles the compromise was so vague as to be meaningless, communion in both kinds was specifically allowed and the moral victory clearly lay with the Czechs. In 1434 the Taborites, who had naturally refused to accept the agreement, were crushed by the strengthened forces of the moderates. Two years later the Bohemian peace was formally ratified and Sigismund, having sworn to support it, was at last admitted to Prague.

During this affair Pope Eugenius had played an inglorious part. He had been compelled to reverse his position regarding the Hussites and to recognize the acts of an assembly which he had thought to dissolve. Whatever the saving theories that might be devised by the legal-minded, the actual sovereign of the church had proved to be not the pope but the council. It was logical, therefore, that the latter should now take up the project of general reform where it had been dropped at Constance. In rapid succession decrees were promulgated to abolish annates,[11] to restrict papal appointments, to reconstitute the cardinal college, and to define the pledges that should be demanded of future popes. Yet, in proportion as the more radical element gained control of the assembly, the more conservative swung over to the papal side—a tendency that was inevitably favored by the pacification of Bohemia. Eugenius, once more the master of Rome, simply awaited a favorable opportunity to renew his defiance of the opposition. By 1438 matters had come to an open breach. The pope refused a summons to defend his conduct at Basel and called a rival council at Florence, where negotiations with the Byzantine emperor led in the next year to an apparent reunion of the Greek and Latin churches.

This triumph of the pope's diplomacy was short-lived, for the treaty failed of ratification at Constantinople. Nevertheless, the trend of events

The papal triumph

[11] A papal tax developed in the fourteenth century. The newly elected prelate had to pay to Rome the first year's income of his office.

CENTRAL AND
EASTERN EUROPE
ABOUT 1475

Burgundian Dominions

Habsburg Dominions

Wittelsbach Dominions

Scale of Miles
0   50   100   150   200

KINGDOM OF NORWAY

KINGDOM OF

KINGDOM OF DENMARK

BALTIC

NORTH SEA

KM. OF ENGLAND

London

Calais

ZEELAND

FLANDERS

ARTOIS

Cambrai

PICARDY

Seine R.

Paris

HOLLAND

Utrecht

GELDER-LAND

HAINAUT

BRABANT

Liége

LUXEM-BURG

Trier

LORRAINE

FRANCE-COMTE

ALSACE

Rhine

Cologne

Mainz

PALAT-OF RHINE

Ems R.

Bremen

Weser R.

Hamburg

Elbe R.

MARK OF BRANDENBURG

Oder R.

SAXONY

SILESIA

KIN

Prague

BOHEMIA

MORAVIA

PALATINATE

Rhine R.

BAVARIA

Danube

AUSTRIA

STYRIA

KING

OF HUN

Drave R.

Save R.

KINGDOM OF BURGUNDY

KINGDOM OF FRANCE

SWISS CONFEDERATION

Rhone R.

SAVOY

DAUPHINÉ

Avignon

PROVENCE

GENOA

MILAN

TYROL

Salzburg

CARINTHIA

CARNIOLA

CROATIA

VENETIAN REPUBLIC

Venice

MANTUA

MODENA

PAPAL STATES

FLORENCE

SIENA

Tiber R.

Rome

ADRIATIC SEA

BOSN

MEDITERRANEAN SEA

CORSICA

Map XVIII

continued to favor the papal cause. In 1439 the fathers at Basel made the
fatal mistake of setting up an anti-pope. A fresh schism was the last thing
Europe desired and thenceforth the credit of the council steadily declined.
The moderates had already deserted; though a dwindling shadow of the
original body lasted on for another ten years, the conciliar movement had
come to a miserable end. None of the temporal princes took any interest
in the anti-pope. Eugenius, by playing off one European power against
another, was able to secure the general recognition of his authority in
preference to that of the discredited council. Finally, in 1449, what was
left of the latter formally dissolved itself, while its protégé resigned all
claim to the papal dignity. Nicholas V, the successor of Eugenius IV, was
thus led to celebrate the restoration of ecclesiastical peace by a great
jubilee at Rome in 1450. Yet one who even glanced at the situation in
the contemporary world could have seen much for which Christendom had
no reason to rejoice.

3. EASTERN EUROPE AND THE NEW MOSLEM OFFENSIVE

**The re-
vival of
Poland**

While the attention of most western Christians had been centered on
the schism and the efforts of the councils to heal it, eastern Europe had
witnessed two important developments, the results of which are still clearly
perceptible. One was a great anti-German campaign launched by a reinvigorated Poland; the other was the victorious advance of the Ottoman
Turks in the Balkan peninsula. The conquest of the southern Baltic coast
by the Teutonic Knights in the thirteenth century has been described in an
earlier chapter.[12] Once that conquest was completed, material prosperity
brought the usual relaxation of primitive discipline and the order rapidly
decayed. During the same time Poland enjoyed a noteworthy revival of
strength. A series of able kings restored the unity of the kingdom, gave it
an improved constitution, and extended its frontiers to include Galicia on
the south. Then, in 1386, the Poles won a great diplomatic victory by
marrying the heiress of their crown to Jagiello of Lithuania, thereafter
known as Ladislas II of Poland. Since Jagiello's father had recently taken
the Ukraine from the Tartars, the incorporation of Lithuania brought the
Polish kingdom to the shore of the Black Sea. It was even more important
that the Lithuanians followed the example of their ruler in accepting
Christianity; for the Poles, without prejudice to holy church, could now
join forces with a people who had long been waging a bitter war against
the Teutonic Knights. The climax in the renewed struggle came with
Jagiello's great victory at Tannenberg in 1410. Although the intervention
of other powers limited the immediate acquisitions of the Poles, the
Prussian order had suffered a fatal blow. The Peace of Thorn, dictated by
Jagiello's grandson in 1466, awarded West Prussia to Poland in full

[12] See above, p. 376.

sovereignty, while the Teutonic Knights were to hold East Prussia merely as a fief of the Polish crown. (See Map XVIII.)

In the Balkans, meanwhile, the Byzantine Empire was entering upon the last dismal stage of its long history. Although a Greek emperor regained the throne at Constantinople in 1261, he could not restore the empire even as it had been in the twelfth century. The control of the Ægean, with its islands and the coasts of the Peloponnesus, was kept by Venice; much of Greece remained in the hands of French barons; and the

The Balkan states

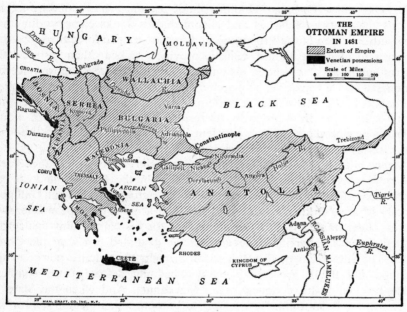

MAP XIX.

emperor's possession of his other European provinces was disputed by the revived kingdoms of Bulgaria and Serbia (see Map XIX). First one and then the other of these states, under rulers who had assumed the imperial title of tsar, threatened to reduce the whole peninsula and to take the city of Constantinople. But each eventually fell back exhausted. Nor could any more Christian co-operation be expected from the Italians, Hungarians, and Poles than from the Bulgars, Serbs, and Byzantines. It had been proved by sad experience that the Latins were quite as willing to fight one another as to fight schismatic Greeks. Like the project of reuniting the eastern and western empires, Innocent III's dream of healing the breach between the two churches had long since faded when the Balkan scene was invaded by the Ottoman Turks.

The rise
of the
Ottoman
Turks

The tremendous drive of the Mongols in the thirteenth century, though checked before Jerusalem by the Mamelukes of Egypt,[13] destroyed the caliphate of Bagdad, together with the last remnants of the Seljuk sultanate. One of the immediate results was a westward migration of nomads from the interior of Asia especially into the borderlands of Christendom, where opportunities for loot and conquest were most promising. Among such invaders of Anatolia was a band of Turkish Moslems who, under a chief named Osman (d. 1326), established themselves to the northwest of Dorylæum (see Map XIX). This was the beginning of the famous dynasty called Osmanli or Ottoman. Orkhan, son of Osman, was even more successful. By the capture of Nicæa and Nicomedia his Turks came to dominate the southern shore of the Propontus, and so were able to force the Byzantine emperor to abandon his last Asiatic province. Orkhan then assumed the title of sultan and, as befitted his enhanced dignity, proceeded to make his conquests into a territorial monarchy. For lack of contemporary sources, the details of his administrative system remain doubtful, but the excellence of his work is amply attested by its results. To him, in particular, would seem to be due the extremely efficient Turkish army, which was soon to win a series of astonishing victories in Europe.

Murad I
(1359-89)

Meanwhile, through employment as imperial mercenaries, the Turks had become very familiar with the situation in the Balkans and so had been encouraged to send raiding expeditions across the strait at Gallipoli. Finally Murad, Orkhan's successor, launched a major European offensive. Taking Adrianople in 1361, he adopted it for his capital and thence delivered a series of terrific blows against the disunited forces of the Christians. The subjection of the Bulgarians brought the sultan's power to the Danube and the Black Sea. The overwhelming defeat of the southern Serbs resulted in his conquest of all Macedonia. And when the Slavs of the northern Balkans finally decided to renounce their jealousies for the sake of a counter-offensive, they suffered the same fate. The little that remained of the Serbian kingdom was now reduced to the position of a tributary state; and the Byzantine Empire, virtually contained within the walls of the capital, was hardly more than that. Wholly isolated by the Turkish encirclement, Constantinople was clearly doomed. Yet, owing to a number of accidents, the fatal day was long postponed.

Bayazid I
(1389-1402)

Up to this point the rulers of western Christendom, though alarmed by Murad's triumphant advance, had done nothing to check it. Indeed, with conditions as they were in the second half of the fourteenth century, what effective action could be expected either from the rival popes or from the rival princes who upheld them? It was only after Sigismund of Hungary,

[13] Originally the slaves who constituted the palace guard of the sultan, the Mamelukes became the rulers of Egypt during the crusade of St. Louis and so remained until the time of Napoleon Bonaparte.

the later emperor, had taken up arms in support of the Serbs and gained certain local successes that one of the Roman popes saw fit to proclaim a crusade against the Turks. As a consequence, Sigismund in 1396 took a miscellaneous force of volunteers down the Danube and prepared to invade Bulgaria. But his brave effort led only to crushing defeat at the hands of Murad's successor, Bayazid I. The latter, having reasserted his dominance of the Balkans, then turned to the reduction of various local emirates in Asia Minor. Finally, in 1402, Bayazid ordered the Byzantine emperor to surrender the city of Constantinople on pain of its total destruction. And he would very likely have carried out his threat if at that juncture he had not been compelled to meet a more formidable enemy.

This was Timur, also a Turk and a Mohammedan, but a conqueror who resembled the Mongol despoilers of the thirteenth century rather than the more statesmanlike Ottoman sultans. Rising to power in Turkestan, Timur in the years following 1380 built up a vast tributary empire that reached from the frontiers of India to those of Syria. By 1402 nomadic hordes were again menacing Anatolia, and when Bayazid advanced to drive them out his army was routed at Angora and he himself was taken prisoner. Momentarily it seemed as if the Ottoman power, which was now further weakened by a war over the succession, would inevitably succumb and on all sides the Christians, rather naïvely, burst into hymns of thanksgiving. Timur, however, chose not to follow up his western victory and died in 1405 while preparing for an expedition into China. Then, as his empire disintegrated, the Ottomans with amazing vigor restored their state and celebrated a fresh series of triumphs. The recovery, begun under Mohammed I, was completed under his son Murad II. Thanks to the useful recruits secured from the fragments of Timur's horde, and to the efficiency of the Ottoman government, Murad was able not only to extend his dominion throughout most of Asia Minor but also to repel a new crusade which, like its predecessor, was led by the Hungarians.

Disaster and recovery

In the ensuing campaigns the Turks quickly regained all they had lost. Before Murad's death in 1451 they were engaged in reducing Bosnia and in extending their raids into southern Greece, where no one of a dozen local princes could effectively withstand them. Then the long reprieve of Constantinople was brought to an end by the new sultan, Mohammed II. In 1453, after a terrific siege in which improved artillery[14] had decisive importance, the great city surrendered to the nation that has since held it. The capture was of obvious value to the Ottomans, who thereby completed their conquest of the Byzantine Empire and acquired a position of commanding strength. In their possession Constantinople once more became the capital of a state that joined two continents and, as such, regained its old military, naval, and commercial importance. So far as Latin

The fall of Constantinople (1453)

[14] See below, pp. 443, 487-89.

Christendom was concerned, the event was one which intelligent men must have long expected. The Turks had already been masters of the Balkans for the better part of a hundred years. By taking Constantinople they destroyed little that had not been moribund for an even greater period. From the standpoint of Christian idealism, of course, the Moslem triumph was eloquent testimony to the degradation of the age—convincing proof that western Europe could not be led by Nicholas V as it had been by Urban II. The true sequel to the crusades was not the feeble Christian war against the Ottoman Turks but the new commercial imperialism that was soon to inspire the voyages of discovery carried out by Portuguese, Spanish, English, and French mariners.

CHAPTER XXIV

Society and Commerce in the Later Middle Ages

1. THE BOURGEOISIE AND THE GROWTH OF CAPITALISM

During the thirteenth century the bourgeois class continued to grow in numbers, in wealth, and in privilege. *Villes neuves* appeared by the hundred, especially in the more backward regions. Since practically all the great towns of Italy, France, Spain, and England had emerged before 1200, the more important of the new foundations were in the northeast of Europe. There, for example, we find Berlin, Dresden, Prague, Rostock, Stralsund, Danzig, Königsberg, Riga, and the other trading communities that were soon combined in the powerful Hansa.[1] As Wales, Scotland, and Ireland had earlier adopted urban models from Norman England, so in the following period the Slavic and Scandinavian countries adopted theirs from Germany. And comparison of municipal charters shows that on all sides bourgeois status remained essentially uniform, implying the elementary liberties sketched in a previous chapter. With regard to the older towns generalization is harder, for by the thirteenth century they had developed widely different institutions. Judged according to their degree of autonomy, they fell into two main groups.[2] In the first were the Italian communes, which now acted like sovereign republics; the Flemish communes, which had come to dominate the whole county; and the German communes (or free cities), which held direction of the weakening empire. In the second group were the towns that, subjected to various kings and princes, enjoyed at most such limited rights of self-government as those of the English boroughs.

The towns and their constitutions

[1] See below, pp. 446-48.
[2] See above, pp. 243-55.

433

In the twelfth century the larger town had ordinarily been governed by a single board of elected magistrates; in the thirteenth it was more usual for such a board to be expanded into a number of courts and councils under the general direction of one principal official. The typical Italian commune thus came to be ruled by a *podesta*, frequently a foreigner installed by rival factions as a means of avoiding civil conflict. The chief municipal magistrate in German-speaking regions was commonly styled *bürgermeister*, in French-speaking regions *maire;* and through French influence the latter title became usual also in the greater English boroughs. The precedent was set by London, which took advantage of Richard's absence on the crusade to regain the self-government lost under Henry II.[3] Thenceforth the city was administered by a mayor, together with aldermen and a common council elected by the citizens in local districts called wards —the custom that was eventually imported from England to our own country. It should be noted, however, that many boroughs continued to prosper without a mayor or an equivalent officer and that, no matter what the precise nature of the constitution, local affairs were normally controlled by the wealthier citizens. Even before it came to be officially recognized, oligarchy was the rule rather than the exception.

Craft gilds

Earlier the more substantial men of a town had often been united in a gild merchant; but that had now been generally superseded by a series of craft gilds, each of which included persons engaged in only one trade. The essence of such a gild's power was its control of a particular industry, the official monopoly that enabled it to exclude outside competition and to prescribe elaborate rules governing production. According to the established practice, a boy entering upon a trade first had to serve as apprentice for a number of years, during which he received at most his board and lodging. Having learned the craft, he became a journeyman, a man working by the day (*journée*), and so he remained until he was able to start in business for himself. To be ranked as a master, he commonly had to produce a masterpiece, a sample of his work that met the standards of the gild. Naturally, too, the master would have to accumulate a certain amount of capital before he could set up an establishment of his own; but his outlay would not be great, and to our eyes his business would remain very small. In any craft that catered solely to the local inhabitants, the number of the latter would determine the number of masters who could make a good living. The gild system, by its intensely conservative regulations, discouraged individual enterprise for the sake of unorthodox gain; so the master could hardly expect to rise above the ordinary standard of bourgeois comfort. Men in one craft usually owned or rented little shops along a single street. There each of them not only produced his wares but also sold

[3] See above, p. 327.

them at retail. And there, in the upper stories that projected over the street, he lived with his family.

What we generally recognize as capitalism is not, therefore, to be found in the business of the ordinary craft gild. Nevertheless, capitalism did develop in the Middle Ages, and on a relatively large scale. The origin of the capital itself is no great mystery. Men seem to have acquired it then precisely as they do now—through savings or earnings of one sort or another. Having acquired it, the more venturesome would seek investment by which to increase their wealth. One good opportunity was already provided by urban real estate; for the physical expansion of mediæval towns rapidly converted arable and waste into building lots that could be leased to individual tradesmen at a handsome figure. The establishment of a *ville neuve* was often made possible by shrewd merchants who furnished the necesary capital and recouped themselves by securing title to the best land about the market place. The foundation of many a bourgeois fortune was· thus laid in the twelfth and thirteenth centuries. But it is ridiculous to assert, as has been done by a certain school of historians, that the sole origin of capital in the Middle Ages was the unearned increment of land. Although most business was then organized on a small scale, numerous merchants were able to make a profit over and above what they needed to live on. Profits of this kind, as well as accumulated rents, could be advantageously invested in a number of new-grown enterprises.

In all such matters the men of northwestern Europe looked for instruction to the Italians; and among them the original experts were the Venetians, who had undoubtedly benefited from their early association with the Byzantine Empire. Through the Norman kingdom of Sicily and the Latin states of the crusaders, Italians had also learned much from the Arabs.[4] Whatever the exact origin of the practices, the following had become well known by the thirteenth century. For the building of ships and the financing of voyages beyond the sea wealthy men often formed companies. Therein every member, by contributing a share of the cost, became entitled to a share of the profit. And the risk was minimized by a system of marine insurance quite like that which is still in common use. Similar arrangements, of course, could be applied to other commercial ventures: the transportation of goods by land, the wholesaling of food and raw materials, manufacturing, and the like. Since Italy had become the foremost distributing center for articles imported from the east, it was natural that before long Italians would try to produce certain of the articles themselves. Frederick II, as we have seen, was keenly interested in projects of this sort; but the greater success was eventually won by the cities to the north, especially Florence. Before the end of the thirteenth century Italian artisans had already developed flourishing industries for the production of glass,

Capital-
istic
enterprise

Italian
influence
in business

[4] See above, pp. 171-76.

silk and linen fabrics, armor, jewelry, and other luxurious wares. The only northern region to witness a comparable development was Flanders, where the larger towns had become world-famous, not only for their usefulness in the transhipment of imports, but also for their manufacture and exportation of woolen cloth.

Money and banking

Activities like these presuppose a ready supply of sound money. During the Carolingian period the standard coin minted in western Europe had been the silver penny (*denarius*); so the shilling, the mark, and the pound had been units of weighed money, and the only gold pieces in circulation had been of Arabic or Byzantine origin.[5] And as princes had constantly debased the silver coinage in order to pay their debts more cheaply, it had gradually been turned into bronze. Just before the end of the twelfth century, accordingly, Venice led the way towards a monetary restoration by minting a penny of fine silver worth twelve of the old ones. This was called a big penny (*denarius grossus*), and in the next hundred years such coins—particularly the *gros tournois*[6] of France and the sterling of England —came to have wide circulation throughout the northwest. Shortly afterwards the coining of gold was resumed by the emperor Frederick II and by the great Italian republics—as familiar words still bear witness, for the ducat was named after the *ducatus* of Venice and the florin after Florence.

The subject of money is today associated with that of banking, and the association goes back at least to the thirteenth century. The Italians, naturally enough, set the example in both. The simplest and oldest of banking transactions was money-changing, for time out of mind travelers had been compelled to convert the currency of one region into that of another. Wherever trade was active, numbers of men came to specialize in that business, and from it they were quickly drawn into credit operations of various kinds. Suppose, for example, that A of Lombardy sold spices to B of Flanders, while C of Lombardy bought cloth from D of Flanders. By canceling B's debt against C's, the actual transfer of cash would be reduced to a minimum. And if agents of the leading importers and exporters met at regular intervals for a mutual balancing of accounts, the result would be what we know as a clearing-house. Activities of this sort became a normal feature of the thirteenth-century fairs—especially those of Champagne, a yearly cycle of six great assemblies for the wholesale distribution of goods, held in Troyes, Provins, and other nearby towns. In all such periodical centers of trade and in all the more important cities the banking firms of Italy, indiscriminately called Lombards, came to maintain regular agents. Through them, as through the international organization of the Knights Templars, financial operations in any country of Europe, or in

---

[5] Hence the name bezant that was applied to such a coin.

[6] I.e., a penny of Tours; cf. the German *groschen*. The derivation of the English sterling is doubtful; but it was not from "easterling," an alleged reference to the Hansa merchants.

almost any country of the Mediterranean, might be readily carried out.
A crusader, for instance, might buy a letter of credit which he could cash
in a Syrian port; a pope could send funds to his legate in Dublin; a king
could pay by draft for crown jewels to be bought in Constantinople. And
despite the prohibitions of ecclesiastical law, the Lombards did a flourishing business in money-lending.

The church, by citing various texts from the Bible, had forbidden the **Money-**
taking of usury. To read certain authors, one would suppose that such **lending**
prohibition tended to paralyze all credit operations in the Middle Ages.
But it is an instructive fact that, even in the days of Innocent III, the
utmost pressure of ecclesiastical authority could not even prevent ordinary
buying and selling on Sunday. And in connection with the lending of
money the church itself taught Christians how to circumvent the canon
law. In the earlier Middle Ages, when a prince needed a loan, he normally
applied to a wealthy prelate, who would be quite willing to provide the
necessary gold or silver in return for a mortgage on good real estate.
During the term of the note the lender enjoyed the income from the land;
then, should the principal remain unpaid, he continued his possession indefinitely. By the thirteenth century, however, the lending business had
been largely taken over by the great merchants. Officially, they never took
usury; instead they collected rents, remuneration for services, or damages
for alleged injury. Eventually they coined the word "interest" to designate
the sum charged for a loan. The rising cost of government, together with
the more luxurious standard of aristocratic life, progressively aided the
cause of the bankers. As always happens, economic necessity made short
work of an inconvenient prohibition, and the law was modified to fit the
facts.

Among the money-lenders of Europe there were many Jews, but their
importance in the financial history of Europe has often been exaggerated.
Since the Carolingian period, when Jews were prominent in what little
trade persisted between Moslem and Christian countries, the situation had
radically changed. The big money-lending business of the thirteenth
century was not in the hands of Jews, whose operations were generally
confined to less progressive regions where banking was not monopolized
by Christians. In such localities the Jews, as long as they remained useful
to the rulers who protected them, enjoyed a dubious security; but they
were herded into particular quarters of the towns, forced to wear a distinctive garb, placed under all sorts of legal restrictions, and periodically
stripped of their earnings. Not infrequently a combination of debtors
would join in buying from the government a cancellation of their notes;
so the unfortunate lender, in order to anticipate the eventual loss of his
principal, had to charge an exorbitant rate for his loans. At best the Jews
were merely tolerated and every now and then religious prejudice, fanned
by economic jealousy, led to savage persecution. For example, the Jews

were driven from England by Edward I, while in France Philip IV proscribed not only them but also the Lombard bankers and the Knights Templars.[7]

Capital-istic industry

Meanwhile the major industries of the Italians and the Flemings had come to depend on an economic organization very different from that of the local craft. Growing in response to widespread demand, these industries depended on wholesale exportation; and undertakings of such large scope required capitalistic management that, for obvious reasons, could not be supplied by the ordinary master of a gild. All the prominent industrial centers thus came to be dominated by big businessmen, who were financiers rather than manufacturers. In Flanders, for instance, the expansion of the cloth industry was made possible by the great wholesalers, or clothiers as they were later known in England. The clothier bought the raw material, paid weavers to make it into cloth, and sold the finished product throughout the markets of the western world. As a class, therefore, the clothiers were capitalistic employers, inevitably affiliated with the bankers and the landed aristocracy of the towns. Under the clothiers the craftsmen were reduced to little more than hired artisans, doomed to a precarious existence which their gilds were powerless to remedy. When, as the result of political disturbance, they were thrown out of work, their only recourse was insurrection. So, in the industrial centers of both Italy and Flanders, the wars of the fourteenth century were constantly embittered by social antagonism.

Urban popula-tions

During the previous three hundred years western Europe had enjoyed an almost uninterrupted advance of prosperity, which can be fairly well measured by the growth of the new urban centers. To our eyes, of course, mediæval towns were not large. Except for Venice and one or two of its Italian rivals, no western city of that age could possibly have had 100,000 inhabitants. The foremost Flemish communes, like Ghent and Bruges, had only half as many and yet were relatively huge. Even London, with about 25,000, was far above the average; for the ordinary town would have a population of from 5,000 to 10,000. However insignificant these figures appear to us, they were very respectable when judged according to Roman standards.[8] By the thirteenth century western Europe had clearly surpassed whatever prosperity it had experienced in ancient times. Later, however, conditions tended to become stabilized. The process of urbanization was halted, and along with that the progress of the bourgeois class. As it became harder for artisans to improve their lot by moving to newly developed regions, their discontent increased. And as the devastations of war and pestilence ruined the European markets, such discontent was fanned into revolutionary activity. This is one of the major factors that must be taken into account when we seek to explain the popular insurrections of the fourteenth century.

[7] See above, p. 325.
[8] See above, p. 35.

2. THE DECAY OF THE MANORIAL SYSTEM AND OF FEUDALISM

In the twelfth century, as already noted,[9] it became increasingly com- **The class** mon for territorial lords to attract settlers of one sort or another by grant- **of hôtes** ing them formal charters of liberty. Under such a grant the peasant, whatever his earlier status, could become free by acquiring a legal residence in some particular place. The town-dwelling class, or bourgeoisie, though engaged in commerce and allied activities, must originally have been recruited, to a large degree, from the rural population. Meanwhile, too, many free villages had been established—though usually without formal charters—in order to bring fresh land under cultivation. The hôtes who inhabited these villages constituted a very superior class within the peasantry. They were customarily exempted from all but a few definite obligations, principally that of paying a money rent. Such a peasant was therefore at liberty to work for wages as well as to sell whatever his land produced; or, whenever he pleased, to dispose of his holding, pack up his chattels, and move to a more favorable locality. All this, obviously, presupposed the cash market that had been created by the growth of urban communities.

The all-important characteristic of these rural colonists was that, whatever their precise occupation and however poor they might be, they were not subjected to anything like the old manorial organization. To that extent they were economically emancipated. By the close of the thirteenth century considerable areas had thus come to be entirely populated by freemen—notably the reclaimed lands along the North Sea and the recently colonized regions beyond the Elbe.[10] Besides, free communities enjoying a variety of special privileges were thickly scattered all through western Europe. The serf who somehow got away to such a community, and stayed there, would quickly cease to be a serf. But what of the old manors, the thousands of agrarian estates that constituted the hereditary wealth of the feudal aristocracy? To have any cultivators left, did the lords have to emancipate them en masse? There is little evidence to support such a conclusion. All fresh demands for labor had been met by natural increase of the population—especially through the migration of younger children to the new centers of employment. Despite the phenomenal growth of the bourgeois class, western Europe remained solidly agrarian except in a few favored regions. And throughout most of the anciently settled land the manorial system had scarcely been changed as late as the fourteenth century.

By that time, of course, an increasing number of serfs had been freed **Economic** by individual charters of manumission, but this is a matter of relative un- **emanci-** importance. Since manorial organization was not invariably, or even **pation**

[9] See above, pp. 243-50.
[10] See above, p. 332.

usually, founded on personal servitude, its decay cannot be explained as the result of personal emancipation. The manor, for reasons set forth in an earlier chapter, must be regarded as an agrarian community whose life depended on a traditional routine of labor and a traditional equalization of the returns. Whether the peasant was legally free or unfree, he contributed his share of the labor and received his share of the returns. Accordingly, there could be no true emancipation of the peasantry as a whole until the ancient manorial organization had been generally abandoned —and that would amount to an economic revolution. Such a revolution did take place, though its course was very gradual and its effects were perceptible at different times in different countries. The key to a fuller understanding of its nature may be found in the fact that serfdom disappeared first in those regions where mercantile development was furthest advanced—as, for example, in Flanders and northern Italy.

It has already been remarked that an immediate result of urban growth in the twelfth century was an increased demand for food and raw materials, which in turn led to the rapid expansion of the cultivated area. From the outset this expansion was largely dominated by capitalistic enterprise. Whether undertaken by the original landlord or by speculators who secured title from him, the reclamation of forest, swamp, and waste was inspired by the hope of profit. The ancient manors had been considered mere sources of goods to be consumed. The new agrarian settlements, on the other hand, were established in order to obtain goods to be sold. Even the individual peasants were engaged in a sort of business. And wherever facilities were best for the sale of agricultural produce in large quantities, it was inevitable that rural estates of the ancient type would be adapted to the new environment. In other words, the manors of the more progressive regions would be turned, essentially, into colonist villages.

Commutation and the end of serfdom

Under these improved economic conditions a great lord, instead of trying to produce everything he needed on his own estates, concentrated on whatever he found most profitable and bought the rest in the urban market. So, in the course of time, whole districts came to be devoted to particular kinds of production: for example, wheat and rye where the soil was richest, butter and cheese where the pasturage was best, wine where the finest grapes could be grown. And since it was now to the interest of the lord to obtain as much as he could at the lowest possible cost, he might decide that he would be better off without the old manorial arrangements. By substituting money rents for all the miscellaneous services of his peasants and hiring laborers with the proceeds, he not only would be relieved of administrative troubles but would also have his work better done. Commutation, thus carried out, necessarily implied the establishment of a cash economy in place of the time-honored routine. The manor ceased to be an agrarian community and became a group of individual tenants. The personal relationship of peasant to lord came to have no importance. As long as the rents were paid, the lord would not care who held the strips. One tenant could accumulate as many as he pleased; everybody was free to sell out and leave if he chose to do so.

Fundamentally, therefore, the emancipation of the peasantry seems to have been brought about through the influence of commercial growth upon the agrarian organization of the Dark Age. So far as western Europe was concerned, we may be sure that such emancipation was well under way by the end of the thirteenth century, but did not reach its culmination for another three hundred years. In both England and France the manorial system was still the rule during the fourteenth century. Then, as those countries recovered from the evils of the early fifteenth century, it rapidly declined and all but disappeared in the sixteenth. Thereafter serfdom was unknown to the English law, and no more than a memory remained in copyhold,[11] a form of hereditary tenure in return for a fixed rent. In most of the French provinces a similar development took place; the Revolution of 1789 found relatively few serfs to free and only vestiges of manorial custom to abrogate. To the eastward emancipation progressed much more slowly. Serfdom was not abolished in Prussia until 1807, in Russia not until fifty years later.

From the view here expressed it follows that in general the improvement of the peasants' condition was hardly the result of their own revolutionary activity. We hear of little such activity during the earlier period, when society was most thoroughly agrarian. Then, in the fourteenth century, there were three great risings, for which peasants were at least in part responsible: the insurrection of 1323-1328 in West Flanders, the Jacquerie of 1357 in northern France, and the Great Revolt of 1381 in England.[12] But discontented artisans were also prominent in all three. In each of them, furthermore, we can readily detect aggravation by local grievances: especially the tyranny of the Flemish aristocracy, the collapse of the royal authority in France after the battle of Poitiers, and the corruption of the English government during the minority of Richard II. More fundamental were a variety of economic ills that now tended to become chronic. By the opening of the fourteenth century the material progress of the previous three hundred years had begun to slacken. As old towns ceased to grow and fewer *villes neuves* were established, the demand for commodities fell off. It became increasingly difficult for a craftsman to rise in his profession, or to secure employment at all. And the worsening of economic conditions in the towns inevitably affected those in rural districts.

Peasants who had been led to hope for improvement in their status were

Peasant insurrections in the fourteenth century

---

[11] So called because the tenure was said to be by copy of court roll—i.e., a manorial record. It has only recently been superseded by a modern form of ownership.

[12] See above, pp. 383, 402, 406.

sharply disappointed when times became harder, and were thoroughly enraged when the governing classes adopted reactionary measures. In England, for example, the Great Revolt of 1381 was the aftermath of the Black Death, the general character of which has already been noted. Whatever may have been the actual mortality, it was so high that food stocks became depleted, prices rose to unprecedented levels, and agricultural labor was at a premium. Parliament thereupon passed the Statute of Laborers, which imposed heavy penalties on runaway villeins and on men who demanded wages beyond what had hitherto prevailed. This policy of the government, together with its notorious inefficiency and its attempts to levy an unpopular tax, precipitated the insurrection. As already remarked, it was a failure; the concessions made to the rebellious serfs were later annulled and emancipation came only in the course of gradual economic improvement. The Great Revolt is of particular interest to historians because it so well illustrates the new social antagonisms of a transitional age.

Decline of the feudal aristocracy

Ultimately, of course, the feudal aristocracy was to be vitally affected by the increased production of gold and silver; for the cheapening of money turned manorial rents into mere token payments. But in the Middle Ages the commutation of villein services, for reasons already seen, worked to the advantage of the landlords. It was rather the undermining of feudal tenure by the growth of a cash economy, supplemented by a revolution in warfare, that weakened their position in society. By the opening of the fourteenth century the rulers of progressive states, such as England and France, had ceased to depend on their ancient feudal and manorial income. Instead they had come to develop a system of regular taxes paid by all classes of subjects. And as an increasing proportion of these taxes came to be taken from the new wealth of the bourgeoisie, it was inevitable that the latter should demand and secure a greater share in the government. The introduction of townsmen into the old feudal councils is a prominent feature of constitutional development in the later thirteenth century.[13] Whatever the precise nature of the representation obtained—in the assemblies of Frederick II, in the *cortes* of the Spanish kings, in the estates general of Philip IV, or in the parliaments of Edward I—the phenomenon was essentially the same. It constituted a legal recognition of bourgeois importance and denoted a proportional decline in the prestige of the feudal aristocracy.

Changes in warfare

With regard to contemporary changes in warfare only a meager outline can be attempted here. Throughout the thirteenth century armies continued to be thoroughly feudal. The knight still fought in the old way, using the weapons of his ancestors, though his defensive armor became increasingly elaborate as mail was extended over his arms and legs and as his head came to be covered by a great helmet with a visor to be pulled up over the face. The castle, too, retained its ancient importance, but palisades and

[13] See above, pp. 380-84.

blockhouses had now been replaced by walls and keeps of solid masonry. The stone keep was at first a square tower placed against the side of the wall that enclosed the bailey.[14] Along the top of this wall ran a parapet, behind which a continuous walk provided advantageous positions for the defenders. Outside was a deep moat, whenever possible filled with water. Such a fortress was an enormous improvement over the eleventh-century castle and yet proved to be vulnerable in many respects. Experience on the crusade taught men the use of battering-rams, catapults, and other siege engines, which were found to be particularly effective when directed against corners. In the thirteenth century, therefore, the old distinctions of motte and bailey and of wall and keep were abandoned. The castle became an integrated structure, with round towers and bastions placed at intervals so as to command every portion of the wall. Even if, by means of scaling-ladders, the enemy took one section, it could be entirely isolated from the rest. And the defenders gained an even greater advantage when fortifications were built in concentric rings.[15]

In the course of the fourteenth century, however, the ancient dominance of the feudal array on the battlefield was definitely broken. Courtrai, Crécy, and Poitiers were noteworthy victories of skillfully used infantry over the best of cavalry forces. And in the following century the *coup de grâce* to the traditional system was administered by the Swiss, when they destroyed the proud armies of Charles the Rash.[16] Although knights—now dressed in entire suits of plate armor—were still fighting at the opening of the six-teenth century, it had come to be recognized that, at least for defense, they had to be reinforced with units of pikemen, archers, and other infantry. Besides, artillery had already proved its effectiveness for certain kinds of warfare. Whatever may be decided with regard to the origin of gunpowder, there seems to be no doubt that the gun was a western invention of the fourteenth century[17] and that its earliest form was a sort of cannon that fired balls of stone. For a long time it was a very crude weapon, almost as dangerous to the attackers as to the attacked. But as cannon were grad-ually improved, they became more useful, especially in besieging fortifica-

[14] See Plate XV: aerial photograph of Portchester Castle, England (reproduced by permission of *Country Life,* London). Note that the Norman castle, with its square keep, was erected in one corner of a Roman fort whose walls yet stand. A parish church came to occupy the opposite corner, but no town grew up here in the Middle Ages.

[15] See Plates XV-XVI: aerial photographs of Kidwelly and Krak-des-Chevaliers. The former was one of many castles built by Edward I in Wales (and this photo-graph is also reproduced by permission of *Country Life*). The latter was the greatest of the crusaders' castles in Syria. Note the aqueduct that brought water from the eastern mountains to the moat inside the outer wall. The main entrance is on the other side of the square gate-house to the right.

[16] See below, p. 472.

[17] See below, pp. 486-89.

tions. By the end of the fifteenth century the feudal castle had lost all military significance. With its moats filled, and with windows cut in its massive walls, it was henceforth to be merely a palatial dwelling—as the word *château* now implies.

Decadent chivalry

In the light of the facts detailed above, it may readily be understood why chivalry became decadent in the later Middle Ages. During the early feudal age the essence of vassalage had been the personal loyalty of a man to a single lord; the fief had been a quite subordinate factor. Subsequently, as one man might accumulate a dozen fiefs and for them owe homage to as many lords, how could he remain a Roland at heart? Lawyers, it is true, invented the saving distinction of liege homage, by which the claims of the chief lord were recognized as paramount; but by this time the spirit of ancient feudalism was already passing. Chivalry, under such conditions, became more and more an aristocratic affectation, overlaid with the *courtoisie* of the fashionable romance. At the opening of the twelfth century *adoubement* was still the barbarian custom of giving arms to the noble youth who had proved his manhood on the field of battle. By the end of the thirteenth it had been made into an elaborate ceremonial—half mystic sacrament, to conform with the ideals of the church, and half courtly pageant, to delight the eyes of high-born ladies. In the fourteenth century it suffered further degradation. The lower the noble sank in real importance, the more extravagantly he flaunted his pride of birth and his feudal traditions. Although men were probably no less brutal in the primitive period, they lived a life that better comported with their character. They were quite frank in their coarseness, not having learned to affect a refinement which they did not possess. The chivalrous ostentation of Philip VI and Edward III ill concealed their actual worthlessness; it was unchivalrous princes like Charles V who set the more useful example for the later age.

3. THE MEDITERRANEAN, THE BALTIC, AND THE NEW ROUTES

The Italian cities

The history of Italy in the thirteenth century, even more fully than earlier, became that of its cities. They, as will be explained in the next chapter, now developed the brilliant secular culture that was eventually to inspire the emulation of all Latin Europe. Economically, however, they merely continued the vigorous life which they had already developed. And politically they maintained their established tradition of resisting every attempt to incorporate them within some larger unit, whatever the title of the ruler. The Papal States, losing all cohesion under the Avignon popes, were resolved into a collection of autonomous cities and petty seigniories. The Two Sicilies[18] in some measure preserved the appearance of territorial kingdoms, but both were decadent. The leadership of the peninsula lay rather with the urban republics of Tuscany and the Po valley.

[18] See above, p. 373.

The political history of these little Italian states is characterized by a bewildering series of local revolutions, no detailed account of which can be attempted here. It may be noted, however, that most of the kaleidoscopic changes affected no more than a few prominent families. Urban wars were carried on no longer by citizen militias but by mercenaries under professional captains, *condottieri*, like those who organized free companies to serve the kings of France and England.[19] Under such conditions the life of the ordinary man was hardly disturbed by the feuds of the great. Besides, in many a city all effective power had now been secured by some kind of despot. The latter might be the descendant of an imperial official, a dictator set up by a form of election, or an adventurer who usurped authority by sheer violence. He was in any case likely to be quite unscrupulous, resorting when he thought best to legal trickery, force of arms, or assassination. Yet, however cruel or vicious, the Italian tyrant might also be a man of exceptional culture, who prided himself on his patronage of art and letters.

Throughout the fourteenth century, for example, Milan was governed **Milan** by the Visconti, who rose from comparative obscurity to be imperial vicars **and** and then dukes, related by marriage to the greatest houses of Germany, **Florence** France, and England. Under the aggressive rule of the Visconti, Milan became the head of a considerable state, extending north to Switzerland and south to Parma. On the east, however, Milan was checked by Venice and in Tuscany by Florence. The latter republic, whose chronic turbulence was aggravated by the increasing distress of the artisan population, ultimately gained political stability through the dictatorship of the richest man in town —the banker, Cosimo de' Medici (d. 1464). Although he held no office, being merely what in America is called a political boss, his ascendancy was unquestioned; and it passed like an actual principality first to his son and then to his grandson. It is a famous irony of history that the Medici coat of arms, an arrangement of "medical" pills, lingers on as the sign of the ordinary pawnbroker.

While Florence had become the greatest industrial center of Italy, its commercial supremacy had long been disputed between Venice and Genoa.[20] Until the second half of the fourteenth century the two republics remained fairly well balanced in strength. Then, in the last of their furious wars, Venice captured a besieging fleet by a heroic counter-attack and was able to dictate terms of peace in 1381. Genoa, progressively weakened by civil disorders, thereafter gave up an ambitious program of mercantile expansion. The Venetians, on the contrary, vigorously pushed their advantage and so completed an imperial structure that to some degree persisted until the time of Napoleon Bonaparte. In this undertaking they were greatly aided by the fact that during all the crises of the previous hundred years their gov-

[19] See above, pp. 400-01.
[20] See above, pp. 384-85.

ernment had continued to function smoothly and efficiently. The Venetians never invoked aid from a foreign prince; they never permitted a despot to assume charge of their city; after the closing of the great council in 1298, they made no radical changes in their constitution. To the student of political science the Venetian republic affords the classic example of oligarchy in its purest and most effective form.

In the course of the fourteenth century, to meet a possible threat to their communications across the Alps, the Venetians adopted a policy of limited territorial conquest. So, by employing mercenaries, they eventually established their control over the Adige valley and the region to the west as far as Brescia and Bergamo (see Map XVIII). Meanwhile their dominance in the eastern Mediterranean had come to be challenged by the Ottoman Turks. The Venetian policy, however, had always opposed fighting the Moslems except when commercial advantage lay in that direction. Even the Turkish conquest of the Balkans failed to inspire them with crusading ardor, for by treaty with the sultan they still retained their privileges in the Levant. It was not until the Ottoman advance endangered their positions on the Adriatic and the Ægean that they actually went to war. This was the beginning of a gradual Venetian decline, for which the Turkish victories were only in part responsible. The decisive factor, as will be seen in the pages immediately following, was rather the diversion of trade to the new Atlantic routes.

The
Hansa

Turning now to the Baltic, we find a significant development of the thirteenth century in the league of German towns called the Hansa. The name had no peculiar significance, for it was often applied in northern countries to any gild or association of merchants. At London, for instance, the men of Cologne had enjoyed special privileges since long before the Norman Conquest; and when their *hansa* was confirmed by Henry II in the twelfth century, it had already been joined by traders from other cities on the Rhine. Similarly, with the extension of German commerce throughout the Baltic, Lübeck became the center of a growing confederation which included the neighboring towns of Hamburg, Stralsund, and Rostock, as well as the German colony of Wisby on the Swedish island of Gothland. By the later thirteenth century this group, or some of its members, had secured valuable concessions in many quarters—notably in connection with the fur trade of Russia, the cloth trade of Flanders, and the fish trade of Norway and Sweden. As, by mutual agreement, the western and eastern groups of German towns now pooled their interests and perfected an organization to administer their common affairs, the combination became *par excellence* the Hansa.

By the early fourteenth century the league had enrolled all the older German towns on rivers flowing into the Baltic or the North Sea, together with the new German towns along the coasts of Prussia, Livonia, and

Estonia. It maintained factories—permanent trading establishments, with warehouses and docks—at Novgorod, Bruges, Bergen, and London; and in each of these places it enjoyed exclusive control over the sale of Baltic products (see Map XVI). Although the Hansa sought to give its members such protection as they failed to obtain from the enfeebled monarchy, it was not a political, much less a national, organization. Held together solely by mercantile interest, it had no formal constitution, no common seal, no official head, and no capital. Its only organ of government was a congress which met in a convenient place whenever the need arose for extraordinary measures. On such occasions Lübeck, by virtue of commercial pre-eminence, was normally deputed to speak for the confederation and so came to be regarded as its chief. Cologne ranked second and was followed in no fixed order by Hamburg, Bremen, and Wisby. We sometimes hear of a Hanseatic congress representing well over fifty towns, but the lesser communities rarely bothered to send deputies and no list of members was ever published. The only penalty that could be inflicted on a rebellious member was exclusion from the monopolies controlled by the league. Conversely, the maintenance of the Hansa's privileges abroad depended on the power of withholding shipping from a recalcitrant port. It was by an embargo on all trade with the Baltic that Bruges in 1307 and Novgorod in 1392 were forced to submit. And the same weapons normally sufficed to preserve favorable relations with foreign princes. The Hansa encountered formidable opposition in only one direction—from the reinvigorated kingdom of Denmark.

At one time or another the Danish kings had claimed portions of the southern Baltic coast, as well as Scania, the tip of the Scandinavian peninsula. The Baltic provinces they had now abandoned to the Teutonic Knights; Scania, on the other hand, they still coveted, for it was of great political and economic importance. Whoever held it and the adjacent islands controlled not only the entrance to the Baltic but also the profitable herring trade. During the earlier years of the Hansa this strategic position formed part of the Swedish kingdom, and there the merchants were quite willing that it should remain, even after Magnus of Sweden (1319-65) inherited the crown of Norway. Then, about the middle of the fourteenth century, the able Waldemar IV of Denmark defeated Magnus, took Scania, and, seizing the island of Gothland, sacked Wisby. Although Waldemar's act was ostensibly directed against the Swedes, the Hansa took the unprecedented step of going to war as the ally of Magnus, and eventually, after taking Copenhagen, dictated the Peace of Stralsund in 1370. Thereby the Hansa obtained free passage of the Sound and free trade throughout Danish territory. Hanseatic commissioners were to have charge of the herring market, as well as possession of four royal castles until the cost of the war had been de-

The Danish war and the height of the Hansa

frayed by the king. It was even agreed that no successor was to be placed on the Danish throne without the consent of the Hansa.

The league, to be sure, soon abandoned its right to interfere in royal elections. Waldemar, dying in 1375, was succeeded by his daughter Margaret, who devoted her long reign to the project of a united Scandinavia. At Calmar in 1397 the three kingdoms finally agreed to union under Margaret—a settlement that was to have lasting consequences; for Norway, detached from Sweden, remained under Danish control for several hundred years. Meanwhile, by rigorously enforcing its commercial privileges, the Hansa long continued to gain in wealth and power. Its decline in the fifteenth century was only in part due to the inevitable hostility of the Baltic states; the fundamental cause was the gradual diversion of trade to the west and south. The Hanseatic towns, like the Italian republics, had attained their height of prosperity while the Baltic and the Mediterranean were two isolated regions. As the two came to be joined by new maritime routes, commercial ascendancy passed to the more convenient ports of the Atlantic seaboard.

The economic decay of Flanders

Another phase of this economic shift is to be seen in the industrial and commercial decay of Flanders. Throughout the thirteenth century, as earlier, the bulk of English wool was exported to the Flemish cities, where it was made into cloth and sold in large quantity—especially to Hanseatic merchants for distribution in the north and to Italian merchants for distribution in the south. During the fourteenth century, however, the Venetians developed the practice of sending convoyed merchant fleets through the Strait of Gibraltar and thence along the coast to England and the Netherlands. Italian merchants thus found it a simple matter to buy wool in London for the benefit of manufacturers in their own cities. Besides, as a political move in the course of the French war, Edward III established colonies of Flemish weavers in England, and within a hundred years English cloth came to be well known in the European market. By the sixteenth century there was no wool to be exported from England; it had all been absorbed by the great English cloth industry that has since led the world. In the meantime, the ship-owners of England, France, Spain, and Portugal had learned to follow the example of the Venetians and, by undertaking Mediterranean voyages of their own, to win profits that had earlier gone to Flemish middlemen. But to appreciate the ultimate significance of these maritime adventures, we must briefly re-examine the economic position of the Moslem world.

Geographic knowledge of the Arabs

The seven centuries that had elapsed since the establishment of the Arab Empire may be said, from the commercial point of view, to fall into two clearly marked divisions. During the first the Moslems enjoyed a virtual monopoly of trade throughout central and western Asia, northern Africa, and the adjoining waters. Then, in the eleventh century, the fleets of the Italian cities—co-operating with Christian hosts in Spain, Sicily, and Syria

—drove the Moslems back and gained dominion over the Mediterranean. Thenceforth it was the Italian merchants who controlled the carrying of oriental products between the ports of the Levant and those of western Europe. The Arabs, however, still maintained their supremacy in the caravan trade across the Asiatic plateau and in the sea trade that linked the

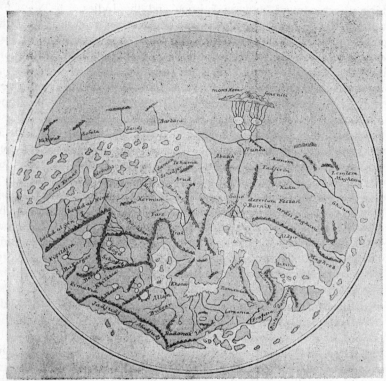

FIG. 30. Al-Idrisi's Map of the World. (South is towards the top of the map.)

coasts of India, Persia, Arabia, and eastern Africa. So al-Idrisi, the Arab geographer of Roger II,[21] could mark these regions on his map, together with the land of Ghana (Guinea) on the western shore of Africa. Such, essentially, remained the extent of geographic knowledge down to the opening of the fifteenth century. Various Christians had crossed Asia—a journey made famous by the writings of the Venetian Marco Polo[22]—and its outline was fairly well known. On the other hand, all of Africa except the

[21] See above, p. 323.

[22] See Marco's famous memoirs of his trip to the court of Kublai Khan, his experiences there, and his return. The story was dictated by Marco during his later imprisonment by the Genoese.

extreme north was only a matter of hearsay to Europeans. Al-Idrisi's map, without offering the possibility of circumnavigation, had shown a westward-flowing river (presumably the Senegal) which had a common source with the Nile. This tradition backed by various legends about a Christian country in the interior (really Ethiopia) might well lead to speculation about establishing direct contact between Europe and the Indies.

Later mediæval navigation

For the undertaking of great voyages, however, more was needed than a speculative interest in the outlying portions of the terrestrial globe. There had to be not only a motive powerful enough to inspire princes to finance the costly enterprises, but also mariners with the necessary training and equipment. In this connection it is obvious that the previous experience of Europeans in the navigation of their local seas was of the greatest importance. Although the direct translation of Ptolemy's geographical works in the fifteenth century[23] led to an improvement in the drawing of maps and the marking of latitude and longitude, theoretical knowledge was of minor value to the master of a ship. Above all he needed sailing directions, and for them he relied on charts that graphically illustrated the information acquired by his predecessors. Such charts, known to the profession as *portolani*, have been preserved in considerable numbers and constitute our best source for later mediæval navigation. Whatever the origin of the magnetic compass,[24] it had come into general use by the thirteenth century; and in the following period all practical maps were covered with lines that diverged from various centers and so described courses along which one might proceed in order to arrive at certain destinations (see Figure 31). Thanks to the *portolani*, drawn by salt-water sailors, the atlases of the later Middle Ages were gradually improved through the addition of newly explored coasts.

Portuguese exploration and the New World

Nevertheless, in spite of all this accumulated wisdom, what fifteenth-century state could be expected to undertake the development of new trade routes? As it happened, only Portugal had the westward outlook and the freedom from other preoccupations to encourage experimentation with African voyages. And Portugal, though recognized by the papacy as a kingdom since 1179, was too small to contemplate an ambitious program of exploration. What ended in revolutionary discovery began very modestly indeed. Prince Henry of Portugal (1394-1460) held two important offices: the headship of the Order of Jesus, which had fallen heir to the local possessions of the Templars[25] and the governorship of Ceuta, a small Portuguese conquest across the strait from Gibraltar. In the former capacity he hoped that his crusaders, like the Teutonic Knights, might win new lands and peoples for Christianity. In the latter he sought to break into the re-

[23] See below, p. 470.
[24] See above, pp. 306-08.
[25] See above, p. 388.

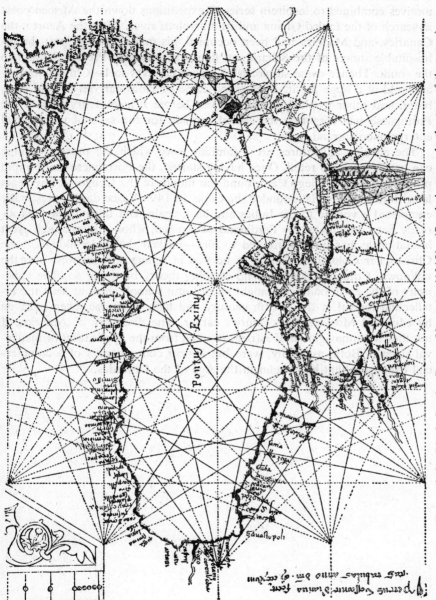

Fig. 31. Chart of the Black Sea by Petrus Vesconte (1318). (South is towards the top of the map.)

munerative slave trade carried on by the Moorish chieftains. These two motives combined to inspire a series of expeditions down the African coast in search of the fabled Ghana and its marvelous river. After the Azores, the Canaries, and Madeira had been occupied, his mariners crept past the inhospitable shores of the Sahara and finally reached the Promised Land to the south. Thence came shiploads of Negro captives to be Christianized— and sold at a huge profit. Thence too came precious cargoes of gold dust, ivory, and other tropical products. Even before Prince Henry's death the Portuguese had forgotten the sacred crusade for the sake of commercial enterprise on a grand scale.

The ensuing adventures are a familiar story which the present volume can hardly begin to retell. Once having started, the Portuguese made rapid progress. In 1482 Diego Cam found the mouth of the Congo. A few years later Bartholomeo Diaz rounded the Cape. In 1498 Vasco da Gama actually completed a voyage to the Indies and back again. But this success had already been anticipated by Ferdinand of Aragon, who—without such great hesitation as has been attributed to him—backed the undertaking of one Christopher Columbus. Daring as he was in sailing straight west into the unknown, Columbus launched no startling theory by doing so. The sphericity of the earth had been taught in all Latin schools since at least the intellectual revival of the twelfth century and had, of course, been believed by educated Moslems for centuries earlier. The discovery of America, if not the circumnavigation of Africa, resulted from the application of mediæval science. Both, assuredly, were but logical consequences of a commercial expansion that had begun in the Age of the Crusades.

CHAPTER XXV

The Advance of Secular Culture

1. VERNACULAR LITERATURE

On approaching the subject of artistic expression in the fourteenth and fifteenth centuries, all writers have long been expected to fix their attention upon a so-called Italian Renaissance. The expression, as first used by historians of a hundred years ago, designated a rebirth of ancient culture which, dispelling the darkness of the mediæval period, ushered in the age called modern. This Renaissance, it was alleged, began with the classical studies of the Italian humanists, was continued by the artists who rediscovered the beauty of antique monuments, and culminated in the great enlightenment of the sixteenth and seventeenth centuries. Today, of course, few historians would subscribe to the theory as stated above. Yet the phrases popularized by the older school remain in common use and, at least when they appear without proper qualification, may still be very misleading. Within the brief scope of the following pages it is proposed to give, not a series of definitions or redefinitions, but a review of actual developments in the various cultural fields.

The fine achievements of the earlier Middle Ages in the field of vernacular literature have been described in the preceding chapters. At the close of the thirteenth century the pre-eminence of the French in prose writing, as well as in all forms of poetic composition, was uncontested; although a number of remarkable works had appeared in German and Spanish, and although Dante Alighieri was about to win imperishable glory for his native Italian. The fourteenth century, with its accumulated miseries for France, brought a marked decline in the quality, if not in the quantity, of French literary production. Too many poems now came to be written according to established formulas and to lack all freshness or sincerity. Prose likewise suffered from the contemporary decadence of feudal society. Froissart's

chronicle of the Hundred Years' War, though pleasing enough as a superficial narrative, never rises above the level of elegant gossip—anecdotes
collected by a Flemish shop-keeper who was utterly dazzled by the false
chivalry of his day. And with the death of Froissart, about 1400, France
entered upon a period of demoralization that hardly ended before the accession of Louis XI.[1] Meanwhile English literature had been introduced
to a new and splendid age by the work of Langland, Chaucer, and Wycliffe;
and in Italy the standard recently set by Dante[2] had been well maintained
by Petrarch and Boccaccio.

**Petrarch
(1304-74)**

Exiled along with Dante was a Florentine notary who established his residence on the papal territory near Avignon. His son, illustrious under the
name of Petrarch,[3] first studied law at Montpellier and Bologna, but abandoned the legal profession to take holy orders. His motive, presumably,
was to obtain means and leisure for a literary career; at any rate, he never
allowed priesthood to interfere with either his love of women or his pursuit
of wordly fame. Petrarch's activities as a humanist will be examined in the
following section; here we are concerned with his early verse—his *Sonnets
in the Life and Death of Laura*. Laura, he tells us, he first saw on April 6,
1327, in a church at Avignon. Who the lady was we do not know. She was
apparently the wife of another, and she paid no attention to Petrarch, who
was left to pen his sonnets at a romantic distance. After alternately cursing
and glorying in his foolish passion, Petrarch thought that the old wound
had been healed when in 1348 it was reopened by the news of Laura's
death. The result was another series of poems, superior to most that had
preceded. Altogether he composed over three hundred sonnets; and although some of them are spoiled by the usual tricks of rhetoric, many are
still ranked among the world's masterpieces of lyric verse.

Petrarch is at his best in such unpretentious songs as praise his lady's
golden hair, bless the grass and flowers that bear the impress of her foot,
or celebrate the glove that has covered her hand—[4]

> O lovely hand that lightly holds my heart,
> That needs but close to press my life away.

In at least one unforgettable sonnet he prays God to deliver him from
his shameful bondage. But with Petrarch the mood of repentance is exceptional. Even when he has realized his love is hopeless, his resignation is not
that of a devout believer.

> Once I besought her mercy with my sighs,
> Striving in love-rime to communicate

[1] See below, pp. 471-74.
[2] See above, pp. 393-97.
[3] In Italian Petrarca—to which the poet changed his father's name, Petracco.
[4] The two following quotations are from Morris Bishop, *Love Rimes of Petrarch*
(Ithaca, N. Y., 1932), and are used by permission.

My pain, to see in that immaculate
Unmelting heart the fires of pity rise.
I longed the freezing cloud that round her lies
In the eloquent winds of love to dissipate—
Or else I'd rouse against her all men's hate
Because she hid from me her lovely eyes.
But now I wish no longer hate for her,
  Nor for me pity; for I know at last
  In vain against my fate I spend my breath.
Only I'll sing how she is lovelier
  Than the divine, that, when my flesh is cast,
  The world may know how happy was my death.

And at Laura's death he finds little consolation in the orthodox faith.[5]

The eyes whose praise I penned with glowing thought,
  And countenance and limbs and all fair worth
  That sundered me from men of mortal birth—
From them dissevered, in myself distraught—
The clustering locks, with golden glory fraught;
  The sudden-shining smile, as angel's mirth,
  Wonted to make a paradise on earth;
Are now a little dust that feels not aught.
Still I have life, who rail and rage at it,
  Lorn of love's light that solely life endears,
  Mastless before the hurricane I flit.
Be this my last of lays to mortal ears;
  Dried is the ancient fountain of my wit,
  And all my music melted into tears.

Of Petrarch's literary associates the most talented was Giovanni Boc- **Boccaccio**
caccio. The son of a Florentine merchant and a Parisian woman, Boccaccio **(1313-75)**
was brought up in his father's trade and for a time lived in France. There
he seems to have interested himself in French literature rather than in business; and as he grew to maturity, he devoted more and more of his time to
writing. In honor of a certain Fiametta he composed a variety of lyrics,
romances, and allegories, largely imitations of the French. It was only after
coming to know the works of Petrarch that Boccaccio despaired of equaling his friend's sonnets and wisely confined his further efforts to prose.
The result was the famous *Decameron*, a collection of stories presumed to
be told by a company of ladies and gentlemen who have isolated themselves
to escape the Black Death. Although Boccaccio's description of the pestilence is one of the classics on the subject, it serves in the *Decameron* merely
to introduce the series of tales that, in large part, he borrowed from the
French *fabliaux* or from such ancient authors as Apuleius. The originality
of the book lies in its graceful smooth-flowing style, which admirably reflects the changing moods of the narrative. The tales, as is well known, vary

[5] The following quotation is from R. Garnett, *CXXIV Sonnets*, p. 78.

from the extremely delicate to quite the reverse. But as yet no one dreamed of expurgating this kind of literature; many generations were to pass before refined language became fashionable even in aristocratic circles. The *Decameron*, whatever may be thought of its subject-matter, is an artistic triumph which, as the first noteworthy composition in Italian prose, deserves mention along with the masterpieces of Dante and Petrarch.

Beginnings of modern English

While Italian was thus acquiring glory as a literary language, what we know as English was just beginning to take form. In the fourteenth century French was still spoken at the royal court of England and was learned as a matter of course by educated persons generally. In both town and country, however, the ancient vernacular had steadily gained among all classes of the people. There were many dialects. That of the north we know as Scottish; that of the south lingers on in rural communities and occasionally appears as a quaint or comic touch in modern novels. Our English is based rather on the speech of the Midlands, the ancient Anglo-Saxon of Mercia modified by and largely mixed with the spoken French of the Normans. It was this English which, after obscure development in various minor books, was brought to splendid maturity by a series of distinguished writers in the latter half of the fourteenth century. One of them was Wycliffe, whose religious teachings have been considered in a preceding chapter. To English literature his great contribution was the Bible that bears his name. Precisely what part he had in the translation remains doubtful, but in the later version of it we find emerging the majestic prose that was to reach such perfection in the Bible of King James two hundred years later.

The Vision of Piers Plowman

One of Wycliffe's contemporaries, and one who shared many of the great preacher's convictions, was the author of the remarkable *Vision of Piers Plowman*. Presumably his name was William Langland, but this is a matter of slight importance; we know him only through his poem, which is written in rather archaic English and employs the ancient alliterative verse of the Anglo-Saxons. This is the beginning, in the modernized English of Skeat.[6]

> In a summer season, when soft was the sun,
> I enshrouded me well in a shepherd's garb,
> And robed as a hermit, unholy of works,
> Went wide through the world, all wonders to hear.
> And on a May morning, on Malvern hills,
> Strange fancies befel me, and fairy-like dreams.
> I was weary of wand'ring, and went to repose
> On a broad green bank, by a burn-side;
> As I lay there and leaned and looked on the waters,
> I slumbered and slept, they sounded so merry.

[6] In *The King's Classics* (Alexander Moring, Ltd.: London, 1905), used by permission of the publisher.

Came moving before me a marvellous vision;
I was lost in a wild waste; but where, I discerned not.
I beheld in the east, on high, near the sun,
A tower on a hill-top, with turrets well wrought;
A deep dale beneath, and a dungeon therein,
With deep ditches and dark, and dreadful to see.
A fair field, full of folk, I found there between,
Of all manner of men, the mean and the rich,
All working or wand'ring, as the world requires.

This was the earth, situated between the Tower of Truth, which was **Allegory** heaven, and the Castle of Care, which was hell. The earth was filled with **of the** all manner of persons, but the rascals seemed to be more prominent. The **earth** dreamer perceived sturdy plowmen, earning "the gain which the great ones in gluttony waste"; prosperous merchants, honest gleemen, devout monks, faithful priests, and other sincere Christians. They were too rare among the hordes of "jugglers and jesters, all Judas's children"; the beggars and beadsmen, intent only on cramming their bags and their bellies; pilgrims and palmers, whose journeys to holy shrines had merely served to make them professional liars; false hermits, "great lubbers and long, that to labor were loath"; friars of all sorts,

Who preached to the people for personal profit;
As it seemed to them good, put a gloss on the gospel,
And explained it at pleasure; they coveted copes.

There was also a pardoner, cheating the poor folk with indulgences under a bull which no prelate worth his two ears would ever have sealed. There appeared bishops and bachelors, masters and doctors, who, though holding parishes, spent their time in London to serve the king or to sing masses for silver. They were almost as mercenary as the lawyers.

I saw then a hundred, in hoods all of silk,
All serjeants, it seemed, that served at the bar,
Pleading their causes for pence or for pounds,
But for love of our Lord their lips moved never!
Sooner measure the mist upon Malvern hills
Than see a mouth mumble ere money be shown!

Nor were the laborers all worthy of their hire. Many were loafers who did **Lady** nothing all day but sing, while the hawkers shouted their wares: "Hot pies, **Meed and** hot!"—"Good geese and good bacon!"—"White wine of Alsace!"—"Red **Piers** Gascony wine!" **Plowman**

This vivid prologue is followed by the allegory of Lady Meed, the personification of unjust reward—what is popularly known as graft. Her proposed marriage to False led to a lawsuit, and all parties proceeded to London to have the case tried before the king. Although Meed had in her train an army of devotees, including all the lawyers, the king was eventually induced to listen to Reason and to put Meed out of his court. So ends the first vision, but the dreamer soon has a second. Conscience appeared in the field full of folk and preached repentance. First one and then another of his listeners was moved to seek forgiveness. The seven deadly sins, each personified by an individual man, made confession of their evil lives. That of Glutton, in particular, remains one of the most graphic passages in English literature, for it includes a realistic picture of the contemporary alehouse and its ribald company. Finally a multitude of repentant sinners set out on a pilgrimage to the shrine of St. Truth, but none knew the way thither. Before long they met a palmer, tricked out with all the symbols of the profession and covered with holy relics. He had been to Sinai, Jerusalem, Bethlehem, Babylon, Armenia, and Alexandria. Could he tell where to find St. Truth?

> "Nay," said the good man, "so God be my guide,
> I saw never palmer with pikestaff or scrip
> That asked for him ever, ere now in this place."

Then the plowman Piers said he knew the answer; he had faithfully served Truth for the past fifty years. The pilgrims thereupon asked Piers to lead them, and he promised to do so if they would help him with his plowing. They agreed and, after much trouble with the lazy and quarrelsome, the work was done. Yet the only result was that Piers became embroiled in an argument with a priest, during which the dreamer awoke, "meatless and moneyless on Malvern hills." The poem, as it has come down to us, includes various other parts: notably the famous satire about a parliament of rats and mice who wanted to bell the cat (i.e., the king) and the mystical addition wherein the Plowman reappears to typify the risen Christ. Whether all this was the work of a single man has been the subject of lively controversy among scholars, though the prevalent opinion now seems to be that at least most of it was. In any case, the *Vision of Piers Plowman* must be recognized as one of the world's classics. The author was not only a great artist but also a penetrating critic of contemporary life. To the student of social history it holds a peculiar interest as an early defense of the common man—an eloquent expression of the discontent that produced the Great Revolt of 1381.

Chaucer (d. 1400) Unlike Langland, Geoffrey Chaucer seems never to have lacked the good things of life. He inherited considerable property from his father, a prosperous vintner of London, received a good education, traveled extensively, held various posts in the royal government, and enjoyed favor at court. Although he composed many works, including numerous translations and adaptations from the French and the Italian, Chaucer remains chiefly famous for the *Canterbury Tales*—like the *Decameron* a collection of retold stories held together by means of a very obvious literary device. Writing in this way, an inferior poet would have produced little more than poor imitations. That Chaucer, despite his borrowing of subject-matter and literary forms, produced a great work of art is sufficient proof of his genius. To the old-fashioned language of *Piers Plowman* Chaucer preferred the colloquial English of the capital, with its rich intermixture of French; and the fact that we can read it with such ease shows how our speech is descended from his rather than from Langland's. Since his own day Chaucer's popularity has never waned; for the *Canterbury Tales* have never been surpassed for graceful, witty, and entertaining narrative. Whatever the special merits of his individual stories, either in prose or in verse, the historian finds particular significance in Chaucer's prologue.

There the poet describes the company assembled in the Tabard Inn at Southwark—the group of persons who are to amuse one another by telling stories while they journey to the shrine of St. Thomas Becket at Canterbury. It is a magnificent series of portraits, deserving all the praise that has been lavished on it for the past five centuries. And it is simple enough to be read by everyone in the original; to attempt a paraphrase would be useless. One or two special points in connection with its vivid portrayal of contemporary society may, however, be indicated. As would be expected in the work of a prosperous bourgeois courtier, no satire is directed against the upper or middle classes. The pictures of the knight and of the squire, his son, are highly idealized; even their servant, the forester-yeoman, is a fine fellow. Nothing unkind is said of the country gentry. The franklin is merely a substantial landowner, fond of good eating. The reeve, to be sure, is hard and avaricious; but so an efficient manager of estates has to be. The merchant, the manciple, and the shipman are worthy people. The various artisans are hardly more than mentioned, unless we include in their number the miller and the inimitable wife of Bath. Both seem like characters drawn from life. The former—red-whiskered and loud-mouthed, with a hairy wart on his nose—is unpleasant merely as an individual. And Chaucer, of course, does not imply that clothiers were usually mannish women who had buried five husbands. The plowman receives hearty praise as a God-fearing laborer who at any time is willing to help out an unfortunate comrade. The serjeant of law is not as he is described by Langland; he is a wise and highly respected man, with merely the foible of liking to appear busier than he really is. Only a little fun is poked at the doctor of physic, who knows his Galen and Avicenna somewhat better than the Bible, and who values gold as a cordial of especial worth.

It is not until he comes to the clergy that Chaucer's gentle irony develops into a rich vein of satire. There is the utterly charming prioress, so tenderhearted that she would weep over a mouse in a trap, delicate and lovely, with manners to grace the royal court. The motto on her brooch is *Amor vincit omnia*, and we are left to wonder whether the reference is to the

The Canterbury Tales: Prologue

love of God. The monk fit to be an abbot is a great hunter and a thorough man of the world, not at all like a fish out of water when away from his cloister. "A lord ful fat and in good poynt," he has nothing monastic about him except his clothes. The friar is more the professional ecclesiastic, with his power of hearing confessions and solemnizing marriages—but what an ecclesiastic! He is a handsome devil, light-spoken and clever. He has a good stock of presents for young wives. He can sing and play. He knows hosts and tapsters much better than beggars and lepers. He enjoys the *entrée* into all the more substantial homes of the country. He hears confession full sweetly and grants pleasant absolution with easy penance, for he can judge of repentance through the sinner's generosity.

> For many a man so harde is of his herte
> He may nat wepe althogh hym soore smerte.
> Therefore, instede of wepynge and preyeres,
> Men moote yeve silver to the poure freres.

Chaucer presents two other clerical rascals, the summoner and the pardoner. The one was a sort of bailiff who served notices on people to appear before the ecclesiastical court—an occupation that gave unlimited opportunities for scandal-mongering and blackmail. The loathsome representative in the prologue is the profession at its worst. The pardoner has already been encountered in *Piers Plowman*. Chaucer's example is an effeminate with a voice "as smal as hath a goot." Yet he is good at his job of selling indulgences, and he also deals in relics: a pillowcase made from Our Lady's veil, as well as a piece of sail from St. Peter's fishing boat—"and in a glas he hadde pigges bones." With this stuff he makes more in a day than an honest priest can get in a year.

> And thus with feyned flaterye and japes
> He made the person and the peple his apes.

To balance these uncomplimentary pictures, we have those of two worthy churchmen. The famous clerk of Oxford is the poverty-stricken scholar who has obtained no benefice, but who does not care as long as he possesses a score of books on Aristotelian philosophy. And the poor parson is all that he should be. He has not hired out his parish and gone to London to find easy money. Instead, he preaches the Gospel to the people, visits the sick and needy in any weather, and shares his meager income with the poor.

> He waited after no pompe and reverence,
> Ne maked him a spiced conscience;
> But Christes loore and his apostles twelve
> He taughte, but first he folwed it hymselve.

It should have been a fact of deep interest to the rulers of the church that in these respects Chaucer agreed with Langland, Wycliffe, Dante, Boccaccio, and a host of other critics, both heretical and orthodox.

2. THE NEW STYLES IN ARCHITECTURE AND THE RELATED ARTS

Looking back over the long development of vernacular literature in mediæval Europe, we may readily see that its later stages were no more inspired by the ancient classics than its earlier ones had been. However original the works of the later writers in Italian, English, and French, none of them were produced in revolt against the traditions of the twelfth and thirteenth centuries. The story is one of continuous growth, rather than one of a revival. To a considerable degree the same generalization holds in the history of architecture and the decorative arts. In those fields, however, another factor must be taken into account—the progress of secularism. Vernacular literature, though largely produced by ecclesiastics, was from the beginning dominated by a secular spirit because it was intended for a secular audience. This was not true of architecture and the allied arts in the earlier period because the great artists, though themselves laymen, were exclusively employed to build and adorn churches. It was only with the decline of ecclesiastical influence and the rise of bourgeois wealth in the thirteenth and following centuries that secular architecture, sculpture, and painting had a chance to flourish.

At the opening of the fourteenth century Gothic still remained the dominant style of architecture in the north, but its great age was past. Simpler forms of construction were superseded by the style known in England as decorated and in France as flamboyant, from the flame-shaped traceries that characterized it (see Figure 12). Although striking effects were occasionally obtained by the use of such ornamentation, it tended, especially in France, to obscure rather than to enhance the structural beauty of the framework.[7] By that time, however, the communes of Flanders and Brabant had begun to raise the splendid civic structures that yet give them such charm and distinction—notably the cloth hall of Bruges (see Plate XIII), the belfry of Ghent, the *hôtels de ville* of Louvain and Oudenarde, and the clustering gild houses of Brussels. The statuary of the fourteenth and fifteenth centuries tells the same story. The radiant beauty of the earlier French sculpture yielded to a naturalism that was better suited to portraits than to expressions of the ideal. So it was characteristic of the later age that some of the best artists were employed in designing memorial statues to the departed great. Even the characters of sacred history came to be represented as persons subject to violent emotion. The pathos of life and the tragedy of death, so prominent in the literature of the fifteenth century, became favorite themes for the sculptor, as well as for the illustrator of books and the painter.

The growth of secular art

[7] Compare the upper façade of Amiens Cathedral (Plate VI) with York Minster (Plate XVII).

Throughout the earlier age painting had been used to decorate ecclesiastical buildings in three principal ways: on glass, on the wooden panels of altars, and on plaster. This last use—the process known as fresco—had scarcely been applicable in Gothic churches for the simple reason that they had no plaster walls. And little remains of such work in other structures north of the Alps. Stained glass, as we have seen, was a highly specialized art which inevitably declined along with Gothic architecture. On the other hand, the painting of altars continued to fascinate artists of the fourteenth century, and in this pursuit they naturally followed the traditions of the illuminators. From an early time it had been customary to adorn the finest manuscripts wtih marginal illustrations. These miniatures, though usually symbolic, might deal with anything. When, for example, a book of devotion was made for a wealthy prince, it might be decorated with realistic scenes from everyday life—as in the case of the Book of Hours illuminated for the duke of Berry, brother of Charles V (see Plate XVIII). Shortly afterwards a famous altar-piece at Ghent was painted by the brothers van Eyck, Flemings in the service of the Burgundian duke. Earlier paintings of this sort had normally been in tempera, pigment mixed with egg or gum. The van Eycks, on the contrary, used oils—a process which they seem to have perfected. The work of Jan van Eyck, in particular, was remarkable for its realism. He was a consummate portrait-painter, as may be realized from his "Man with the Pink" (see Plate XVIII) or the figures of the donors in his larger compositions. He also excelled in the painting of domestic interiors, reproducing with amazing skill the textures of rich fabrics, the sheen of polished wood and metal, a landscape seen through a window, or the depth of reflection in a mirror. Effects like this had never before been achieved by smearing paint on a flat surface; and the art was essentially a native product, untouched by classic influence.

Italy, meanwhile, had witnessed remarkable developments, not only in painting, but also in sculpture and architecture; and to some degree they were inspired by antique models. The craze for Roman writings begun by the humanists[8] was accompanied by a craze for the remains of Roman art. Since to the collector of antiquities everything mediæval was barbarous or "Gothic," a reaction set in against the exuberant and often meaningless style that had been imported from the north. Italians generally sought to restore their buildings to classic purity. Knowing nothing of Greek architecture, they tended to imitate such Roman monuments as the triumphal arches and the Colosseum, which had never been examples of perfect taste. Too often they were satisfied with the addition, to a Romanesque or Gothic structure, of pilasters, entablatures, and other superficial features. The first great church to be hailed as an expression of the new movement was the cathedral of Florence, on which Brunelleschi placed a

[8] See below, pp. 468-70.

dome some three hundred feet high. Constructed like a cupola on an octagonal base, it was a fine and original work, though hardly Roman in design. More Italian than classic were likewise the civic buildings and private residences, the best of which owe their beauty to graceful proportions rather than to pseudo-Roman decoration. What is called Renaissance architecture thus began as a very haphazard style, resting on no logical development of structural principles. It was not until later that Italian architects sought to work out a complete system, and then they adopted the mathematical formulas of Vitruvius.[9] The results were not altogether happy, but the continuation of the story must be left to others.

On the whole, Italian contributions in sculpture and painting were superior to those in architecture, and as late as the fifteenth century the former owed little to classic art. Perhaps it was fortunate that there were no antique pictures and, for a while, very few antique statues to be copied. The first of the great Italian sculptors was the Florentine Ghiberti, whose masterpiece was the set of bronze doors for the baptistery of the local cathedral (see Plate XX). His magnificent reliefs, to be sure, reveal touches of Roman ornamentation; yet the total effect is anything but classical. The scenes from the Old and New Testaments are infused with religious feeling, while much of the decoration is naturalistic. In the work of the slightly younger Donatello this latter characteristic is even more pronounced. His statues of saints, instead of being attempts to represent ideal Christian virtues, are individual men and women, modeled from life with all their peculiarities and imperfections. His angels are smiling robust children. His David is a graceful Florentine boy who, it must be admitted, looks more like a dancer than the slayer of Goliath. Such an artist was primarily a master of portraiture. His equestrian statue of the mercenary captain Gattamelata (see Plate XX) set a new standard for the representation in bronze of a horse as well as a rider. This was the beginning of an art that, with the better appreciation of antique sculpture, was to attain fresh glory under the hands of Michelangelo. *Italian sculpture*

The history of Italian painting is a much more complicated subject, and one that can be no more than touched here. The man who laid the foundations for the splendid advance of this art in the following centuries was Giotto, the compatriot and friend of Dante. Breaking with Byzantine tradition, he covered walls with frescoes that sought to tell a story by direct expression in pictures. Such, for example, are his famous decorations at Assisi, which deal with the life of St. Francis. Each scene is in itself a dramatic episode, portrayed with what was intended for realism. Giotto's *Italian painting*

[9] A Roman engineer of the Augustan age. His work, preserved in a tenth-century manuscript, was rediscovered in the fifteenth century and was thenceforth regarded as a great authority by architects, though it was much better on practical details of construction than on æsthetics.

skill in drawing was limited, but the pictorial value of his compositions made him the founder of a new school (see Plate XIX). The rest of the century saw little more than imitations of Giotto; then Florence produced the astonishing Masaccio, who died at the age of only twenty-seven. The vivid realism of his pictures became the inspiration of all the great Florentine masters who followed (see Plate XIX). By way of conclusion, it may only be mentioned that Verrochio, a disciple of Masaccio and a pupil of Donatello, helped to develop the surpassing genius of Leonardo da Vinci.

These facts should at least indicate that the rich vein of naturalism in Renaissance art was independent of all classic influence and had its source in the later Gothic art of the thirteenth and fourteenth centuries. It was not that the Italians borrowed from the Flemings or vice versa; both groups started with a common inspiration and up to a certain point progressed together. That the van Eycks were of the same generation as Masaccio, Ghiberti, and Donatello is more than coincidence. Whatever may be decided concerning the mutual influence of the two schools, it must be admitted that the Flemings led the way in realistic portraiture and landscape painting, and that they improved the technique of mixing pigment with oil. On their side the Italians excelled in fresco, and from them all Europe learned the art of pictorial composition. Although ecclesiastical influence remained, the old religious feeling that had inspired Dante and Giotto all but died under their successors. The art of fifteenth-century Italy was secular in spirit. The madonnas and saints of the great Italian masters were hardly less fleshly, though more fully clothed, than their Roman gods and goddesses. The Italian theorists, who wished to derive everything fine in their civilization from the antique, were right in at least one particular: their art was essentially pagan. Eventually, as the artists became more expert, they were better able to appreciate the finer qualities of classic work and to draw from it lessons of value for their own age. There was, nevertheless, no rebirth of ancient art, no sharp contrast between that said to be of the Renaissance and that said to be of the Middle Ages.

3. SCHOLASTICISM, SCIENCE, AND HUMANISM

Later scholastic controversy

At the opening of the fourteenth century the problem of dominant concern in university education was the interpretation of Aristotle—and it is one on which present-day scholars by no means agree. Aristotle's authentic writings are not wholly consistent; while his earlier books maintain a Platonic interest in metaphysics, his later books, especially those dealing with biology, shift their emphasis to science and what we definitely recognize as a scientific method of research. In the thirteenth century, however, the accepted works of Aristotle included much that is now known to be spurious, and the task of anyone who attempted to study them was further complicated by the fact that so many of his authorities were Neoplatonists. Such assuredly were Porphyry, the author of the *Isagoge*, and also Boëthius, the first to translate a portion of Aristotle's logic into Latin. The fathers of the church, notably St. Augustine, had been strongly influenced by Neo-Platonism, and so had the Arab commentators, such as Avicenna and Averroës. More recently, as we have seen, the *Summa Theologiæ* of Thomas Aquinas had attempted a definitive reconciliation of Aristotelian philosophy and traditional Christianity. Yet, so far as the contemporary world was concerned, his exposition seemed only to provoke fresh controversy.

The formal acceptance of the Thomist doctrine by the Dominican order naturally invited the Franciscans to reject it, and the center of their opposition continued to be Oxford University. There, and later at Paris, Duns Scotus won the designation of *Doctor Subtilis* by defending the thesis that such dogmas as the existence of God and the immortality of the soul cannot be proved by reason. Logically carried out, this argument would have denied much of the Thomist system. Duns, however, died prematurely in 1308 and within a few years his fame had been eclipsed by that of another Oxford Franciscan. William of Ockham was an Englishman, named for the village of his birth. As already remarked, his academic career was interrupted by a summons to the papal court at Avignon, where he was eventually excommunicated for supporting the Franciscan tenet of apostolic poverty against Pope John XXII.[10] In spite of his condemnation, he continued to enjoy great renown, not only as an antagonist of the papacy, but also as the author of many scholarly books. *Duns Scotus and William of Ockham*

The precise force of Ockham's teaching has been much disputed. Earlier historians generally declared that, by reviving nominalism, he opposed the current Aristotelianism of the schools. On the other hand, more recent critics have pointed out that Ockham published his logic as a mere commentary on Aristotle, leaving readers to describe his doctrine in any way they chose. Whether or not Ockham should be called a nominalist depends altogether on how that term is defined.[11] Since the days of Abelard a multitude of scholars had devoted their lives to the study of dialectic, and yet the problem of universals remained a subject of endless argumentation. This problem—it now appears sensible to conclude—Ockham summarily disposed of by reasserting the original view of Aristotle. Logic, as had been asserted by John of Salisbury,[12] is not a means of ascertaining absolute truth, but a useful tool for explaining facts otherwise learned. The universals of Porphyry have no existence apart from the mind that conceives them. They are only general ideas, which have no rational *Ockham's logic and the scientific method*

[10] See above, pp. 392-93.
[11] See above, pp. 259-63.
[12] See above, p. 265.

validity except in so far as they are derived from the experience of the individual. The articles of the Christian faith, Ockham declared, should be accepted as such. They cannot be proved by reason; nor can they be made the basis of all knowledge. In other words, science is science and theology is theology; the two are essentially different and must not be confused.

Thus understood, Ockham's logic was not so much an attack on the Thomist system as a limitation of its scope. Sixteen centuries earlier the disciples of Aristotle had tended to desert metaphysical speculation for the sake of scientific research. It is very significant that the disciples of Ockham now displayed the same tendency. Men whom contemporaries knew as Ockhamists became a dominant force in the university of Paris, and so in Latin Europe as a whole. Among them, about the middle of the fourteenth century, were Jean Buridan, Oresme, and Albert of Saxony, whose writings have been hailed as anticipating those of many great scientists in the seventeenth century. Without entirely accepting so enthusiastic an appraisal, we may yet agree on a few facts. All three of these Ockhamists were deeply interested in problems of celestial mechanics and seem to have concluded, however vaguely, that such problems might be solved through a fuller understanding of terrestrial mechanics. Thus, at least, they did give thought to the phenomena that were eventually to be explained by Newton's law of gravitation. And the work of Oresme, in particular, had two important influences: it helped Galileo to describe the uniform acceleration of falling bodies and it helped Descartes to establish the principles of analytical geometry. We may therefore be certain that, by re-emphasizing the necessity for scientific observation, Ockham and his disciples laid part of the foundation on which were to rise imposing structures of the later age.

Medicine and anatomy

The fourteenth century also witnessed a noteworthy development of medicine. Up to this point the Latin schools had added little if anything to the medical wisdom which they had inherited from the Greeks and Arabs. Especially Galen and Avicenna were held in such reverence that originality was somewhat discouraged. Practicing physicians nevertheless found it advisable to supplement their book-learning with direct observation—and that, in the case of anatomy, meant dissection of the human body. Precisely how and when such study began in the west we do not know. But it had proceeded far enough by the end of the thirteenth century to encourage a teacher of medicine at Bologna, Mondino dei Luzzi (d. 1326), to publish a textbook on the subject. Disclaiming all ambition to write in an elevated style, the author gives practical directions as to how one seeking to learn about human anatomy should proceed to cut up a cadaver. The book enjoyed enormous success and eventually appeared in many printed editions. As a consequence, its original illustrations have long since been lost. To gain some idea of Mondino's own drawings, the best we can do

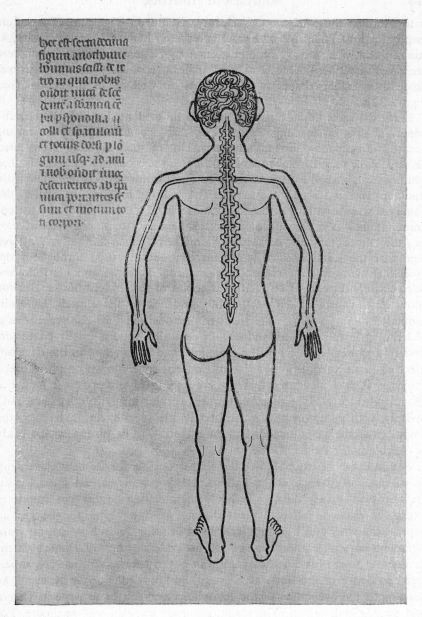

FIG. 32. Anatomical Drawing by Guido da Vigevano.

is to examine those of a contemporary, Guido da Vigevano. The latter, as physician to Philip VI of France, presented him with various writings, one of which was an essay on human anatomy. The manuscript, fortunately preserved, contains eighteen colored plates, graphically showing various procedures in the diagnosis of ailments as well as in dissection (see Figure 32).

From the facts already noted it should be evident that the other traditional subjects of academic instruction, theology and law, by no means decayed during the fourteenth century. But of them nothing more need be said here; they continued to be developed according to standards that had been established earlier. Essentially a newer interest was the humanistic study revived in Italy by the famous Petrarch. In his time, as earlier, the humanist was essentially one who remained loyal to the ideal of the ancient grammarians—one who devoted himself primarily to *litteræ humaniores*, i.e., the "more humane" or secular literature of pagan antiquity. We have seen that the Latin classics had been continuously used throughout the preceding centuries; for such classics, indeed, Petrarch and his followers were entirely dependent on mediæval copies of the ancient books. But the educational system of the west, being governed by the church, had subordinated literary study to the needs of practical religion. The great revival of learning in the eleventh and twelfth centuries, though briefly characterized by renewed enthusiasm for grammar, had culminated in the development of the universities, where instruction was concentrated on professional subjects. It was inevitable that the weakening of ecclesiastical influence should produce a sharp reaction towards secular ideals in education. And in Italy, with its urban civilization and its pleasure-loving aristocracy, the emphasis of the schools tended to be æsthetic—to be placed on the study of literature for its own sake.

Petrarch, whose example was largely responsible for the new movement, was a man of strange contradictions. Having won merited fame by his Italian verse, which displays a lively appreciation of the contemporary world, he came to affect a great disdain for the vulgar tongue and to express the wish that he could have lived in some age other than his own. Although he was a priest, he showed no understanding of Dante's Christianity and found his chief inspiration in pagan letters. With a very imperfect knowledge of the Latin classics and no knowledge of Greek at all, he denounced the barbarism of the schoolmen and sought to write as Cicero and Seneca had written. The result, naturally enough, was mediocre. For the sake of sheer delight, who today would read any of Petrarch's works except his sonnets? And much the same criticism holds for Boccaccio, who ranks among the immortals on account of his stories in the vernacular, not on account of his later attempts at elegant Greek and Latin.

A cause, however, should not be judged by the foibles of its leaders. **Humanism** The humanist enthusiasm for classical study, despite the extremes to which **and** it was sometimes carried, was in itself admirable—as all lovers of great **literary** art will surely admit. Within the field of Latin literature it led to the redis- **apprecia-** covery of many forgotten books and the truer appreciation of many that **tion** had been neglected. Within the field of Greek literature—so far as the western schools were concerned—it produced a revolution. Such of the ancient authors as had generally been known through poor translations now came to be used in the original, and beside them were now placed the masterpieces of prose and verse that the Latins, following the Arabs, had hitherto ignored. Study of this sort was a thousand years old, or more, in the cities of the eastern Mediterranean; but to the Italians of the later fourteenth century it was an exciting novelty. Once launched, the humanist education quickly became an academic craze. To satisfy the demands of students, old professorships were reformed and new ones were established. Great libraries were erected to house the treasures that were eagerly col- lected on all sides. Improved editions of Greek and Latin authors were brought out in beautiful handwriting. Scholars produced more adequate grammars, dictionaries, and other manuals. And as men sought to read the classics with a fuller understanding, they gained a better knowledge of the ancient world generally and so broadened their intellectual horizon. All this, it will be agreed, places us under deep obligation to the humanists, who came to dominate the universities of Italy in the fifteenth century and those of other countries in the centuries following.

To praise the humanism of the later Middle Ages as an æsthetic revival **Humanism** is by no means to admit the once-honored thesis of the Italian Renaissance. **and** However important in the field of education, humanism was no magical **science** element by which mediæval culture could be transformed into modern culture. Will anyone today care to assert that a finer appreciation of ancient literature produced the glorious arts of the fifteenth century, the growth of capitalism, the opening of the New World, the Protestant Revolution, or the triumphs of experimental science? Repetition of what has already been said about some of these developments will hardly be necessary. So far as architecture, sculpture, and painting are concerned, the influence of humanism was at most secondary. Vernacular literature, it may easily be perceived, progressed not by virtue of humanism but in spite of it. Economic development had absolutely nothing to do with chang- ing academic fashions, and it was the former rather than the latter that determined the course of ecclesiastical history. There remains the question of scientific progress, and in this connection it must be granted that the chief credit goes to the later scholastics.

The early humanists, by rejecting both the vernacular and the contem- porary Latin for literary composition, made it difficult for their disciples to be more than antiquarians. Along with scholastic theology, they condemned original advance in law, mathematics, and the study of natural phenomena. Their zeal to extol Plato was in itself admirable, but in so doing they tended to depreciate Aristotle together with all that he and his mediæval commentators had contributed towards the definition of scientific method. The later humanists, fortunately, tended to acquire a broader vision. Many of them did not disdain the study of useful arts in the contemporary world or the accurate translation of such Greek classics as might be needed by engineers and other non-academic persons. So, for example, the fifteenth century witnessed the appearance in Latin of Ptolemy's *Geography,* as well as of various books by Archimedes, which had hitherto been somewhat neglected. How the new Ptolemy supplemented the work of actual navigators has been seen in the preceding chapter; how the mechanics of Archimedes supplemented the work of actual technicians will be seen in the one following.

CHAPTER XXVI

Europe in the Later Fifteenth Century

1. THE NEW DESPOTS

Judged according to political success, the outstanding figure in the west **Louis XI** during the second half of the fifteen century was assuredly Louis XI of **(1461-83)** France. Charles VII, the king who owed his crown to Jeanne d'Arc, lived on until 1461. He was cordially detested by many persons, including his son Louis, who eventually ran away to the court of the magnificent Philip the Good, duke of Burgundy.[1] In return for his splendid entertainment of the future king, Philip doubtless expected a handsome reward, but in that he was disappointed. The dauphin was quite willing that someone else should pay his expenses until he came to the throne; when that happy moment arrived, he assumed the position of an absolute monarch who required no advice from a ducal cousin.

Physically, Louis XI inherited the feebleness of his Valois ancestors. He was small and weak. His legs were hardly strong enough to hold him up. His face was singularly unattractive—almost cadaverous with its sunken eyes, long thin nose, and prominent bones. To make up for these deficiencies, his intelligence was unsurpassed and, in spite of his unhappy youth, he had received a good education. Clear-sighted, indefatigable, and relentless, the king knew precisely what he wanted and, to attain his ends, willingly sacrificed every other consideration. Disliking war, he used his army only as a last resort. Customarily he relied rather on diplomacy, in which he proved himself a master of consummate skill. All who opposed his will were to find him a hateful tyrant; even his loyal subjects might complain of his harsh and grasping administration. Yet Louis XI was not senselessly cruel. Men who served him faithfully had just treatment. And although he was extremely parsimonious in little ways, he spared no expense when vital issues were at stake.

[1] See above, p. 413.

Such a king, obviously, was not a paragon of chivalry. He seemed, in fact, deliberately to make himself as little the gallant gentleman as possible. Immediately after the funeral of Charles VII had been concluded with fitting pomp, Louis put aside all the trappings of royalty and thenceforth appeared in a cheap traveling costume—a long coat of fustian and a wide-brimmed pilgrim's hat, decorated with small pewter figures of the Virgin and the saints. On appropriate occasions one of these would be removed for the sake of a short prayer; then it would be clapped back into place. For the king was superficially very pious, attending mass every day and by other conventional acts always seeking the aid of heaven in his enterprises, both honest and dishonest. Normally his days were spent in constant journeys about his kingdom, in every corner of which he took a proprietary interest. Detesting all lavish entertainment, he moved about with a few servants and commonly stayed at a public inn or with some local merchant. His bourgeois tastes and sympathies were shown in many other ways. The towns, in return for heavy taxes, received his especial protection and encouragement. The feudal class he jealously kept from all power in the state. As ministers he chose only men who owed everything to his patronage. For confidential agents he often preferred low-born rascals, sometimes even convicts let out of jail for that particular purpose.

Charles the Rash of Burgundy

Since Philip the Good was now too old to engage in active reprisals against his faithless guest, that task devolved upon his son Charles, who finally inherited the ducal crown in 1467. The young prince was a dashing figure. Athletic, handsome, and likable, he was not only a brave knight but also an able and intelligent ruler. Though living in great magnificence, he was sober, chaste, and sincerely religious. The fatal flaw in his character was indicated by the name he came to bear, Charles the Rash (*le Téméraire*). Goaded by ambition, he was never satisfied with a moderate program of achievement. Instead, he recklessly threw himself into a series of grandiose projects, refusing in his pride ever to retreat before superior strength or ever to heed the advice of the cautious. The striking contrast between him and the king of France gave to their prolonged conflict a certain epic character—made it a worthy theme for the great chronicler who happened to be present.

Commines

Philippe de Commines was a Flemish nobleman who rose to be councilor and chamberlain at the Burgundian court. Later prevailed on by Louis XI to enter the royal service, he remained in it until the king's death. Being then removed from political office, Commines devoted his last years to the writing of the memoirs that, ever since, have been justly famous. Unlike Froissart, Commines never contented himself with superficial description. The comings and goings of men were in themselves, he felt, of subordinate interest; what fascinated him was the interplay of motives behind the scenes. He saw in war and politics a game played by statesmen. Which were the best moves? How did they come to be taken? Specifically, what were the qualities of Louis XI that brought him victory over an apparently superior adversary? Though preoccupied with state-craft rather than with feudal adventure, Commines owed nothing to the humanism of Italy. His mental horizon was that of a fifteenth-century Frenchman who followed the honest example of Villehardouin by report-ing what he had himself observed.

During the first decade of his reign Louis had to withstand as best he could a combination of discontented princes led by the duke of Burgundy. Time and again, as Commines so graphically tells us, the king accepted defeat and signed a humiliating peace, only by some kind of chicanery to slip out of his commitments. Eventually he escaped reprisal because the duke had evolved the magnificent design of uniting his scattered territories and so of reconstituting the ancient Lotharingia.[2] By 1475 Charles had almost realized his ambition. But the diplomacy of Louis XI frightened the Habsburg emperor[3] into refusing a Burgundian alliance and built up a coalition to defend the local states of Alsace and Lorraine. Foremost among the French allies were the Swiss who, having gained their independ-ence through the paralysis of the royal power in Germany, had no liking for the new and powerful monarchy that was emerging on their western border. In their earlier wars they had found that massed infantry armed with long pikes could successfully oppose charging cavalry, and through similar tactics they now astonished Europe by breaking the military power of Burgundy. Twice in 1476 Charles sought to punish the troublesome mountaineers, and twice he was defeated. Before the walls of Nancy in the next year he insisted on again attacking a Swiss position. The result was the same, except that on this occasion the duke himself remained on the stricken field.

The delight of Louis XI and the dismay of certain French nobles when they heard the news are vividly described by Commines. The emotions were justified, for thenceforth the king was to be undisputed master of his realm. Despite the fact that Charles had left an heiress, Louis proceeded to confiscate his fiefs as escheat to the crown. Without difficulty the royal troops occupied Picardy, Artois, Burgundy, and Franche-Comté, although the last was imperial territory. He likewise sought to take Flanders, but there he overreached himself. The Flemings rallied to the support of Charles's daughter Mary, who was a native of their country, and she, in revenge for the royal perfidy, accepted marriage with Maximilian of Austria (see Table VIII). Thus a Habsburg prince was installed as ruler of the Netherlands and claimant of the whole Burgundian heritage—an event of prime importance for the future of Europe. Meanwhile, however,

The fall of Burgundy

[2] See above, p. 157.
[3] Frederick III, father of Maximilian; see Table VIII.

Louis had obtained another windfall. The extinction of the Angevin house, descended from a brother of Charles V (see Table VII), gave the king the duchy of Anjou and the counties of Maine, Bar, and Provence (see Map XVII). Aside from Flanders, only one of the great French fiefs was still independent of royal control—the duchy of Brittany, which was to be acquired through marriage by Louis's son, Charles VIII.

Govern-
ment of
Louis XI So far as internal government was concerned, Louis XI ruled France as the unrestricted heir of Charles V. There was, in fact, no substitute for royal absolutism; a parliamentary government like that of England had no place in a kingdom devoid of institutional unity. Louis XI called only one meeting of the estates general—when, during his early years, he needed support against a feudal coalition. Later, as resistance to the king's will utterly collapsed, he used only provincial estates and assemblies of notables who could be counted on not to oppose him. Thanks to his control of the permanent taxes that have earlier been described,[4] he was able to ignore divergencies of local custom and to maintain a despotic system of finance. A similar conclusion may be drawn with regard to his administration of justice. The *parlement* at Paris normally acted as a supreme court for all France, but the variation of the law from region to region made complete centralization impossible. Charles VII had established a local *parlement* for Languedoc at Toulouse, and one for Dauphiné at Grenoble; Louis XI added one for Guienne at Bordeaux and one for Burgundy at Dijon. Much the same functions had already come to be exercised by ancient courts in Normandy and Champagne. These tribunals all administered ordinary law, following established precedents and observing a regular procedure. Cases of treason and other trials in which the king took a particular interest he removed for arbitrary judgment before his council. As may be seen from such examples, the one institution that was common to all France was the monarchy.

Despite his oppressive taxation and tyrannical ways, Louis XI deserved well of his country, for he made its interests his own. The flood of money that he brought into the treasury he spent not for sumptuous entertainment and vainglorious wars but for the defense and consolidation of the state. The standing army of his father—organized in regular companies of cavalry, infantry, and artillery—he increased and improved at heavy expense. Yet he used it only when he had to, regarding it as a valuable tool rather than a plaything. Goodly sums were also devoted to the needs of diplomacy: the subsidies, bribes, and pensions lavished by the king on all useful allies, together with the salaries paid to the host of agents whom he dispatched all over Europe. That such expenditure was amply justified by its results has already been seen. And the growing burden of taxation was more than offset by the revived prosperity of the countryside. Thanks

---

[4] See above, p. 412,

to the king's despotic government, France at large remained at peace. The destruction of the Burgundian power removed a constant incentive to feudal disorders within the kingdom. The subjection of the nobility, though cruel, proved a blessing to the other classes. The brigandage of discharged troops, which had once more grown to alarming proportions under Charles VII, was finally ended. Wise economic measures stimulated the repopulation of devastated regions and a noteworthy advance in commerce. The restored brilliance of French civilization in the following century was largely due to the tireless energy of the mean-looking but masterful Louis XI.

In England, as we have seen, the duke of Burgundy had helped to place the Yorkist Edward IV on the throne;[5] so it was quite natural that the French king should lend support to a Lancastrian adventurer named Henry Tudor, although his claim to the throne was somewhat dubious (see Table III). Shortly after the death of Edward IV in 1483 his two sons were murdered at the instigation of their uncle, who was crowned as Richard III. Encouraged by this act of violence, Henry Tudor landed in Wales with a small army. There he gained other recruits and before a month had passed was fortunate enough to win the battle of Bosworth Field, in which Richard was slain (1485). Henry's victory in the field, confirmed by his marriage to a daughter of Edward IV, by the ratification of parliament, and by the judicious execution of rival claimants, assured the triumph of the new dynasty. The later fortunes of the Tudors lie beyond the scope of the present study. It should, however, be remarked that under them the English monarchy became virtually absolute. Parliament, to be sure, did not disappear; but that was because, reflecting the public demand for a strong kingship, it served merely to register the royal will. And through a process like that adopted by Louis XI, the Tudors gradually subordinated the courts of common law to their own arbitrary justice administered through a branch of the privy council. Whatever the traditional theory of the constitution, for the next hundred years England was to be as thoroughgoing a despotism as France.

The third of the great western monarchies at the close of the fifteenth century was Spain, a much more recent creation. In the preceding pages it has been seen how Aragon became an important state through union with Catalonia and the conquest of the Moorish territory to the south. At the same time the kingdom of Castile, finally combined with León, had pushed its dominion to the Mediterranean at Murcia and to the Atlantic at Cadiz, thus restricting the Mohammedans to the little territory of Granada (see Map XV). On the west coast Portugal had established itself as an independent kingdom, and to the north Navarre had come to be ruled by a series of French princes. This was the situation at the end of

The Tudor accession in England

The new monarchy of Spain

[5] See above, pp. 412-13.

the thirteenth century, and in general it remained unchanged for the better part of two hundred years. Taking advantage of the chronic civil wars in Spain, Louis XI obtained possession of two Catalonian provinces, Roussillon and Cerdagne, and so brought his frontier to the crest of the Pyrenees. But in another affair he was taken by surprise. In 1468 a group of Castilian rebels submitted on condition that Isabella, the sister of their unpopular king, be recognized as heiress of the crown, and in the following year she married Ferdinand, the prince apparent in Aragon. First brought together by personal union in 1479, the two kingdoms were finally made into one, the kingdom of Spain. Its territory, as Ferdinand conquered Granada and the southern half of Navarre, came to include the entire peninsula with the exception of Portugal. Its government, as Ferdinand made himself independent of the local estates, or *cortes*, became an absolute monarchy. Its anti-French policy, as Ferdinand arranged a momentous alliance with the house of Habsburg, was to remain a dominant factor in the European wars of the sixteenth and seventeenth centuries.

Cultural revival under the despots

That the political developments just described were intimately connected with the revival of culture in western Europe is quite evident. What is hailed as the classic age of Spanish arts and letters began with the foundation of the unified monarchy by Ferdinand and Isabella. The successful rule of the Tudors was the immediate cause of the so-called English Renaissance. In both kingdoms the influence of the Italian humanists became increasingly important during the sixteenth century. Yet, on the whole, the finest accomplishments of either the Spanish or the English at that time will be found to rest on long-established precedents of the Middle Ages. A similar generalization holds true in the case of France. Throughout the fifteenth century the French architects, sculptors, and painters generally followed the Gothic tradition; and even later there was no absolute desertion of the older styles. So far as literature was concerned, the reign of Louis XI was chiefly remarkable for the renewal of an ancient glory. It is no exaggeration to say that in the field of political memoirs the standard set by Commines has never been surpassed, and that, as a balladwriter, François Villon has hardly been equaled.

François Villon

Villon is certainly one of the most famous characters in literary history. Born of a poor Parisian family in 1431, the boy was adopted by a certain Guillaume de Villon, a chaplain attached to the church of Saint-Benoît near the Sorbonne. Thanks to this worthy man, François acquired not only the name of Villon but also a superior education. In due course he became a master of arts at Paris and then took up the study of theology. Meanwhile, however, he had developed the roistering habits that were to debar him from any superior degree, as well as from ecclesiastical preferment. The discipline of the university, never very strict, had suffered from the general confusion of the kingdom. Paris, like the countryside, was filled with bands of thieves and cut-throats, and the students were often no better. Villon found in the taverns a more congenial society than in the cloister of Saint-Benoît; so the spiders, he tells us, spun their webs over the bed where he was supposed to be sleeping. In 1455 his academic career, such as it was, came to a sudden end with his killing of a priest in a fight over a girl of the streets. While the police investigated the affair, Villon hurriedly left Paris. Then, after his friends had proved that his act had been in self-defense, he returned to his old lodgings. But in the meantime he had apparently joined a gang of professional robbers, in whose jargon he wrote a number of ballads.

There now ensued a number of housebreakings, ending in the theft of **The** a considerable sum from one of the Parisian colleges. Villon, implicated ***Petit*** through the blabbing of a drunken comrade, again left the city in haste. ***Testament*** He had time only to finish a last will in verse, the poem known as the *Petit Testament*. Therein, posing as a victim of love, he makes a number of humorous bequests: his fame to Guillaume de Villon, his heart to the girl who had jilted him, his right of preferment to certain canons of Notre-Dame, his sword to a friend who is to pay the sum for which it is now in pawn. But while he is writing, he hears the bells of the Sorbonne, and they bring to mind the scholastic drudgery in which he has been so long engaged. The thought paralyzes his brain and he goes to bed. Already famous in student circles as a writer of ballads, Villon gained wide renown through the *Petit Testament* and, while exiled from the capital, enjoyed the hospitality of various distinguished patrons. Nevertheless, he seems to have continued his old avocation; for the year 1460 found him jailed as a thief by the bishop of Orleans.

At that particular moment Louis XI celebrated his accession in the **The** usual fashion by releasing prisoners in the course of a triumphal procession ***Grand*** throughout the kingdom. And since the king happened to come in the ***Testament*** right direction, Villon once more found himself at liberty. Returning to Paris in a chastened mood, he wrote his *Grand Testament*, one of the greatest poems in any language. It is not merely clever and amusing; fundamentally, it is the poet's lament for a wasted life—as sincere and moving as if told in the confessional. Villon begins with a bitter song against the bishop who threw him into a dungeon; then turns to bless Louis XI. May he live to be as old as Methuselah and have twelve children, all sons! This theme brings him to the story of King Alexander and the thief—and so to himself. He is now thirty and has little to show for the years but disillusionment.[6]

---

[6] The following quotations are from John Payne's translation, which has appeared in many editions.

My time of youth I do bewail,
  That more than most lived merrily,
Until old age 'gan me assail,
  For youth had passed unconsciously.
  It wended not afoot from me,
Nor yet on horseback. Ah, how then?
  It fled away all suddenly
And never will return again.

He is left with no money and little learning. Even love has lost its
savor. If he had applied himself to study, he might have a chance to sleep
warm in his old age. But the precious hours had been spent with boon
companions—and what has become of them?

Where are the gracious gallants now
  That of old time I did frequent,
So fair of fashion and of show,
  In song and speech so excellent?
  Stark dead are some, their lives are spent;
There rests of them nor mark nor trace;
  May they in heaven have content;
God keep the others of His grace!

Of the rest some are beggars; some, on the other hand, are great lords,
who drink noble wines and eat grand meats every day. Himself, he has had
no such luck. He is descended from poor folk, whose tombs bear neither
crowns nor scepters. There is only one consolation.

When I of poverty complain,
  Ofttimes my heart to me hath said,
"Man, wherefore murmur thus in vain
  If thou hast no such plentihead
  As had Jacques Cœur,[7] be comforted:
Better to live and rags to wear
  Than to have been a lord and, dead,
Rot in a splendid sepulchre."

Yet want follows on his track and death comes after. His father has
long been gone; his mother, as she well knows, must soon go. His turn
will come. There is no escape. Even the fairest of the fair go the way of
all flesh. So he writes on that hackneyed theme his *Ballad of Dead Ladies*
—surpassingly beautiful, though little more than a list of names and the
refrain, *Mais où sont les neiges d'antan?*[8] After similar poems to the lords
of old time, Villon inserts in the testament his very famous *Complaint of
the Fair Armoress.* Then the *Double Ballad of Good Counsel* strikes a
livelier note, giving to young men the vain advice of keeping away from

---

[7] A merchant of Bourges, famous for his wealth.
[8] Cf. Rossetti's translation: "But where are the snows of yesteryear?"

the girls—"Good luck has he that deals with none."[9] And he adds the jingling verses that celebrate the speech of the Parisian women.

> Prince, give praise to our French ladies
> For the sweet sound their speaking carries;
> 'Twixt Rome and Cadiz many a maid is,
> But no good girl's lip out of Paris.

Eventually, with a solemn invocation and a legal preamble, he comes to the testament proper—an appealing combination of humor and tender seriousness, as in the lovely prayer to the Virgin which he bequeaths to his mother, herself unable to write. At the end he provides a mock epitaph for himself, asking that he be buried in a nunnery and that the great bells of Notre-Dame be rung for his funeral! Like the life of the poet, the *Grand Testament* is a constant alternation of the grim and the gay.

None of Villon's good resolutions were kept. In 1462 he was again in prison. Let out on bail, he became involved in another stabbing affray and was sentenced to be hanged. It was on this occasion that he characteristically wrote two poems, one a coarse joke and the other a touching appeal on behalf of himself and his fellow convicts.

Last years

> Men, brother men, that after us yet live,
>   Let not your hearts too hard against us be;
> For if some pity of us poor men ye give,
>   The sooner God shall take of you pity.
> Here are we five or six strung up, you see,
> And here the flesh that all too well we fed
> Bit by bit eaten and rotten, rent and shred,
>   And we the bones grov dust and ash withal;
> Let no man laugh at us discomforted,
>   But pray to God that he forgive us all.

Actually, he was saved from the gallows but banished from Paris. When or where he died we do not know. That we should not was perhaps his final jest.

2. The Church and the Witchcraft Delusion

Unhappily for the church, the prospect of reform in the fifteenth century died with the councils. The decrees of Basel were ignored except as the princes of Europe chose to re-enact them. In this respect, as in so many others, the example was set by the king of France, who in 1438 induced the French clergy to formulate the Pragmatic Sanction of Bourges. It declared the authority of a general council superior to that of a pope, ordered that no papal bull should take effect in France until it had been promulgated by the king, forbade the collection of annates from French

The relapse of the papacy

---

[9] This and the following quotations are from the incomparable translations of Swinburne.

prelates, and prohibited the filling of ecclesiastical offices in the kingdom by papal appointment. The Pragmatic Sanction, although it was not continuously enforced, remained the cornerstone of the Gallican Liberties[10] for the next three hundred years. Similar legislation in England was prevented by the civil war between the Lancastrians and the Yorkists. In Germany, where the imperial authority was only a memory, no concerted action could be expected from the rulers of the local states. And much the same conditions prevailed in Italy and Spain.

Meanwhile the papacy, to the great distress of many loyal supporters, not only failed to extirpate the ancient abuses but allowed them to be aggravated. Apparently secure in the enjoyment of absolute monarchy, the popes in the closing decades of the fifteenth century once more became submerged in Italian politics. Distinguished as temporal rulers and as devotees of the new secular culture, they forfeited all respect as leaders of Christendom and even as exponents of common decency. The final result was the Protestant Revolution, the story of which must be left to other volumes, which deal with the sixteenth and following centuries. Here it need only be pointed out that Protestantism brought few if any theoretical innovations; that as Martin Luther was the successor of John Hus, so the latter was the successor of Wycliffe, Marsiglio, the Spiritual Franciscans, and the Waldensians. To understand any one man in this series of more or less heretical agitators, we have to take into account all phases of European history throughout the later Middle Ages.

The influence of evil times

In so far as the church had been the dominant institution of the earlier period, its decline was the crucial event during the years that ensued. Indeed, no phase of European civilization in the fourteenth and fifteenth centuries remained unaffected by the fading of the old ecclesiastical ideals. The thirteenth century was hardly a golden age when everybody did as he should and all men lived in Christian concord. Yet, to judge from contemporary arts and letters, it was a time of general contentment. Then came one of mounting trouble and unrest. The gradual submergence of the papacy in secular affairs culminated in the Babylonian Captivity, which was followed by the scandal of the Great Schism. Meanwhile the western world was devastated by pestilence, war, and insurrection. The proudest states of Christendom fell prey to anarchy as the Turks, after undoing the work of the crusades, resumed the offensive and conquered a large section of Europe. Under such circumstances it is not surprising that vernacular literature came to be marked by a tone of pessimism and that the calm of early Gothic art gave way to a highly emotional expression of the tragic and the pathetic. At the same time the revolt against ecclesiastical education led to a new emphasis on secular study, as is particularly shown by the popularity of humanism in Italy. So too thousands of men and women,

---

[10] See above, p. 416.

to whom the traditional religion no longer brought spiritual satisfaction, were attracted by various mystic cults, only some of which were thoroughly orthodox.[11]

Another characteristic feature of the age, and one that should not be forgotten in appraising its alleged enlightenment, was the enormous growth of belief in witchcraft. To understand the beginnings of this strange delusion, it is necessary to keep in mind the distinction between the official doctrine of the early church and the unofficial folklore that accompanied it. One who accepts the authority of the New Testament must, of course, accept a variety of ideas concerned with diabolism. Satan, the chief of the fallen angels, tempted Christ and continually sought to lure all men to destruction. In his nefarious schemes he was supported by a host of lesser devils, whose ranks included the pagan deities of the ancient world. Such a demon could enter into possession of a man's body and so cause madness, but could be cast out by divine intervention. One grade of the lower clergy had thus come to be that of exorcist. Satan's power, though subordinate to the omnipotence of God, was the source of many noxious things, ranging from petty mischief to major calamities like storms and pestilences. Especially since the time of Gregory the Great, Christian literature had been filled with stories of diabolic malice and its nullification by saintly act.

The Middle Ages also inherited much lore about magic from the Old Testament, as well as from the works of pagans. The Hebrews, like other ancient peoples, had believed in clairvoyants and mediums—particularly women who, through incantation, called up the spirits of the dead. Such was the witch of Endor consulted by Saul, and such presumably were the witches for whom the sacred law prescribed the death penalty.[12] The Romans, on the other hand, had not tried to prohibit magical practices as long as they did not result in crimes otherwise punishable by the state. Murder, for example, led to prosecution before the courts, whether it was alleged to have been committed by natural or supernatural means. In matters of this kind even the educated classes were commonly superstitious, fearing the sorcerer who could produce death or disease by applying malevolent charms to wax images, locks of hair, nail-parings, and the like. Besides, the Latin classics contain marvelous stories of men who could change themselves into animals (e.g., werewolves); and of night-hags who could assume the form of owls or mice, who rode on the storm-wind along with the sinister goddess Hecate, and who prowled about after dark to steal bits of corpses for use in their infernal rites.

Demonology and magic

[11] See above, p. 417.

[12] *I Samuel*, xxviii; *Exodus*, xxii, 18. "Witch," of course, is merely the translation of a Hebrew word.

Similar beliefs are occasionally heard of in the Christian writings, where black magic, as distinguished from the holy miracles of the church, is attributed to Satanic influence. By a compact with the devil one might become a sorcerer and thus learn how to make love-charms or to injure one's enemies in mysterious ways. But the best authorities were inclined to deprecate such notions as that men or women could change themselves into animals, could ride through the air on broomsticks, or perform many of the other marvels popularly attributed to them. The canons of ecclesiastical councils generally assessed penance on anyone who was foolish enough to hold that deeds of this sort were possible. Following the example of St. Augustine and other fathers of the church, the schoolmen of the twelfth and thirteenth centuries wrote at great length on the origin of evil, the fall of the angels, and the power of the devil. Some were more willing than others to accept popular tales about witches and the like; yet in general they tended to support the conservative opinions of the earlier authorities. For instance, Thomas Aquinas declared that neither Satan nor his agents could in any way contravene the divine order of nature, as by transforming a man into a beast.[13] Whoever believed the opposite was sinfully yielding to Satanic deceit. But what, in the absence of saintly advice, might not such deceit accomplish?

It was not until the fourteenth century that charges of sorcery began to be prominent in trials before secular courts and that the Inquisition began to take cognizance of witchcraft as a form of heresy. In this connection the prosecution of the Templars under Philip IV established a baneful precedent, which led straight to the burning of Jeanne d'Arc in 1431.[14] By such acts state and church combined to justify a fear that had already secured firm hold of the popular imagination. Although various historians have denounced the scholastics for contributing to the witchcraft mania of the following centuries, it is hard to see how their academic learning could have greatly influenced opinion throughout the countryside. Was it not rather the experts who followed the masses? Psychologically, the growth of belief in witchcraft may well be explained as resulting from the increased misery and discontent of the later Middle Ages. Universal dread and suspicion, fostered by the evil times, found expression in the denunciation of witches. And, once started, the delusion of a vast Satanic conspiracy for the ruin of the world gained crushing headway.

How far that delusion had advanced by the latter half of the fifteenth century is shown by the famous witch bull of Innocent VIII[15] in 1484. Therein the pope declares he has heard that in certain districts of Germany

---

[13] See above, p. 355.
[14] See above, pp. 388, 411.
[15] One of the "Renaissance popes," who reigned from 1484 to 1492—a man of dubious private morals, but a distinguished patron of the arts.

many persons of both sexes, heedless of their own salvation and forsaking the catholic faith, give themselves over to devils male and female, and by their incantations, charms, and conjurings, and by other abominable superstitions and sortileges, offenses, crimes and misdeeds, ruin and cause to perish the off-spring of women, the foal of animals, the products of the earth, the grapes of vines, and the fruits of trees, as well as men and women, cattle and flocks and herds and animals of every kind, vineyards also and orchards, meadows, pas-tures, harvests, grains, and other fruits of the earth; that they afflict and torture with dire pains and anguish, both internal and external, these men, women, cattle, flocks, herds, and animals, and hinder men from begetting and women from conceiving, and prevent all consummation of marriage; that, moreover, they deny with sacrilegious lips the faith they received in holy baptism; and that, at the instigation of the enemy of mankind, they do not fear to commit and perpetrate many other abominable offenses and crimes, at the risk of their own souls, to the insult of the divine majesty, and to the pernicious example and scandal of multitudes.

And since it appears that the two inquisitors deputed to punish heresy in these districts have been hindered in their activity by misguided persons, the pope explicitly confirms their authority with regard to the extirpation of witchcraft. All clergy and laity, under threat of severe penalty, are prohibited from in any way interfering with their holy work.

Innocent's bull, of course, did not enjoin belief in witchcraft as an article of Christian faith. By enumerating the acts of sorcery being committed in Germany, it merely stated the views shared even by the educated of that time. The pope issued the document as a routine matter, to confirm the principle that witchcraft was a form of heresy. Thus encouraged, the two Dominican inquisitors, Kramer and Sprenger, proceeded to write for their colleagues a manual called *Malleus Maleficarum* (The Hammer of Witches). Dealing with what the pope had apparently taken for granted, it is divided into three parts. The first expounds the doctrinal basis, present-ing a scholastic argument under eighteen questions to prove that Christians must believe in the numerous manifestations of witchcraft. The second describes the wicked things that may be done by sorcerers and the remedies by which Satanic guile may be effectively counteracted. The third then explains the procedure to be followed in the detection and trial of suspects. On the whole, the book contained little that was new; but, as a convenient summary of established belief and practice, it was widely used during the intensive witch-hunt of the ensuing period and by its legalistic precision undoubtedly helped to crystallize scholarly opinion.

Unfortunately, nobody at that time thought of denying the assumptions of the *Malleus Maleficarum* or of condemning the heartless procedure which it so coolly advocated; nor did any of the reformers who attacked the organized church in the next century. It was only gradually that Catholic and Protestant ceased to vie with one another in the persecution

of alleged witches—though, as they now agree, at least three-fourths of
it was sheer hysteria.

3. Material Conditions of Life

This last chapter may very well close with a section bearing the same
title as the one that closed the first; for material conditions of life tend
to govern civilization, and civilization is what every general history is
mainly concerned with. The present section, like the previous one, can
give no complete sketch of such material conditions. All that will be
attempted is a brief description of certain outstanding developments,
together with a few remarks by way of comparing the later with the
earlier age.

On the whole, we may be sure, the standard of living in fifteenth-century
Europe was superior to that in the Roman Empire. The important consideration is not that the luxury enjoyed by wealthy men about 1450 was
probably equal to whatever had been enjoyed by their Roman predecessors,
but that the masses were undoubtedly better off. Most peasants had long
since attained economic if not legal freedom, and even those who were still
serfs had no reason to envy the *coloni* of the ancient empire. Besides, we
have to take into account the prosperous and powerful bourgeoisie, a class
that greatly outnumbered the Roman *curiales*. The old imperial provinces
now contained many more towns than before, and these towns were on the
average much more populous. Mediæval commerce and industry had far
surpassed anything known to the earlier population of the west, while agriculture had been definitely improved on being extended into new lands.
And increase of economic production meant increase of total wealth—
chiefly represented by goods which people used.

So far as dress was concerned, it will hardly be necessary to give many
details, for such matters have been rendered very familiar by contemporary
painting. Although the principal articles of clothing were fundamentally the
same as before, there was now much greater variety both in materials and
in styles. Not only the robes and cloaks of women but also the capes, tunics,
and hose of men had come to be made of brilliantly colored stuffs which, at
least for the upper classes, were cut in constantly changing ways to suit the
whims of fashion. Thanks to the influence of the Arabs, and to the improvement of manufacturing technique in the west, the older woolens and linens
had been supplemented by silks and cottons, and all fabrics had come to be
more finely woven, more effectively dyed, and more delicately ornamented
—especially in patterns borrowed from the orient. Shoes and hats, as well
as numerous other articles, reflected the improved skill of craftsmen who
worked with leather and felt. Jewelry, whether or not the design was inspired
by the antique, was extraordinarily beautiful. Indeed, the costume of the
fifteenth century was in general so picturesque that it has remained a favorite

subject of the antiquarian and is still used to enhance the pageantry of various modern courts.

In matters of diet western Europe continued to follow long-established **Food and** precedents: that of the Mediterranean peoples was essentially Roman, that **drink** of the northern peoples essentially barbarian. Although the church prescribed eggs and fish on Fridays and during Lent, the typical member of the feudal aristocracy was a great eater of meat. And although he might be very fond of wine, his more usual drink was likely to be beer. Distillation, known to the Arab alchemists and to their Latin disciples, was as yet scarcely used for the production of potable liquors. Of greater importance to the average European was the introduction from the east of various grains, fruits, and vegetables, together with sugar, pepper, and other spices which, with the opening of the new trade routes, ceased to be luxuries reserved to the very rich. Tea, coffee, and chocolate were of course still unknown in the western lands; as were also the products—among them potatoes, squash, Indian corn, and tomatoes—that were later to be brought from the Americas. Otherwise the well-to-do man of the fifteenth century could, if he chose, enjoy as varied a diet as we do today.

With regard to housing, the later mediæval standard was quite compa- **Houses** rable with that of antiquity. Building materials and methods of construction **and fur-** were, in fact, the same as had been used in the Roman Empire. Since at **nishings** least the eleventh century carpenters and masons had begun to recover whatever of the ancient skills had been lost during the troubled years that followed the barbarian invasions. As already seen, the fourteenth and fifteenth centuries were remarkable for the development of secular architecture—for the erection not only of great civic buildings but also of splendid private residences. In this respect the grandees of the Italian cities undoubtedly led the way; yet the wealthier classes in France, Flanders, England, and other countries now came to put up increasingly fine houses, a few of which have persisted to our own day. In any such home the furnishings—chairs, tables, beds, sideboards, rugs, tapestries, tableware, and the like—would be generally sumptuous. Light, to be sure, would be provided by candles and primitive lamps; heat by old-fashioned braziers, stoves, and fireplaces, though the latter had come to be usually fitted with chimneys. Windows would be glazed. Sanitation, however inadequate to our eyes, would equal that in the gorgeous palaces of Louis XIV. Time would still be recorded by a sun-dial or water-clock. The huge mechanical clocks that had been invented as early as the thirteenth century would be found only in church-towers or other great buildings, and were very inaccurate. It was left for later generations to perfect the pendulum-clock and the chronometer run by coiled springs.

Although most tools of the manual laborer were about the same as those used in antiquity, there had been considerable improvement in agricultural

Industry
and
machines

implements—especially the plow and the harness that enabled it or a heavy wagon to be pulled by horses. Among the other outstanding inventions of the later Middle Ages were the flail and the wheelbarrow. Windmills were a common sight in many regions, and water-power was frequently applied not only to the grinding of corn, but also to the sawing of logs, the crushing of bark, and the fulling of cloth.[16] Contemporary developments in spinning and weaving remain a matter of considerable obscurity. It would appear, however, that both the spinning-wheel and the draw-loom[17] were brought to Italy from the orient as necessary adjuncts of the silk industry in the thirteenth and fourteenth centuries, and thus were eventually adapted to the manufacture of other textiles. In such cases our principal trouble lies in the fact that our only sources are usually vague references in written documents. We are indeed fortunate in having a few sets of drawings made by engineers of that age to illustrate the machines in which they happened to be interested.

Military
engineer-
ing

Since the time of Villard de Honnecourt and Pierre de Maricourt[18] the interest of military engineers had more and more been turned to the use of explosives. This interest is already apparent in the *Bellifortis* of Konrad Kyeser, written between 1395 and 1405. The author was a German engineer who had evidently served in the wars of eastern Europe and who, by his own account, was a distinguished inventor. His book is most curious, being essentially a series of drawings with comments in bad Latin verse that often lapses into prose. And his drawings are a strange mixture. Alongside weapons and engines of war we find siphons and wheels for raising water, equipment for swimmers and divers, pontoon bridges, a device for pulling horses across a stream, a boat propelled by paddle-wheels, heating arrangements for baths, the blasting of a tree, hot-air balloons, fireworks, and miscellaneous tools. Most of Kyeser's military appliances are of the old type: crossbows, catapults, siege apparatus, and the like. Yet among his war chariots we observe some armed with cannon. He has good pictures of bombards, both small and large (see Figure 33); and he proves that, even in his age, men were beginning to experiment with multiple guns arranged in the form of a revolver.

During the next fifty years Kyeser's work was continued by various writers, among whom the most noteworthy were an anonymous Hussite engineer and a certain Iacopo Mariano of Siena. The sketchbook of the former, with a running commentary in German, seems to have been based

[16] I.e., the beating and cleansing of woolens to remove the natural oil and so increase the thickness of the fabric.

[17] The improved loom on which a pattern could be woven into cloth by pulling aside the threads of the warp in a certain fixed order.

[18] See above, pp. 308-09.

FIG. 33. A Primitive Cannon (Drawing by Konrad Kyeser) and a
Primitive Tank (Drawing by the Hussite Engineer).

on actual experience in the Bohemian campaigns.[19] The author devotes little space to the older methods of siege and attack. Instead he shows in detail how cannon may be lifted by compound pulleys, set into position, and used for offense or defense; particularly how they may be singly mounted, with or without wheels, and how in combination they may serve as armament for wagons, boats, and wooden towers. He also has remarkable illustrations of a diving-suit fitted with a tube for respiration and of machines for boring tree-trunks, mixing powder, and polishing gems. Mariano, a better artist, provides us with admirable pictures not only of guns but also of projectiles. And he, even more than his Hussite predecessor, pays great attention to mechanical contrivances of all kinds: water-wheels, screws, capstans, cranes, boats, bridges, chimneys, wells, furnaces, and much else (see Figure 34). No-one who has looked at these drawings can fail to realize that they anticipated a great deal for which the famous Leonardo da Vinci has usually received the sole credit.

Mediæval technology and the printing-press

From the few facts noted above it should be quite apparent that the progress of the industrial arts and applied science owed vastly more to the experience of mediæval technicians than to the revival of humanistic study. Although valuable information could be obtained from the recovered books of Archimedes and Vitruvius, the engineers and architects of the fifteenth century were as little dependent on them as contemporary navigators were on the newly translated *Geography* of Ptolemy.[20] Admiration of Greek and Roman art might lead to the refinement of æsthetic standards; it could not teach men how to carve stone, cast bronze, or paint on canvas. Such techniques were perfected through long and obscure experimentation, as were the making of fine fabrics, the designing of musical instruments, the grinding of lenses (whether for eye-glasses or for telescopes), and the mining, smelting, and working of metals. The technological advance of western Europe between 1000 and 1500 is just beginning to be appreciated. But it has long been acknowledged that at least three momentous inventions must be accredited to the later Middle Ages: the magnetic compass, the gun, and the printing-press. Of these only the third has ever been attributed to the influence of humanism. The present study may well conclude with a consideration of that important subject.

What we know as printing is a rather complex process that involves the use of paper, ink, metal type, and a mechanical press. To understand the nature of the fifteenth-century invention, we must take all four elements into account. The matter of ink need not detain us, for printers had merely to improve various compounds that had long been familiar to writers and

[19] See Figure 33. The inscription attached to the upper drawing is to the following effect: "Item, this is the Hussites' wagon-fort. On it the Hussites fight. It is good and efficient."

[20] See above, p. 450.

FIG. 34. Field Gun Firing an Incendiary Bomb, Knight Armed with a Hand Gun (Drawings by Iacopo Mariano).

painters. The press, too, may be quickly disposed of. As employed for early printing, it was simply an adaptation of a very ancient device for crushing grapes, smoothing cloth, and performing other operations. Paper, on the other hand, was a more recent acquisition. First introduced into Europe by the Arabs,[21] the art of paper-making was not generally known to the western peoples until the thirteenth century. Then, together with the use of paper, they seem to have learned the rudiments of printing—the transfer of designs by means of ink smeared on carved wooden blocks. Ordinarily such woodcuts were pictures, for which the scribe left blank spaces in his manuscript. But lettering was occasionally added to explain the illustrations, and by an easy extension whole books came to be thus printed, each page from a separate block. Who first thought of casting metal type, which could be set in a frame and repeatedly used, has been a hotly disputed question. On the whole, we may conclude that, although some practice of the sort was apparently developed by Dutch printers in the first half of the fifteenth century, credit for the perfected invention must be awarded to Johann Gutenberg of Mainz (d. 1468). He assuredly was the man who first published great printed books and so became the recognized founder of the new trade.

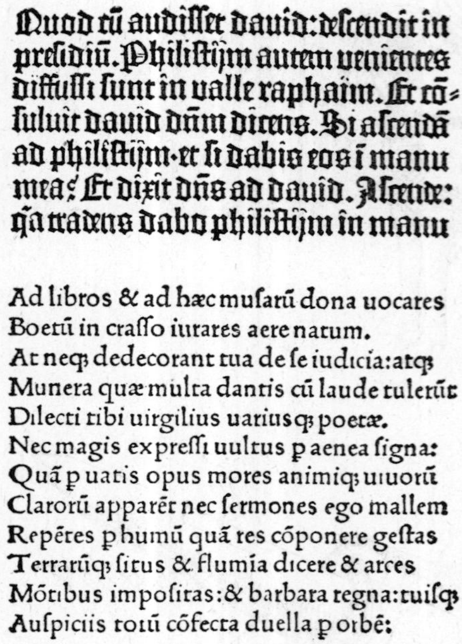

Quod cū audiſſet dauid:deſcendit in preſidiū.Philiſtijm autem venientes diffuſſi ſunt in valle raphaim.Et cō-ſuluit dauid dūm dicens.Si aſcendā ad philiſtijm·et ſi dabis eos ī manu mea? Et dixit dūs ad dauid. Aſcende: ŋa tradens dabo philiſtijm in manu

Ad libros & ad hæc muſarū dona uocares
Boetū in craſſo iurares aere natum.
At neq; dedecorant tua de ſe iudicia:atq;
Munera quæ multa dantis cū laude tulerūt
Dilecti tibi uirgilius uarius q; poetæ.
Nec magis expreſſi uultus p aenea ſigna:
Quā p uatis opus mores animiq; uiuorū
Clarorū apparēt nec ſermones ego mallem
Repētes p humū quā res cōponere geſtas
Terrarūq; ſitus & flumia dicere & arces
Mōtibus impoſitas:& barbara regna:tuiſq;
Auſpiciis totū cōfecta duella p orbē:

FIG. 35. Examples of Early Printing: (Gothic) *Bible* of Gutenberg, *c.* 1455; (Roman) *Horace* of Miscomini, 1482.

Significance of the invention

It has often been stated that the demand for books created by the humanists led directly to the invention of the printing-press. Yet the first books to be printed were Bibles, psalters, and scholastic texts, rather than editions of the classics. Moreover, the earliest type to be used was that called Gothic, a reproduction of the decorated handwriting of the later Middle Ages. This the humanists disliked, and it was largely through their influence that printers came to adopt the so-called Roman type, which was actually copied from the Carolingian minuscule.[22] That the appearance of the printing-press revolutionized the intellectual history of mankind is another familiar

[21] See above, p. 175.
[22] See Figures 10, 35.

statement. If taken generally to apply to a very slow process, it is true enough. It does not, however, hold for the fifteenth and sixteenth centuries alone. Although the invention was welcomed as a useful method of producing books cheaply, it hardly induced anybody to read what he would not otherwise have read and it left unchanged the ideas of the illiterate masses. Here, as always, the historian finds that his epoch-making event was a gradual development rather than a sudden innovation.

CONCLUSION

The Significance of the
Mediæval Periods

One who writes a book on the Middle Ages necessarily stops with the close of the fifteenth century, when he reaches the time-honored boundary between the mediæval and modern periods. Although that boundary is in some respects unsatisfactory, it is no worse than most of the arbitrary divisions that have come to be accepted, and it has the advantage of leaving to other volumes such excellent starting-points as the discovery of the New World and the outbreak of the Protestant Revolution. To say this, however, is merely to adopt a convenience in historical narration; it is not to attribute a peculiarly modern character to voyages of exploration or to attacks upon the organized church. Without serious distortion of the truth, the Protestant Revolution might be called a chapter in the history of mediæval religion, the opening of the New World a chapter in the history of mediæval commerce. When used with more than a chronological implication, the terms "mediæval" and "modern" become only a source of confusion.

The historian cannot, for example, hold that the essence of mediævalism was feudal society without concluding that a good part of western Europe ceased to be mediæval in the thirteenth century; or hold that such essence was devotion to the papacy without concluding that a large section of mankind is still mediæval. We are told about a mediæval mind, perpetually fascinated by abstractions, merely to discover that few men outside the cloister ever thought in that fashion at all. It would really seem more sensible to forget such generalizations and to realize that in the so-called Middle Ages, as in other ages, ideas and habits and institutions varied enormously. To call anything mediæval is not to describe it. No single word should be expected to give precise information about peoples and customs throughout a span of a thousand years. A book on the period after 1500 can cover only a little more than four centuries; yet who will attempt a brief definition of "modernity" or a summary characterization of the "modern mind"? The search for the first modern man is as vain as that for the last man of antiquity.

As historical students, we cannot hope to isolate the typically mediæval or the typically modern; we can only try to explain what happened in a given period. If, without presupposing an Italian Renaissance or other miraculous transformation, we turn from the mediæval centuries to the sixteenth and seventeenth, we find in political history a mere continuation of what we have already observed. For instance, we may see that the Habsburg inheritance of the Spanish throne was the lucky consequence of a policy that had been followed by every feudal house in Europe; that, by fighting the French kings for two hundred years, the Habsburgs prolonged an ancient feud which they had taken over along with the Burgundian dominions. Indeed, European politics are still permeated by traditions of the Middle Ages. The newspapers of the early 1940's may not have referred to the Holy Roman Empire, but contemporary events momentarily served to replace it on the map. The continuing rivalries of nations in the Balkans, along the German-Slavic frontier, on the Baltic, and throughout the lands to the west generally carry us back to the days of Jeanne d'Arc or earlier. To explain even the development of modern imperialism in Asia and Africa, we have to consider the precedents set by knights and traders during the Age of the Crusades.

In other fields the importance of the mediæval period is yet clearer. The constitutions of both England and France, as they were to be retained for centuries, had substantially appeared long before the end of the Hundred Years' War. It is primarily from the towns of the twelfth century that we derive such important features of our modern civilization as local self-government, the free tenure of land, everyday business organization, banking practice, and other varieties of capitalistic enterprise. And the so-called emancipation of the peasantry, which made possible our modern nationalism, undoubtedly resulted from economic transformation during the Middle Ages. In navigation, warfare, and book-making the importance of mediæval invention has long been recognized. Besides, scholars are now coming to realize that in many additional respects—especially in the fields we know as engineering and other applied sciences—the period between 1000 and 1500 witnessed the true beginnings of the machine age which we now take for granted.

Yet a greater glory of the Middle Ages will probably continue to be seen in such cultural developments as the creation of a rich vernacular literature, the perfection of a splendid native art, and the revival of learning that gave birth to our first universities. For beauty and originality the monuments of the Romanesque and Gothic styles, the feudal epics, the songs of the troubadours, and the cycles of romances rank among the world's master-pieces. Many of them—together with the memoirs of Joinville and Com-mines, the stories of Boccaccio, and the immortal verse of Dante, Petrarch, Chaucer, and Villon—have held an unfailing charm for countless genera-tions. Scholasticism, in view of the facts cited above, can hardly be dis-dained as mere academic futility. The logic and mathematics of the thir-teenth century, so far as they go, are still valid. The theology of Peter Lombard and Thomas Aquinas, though rejected by Protestants, continues official in the Roman Church. The study of law, with its necessary reliance on deduction from authoritative precepts, has never ceased to be funda-mentally scholastic. The natural science of the schoolmen, for all its short-comings, was the best the world could then offer and prepared the way for the triumphs of the seventeenth and eighteenth centuries.

The traditional distinction between the modern and the mediæval is not, therefore, a distinction between the vital and the defunct. Many an institu-tion that flourished after 1500 is today as dead as chivalry, while much from the Middle Ages remains a living heritage of the present.

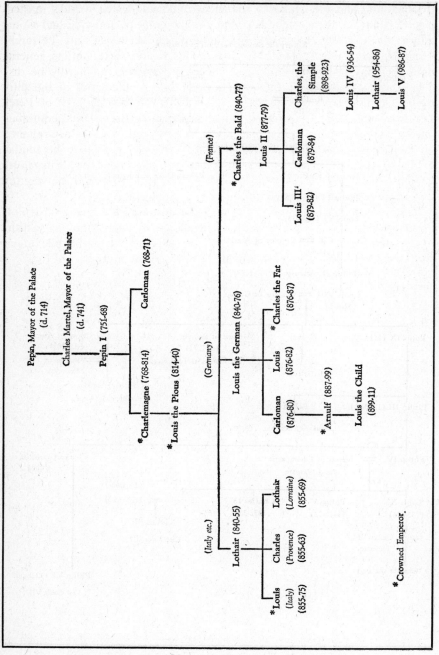

TABLE I. THE CAROLINGIANS.

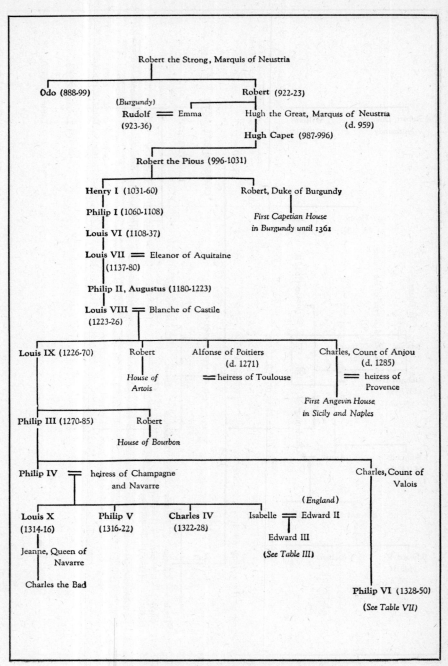

Robert the Strong, Marquis of Neustria

Odo (888-99)　　　　　　　　　　Robert (922-23)

(Burgundy)
Rudolf ═══ Emma　　　Hugh the Great, Marquis of Neustria
(923-36)　　　　　　　　　　　　　　　　(d. 959)

Hugh Capet (987-996)

Robert the Pious (996-1031)

Henry I (1031-60)　　　　　　Robert, Duke of Burgundy

Philip I (1060-1108)　　　　　First Capetian House
　　　　　　　　　　　　　　in Burgundy until 1361
Louis VI (1108-37)

Louis VII ═══ Eleanor of Aquitaine
(1137-80)

Philip II, Augustus (1180-1223)

Louis VIII ═══ Blanche of Castile
(1223-26)

Louis IX (1226-70)　　Robert　　　Alfonse of Poitiers　　　Charles, Count of Anjou
　　　　　　　　　　　　　　　　　　(d. 1271)　　　　　　　　(d. 1285)
　　　　　　　House of　　　═══ heiress of Toulouse　　═══ heiress of
　　　　　　　Artois　　　　　　　　　　　　　　　　　　　Provence

　　　　　　　　　　　　　　　　　　　　　　　　First Angevin House
　　　　　　　　　　　　　　　　　　　　　　　in Sicily and Naples

Philip III (1270-85)　　　Robert

　　　　　　　　House of Bourbon

Philip IV ═══ heiress of Champagne　　　　　　　　Charles, Count of
　　　　　　　and Navarre　　　　　　　　　　　　　　Valois

　　　　　　　　　　　　　　　　　　　　(England)
Louis X　　　Philip V　　Charles IV　　Isabelle ═══ Edward II
(1314-16)　　(1316-22)　　(1322-28)
　　　　　　　　　　　　　　　　　　　　Edward III
Jeanne, Queen of　　　　　　　　　　　　(See Table III)
Navarre

Charles the Bad　　　　　　　　　　　　　　　　　Philip VI (1328-50)

　　　　　　　　　　　　　　　　　　　　　　　　(See Table VII)

TABLE II. THE CAPETIAN HOUSE TO 1328.

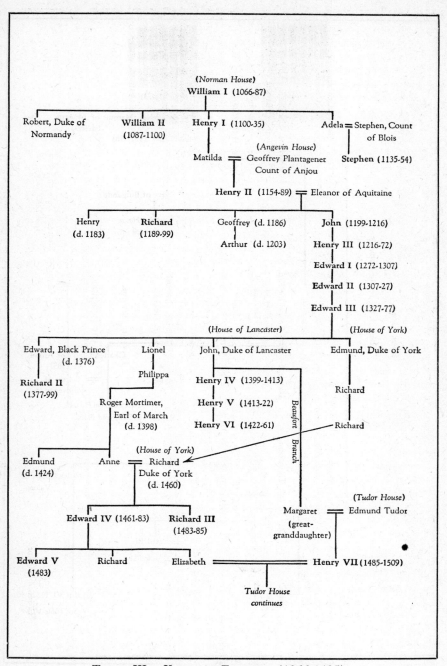

TABLE III.   KINGS OF ENGLAND (1066-1485).

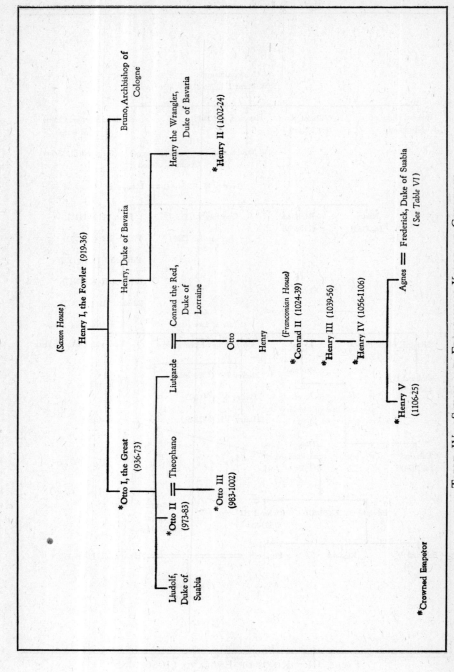

TABLE IV. SAXON AND FRANCONIAN KINGS OF GERMANY.

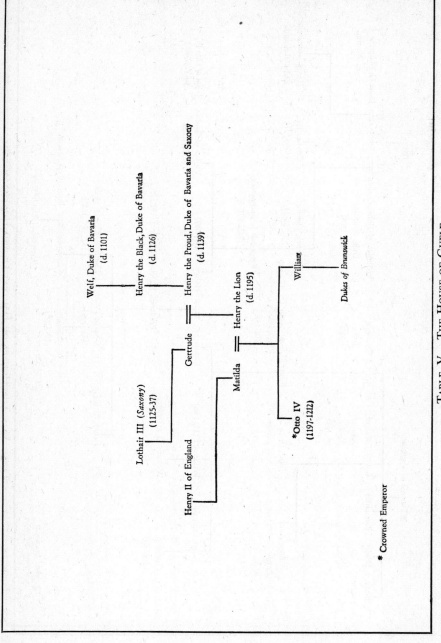

TABLE V. THE HOUSE OF GUELF.

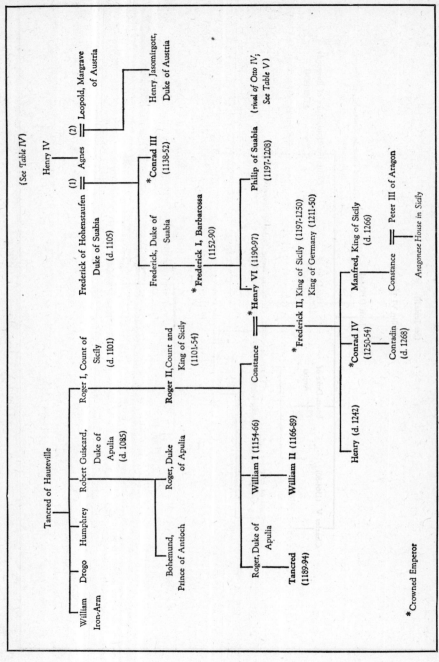

TABLE VI. THE HOUSES OF HAUTEVILLE AND HOHENSTAUFEN.

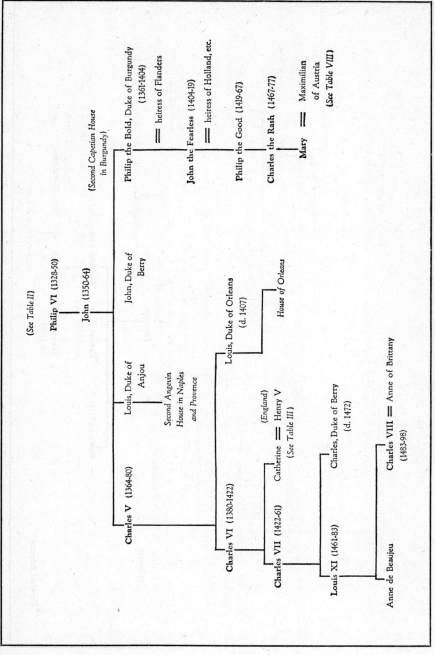

TABLE VII. THE VALOIS HOUSE (1328-1498).

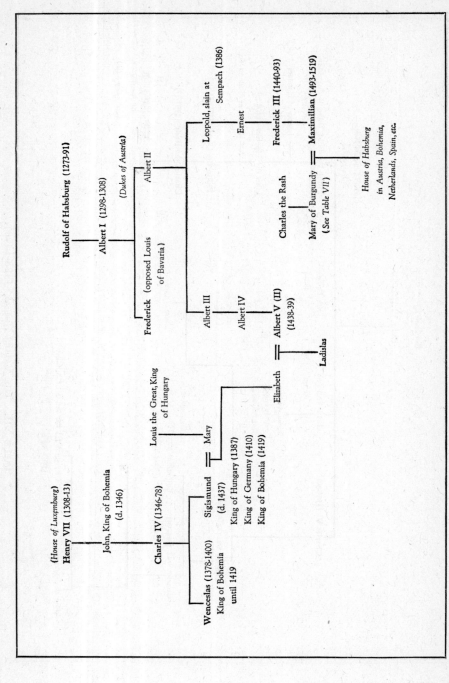

TABLE VIII. THE HOUSES OF LUXEMBURG AND HABSBURG TO 1493

(House of Luxemburg)
Henry VII (1308-13)
|
John, King of Bohemia
(d. 1346)
|
Charles IV (1346-78)
|
┌─────────┴─────────┐
Wenceslas (1378-1400)   **Sigismund**
King of Bohemia   (d. 1437)
until 1419   King of Hungary (1387)
                                 King of Germany (1410)
                                 King of Bohemia (1419)
                                 ═══ Mary
                                      |
Louis the Great, King
of Hungary
                                 Elizabeth
                                 ═══ Albert V (II)
                                     (1438-39)
                                     |
                                 Ladislas

Rudolf of Habsburg (1273-91)
|
Albert I (1298-1308)
|
(Dukes of Austria)
Albert II
|
┌──────────────┴──────────────┐
Frederick (opposed Louis   Leopold, slain at
of Bavaria)   Sempach (1386)
                                |
Albert III   Ernest
| |
Albert IV   **Frederick III** (1440-93)
| |
Albert V (II)   **Maximilian** (1493-1519)
(1438-39)   ═══ Mary of Burgundy
                                    (See Table VII)
                                    |
                                Charles the Rash
                                |
                        *House of Habsburg
                        in Austria, Bohemia,
                        Netherlands, Spain, etc.*

Abbreviations for
CHRONOLOGICAL CHARTS

K...King

D...Duke

C...Count

P...Pope

ÆB...Archbishop

B...Bishop

d...died

m...married

†...murdered

✂...Battle of

FOURTH CENTURY

Date	ARTS AND LETTERS	THE CHURCH	ROMAN EMPIRE (WEST)	ROMAN EMPIRE (EAST)	THE BARBARIANS
300	Porphyry			Diocletian (284–305)	Franks and Alamans on the Rhine
10		Grant of toleration to Christians	Constantius (d. 306)	Galerius (d. 311)	Goths and other Germans on the Danube
			Constantine (306–37)	Licinius (d. 324)	
			✗Milvian Bridge (312)	Founding of Constantinople	
20		Arian heresy			
30		Council of Nicaea (325)			
40		St. Anthony of Egypt	Sons of Constantine (337–61)		
350		St. Pachomius (d. 346)			Invasion of Europe by the Huns
60					
		P. Damasus I (366–84)	Valentinian I (364–75)	Valens (364–78)	
70	Vulgate of St. Jerome				
		St. Basil (d. 379)	Gratian (375–83)	Theodosius I (379–95)	✗Adrianople (378)
80	Gothic Bible of Ulfilas (d. 383)	P. Siricius (384–99)	Valentinian II (383–92)		The Visigoths in the Empire
	Ammianus Marcellinus		Theodosius I (d. 395)		Rise of Alaric
	Ausonius				
90		St. Ambrose (d. 397)	Honorius (395–423)	Arcadius (395–408)	
400	St. Augustine's *Confessions*				

FIFTH CENTURY

ARTS AND LETTERS

- Claudian
  Symmachus
  Capella
  Macrobius
- St. Jerome (d. 420)
  St. Augustine (d. 430)
  City of God
- *Theodosian Code*
- Orosius
- Byzantine architecture in the east and at Ravenna
- Apollinaris Sidonius (d. 488)

THE CHURCH

- P. Innocent I (402-17)
- Nestorian heresy
- P. Leo the Great (440-61)
- Monophysite heresy
- Council of Chalcedon (451)
- St. Patrick (d. 461)
- Schism between East and West

ROMAN EMPIRE

EAST

- Arcadius (d. 408)
- Theodosius II (408-50)
- Invasion by Huns under Attila (d. 453)
- Marcian (450-57)
- Leo I (457-74)
- Zeno (474-91)
- Rise of Theodoric the Ostrogoth
- Anastasius I (491-518)

WEST

- Honorius (d. 423)
  Stilicho (d. 408)
- Sack of Rome by Alaric (410)
- Valentinian III (425-55)
- Aëtius (d. 454)
- Catalaunian Fields (451)
- Puppet Emperors (455-76)
- Odoacer (476-93)
- OSTROGOTHS
- Theodoric (493-526)

THE BARBARIANS IN THE WESTERN PROVINCES

Franks, Alamans, Burgundians, Vandals, and others cross the Rhine into Gaul
Angles and Saxons invade Britain

Visigoths enter Gaul (412)

Visigoths conquer Spain from the Vandals, who cross into Africa under Gaiseric (429)

BURGUNDIANS	ALAMANS	FRANKS	VISIGOTHS	VANDALS	ANGLO-SAXONS
Rhone Valley	Alsace and upper Danube	North Gaul	South Gaul and Spain	Africa	Britain
		Salian and Ripuarian Kingdoms	Theodoric	Kingdom under Gaiseric (d. 477)	Permanent settlement begins
Conquered by Franks in Sixth Century	Conquered by Franks in Sixth Century	Clovis (481-511) Soissons (486) Conversion	Kingdom in Spain continues until 711	Conquered by Justinian in Sixth Century	Various small kingdoms continue

Time scale: 400 — 10 — 20 — 30 — 40 — 450 — 60 — 70 — 80 — 90 — 500

SIXTH CENTURY

Date	BRITISH ISLES	SPAIN AND AFRICA	FRANKISH KINGDOM	ITALY	BYZANTINE EMPIRE	ASIA	ARTS AND LETTERS
500	Continuation of Anglo-Saxon conquest	Vandals in Africa / Visigoths in Spain	Clovis (d. 511) Conquest of Aquitaine	Theodoric (d. 526)	Anastasius (d. 518)	Renewal of the Persian offensive	The *Salic Law*
10			**Sons of Clovis** (511–61)				Boëthius (d. 524) Cassiodorus
20			Conquest of Burgundy Provence Alamania Bavaria Thuringia		**Justin I** (518–27)		St. Benedict's reform of monasticism
30					**Justinian** (527–65) Theodora Belisarius Narses		Justinian's *Corpus Iuris Civilis*
40		Justinian's reconquest of Africa and part of Spain		Justinian's reconquest (535–53)		Persistence of Nestorian and Monophysite (Jacobite) Churches	Splendor of Byzantine architecture
550				Exarchate of Ravenna	**Successors of Justinian** Wars with Avars and Persians	Invasion of Europe by the Avars, who conquer the Slavs, Bulgars, and other peoples	Santa Sophia Procopius
60	St. Columba (d. 597) at Iona		**Grandsons of Clovis**				
70			Decline of Merovingian power	Lombard invasion under Alboin			Gregory of Tours (d. 594) *Ecclesiastical History of the Franks*
80	St. Columban (d. 615) to Gaul		Civil wars Austrasia vs. Neustria	Political chaos	**Maurice** (582–602)		
90	Mission of Augustine (597)	Visigoths recognize Roman Church		P. Gregory the Gt. (590–604) Extension of papal authority			Gregory the Great *Pastoral Care Dialogues*, etc.
600							

Year	BRITISH ISLES	SPAIN AND AFRICA	FRANKISH KINGDOM	ITALY	BYZANTINE EMPIRE	THE ARABS	ARTS AND LETTERS
600	Northumbria the dominant Anglo-Saxon kingdom		Great-Grandsons of Clovis	Gregory the Great (d. 604) Successors Papacy remains strong	Loss of Balkans to Avars and Slavs Phocas (602-10)	Mohammed (d. 632) Preaching of Islam	Isidore of Seville (d. 636) *Etymologies*
10		Byzantine loss of Spanish coast			Heraclius (610-41)		
20				Lombards split into many small principalities	Successful offensive against Persia (622-29)	The Hegira (622)	
30				Byzantine control rapidly weakens	Defeat by Moslems	CALIPHATE Abu-Bakr (632-34) Omar (634-44) Conquest of Syria, Persia, Egypt.	The *Koran*
40		Arab conquest of Egypt	Dagobert (d. 639) *Rois Fainéants*		×The Yarmuk (636) Successors of Heraclius	Othman (644-55) Civil War	
650			Mayors of the Palace		Collapse of the Byzantine Power Losses: Syria Egypt North Africa Spanish coast Islands of the Mediterranean Most of Italy Interior of the Balkan peninsula	Ali (655-61)	Learning of the Irish monks
60						Muawiya (661-80) Ommiad Caliphs at Damascus until 750	Illuminated manuscripts
70	Council of Whitby (664)	Arab campaigns into Tunisia				Further conquests in Asia and North Africa	
80						Control of the Mediterranean	
90		Arab conquest of North Africa	Willibrord's mission in Frisia		Defense of Asia Minor and Constantinople		
700							

SEVENTH CENTURY

EIGHTH CENTURY

	BRITISH ISLES	SPAIN AND AFRICA	FRANKISH KINGDOM	ITALY	BYZANTINE EMPIRE	THE ARABS	ARTS AND LETTERS
700	Mercia the dominant Anglo-Saxon Kingdom		Pepin II, Mayor of Palace in Neustria and Austrasia (d. 714)	Successors of Gregory the Great	Revival of Byzantine strength		Bede (d. 735) *Ecc. Hist. of the English People*
10		Moslem conquest of Visigothic kingdom	Charles Martel M. of P. (714-41)	Liutprand, K. of Lombards (712-44) attacks Ravenna	Leo III (717-40) Iconoclastic Controversy	Siege of Constantinople fails (718)	Learning of Irish and Anglo-Saxon monks brought to continent by missionaries
20		Moslem raids in Gaul	Pacification of Aquitaine Burgundy Alamania Bavaria Thuringia Frisia	Popes condemn iconoclasts and appeal to Franks	Schism between East and West		
30		X Tours (Poitiers) (732)					St. Boniface (d. 754) Influence upon education
40			Pepin III, M. of P. (741-68)				
750				Aistulf, K. of L. (750-56)	Successors of Leo III Palace revolutions	Fall of Ommiads (750)	Beginnings of Arabic Science
60		Ommiad Emir at Cordova later styled Caliph	Pepin, K., with papal support (751) Conquest of Septimania	Takes Ravenna P. Stephen II (752-57) Frankish intervention	Religious strife Bulgarian wars Loss of all authority in Rome and North Italy	Abbasid Caliphs at Bagdad until 1258 al-Mansur (754-75)	Translations from Greek
70			Charlemagne (768-814) Conquest of Lombard Kingdom and Saxony	Donation of Pepin Papal States Desiderius (757-74) last of the Lombard kings			Libraries
80	Viking raids along coasts of Britain and Ireland	Morocco becomes independent	Reconquest of Bavaria Defeat of Avars Creation of Eastern Marches Spanish March			Harun-al-Rashid (786-809)	Moslem architecture and decorative arts
90			Imperial coronation (Xmas, 800)	P. Leo III (795-816)			Carolingian Revival of Learning Alcuin (d. 804) Paul the Deacon
800							

NINTH CENTURY

	BRITISH ISLES	CAROLINGIAN EMPIRE	BYZANTINE EMPIRE	THE ARABS	ARTS AND LETTERS
800	Wessex the dominant Anglo-Saxon Kingdom	Charlemagne (d. 814) Emperor. The Frankish Kingdom at its height	Paralysis under weak emperors	Harun-al-Rashid (d. 809)	Einhard (d. 840) Rabanus Maurus
10	Increase of Viking raids throughout British Isles	Louis the Pious (814-40) Emperor. Weakening of the monarchy			John the Scot. Carolingian minuscule
20			Rise of Bulgaria	al-Mamun (813-33)	
30					Vernacular languages; *lingua romana* and *lingua teudesca*
40	Viking conquests: E. Ireland W. Scotland	Civil war among sons. Lothair (840-55) (Emperor) Peace of Verdun (843). Louis the German (840-76) [GERMANY]. Charles the Bald (840-77) [FRANCE]	Michael III (842-67)	Disintegration of Arab Empire under rival caliphs and independent governors	Arabic culture Literature Music Fine Arts Commerce Geography
850	Most of Northumbria, Mercia, and E. Anglia	**GERMANY:** Viking raids. **CENTRAL KGDM.:** Division among three sons (855). **FRANCE:** Viking raids. Settlement of Normandy	Viking raids down Dneiper to Black Sea; Russians		Mathematics Astronomy Medicine, etc.
60		*Germany:* Increasing power of dukes. *Central Kgdm.:* P. Nicholas I (858-67) Extension of papal power. *France:* Feudalization of kingdom. Great duchies	MACEDONIAN HOUSE. Basil I (867-86)	Sea power of Tunisian emirs	
70	Alfred, K. of Wessex (871-901)	*Central Kgdm.:* Italy, Provence, Lorraine → Charles the Fat (881). Emperor (881)	Religious peace between East and West	Capture of Sicily, Crete, Sardinia, Corsica, and Balearic Is.	Hunain al-Kindi al-Farghani al-Khwarizmi
80	Defense of Wessex, which comes to include all territory south of Thames; also W. Mercia	*Germany:* Charles the Fat (876-87). *France:* Emperor (875). Various Carolingians (877-85). Charles the Fat	Bulgarians under Boris I (852-84) accept Greek Christianity		
90		*Germany:* Arnulf (887-99). Emperor (896). *Central Kgdm.:* Deposed (887). *France:* Odo of Paris (888-98)		Continuous raids along European coasts	Slavic alphabet invented by Cyril, missionary to Bohemia. Adopted by Bulgarians
900		Political disintegration. Civil Wars. Invasions of Vikings, Hungarians, and Saracens.			

	ENGLAND	FRANCE (SPAIN)	GERMANY	ITALY	BYZANTINE EMPIRE	THE ARABS	ARTS AND LETTERS
900	Alfred (d. 901) Edward the Elder (901–25)	Charles the Simple (898–923)	Louis the Child (899–911)	Degradation of the Papacy Control by local nobles	Macedonian Dynasty Hungarians in Pannonia	Caliphs at Bagdad become controlled by military chieftains	Advance of Arabic Culture
10	Conquest of Danelaw begun	Recognizes duchy of Normandy (911) Acquires Lorraine	Conrad I (911–18) SAXON HOUSE Henry I (919–36) Reorganizes kingdom Acquires Lorraine		Bulgarian Empire under Tsar Simeon (d. 927); then decline		al-Razi al-Farabi al-Haitham al-Battani
20	Aethelstan (925–37)	Kings of the Parisian House (922–36)		Rise of Venice as an independent city state			
30	Conquest of Danelaw completed	Kings of the Carolingian House (936–87)	X The Unstrut (933) Otto the Great (936–73)		Rise of Russia under Princes of Kiev		Anglo-Saxon literature Beowulf Song of Maldon Anglo-Saxon Chronicle Translations
40	The Kingdom of England		Lordship of Arles and Bohemia Redistribution of duchies	Assumes crown of Italy (951)	Attack Constantinople and overrun Bulgaria		
950	Edgar (959–75) Lordship of all Britain	SPAIN Caliphate of Cordova at height Five Christian states in north: León, Castile, Navarre, Aragon, Catalonia (County of Barcelona)	X The Lech; final Hungarian defeat Imperial coronation (962) The Holy Roman Empire	P. John XII (955–63)	Byzantine offensive in Cilcia Nicephorus Phocas (963–69)	Byzantine conquest of Antioch and Cyprus	Revival of Learning under Otto I German schools and scholars
60							
70			Byzantine alliance Otto II (973–83) m. Theophano	Fails to conquer South Italy	John Tzimisces (969–76) Defeats Russians		Scientific works of Gerbert (Silvester II)
80	Aethelred (979–1016)		Otto III (983–1002)	Imperial dreams Neglect of Germany	Basil II (976–1025)		Abacus, armillary sphere, astrolabe, etc.
90	Renewal of Danish raids Danegeld	Hugh Capet (987–96) Robert (996–1031)	Hungary Christian under Stephen I (997–1038) Poland under Boleslav I (992–1025)	P. Silvester II (999–1003)	Russians under Vladimir (d. 1015) accept Greek Christianity		
1000							

	ENGLAND	FRANCE (SPAIN)	GERMANY	ITALY	BYZANTINE EMPIRE	ARABS AND TURKS	ARTS AND LETTERS
1000	**Aethelred** (d. 1016)	**Robert** (d. 1031)	**Otto III** (d. 1002)	**Silvester II** (d. 1003) Papacy weakens Cluniac Reform	**Basil II** (d. 1025) conquers Bulgaria after long war	Emergence of **Seljuk Turks**	**Continuance of Arabic culture**
10	DANISH CONQUEST **Canute** (1016-35) K. of Denmark and Norway	The Capetian kings accomplish little, but the French nobility is very active, especially the Normans in Italy and England	**Henry II** (1002-24) Slavic offensive led by Poland German control of Bohemia				Avicenna (d. 1037) al-Biruni (d. 1048)
20			(FRANCONIAN HOUSE)	**Pisa and Genoa** lead offensive against Moslems on the sea			
30	Peace with Scots; cession of Lothian		**Conrad II** (1024-39)		Decline under successors of Basil II; Macedonian house ends (1056)		
	Sons of Canute (1035-42)	**Henry I** (1031-60) French recruits make possible Christian offensive in Spain Noteworthy expansion of León, Castile, and Aragon	Acquires Kingdom of Arles (1032)	Rise of the **Lombard Communes**		Turkish advance into Persia	
40	**Edward Confessor** (1042-66) (Son of Aethelred)		**Henry III** (1039-56) Reform of church Control of papacy Height of the H. R. E.	Four German popes **P. Leo IX** (1048-54) Reform councils			
1050	Advancing influence of Normans		**Henry IV** (1056-1106) Regency to 1066	Alliance with Normans **P. Nicholas II** (1058-61)	Final schism between East and West (1054)	Sultan **Togrul Beg** takes Bagdad (1055)	**Revival of Culture in Western Europe**
60		**Philip I** (1060-1108) ✕ Barbastro in Spain (1065)	Papal autonomy Cardinal College **Robt. Guiscard** D. of Apulia (1059-85)	**P. Alexander II** (1061-73)	Loss of South Italy **Romanus IV**		Dialectic Nominalism vs. Realism
70	NORMAN CONQUEST **William I** (1066-87) Introduction of feudal tenures French culture		Saxon Wars Investiture Controversy	Rise of Hildebrand **P. Gregory VII** (1073-85) Canossa (1077)	✕ Manzikert (1071) Loss of Asia Minor	**Alp Arslan** (1063-72) Conquest of Persia and Armenia **Malik Shah** (1072-92) Conquest of Asia Minor and Syria	Roscellinus Berengar of Tours
80	*Domesday Book* **William II** (1087-1100)		Constant civil war	Henry IV takes Rome (1084)	**Alexius Comnenus** (1081-1118) Norman War		Development of Romanesque architecture
90	Anselm, Æ B of Canterbury	Council of Clermont (1095); Crusade proclaimed	Henry abandons Italy	**P. Urban II** (1088-99) **C. Roger** (d. 1101) conquers Sicily	FIRST CRUSADE 1096 Arrival at Constantinople 1098 Capture of Antioch 1099 Capture of Jerusalem		Bayeux Tapestry *Song of Roland*
1100							

ELEVENTH CENTURY

TWELFTH CENTURY

	ENGLAND	FRANCE	GERMANY	ITALY	EASTERN EUROPE	THE TURKS	ARTS AND LETTERS
1100	Henry I (1100-35) Coronation Charter Takes Normandy from brother Improved central government Exchequer Privileged boroughs Angevin alliance	Philip I (d. 1108) Louis VI (1108-37) Consolidation of Capetian domain Communes and privileged towns Suger (d. 1151)	Henry IV (d. 1106) Henry V (1106-25) Continued strife between Papacy and Empire Investiture Controversy ended by Concordat of Worms (1122)	Roger II (1101-54) Inherits Sicily	Alexius Comnenus (d. 1118) Recovers coast of Asia Minor War with crusaders over Antioch Comneni continue until 1185	Results of Crusade: Latin Kingdom of Jerusalem County of Edessa Princ. of Antioch County of Tripoli Templars and Hospitallers	Omar Khayyam Idrisi Averroës Rise of the Universities
20			Acquires Apulia and Calabria		Trade concessions to Pisa, Genoa, Venice	Scholastic theology Abelard Peter Lombard	
30	Stephen (1135-54) The Anarchy Angevin War	Louis VII (1137-80) Rise of Angevins Geoffrey Plantagenet	Lothair III (1125-37) Guelf (G) vs. Hohenstaufen (H) (H) Conrad III (1138-52) (G) Henry the Lion	K. of Sicily (1130) Anticlerical agitation Arnold of Brescia Peter Waldo Cathari (Albigensians)	Hungary remains strong; holds Croatia Poland weakens Intermittent German lordship Bohemia loyal part of H. R. E.	Zangi, Gov. of Mosul takes Edessa (1144)	Canon Law Gratian Revival of Roman Law Translations of Greek and Arabic science Adelard of Bath John of Salisbury
1150	Second Crusade (1147) Henry II (1154-89) m. Eleanor of Aquit. Constitutional reforms Common Law New taxes	Second Crusade Eleanor of Aquit. divorced (1152) SPAIN C. of Portugal recognized as K. by pope (1179) C. of Barcelona acquires crown of Aragon (1150)	Second Crusade (1147) (H) Frederick Barbarossa (1152-90) Italian expeditions; conflict with papacy and communes	P. Hadrian IV (1154-59) P. Alexander III (1159-81) Fall of Milan (1162) Lombard League X Legnano (1176) Peace of Constance (1183)	Eastward expansion of Germans Slavic Marches: Pomerania to Austria	Second Crusade (1147-49) fails Nur-ed-Din (1146-74) takes Damascus	St. Bernard Vernacular Lit. Chansons de Geste Lyrics of troubadours
70	†Becket (1170) Norman expansion in Wales Irish conquests Wars with sons	Philip Augustus (1180-1223) acquires Picardy (1189-92)	Old duchies broken up Fall of Henry the Lion (1181) Sicilian alliance (H) Henry VI ('90-'97) Acquisition of Sicilian Kingdom		Henry the Lion founds Lübeck Russia disintegrates	Saladin, Sultan of Egypt (1171-93) Acquires Mosul, Aleppo, Damascus Takes Jerusalem (1187)	Romances of Marie de France and Chrétien de Troyes Drama and music Icelandic sagas The Cid; Goliardi Transition to Gothic Arts Architecture
90	Richard I (1189-99) → Third Crusade Angevin-Capetian War Contest with pope over divorce	Angevin-Capetian War Contest with pope over divorce	(G) Otto IV vs. (H) Philip of Suabia	P. Celestine III ('91-'98) P. Innocent III (1198-1216)	Isaac II (1185-95) Bulgaria again independent Alexius III (1195-1203)	Third Crusade (1190-92) fails Teutonic Knights	Sculpture Stained glass
1200	John (1199-1216)						

Year	ENGLAND	FRANCE	GERMANY	ITALY	EASTERN EUROPE	THE TURKS	ARTS AND LETTERS
1200	John (d. 1216) Loss of Normandy, etc. Quarrel with Pope (1207-13)	Philip Aug. (d. 1223) Conquest of Normandy, Anjou, Poitou, etc. ×Bouvines (1214)	Frederick II, K. of Sicily (1197-1250) Philip of Suabia (d. 1208) Otto IV put out by Frederick II (1215) Emperor (1220)	Innocent III (d. 1216) Height of the Papacy Franciscan order Lateran Council (1215) P. Honorius III (1216-27) Dominican order	→Fourth Crusade Capture of Constantinople (1204) Latin Empire (1204-61) Maritime supremacy of Venice	Rise of Mongols under Jenghis Kahn (1206-27) Conquer all central Asia and Persia	Perfection of Gothic Arts French Literature Villehardouin *Fabliaux* Later romances
10	Magna Carta (1215) Henry III (1216-72) Minority to 1227	Albigensian Crusade (1208-29)					
20	SPAIN James the Conqueror of Aragon (1213-76) takes Valencia Final union of León and Castile under Ferdinand III (1230) Takes Murcia, Cordova, Seville						
30		Louis VIII (1223-26) Louis IX (1226-70) Blanche of Castile Regent to 1234 Secures half of Languedoc Constitutional advance Crusade (1248-54) disastrous	Crusade (1228-29) Sicilian Code Contest with Gregory IX Italian Wars Germany left to princes	Renewal of Lombard League P. Gregory IX (1227-41) Canon Law Papal Inquisition ×Cortenuova (1237) P. Innocent IV (1243-54)	Teutonic Knights in Prussia (1230) Union with Livonian order (1237) Mongols invade Bohemia and Hungary	Frederick II recovers Jerusalem Mongols conquer Russia; Kiev destroyed Fall of Jerusalem Louis IX's Crusade in Egypt	German Literature *Nibelungenlied* Walther von der Vogelweide Scholastic learning
1250			Conrad IV (1250-54) Disputed-Election (1257) Interregnum until 1273	Manfred, Regent, then K. of Sicily (1258-66)	Republic of Novgorod prosperous	Mongols end Caliphate of Bagdad (1258); checked in Syria by Mamelukes, who take Antioch (1268)	Robert Grosseteste Albertus Magnus
60	Provisions of Oxford (1258) Simon de Montfort Barons' War (1264-65)	Peace with England (1259)		P. Urban IV (1261-64) P.Clement IV (1265-68)	Michael Palaeologus (1261-82) Restored Byzantine Empire		Thomas Aquinas Roger Bacon
70	Edward I (1272-1307)	Philip III (1270-85) Secures all Languedoc	Rudolf of Habsburg (1273-91) Takes Austria from Ottokar of Bohemia	Charles of Anjou K. of Sicily (1266-85) Ruin of Pisa Rise of Florence	Bitter rivalry of Venice and Genoa for Black Sea	Kublai Khan (1259-94) Marco Polo's travels	Architecture and technology Many new inventions or importations from the east Villard de Honnecourt
80	Conquest of Wales (1282-84)			P. Martin IV (1281-85) Sicilian Vespers (1282) Island acquired by K. of Aragon	Second Bulgarian Empire		Pierre de Maricourt
90	Statutes Scottish Wars Model Parl. (1295) ×Falkirk (1298)	Philip IV (1285-1314) m. heiress of Champagne War with Edward I (1294-98)	Origin of Swiss Confederation (1291) Albert of Austria (1298-1308)	P. Boniface VIII (1294-1303) *Clericis Laicos* (1296)		Fall of Acre (1291) End of the original crusade	French literature Joinville *Romance of the Rose*
1300							

THIRTEENTH CENTURY

FOURTEENTH CENTURY

	ENGLAND	FRANCE	ITALY	GERMANY	EASTERN EUROPE	THE OTTOMAN TURKS AND THE BALKANS	ARTS AND LETTERS
1300	Edward I (d. 1307) Conquers Scotland Edward II (1307-27)	Philip IV (d. 1314) {Estates General ✕ Courtrai (1302) Trial of Templars (1307-14)	Unam Sanctam Anagni (1303) P. Clement V (1305-14)	Wars of Habsburg (H), Luxemburg (L), Wittelsbach (W) (L) Henry VII (1308-13)	Teutonic Knights Headquarters to Prussia (1309) John, K. of Bohemia (1310-46)	Osman (1299-1326) and his Turks capture Brusa	Scholastic learning Pierre Dubois Mondino
10	Robert Bruce K. of Scotland ✕ Bannockburn Scottish independence	Sons of Philip IV (1314-28) Law of Succession	P. John XXII (1314-34) Contest with Franciscans and Louis of Bavaria	(W) Louis of Bavaria (1314-47) Growth of the Swiss Confederation	Angevin House in Hungary (1309)	Orkhan (1326-59) Takes Nicaea and Nicomedia Organizes state	Duns Scotus William of Ockham Marsiglio of Padua
20	Edward III (1327-77)	VALOIS HOUSE Philip VI (1328-50)	Development of Canon Law	Rise of the Hansa Independence of princes and Free Cities			Italian literature Dante (d. 1321) *Divine Comedy* Petrarch (d. 1374) *Sonnets*
30	Opening of the Hundred Years' War (1337)		Papal Taxation				Boccaccio (d. 1375) *Decameron*
40	✕ Sluys (1340) ✕ Crécy (1346)	Acquisition of Dauphiné	The Black Death	(L) Charles IV (1346-78) Abandons Italy	also K. of Bohemia Founds U. of Prague	Decline of Bulgaria	Painting Miniatures Giotto (d. 1336)
1350	The Black Prince ✕ Poitiers (1356)	John (1350-64) [Estates at Paris Etienne Marcel Jacquerie (1358)]	Revival of mysticism Brothers of the Common Life	Golden Bull (1356) Seven Electors	Revival of Poland	Turks enter Europe (1356) Murad I (1359-89) Takes Adrianople Conquers Bulgars	Revival of humanism Petrarch and his disciples
60	Anti-papal statutes	Victory of Charles V (1364-80)	St. Catherine of Siena	War of Hansa with Waldemar of Denmark			But of Paris Ockhamists maintain scholastic tradition
70	The English all but driven from France	Foundation of absolute monarchy Du Guesclin	P. Gregory XI (1371-78) Returns to Rome	Peace of Stralsund (1370) Height of Hansa	also K. of Bohemia (1378-1419)	Defeat of Serbs	Architecture Flamboyant style of Gothic
80	Richard II (1377-99) Great Revolt (1381)	Charles VI (1380-1422) Philip of Burgundy acquires Flanders (1384)	The Great Schism (1378-1417) Clement VII (d. '94) VI (d. '89) — Urban [Rome] Boniface IX (d. 1404) — [Avignon]	(L) Wenceslas ('78-1400) Sigismund (brother) K. of Hungary (1387-1437)	Jagiello of Lithuania acquires Polish crown (1386)	Vassalage of Byzantine Emperor (1381) Bayazid I (1389-1402)	Secular buildings of Flanders and Italy English Literature Chaucer (d. 1400) *Canterbury Tales*
90	Growth of Lollardy Attempted royal absolutism Revolution	Insanity of king Orleans *vs.* Burgundy	Benedict XIII (1394-1417)	Final Swiss victory Wenceslas deposed, keeps Bohemia	Union of Calmar (1397)		Wycliffe's *Bible* Langland *Piers Plowman*
1400							

Papacy at Avignon until 1376

(son)

Year	ENGLAND	FRANCE	ITALY	GERMANY	EASTERN EUROPE	THE OTTOMAN TURKS AND THE BALKANS	ARTS AND LETTERS
1400	HOUSE OF LANCASTER Henry IV (1399-1413) Parliamentary government	Charles VI (d. 1422) John of Burgundy (1404-19) Civil War	Innocent VII (d. 1406) Gregory XII (1406-15)	Preaching of Hus in Bohemia	Wenceslas, King of Bohemia (d. 1419) Sigismund K. of Hungary (d. 1437)	✗Angora (1402) Victory of Timur (d. 1405) Civil War	**Painting** Van Eyck brothers Masaccio (d. 1428)
10	Henry V (1413-22) ✗Agincourt (1415)	†Orleans (1407)	Council of Pisa (1409) Council of Constance (1414-18)	(L) Sigismund Hus burned (1415)	✗Tannenberg (1410) Decline of Teutonic Knights	Mohammed I (1413-21) Turkish recovery	
20	Henry VI (1422-61) Regency of Gloucester and	Invades France †Burgundy (1419) Peace of Troyes (1420) Charles VII (1422-61) Bedford	P. Martin V (1417-31) Restoration of papal monarchy		Sigismund, K. of Bohemia (d. 1437) Hussite War (1420-36) ·John Zizka (d. 1424)	Murad II (1421-51)	**Sculpture** Ghiberti (d. 1455) Donatello (d. 1466)
30		Career of Jeanne d'Arc (1429-31) Peace of Arras (1435)	P. Eugenius IV (1431-47) Contest with Council of Basel	Council of Basel (1431-49) Religious peace with Hussites (1434) Germany and Bohemia to Habsburg house (1437)			**Architecture** Brunelleschi (d. 1466)
40	Defeat in France	Restoration of Charles V's government		Frederick III (1440-93) Failure of Conciliar Movement		Turks subdue all Balkans	**Technology** Konrad Keyser The Hussite Engineer
1450	Insanity of king Yorkist rising	Fall of Guienne End of Hundred Years' War (1453)	P. Nicholas V (1447-55) Papal triumph	BURGUNDY Philip the Good (d. 1467) unites Netherlands	Revival of Russia under Princes of Moscow	Mohammed II (51-81) Fall of Constantinople (1453)	Iacopo Mariano Gutenberg
60	HOUSE OF YORK Edward IV (1461-83)	Louis XI (1461-83)	Relapse of Roman Church under Renaissance popes	War with Louis XI Charles the Rash (1467-77)		EXPLORATION Portuguese voyages under Prince Henry (d. 1460)	**French literature** Commines
70	Warwick the King-Maker Extermination of Lancastrians	League of Public Weal (1465)	SPAIN Isabella of Castile m. Ferdinand of Aragon (1469) Latter inherits crown (1479)	Occupation of Alsace, Lorraine Defeat by Swiss	Peace of Thorn (1466) Polish dominance in Prussia		Villon
80	Richard III (1483-85) HOUSE OF TUDOR Henry VII (1485-1509)	Royal absolutism; acquires Burgundy, Provence, etc. Charles VIII (1483-98) Anne de Beaujeu Regent	Establishment of royal absolutism	Mary of Burgundy m. Maximilian son of Philip III(1477)	Discovery of Senegal, Niger, etc. Diego Cam discovers Congo (1482) Diaz rounds Cape (1486)		**Witchcraft delusion** Bull of Innocent VIII (1484) *Malleus Maleficarum* (1486)
90	Establishment of royal absolutism	Charles m. to heiress of Brittany	Conquest of Granada (1492)	Foundation of Habsburg greatness	Columbus discovers America (1492) Vasco da Gama circumnavigates Africa (1498)		Further development of secular arts and humanistic study in Italy and elsewhere
1500							

FIFTEENTH CENTURY

Suggested Readings

The following lists are not intended to serve as bibliographies of the subjects treated in the various chapters, but merely to provide a few suggestions of supplementary reading, principally source material in English and somewhat general discussions by modern writers. Anyone who desires additional references should consult L. J. Paetow, *Guide to the Study of Mediæval History*, Second Edition (New York, 1931); J. W. Thompson, *Reference Studies in Mediæval History,* 3 vols. (Chicago, 1925-30); and the bibliographies attached to the chapters in *The Cambridge Medieval History,* 8 vols. (Cambridge, 1911-36). This collaborative work is the most comprehensive survey of the mediæval period in English. It can usually be relied on for a scholarly narrative of political events and it includes occasional essays on particular phases of civilizations; but such essays, unfortunately, provide no continuous account of cultural development. J. W. Thompson's *Middle Ages,* 2 vols. (New York, 1932), is considerably larger than the ordinary textbook and contains interesting chapters on arts, letters, and social conditions. Warmly recommended, to supplement whatever appears below in that connection, is Herbert Heaton's *Economic History of Europe*, Revised Edition (New York, 1948). And for many details of political history that are here omitted—especially those concerned with the Byzantine Empire and adjacent regions—the interested student should consult *The World of the Middle Ages* by J. L. LaMonte (New York, 1949). See also E. P. Cheyney, *The Dawn of a New Era, 1250-1453* (New York, 1936); and G. C. Sellery, *The Renaissance: Its Nature and Origins* (Madison, 1950)—a fine essay that includes suggestive comment on many phases of mediæval culture.

Useful collections of documents and other materials for study are the following: *Translations and Reprints from the Original Sources of European History,* University of Pennsylvania Press (Philadelphia, 1897 ff.); E. F. Henderson, *Select Historical Documents of the Middle Ages* (London, 1896); O. J. Thatcher and E. M. McNeal, *A Source Book for Mediæval History* (New York, 1905); F. A. Ogg, *A Source Book of Mediæval History* (New York, 1907); J. H. Robinson, *Readings in European History* (Boston, 1904); J. F. Scott, A. Hyma, and A. H. Noyes, *Readings in Medieval History* (New York, 1933); R. C. Cave and H. H. Coulson, *A Source Book for Mediæval Economic History* (Milwaukee, 1936); F. Duncalf and A. C. Krey, *Parallel Source Problems in Mediæval History* (New York, 1912). The first volume of Henry Guerlac's *Readings in the History of Science,* soon to be published in three parts, includes much valuable material for the mediæval, as well as the ancient, period. Numerous extracts from mediæval sources are also provided by *Chapters in Western Civilization*, published for the Columbia course on the history of civilization (New York, 1946). More specific references to some of these translations will be given below; likewise to the *Berkshire Studies in European History*—a series of small but comprehensive books edited by R. A. Newhall, L. B. Packard, and S. R. Packard.

INTRODUCTION

W. Z. Ripley's *Races of Europe* (New York, 1899), long the standard book on the so-called Nordic, Alpine, and Mediterranean races, has now been completely rewritten by C. S. Coon (New York, 1939). The classic interpretation of European history in terms of racial superiority and inferiority is the work of J. A. Gobineau, *Essai sur l'inégalité des races humaines*, which has been translated by A. Collins (New York, 1915). For a good review of this question in the light of political controversy see the article by V. G. Childe in *History*, vol. XVII (1933). Cf. J. S. Huxley, A. C. Haddon, and A. M. Carr-Saunders, *We Europeans* (New York, 1936).

CHAPTER I. THE ROMAN WORLD

For adequate citation of readings on Græco-Roman institutions and culture the reader must be referred to histories of the ancient world; especially *The Cambridge Ancient History* (Cambridge, 1923-39), the last three volumes of which deal with the Roman Empire and are supplied with scholarly bibliographies. Brief and generally reliable essays on particular aspects of ancient civilization will be found in *The Legacy of Greece*, edited by R. W. Livingstone (Oxford, 1921), and *The Legacy of Rome*, edited by C. Bailey (Oxford, 1923). The former includes good sketches of Hellenistic science. And on this same subject see J. L. E. Dreyer, *History of the Planetary Systems from Thales to Kepler* (Cambridge, 1906); F. Cajori, *History of Mathematics* (New York, 1919); C. J. Singer, *History of Biology* (New York, 1950), *From Magic to Science* (London, 1928), and *A Short History of Medicine* (New York, 1928); F. H. Garrison, *An Introduction to the History of Medicine* (Philadelphia, 1929); A. Castiglioni, *History of Medicine* (New York, 1941). Extracts from the medical writers will be found in A. J. Brock's *Greek Medicine* (New York, 1929) and L. Clendening's *Source Book of Medical History* (New York, 1942).

In order to appreciate the teachings of the later Stoics, the student can do no better than read the works of Epicteus and Marcus Aurelius, which are available in many translations. Illustrations of life in the ancient world from contemporary sculpture and painting have been collected in various dictionaries of antiquities, albums of classical art, and the like. Useful commentaries based on these illustrations, as well as on literary sources, have been produced by numerous authors: e.g., H. W. Johnston, *The Private Life of the Romans* (Chicago, 1932); M. Cary and T. J. Haarhof, *Life and Thought in the Greek and Roman World* (New York, 1940). See also S. Dill, *Roman Society from Nero to Marcus Aurelius* (London, 1905). The best general book on the social and economic history of the Roman Empire is the one bearing that title by M. I. Rostovtzeff (Oxford, 1926). The second chapter in *The Cambridge Economic History*, vol. 1 (Cambridge, 1941), by C. E. Stevens gives an admirable account of Roman agriculture. A. P. Usher's *History of Mechanical Inventions* (New York, 1929), pp. 32 ff., clearly sketches the principal achievements of the ancient world in the field of technology.

CHAPTER II. THE DECLINE OF THE ROMAN EMPIRE

There are good chapters on many phases of the later Roman Empire in *The Cambridge Ancient History*, vol. XII. *The End of the Ancient World and the*

Beginnings of the Middle Ages, by F. Lot (New York, 1931), graphically treats the decline of the empire and raises a number of interesting questions in that connection. See also Rostovtzeff's work cited above and S. Dill, *Roman Society in the Last Century of the Western Empire* (London, 1899). The best source for early Christianity is, of course, the New Testament, which should be read— if for no other reason—as part of a historical education. Documents concerning the Christian persecutions have been published in the Pennsylvania *Translations and Reprints,* IV, no. 1. See also H. B. Workman, *Persecution in the Early Church* (London, 1906); N. H. Baynes, *Constantine the Great and the Christian Church* (London, 1930); A. H. M. Jones, *Constantine and the Conversion of Europe* (London, 1948); and (in the *Berkshire Studies*) E. R. Goodenough, *The Church in the Roman Empire* (New York, 1931). The religious background of Christianity is set forth by T. R. Glover, *The Conflict of Religions in the Roman Empire* (London, 1909), and W. R. Halliday, *The Pagan Background of Christianity* (London, 1925). Cf. A. D. Nock, *Conversion* (London, 1933), and *St. Paul* (London, 1938). Anyone who wants a taste of Neo-Platonism can obtain it from the work of Plotinus, which has been translated in the *Bohn Library.*

Chapter III.   The Barbarization of the West

The best description of the Ural-Altaic nomads in English is that of J. Peisker in *The Cambridge Medieval History,* I, ch. xii. For accounts of the barbarian invasions see the other chapters in the same volume and those in Lot's *End of the Ancient World*; also J. B. Bury, *History of the Later Roman Empire,* 2 vols. (London, 1923). Every student of mediæval history should read the *Germania* of Tacitus—preferably in a recent translation, for the older ones are likely to be inaccurate. The *Salic Law* has been partly translated in Henderson's *Select Documents*; the Anglo-Saxon dooms have been fully translated in F. L. Attenborough's *Laws of the Earliest English Kings* (Cambridge, 1922). Selections from the latter are given in various source books, as in C. Stephenson and F. G. Marcham, *Sources of English Constitutional History* (New York, 1937). See, too, Katherine Fischer's *Burgundian Code* in the Pennsylvania *Translations and Reprints* (Philadelphia, 1949). The famous *History of the Franks* by Gregory of Tours graphically describes life in Merovingian Gaul: translated with an admirable introduction by O. M. Dalton (Oxford, 1927), and in part by E. Brehaut for the Columbia *Records of Civilization* (1916). Two famous books on the subject of Germanic law are those of E. Jenks, *Law and Politics in the Middle Ages* (London, 1913), and H. C. Lea, *Superstition and Force* (Philadelphia, 1892). For additional references see the following chapters.

Chapter IV.   The Church After Constantine

Innumerable books on the history of the Christian Church deal with the controversial subject of the episcopate. A clear sketch from the Protestant point of view is that contributed to the *Berkshire Studies* by S. Baldwin, *The Organization of Mediæval Christianity* (New York, 1929). A more comprehensive work, now in process of translation, is Hans Lietzmann's *History of the Early Church* (New York, 1937 ff.). For the Catholic tradition see P. Batiffol, *Primitive Catholicism* (London, 1911); also J. Lebreton and J. Zeiler, *The History of the Primitive Church,* 2 vols. (New York, 1949). Of the utmost value to the student of the mediæval church is the *Rule of St. Benedict,* of which an inexpensive translation has been published by the Society for the Promotion of Christian Knowledge (London, 1931). For interpretation see especially E. C.

Butler, *Benedictine Monachism* (London, 1919), and J. Chapman, *St. Benedict and the Sixth Century* (New York, 1929). The life of a pre-Benedictine monk, St. Columban, appears in the Pennsylvania *Translations and Reprints*, II, no. 7; cf. Maud Joynt, *Life of St. Gall* (New York, 1927). Also invaluable as historical sources are the works of the great church fathers. St. Augustine's *Confessions* and *Civitas Dei* are obtainable in various translations. Selected letters of St. Jerome have been translated by F. A. Wright for the *Loeb Classical Library* (London, 1933). Biographies of these authors, as well as commentaries on their doctrines, are numerous. But this list will close with the mention of two excellent books that deal primarily with early mediæval education: E. K. Rand, *Founders of the Middle Ages* (Cambridge, Mass., 1928), and M. L. W. Laistner, *Thought and Letters in Western Europe, A.D. 500 to 900* (London, 1931).

CHAPTER V.   THE EMPIRE IN THE SIXTH CENTURY

Practically every phase of Byzantine history receives detailed treatment in *The Cambridge Medieval History*, vols. II and IV. Briefer sketches will be found in C. Diehl, *History of the Byzantine Empire* (Princeton, 1925); N. H. Baynes, *The Byzantine Empire* (London, 1925); and S. Runciman, *Byzantine Civilization* (London, 1933). The second volume of *The Cambridge Medieval History* also includes good chapters on the Slavs and the Avars by J. Peisker and on the Roman law by H. J. Roby. For a fuller account of Roman legal development see F. P. Walton, *Historical Introduction to the Roman Law* (Edinburgh, 1912). *The History of the Wars* by Procopius has been translated by H. B. Dewing in the *Loeb Classical Library*, 5 vols. (London, 1914-28); Paul the Deacon's *History of the Lombards* by W. D. Foulke in the Pennsylvania *Translations and Reprints* (Philadelphia, 1907). On Persia see P. M. Sykes, *History of Persia*, 2 vols. (London, 1930).

Any one of a dozen histories of architecture will provide information about the Byzantine style, with adequate illustrations. But the student is referred in particular to T. G. Jackson's *Byzantine and Romanesque Architecture*, vol. I (Cambridge, 1913), which contains a wealth of drawings by the author, including reproductions of famous mosaics in color. See also J. A. Hamilton, *Byzantine Architecture and Decoration* (London, 1933); D. T. Rice, *Byzantine Art* (Oxford, 1935); E. W. Anthony, *A History of Mosaics* (Boston, 1936); E. H. Swift, *Hagia Sophia* (New York, 1940).

CHAPTER VI.   THE RISE OF ISLAM

The career of Mohammed and the growth of the Arab Empire are clearly sketched by A. A. Bevan and C. H. Becker in *The Cambridge Medieval History*, vol. II. A fuller account is given in the recent and scholarly *History of the Arabs* by P. K. Hitti, Fourth Edition (New York, 1949); cf. his *Short History* (Princeton, 1947). The indispensable source for a study of Mohammedanism is, of course, the Koran. The best translation is that of M. Pickthall, *The Meaning of the Glorious Koran* (New York, 1930), but there are numerous others, including the volume of selections by S. Lane-Poole, entitled *The Speeches and Table-Talk of the Prophet Mohammed* (London, 1882). For books dealing with Moslem culture see below, under Chapter IX.

CHAPTER VII.   THE PAPACY AND THE BARBARIAN WEST

On Merovingian Gaul see Lot's *End of the Ancient World*, pt. iii; C. Pfister's chapters in *The Cambridge Medieval History*, vol. II; S. Dill, *Roman Society in Gaul in the Merovingian Age* (London, 1926); and the work of Gregory of

Tours, cited above p. 126. *The Pastoral Care* and various other writings of Gregory the Great are included in the collection of *Nicene and Post-Nicene Fathers*, Second Series, vol. XII. Gregory's *Dialogues* in translation have been edited by E. G. Gardner (London, 1911). F. H. Dudden's *Gregory the Great*, 2 vols. (New York, 1905), is an excellent biography. *An Encyclopedist of the Dark Ages,* by E. Brehaut (New York, 1912), summarizes Isidore's *Etymologies* and gives examples in translation. The more famous works of Bede are available in various English editions. See also *The Letters of St. Boniface*, translated by E. Emerton for the Columbia *Records of Civilization* (New York, 1940), and Willibald's *Life of St. Boniface*, translated by G. W. Robinson (Cambridge, Mass., 1916). Numerous other works on the spread of Christianity are cited in *The Cambridge Medieval History*, vol. II, which also has good chapters on the rise of the Carolingians.

CHAPTER VIII. THE CAROLINGIAN EMPIRE

The best review in English of the Carolingian Empire and its institutions is that of G. Seeliger in *The Cambridge Medieval History*, II, chs. xix, xxi. More illuminating than much of the modern writing about Charlemagne are the biography by Einhard, which has been translated a number of times, and the emperor's capitularies, some of which may be found in the Pennsylvania *Translations and Reprints*, III, no. 2, and VI, no. 5. On the imperial coronation of 800 see Duncalf and Krey, *Parallel Source Problems*. The outstanding book on Latin education during the Carolingian age is Laistner's *Thought and Letters*, which includes a full bibliography. See also H. O. Taylor, *The Mediæval Mind* Fourth Edition (Cambridge, Mass., 1949), I, chs. x-xi; and C. H. Haskins, *The Renaissance of the Twelfth Century* (Cambridge, Mass., 1927), introductory chapters. E. A. Lowe in *The Legacy of the Middle Ages*, edited by C. G. Crump and E. F. Jacob (Oxford, 1926), sketches concisely the difficult subject of mediæval handwriting. Among the many books written about the Vikings may be mentioned the following: T. D. Kendrick, *History of the Vikings* (New York, 1930); A. Mawer, *The Vikings* (Cambridge, 1913); A. Olrik, *Viking Civilization* (New York, 1930); M. W. Williams, *Social Scandinavia in the Viking Age* (New York, 1920).

CHAPTER IX. THE GREEK AND MOSLEM WORLDS

Standard works on the Byzantine and Arab Empires have been cited above under Chapters V and VI. The best survey of Moslem civilization is to be found in the pertinent chapters of Hitti's *History of the Arabs*, which contains references to many special studies. See also the admirable summaries in *The Legacy of Islam*, edited by T. W. Arnold and A. Guillaume (Oxford, 1931); G. Sarton's *Introduction to the History of Science*, Vols. I-II (Baltimore, 1927-31). To the histories of particular sciences noted above under Chapter I may be added David Reisman, *The Story of Medicine in the Middle Ages* (New York, 1935). A magnificent work on *Early Muslim Architecture* has been produced by K. A. C. Creswell, 2 vols. (Oxford, 1922-40). Good general discussions are given by C. T. Rivoira, *Moslem Architecture* (Oxford, 1918), and M. S. Briggs, *Muhammadan Architecture* (Oxford, 1924).

CHAPTER X. THE DEVELOPMENT OF FEUDALISM

Political reconstruction following the collapse of the Carolingian Empire is adequately treated in *The Cambridge Medieval History*, vol. III; the chapters on France and England are particularly good. In addition, see the exceptionally readable volume by C. H. Haskins, *The Normans in European History* (Boston, 1915). C. Stephenson's *Mediæval Feudalism*, published by the Cornell University Press (Ithaca, 1942), is the only recent book on that subject in English. Feudal documents have been included in the Pennsylvania *Translations and Reprints*, IV, no. 3; and by Stephenson and Marcham, *Sources of English Constitutional History*, sect. ii. For additional references to books on the working of feudal institutions see below under Chapter XVII.

CHAPTER XI. AGRARIAN AND MILITARY SOCIETY

Nellie Neilson's *Medieval Agrarian Economy*, in the *Berkshire Studies* (New York, 1936), is the best brief account of the manorial system in English. Much additional information, together with elaborate bibliographies, will be found in *The Cambridge Economic History*, vol. I. See also Eileen Power's *Medieval People* (London, 1924); her chapter in *The Cambridge Medieval History*, vol. VII; and Heaton's *Economic History of Europe*, ch. v. Numerous translations of manorial documents are available, but they are usually hard to understand without the help of an expert. Far superior to the older books on the subject is S. Painter's *French Chivalry* (Baltimore, 1940); cf. Stephenson's *Mediæval Feudalism*, chs. iii-iv. *Social France in the Age of Philip Augustus*, by A. Luchaire (New York, 1912), contains much interesting detail largely drawn from contemporary literature. The Bayeux Tapestry has been reproduced several times—excellently in H. Belloc's *Book of the Bayeux Tapestry* (London, 1914), though his comments are not always reliable.

There are many translations of the Icelandic sagas, on which in general see W. A. Craigie, *The Icelandic Sagas* (Cambridge, 1913), and Bertha S. Phillpotts, *Edda and Saga* (London, 1931). C. K. Scott-Moncrieff's metrical versions of *Beowulf* (London, 1921) and *The Song of Roland* (London, 1920) are especially recommended. Cf. C. W. Kennedy's translation of *Beowulf* (New York, 1940). Good introductions to the vernacular literatures of western Europe are provided by *The Cambridge History of English Literature*, vol. I (Cambridge, 1932); G. Paris, *Mediæval French Literature* (London, 1903); and K. Francke, *A History of German Literature* (New York, 1913). See also W. P. Ker, *The Dark Ages* (New York, 1904), and *Epic and Romance* (London, 1908).

CHAPTER XII. THE EMPIRE, THE PAPACY, AND THE CRUSADE

All the standard works on mediæval history tend to emphasize the conflict of the empire and the papacy, and many source books include excerpts from the contemporary writings. But see especially the chapters in *The Cambridge Medieval History*, vols. III and V; Duncalf and Krey, *Parallel Source Problems;* and *The Correspondence of Pope Gregory VII*, translated by E. Emerton for the Columbia *Records of Civilization* (New York, 1932). Political theory in the Middle Ages is excellently set forth in these two books: C. H. McIlwain, *The Growth of Political Thought* (New York, 1932), and G. H. Sabine, *A History of Political Theory* (New York, 1937). *The Cambridge Medieval History*, vols. IV and V, gives full treatment to all aspects of the crusade, including the relations between the Roman and Greek Churches. Interesting source material will be found in A. C. Krey's *First Crusade* (Princeton, 1921) and in the Pennsylvania *Translations and Reprints*, I, nos. 2, 4; also, in the Third Series, Fulcher of Chartres, *Chronicle of the First Crusade*, translated by M. E. McGinty (Philadelphia, 1941). Cf. William of Tyre, *A History of Deeds Done beyond the Seas*, translated by E. A. Babcock and A. C. Krey for the Columbia

Records of Civilization (New York, 1943). A good brief account of the whole crusading movement is provided by R. A. Newhall's volume, *The Crusades* in the *Berkshire Studies* (New York, 1927), which contains a useful bibliography. For many additional references see LaMonte, *The World of the Middle Ages*, pp. 778-779.

CHAPTER XIII. THE GROWTH OF THE TOWNS

Our finest survey of mediæval economic development is H. Pirenne's *Economic and Social History of Medieval Europe* (New York, 1937), which is to be supplemented by his *Mediæval Cities* (Princeton, 1925) and his chapter in *The Cambridge Medieval History*, vol. VI. The best sketch in English of the early Italian communes is that of C. W. Previté-Orton in vol. V of *The Cambridge Medieval History*. C. Stephenson's *Borough and Town* (Cambridge, Mass., 1933) is in the main a technical study, but reviews some typical urban liberties on the continent. For additional references see Heaton's *Economic History of Europe*, chs. vii-x. Few illustrative documents have been translated except those pertaining to the English boroughs; see, for example, Stephenson and Marcham, *Sources of English Constitutional History*. Additional references to later economic developments will be found below under Chapter XXIV.

CHAPTER XIV. THE DEVELOPMENT OF UNIVERSITY EDUCATION

A splendid introduction to the mediæval revival of learning in general is provided by C. H. Haskins, *The Renaissance of the Twelfth Century*. On the early universities see the same author's *Rise of the Universities* (New York, 1923) and H. Rashdall's *Universities of Europe in the Middle Ages*, Revised Edition, 3 vols. (Oxford, 1936). Highly entertaining letters of students have been translated by Haskins in his *Studies in Mediæval Culture* (Oxford, 1929). Numerous quotations from mediæval scholars can be found in H. O. Taylor's *Mediæval Mind* and in R. L. Poole's *Illustrations of the History of Mediæval Thought and Learning* (London, 1920). There are many books about Abelard and Héloïse, but their famous story can best be read in their own letters, translated by Scott-Moncrieff (New York, 1929). The student is warned against older books entitled *Letters of Abelard and Héloïse*, which are largely falsification.

On particular subjects of study in the mediæval schools there are chapters, not always adequate, in *The Cambridge Medieval History*, vol. V; in Crump and Jacob, *The Legacy of the Middle Ages;* and in F. J. C. Hearnshaw, *Mediæval Contributions to Modern Civilization* (London, 1921). Mediæval dialectic, theology, jurisprudence, mathematics, and natural science can scarcely be understood except by advanced students; for few scholarly works of the Middle Ages have been translated and even good summaries of them are hard to find in English. Popular histories of science are exasperatingly brief on the Middle Ages. L. Thorndike's *History of Magic and Experimental Science*, 4 vols. (New York, 1923-34), is for the specialist rather than for the beginner. But see the histories of particular sciences noted above, pp. 518, 521; also Beryl Smalley, *The Study of the Bible in the Middle Ages* (Oxford, 1941).

CHAPTER XV. DEVELOPMENTS IN LITERATURE

The best review of Latin literature in the twelfth century is that of Haskins in his *Renaissance of the Twelfth Century*, where reference is made to various other works on the subject. On the Goliardi see especially Helen Waddell's *Wandering Scholars* (London, 1934) and her charming translations in *Mediæval*

Latin Lyrics (London, 1933), some of which have been quoted in the text. *Wine, Women and Song,* by J. A. Symonds (London, 1925), is an older collection of the same sort. There are many works on the troubadours and their music. See particularly H. J. Chaytor, *The Troubadours* (Cambridge, 1912); P. Aubry, *Trouvères and Troubadours* (New York, 1914); and G. Reese, *Music in the Middle Ages* (New York, 1940). General books on vernacular literature have already been cited above under Chapter XI; but in preference to them the student is urged to read the actual compositions of mediæval authors. The romances of Marie de France, Chrétien de Troyes, and others are available in many translations, including several convenient volumes in the *Everyman Library.* The *Romance of Reynard* can likewise be had in a number of versions. The best translation of *Aucassin et Nicolette* is that of Andrew Lang. The *Poema del Cid* has been put into English verse by A. M. Huntington (Hispanic Society of America, 1921); also by R. S. Rose and L. Bacon (U. of California Press, 1919). The existing translations of Walther von der Vogelweide are not remarkable as poetry, but give some idea of the author's thought. See, for example, W. A. Phillips, *Selected Poems of Walther von der Vogelweide* (London, 1896). The *Nibelungenlied* can be read in numerous translations, both prose and verse.

CHAPTER XVI.   DEVELOPMENTS IN THE STRUCTURAL AND DECORATIVE ARTS

Two interpretative studies of mediæval art are highly recommended to anyone who has a real interest in the Middle Ages: E. Mâle, *Religious Art in France, Thirteenth Century* (London, 1913), and Henry Adams, *Mont-Saint-Michel and Chartres* (Washington, 1904). Among the numerous other works that could be listed, the following are outstanding: T. G. Jackson, *Byzantine and Romanesque Architecture,* 2 vols. (Cambridge, 1913), and *Gothic Architecture,* 2 vols. (Cambridge, 1915); A. W. Clapham, *Romanesque Architecture in Western Europe* (Oxford, 1936); A. K. Porter, *Medieval Architecture,* 2 vols. (New Haven, 1912); Alice Gardner, *Medieval Sculpture in France* (Cambridge, 1931); L. F. Day, *Windows* (London, 1909); H. Arnold, *Stained Glass of the Middle Ages in England and France* (London, 1939); C. R. Morey, *Mediæval Art* (New York, 1942); Joan Evans, *Art in Mediæval France* (London, 1948).

There is extremely little in English on mediæval technology but the following books are good on particular phases of the subject: Usher, *History of Mechanical Inventions;* C. W. C. Oman, *The Art of War in the Middle Ages* (London, 1924); M. S. Briggs, *The Architect in History* (Oxford, 1927); E. K. Chatterton, *Ships and Ways of Other Days* (London, 1913). For additional references see Carl Stephenson, "In Praise of Medieval Tinkers," *Journal of Economic History,* VIII (1948), 26-42. The album of Villard de Honnecourt has been twice edited: by J. B. A. Lassus (Paris, 1858) and by R. H. Hahnloser (Vienna, 1935). The letter of Pierre de Maricourt about the magnetic compass is summarized by S. P. Thomson in *Proceedings of the British Academy,* II, 384 ff. A translation was published by Brother Arnold, M. Sc. (New York, 1904).

CHAPTER XVII.   THE LATIN WORLD AFTER THE FIRST CRUSADE

The best book on the working of feudal institutions in England is that of F. M. Stenton, *The First Century of English Feudalism* (Oxford, 1932). See also A. B. White, *The Making of the English Constitution* (New York, 1925); W. A. Morris, *The Constitutional History of England to 1216* (New York, 1930); G. B. Adams, *Constitutional History of England* (New York, 1921); Stephenson and Marcham, *Sources of English Constitutional History,* sect. ii;

Stephenson, *Mediæval Feudalism*, ch. v. Contemporary developments in France and other countries are well covered in *The Cambridge Medieval History,* vols. V and VI. The feudalization of Germany and the eastward expansion of the Germans are emphasized in J. W. Thompson's *Feudal Germany* (Chicago, 1928). For references to books on the crusades see above under Chapter XII.

CHAPTER XVIII. THE TRIUMPH OF THE PAPACY

In addition to the books cited above under Chapters XII and XVII, see S. R. Packard's volume in the *Berkshire Series,* entitled *Europe and the Church under Innocent III* (New York, 1927), which contains a useful bibliography—as does E. F. Jacob's brilliant chapter in *The Cambridge Medieval History,* vol. VI. For reasons stated in the text, there is no better reading on the Fourth Crusade than the famous account of Villehardouin, conveniently edited in a volume of the *Everyman Library* called *Memoirs of the Crusades.* Cf. the chronicle by Robert of Clari, translated by E. H. McNeal for the Columbia *Records of Civilizations* (1936). And on the Third Crusade see Ambroise, *The Crusade of Richard Lion-Heart,* translated by M. J. Hubert in the same series (1941). Especially valuable, to illustrate contemporary feudalism as well as the results of the Fourth Crusade, is P. W. Topping's *Assizes of Romania,* Pennsylvania *Translations and Reprints* (Philadelphia, 1949).

CHAPTER XIX. HERESY, THE FRIARS, AND THE UNIVERSITIES

For most of the subjects treated in this chapter *The Cambridge Medieval History* again furnishes scholarly guidance; one who wishes to become familiar with the controversial literature on mediæval heresies, the inquisition, and the like is advised to consult the bibliographies attached to vol. VI. Relevant documents may be found in the Pennsylvania *Translations and Reprints,* III, no. 6. The best sources for the life of St. Francis are his own writings, translated by P. Robinson (Philadelphia, 1906) and the biography by Thomas of Celano, translated by A. G. F. Howell (London, 1908). For additional references and criticism see F. C. Burkett's chapter in *Franciscan Essays,* vol. II (Manchester, 1932), and that by A. G. Little in *The Cambridge Medieval History,* vol. VI. The material in English on the Dominicans is not so plentiful; but see G. R. Galbraith, *The Constitution of the Dominican Order* (Manchester, 1925) and B. E. R. Formoy, *The Dominican Order in England* (London, 1925).

Although the *Summa Theologiæ* of Aquinas has been translated, most students will probably get a clearer idea of his teaching from modern works about him: e.g., E. H. Gilson, *The Philosophy of St. Thomas Aquinas* (Cambridge, 1924); M. Grabmann, *Thomas Aquinas* (New York, 1928); and M. C. D'Arcy, *Thomas Aquinas* (London, 1930). Aside from the rather scattering remarks of Thorndike in the second volume of *A History of Magic and Experimental Science,* there is nothing very good in English on the scientific work of Albertus Magnus and his contemporaries. Roger Bacon's *Opus Maius* has been translated by R. B. Burke (Philadelphia, 1928). The theory of Bacon's cipher, as set forth by W. R. Newbold (Philadelphia, 1928), has been proved entirely false by recent studies too numerous to cite here.

CHAPTER XX. CHURCH AND STATE AFTER INNOCENT III

On Frederick II see especially C. H. Haskins, *The Normans in European History,* ch. viii, and the special articles in the same author's *Studies in the History of Mediæval Science* (Cambridge, Mass., 1927); also E. Kantorowicz, *Frederick II* (London, 1931). But for Frederick's own work on birds anyone interested should by all means read the translation by C. A. Wood and F. Marjorie Fife, published as *The Art of Falconry* (Stanford University, 1943). On Louis IX and his crusade the classic work is Joinville's biography, which can be found in several translations, including one in the *Everyman Library*. On Louis IX and his crusade the one work that should be read by everybody is Joinville's biography, which can be found in several translations including one in the *Everyman Library* (*Memoirs of the Crusades*). On other outstanding features of European history in the thirteenth century the student is referred to the books cited above under Chapter XVII and to *The Cambridge Medieval History*, vols. VI and VII.

CHAPTER XXI. THE GROWTH OF OPPOSITION TO THE PAPACY

The general reference given immediately above holds good for the present chapter also. There is, unfortunately, no good English translation of the *Romance of the Rose*; but see the modern French version by A. Mary (Paris, 1928). An excellent introduction to the study of Dante is provided by K. Vossler's *Mediæval Culture*, 2 vols. (London, 1929). All of Dante's works may be readily found in English; C. E. Norton's prose translation of the *Divine Comedy* is especially recommended. The ideas of Ockham, Marsiglio, and other writers of the later Middle Ages are well discussed in McIlwain's *Growth of Political Thought* and in Sabine's *History of Political Theory*. See also D. S. Muzzey, *The Spiritual Franciscans* (New York, 1907), and J. N. Figgis, *Studies of Political Thought from Gerson to Grotius* (Cambridge, 1923). The *Defensor Pacis* of Marsiglio has been discussed, with quotations, by E. Emerton (Cambridge, Mass., 1920). There is, unfortunately, no complete English translation.

CHAPTER XXII. FRANCE AND ENGLAND DURING THE HUNDRED YEARS' WAR

A profusion of books about England in the fourteenth and fifteenth centuries can be found in any good library, including many that deal with the contemporary writings of Englishmen (see below, under Chapter XXV). So far as fourteenth-century France is concerned, there is little in English aside from chapters in general books, as in *The Cambridge Medieval History*, vol. VII. Within its limitations (see above, p. 454), the latter part of Froissart's chronicle is a valuable source for certain phases of the war. It is available in many editions, either full or condensed, like that in the *Everyman Library*. The life of Jeanne d'Arc has often been told, as by F. C. Lowell (Boston, 1896) and by Andrew Lang (London, 1908). All students, however, are especially urged to read the records of her trial, translated by T. D. Murray (New York, 1902) and W. P. Barrett (New York, 1932). These records, it should be noted, are a fine source not only for the life of the maid but also for contemporary belief in witchcraft and for inquisitorial procedure in ecclesiastical courts.

CHAPTER XXIII. THE DECLINE OF THE CHURCH

All phases of ecclesiastical history in the fourteenth and fifteenth centuries are well treated in *The Cambridge Medieval History*, vols. VII and VIII, which contain exhaustive bibliographies on Wycliffe, Hus, and the various groups of mystics. The works of Wycliffe are practically all obtainable in English, as are some of those of Hus. Such mystics as Richard Rolle and Juliana of Norwich can best be understood by studying their own writings. See also *The Book of Margery Kempe, 1436*, a modern version by W. Butler-Bowdon (London, 1936); V. D. Scudder, *St. Catherine as Seen in Her Letters* (London, 1905); and A. Hyma, *The Christian Renaissance* (Grand Rapids, 1924), which is particularly concerned with the mystics of the Low Countries. Chapters devoted to the Mongols, the Balkan peoples, and the Ottoman Turks will be found in *The Cambridge Medieval History*, vol. IV. A. H. Lybyer's *Government of the Ottoman Empire in the Time of Suleiman the Magnificent* (Cambridge, Mass., 1913) describes the Ottoman system of administration, both civil and military, as it had come to be established long before the sixteenth century.

CHAPTER XXIV. SOCIETY AND COMMERCE IN THE LATER MIDDLE AGES

Industrial and commercial developments in the later Middle Ages are brilliantly explained by Pirenne in his *Economic and Social History of Medieval Europe*; cf. Heaton's *Economic History of Europe,* chs. vi-x. On the Italian cities and the Hansa see also the pertinent chapters in *The Cambridge Medieval History*, vols. VII and VIII; on the Jews in Mediæval Europe, *The Legacy of Israel*, edited by I. Abrahams and others (Oxford, 1927), and ch. xxii in the seventh volume of *The Cambridge Medieval History*; on changes in warfare, Oman's *Art of War in the Middle Ages*, A. H. Thompson's chapters in the sixth volume of *The Cambridge Medieval History*, and C. H. Ashdown's *Armour and Weapons in the Middle Ages* (London, 1925). The geographical background of the great explorations is admirably sketched by G. H. T. Kimble, *Geography in the Middle Ages* (London, 1938). To supplement the plates included in Kimble's book, the reader is particularly referred to A. E. Nordenskiöld, *Facsimile-Atlas* (Stockholm, 1889), and *Periplus* (Stockholm, 1897), both in English translation.

CHAPTER XXV. THE ADVANCE OF SECULAR CULTURE

The older view of the Italian Renaissance is eloquently set forth by J. A. Symonds in his famous book on that subject. With it may be compared a number of more recent studies, including one by H. S. Lucas in this same historical series. Arthur Tilley's chapters in *The Cambridge Medieval History*, vols. VII and VIII, give the main facts about the Italian humanists, though he repeats too many catchphrases about the "mediæval" and the "modern." W. G. Constable's chapter in vol. VIII excellently summarizes the development of Gothic art and its relation to Renaissance art; cf. Morey, *Mediæval Art*. But every student of the subject is especially urged to read Sellery's new and admirable summary, *The Renaissance* (see above, p. 517)—which confirms and amplifies the opinions tentatively expressed in the preceding chapters.

The works of Chaucer and Boccaccio are too familiar to need citation of particular editions here. For really poetic translations of Petrarch, and a fine modernized version of Langland, see the books referred to above, pp. 454, 456. The view concerning Ockham accepted in the text is that of A. A. Moody, *The Logic of William of Ockham* (New York, 1935). On the works of the Ockhamists an invaluable commentary has now been provided by Sarton's *Introduction to the History of Science,* vol. III (Baltimore, 1949)—see his index. The plate reproduced above on p. 467 is one of many in E. Wickersheimer, *Anatomies de Mondino dei Luzzi et de Guido de Vigevano* (Paris, 1926). On the advance of medical study in the fourteenth and fifteenth centuries see the works referred to above, pp. 518, 521; also C. J. Singer, *The Evolution of Anatomy* (London, 1925).

CHAPTER XXVI. EUROPE IN THE LATER FIFTEENTH CENTURY

On Charles VII and Louis XI there is nothing better in English than the chapters in *The Cambridge Medieval History*, vol. VIII. To supplement them, the student may well turn to the memoirs of Commines, translated in the *Bohn Library*, and to the poems of Villon. John Payne's translation of the latter is superior to many of the more recent attempts, but finest of all are the few ballads that were put into English verse by Swinburne. A scholarly history of witchcraft in English remains to be written; see, however, the scattered papers of G. L. Burr, which are reprinted in a volume published by the Cornell University Press (Ithaca, 1943). A number of documents on witchcraft are included in the Pennsylvania *Translations and Reprints*, III, no. 4. The *Malleus Maleficarum* has been translated and edited with an amazing introduction by Montague Summers (London, 1928). See also Thorndike's useful summary in *The Cambridge Medieval History*, vol. VIII. As to technology in the latter Middle Ages, there are no general accounts to be recommended, though Usher's *History of Mechanical Inventions* contains admirable sections on clocks, water-wheels, windmills, spinning and weaving machines, and the printing-press. On this last subject see also G. P. Winship, *Printing in the Fifteenth Century* (Philadelphia, 1940), and D. B. Updike, *Printing Types*, 2 vols. (Cambridge, Mass., 1937). Many other drawings like those reproduced in Figures 33 and 34 will be found in the articles of M. Berthelot, *Annales de chimie et de physique*, for the years 1891 and 1900.

Index

NOTE: In the following pages, as a matter of convenience, Roman emperors in the east after Justinian are called Byzantine emperors; kings of the West Franks after 843 are called kings of France; kings of the East Franks after 843 are called kings of Germany. Absolute uniformity in indexing personal names is impossible, but in general a man will be found under that portion of his name by which he is commonly known: e.g., John of Salisbury; Hus, John. Titles of books have ordinarily been omitted except those whose authors are unknown. For a large number of things which are not separately listed the student is referred to such comprehensive topics as Arms and armor, Cloth-making, Costume, Domestic animals, Food and drink, Fowls, Fruits, Grain, Harness, Houses and furnishings, Metal-working, Music, Tools, Vegetables, Writing materials.